Magician and Mechanic

Magician and Mechanic

The Roots of "Spiritual but Not Religious" from the Renaissance to the Scientific Revolution

MICHAEL HORTON

William B. Eerdmans Publishing Company
Grand Rapids, Michigan

Wm. B. Eerdmans Publishing Co.
2006 44th Street SE, Grand Rapids, MI 49508
www.eerdmans.com

Published 2026

Book design by Lydia Hall

Printed in the United States of America

32 31 30 29 28 27 26 1 2 3 4 5 6 7

ISBN 978-0-8028-7712-3

Library of Congress Cataloging-in-Publication Data

A catalog record for this book is available from the Library of Congress.

Contents

Abbreviations

LCL	Loeb Classical Library
LW	*Luther's Works*. 55 vols. Edited by Jaroslav Pelikan and Helmut T. Lehmann. Philadelphia: Fortress; St. Louis: Concordia, 1955–1986
WA	Martin Luther, *Dr. Martin Luthers Werke: Kritische Gesamtausgabe* [Weimarer Ausgabe; Schriften], 65 vols. Weimar: H. Böhlau, 1883–1993
WA TR	*Tischreden*

INTRODUCTION

Fullness and the Future

Modernity's Search for the Sacred

Know yourself, offspring of God in mortal clothing.

—Marsilio Ficino[1]

My first volume in this series explored the epicenter of the so-called Axial Age.[2] Across various civilizations during the sixth century BCE one discerns a shift from myths that justify rituals to ones that teach philosophical truths in allegorical garb. Whatever we call it, this transition is represented by a recognizable turn from the local, oral, and embedded life of a locative outlook to a universal, literate, and utopian perspective. During this century there is a widespread interest in the self and its afterlife. It coincides with the rapid rise and spread of the Achaemenid (Persian) Empire. Late Period Egypt reflects a more metaphysical attitude, and during this same period we also see the birth of philosophical religions like Hinduism, Buddhism, Jainism, Taoism, Confucianism, and Zoroastrianism. In Greece it begins to appear in the work of Pherecydes, Epimenides, Pythagoras, and Parmenides, introducing foreign doctrines like reincarnation.

1. Ficino, *Meditations on the Soul*, 78–79.

2. Coining the term, Jaspers's *Origin and Goal of History* represents the most sweeping construal of an Axial Age. A more recent but no less ideologically driven account is found in Armstrong, *Great Transformation*. At the other extreme, Iain Provan rejects the paradigm in *Convenient Myths*, 1–40. The first interpretation is an example of making historical facts fit the paradigm, especially by incorporating the Hebrew prophets. If anything, the prophets indicted Israel for violating the covenant with Yahweh by following after these other gods. However, there is considerable evidence of such a broad transition beginning in the sixth century BCE. Regardless, I prefer Jan Assmann's flexible term "axiality" and especially J. Z. Smith's dialectic between locative and utopian societies. For both, there are discernible features, but they can be present or recede in favor of the other in any age. For a fuller description of this thesis, see the early chapters of my first volume.

The idea of the "divine self" emerged as a unifying core of "axiality" across these diverse cultures. Pre-axial religions were, for the most part, this-worldly, public, centered on rituals to keep the city in harmony with the realm of the gods who founded it. Flourishing here and now, living within inherited boundaries, and giving due honors to the gods were the focus. Generally, there was no concept of a personal afterlife, except in one's reputation and offspring. The individual was embedded in the family, the family in a kinship group, the kinship group in the city, and the city in the king.

What changes gradually in the Axial revolution is a discovery of the self, concomitant with personal survival after death, and a more otherworldly dimension. It is in this utopian environment that the idea of the "divine self" appears. Alongside the continuing public religion we see mystery religions that are more esoteric and encourage a sense of being an individual—not merely a subject in a stable order but a self-transforming and world-transforming agent. Strange myths appear, which in Greece have been called Orphic. But instead of being the basis for public rites, they encode philosophical mysteries about the One from which all reality emanates in appearance and to which it returns. The divine self wants to break free of all limits and boundaries of the body as well as the laws of the physical world. This Axial Age dawns first in the vast territory of the Persian Empire and comes to the Greek world about a century or two later.

Whether or not we adopt the Axial Age thesis, the Greeks seem to have embraced with gusto something very much like this theory. Journeys to the East for spiritual enlightenment lent credibility to a sage's resume. Genealogies of a perennial philosophy encompassed those peoples—Iranian magi, Egyptian priests, Indian gymnosophists, Thracians—from whom they believed the Greeks derived philosophy. In classical Greece, such philosophical religion attached itself to the legendary Orpheus, who reconciled Apollo and Dionysus, reason and divine madness. I argued in *The Shaman and the Sage* that much of this "Orphic" literature was composed in Pythagorean circles. Plato appealed to Orphic myths to ground his distinctive doctrines, and centuries later Neoplatonists would seek to create a canon of Orphic mysteries and rituals. The philosophical religions mentioned above were also canonizing sacred texts in a process that would continue in Hinduism and Buddhism well into the medieval era. Whatever one makes of the Axial Age thesis itself, scholars agree widely on the features of "axiality" I have mentioned. There is also wide agreement that these features characterize what we call modernity.[3] Indeed, we might call the Orphic tradition the natural religion

3. For example, without referring to the Axial Age, Stephen Toulmin highlights these transitions in *Cosmopolis*, 5–44.

of Western civilization. Its encounters with Judaism and Christianity (and later, Islam) ranged from fierce opposition to relative absorption in one direction or the other. In fact, the history of these oppositions and assimilations forms a larger part of modernity than is usually acknowledged. Even today, the rise of spirituality without religion is mainly a reaction against Christian monotheism rather than a sudden burst of rationalistic atheism. It is not surprising, therefore, that heresy in the West, even when it has been called "atheism," has been pantheistic in tendency.

I use several nicknames I have borrowed from others for this "Orphic" phenomenon: natural supernaturalism, philosophical religion, "spiritual but not religious," cosmotheology, and perennial philosophy. I refer readers to my introduction to volume 1 for definitions of these terms. Here I introduce two questions that become especially acute in the modern age and will be raised at various points in this volume: Where do I find fullness? And where is history going?

Where Do We Find Fullness?

Charles Taylor defines fullness as what one experiences when "in that place (activity or condition), life is fuller, richer, deeper, more worth while, more admirable, more what it should be."[4] The Renaissance represents a major eruption of pagan spirituality within a broader landscape of official, locative, public religion. One need not (indeed, could not) renounce the latter. Yet in the search for fullness, many sought at least to appropriate pre-Christian myths, imagery, art, and ideas as anticipations of Christianity.

Comparisons of Quattrocento Florence with ancient Alexandria are easy to draw, especially since the pioneers of the Renaissance claimed explicitly to be reviving the Orphic heritage. Turning from the public religion focused on securing divine favor in this life, Socrates had drawn upon the otherworldly myths of mystery religions. One may see the whole philosophy of Plato's Socrates as a discourse, occasioned by Socrates's impending execution, on death as liberation. We have seen how the resurgence of Orphic theology in ancient Roman Alexandria was provoked by existential anxiety over tormenting demons that haunt

4. Taylor, *Secular Age*, 5; cf. 6–27. Taylor somewhat idealizes medieval Christendom, I think, and focuses the blame for secularization on nominalism, which reaches its apogee in the Reformation. This narrative is associated today especially with John Milbank and his circle of Radical Orthodoxy. Taylor acknowledges similarities (*Secular Age*, 295), adding, in reference to Milbank and Catherine Pickstock, "There is one such current today, with which I have great deal of sympathy" (773).

daily life and impede the soul's celestial journey. George Sarton in his *History of Science* reminds us,

> The Hellenistic nations were ready to welcome foreign sages, such as the Iranian magi, the Indian gymnosophists, and many others, because of their spiritual curiosity and even more because of a kind of religious starvation. The orientalizing Greeks were opening their hearts to the Great Mother of Phrygia, to Mithras, or to the gods of Egypt, especially Isis and Osiris. We should remember that the desire for living forms of religion had existed in Greece from early times; witness the existence and popularity of mystery cults like the Eleusinian, Orphic, and Dionysiac ones. Since the time of Aristotle and Epicurus, the old mythology had lost favor; on the other hand, the astral religion that had to some extent replaced it was too learned and too cold to satisfy the plain people. The Greeks established in Asia or Egypt were far away from their old sanctuaries, and their religious hunger caused them to be very susceptible to the Oriental mysteries.[5]

Even in the ancient world, the turn inward to the inmost self was a common denominator. "Cynicism and Skepticism favored quietist tendencies," notes Sarton, "even as Stoicism and Epicureanism did. It is not strange that so many philosophers of various sects were united on this, the need of dispassionateness and disinterestedness, even of indifference, for the whole world around them was cruel and no peace was possible without withdrawal from the circumambient chaos. Peace was nowhere to be found save in one's soul."[6]

Late medieval piety seems to have offered less "fullness" than many assume, including Taylor. The Fourth Lateran Council felt obliged to require confession to a priest and attendance at Mass at least once a year. The church seemed to realize this diminished interest in its public rituals by ramping up its own quasi-magical talismans. Sacramentals proliferated: blessed cards and cloths, holy water, pilgrimages to touch relics of the saints, and the infamous sale of papal indulgences. Processions and Masses became more theatrical to attract worshipers.

Scholars were, if anything, even more cynical. Most humanists were employed by the church. "Familiarity, if not breeding contempt," says Alison Brown, "bred a spirit of nonsubservience and 'equivocal disillusionment' towards the papacy . . . that helped the new ideas of the avant-garde to grow."[7] The reforms of Pope

5. Sarton, *History of Science*, 17.
6. Sarton, *History of Science*, 162.
7. Brown, *Return of Lucretius*, 5, quoting Holmes, *Florentine Enlightenment*, 53.

Gregory VI in the eleventh century sought to correct abuses. However, by not only condemning wicked priests but also declaring that their ministrations were null and void, he raised anxieties about the efficacy of the sacraments. While it was common for priests and popes to have mistresses, Rodrigo Borgia—Pope Alexander VI—gained peculiar recognition for profligacy. Roger Gill relates, "The most famous account of his licentiousness while a cardinal was in a letter sent to him by Pope Pius II, a man who had himself two illegitimate children but admitted to having given up sex for drinking."[8] Alexander managed to have his favorite son, Cesare, ordained at seven years of age, and at eighteen Cesare was made a cardinal alongside Alessandro Farnese, the future Pope Paul III, whose sister Giulia (though married to Orsino Orsini) was Alexander's favorite mistress. The divisions within the church—before the Reformation—and the profligacy of its clergy, including the popes, led to widespread anxiety and cynicism. "What greater enemies could the church have," says Erasmus daringly in section 33 of *The Praise of Folly*, "than these charlatan popes who encourage the disregard of Christ, who depict Him as a mercenary, who corrupt His teachings by forced interpretations, who scandalize Him by their infamous lives."[9]

It is this lack of fullness that Greek and Roman myths and art were thought to fill. In fact, pagan themes did not raise curial eyebrows as long as they were properly glossed by their creators as prophetic allusions to Christ's advent rather than an alternative religion. Yet, there was a thin line—quite literally in the case of the Ducal Palace of Urbino with twin chapels, where an inscription reads, "You see two chapels joined by a slight divide; one is sacred to the Muses, the other to God."[10]

Marsilio Ficino more than anyone else inspired the Orphic renaissance. From the "divine self" at the center of his thought, he created an exotic elixir all his own, combining a more original Neoplatonism with alchemy, astrology, and, with the influence of Giovanni Pico della Mirandola, kabbalah. "Know yourself," he exhorts, "offspring of God in mortal clothing."[11] Hanegraaff reminds us that this tradition "focused on attainment of a salvational gnosis by which the soul could

8. Gill, "Pinturicchio's Frescoes."

9. Dolan, *Essential Erasmus*, 158.

10. Joscelyn Godwin, *Pagan Dream*, 91.

11. Ficino, *Meditations on the Soul*, 78–79. "Knowledge and reverence of oneself are best of all," he continues. "I pray you uncover yourself. Separate the soul from the body, reason from sensual desires; separate them as much as you can; your ability depends on your endeavor. When the earthly grime has been removed you will at once see pure gold, and when the clouds have been dispersed, you will see the clear sky. Then, believe me, you will revere yourself as an eternal ray of the divine sun and, moreover, you will not venture to contemplate or undertake

be liberated from its material entanglement and regain its unity with the divine Mind." He adds, "Allowing for the great differences between various systems, this is what the gnostic, hermetic, and theurgical currents of late antiquity all had in common; and to an extent that has not always been sufficiently recognized, this is what Platonism came to mean for its Renaissance admirers."[12]

Ficino and his ilk drew inspiration not only from Plato's metaphysics but also from the Hermetic magic and rituals that Dodds saw as the epitome of "irrationalism."[13] Such magic, not always of the "white" variety, reached into the papal apartments and cathedrals, Elizabeth's court, Shakespeare's Prospero, and the Faust of Marlowe and Goethe. As Gilles Quispel observes, the Renaissance was less the birth of modern reason than "the rebirth of occultism: ostensibly it was a sort of Platonic philosophy, which in reality, however, included a Hermetic magical core which leavened the whole movement." Quispel shows that the lesson of the Asclepius was well-understood by Ficino: "*omnia unius esse aut unum esse omnia* [The All is from the One and All is one]."[14]

At the same time, Orpheus long ago had reconciled the brothers. Apollonian reason and Dionysian madness are knitted together in the Western psyche. Nietzsche rightly saw that "Orpheus" (Socrates) synthesized these rational and irrational personalities. And after the Renaissance, Orphic philosophical religion (or spirituality) would be equated with reason itself, loosening the foundations of Christian monotheism.

Although the Florentine Renaissance is seen usually as the rebirth of learning and reason, it was just as obsessed with "divine frenzy" as Plato. Reason takes us only so far, Ficino writes to a friend, but divine madness returns the divine soul to its origin. "Without this, say Democritus and Plato, no man has ever been great . . . you are inspired and inwardly possessed by that frenzy."[15] Ficino even assimilates Epicureanism to Plato: "Elsewhere [Plato] describes this love as the ardent desire of a soul that in a way is dead in its own body, while alive in another. He then says that the soul of a lover leads its life in another body. This the Epicureans follow when they say that love is a union of small particles, which they call atoms, made to penetrate the person from whom the images of beauty have been taken. . . . This first attempt at flight Plato calls divine ecstasy and frenzy."[16] To make any

---

any base or worthless action in your own presence . . . the soul, which is by nature divine. . . . Therefore, seek yourself beyond the world."

12. Hanegraaff, *Esotericism and the Academy*, 12.

13. Dodds, *Greeks and the Irrational*, 283–314.

14. Quispel, "Reincarnation and Magic," 168–69.

15. Marsilio Ficino to Peregrino Agli, in Ficino, *Meditations*, 64–69.

16. Marsilio Ficino to Peregrino Agli in Ficino, *Meditations*, 64–69.

progress, he advises, "we remember what we knew before when we existed outside the prison of our body. The soul is fired by this memory and, shaking its wings, by degrees purges itself from contact with the body and its filth and becomes wholly possessed by divine frenzy."[17] We saw in volume 1 that across Mesopotamian and Mediterranean cultures a sign of true inspiration was divine possession (*enthysiasmos*). While in this state the poet was out of his wits. The Renaissance thus awakened the Dionysian spirit.

The development to this point more than justified the decoration of Duke Orbino's palace mentioned above, completed before 1470, with scenes from Hermetic mythology. By the 1480s, the floor of the Siena Cathedral included an inlay of Hermes Trismegistus surrounded by sybils, with Moses handing him the tablets prophesying Christ's advent. And then there is the Vatican Palace itself, where Pope Alexander VI employed Pinturicchio to paint Osiris, Hermes Trismegistus, and the bull of Apis on the walls of the papal apartments, where he conducted Hermetic rituals and sometimes orgies.[18] Alexander created a myth of himself as having been descended from Alexandrian sages and dreamed of turning Christendom into a theocracy based on Hermetic religion. Ralph Bauer notes, "For Alexander, Hellenistic-Egypt, and Alexandria especially, was the cradle of civilization and true religion."[19] His successor, Julius II, said he would never live in the Borgia apartments, which were sealed until the nineteenth century. "He desecrated the Holy Church as none before," Julius declared.[20] Infuriated by the preaching of Savonarola, particularly the direct criticisms toward himself, Alexander had Savonarola tortured and hanged in 1497.

Importantly, Paul Kristeller points out that the condition was indifference and "merely nominal adherence to the doctrines of the Church," rather than outright neo-paganism. Such indifference could be found among the highest ranks of clergy.[21] Kristeller is correct when he says, "The view that the humanist movement was essentially pagan or anti-Christian cannot be sustained."[22] Many humanists in fact wanted to reform the church and society along more Christ-like lines. However, Kristeller tends to underappreciate the extent to which pagan and Christian influences blended in a free play of imagination, as humanists sought to enrich and reform Christianity with freshly available material from the suppressed wing

17. Marsilio Ficino to Peregrino Agli in Ficino, *Meditations*, 64–69.
18. Gill, "Pinturicchio's Frescoes," 35–36.
19. Bauer, *Alchemy of Conquest*, 82.
20. Quoted in Cawthorne, *Sex Lives*, 219.
21. Kristeller, *Renaissance Thought*, 67.
22. Kristeller, *Renaissance Thought*, 69.

of the cultural library. Humanism reflects an intertextual imagination. Joscelyn Godwin builds a compelling case for an "imaginal paganism," more visual than literary, a "state of mind and soul that arose in fifteenth-century Italy, spread through Europe along certain clearly defined fault-lines, and persisted for about two hundred years, during which, although no one believed in the gods, many people acted as though they existed. . . . The 'gods,' who had to receive their ceremonial dues, were none other than the Holy Trinity and the Christian saints. The 'other things' that one could go on to enjoy after duty was done, were the unchristian activities, ranging from killing one's neighbors to making images of heathen gods and delighting in them."[23] This is a crucial distinction: duty and delight. One may continue in a loveless marriage while entertaining mistresses on the side.

In fact, the most extravagant examples of pagan-themed villas and gardens are found in the Viterbo region and belonged to cardinals who were close friends and central players in the Counter Reformation. One such figure was Cardinal Ippolito II d'Este, Duke of Ferrara, governor of Tivoli, and Pope Alexander VI's grandson, who commissioned the famous Tivoli Gardens. As in other gardens, there were grottos under fountains in the Tivoli Gardens where guests were led on a journey similar to those of initiates in the Eleusinian mysteries. This "esoteric itinerary," we are told, "was reserved for the Cardinal's intimates. This plunges us into 'the middle of a Hesiodic cosmogony, re-seeded by Neoplatonic Orphism and historicized in honor of the genius loci.' . . . Another pervasive myth of the garden . . . is that of Dionysus, who fits into the family as the son of Harmonia's other daughter, Semele. . . . For this reason, Dionysus or Bacchus is a god of the mysteries of spiritual rebirth." It is known as the Grotto of Bacchus.[24]

Cardinal Alessandro Farnese, educated in the court of Lorenzo de' Medici, erected his Villa Farnese at Caprarola along similar lines. Alessandro's sister Giulia, Pope Alexander's favorite mistress, helped him to climb the curial ladder. As Pope Paul III, Farnese convoked the Council of Trent and launched the wars of religion. He was known for his illegitimate children, whom he managed to make cardinals and dukes as teenagers. After visiting the Villa Farnese, the recently converted Christina of Sweden exclaimed in horror, "It is as if our Savior had never breathed!"[25] Cardinal Cristoforo Madruzzo, bishop of Trent during the momentous council there, created his villa along similar lines, and the extravagant

23. Godwin, *Pagan Dream*, 1–2.

24. Godwin, *Pagan Dream*, 164–65, quoting Madonna, "Il Genius Loci di Villa d'Este," 194.

25. Godwin, *Pagan Dream*, 180.

gardens and pavilions of Cardinal Gianfrancesco Gambara, delegate to Trent and inquisitor general, also hold similar charms. Regardless of what they held officially, comments Godwin, "these clerics certainly cultivated another myth with all the intensity of an alternative religion."[26]

Duke Vicino Orsini accompanied the Farnese family in the war against the Protestant League of Schmalkald, returning to build his Sacro Bosco (sacred wood). "It has been explained as a Neoplatonic sanctuary, a creation of Epicurean philosophy, the itinerary of the soul from human to divine love, and a hieroglyph of the alchemical work."[27] By day, one could be a contemplative mystic and by night engage in Bacchanalian revelry. Some scholars go so far as to suggest that this circle of friends formed part of "a secret society of Hermeticists and neopagans who were not merely in love with Antiquity, but also in revolt against Christianity." Resisting such conspiracy theories, Godwin concludes sensibly, "Impatience with the Church does not preclude working for it, and for Christian principles as one chooses to see them. Nor does religious skepticism exclude esoteric activities, such as alchemy and astrology in which Vicino Orsini was engaged."[28]

Much of the Greek philosophy as well as esoteric writings available in the Latin West had been translated by Arab scholars in Baghdad during the eighth and ninth centuries. Margaret Osler notes, "The translation movement received support from the caliphs (the chief civil and religious leaders, as successors of Muhammad), who believed that the Greek writings were originally part of the canon of Zoroastrianism (the chief religion of the Persian Empire) that came to be known among the Greeks as a result of Alexander the Great's pillage of Persia (modern-day Iran)."[29] She adds,

> Chemistry and alchemy originated in Hellenistic Egypt, where the city of Alexandria, established as the capital of the Greek colony of Egypt by Alexander the Great, became an important center of learning and research in the sciences. Manuscripts from the third century AD contain recipes for a variety of chemical and metallurgical processes, including recipes for making alloys that look like gold and silver and for making artificial gems. . . . In addition to describing techniques for making imitations of gold and silver, the Alexandrian writers began to describe procedures for actually making gold and silver from base metals

26. Godwin, *Pagan Dream*, 153.
27. Godwin, *Pagan Dream*, 170–72.
28. Godwin, *Pagan Dream*, 172–73, quoting P. L. Wilson, "Oneiriconographia," 404.
29. Osler, *Reconfiguring the World*, 4.

> such as lead and copper. The manuscripts instructed the practitioner to start by making a substance, usually a powder, called the "philosopher's stone."[30]

For the most part, the Hermetic tradition was mediated to medieval adepts by Arab philosophers, especially the ninth-century alchemists Jabir ibn-Hayyan (Geber) and Muhammad ibn-Zakariya ar-Razi (Rhazes).[31]

The church condemned judicial astrology (divining the future), but the boundary was crossed at times even by theologians such as Roger Bacon. Paolo Rossi observes, "Even William of Auvergne and Albertus Magnus—who advocated the distinction between natural and demonic magic—finally accepted the rulings of the Church and admitted the dangers of all magic and its implicit idolatry."[32] Anthony Grafton and Nancy Siraisi point out, "Trying to erect figures in order to influence the heavens was, as Aquinas had said, mere superstition."[33] Yet it may have been difficult to convince an average person that this was different from common devotion to statues of Mary and the saints. "But during the Middle Ages," Bauer observes, "it was the Franciscans and their sympathizers who were the most fervent promoters of alchemy," including Roger Bacon, Bonaventure, Arnald of Villanova, Johannis de Rupescissa, and Ramon Llull.[34]

Ficino opened up to Europe the possibility of a natural magic that could not only provide spiritual, wing-mending therapy but also bring down celestial powers to improve and extend human life, as Epicureans desired, but abandoned Epicurus for Plato in his search for the means of such fullness. Giovanni Pico della Mirandola offered the bold proposal of human individuals even choosing their own nature. The search for fullness was palpable. Not just in an afterlife, but here and now, one made the transcendent immanent. After Cosimo de Medici brought to Ficino Greek manuscripts of the Corpus Hermeticum, the young translator dropped everything for the project. Through these and other writings from later Neoplatonism, Ficino concocted his own mixture of Orphic Hermeticism, to which Pico added mystical kabbalah while rejecting astrology, as we see in chapter 6. Germana Ernst explains, "From the time of Pico onward, sharp attacks

30. Osler, *Reconfiguring the World*, 21–22.

31. Osler, *Reconfiguring the World*, 21–22. "Jabir probably did not write all of the 2,000 books ascribed to him; later authors likely attributed their own writings to him. In fact, his name may not even refer to a real person. In fact, recent scholarship has established that an obscure Italian Franciscan monk, Paul of Taranto (thirteenth century), was actually the author of some of the most influential treatises attributed to Geber [Jabir]."

32. Rossi, *Francis Bacon*, 17.

33. Anthony and Siraisi, "Between the Election and My Hopes," 76.

34. Bauer, *Alchemy of Conquest*, 82–84.

on astrology had tried not only to undermine its claims to possess a 'scientific' foundation, by insisting repeatedly that its principles lacked any foundation or consistency, but also to denounce and condemn any effort to reconcile astrology with theology." Even the French cardinal Pierre d'Ailly (1351–1420) had tried in vain to convince the church that they could be reconciled.[35] Astrology could not predict the end of the world, he argued, since that is a direct act of divine intervention. However, one could at least predict the advent of the antichrist.[36]

However, the Italian polymath Gerolamo Cardano (1501–1576), a pioneer of mathematics and both an astrologer and alchemist, even followed the theurgic Neoplatonists in believing in the celestial efficacy of statues. He went so far as to cast Christ's horoscope, but upon publishing the geniture of Christ he encountered stern opposition from ecclesiastical authorities. Cardano insisted that it was only according to his human nature.[37] But Gaurico, whom Cardano considered a charlatan, was made a bishop after making a positive geniture for Farnese, Pope Paul III.[38] Conversely, unflattering horoscopes may have been partially responsible for papal measures against astrology.[39] Though a close friend of Cardano's (and an early teacher of Calvin), Andrea Alciato "was also the declared enemy of all occult interests . . . a sharp opponent of astrology."[40]

The Swiss physician and alchemist Paracelsus (1493–1541) put his personal stamp on Renaissance Hermeticism, giving natural supernaturalism its basic form all the way down to Newton. Accepting to some degree a gnostic antithesis between incorporeal and corporeal, Hermeticists ancient and modern added another stage of synthesis, uniting opposites to produce a "third thing." Thus, located at the intersection of the two worlds, the *magus* held the power of transforming the natural into the supernatural.

The Hermetic interests of Kepler, Boyle, Leibniz, and Newton are well known, although their physics contributed to the waning of an alchemical worldview that

35. Ernst, "Veritatis amor dulcissimus," 55.

36. Bauer, *Alchemy of Conquest*, 162.

37. Ernst, "Veritatis amor dulcissimus," 52, 54.

38. Ernst, "Veritatis amor dulcissimus," 57–58.

39. "The ninth rule of the Tridentine Index condemned divinatory practices and theories. In the solemn preamble to his bull *Coeli et terrae* of 1586, Sixtus V proclaimed that knowledge of future events was reserved exclusively for God. All theories that aspired to such knowledge, including astrology, were to be rejected as deceptive." See Ernst, "Veritatis amor dulcissimus," 61. "In 1636, on the eve of the trail of Galileo, Urban VIII—who, 'though very expert in astrology, forbade others to pursue it'—confirmed in his bull *Inscrutabilis* that the human intellect, 'imprisoned in the shadows of the human body,' was prohibited from raising itself to the 'secrets' of God" (45).

40. Ernst, "Veritatis amor dulcissimus," 45.

they ardently defended and practiced. It is implausible to conclude on historical grounds that the Hermetic outlook just happens to reappear at such critical episodes as embarrassing but epiphenomenal hobbies. According to Edward Rosen, "Out of Renaissance magic and astrology came not modern science, but modern magic and astrology."[41] That was certainly the view of Father Marin Mersenne, a key player in the Scientific Revolution.[42] Yet this assumes a clear separation that was only beginning to emerge in Mersenne's day. In fact, the antithesis may have been drawn more sharply in this polemical atmosphere (exhibited in his feud with Robert Fludd) than it is even today.

Precisely because of the prominent role that Hermeticism had played thus far in natural philosophy, the new mechanistic science had to conduct a relentless campaign of "de-magification." However, we shall see that this expulsion of a magical cosmos by mechanical philosophers could be called a "re-Christianization," emphasizing the distinction between the Creator and his creation and opening up space for the birth of modern science. Herbert Butterfield writes of the seventeenth century, "Because of science, the face of the earth and the activities of men were to alter more in a century than they had previously done in a thousand years."[43] However, what we discover is far from the familiar modern narrative. Instead of being a war between science and religion, the pioneers of the Scientific Revolution emancipated natural investigation from cosmotheology on the grounds of Christian orthodoxy.

With notable exceptions, especially in German scholarship, documentary evidence of a genealogical relationship of modern science to Renaissance Hermeticism rested quietly in the basement of the cultural library. Ebeling observes that the modern story of science's march "from myth to reason . . . saw the *Ars Hermetica* as merely 'an aberration in cultural history.'"[44] After the wave of scholarship over the last half century, it is no longer possible to ignore obvious connections, but there are lively debates today over whether the Scientific Revolution arose because of Hermeticism or in spite of it. I argue that the relationship is more complicated with influences in every direction. It is not the shaman *or* the sage, or a transition from the shaman *to* the sage, but the shaman *in* the sage that characterizes the narrative explored in my first volume. Similarly, it is the magician *in* the mechanic—the enduring mysticism even in modern science—that appears in this part of the story.

41. Rosen, "Was Copernicus a Hermetist?," 171.

42. Lenoble, *Mersenne*, 41.

43. Quoted in Nebelsick, *Renaissance*, xiv.

44. Ebeling, *Secret History*, 101, citing Kopp, *Die Alchemie*, vii.

Plato was not the only source of this search for the divine self, however. Although the Florentine Renaissance is associated primarily with Plato, the initial flourish of humanist fascination was with the lengthy philosophical poem, *De rerum natura* (On the nature of things) by the Roman Epicurean Lucretius (99–55 BCE). Epicureans were certainly hedonists, but not champions of vice.[45] The goal of life is happiness and pleasure—and the avoidance of pain, which comes with overindulgence. The main source of misery is the fear of death, which depends on the fear of the gods. Once one realizes the gods do not care, one also discovers freedom from the pain caused by the fear of death. The soul simply perishes with the body. Do you want to be happy? Then "Don't fear God, don't worry about death; what's good is easy to get, and what's terrible is easy to endure."[46] If there are no gods to worry about interfering with our lives, we become gods ourselves, free to create our own meaning and purpose in this life.

Brown observes that these copies of Lucretius's poem "sparked the 'radical naturalism' and 'new vision of the world' that has traditionally marked the Renaissance period, Lucretius's opening invocation to Venus, goddess of love and mother of burgeoning nature, being an inspiration not only to Virgil in his own day but to Renaissance poets and artists as well."[47] At the same time, with death still very much on everyone's mind, the Council of Florence declared:

> "Those souls who die in the state of Deadly Sin, or with the sole Original Sin, will go down into Hell." The message was later reinforced by sermons of the Mendicants and Savonarola on "the art of dying well," which urged people to "go often to see the dead being buried" and to take pleasure in watching relatives die and be buried. Although the "explosion of masses" in Florence and elsewhere in the fourteenth century demonstrated the evident success of this campaign to save souls, it is also evidence of a heightened anxiety about death.[48]

Brown quotes several anxious women especially, who sat at the feet of friars because they did not know where they were going after they died.[49] Lucretius appeared at just the right time, offering his therapy against fear.

Palmer contends that the influence of Lucretius led to a "secularized natural

45. Sarton, *History of Science*, 168.
46. Inwood and Gerson, *Epicurus Reader*, vii.
47. Brown, *Return of Lucretius*, 2.
48. Brown, *Return of Lucretius*, 13.
49. Brown, *Return of Lucretius*, 13.

philosophy."[50] It is true that some did adopt the whole Lucretian package, sowing seeds of religious skepticism that would blossom in the Radical Enlightenment. However, we should not view Renaissance Neoepicureanism as a sort of left wing juxtaposed to Platonism and Aristotelianism on the right. After all, insufficiently filtered versions of both schools generated their own heterodoxies. We may recall the tempest in thirteenth-century Paris over Aristotelianism, especially as mediated by Averroes. Aquinas himself fell under suspicion until he scrubbed the philosopher of pagan error and introduced a scholastic Aristotelianism that many humanists came to regard as a moribund project. Introduced by John Argyropoulos, the Renaissance Aristotle was more "original," although it was intended as a literary rather than theological project.[51] Compared with Plato, Aristotle was not difficult to reconcile with Epicureanism. Although Aristotle rejected atomism, his universe did not require an effectual cause or providential guidance; he taught the mortality of the soul and the eternity of the world. It was this uncensored Aristotle who attracted Pietro Pomponazzi (1462–1525). Pomponazzi represents a "secularized natural philosophy" as much as Lucretius.[52] Whatever school one preferred, many humanists were seeking alternative sources of fullness. Like modern societies today, the Renaissance age was far from disenchanted, but it looked for its enchantment increasingly in the occult basement of the cultural library.

The revival of Pyrrhonic skepticism through Sextus Empiricus carved another powerful tributary, as we will see. The publication of all these schools "generated a dizzying moment in the history of heterodoxy," Palmer observes. "Thus, the process of rehabilitating Epicurus, and the hostility that project faced, is not merely a moment in the history of humanism, but a critical intersection between humanism and the history of unbelief."[53] Yet these ancient sources were not imbibed

50. Palmer, *Reading Lucretius*, 23. She adds, "The six arguments made by Lucretius that I identify as proto-atheist are closely interrelated. These are, first, creation from chaos, or emergent order, the idea that the cosmos, Earth, nature, life, and human civilization developed gradually from an unplanned and chaotic system. This is closely related to the second thesis, denial of Providence or any kind of design or purpose in nature or human life, history, or experience. The third thesis, denial of divine participation in everyday functioning of the natural world, is closely related to the fourth, denial of miraculous intervention or any other action by the gods affecting the natural world or human experience, and to the fifth, the argument that the gods do not hear human prayer and never act upon it. The last of the six is the denial of the immortality of the soul and the rejection of any afterlife" (25).

51. Besides translating Aristotle's whole corpus, Argyropoulos was a teacher of Ficino, Pico, Lefèvre d'Étaples, Lorenzo de' Medici, Johannes Reuchlin, and Leonardo da Vinci.

52. See Celenza, "Pythagoras in the Renaissance," 668–69 n. 6, and Celenza, "'Post-Plotinian' Ficino," 72–73.

53. Palmer, *Reading Lucretius*, 20, 22.

straight-up but were blended in novel concoctions that would have offended the taste of the original authors. Rather than carving different tributaries into modernity, the streams of Platonism, Epicureanism, and skepticism wove in and out of each other.

Renaissance villas were also emblems of philosophical eclecticism, sometimes even playful skepticism. Inscriptions on a terrace of Duke Vicino Orsini's palace offer what seems like an intentionally ambiguous juxtaposition of maxims from Socrates, Aristotle, Epicureanism, and Platonism: "Live well and rejoice," "Blessed are they who keep to the mean," "Eat, drink, and be merry; after death, no more pleasure," and "Spurn the earth; after death, true pleasure." Godwin adds, "On the west face is a similar ensemble" that reads, "direct my steps, Lord," "what, therefore?," "the wise man dominates the stars," and "wisdom is less than fate."[54] As with the twin chapels in the Duke of Urbino's palace, it seemed possible to participate sincerely in two cults: public religion and pagan spirituality.

Luther and Calvin considered Plato the best of the pagan philosophers, but they considered Erasmus and Zwingli to be too enamored of him. There was a limit to what could be appropriated from the Greek tradition. Osler summarizes well that "the roots of European intellectual life grew from the seeds planted by both the biblical religions and the ancient Greeks. Biblical religions emphasized the unrestrained will of an all-powerful God, while the Greek approach emphasized a world ruled by impersonal principles of unity and harmony."[55] She adds, "The Hebrew Bible, which Christians call the Old Testament, describes a world that God created and with which he continues to interact. . . . The existence of the world as well as the conditions of human life remain contingent on divine will." The Bible presents a narrative from creation and the fall to redemption in Christ who will return at the end to judge the living and the dead. In contrast, according to Osler:

> Greek accounts of the world are very different. Unlike the biblical writings, they emphasize unchanging principles that provide the foundation and order of the natural world. . . . Thus, where the Bible recounts nature and humankind as subject to the willful actions of an all-powerful God, the Greek philosophers focused on the regularity and order they perceived in the natural world. Moreover, the Greeks viewed the world as eternal, having neither beginning nor end.[56]

54. Godwin, *Pagan Dream*, 173.
55. Osler, *Reconfiguring the World*, 1.
56. Osler, *Reconfiguring the World*, 2.

Breaking out of the Greek worldview was essential for the birth of modern science. We see during the seventeenth century a fascinating intersection of diverse streams, calling into question dogmatic distinctions between reason and enthusiasm, science and religion, orthodoxy and heterodoxy, pantheism and atheism.

The search for fullness in Christianity is extrospective, the Magisterial Reformers emphasized. True happiness is found not by looking deeper into oneself but by turning outward, looking up to God in faith and out to the neighbor in love and good works. The Reformers wanted to return to the biblical outlook that Osler highlights above. The focus was on the historical Christ and his acts of salvation, proclaimed now by the external word and sacraments, drawing people outside of themselves to find fullness in Christ's redemptive work.

Divine frenzy was "enthusiasm" (god-within-ism) of the sort that Luther identified in the radicals whom he dubbed *Schwärmerei*, that is, swarmers (like bees).[57] However, Luther and Calvin came to associate this spiritual illness with Rome and Anabaptists alike. Both corrupt the gospel, turning the sinner from Christ outside of us (*extra nos*) to the inner Christ, who is really the inner self in its ascent through mystical experience and good works. Does not the pope also pretend to receive new revelations and deceive followers with false miracles?

Following late medieval mystics like Eckhart, radical spiritualists turned inward to discover fullness. As in Neoplatonism generally, the highest divinity is the innermost self. Advancing a radical dualism between inner and outer, invisible and visible, body and soul, letter and spirit, the Jesus of history and the Christ of faith, these writers shifted the locus of authority from both the external church and the scriptures to the inner light of the autonomous individual. Fullness was to be found in the process of being absorbed into God by a surrender of the will. Designated by Hegel as "the first German philosopher," the radical pietist Jakob Böhme developed an elaborate system of kabbalistic cosmology in which God himself and the world emerge from a struggle between evil and good, darkness and light, wrath and love.

Given such variety, it is all the more striking that these features—doctrines, if you will—remain remarkably similar across time and space from the civilizations shaped by the transitions of the sixth century BCE. To my mind, this cannot be explained apart from the imaginative force of the "divine self." In more familiar terms, it is the dogma of autonomy. We may compare the phenomenon to a hurricane. Such storms go by many names, but the Atlantic hurricane exhibits typical features and patterns. Like atmospheric rivers, many of the features of axiality create favorable conditions, but it is only when the idea of the "divine self" becomes

57. Luther, *WA* 18:135,24–139,26.

a well-defined eye that its enormous energy creates its own weather system. And, like wind shear from October westerlies, cultural counterforces break up these systems until another season rolls around and a new storm is formed—the same basic phenomenon but with its own name, character, and intensity.

Where Is History Going?

This volume contains considerably more evidence of the impact of the twelfth-century monk Joachim of Fiore. The Axial tendency to return the soul to the One through ascetic practice (purgation, contemplation, union) was a ladder laid on its side, as a historical process. From now on, Joachite eschatology was the most influential current in early modern history. Figures as diverse as Columbus, Quaker George Fox, and a host of radical puritans and pietists who shaped the modern age agreed. This eschatology is the main engine of modern utopianism. Indeed, the transition from a locative premodern condition to a utopian "axiality" reaches heretofore unknown heights. Perhaps only in ancient Gnosticism was the divine self ever more reflective on its own transcendence and unwilling to live in the present. The historical sensibility of the Renaissance *magus* is something unprecedented in previous "leaps of consciousness."

Outside Judaism and Christianity, the dominant view of time was cyclical, from a golden age of innocence to a point of gradual decline and catastrophe until the rebirth of a new utopian age. The emanation-return schema of Orphic cosmology rendered history merely a moving picture of eternity. "The end is like the beginning" was the motto that Hermeticism symbolized by a snake eating its tail.[58] In contrast, biblical faith breaks the circle into a line from promise to fulfillment. It is always a "new thing" that God will accomplish in the future (e.g., Isa 43:19), a new covenant (e.g., Jer 31), something that "no eye has seen, nor ear heard, nor the heart of man imagined" (1 Cor 2:9). According to early Christian teaching, some of these prophecies are fulfilled in Christ's first advent and others will be in his

58. Ovid's *Metamorphoses* (1.109–201) bequeathed the return of a golden age to the West, but it was enriched by the rediscovery of earlier sources. In his five ages of man, Hesiod measured his own age of iron against the golden age ruled by Cronus, when people lived as divine offspring. Some Orphic theogonies identified this age with Phanes, that is, before Cronus and the Titans. Stoics taught that the cosmos, as a single divine being, expands and contracts until a periodic conflagration in which all reality is reduced to its original element and the whole process starts all over again. According to the Stoic doctrine of *apokatastasis*, there are periodic conflagrations in which reality is reduced to its original element and then expands again: the end is like the beginning, which ancient Hermeticists illustrated with the Ouroboros serpent eating its tail.

second, but all of them turn on Christ. Like other apocalyptic figures in the book of Revelation, the "thousand years" (Rev 20:7) is symbolic of the entire age of Christ between his two advents. For now, he is conquering the nations, not through the secular sword but by his word and Spirit, until he returns in final judgment and salvation to consummate his everlasting reign.[59]

Adopting a literal interpretation of the millennium, however, the leaders of a second-century movement called the New Prophecy—Montanus together with his assistants, Prisca and Maximilla—claimed to be inspired prophets ushering in a new Pentecost centered in their native Phrygia. Opposed by churches in the East and the West, Montanism was declared a heresy, and in 431 the Council of Ephesus officially rejected the idea of a literal millennium before Christ's return. At about the same time of this council, Augustine defended a symbolic interpretation of the "thousand years" in Revelation 20. Representing completion, the thousand years symbolizes the whole period between Christ's two advents. According to this interpretation, which was shared by leaders in the Christian East, this era is marked by tribulation for the saints yet progress of the gospel to the ends of the earth. The next apocalyptic event is Christ's return, the resurrection and last judgment, followed by the everlasting Sabbath.[60]

However, the twelfth-century Calabrian monk, Joachim of Fiore, redrew the eschatological map. Similar to Montanism's announcement of a new Pentecost, Joachim taught that a utopian "age of the Spirit" was about to dawn in the middle of history before the return of Christ.[61] The age of the Father (law; the order of the married) was superseded by the age of the Son (grace; the order of the clergy). And the age of the Spirit (immediate gnosis; the order of the monk) will replace the church and its ministry. The new covenant (age of the Son), advancing through the ministry of the visible church, will be as obsolete as the age of the Father. Joachim was familiar as a monk with the three stages of ascent from purgation to contemplation and union. At the first stage, one depends on authorities and an elaborate system of physical rites, but then recognizes them as pictures of higher

59. For a substantial investigation of primary sources, see C. E. Hill, *Regnum Caelorum.*

60. Augustine, *On Catechizing the Uninitiated* 22. He divided history into seven ages. After the six days of God's creative work, God entered his royal session. As his image, Adam and Eve were commanded to work (i.e., ruling and subduing) and then enter God's Sabbath rest. Having forfeited this blessing, God opened up space within history for a new promise of entering his rest through a new Adam, Jesus Christ. Augustine argued that this seventh age is not a millennial era within history but the everlasting Sabbath. Thus, the sixth age ends with the resurrection of the dead and final judgment.

61. I summarize Joachim's program and the aftermath with the Spiritual Franciscans in volume 1.

truths. Finally, one transcends reason as well, surrendering to the mystical ecstasy of union with God.

Yet, what is utterly new in Joachim is that he places this ladder on its side, fusing the vertical ascent of the soul with the historical orientation of Christianity. This direct union with God, apart from any mediation, will not only be the experience of a few spiritual athletes, but the whole world will be a vast monastery. The movement from the purgation (age of the Father) to union (age of the Spirit) is a growth from childhood dependence on authority to the maturity of autonomy based on the inner light.

Joachim predicted this new age, which began with St. Francis, would reach its apex in the year 1260. Rather than look for Jesus at the end of the age, attention was drawn to a golden age under the leadership of an angelic pope and a final world emperor. However, this would not occur without the active participation of the godly. After a terrible persecution, they would triumph over a false pope and emperor. For many, the questions "Where can I find fullness?" and "Where is history going?" received a single answer in Joachite prophecy. People are not victims of cruelty, playthings of despots and death, or passive spectators to the decline of civilization and the church simply waiting for Jesus to return. Rather, they have a decisive role to play in the triumph of the saints here and now.[62]

Aquinas criticized Joachim's view of the Trinity as heretical tritheism, as the Fourth Lateran Council had in 1215, which was followed in suit by the Synod of Arles in 1263, but Dante placed the abbot in the sun heaven of his paradise along with Lombard, Aquinas, and Bonaventure. Already in the late medieval period, Bauer notes, Hermeticism was absorbed into the "millenarian prophecy inspired by Joachim of Fiore." Especially in Franciscan circles, "the alchemists enveloped their theories of matter in prophetic spiritualism."[63] Bauer adds that

> in 1317, Pope John XXII—the same pope who would later rule against Franciscan poverty—outlawed alchemy, in his decretal *Spondent quas non exhibent*. Although the alchemists launched a counteroffensive against Avicenna's and the Thomists' attacks, the philosophical debate about the efficacy of alchemy henceforth assumed distinctly theological implications about the borderline between religious orthodoxy and heterodoxy.[64]

62. Graziano, *Millennial Kingdom*, 22.
63. Bauer, *Alchemy of Conquest*, 82–84.
64. Bauer, *Alchemy of Conquest*, 81.

Alongside the Epicurean and Platonic revivals, we discover in Renaissance Florence a resurgence of Joachite prophecy in the person of Girolamo Savonarola. Though it survived and even flourished in some places through the Spiritual Franciscans, the Joachite eschatology exercised a significant impact from Christopher Columbus to Isaac Newton.

As we will see, Joachite prophecy was particularly formative in Anabaptist circles. The expectation of an age of the Spirit, leaving behind the visible church and its ministry of preaching and sacraments, fit well with spiritualist emphases. By the seventeenth century, millennialism had suffused the European imagination, in both Roman Catholic and Protestant lands, and had contributed significantly to utopian ideals of universal progress and enlightenment. Combined with Hermeticism, alchemy now becomes a historical process of transmuting base metals into gold. Roger Garaudy observes that of "the first revolutionary movements in Europe, all were more or less imbued with the ideas of Joachim of Fiore."[65] Contrary to the usual lamentations, history was not growing old; it was about to reach its apotheosis. "Here history is theophany," notes Frank Graziano, "the mood is constructive, and the actions are decisive, with human efficacy guided by divine will as the cosmic plan unfolds. God and his creation collaborate in the progression, perfection, and culmination of history; enterprise becomes eschatology."[66]

Conclusion

The march of history and the perennial tradition are metanarratives that presuppose an ideal—a golden age in the future or the past—by which historical advancement and decline are judged. These narratives often presuppose an origin and a *telos* that plot everything in between as either development or decay, an inexorable cultural evolution toward utopia or dystopia. Both presuppose a model of cultural evolution in which modern definitions and antitheses of science and magic, reason and religion, are given a normative status. As Burkert points out, the study of ancient cults is "a battlefield between rationalists and mystics since the beginning of the nineteenth century."[67] Indeed, the battle between these metanarratives is bound up with modern and antimodern sensibilities.[68]

65. Garaudy, "Faith and Revolution," 66.

66. Graziano, *Millennial Kingdom*, 22.

67. Burkert, *Babylon*, 74.

68. For a fascinating exploration of antimodernism as a part of modernity itself, see S. Smith, *Modernity and Its Discontents*.

The march of history orientation strikes most of us as a straightforward explanation of the facts. Its basic outline unfolds in familiar chapters, leading from the childhood of religious dogmatism and superstition to the maturity of autonomous reason and science. Whether valorized or vilified, "modernity" is not merely a convenient periodization or description of common features but an ideological construction. The very idea of progress from authority to autonomy belongs to the history of modernity itself rather than standing outside it like a natural fact. In other words, the concept of "modernity" is a utopian script that has been written by Orphic bricoleurs, bound up with the enduring impact of a fertile dogma: the "divine self."

It is difficult for us to imagine a time when writers had to articulate and defend the thesis of Lessing's 1780 treatise, *The Education of the Human Race*, which begins with a nod to Joachim of Fiore. In fact, the Enlightenment metanarrative is projected back onto the so-called Greek Enlightenment with the triumph of science and reason from Thales to Socrates, Plato, and Aristotle. Reading through thick post-Enlightenment glasses, the modernist version views Presocratic natural philosophers as the first cry of science emancipating itself from superstition. Accordingly, the mythic and mystical outlook of pioneering scientists and their uncanny resemblance to magicians is suppressed or attributed to early childhood development that would be transcended. However, even if this metanarrative is adopted for the so-called Greek miracle, it fails to account for the fact that the rational and mystical were intertwined precisely at the beginning of every noteworthy "breakthrough" toward modernity not only in science and technology but in politics and law, economics, theology, the arts, and so forth.

My first volume sought to demonstrate the implausibility of this way of interpreting ancient Greece. In fact, the philosophical religion that emerged in the classical period represents an intense spiritualization of myths and rites related to mystery cults associated particularly with Dionysus and Orpheus. The prevailing metaphysics was pantheism or panentheism (to borrow modern terminology) and not atheism, natural supernaturalism and not naturalism. The true mystics, said Plato's Socrates, are those who practice philosophy in the right way. This includes belief in the immortal and therefore divine soul, disdain for its bodily incarceration, reincarnation through many lives, and eventual reunion with the One (*Phaedo* 64–77). It is difficult to see how this is less theological or dogmatic than other religions, yet eventually it became identified simply as reason.

It is striking, therefore, that early modern scientists saw their program not as part of some emergence from childhood religion and superstition but as a return to Greek thought. The Renaissance originates in the "rebirth" of Neoplatonic-Hermetic gnosis. On the first page of his famous *De revolutionibus orbium coe-*

lestium, Copernicus credits Pythagoreans (especially Philolaus) as architects of his cosmology. Humanists vilified scholasticism, and experimental philosophers wrote sweeping diatribes against both, although they were heavily dependent on scholastic categories and their humanist education. Especially since the Renaissance, the cultural library is always open, and people are free to check out whatever books they like, from which new interpretations and syntheses emerge.

Instead of adopting either metanarrative—the march of history (rationalism) or the anti-modern (mystical) views—my project focuses on the locative zigs and utopian zags that condition these different expressions of the divine self. There are many "Platonisms" and "Aristotelianisms" during this period, not to mention varieties of skepticism and Epicureanism. Or, better put, there are many Renaissance appropriations of these ancient schools. Dmitri Levitin observes, "One need hardly delve deep into linguistic philosophy to make the obvious point that there was no such thing as 'Epicureanism' in seventeenth-century England, only attitudes to Epicurus."[69] Craftsmen of the sacred are not just curators of an unchanging truth but are bricoleurs, borrowing whatever materials are near at hand to fashion their own versions of received texts.[70] Nevertheless, the generally accepted features of axiality are strikingly evident along this course toward modernity: individualism, distancing, disembedding, criticism, and utopianism.

69. Levitin, *Ancient Wisdom*, 4.

70. Lévi-Strauss, *Savage Mind*, 24.

1

Renaissance

Visitation of the Magi and Rebirth of the Divine Self

They called him Trismegistus or thrice-greatest because he was the greatest philosopher and the greatest priest and the greatest king. . . . Among philosophers he first turned from physical and mathematical topics to contemplation of things divine, and he was the first to discuss with great wisdom the majesty of God, the order of demons and the transformations of souls. Thus, he was called the first author of theology, and Orpheus followed him, taking second place in ancient philosophy. After Aglaophemus, Pythagoras came next in theological succession, having been initiated into the rites of Orpheus, and he was followed by Philolaus, teacher of our divine Plato. In this way, from a wondrous line of six theologians emerged a single system of ancient theology, harmonious in every way, which traced its origins to Mercurius and reached its absolute perfection in the divine Plato.

—Marsilio Ficino[1]

One doubt still troubles me. I fear that under cover of the rebirth of ancient learning paganism may seek to rear its head, as even among Christians there are those who acknowledge Christ in name only, but in their hearts are Gentiles.

—Erasmus of Rotterdam[2]

1. Marsilio Ficino, preface to Latin translation of *Hermetic Corpus* in Copenhaver and Schmitt, *Renaissance Philosophy*, 147. Quoted in Ebeling, *Secret History*, 62–63.

2. Erasmus, "To Wolfgang Capito," in Huizinga, *Erasmus*, 220–21.

Covering the walls of the Magi Chapel in the Palazzo Medici Riccardi are Benozzo Gozzoli's opulent frescoes, entitled *Journey of the Magi*. The paintings celebrate the arrival of Greek dignitaries for the Council of Florence. Although the momentous meeting did not seal a lasting reunion of the churches of the East and West, it did spark the Renaissance. Along with the two emperors and Medici hosts appear three churchmen-philosophers who figure prominently in this narrative: Gemistos Plethon, Nicholas of Cusa, and a young Marsilio Ficino.[3]

It was a personal as well as public coup for Cosimo de Medici to win the honor of hosting the council (1438–1445). Besides the historic opportunity it afforded for reuniting Christendom, the council filled the city with nearly a thousand Greek-speaking guests. Poggio Bracciolini (1380–1459) recalled that it seemed as if Plato and Aristotle had returned, coming to Florence "from almost outside the world itself."[4] Poggio himself had rediscovered Greek manuscripts, including Lucretius's Epicurean poem. Now, as papal secretary, he had a front-row seat. The experience must have been something like that of an orphaned adult meeting long-lost siblings raised on the family estate. Manuscripts were busily copied and translated. Besides texts attributed to Plato and Aristotle, writings from ancient schools barely known previously (such as Epicureanism, Stoicism, and skepticism) were now suddenly accessible, although for the Byzantine guests present, these texts had always been available. More than this, the Greek visitors were heir to centuries of internal and external engagement that created these diverse schools. Now, all of a sudden these manuscripts mediated to Latin speakers a half-forgotten and sometimes suppressed part of the cultural memory.[5]

These manuscripts from a lost world arrived at a time of widespread existential anxiety. In many respects, the eclectic milieu of fifteenth-century Florence was similar to that of the ancient Alexandrian culture that produced many of these writings. Through the course of the fourteenth century, the Black Death claimed half of the population in what had been one of Europe's largest and most prosperous cities. In addition to food shortages, attempted coups, and the threat of invasion, the republic's famous banks collapsed.

More importantly for late medieval people, this was also a time of spir-

3. Thomson, "Manuel Chrysoloras," 63–82. Besides Salutati and Poggio, students included Leonardo Bruni, Ambrogio Traversari, and Niccolò de Niccoli.

4. Poggio Bracciolini in Fubini, *Poggius Bracciolini*, 2:628. Quoted in Brown, *Return of Lucretius*, 8.

5. A superbly annotated list of medieval translations is found in Grafton, "Availability," 767–91. Umberto Eco invites us to "imagine what the Latin reader was able to make of Aristotle with the aid of Hermann the German's Latin translation of an Arabic text, based in turn on an attempt to fathom the Syriac version of an unknown Greek original!" (*Labyrinth*, 98).

itual insecurity. The Western Schism provoked larger questions, as Pope Benedict XVI explains:

> For nearly half a century, the Church was split into two or three obediences that excommunicated one another, so that every Catholic lived under excommunication by one pope or another, and, in the last analysis, no one could say with certainty which of the contenders had right on his side. The Church no longer offered certainty of salvation; she had become questionable in her whole objective form—the true Church, the true pledge of salvation, had to be sought outside the institution.[6]

Moreover, the reforming pope Gregory VII had condemned wicked priests and declared their ministrations null and void. Understandably, there were periodic uprisings against the "wicked priests." The Borgia and Medici popes of the late fifteenth and early sixteenth centuries led openly scandalous lives and destabilized European politics for their personal gain. "A pope like Alexander VI, by his conspicuously impious behavior, suggested to the public that even the *pontifex maximus* did not himself fear (or believe in) God, thereby leading others to doubt."[7] And since priestly corruption was so widespread, what confidence could one have in attaining eternal bliss? Nor was skepticism about revealed religion confined to upper-class families like the Pulci. A Dominican sermon in Florence's cathedral in 1305 claimed that people no longer believed either in paradise or hell, and six years earlier a Tuscan businessman denied the possibility of resurrection.[8]

As Alison Brown observes, "Another facet of this openness was Florence's religious heterodoxy, which encouraged the early outburst of hedonism and Epicureanism, as well as Catharism, in the thirteenth and fourteenth centuries."[9] Cathars ("The Pure") or Albigensians were part of a gnostic movement that mushroomed in the later Middle Ages and was brutally repressed by a series of crusades but still had its followers in the region of Florence.[10] The Petrobrusians, led by Peter of

6. Prior to becoming pope, Ratzinger, *Principles*, 196.

7. Palmer, *Reading Lucretius*, 20, 22.

8. Brown, *Return of Lucretius*, 10–11.

9. Brown, *Return of Lucretius*, 10–11.

10. Identifying evil with matter and the God of creation, Cathars rejected not only the sacraments but marriage. Their only ritual was the *consolamentum*: laying on of hands to receive the Spirit with the evidence of glossolalia. The material world could only be transcended through intense prayer. Italian Cathars were drawn from minor elites, traders and merchants, as well as artists and some popular politicians. See Lansing, *Power and Purity*, 60–78. Although Catharism-Albigensianism is associated with southern France, it came to Italy by Bogomil missionaries

Bruys, went so far as to condemn not only crosses and relics but the sacraments. They ransacked monasteries and forced marriages of the religious.

> And what was true of the thirteenth and fourteenth centuries is also true of the fifteenth. Among the heresies that Cristoforo Landino listed as alive in his day, in his 1481 Dante Commentary, was the Patarine belief that 'our bodies won't rise again,' that it is 'a mortal sin to kill any animal excepting fish, fleas and lice,' and that 'usury is not a sin if done without fraud'—suggesting perhaps some continuity between the early Catharism of merchant and banking families in Florence like the Pulci and the heretical views of the Medici poet Luigi Pulci in the fifteenth century.[11]

The story of modernity, particularly its central dogma of the divine self, is less the product of a disenchanting naturalism than the "divine madness" of natural supernaturalism. Ever surging beneath the crust of Christendom, such ecstasy erupts in novel gushers. And in Florence, it was triggered by the literature of Alexandrian gnosis itself as well as the apocalypticism of Savonarola and the more "atheistic" Neoepicurean reaction. Although far from comprehensive, these three streams reshaped the European landscape for centuries to come.

In the Renaissance, the West returned to ancient sources of the divine self. Through the study of Plato and other Orphic manuscripts, figures like Marsilio Ficino and Giovanni Pico della Mirandola (hereafter Pico) revived Roman Alexandria. But, as Bard Thompson observes, they also transformed the sacred self: "Seeking to reconcile Christianity with their own versions of the perennial philosophy, these thinkers focused especially on a new vision of human divinity: man as a history-bending magus who, through magic, can recreate both himself and the world."[12]

---

where gnostic communities were given sanctuary. Massacres in France led many to seek safety in northern Italy, but the Inquisition came to these independent republics in the late fourteenth century. See Stephens, "Heresy," 25–60, and Stoyanov, *Other God*, 188–259.

11. Brown, *Return of Lucretius*, 10–11. Pulci "was deprived of a Christian burial *ob scripta prophana prophano in loco*, that is, for decrying miracles and describing the soul as 'no more than a pine nut in hot white bread'" (12). See Pulci, *Morgante*.

12. Thompson, *Humanists and Reformers*, 13.

Plethon's Spark

We think of the Renaissance as a Platonic revival, and it was, but we have seen that Plato had been a welcome guest all along.[13] Even the Aristotelianism of Arab philosophy that influenced scholastics like Aquinas was considerably Neoplatonized. What distinguishes the Renaissance from medieval appropriations of Arabic Aristotelianism and Platonism is the profusion of primary texts, translations, and interpreters. At the headwaters of this Platonic revival stands Georgios Gemistos (1355/60–1452/54).[14] After his Florentine auditors dubbed him a second Plato, he adopted the name Plethon.

To prominent Greek delegates such as George of Trebizond and Gennadius Scholarios, it was a mystery that their emperor had invited Plethon in the first place.[15] Critical of Plato, they preferred Aristotle and, sympathetic to Latin theo-

13. In fact, a commentary on the Dionysian corpus was *de rigueur* for mature theologians. Christian Platonism infused the Middle Ages, from Franciscans such as Bonaventure to Dominicans such as Albert the Great (who was more than a dabbler in magic). Ambrose and Augustine drew liberally, though not uncritically, from "the Platonist books," mainly Plotinus as translated in summary form by Marius Victorinus. Since Boethius, Aristotle had been reconciled with his master, and the Arab philosophers who mediated Aristotelianism to medieval scholasticism were essentially Neoplatonists attached to the hoary lineage of Hermes Trismegistus. See Kristeller, *Renaissance Thought*, 35, 44. The ninth-century Carolingian renaissance, propelled by John Scotus Eriugena, and the School of Chartres in the eleventh and twelfth centuries, centered on Plato and a distinctively Eriugenist reading of Pseudo-Dionysius. Aquinas, a pupil of Albert's, was influenced by the Christian Neoplatonism of Augustine as well as the Neoplatonized Aristotelianism of Arab philosophers. Having assisted Albert in his Dionysius commentaries, Aquinas contributed his own. Besides these influences, there was the more pantheistic trajectory of Rhineland mysticism leading from Eriugena to Eckhart.

14. I trace his fascinating heritage in chapter 11 of volume 1 of this series. The most helpful monographs I have found are the following: Woodhouse, *Gemistos Plethon*; Sinossoglou, *Radical Platonism*; Hladký, *Philosophy of Gemistos Plethon*. Hladký over-Christianizes Plethon while Sinossoglou overrationalizes him. Nevertheless, both are the fruit of considerable research and are well worth reading together.

15. Perhaps even more puzzling than the invitation was why Plethon would be interested in a conference focused on the procession of the Spirit in the Trinity. It may be that the full designs of his program were not yet known or even developed. The most persuasive argument I have found is that his repaganizing program back home could get off the ground in a crumbling Byzantine empire much better than in a scholastic Latin world headed by the Roman pontiff. See Sinossoglou, *Radical Platonism*, 119. Opposition to reunion does not distinguish Plethon: after brutal invasions and occupations by the West, many Greek Christians were disposed more favorably toward the comparatively gentle yoke of the Ottomans. Yet, Darien C. DeBolt argues convincingly that Plethon knew his revival was more likely to flourish in the Christian East, particularly in its weakened condition, than in the scholastic West with a powerful pope. Thus,

logians Aquinas and Scotus, they favored reunion. In sharp contrast, Plethon proposed a Platonic religion around Zoroaster, the Persian magi, and the Chaldean Oracles. At the same time, he envisioned something new: a *magus* capable of bringing utopia into this world through reason. Sinossoglou sees Plethon's "epistemic optimism" as the main engine of his utopian neo-paganism.[16]

Plethon appears to have lost interest in the council's lengthy discussions of the Trinity. "By that time Plethon . . . had found new company: the Florentine intellectuals. As an eyewitness, a horrified Trebizond quoted Plethon as claiming that the rise of a new religion no different from paganism was only a question of time." But rather than openly clash with his delegation, Plethon turned to his commentary on the Chaldean Oracles as a way of quietly advancing his cause. During this time he also composed his polemical work, *On the Differences of Aristotle from Plato* (1439), which provoked a *Defense of Aristotle* from Scholarios.[17] According to the standard account, Plethon inspired Cosimo to found the Platonic Academy.[18]

Returning to the Peloponnese, Plethon had scarcely unpacked his bags before he criticized the dogma of the Trinity and composed the *Nomoi* (Laws): his blueprint for a revived paganism based on the teachings of Plato, the Zoroastrian magi, Orphic literature, along with Stoic and Islamic fatalism.[19] The chapter on fate (*De fato*), rejecting the belief in God's freedom in *ex nihilo* creation, circulated widely.[20] He also produced an edition of the Orphic Hymns.[21] Emphasizing religious disagreement, his *Nomoi* advances religious skepticism in the interest of Platonic rationalism.[22] As in Plato's *Republic*, the totalitarian state envisioned in his *Nomoi* would hold all property in common. With Mistra as the capital, Platonism would be the official religion, with appropriate philosophical rites, emperor-worship, and an astrology-based liturgical calendar. Enemies—especially Christians and homosexuals—would be executed.[23] He also wrote *Recapitulation of Zoroastrian and*

---

it seems, he defended Greek Orthodoxy in the interest of heterodoxy and staunchly opposed any union. DeBolt, "George Gemistos Plethon."

16. Sinossoglou, *Radical Platonism*, chapters 4, 7, and 9.

17. Hladký, *Philosophy of Gemistos Plethon*, 41; cf. 190, 235–38.

18. This account is challenged to some extent by Hanegraaff, *Esotericism and the Academy*, 41. See also Hankins, "Cosimo de' Medici," 144.

19. Hanegraaff, *Esotericism and the Academy*, 38.

20. Sinossoglou, *Radical Platonism*, 146.

21. Hladký, *Philosophy of Gemistos Plethon*, 43.

22. See especially Plethon's *Laws* 22.4 through 24.6 (I, 1), as summarized by Hladký, *Philosophy of Gemistos Plethon*, 52–53.

23. Hladký argues that neither Plato nor Plethon intended their ideal state to be anything more than "a kind of fiction about the perfect government which, nonetheless, cannot be realized in practice" (*Philosophy of Gemistos Plethon*, 278). I took this view of Plato's *Republic* (and

Platonic Doctrines.[24] Plethon does not try to insert Christianity into the perennial tradition but simply ignores it as a corruption of Platonic truth.[25]

Like Socrates's ideal republic, Plethon's neo-pagan monastery never materialized. He died in Mistra in 1452 just before the fall of Constantinople, but his fame endured, particularly through his star pupil Bessarion who remained in Italy to defend his master's reputation and ideas, including astrology and Pythagorean number-mysticism.[26] Plethon's old nemesis, George of Trebizond never left Italy. Teaching in Rome, where he served as papal secretary to Nicholas V, he wrote *Comparisons of Plato and Aristotle* in which he attacked Plethon at length, provoking Bessarion's lengthy response.[27]

Bessarion's gift of 482 Greek manuscripts formed the nucleus of the famous San Marco Convent library in Florence. Seeing more favorable fortunes for a Plato renaissance in the West, he reversed his position on reunion of the churches and was made a cardinal in 1434, even being considered twice for the papacy.[28] Bessarion defended Nicholas of Cusa from charges of heresy and formed a small circle of students that included Ficino and Pico.[29] Without Bessarion it is unlikely that Plethon's spark would have turned into a flame.

Ficino's Flame: The Egyptian Moses and the Perennial Philosophy

The son of Cosimo's physician, Marsilio Ficino was six years old when Plethon arrived, but Bessarion took him under his wing. In 1456 Ficino tried to accommodate Platonism to Lucretius's guide to happiness.[30] After all, Plethon's enthusiastic reception in Florence was encouraged by his modern way of merging an Epicurean goal of life (viz., happiness) with a Platonic means of attaining it. But by the next

---

therefore his *Laws*) in volume 1. Whether it applies to Plethon remains an open question in view of the slender evidence Hladký offers.

24. Sinossoglou, *Radical Platonism*, 5.

25. Hladký, *Philosophy of Gemistos Plethon*, 273.

26. Woodhouse, *Gemistos Plethon*, 33.

27. Bessarion, *Bessarionis in calumniatorem Platonis Libri IV.* For an English translation, see Monfasani, *Liber Defensionum*. Monfasani has also provided an English edition of George of Trebizond's *Vindicatio Aristotelis* (Monfasani, *Vindicatio Aristotelis*).

28. Woodhouse, *Gemistos Plethon*, 32–33.

29. Hladký, *Philosophy of Gemistos Plethon*, 213–14.

30. Epicurus flourished between 341 and 270 BCE and Lucretius between the mid-nineties and mid-fifties BCE.

year, Ficino began to write to friends about his suspicions concerning Lucretius.[31] How can the body be freed from pain? Either it is through Lucretius's therapy of accepting mortality or the Platonic hope of the soul's immortality. At this point, the turn is sharp.[32] Ficino rued his youthful enthusiasm for Lucretius and turned his face devoutly toward Plato, burning his *commentariola* ("little commentaries") on the poem, in a severe version of Plato's devaluation of everything bodily.[33]

In 1462 Cosimo gave Ficino Plato manuscripts to translate and gave him the house at Careggi for his Platonic Academy. Marsilio celebrated the event by singing an Orphic hymn to the Cosmos.[34] Cosimo was elated when a monk returned with a copy of seventeen philosophical treatises known as the Corpus Hermeticum. Ficino had already been translating Plato's corpus into Latin throughout the 1460s, but he was only too happy to obey his patron's order to drop everything for this prized acquisition. After all, Hermes Trismegistus was the fountainhead of the wisdom that Plato inherited.

After the five-year reign of Piero, Cosimo's grandson Lorenzo the Magnificent became the father of the republic and patron of the Renaissance. Lorenzo seems to have been weighing Epicurean and Platonic philosophies, discussing the true goal of happiness with Ficino at Careggi. Following up in a letter, Ficino turns over various options—Stoic duty and "Epicurean peace"—but directs Lorenzo instead to union with God as the highest aim: "So, according to Plato, true happiness is the property of the soul that, when freed from the body, contemplates the divine."[35]

With Bessarion's encouragement, Ficino became a priest in 1473. In the following year, he wrote his *Platonic Theology* and *On the Christian Religion*. From his youthful dalliance, he knew Epicureanism well and it was always the foil for his defense of the soul's immortality.[36] Ficino's efforts no doubt contributed to the decision of the Fifth Lateran Council (1512–1517) to define the immortality of

31. Brown, *Return of Lucretius*, 17.

32. Brown, *Return of Lucretius*, 18–19.

33. Such thoughts he wrote down in his lost *commentariola in Lucretium*, "which must have been written at this time, 'when still a boy,' before he 'consigned it to the flames' when more mature" (Brown, *Return of Lucretius*, 20). Elena Nicoli argues that Ficino did not literally burn his notes on Lucretius's poem, but that it was a trope from Plato who wanted to burn all copies of Democritus's works (according to Diogenes Laertius). See Nicoli, "Ficino," 330–61.

34. "Cosimo de' Medici to Marsilio Ficino," in Ficino, *Meditations*, 122. Here the ruler of the republic eagerly asks for Ficino to come to his Careggi estate—"and bring your Orphic lyre." He tells Ficino he wants to find the path to true happiness. Thereafter, Careggi was the center of Ficino's life and labors. See Kristeller, "Marsilio Ficino," esp. 43. Cf. Klustein, *Marsilio Ficino*.

35. "Cosimo de' Medici to Marsilio Ficino," in Ficino, *Meditations*, 127.

36. Brown, *Return of Lucretius*, 23.

the soul as official dogma.[37] In 1516 Lucretius's *De rerum natura* was prohibited in Florentine schools.[38] However, Platonism and Epicureanism combined in fascinating, if inconsistent, ways throughout the sixteenth century, as both did with Stoic, Aristotelian, and Skeptic ideas.

As we see in the epitaph above, Ficino's renaissance was a revival of a hoary perennial philosophy, the original theology (*prisca theologia*) descending from Hermes Trismegistus, Zoroaster, Orpheus, and Indian sages to Pythagoras and Plato. This golden genealogy flooded the humanist imagination, as in Raphael's "School of Athens," with Zoroaster holding the celestial orb.[39] As Grafton notes, "Marsilio Ficino considered the Hermetic matter a vital element, perhaps *the* vital element, in the Platonic tradition."[40]

Theurgic Neoplatonism, exhibited in the *Chaldean Oracles* that Porphyry was the first to consider divinely inspired, saw magic and ritual as a way of freeing the soul.[41] Hanegraaff reminds us that it "focused on attainment of a salvational gnosis by which the soul could be liberated from its material entanglement and regain its unity with the divine Mind." He adds, "Allowing for the great differences between various systems, this is what the gnostic, hermetic, and theurgical currents of late antiquity all had in common; and to an extent that has not always been sufficiently recognized, this is what Platonism came to mean for its Renaissance admirers."[42] Hankins observes,

> Ficino's Platonism is broadly speaking that of late antiquity, but he has imported it into the very different world of fifteenth-century Europe. This is a world that is suffering from a religious identity crisis that will in a few years lead to the Reformation and engulf Europe in centuries of religious war. Ficino's Platonism is very much a part of that crisis, and one of his goals is to use Platonism to dramatically reshape Christianity.[43]

The Renaissance held "potential for instigating a revival of paganism in one form or another, implicitly or explicitly, within Christianity itself or perhaps even in

37. Palmer, *Reading Lucretius*, 29.

38. Febvre, *Problem of Unbelief*; Kristeller, *Renaissance Thought*, 66–81. Wootton, "Lucien Febvre," 695–730; Wootton, "New Histories," 13–53, esp. 16–17, 9, 27, 31; Davidson, "Unbelief and Atheism," 55–85, esp. 61–62.

39. Seznec, *Survival*, 56.

40. Grafton, "Availability," 783.

41. Majercik, *Chaldean Oracles*, 4–5. Porphyry rejected theurgy in his debate with his student Iamblichus, but had been moving in that direction prior to the debate and was a staunch advocate of religious oracles. Besides the recently written *Chaldean Oracles*, he sought to unite all philosophical religions (except for Christianity) in *Philosophy from Oracles*.

42. Hanegraaff, *Esotericism and the Academy*, 12.

43. Hankins, "Cosimo de' Medici," 2.

competition with it."[44] The latter was Plethon's explicit intention, repeated with fateful consequences in the case of Giordano Bruno more than a century later.[45] Ficino and Pico experienced close calls with the papal curia, but they insisted that their aim was to bring the treasures of the East to the feet of Christ.

As Ficino rhapsodized, "For this century, like a golden age," has restored all art and culture, including "our Plato," and the "ancient singing of songs to the Orphic lyre, and all this in Florence."[46] He stated that the philosophical gold was refined by Iamblichus and eventually Proclus.

> But Bessarion, the light of the Academy, swiftly applied an effective medicine for these dim and feeble eyes, so that the gold would be not only pure and shining, but malleable for the hands and harmless to the sight. This Plato foretold; he said to King Dionysius that a time would come after many generations, when the mysteries of theology would be purified by penetrating discussion, as gold is purified by fire. This time has come indeed, Bessarion! May the spirit of Plato, we, and all his followers rejoice at this exceedingly![47]

Surely Ficino was aware that Augustine had condemned Hermes Trismegistus (Latin: *Mercurius ter Maximus*), but he nevertheless enlists the bishop of Hippo to support the shocking thesis that the Egyptian Hermes was the "founder of 'theology.'"[48] He built Hermopolis and was the priest-king of Egypt when Moses was the philosopher-ruler of the Hebrews. Ficino even devoted a treatise to the fictitious sage in 1471.[49] Through Plethon's influence, reinforced by Bessarion, Ficino developed a passionate interest in Orphic mysteries as mediated by later Neoplatonists.[50] Instead of taking Plethon's line of outright neo-paganism, however, Ficino followed Lactantius in grafting the *philosophia perennis* (or *prisca theologia*, ancient theology) onto biblical history.[51] Not without some controversy, he wel-

44. Hanegraaff, *Esotericism and the Academy*, 298.

45. See the introduction in Ficino, *Platonic Theology*, 1:vii.

46. Ficino, "To Paul of Middelburg" (1492), in Ross and McLaughlin, *Renaissance Reader*, 79.

47. Ficino, "To Cardinal Bessarion: In Praise of Those Who Expound Plato," in Ficino, *Meditations*, 83.

48. Gandillac, "Neoplatonism," 158. Only a little context shows that Augustine understood "theology" to be borrowed from ancient Greek philosophy, not that it was incipient Christianity.

49. Ficino, *Mercurii Trismegistis.*

50. See Merry, "George Gemistos Plethon," 127–30.

51. Yates, *Giordano Bruno*, 117, 119, points out that "he was directly dependent on Dionysius (and Aquinas's commentary) in his *Theologia Platonica* and *De Christiana Religione*." See Aquinas, *Summa theologia*, I, q. 108, a. 5–6. Dante's *Convivio*, but especially *Paradiso* "sets out the souls of the blest on the spheres of the seven planets; places the Apostles and the Church

comed not only Orphic theology but also theurgic rites attributed to Orpheus, Hermes Trismegistus, and Zoroaster.[52]

Orphic philosophy easily assimilates particular religions, allegorizing their scriptures as myths that point to its own higher truths of reason.[53] Moses could be understood as a Hebrew Hermes and Plato's philosopher-king. The early Jewish historian Eupolemus calls Moses "the first wise man," and Artapanus "calls him the master of Orpheus" who "gave the Egyptians their hieroglyphs" and because of his skill they styled him "Hermes."[54] Philo's reconciliation of Plato with "the Mosaic philosophy" was approved by gentile philosophers, such as the second-century Pythagorean Numenius of Apamea. After all, he said, "What is Plato but a Greek-speaking Moses?" (fr. 8.13). Both were philosopher-rulers, givers of laws as well as of secrets. Similarly, Christian apologists in the second and third centuries—such as Tatian and the Alexandrian theologians Clement and Origen—argued that the Greeks had stolen the best wisdom of the "barbarians," including Moses and the Hebrew prophets.[55]

Rather than the prophet of strict monotheism, Moses becomes the pupil of Egyptian wisdom and magic.[56] What I am calling "natural supernaturalism," Assmann designates "cosmotheism." He says, "The Renaissance rediscovery of the worldview of antique cosmotheism, along with classical texts and works of art, already had all the impact of a return of the repressed. The figure of Moses the Egyptian stands for this return."[57] And, following Lactantius, Ficino adopts Hermes Trismegistus as a gentile prophet of Christ.[58]

After 1469, Ficino added Zoroaster the Iranian priest to the genealogy, making him the author of the Chaldean Oracles and fountainhead of the magi who visited

---

Triumphant in the eighth sphere; in the ninth sphere ranges the nine angelic hierarchies; and crowns all with the Trinity in the Empyrean. Ficino was a great student of Dante, and was certainly thinking of the *Paradiso* in the passage on the hierarchies analysed above for he makes a reference to Dante's poem in it."

52. Yates, *Giordano Bruno*, 119.

53. Hanegraaff, *Esotericism and the Academy*, 18.

54. Hanegraaff, *Esotericism and the Academy*, 18–19.

55. Hanegraaff, *Esotericism and the Academy*, 26.

56. See Assmann, *Moses the Egyptian*.

57. Assmann, *Price of Monotheism*, 43.

58. Another way of grafting biblical figures onto the perennial tree, as found in a twelfth-century alchemical text, was to give precedence to Hermes Trismegistus as the grandson not of the Greek god Hermes but of Enoch, the son of Noah, the first Hermes. See Schmidt-Biggemann, *Philosophia Perennis*, 85. In this way, the Egyptian Hermes could be the fountainhead rather than Moses, yet still be received as a biblical prophet. To the thirteenth-century Oxford scientist, philosopher, and theologian Roger Bacon, the Egyptian Hermes was the "Father of Philosophy."

the infant Jesus.[59] Like Plethon, he made Zoroaster the equal of Plato himself. Anticipating nineteenth-century comparative religion, Ficino suggests that "Abraham himself had already taken the Zoroastrian wisdom with him when he set out from the city of Ur of the Chaldaeans in quest of the promised land."[60] According to Schmidt-Biggemann, it was precisely this synthesis that the Corpus Hermeticum had already achieved in Alexandrian antiquity. The visitation of the magi to Jesus, following a star to Bethlehem, was an obvious testimony to the fusion of Christianity and paganism in the imagination of Medici Florence.

Consequently, for Ficino theology encompasses all wisdom. Plato is "the father of philosophers. . . . And that is why he has been considered indisputably divine and his teaching called 'theology' among all peoples."[61] Thus, by "theology" Ficino means the perennial tradition or *prisca theologia.* Like all intelligible realities themselves, general and special revelation differ only in degree. Pythagoras, Philolaus, and especially Plato "were thus elaborating what we can call *revealed philosophies*."[62] He let go of the division drawn by Aquinas between natural and revealed theology. Ficino believed that the mysteries of Christianity, foreshadowed by the Hebrew prophets, found confirmation in the perennial wisdom of gentile sages. He invokes this tradition as testifying to both the true Son of God and the Spirit, but assimilation flowed in the other direction as well. As Yates observes, he treats Ormuzd, Mithras, and Ahriman "to be the expression among the Magi of Persia of the truth pervading all religions that God is a Trinity," apparently unaware that "Ahriman is the evil principle in the uncompromisingly dualist Zoroastrian system."[63]

Pico also adopted the concept of philosophy as "participation in divine wisdom" from Moses to Orpheus and the Egyptian Hermes to Indian philosophers and Greeks, including Pythagoras, Plato, and the Neoplatonists.[64] In fact, as we will see, Pico is more likely Ficino's teacher than a pupil. Both are convinced that Hermetic Neoplatonism and kabbalah prove the doctrine. It is by reading the Gospel of John and Dionysius, says Ficino, that the Neoplatonists discovered the Trinity.[65]

59. Schmidt-Biggemann, *Philosophia Perennis*, 85.

60. Hanegraaff, *Esoterism and the Academy*, 45–46.

61. Ficino, *Platonic Theology*, 1:9.

62. Hankins, "Marsilio Ficino."

63. Yates, *Giordano Bruno*, 128–29.

64. Schmidt-Biggemann, *Philosophia Perennis*, 35–36.

65. Ficino, *Dionysius*, xvii. Ficino accepted the common belief that Dionysius was St. Paul's convert in Acts 17.

Christianity and Philosophical Religion

Even when defending specifically Christian doctrines, as in *On the Christian Religion*, Ficino tends to assimilate them to Neoplatonism. "The historical forms of religion—paganism, Brahmanism, Zoroastrianism, Hermetism, Orphism and Judaism—as well as more recent phenomena like Christianity and Islam, all capture that revelation in different degrees."[66] Like the natural sun, the One sheds its light in a multiplicity of rays, but the reality is always a unity above historical and bodily diversity. It did not really matter whether Zoroaster or Moses came first, since both were inspired directly by God and taught the same doctrines.

Significantly, by the time Ficino wrote the introduction to his Plotinus translation, Moses had dropped out completely. Gandillac notes that "he presents a genealogy that does not introduce any biblical authority."[67] Philosophy is not itself a religion but a spiritual path of contemplation and union with the divine self within. As the body is to the soul, so the historical is to the allegorical, and religion is to spirituality. This idea grounds what Carlos Fraenkel describes as "philosophical religions."[68] The content of this perennial wisdom was Orphic metaphysics, which was considered synonymous with cosmic Reason (i.e., God).

Ficino explicitly upholds distinctively Christian doctrines, yet they seem to play no constitutive role in his thinking, and one wonders at many points how his speculations can be consistent with Christianity. Hankins explains, "In the case of Judaism and Christianity, a narrative can be told about [God's] interactions with the human race and with individual lives." However, Platonists see such stories as mythological representations of eternal truths that philosophers recognize as such.[69] Hankins adds, "The unphilosophical require religious law and fear of punishment to regulate their behavior. They require myth, cult, liturgy and rituals of various kinds to communicate to their limited understandings something of the divine nature. The philosophical on the other hand have a rational understanding of divinity and do not require laws, customs and rituals to regulate their behavior

66. Hankins, "Marsilio Ficino," 102–3. "Contact with the divine empowered weak human souls to pass beyond their normal sphere, remit their presence in the body and gain a glimpse of the utterly real, the *ontôs ôn*, in Plato's phrase. . . . They descend from a number of sources mostly independent of Judaism: Zoroaster, Hermes Trismegistus and Orpheus principally, each representing one of the three continents known to the premodern world."

67. Gandillac, "Neoplatonism," 158. Gandillac points out that this chain from Hermes Trismegistus and from there to Orpheus, Pythagoras, and "our divine Plato" is "following a tradition coming doubtless from Syrianus."

68. Fraenkel, *Philosophical Religion*; cf. Hankins, "Marsilio Ficino," 121–22.

69. Hankins, "Marsilio Ficino," 106.

and guide their understanding."[70] Yet this is where they often come into conflict with the public religion—in this case, the church. "The wisest course is to conform outwardly to the beliefs of the multitude, but philosophy allows one to remain free inwardly. *Intus ut libet, foris ut mos est*," that is, "In private think what you wish, in public behave as is the custom." Aspiring philosophers would eventually discover, through *askēsis* and contemplation, a divine nature very different from that of traditional religion. They would discover that God was a metaphysical principle, eternal and unchanging, who functions as an integral and animating part of the natural order.[71]

Bearing the same title as Proclus's major work, Ficino's *Platonic Theology* is more of an "open-ended dialogue" than a systematic theology.[72] Ficino saw himself as something like an Orpheus *redivivus*, delivering the perennial wisdom to the philosopher-king of his own age. Priority is given in his work to natural revelation, because the reason that suffuses nature indwells the inmost self. His view of miracles as a "violent or coercive proof" underscores his natural supernaturalism. The picture of divinity surging throughout the cosmos takes precedence over that of a personal God who is distinguished qualitatively from creation.

Correspondence of All Things with Soul in the Middle

As in Plato, Ficino emphasizes the importance of soul being in the middle between the intelligible and sensory worlds.[73] No Renaissance figure exhibits better the notion of the divine self as *magus*, uniting heaven and earth through mar-

70. Hankins, "Marsilio Ficino," 104–5.

71. Hankins, "Marsilio Ficino," 104–5.

72. Ficino, *Platonic Theology*, 1:11. He was working on this magnum opus between 1469 and 1474, the same year he finished *De religione christiana* and after he had translated Plato's corpus, Iamblichus, and the Corpus Hermeticum. Though dependent on Aquinas at certain (usually unacknowledged) points, and with its own "grand architecture," the *Platonic Theology* is more like an open-ended Platonic dialogue. See the introduction in Ficino, *Platonic Theology*, 1:xiii. Ficino also wrote a commentary on the Pseudo-Dionysian corpus. Interestingly, after praising Dionysius as the greatest of the Platonic theologians, he adds that the Platonists actually followed him (Ficino, *Dionysius*, 1:3). Lorenzo Valla (1407–1457) had raised some questions about its authorship. Luther and Calvin denied that Paul's Areopagite convert was the author but so did Catholic humanists like Erasmus, Beatus Rhenanus, and Cajetan. See the introduction in Ficino, *Dionysius*, xi.

73. Ficino, *Platonic Theology*, 1:231–47. It is expounded also by Plotinus in *Enneads* 5.2.1. On this idea, see Schmidt-Biggemann, *Philosophia Perennis*, 86–87; cf. Celenza, "Revival," 88.

velous natural operations.[74] Ficino tries unsuccessfully to reconcile the Platonic idea of the One as necessarily emanating the world and the Christian belief in creation.[75]

Like the ancient shaman, the *magus* is the one who knows how to bring the power of the heavens down to the natural world.[76] Ficino's astrological explanation may seem remote, but when he discusses the way in which black bile *makes* people intelligent, he takes the theory of correspondences to new heights. If you want to feed your brain, he advises, eat more animal brains; if you desire a healthier liver, eat more animal liver, and so on.[77] We are reminded of Pythagoras's prohibition against eating fava beans, since their shape and texture resemble a human fetus and could be vessels carrying a human soul, thus representing a form of cannibalism. In the Orphic imagination, things in nature are not simply *like* but *are* their celestial archetype. Rather than analogy, the relation of things below and above is identity, with soul in the middle.

Given such identity between things above and below, Ficino never contemplates one aspect of reality in isolation from the whole. He glides effortlessly between astrology, alchemy, medicine, music, psychology, and theology because these are simply different facets of a single world full of correspondences. Matter is completely inert in Ficino's thinking; all motion in the cosmos is an interaction of souls.[78] He explains to fellow priest Sebastiano Foresi that eminent souls love music because its harmony stimulates the part of the brain that controls judg-

74. Ficino, *Platonic Theology*, 1:29–53.

75. On the one hand, God transcends being itself (Ficino, *Platonic Theology*, 1:19). God alone is necessary, preserving all things (1:133–37). Mind and matter have existed eternally but not independently of God (1:139). "We find the same view expressed time and again in Mercury Trismegistus," namely, that God disposes all things "by His free will" (1:179). God's ideas "are *not* forms by which as by some natural necessity He would be led to act, *as a fire to burn*" (1:165, emphasis added). On the other hand, "Whatever God does He does through His own being . . . *Is it through choice* rather than through being that the Sun gives light to the world, *that fire heats*, that the soul nourishes the body?" (1:145, emphasis added). Thus, he even contradicts the analogy of a fire. "Hence the Orphic saying: 'Jupiter, form of all.' . . . Similarly, in pure act, which is God, exist all the forms distinctly and actually," though without differentiation in God (1:163). All things that God wills to exist, "to the extent that they are in God, *are God Himself*; and to the extent that they emanate from God, are images of the divine countenance" (1:187, emphasis added). Allen and Warden point out that although Ficino knows his Aquinas well, he reverts to a thoroughly Platonic conception. His Pseudo-Dionysius is closer to Eriugena's (Ficino, *Platonic Theology*, 1:x–xv).

76. Ficino, *Three Books*, 377 (3.24).

77. Ficino, *Three Books*, 247–49 (3.1).

78. Ficino, *Platonic Theology*, 1:23.

ment, which is then "wonderfully moved by the universal harmony."[79] The same harmony in the microcosm is evident in the macrocosm, which is why astrology is a crucial aspect of Ficino's wing-mending therapy.[80] Echoing Plato, Ficino views humanity as needing gnosis—not external salvation from sin as much as internal correspondence between individual soul and the World Soul: "Not atonement, but attunement," as Noel Cobb describes it. "Know thyself, becomes: 'know the stars!' Astrology as a way of living one's life in accord with the heavens." According to Cobb, from this perspective every phenomenon—"pomegranate, grape, starfish, python, raincloud, rose, emerald, Oaktree, waterfall, zebra, orchid, earthquake, etc., has an archetypal home: Saturn, Mars, Jupiter, Mercury, Sol or Luna."[81]

> [Ficino sees] the Zodiac as a theatre of soul, a Memory Theatre-in-the-Round, an alchemical vessel for the planetary workings of the imagination and a container for the sufferings of psyche—psychological not just in the introverted, introspective sense. Psyche, as World Soul, according to Ficino, and following Plato, is scattered throughout everything; everything manifests soul's interiority and depth . . . The Gods are embodied, astronomically, in the planets, but psychologically in the myths and in the phenomenological texture of the sensible world. Ficino's psychology is one which would imagine the divinity within each thing, the God in each event. . . . We are in psyche, not psyche in us, as C. G. Jung so often pointed out.[82]

Reflecting the more world-affirming texts within the Corpus Hermeticum, Ficino understands the *magus* as the unifier of heaven and earth: the psychologist-priest-physician-astrologist-musician. Yet, as with his ancient predecessors, such unifying activity presupposes a deep ontological wound that must be healed. To some extent, what Yates calls "optimistic Gnostics" depend on the outlook of "pessimistic Gnostics," and that is what we find in Ficino. Viewing himself as a physician-priest, an aged Marsilio wrote *Three Books on Life* (*De vita libri tres*, 1480–1489). After the success of this work, with thirty editions in other languages by 1647, the legitimacy of natural magic was established. However, his advocacy of astrology and alchemy in this work brought him before Pope Innocent VIII on the charge of heresy, though he was acquitted. The revival of Ficino's Plato, in the noble train of hoary predecessors, was religious and theurgic, not merely theoret-

79. Ficino to Sebastiono Foresi in Ficino, *Meditations*, 59–60.
80. Cobb, foreword to Moore, *Planets Within*, ii.
81. Cobb, foreword to Moore, *Planets Within*, ii–iii.
82. Cobb, foreword to Moore, *Planets Within*, ii–iii.

ical.[83] For example, one chapter of *Three Books on Life* is entitled "Astronomical Care to Be Taken in Procreating Children, in Preparing Meals, in Buildings, and in One's Dwelling-Place and Clothing; and How Much It Is Permissible to Care about Such Things."[84]

Book 3 of *Three Books on Life* goes to the heart of Ficino's theurgy. Since everything in the visible world has a sympathetic correspondence to each god embodied in the Zodiac, healing requires precisely the right ritual, at the right time, wearing the right clothes and amulets, singing the right song.[85] It also requires taking the right pill, compounded from the right myrobalans or plants. "The first pills can be called golden or magical, composed partly in imitation of the Magi, and partly through my own invention under the influence of Jupiter and Venus; they draw out phlegm, choler, and black bile without difficulty, strengthen the individual bodily parts, and sharpen and illumine the spirits." Essentially, these pills are anti-depressants and improve memory function.[86]

One might wonder why Ficino would concentrate on physical healing and extending life while insisting that true happiness is found only when the soul is finally separated from the body. Didn't Socrates tell his friends the judges were doing him the greatest favor by sentencing him to death? However, Ficino is closer at this point to the Stoicized Platonism of the Corpus Hermeticum. Since everything is related as part of a single divine body, Stoics emphasized the theory of sympathetic correspondences. The major difference between Platonists and Stoics is whether all that is real is corporeal or incorporeal. On that question, Ficino is definitely a Platonist—at certain points he is even radical in his ontological idealism. Nevertheless, as the soul is in the middle, so too is the *magus*, who brings down the celestial gifts from their fate-ruled sphere to the realm that is overseen by nature.

Is God involved? Given his anti-Epicurean polemic, one would assume so. Yet, Ficino's natural supernaturalism resists traditional theology. God's providence guides the whole, not the parts, and providence is limited to the realm of intellect rather than the fate-ruled celestial and natural realms. Hence, he insists on calling his work "natural magic."[87] It is not cavorting with the devil but discerning the

83. Gandillac, "Neoplatonism," 164.

84. Ficino, *Three Books*, 381–83 (3.25).

85. Ficino, *Three Books*, 387–89 (3.25.35–100), but throughout the third book.

86. Ficino, *Three Books*, 149 (1.5–20).

87. Copenhaver, "How to Do Magic," 140. Copenhaver adds, "At the level of *physics*, the concept governing this medicine is physical temperament, the mixture—balanced or unbalanced—of material elements (fire, air, water, earth) and their qualities (hot, cold, wet, dry), the basic components of all earthly things, including human bodies. . . . At the level of *physiology*, the same principle of balance governs the primary fluids that the body needs to live, eat, grow,

secrets of divinity embedded in nature itself: natural supernaturalism. There is still room for God's general providence as well as human freedom in the physical sphere. Whatever problems and inconsistencies in his formulations, this outlook raises the role of the *magus*-healer. Paradoxically, Ficino spreads the message of mending wings to take flight from the body while, at the same time, exhibiting an Epicurean preoccupation with repairing the body through celestial powers.

It is the *spiritus* in the blood that mediates between corporeal and incorporeal realms. Ficino explains, "The body is indeed healed by the remedies of medicine; but spirit [*spiritus*], which is the airy vapor of our blood and the link between body and soul, is tempered and nourished by airy smells, by sounds, and by song. Finally, the soul, as it is divine, is purified by the divine mysteries of theology. In nature, a union is made from soul, body, and spirit. To the Egyptian priests, medicine, music, and the mysteries were one and the same study. Would that we could master this natural and Egyptian art as successfully as we tenaciously and wholeheartedly apply ourselves to it!"[88]

Blood, stars, music, gems, plants, colors, smells, tastes: all combine in a unified theory of natural magic. Addressing "literary people," Ficino explains,

> Every one of you, therefore, is almost wholly spirit—"spiritual" man, I say, disguised in this little earthly body, wearying his spirit with constant labor more than others do, so that more than theirs his spirit must be constantly renewed. . . . By somehow having started first with Apollo, we immediately fall into mention of Bacchus [Dionysus]. And justly indeed from light we proceed to heat, from ambrosia to nectar, from intuition of truth to ardent love of truth.[89]

The principal enemies of scholars are phlegm, black bile, sexual intercourse, gluttony and sleeping in the morning. All of this he explains in detail and, if one accepts the premises, the conclusions follow quite logically.[90] Elaborate and (to us) absurd concoctions are prescribed as remedies.[91]

---

reproduce, and stay healthy. These four *humors* are products of ingested food, but they also enable the body to take nourishment from what it eats and drinks . . . The *blood* in the veins is mainly humoral blood, but it is mixed with the three other humors: *phlegm*, a secretion coming mainly from the brain, like mucus in color and consistency; *yellow bile*, made by the liver and found in the gall bladder; and *black bile*, whose organ is the spleen."

88. Ficino, *Meditations*, 64.

89. Ficino, *Three Books*, 379 (3.24).

90. Ficino, *Three Books*, 129 (1.9).

91. Ficino, *Three Books*, 155–61 (1.23–26).

According to Ficino, astrology, music, and medicine are all part of a single therapy for improving life. "You ask, Canigiani, why I so often combine the study of medicine with that of music. What, you say, has the trade of pharmacy to do with the lyre?" Ficino answers:

> Astrologers might relate these two, Canigiani, to a conjunction of Jupiter with Mercury and Venus. They consider that medicine comes from Jupiter and music from Mercury and Venus. Followers of Plato, on the other hand, ascribe them both to one god, Apollo, whom the ancient theologians thought was the inventor of medicine and lord of the sounding lyre. Orpheus, in his book of hymns, asserts that Apollo, by his vital rays, bestows health and life on all and drives away diseases. . . . So, since the patron of music and the discoverer of medicine are one and the same god, it is hardly surprising that both arts are often practiced by the same man.[92]

Moreover, these arts correspond to different parts of the human person:

> Plato and Aristotle taught, as we have often found from our own experience, that serious music maintains and restores this harmony to the parts of the soul, while medicine restores harmony to the parts of the body . . . not to mention the miracles of Pythagoras and Empedocles who could quickly quell lust, anger, or madness by serious music. . . . Finally, anyone who has learned from the Pythagoreans, from the Platonists, Mercurius [Trismegistus], and Aristoxenus, that the universal soul and body, as well as each living being, conform to musical proportion, or who has learnt from the sacred writings of the Hebrews that God has ordered everything according to number, weight, and measure, will not be surprised that nearly all living beings are made captive by harmony—nor will he blame Pythagoras, Empedocles, and Socrates in his old age, for playing the lyre.[93]

This remarkable intersection of music, medicine, magic, astrology and kabbalah is not occasional but instead pervasive in Ficino's writings.

What is important for modernity is Ficino's naturalizing of causes—a medicalizing of what were accounted for previously by God's providence or human misuse of free will. Already we see a secularizing of the world in the name of reenchantment. Dag Nikolaus Hasse notes that the *Platonic Theology* "presents a theory of

92. Ficino, *Meditations*, 61–63.
93. Ficino, *Meditations*, 61–63.

long-distance effects of the soul which owes much to Avicenna without naming him." Avicenna (Ibn Sina) offered a naturalistic explanation of prophecy, healings, dreams, and visions, and this view was adopted by later Renaissance thinkers such as Pietro Pomponazzi in his *On the Causes of Natural Effects* (also known as *On Incantations*; 1520).[94] The upshot of these thoughts is natural supernaturalism: a magic that is inherent in nature itself rather than a miracle intervening in nature. In other words, the fact that supernatural events may be explained in naturalistic terms does not count against his magical realism but substantiates it. On the one hand, Ficino's methods and therapies seem ludicrous. His animism is radically different from a naturalistic method. When we speak of people who are saturnalian, mercurial, or jovial, it is a figure of speech and not literally caused by the influence of a particular celestial body. On the other hand, he is naturalizing the supernatural as much as supernaturalizing nature. Transcendence can be made immanent through spiritual technology.

Images and Talismans

The third book of the *Three Books on Life* brought Ficino to the attention of the Inquisition. It was Ficino's appeal to magical talismans—that is, his attempt to change and control astral powers—that provoked the Vatican's suspicion.[95] Herodotus had pioneered the Greek view that other gods were simply different names for the Greek ones. Yet it is one thing to endorse a Hermetic cosmology and quite another to practice Hermetic theurgy. After all, to whom is one offering invocations, appealing to for protection, and for weal or for woe? The Orphic Hymns praise Zeus, Dionysus, and Phanes, not the Father, Son, and Holy Spirit. Yet we must not forget that throughout the Middle Ages relics of the saints and medallions were touched and worn to ward off evil spirits. Statues were said to weep. The question for the church was not whether images were in some sense alive with a glorified soul but whether the gods of Greece and Rome could replace Mary and the saints.[96]

94. Hasse, "Arabic Philosophy," 124.

95. Yates, *Giordano Bruno*, 62.

96. Quispel notes, "And when about 300 AD Catholics mocked certain *novi viri* (New Age Men) in Africa, because they venerated idols, they answered: 'We do not believe that bronze, golden, silver or other effigies as such are gods, and we do not attribute to them any religious meaning, but we honour and venerate beings that are in them, because owing to the consecration they were forced to dwell in handmade statues." See Quispel, "Reincarnation and Magic," 199, quoting Arnobius, *Against the Gentiles* 6.17. The earliest icons of the Eastern Orthodox

So there was not only a Hellenization of Egypt but an Egyptianization of the Greeks, whose transpositions Herodotus documented in the fifth century BCE. Again, the Asclepius attributed to Hermes Trismegistus is an example. "The icon participates in the archetype," Tat explains to the king in treatise seventeen of the Corpus Hermeticum, just as John of Damascus did in the seventh century.[97] "With these rationalisations," notes Quispel, "the Hermeticists offered a seemingly philosophical, Platonic interpretation of their magical religion. It was to have a great future."[98] And how could one condemn Hermes's magic when so much of it had already been incorporated into medieval ritual? What contempt for the heavens would one have to acknowledge life in the tiniest worm and leaf below, and deny a soul to celestial bodies![99] Ficino is convinced that the *spiritus* of the higher entities can cure the *spiritus* of the lower.[100] Moore notes, "In Ficino's theory *spiritus* is the means of magical effect between planetary daimons and the physical world or the life of the individual. The method by which this *spiritus* is conveyed from planets to the individual is described in *The Asclepius* as a matter of image-making."[101]

Here also Ficino tends to naturalize the magic. The *Asclepius* explains the "art of making gods." It is nothing less than a statue made of sympathetic materials that attract a god to descend into it during the ritual. While Ficino includes sympathetic materials, they serve merely to stimulate the imagination. It is in the imagination where the healing *magus* brings down the curative powers of the heavens. "I do not quite understand, however, how images have any force upon a distant target," he says, "but I suspect that they have some force on the wearer." This is where his notion of the imagination enters. Far from being mere fiction, imagination mediates between cosmic intellect and individual souls. "Yet the Arabs and the Egyptians ascribe so much power to statues and images fashioned by

Church are remarkably similar to Egyptian images, and as such Quispel points out the contrast between "Egyptian magical realism" and Greek representational realism (201–4).

97. Corpus Hermeticum, Treatise 17, "To Asclepius." See Quispel, "Reincarnation and Magic," 203–4.

98. Quispel, "Reincarnatiuon and Magic," 205. Quispel adds, "Until this day the Orthodox Christians of Eastern Europe do believe that the saints are really present in the icons that represent them. . . . [An icon] should be dedicated with a special religious rite by a priest and sprinkled with holy water under invocation of the Holy Spirit." Quispel continues, stating that "this was a legacy of Egypt. Just as the Hermeticist created his god, so the Orthodox Christian of Eastern Europe created his saints."

99. Ficino, *Three Books*, Apology, 399.

100. Chapter 26 of Ficino, *Three Books*, Book 3, is titled "How by Exposing Lower Things to Higher Things, You Can Bring Down the Higher, and Cosmic Gifts Especially through Cosmic Materials" (385).

101. Moore, *Planets Within*, 38–39.

astronomical and magical art that they believe the spirits of the stars are enclosed in them." Tantalizingly, he concludes, "This *could* be done, I believe, by daemons, but not so much because they have been constrained by a particular material as because they enjoy being worshipped."[102]

"Why wear an amulet signifying the speed of Mercury except to keep that quality of the soul in mind? For Ficino the gods themselves are facets of the soul requiring attention." It's "psychopoetics," says Moore, as if his words "were the products of a dream."[103] Merging Plotinus with later Neoplatonism, Ficino says that, according to Hermes Trismegistus, the magi, through their statues, captured merely cosmic deities rather than those "wholly separate from matter, . . . cosmic, I say, that is, a life or something vital from the Anima Mundi [World Soul] and the souls of the spheres and of the stars or even a motion and, as it were, a vital presence from the daemons [13.37–38 and 8.24a]."[104] According to Ficino in what may be his main *apologia*:

> Indeed, the same Hermes, whom Plotinus follows, holds that daemons of this kind—airy ones, not celestial, let alone any higher—are themselves present all along in the materials and that Hermes himself put together statues from herbs, trees, stones, and spices, which had within themselves, he says, a natural force of divinity [13.38]. He added songs resembling the heavenly bodies [as in 3.21]; he says the divinities take delight in such songs and so stay a longer time in the statues and help people or harm them. He adds that once the wise men of Egypt, who were also priests, since they were unable to persuade the people by reasoning that there were gods, that is, certain spirits superior to mankind, thought up this magical lure through which they could allure daemons into the statues and thereby show that divinities exist [13.37]. But Iamblichus condemns the Egyptians because they not only accepted daemons as steps in the search for the higher gods but frequently also worshiped them. Rather than the Egyptians he prefers the Chaldeans, who were not preoccupied with daemons—the Chaldean priests of religion.[105]

Ficino of course is treading on dangerous territory at this point. But he continues by arguing with Aquinas that "if they made speaking statues at all [8.24a, 13.37], it was not the mere influence of the stars itself that formed the words

102. Ficino, *Three Books*, 351 (3.20), emphasis added.
103. Moore, *Planets Within*, 38–39.
104. Ficino, *Three Books*, 389–91 (3.26).
105. Ficino, *Three Books*, 389–91 (3.26).

within, but daemons" (that is, demons in the Christian sense). "I say, for I suspect the astrologers, both Chaldean and Egyptian, somehow tried to draw daemons through celestial harmony into earthen statues."[106] A charitable interpretation is that Ficino, a Catholic priest, is distancing himself from Iamblichus; a more critical conclusion is that he is hiding his esoterism in the above-ground esoterism of the Catholic faith. In any case, once again his overall outlook depends on theurgic Neoplatonism at every step.[107] Under increasing scrutiny, Ficino explains further that there are two kinds of magic. "The first is practiced by those who unite themselves to daemons by a specific religious rite, and, relying on their help, often contrive portents. This, however, was thoroughly rejected when the Prince of this World was cast out. But the other kind of magic is practiced by *those who seasonably subject natural materials to natural causes to be formed in a wondrous way*."[108] These "natural materials" and "causes" in a "wondrous way" is what I'm calling natural supernaturalism.

To avoid the church's censure, Ficino had to draw a careful distinction between white and black magic. According to Yates, Ficino "again worries over what Thomas Aquinas has said in the Contra Gentiles, finally reaching a position which he imagines is near to that of Thomas, namely that the talismans have their power mainly from the materials of which they are made, not from the images." "Yet," in a departure from Aquinas, Ficino argues that "if they are made under the influence of a harmony, similar to the celestial harmony, this excites their virtue." "In short," Yates concludes, "by devious means, Ficino has extracted his use of talismans from blame."[109] Whether by deception or sincere belief, Ficino grew increasingly defensive:

> Someone therefore will say: Marsilio is a priest, isn't he? Indeed he is. What business then do priests have with medicine or, again, with astrology? Another will say: What does a Christian have to do with magic and images? And someone else, unworthy of life, will begrudge life to the heavens. Finally, all who feel this way will be quite ungrateful for my service toward them; and they will not be ashamed to be cruel in the face of my charity, with which I looked to the life and prosperity of all citizens to the best of my ability.[110]

106. Ficino, *Three Books*, 389–91 (3.26).
107. Examples of these tensions appear in Ficino, *Three Books*, 245–391 (3.23–26).
108. Ficino, *Three Books*, Apology, 399, emphasis added.
109. Yates, *Giordano Bruno*, 73.
110. Ficino, *Three Books*, 395–97.

Ficino called for assistance from his "most beloved brothers in the pursuit of truth, the three Pieros: Nero, Guicciardini, and Soderini."

> The most outstanding duty without a doubt, most necessary and especially desired by all, is to see to it that men have a sound mind in a sound body. This we can accomplish only if we join medicine with the priesthood. . . . After this, you too rise, O mighty Guicciardini, and reply to intellectual busy-bodies that Marsilio is not approving magic and images but recounting them in the course of an interpretation of Plotinus. And my writings make this quite clear, if they are read impartially. Nor do I affirm here a single word about profane magic, which depends upon the worship of daemons, but I mention natural magic, which, by natural things, seeks to obtain the services of the celestials for the prosperous health of our bodies. . . . From this worship, the Magi, the first of all, adored the newborn Christ. Why then are you so dreadfully afraid of the name Magus, a name pleasing to the Gospel, which signifies not an enchanter and a sorcerer, but a wise priest?[111]

Pico: Pioneer of Christian Kabbalism

Across his own corpus, Ficino typifies the tension between competing worldviews that he inherited from a long train of predecessors. Assmann observes that in the Middle Ages, "The opposition between cosmotheism and monotheism, or between nature and revelation, was never resolved but merely suppressed in the victorious development of the church."[112] Ficino's Pseudo-Dionysius was that of John Scotus Eriugena, but it was also influenced by his own translation of Proclus.[113] While affirming creation *ex nihilo*, his operative metaphysics is Neoplatonic emanation. He affirms the resurrection, but it plays no constitutive role in an eschatology, in which physical bodies are unreal at best and the soul's only blessedness is in being freed finally and forever from its sluggish carapace.

This tension marks at least one side of the secularizing tendency of modernity. Eriugena, Eckhart, and gnostic sects drew the attention of the magisterium to the threat of pantheism. And this is precisely what the Vatican suspected in the Christian kabbalism of Pico's *Nine-Hundred Theses*. Ficino was viewed with some suspicion, but Pico's case brought crystal clarity to how far the church would allow the incursion of theosophy. Pico was less willing than Ficino to conceal occult doc-

111. Ficino, *Three Books*, 395–97.

112. Assmann, *Moses the Egyptian*, 47.

113. The English edition of Ficino's *Commentary* on the Dionysian corpus covers two volumes.

trines, though he was more suspicious of astrology. Both figures seem sincerely to have felt that Christianity was the fuller revelation of the perennial philosophy.

Although thirty years younger than Ficino, Pico (1463–1494) was less Ficino's pupil than his instructor. In fact, a couple years prior to Ficino's books on natural magic, Pico declared, "Nothing is more effective in natural magic than the Orphic hymns. The names of the gods that Orpheus sings are not the names of deceiving demons, from whom evil and not good comes, but of *natural and divine* powers, distributing in the world by the true God for the great utility of man—if he knows how to use them."[114] Pico goes on to correlate Orphic and kabbalistic theology at key points.[115] "There is no science that gives us more certainty of Christ's divinity than magic and Cabala," Pico ventured to say.[116] It was Pico who hounded Ficino to translate Neoplatonists. However, there was some tension between them over Ficino's insistence with Plotinus (and the early church fathers) that God is above being. In contrast, Pico followed Aristotelians in denying the distinction.[117] Pico sought to reconcile Aristotle and Plato, Averroes and Avicenna, Aquinas and Scotus, not to mention pagan and Christian wisdom.[118] Touching briefly on a Jewish kabbalistic notion of sacrifice, Ficino concluded, "But we leave these things for our friend Pico to explore."[119]

He was introduced to Judaic literature in Padua from 1480 to 1482 by Elia del Medigo, a staunch Averroist who bequeathed to Pico the doctrine of panpsychism, the belief that all intellective souls share in a single divine mind.[120] In autumn of 1486, recovering in Perugia from injuries caused by an angry husband after an affair with his wife, Pico wrote Ficino, "Divine Providence . . . caused certain books to fall into my hands. They are Chaldean books . . . of Esdras, of Zoroaster and of Melchior, oracles of the magi, which contain brief and dry interpretation of Chaldean philosophy, but full of mystery."[121] With additional assistance from Rabbi Johannan Alemanno and the converted Sicilian rabbi Flavius Mithridates, Pico

114. Pico, "Thirty-One Conclusions According to My Own Opinion on Understanding the Orphic Hymns according to Magic, that is, the Secret Wisdom of Divine and Natural Things First Discovered in Them by Me," 10.2 and 10.3, in Farmer, *Syncretism*, 505. Farmer notes the priority of Pico's magical works on 115–32. Overreacting against Yates's thesis at some points, he nevertheless offers crucial correctives.

115. Pico, "Cabalistic Conclusions Confirming the Christian Religion," 11.1–72, in Farmer, *Syncretism*, 519–53.

116. Pico, *Conclusiones*, 79, quoted by Copenhaver and Schmitt, *Renaissance Philosophy*, 168.

117. Copenhaver and Schmitt, *Renaissance Philosophy*, 175.

118. Copenhaver and Schmitt, *Renaissance Philosophy*, 168.

119. Ficino, *Three Books*, 369 (3.22).

120. Pico, *Conclusiones*, 34, quoted by Copenhaver and Schmitt, *Renaissance Philosophy*, 170.

121. Pico, *Opera*, 367, quoted in Farmer, *Syncretism*, 13.

grafted Jewish gnosis onto the perennial tradition in service to Christian apologetics.[122] Though wary of astrology, Pico became a founder of Christian kabbalah.

Kabbalah means tradition and, more specifically, belief in an esoteric oral tradition of Moses's teaching distinct from the Hebrew scriptures. With roots in Alexandrian Jewish gnosis, it appears as a distinct movement with Abraham Abulafia. Born in Zaragoza, Spain, in 1240, he experienced visions of a decidedly messianic stamp. Abulafia's visions convinced him that he was the messiah, and in 1280 he came to Rome on a mission to convert Pope Nicholas III. On hearing of his approach, the pope issued the command to "burn the fanatic." Instead, however, the pope died two days later and Abulafia took up residence in Sicily and southern Italy. Here he became involved with the followers of Joachim of Fiore. In the year 1290, he declared, Jews and gentiles would be united in the age of the Spirit.[123]

It is not surprising that Pico, Ficino's prophetic Apollo, became a devoted friend and follower of Savonarola, the prophet of Florence whose purported revelations were drawn from Joachim's writings. Abulafia's prophetic kabbalah made its way to Palestine, where it was combined with Sufism, and then returned to Europe.[124] "In Venice," Johnson relates, "the Franciscan monk Francesco Giorgi (1466–1540), who had access to a wider range of Hebrew literature than the Florentines, taught a Cabalist theology which was unequivocally Christian, yet rested squarely on micro-macrocosmic principles." The rush of great humanists to kabbalah included Johannes Reuchlin (1455–1522).[125]

As in Stoic cosmology, kabbalah sees expansion and contraction as forming the cycle of creation. The Ten Sephiroth are then related to the ten spheres of the cosmos.[126] Yates points out, "A striking feature of Cabalism is the importance

122. Farmer, *Syncretism*, 13; cf. Copenhaver and Schmitt, *Renaissance Philosophy*, 171.

123. Hames, *Jacob's Ladder*.

124. Moses de León claimed it was written by the early second-century rabbi Simeon ben Yochai, but most scholars believe Moses is the author, perhaps with other writers. See Scholem, *Major Trends*, 163–65.

125. Johnson, "Neoplatonists," 157–58.

126. Eco, *Labyrinth*, 301–2: "The so-called theosophical Kabbalah, while making occasional recourse to practices of numerological reading through acrostics or anagrams, remained basically respectful of the sacred text. The Kabbalah of names, on the other hand, alters, rearranges, dismantles, and recombines the surface of the text and its syntagmatic structures, all the way down to the linguistic atoms constituted by the individual letters, in a process of continuous linguistic re-creation. If, in the theosophical Kabbalah, the text still stands between God and the interpreter, in the ecstatic Kabbalah, the interpreter stands between the text and God. The practice of reading by permutation tends to provoke ecstatic effects. . . . As Abulafia himself says: 'And begin by combining this name, namely *YHWH*, at the beginning alone, and examine all its combinations and move it and turn it about, like a wheel returning around, front and

assigned to angels or divine spirits as intermediaries throughout this system, arranged in hierarchies corresponding to the other hierarchies. . . . Creation from the point of view of God is the expression of His hidden self that gives Itself a name, the holy Name of God, the perpetual act of creation."[127] From its origins in Jewish gnosis, kabbalah had been intertwined with gnostic and Hermetic strands.[128] For example, the mid-eleventh-century Arabic Hermetic text, *Picatrix*, includes Jewish angels.[129]

By deciphering the code of Hebrew letters and numbers by which God made the world, one becomes a co-creator. There is magic in kabbalah, Eco explains, "because the letters the mystic combines are the same sounds with which God created the world . . . the symbolic cargo of language was transformed into a kind of quasi-mathematical command. Kabbalistic symbolism thus turned into—or perhaps returned to—a magical language of incantation."[130] Just as Ficino was convinced that natural magic demonstrated the truth of Christianity, Pico was convinced that kabbalah proved the miracles of Christ.[131] Kabbalism is the apex of natural philosophy, but Christ's miracles are the apex of revealed theology.[132] Among his *Nine-Hundred Theses* (1486), Pico included thirty-one on the Orphic hymns "according to magic," a kabbalistic way of predicting the end of the world.[133]

Invoking angels could hardly be suspicious in medieval piety, but here they were implored in a context of spiritual technology that savored of magic. The names of God were in effect talismans, and this arranging of Hebrew letters into incantations aroused the Holy Office to investigate and, finally, condemn Pico's

back, like a scroll, and do not let it rest. . . . Afterwards go on to the second one from it, *Adonay*, and ask of it its foundation [*yesodo*] and it will reveal to you its secret [*sodo*]. And then you will apprehend its matter in the truth of its language. Then join and combine the two of them [*YHWH* and *Adonay*], and study them and ask them, and they will reveal to you the secrets of wisdom. . . . Afterwards combine Elohim, and it will also grant you wisdom.'"

127. Yates, *Giordano Bruno*, 92–93. Abraham Abulafia was a thirteenth-century Spanish Jew "who developed a most complex technique of meditation through a system for combining Hebrew letters in endless varieties of permutations and combinations." Numerical values were assigned to each Hebrew letter. "There are, for example, seventy-two angels through whom the Sephiroth themselves can be approached, or invoked, by one who knows their names and numbers."

128. Gershom Scholem traces these roots in Scholem, *Jewish Gnosticism*.

129. Yates, *Giordano Bruno*, 108.

130. Eco, *Labyrinth*, 302.

131. Pico, "Cabalistic Conclusions Confirming the Christian Religion," 11.1–72, in Farmer, *Syncretism*, 519–53.

132. Pico, *Opera*, 171–72; see Farmer, *Syncretism*, 127.

133. Farmer, *Syncretism*, 435; cf. 129.

Theses to the flames. "It is thus a much more ambitious kind of magic than Ficino's natural magic, and one which it would be impossible to keep apart from religion," Yates observes. "For the Renaissance mind, which loved symmetrical arrangements, there was a certain parallelism between the writings of Hermes Trismegistus, the Egyptian Moses, and Cabala which was a Jewish mystical tradition supposed to have been handed down orally from Moses himself."[134]

Moses played a walk-on role in Ficino's saga of the *prisca theologia*, which was basically assimilated to Hermes Trismegistus. However, kabbalah took its bearings from the biblical philosopher-ruler Moses, albeit the secret occult version of him. Pico's magic unites heaven and earth or, as he put it, "marries the world."[135] However, as Yates notes, "natural magic, according to Pico, is but a weak thing, and no really efficacious magic can be done with it, unless cabalistic magic is added to it."[136] In his *Orations*, Pico placed this occult Moses at the head of the perennial philosophy.[137] Linked to both the idea of a perennial philosophy and to magic, kabbalah was viewed as a code for a secret "language" that went all the way back to Adam and Eve in the garden. The search for this primordial language to unite humanity in the present occupied the minds of Hermeticists all the way to Leibniz and, one might even say, the early Wittgenstein.[138]

Manifesto of Modernity

No other fifteenth-century writing is as well known as Pico's 1486 *Oration on the Dignity of Man*, which he intended as the introduction to his defense of the *Nine-Hundred Theses* before the papal court. Sometimes called the "charter of modernity" and the "manifesto of the Renaissance," the *Oration* begins with an allusion to the Asclepius:

134. Yates, *Giordano Bruno*, 84.

135. Yates, *Giordano Bruno*, 88. See above.

136. Yates, *Giordano Bruno*, 91.

137. Hanegraaff, *Esoterism and the Academy*, 59–61.

138. Eco, *Labyrinth*, 293–97. Already in Dante there is an almost modern obsession with language and the search for a universal language that will reunite humankind. Adam and Eve spoke Hebrew, Dante believed. As Eco points out here, "Dante pursues the dream of a restoration of the Edenic *forma locutionis*, which is both natural and universal. Unlike many men of the Renaissance, however, who will go in search of a Hebrew language restored to its revelatory and magical powers, Dante's goal is to recreate the original conditions with an act of modern invention." It will be a poetic language to heal the wound of Babel.

> Most esteemed Fathers, I have read in the ancient writings of the Arabians that Abdala the Saracen on being asked what, on this stage, so to say, of the world, seemed to him most evocative of wonder, replied that there was nothing to be seen more marvelous than man. And that celebrated exclamation of Hermes Trismegistus, "What a great miracle is man, Asclepius," confirms this opinion.[139]

Nevertheless, he was not satisfied with the reasons for this opinion: humans were created a little below the angels (Psalm 8) or standing midway between God and creatures as a marriage between upper and lower worlds. Though these reasons are "of great weight," he says, "they do not touch the principal reasons, those, that is to say, which justify man's unique right to such unbounded admiration. Why, I asked, should we not admire the angels themselves and the beatific choirs more?"[140] Humans rise above the angels and all intelligible beings themselves in admiration. After God created his cosmic temple, filled with spiritual beings, he populated this "dung heap of the inferior world teeming with every form of animal life."

> But when this work was done, the Divine Artificer still longed for some creature which might comprehend the meaning of so vast an achievement, which might be moved with love at its beauty and smitten with awe at its grandeur. When, consequently, all else had been completed (as both Moses and Timaeus testify), in the very last place, He bethought Himself of bringing forth man.[141]

In traditional theology, humanity was the ectype of the divine archetype. Human nature was defined by being created in God's image. But according to Pico,

> Truth was, however, that there remained no archetype according to which He might fashion a new offspring. . . . At last, the Supreme Maker decreed that this creature, to whom He could give nothing wholly his own, should have a share in the particular endowment of every other creature. Taking man, therefore, this creature of indeterminate image, He set him in the middle of the world and thus spoke to him: "We have given you, Oh Adam; no visage proper to yourself, nor any endowment properly your own, in order that whatever place, whatever form, whatever gifts you may, with premeditation, select, these same you may

139. Pico, *Oration*, 3.
140. Pico, *Oration*, 4.
141. Pico, *Oration*, 5.

> have and possess through your own judgment and decision. The nature of all other creatures is defined and restricted within laws which We have laid down; you, by contrast, impeded by no such restrictions, may, by your own free will, to whose custody We have assigned you, trace for yourself the lineaments of your own nature. I have placed you at the very center of the world, so that from that vantage point you may with greater ease glance round about you on all that the world contains. We have made you a creature neither of heaven nor of earth, neither mortal nor immortal, in order that you may, as the free and proud shaper of your nature, be granted to have what you choose, to be what you will to be!" [142]

Animals bring from their mother's womb "all they will ever possess," and even "the highest spiritual beings" have a fixed mode of being."[143] But only humans were given the choice of determining their own nature. "And if dissatisfied of your own being, fashion yourself in the form you may prefer. It will be in your power to descend to the lower, brutish forms of life; you will be able, through your own decision, to rise again to the superior orders whose life is divine."[144] Pico exults, "Oh unsurpassed generosity of God the Father, Oh wondrous and unsurpassable felicity of man, to whom if with the lot of all creatures, he should recollect himself into the center of his own unity, he will there become one spirit with God, and in the solitary darkness of the Father, Who is set above all things, himself transcend all creatures."[145] The rest of the *Oration* attempts to graft the Bible onto the perennial tradition and kabbalah, with humans identified as "divinity clothed in flesh." "Let us be driven, Oh Fathers, by those Socratic frenzies which lift us to such ecstasy that our intellects and our very selves are united to God."[146] The Dionysian and Orphic mysteries become assimilated to the secret Moses and allegorized allusions to the Bible. Pico says that "the sayings of Pythagoras are called sacred, because, and to the degree that, they derive from the Orphic teachings."[147]

Pico's descriptions of the human being remind one of the shaman who traverses all worlds and transforms himself into whatever nature he prefers. In fact, kabbalah celebrates "this nature capable of transforming itself," which for Greeks was "symbolized by the figure of Proteus."[148] And, over against demonic sorcery,

142. Pico, *Oration*, 5–8.
143. Pico, *Oration*, 8.
144. Pico, *Oration*, 8.
145. Pico, *Oration*, 8.
146. Pico, *Oration*, 26.
147. Pico, *Oration*, 66.
148. Pico, *Oration*, 9.

true magic is simply "the highest realization of natural philosophy."[149] Yet, far from representing an Epicurean license, Pico's manifesto calls for humans to choose the highest nature, union with divinity itself:

> Let us disdain the things of earth, hold as little worth even the astral orders and, putting behind us all the things of this world, hasten to that court beyond the world, closest to the most exalted Godhead. There, as the sacred mysteries tell us, the Seraphim, Cherubim and Thrones occupy the first places; but, unable to yield to them, and impatient of any second place, let us emulate their dignity and glory. And, if we will it, we shall be inferior to them in nothing.[150]

Pico repeated these sentiments in his 1489 *Heptaplus*, a commentary on Genesis 1:1–27, after being influenced further by Alemanno. Like Origen, he interprets the "waters above" and "waters below" as signifying allegorically the three worlds (terrestrial, celestial, intelligible). Humans do not fit neatly in the hierarchy but contain both worlds in themselves.[151] These ideas were already present in Nicholas of Cusa.[152]

The Spanish bishop Pero Garcia wrote a treatise against Pico, but Garcia had to face the argument of those who wondered why Pico's magical statues and amulets would be proscribed even while statues, saints' relics, and "wax lambs blessed by the pope, or the blessing of bells" could be central to official piety. After a bull condemned all of the *Nine-Hundred Theses* and forbade their publication, Pico was welcomed by Lorenzo de' Medici, whose patronage encouraged the pope to allow him to live in Florence.[153] There he came under the spell of the Dominican friar Savonarola and abandoned all magic in favor of the preacher's prophecies of the imminent end of days. It is to that episode that we turn next.

149. Pico, *Oration*, 53.

150. Pico, *Oration*, 12–13.

151. Copenhaver and Schmitt, *Renaissance Philosophy*, 174.

152. Copenhaver and Schmitt point out similarities with Nicholas of Cusa (*De conjecturis* 1.173) in *Renaissance Philosophy*, 182.

153. Yates, *Giordano Bruno*, 112.

2

Prophet of Florence

Savonarola and the Age of the Spirit

> [Joachim of Fiore is] not only the most important author of the Middle Ages, but one of the most significant theorists of history in the Western tradition.
>
> —Bernard McGinn[1]

> In the age of the Florentine Platonists and Savonarola the elements of exaltation and apprehension were strangely mixed in their outlook on the future, just as in their view of knowledge rational and mystical approaches mingled. The Platonists were swept to a high excitement by the sense that the *plenitudo temporum* had arrived, yet at the same time were assailed by anxious expectations of Antichrist.
>
> —Marjorie Reeves[2]

Pompanazzi was reviving the pagan Aristotle, Coluccio Salutati and his apprentice Machiavelli were spreading Epicurean ideas, and the imaginative paganism that thrilled popes and poets was creating what some preachers, especially Dominicans, saw as the end of Christendom. In this context, the Dominican preacher Girolamo Savonarola (1452–1498) appeared with tremendous urgency. In the writings of Savonarola, as in those of Joachim of Fiore, the two questions I posed in the introduction intersect: Where do we find fullness? And where is

1. McGinn, *Visions of the End*, 126.
2. Reeves, *Joachim of Fiore*, 82.

history going? Through the preaching of Savonarola, Ficino's age of gold is fused with Joachim's age of the Spirit.[3]

Savonarola: Joachite Prophet of Florence

As Plethon brought Plato's flame to Florence, Girolamo Savonarola seemed to channel Joachim in a setting that was fertile for apocalyptic politics. Yet from the beginning we detect a distinctly modern naturalization of the supernatural. As Ficino's magic brought the healing powers of the heavens and placed them in human control, Savonarola's Joachite prophecy contributed to an immanentizing of the eschaton.

Born in Ferrara, Savonarola wrote *On the Ruin of the World* at the age of twenty, followed three years later by *On the Ruin of the Church*. After this he joined the Dominican Order but was embroiled in successive controversies. In 1490 Lorenzo de' Medici, largely through the ministrations of Pico, intervened to call the Dominican to the esteemed San Marco Convent that had already been so richly supplied by Bessarion's personal library. Savonarola began lecturing in the very halls in which Plethon had cast his spell, but soon he attacked everything for which the Renaissance stood. In fact, the perceived doublemindedness of Florentines—half pagan and half Christian—became the irritant that formed the pearl of his Joachite program.

Echoing a trail of Christian writers as far back as Tertullian, Plethon's nemesis, George of Trebizond, called Plato "the very fountainhead of all heresies."[4] Along with Scholarios, Patriarch of Constantinople, Trebizond was aghast at the possibility that the revival of pagan Platonism in the East was poised to conquer the Latins through Plethon, the very harbinger of the antichrist. Hanegraaff summarizes, "Muhammad was the second Plato, Plethon the third, and George's *Comparatio* culminated in dire warnings against Cardinal Bessarion, the fourth Plato, who wanted to become pope and might very well succeed. . . . Among the sympathetic early readers of George of Trebizond's *Comparatio*—attacking Plethon's revival of Plato—was the famous Florentine prophet Savonarola, and his follower, Gianfrancesco Pico della Mirandola, Giovanni's nephew."[5]

Far from being an obscurantist, Savonarola lectured on grammar, law, theology, spirituality, and philosophy. However, he began not with Aristotle or Plato

3. See the introduction for a description of Joachim's interpretation of history.

4. Hanegraaff, *Esoterism and the Academy*, 79.

5. Hanegraaff, *Esoterism and the Academy*, 79.

but with the ancient Roman mediator of the radical skepticism, Sextus Empiricus, whose Greek *Outlines of Pyrrhonism* arrived from Constantinople in 1427.[6] Even skepticism was affiliated with the Orphic lineage according to Diogenes Laertius. Ancient reports tell that Pyrrho of Elis accompanied Alexander the Great in his campaign in India and spent eighteen months with the "naked philosophers" (*gymnosophistai*), Buddhist monks, and Zoroastrian magi.[7] In agreement with Stoics and Epicureans alike, Pyrrhonic Skepticism maintained that happiness (*eudaimonia*) is only attained by tranquility of mind (*ataraxia*).[8] Yet, closer to Buddhism, it taught that such rest comes only by recognizing that every argument reaches an impasse (*aporia*), requiring suspension of judgment (*epochē*). Pyrrhonists criticized not only the dogmas of the schools but even their own dogmatism, showing how the schools cancel each other out so that nothing can be truly known.

Radical doubt may seem an odd philosophical tool for a revivalist preacher, but we must bear in mind that ancient schools were not being encountered from the inside in face-to-face engagement over centuries but through the medium of written texts. It was not a renaissance as much as a reconstruction. Everyone had a very contemporary agenda for their selections and interpretations. Like Ficino's use of theurgic Neoplatonism and Adriani's Epicureanism, Savonarola's propaedeutic immersion of students in Sextus Empiricus was driven not by antiquarian fascination but by immediate needs. At the end of the day, he was not actually a skeptic. His goal was not the suspension of all judgment. Rather, he used skepticism to disprove all other schools in order to show that Christianity escaped such searing criticism unscathed. All human learning is vain, leaving no choice but to surrender to the inerrant scriptures and, as we will see below, to Savonarola's own prophetic unction. Soon the same strategy would be followed by radical Anabaptist spiritualists to privilege the inner light, by Counter Reformation apologists to lodge the only certainty in the magisterium, and by Descartes to eliminate everything uncertain in order to build a new system of truth on a single indubitable foundation. It is skepticism in service of rationalism: the one

6. His major works in English translation appear in the Loeb series (Harvard University Press): *Outlines of Pyrrhonism*; *Against the Logicians*; *Against the Physicists and Against the Ethicists*; *Against the Professors*. As stated by Copenhaver and Schmitt, *Renaissance Philosophy*, 241: "Until Francesco Filefo brought Greek manuscripts of Sextus from Constantinople in 1427, the only Latin text was a fourteenth-century version of the *Outlines* that survives in just three manuscripts; two partial Latin translations followed in the fifteenth century but attracted little interest." Even after this, there was not much interest until Savonarola and Gianfrancesco Pico.

7. Diogenes Laertius, *Lives of Eminent Philosophers* 9.11, 61. See Beckwith, *Greek Buddha*.

8. Warren, *Epicurus and Democritean Ethics*, 1.

indubitable foundation. However, Montaigne and Bayle would later adopt a thoroughgoing skepticism, more original as well as modern, to relativize all claims to absolute truth. Yet, this methodological strategy was introduced by the prophet of Florence.[9]

The period and place of Savonarola's greatest influence coincided with a revival of Hermeticism and magical arts. Evidently, the same people who admired Ficino and Pico as civic heroes also flocked for a time to Savonarola's sermons. One day they might have been making statues and talismans, the next casting them into the fire.[10] Marjorie Reeves writes,

> In the age of the Florentine Platonists and Savonarola the elements of exaltation and apprehension were strangely mixed in their outlook on the future, just as in their view of knowledge rational and mystical approaches mingled. The Platonists were swept to a high excitement by the sense that the *plenitudo temporum* had arrived, yet at the same time were assailed by anxious expectations of Antichrist. It is to the astrologer Paul of Middelburg that Marsilio Ficino in 1492 wrote his famous letter proclaiming the Age of Gold to have arrived and listing all its manifestations. . . . Yet at the same time general anxiety concerning the future was building up to a peak. . . . Various prophets appeared with strange foreboding messages in the streets of Rome.[11]

Soon, the lecture hall could not contain the swelling crowds, so the Dominican began to preach regularly in the cathedral. His pointed jeremiads against the worldliness of Florence wore thin on the Medici family, but the palpable sense of imminent judgment and health and wealth for all who repent rendered political opposition to Savonarola hazardous. Allison Brown relates,

> The fear aroused by Savonarola's sermons is well documented. Ser Niccolo Michelozzi's wife, for example, who heard his famous Lent sermon in San Lorenzo in 1492 threatening that God's vengeance would come, "Quickly, quickly, and speedily, speedily" . . . then believed "that any day now, indeed, at any hour, the heavens and the earth are going to collapse." "She's so frightened, it's too much,"

9. See Floridi, *Sextus Empiricus* and, especially for our scope, Popkin, *History of Skepticism*.

10. McGinn, *Apocalyptic Spirituality*, 306 n. 61: "Although a number of authors at the end of the fifteenth century mixed apocalypticism and astrology, such as Johannes Lichtenberger, the court astrologer of Frederick III, and the Dominican Giovanni Nanni of Veterbo, Savonarola, in line with traditional Thomistic teachings, makes his opposition to astrology clear."

11. Reeves, *Joachim of Fiore*, 82.

> Ser Pace Bambello told his friend Niccolo, urging him to write to his wife and comfort her as he best knew how to do.[12]

Living in Lorenzo de' Medici's palazzo along with Pico and Ficino, Michelangelo regularly attended Savonarola's sermons, whose influence is evident in *The Last Judgment* he painted in the Sistine Chapel.

Savonarola began to divulge his purported visions, which he later composed in his *Compendium of Revelations*. "For a long time by divine inspiration I have predicted many future events in various ways," he declared. "Now necessity compels me to write down the coming events I publicly preached about, especially those that are more important and of greater weight."[13] These visions proclaimed an imminent judgment, "the sword of the Lord"—indeed, a great flood—that had been revealed to him. Yet for those who repent, a glorious age will dawn. Following Joachim of Fiore, he taught that a "Cyrus from the north" would descend, an interesting figure who would be both a scourge and a catalyst for the reformation of the church and society.[14] "I frequently repeated that Italy, especially Rome, would be destroyed," he reminds them. Yet, he adds, such conditional prophecies are always capable of being averted by repentance.[15]

This prophecy Savonarola claims to have received from the Virgin Mary, as he ascended the ladder beyond the stars to the seraphim and, beyond them, to the throne of the mother of God. In this conversation, at once officious diplomacy and intimate familiarity, Mary promises Savonarola that Florence will be the center of a reformation that will spread to the world. As a consequence of its repentance, it will enjoy riches beyond anything it has yet seen.[16] It will be an age of universal peace, with Florence as the new Jerusalem:

> I announce this good news to the city, that Florence will be more glorious, richer, more powerful than she has ever been; First, glorious in the sight of God as well as of men: and you, O Florence will be the reformation of all Italy, and from here the renewal will begin and spread everywhere, because this is the navel of Italy. Your counsels will reform all by the light and grace that God will give you. Second, O Florence, you will have innumerable riches, and God will

12. Brown, *Return of Lucretius*, 54.

13. Savonarola, *Compendium*, 192. Page citations of Savonarola, *Compendium of Revelations*, are from McGinn, *Apocalyptic Spirituality*, 192–276.

14. Savonarola, *Compendium*, 201.

15. Savonarola, *Compendium*, 202.

16. Savonarola, *Compendium*, 261–70.

> multiply all things for you. Third, you will spread your empire, and thus you will have power temporal and spiritual.[17]

"In these years Italy was prey to uncertainty," and ripe for such visions, writes McGinn. Savonarola blended "Florentine civic patriotism into a new kind of apocalyptic vision."[18] This prophecy pronounced by Savonarola over a repentant Florence would be repeated by his legatees over Spain, Portugal, England, and New England, and over the inhabitants of territories they conquered.

As late as 1492, Lorenzo de' Medici seemed to support Savonarola, calling for him to perform the last rites, although traditions differ regarding whether the preacher granted absolution.[19] Reeves relates that

> by the end of 1494 Savonarola was proclaiming unequivocally the full role of Florence as the new Jerusalem, God's elected instrument for world renewal, the centre of a new and glorious age . . . the people of Florence were the new Israel to be led through tribulation to felicity by their new Moses. In his first prophetic sermons in Florence in 1490 he cited the Abbot Joachim and St Vincent Ferrer as authorities. . . . In his juxtaposition of tribulation and renewal, in his vision of the Sabbath Age of peace and world unity, in his emphasis on human agencies to carry out this divine programme, and especially on the Angelic Pope and Second Charlemagne, Savonarola was clearly drawing on the Joachimist vision as developed in the fourteenth century, and, as we have seen, the source material for this was plentiful round about him.[20]

We have encountered this identification with Moses before: the ideal philosopher-king in the line of Zoroaster, Orpheus, and Hermes Trismegistus. Ever since Pythagoras, the philosopher-ruler was idealized as the spiritual leader and giver of laws.

Fortunes turned, at least for the time, in the Dominican's favor. Having laid waste to Italy, Charles VIII of France invaded Florence in 1494. While the populace evicted Lorenzo's son and successor, Piero the Unfortunate, Savonarola interceded outside the city and negotiated a truce—encouraging Charles to assume his new

17. Quoted in Weinstein, *Savonarola and Florence*, 143. See also Weinstein, *Savonarola*.

18. McGinn, *Apocalyptic Spirituality*, 186.

19. Kadir, *Columbus*, 46–47.

20. Reeves, *Joachim of Fiore*, 88. Reeves notes also that later Savonarola pretended not to have read these authorities. While his eschatology focused on a climactic era, Reeves notes that on some occasions he seems to have also a more cyclical view of history as "periodic decline and renewal" (89).

role as the Last World Emperor, the Cyrus from the north predicted by Joachim. After making a compensatory payment, Florence was spared, and it seemed that Savonarola really was a prophet after all. Sparing the republic, Charles continued his march south. It seemed now that the tide had turned, and God would repay Florence's faithfulness by making it the rich capital of the new Jerusalem. With the Medici exiled, Savonarola presided from 1494 to 1498 over an austere "people's republic," declaring Christ the king of Florence.

The recent events surrounding the French monarch as the "Cyrus of the north" seemed to have confirmed Savonarola's prophetic inspiration, not to mention his diplomatic skill. Despite such theocratic resonances, Savonarola's reformed Florence rejected the lordship of a single ruler and even an aristocratic oligarchy. Christ's kingship ruled out all secular authorities, just as the Franciscans would argue in New Spain.[21] Essentially, Florence would become a monastery. Savonarola drafted a new constitution with the election of a general council drawn from three thousand eligible citizens who were committed to a godly commonwealth. Christ may have been acclaimed king of Florence, but Savonarola was definitely his earthly viceroy.[22]

Assured of his position, the friar became more vehement, mocking those pursuing secular studies.[23] When Satan told him that his predictions were due to his birth star, Savonarola replied by citing the prophets and apostles, concluding "that astrology is condemned in many places in sacred Scripture." It is sheer "superstition." In fact, "Those who pursue divinatory astronomy are not only fools and men of weak minds and no judgment, but also bad Christians."[24] Brown explains, "Gone were the certainties of the hierarchical neoplatonism of Lorenzo de' Medici's circle, to be replaced by the cultural austerity of the new regime." Many in Lorenzo's circle of humanists left, but others such as Bartolomeo Scala and Ficino continued to represent the old guard.[25]

Savonarola found his implacable foe in Marcello Adriani, a restorer of the university who was partial to the earlier Epicurean renaissance. Not particularly interested in stirring a hornet's nest, Adriani at first gave purely secular lectures with carefully veiled criticisms of Savonarola.[26] He agreed with Lucretius's theory that religious leaders, in league with the state, use the fear of death to compel obedience. Nevertheless, Adriani took a more cynical position that such moderate

21. Phelan, *Millennial Kingdom*, remains a classic narrative. Important also is Graziano, *Millennial Kingdom*, especially 42–56.

22. Graziano, *Millennial Kingdom*, 42.

23. Brown, *Return of Lucretius*, 49–50.

24. Savonarola, *Compendium*, 214–15.

25. Brown, *Return of Lucretius*, 42–43.

26. Brown, *Return of Lucretius*, 45–46.

political religion was expedient for good rule. However, the success of Savonarola's Pyrrhonic attack on the arts and sciences had to be challenged. Perceiving the Dominican preacher as a charlatan, Adriani advanced Horace's attitude: *Nil admirari* "Marvel at nothing." To do so, he said, "is perhaps the one and only thing . . . that can make a man happy and keep him so." He also paraphrased Vergil's line: "They are indeed happy beyond measure who do not wonder at the majesty of nature because they know its causes."[27] And if people understood that the cause of fear was preachers like Savonarola, the phantom would vanish. Attacking papal indulgences, along with Savonarola's invocation of Florence's contract with God, Adriani contrasted the "pawnbroker" deity with "the pharmacist. . . . Nor was God to be feared, since 'it is his nature to bestow benefits for nothing,' and if you should want to propitiate him, good behavior is more effective than incense."[28]

It is surprising how widely Savonarola was respected, at least initially, even by the Neoplatonist philosophers and artists. Some recent scholars have challenged Savonarola's influence on Pico.[29] It may seem strange that Giovanni Pico della Mirandola and his nephew Gianfrancesco Pico were influenced by Neoplatonic philosophy and kabbalah even as they polemicized against "the vanity of the arts and science."[30] Nevertheless, the elder Pico's role in the prophet's rise is well documented. Not only did Pico secure Savonarola's teaching position under Lorenzo but, as Reeves points out, "Giovanni Pico della Mirandola studied the cabbala and knew the works of Joachim."[31]

We hear explicit Joachimist echoes of the Third Age. There is the dawn of the new age, led by a "Cyrus from the north," preceded by cataclysm and the antichrist. "The significant point to grasp is that we are not dealing here with two opposed viewpoints—optimistic humanists hailing the Age of Gold on the one hand, and medieval-style prophets proclaiming Woe! on the other. Foreboding and great hope live side by side in the same people."[32] Pico fell under Savonarola's spell especially in his last five years (1490–1494). However, his nephew, Gianfrancesco Pico, became a devoted follower and wrote biographies of both his uncle and Savonarola.[33] Although Gianfrancesco was only seven years younger than his uncle,

27. Brown, *Return of Lucretius*, 51.

28. Brown, *Return of Lucretius*, 53–54.

29. According to Steven Farmer, Gianfrancesco appears to have doctored his uncle's work to conform more closely with Savonarola. See Farmer, *Syncretism*, 81.

30. Gianfrancesco Pico della Mirandola, *Examen vanitatis doctrinae gentium et veritatis Christianae disciplinae* (Examination of the vanity of the doctrines of the gentiles and of the truth of the Christian teaching, 1520).

31. Reeves, *Joachim of Fiore*, 84.

32. Reeves, *Joachim of Fiore*, 83–84.

33. Pico's antipathy toward astrology reflects the influence of the Dominican preacher, who

Pico took great interest in his intellectual and spiritual development.[34] Turning more to scripture and practical piety, the elder Pico no longer speaks of uniting all philosophies in his grand system.[35] He died in 1494, when Savonarola was at his peak after the routing of Charles VIII.

Though all schools are scorned in his *Examen vanitatis doctrinae gentium*, Gianfrancesco directs most of his arrows toward Aristotle and Aristotelianism and reflects his background in Christian Neoplatonism. He also stands with Ficino against Epicureanism in defense of God's providence and the soul's immortality. On all these points, not only Pico but also Savonarola would have sympathized. Yet when it comes to the vanity of arts and sciences, and of astrology in particular, Gianfrancesco shows himself an ardent disciple of the Dominican friar. On the one hand, Gianfrancesco is a reactionary; on the other hand, many of the criticisms of Aristotle and Aristotelian philosophy anticipated those of Galileo and of many modern thinkers afterward.[36]

> Whereas Giovanni Pico had often argued that all philosophies and all religions have attained a portion of the truth, Gianfrancesco said, in effect, that all religions and all philosophies—save the Christian religion alone—are mere collections of confused and internally inconsistent falsehoods. In holding such a view, he sided not only with Savonarola, but with certain of the Fathers and with the Reformers as well.[37]

Yet more than the rest, he sought neither to advance nor to reform philosophy but "to demolish it."[38] The strategy of relentless criticism, Pyrrhonic skepticism, was deployed in service to returning to faith in scripture.

---

wrote a treatise titled *Trattato contra li astrologi*. Regardless, Gianfrancesco's sweeping denunciation of "the vanity of philosophy," including Platonism, seems inimical to his uncle's entire program. While Pico was convinced that kabbalah mediated oral traditions that could restore the universal language and lost knowledge, Savonarola and Gianfrancesco held that an inerrant scripture is sufficient. See Hanegraaff, *Esoterism and the Academy*, 81. He adds, "See the opening sentences of Savonarola's treatise against astrology (*Trattato contra li astrologi*, 1.1, in Savonarola, *Scritti filosofici*, vol. 1, 278): 'The foundation of the Christian religion is the sacred Scripture of the New and Old Testament, which we are obliged to believe to be true down to the smallest iota, and we must approve all that it approves, and disapprove of all that it disapproves of, since it is made by God, who cannot err'" (81 n. 14).

34. Schmitt, *Gianfrancesco*, 32.

35. Schmitt, *Gianfrancesco*, 32.

36. Schmitt, *Gianfrancesco*, 31.

37. Schmitt, *Gianfrancesco*, 31–54.

38. Schmitt, *Gianfrancesco*, 31–54.

As for Ficino, it was merely a week into 1494 when he experienced a change of heart about Savonarola. Initially, the preacher was open to astrology and pagan wisdom. He even spoke of a "doctor of souls" who would soon come to heal spiritual illnesses, likely alluding to Ficino (or so Ficino assumed).[39] He wrote a letter on the same day to his close friend Giovanni Calvacanti gushing about Savonarola as "God's chosen instrument," possessing "sanctity and wisdom." Then, two days later, Savonarola delivered a sermon attacking astrologers and those who rely on pagan wisdom, which Ficino took as targeting him.[40] On the same day Ficino wrote another letter to Calvacanti, this time concluding that the Dominican preacher was a less than pure vehicle of truth.[41]

Savonarola declined a summons to Rome in 1495. Instead, he sent his nemesis, Pope Alexander VI, a copy of his *Compendium of Revelations*, in which he claimed to have prophesied the death of Lorenzo de' Medici and Pope Innocent VIII, not to mention the invasion of Charles of France, which turned out to be a blessing after all.[42] And how could Savonarola accede to the demand of a false pope that Florence should enter a holy alliance against Charles VIII, the Dominican's "Last World Emperor," with whom he had signed a concordat? "With divine inspiration," he insisted, "I recommended things that were necessary and useful for public safety to the citizens, but I did not compel them."[43] He assured the pope, "The reformation of the city (something that everyone thought was impossible) was brought off by the admonitions of my sermons."[44]

Banned by the Vatican from preaching, Savonarola nevertheless continued even after the pope excommunicated him and threatened to place Florence under an interdict. His sermons became more defensive. He was not simply interpreting scripture, he insisted, but was receiving new revelations.[45] In his *Compendium of Revelations*, in fact, Savonarola declared that his words "are not from the Holy Scriptures, as some thought, but have newly come forth from heavens just at that time."[46] Two years later, in 1497, Ficino's *Commentary on St. Paul's Epistle to the Romans* included a not so veiled polemic focusing on false views of vision and prophecy.[47] Like the magi and Plato's "divine madness," biblical prophets are given

39. Vanhaelen, "Ficino's Commentary," 212.
40. Vanhaelen, "Ficino's Commentary," 212–13.
41. Vanhaelen, "Ficino's Commentary," 210–11.
42. Savonarola, *Compendium*.
43. Savonarola, *Compendium*, 236.
44. Savonarola, *Compendium*, 239.
45. Vanhaelen, "Ficino's Commentary," 218.
46. Quoted in Vanhaelen, "Ficino's Commentary," 220.
47. Vanhaelen, "Ficino's Commentary," 213. Oddly, the focus is on Paul's passing comment—

a direct vision of God. "Later on, in Book XVI," says Vanhaelen, "Ficino goes as far as to compare the Neoplatonic rituals of magic, sacrifice and demonology with the Christian rituals of prayer and fasting, indeed reconsidering Christian rituals in the light of Neoplatonic mysticism."[48]

With one stroke Ficino challenges Savonarola's pretensions and justifies his own Platonic renaissance by ranking the Orphic sages as recipients of direct revelation even above prophets, following Plato's *Phaedrus*. Savonarola boasted that he preached "new things in new ways" (*nova dicere et nova modos*), while Ficino argues that genuine prophets based their teaching on ancient truth.[49] In Ficino's perspective, we also may actually ascend to the third heaven as Paul did—and as had Zoroaster, Orpheus, Hermes Trismegistus, Moses, and "our divine Plato." We may behold the Truth itself, God's essence, instead of relying on interpretations masquerading as revelation.[50] If truth is accessible to philosophers—even non-Christian ones—then the philosophical religion may continue. God manifested himself to the Hebrews through the prophets and to the gentiles through the philosophers.[51] Philosophers alone should be entrusted with the "divine mysteries," as he wrote in his preface to Lorenzo in *The Christian Religion*, and what Paul condemns in the first chapter of Romans is not pagan wisdom as such, but the same idolatry and superstition that Apollonius of Tyana, Porphyry, and Iamblichus also rejected.[52]

Toward the end of Carnival (February 7, 1498), Savonarola summoned the citizens to the "bonfire of vanities" in the piazza. Persuaded by his visions, Florentines cast into the flames their secular art and books, dice and cards, not to mention ostentatious clothing, pictures, and song-sheets, waiting for a sign of divine approbation. Savonarola not only claimed to be interpreting Holy Scripture faithfully but to be an agent of prophetic revelation. Indeed, he bound God's

not even in Romans, but in 2 Corinthians 12—about having been "caught up to the third heaven" to be told "inexpressible things" (vv. 2–4). This apostolic experience was a lodestar also for Pseudo-Dionysius, and Ficino appeals to it in order to contrast Paul's "rapture" (*raptus*) to the third heaven—where the divine essence is beheld—with the second heaven that Ficino believes is beheld by mere prophets, alluding to Plato's distinction between various forms of divine madness.

48. Vanhaelen, "Ficino's Commentary," 215.

49. Vanhaelen, "Ficino's Commentary," 218.

50. Vanhaelen, "Ficino's Commentary," 226–27.

51. Vanhaelen, "Ficino's Commentary," 229.

52. Vanhaelen, "Ficino's Commentary," 231. This is ironic, especially in the case of Apollonius of Tyana, who was a charlatan who was viewed by many contemporaries as a pagan counterpart to Jesus.

reputation to his own, insisting with the circular argument, "He has made me say it and if He errs, I too err; but He cannot err, so neither do I in telling you what God says."[53]

Lucretius's Revenge

Targeting "the high priests of the Christian religion," Adriani's 1497 lecture gave greater liberty and frankness to his Lucretian polemic. Far from corrupting Christianity, ancient philosophers were more sanctified than Christians. This shaming of contemporary Christians by pious pagans was a familiar motif of Renaissance utopias. Savonarola had played on the long-established gift relationship between Florence and God "by promising the Florentines that they would become richer and more powerful if they accepted the reforms that he, as God's mouthpiece, urged on them." So, long before Nietzsche and Freud, Adriani offered a psychological explanation going back to Roman Epicureanism: "According to Lucretius, we create figures of power as a projection of our own fantasies, hoping to become as powerful as they are by propitiating them with prayers and 'stocking our cities with altars.' 'Unhappy human race, to grant such feats / to Gods, and then to add vindictiveness!'"[54]

The preacher's bonfires, holy plays, and fiery sermons continued until he was challenged by a rival preacher to put his prophecies to the test. Claiming to have certified his gift by miracles, he was challenged to a trial by fire, passing through the flames. A sudden rainstorm drenched the crowd, aborting the trial, but emotions turned against the Dominican for failing to prove himself. He was arrested and under torture confessed that he had indulged in fabrication. On May 27, 1498, just three months after he had overseen the "bonfire of vanities," Savonarola himself was brought before an ecclesiastical and civil court and, under the direct order of Pope Alexander VI, was defrocked and hanged, and then his body was burned along with three fellow friars in the same piazza. In Ficino's *Apology*, addressed to the College of Cardinals just after the execution, Savonarola becomes an antichrist misled by evil daimons.[55]

While Savonarola was burned as a heretic, Ficino, though investigated, never came before the Inquisition. Surviving the political turmoil mostly by ignoring

53. Brown, *Return of Lucretius*, 54, from Savonarola, *Prediche* (May 8, 1496).

54. Brown, *Return of Lucretius*, 54–55, from Savonarola, *Prediche* (May 8, 1496).

55. Vanhaelen, "Ficino's Commentary," 209.

it, he continued his work and was assured of a peaceful death by a succession of Medici popes. Lorenzo de' Medici's second son became Pope Leo X, Luther's nemesis. Made a cardinal at fourteen, Lorenzo's nephew became Pope Clement VII and restored his relatives to power in Florence.

With Savonarola gone, Lucretius returned with the Medicis. It was in 1497, while still in the chancery, that a young Machiavelli transcribed his copy of Lucretius's *De rerum natura*, and his notes are revealing.[56] When the Medicis returned in 1512, Adriani was able to keep his job, while Machiavelli was sacked for teaching the same doctrines: the origin of institutional religion in fear.[57] The following year, the Fifth Lateran Council declared Epicureans and Averroists heretical "for believing 'in the mortality or in the unity of the soul and the eternity of the world.'"[58]

We need not digress into the dissimulation of Adriani, which was driven by survival as much as by conviction. Ficino was no comfort, given his disdain of Epicureanism at this point. Yet Savonarola's manipulative and egomaniacal pretensions provided exactly the sort of backdrop for the Epicureanism of Adriani and its cynical development by Machiavelli, but Adriani had to be careful. Like Adriani and anticipating Hobbes, Machiavelli adopted the Lucretian critique of religion as crowd control, but instead of justifying liberation from fear he used it to reinforce secular power.[59] This is similar to the use of skepticism by Savonarola. Adriani adopts Lucretius's critique but instead of concluding with the philosopher that the public religion is a threat to happiness, he argues that an undogmatic religion is extremely valuable to keep the masses in check. In *The Golden Ass*, Machiavelli oscillates between two poles, criticizing "propitiatory religion (and with it, the legacy of Savonarola)" and religion as useful to the prince and the unity of a people. As we will see, this is essentially Kant's "religions of rogation" versus "religions of morality," corresponding to "ecclesiastical faiths" and "universal morality." Machiavelli's reading of Lucretius is distinctly modern. The naive religious views of the masses are not just to be criticized but used. Even for many contemporaries, Epicureanism was not rejected on theological grounds, but because it undermined civic morality. Theology is one thing, but social morals and politics are another. Once this totally instrumental view of religion was acknowledged, there was very little that metaphysicians and theologians could do about it. Humans are basically

56. Brown, *Return of Lucretius*, 69.

57. Brown, *Return of Lucretius*, 71.

58. Brown, *Return of Lucretius*, 77–78.

59. See especially Machiavelli, *Discourses* 1.11 and chapter 17 of *The Prince*. Cf. Brown, *Return of Lucretius*, 78.

animals that, by a sheer act of will, consent to the prince—a view that Hobbes would later perfect.[60]

Savonarola's reign depended on the people's fear of punishment. Machiavelli admired Savonarola for using appeals to divine revelation and, according to Brown, "in reading the Bible 'judiciously' when it was necessary to break its commandments." As Brown also observes:

> But he criticized Savonarola for misusing his influence with the people, since instead of preaching boldness, he encouraged passivity by suggesting that they would be saved through fasting and through their prayers alone, "idle and on their knees," and, worse, he lost their respect through his hypocrisy over the law of appeal. There is little in the evidence of his friends' or his own writings to suggest that Machiavelli believed in Christian revelation, or even in the special authority accorded to religious states and holy men. Despite calling Christianity "our religion" that "teaches us the truth and the true way," he also treated it "relativistically" as a form of power, one of a succession of religions with a limited life cycle, just as Bartolomeo Scala had done when discussing religion in his *Dialogue on Laws* and his *Defense* of Savonarola.[61]

Imagination also played a large role in Ficino's psychology, just as Pico emphasized the power of the individual to determine his or her own nature. Machiavelli coins a distinctively modern term for this—"self-fashioning" (*prosopoeia*)—and often appeals (like Lucretius) to the metaphor of the theater, appearance, and reality.[62] Machiavelli, like Adriani, never tires of extolling the animals above the humans. Anticipating Rousseau's "noble savage," Machiavelli's primitive human is, like the First Human of Plato and Philo, the archetype for the fleshly Adam, who turns out to be a poor copy. As Brown puts it, "Like the centaur Chiron in *The Prince*, who is said to reflect a Lucretian 'taste for the primitive and savage,' animals in [Machiavelli's] *The Golden Ass* are closer to nature than man is; they are more philanthropic to each other and better equipped for survival than man, who (following another familiar Lucretian theme) is alone born nude and helpless, his life beginning in tears."[63] The interactions of Epicureanism, Hermeticism, and Joachite prophetism are a large part of the making of modernity.

60. Brown, *Return of Lucretius*, 87.

61. Brown, *Return of Lucretius*, 80. Machiavelli even "said he never made a practice of listening to sermons himself," and his friends attested to his lack of interest in religious practice (81).

62. Brown, *Return of Lucretius*, 82.

63. Brown, *Return of Lucretius*, 84.

Conclusion

We miss a lot if we restrict secularizing trends to Epicurean naturalism. The Florentine Renaissance was domesticating transcendence to nature even as Savonarola was immanentizing the eschaton. Whether in the realm of nature or history, fullness is to be found here and now. Who we are and where history is going is up to us. There is no specific nature; it is a locative and therefore limited, bounded, and defined personhood. It is up to us to choose our identity.

As in nature, so in history we are authors of our own destiny. Renaissance writers referred often to the *plenitudo temporum*, the culmination of history in the near future tied to marvelous but natural historical events. Interestingly, the phrase itself, taken from the Latin translation of Galatians 4:4, refers to Christ's advent ("But when the fullness of time had come, God sent forth his Son"). This is a good example of how traditional typological exegesis became replaced with a millennialist interpretation. Moreover, ever since Joachim biblical prophecy was tied to the daily news. With an allegorical spin, Gog and Magog could be the Ottomans or the Muslims and Jews of the Iberian Peninsula. Columbus could assume to himself the fulfillment of Isaiah 42:1 that Jesus claimed for himself in Luke 4:18: "The Spirit of the Lord is upon me, because he has anointed me to proclaim good news to the poor. He has sent me to proclaim liberty to the captives and recovering of sight to the blind, to set at liberty those who are oppressed." Ironically, Columbus assumed this prophecy to his agenda of Spanish oppression. Christ has been displaced from Christianity. Unwilling to wait for Jesus to return, the eschatological sights were set on a Joachite drama in the present with the reign of the spirituals.

3

Radicals
The Revolution of the Saints

> The saint is a Gnostic who will not leave the transfiguration of the world to the grace of God beyond history but will do the work of God himself, right here and now, in history.
>
> —Eric Voegelin[1]

> The first revolutionary movements in Europe [were] all more or less imbued with the ideas of Joachim of Fiore.
>
> —Roger Garaudy[2]

> The revolutionary opposition to feudalism was alive throughout the Middle Ages. It took the shape of mysticism, open heresy, or armed insurrection. . . . Müntzer himself was indebted to it. . . . The medieval mystics, and particularly the chilastic works of Joachim the Calabrian, were the main subjects of his studies.
>
> —Friederick Engels[3]

Luther rebuffed those who saw him as Joachim's "angelic pope." In fact, as Engels relates, when Ulrich von Hutten intercepted Luther to offer the defense of the Teutonic Knights, Luther replied, "I do not wish the Gospel defended by force

1. Voegelin, *New Science*, 147.
2. Garaudy, "Faith and Revolution," 66.
3. Engels, *Peasant War*, 14, 21.

and bloodshed. The World was conquered by the Word, the Church is maintained by the Word, the Word will also put the Church back into its own, and Antichrist, who gained his own without violence, will fall without violence."[4]

Some of these early admirers and even students of the German reformer grew increasingly dissatisfied with the direction, not just the pace, of Luther's reform. The name Anabaptist or Catabaptist was given by detractors to "rebaptizers." Although its bearers believed they were actually baptizing people the first time, the label stuck. When it comes to Anabaptist history, the view on the ground becomes "as complex as a street map of Tokyo," notes Hillerbrand.[5] "Anabaptism" became a catch-all title for disparate groups.[6] Some who were so labeled did not reject infant baptism, and others who did reject it remained otherwise more traditional doctrinally. Yet, with a wide-angle lens we see clear markers identifying distinct territories and boundaries. As contemporary Anabaptist scholar Leonard Verduin notes, "They were not interested in any continuity with the Church of the past; for them that Church was a 'fallen' creature."[7] To them, Luther, Bucer, Calvin, and their ilk were "the scribes" and "false preachers" who opposed Christ in the New Testament, armed with "the word that merely beats the air" rather than "the secret, inborn word."[8]

Moreover, Anabaptists were united sufficiently to produce the Schleitheim Confession in 1527. In varying degrees of intensity, common emphases among these groups included (1) restorationism, that is, the idea that the true church apostatized after the apostles and will soon be restored; (2) Joachite eschatology; (3) discipleship, with emphasis falling upon salvation by following Christ's example, which precludes infant baptism; (4) the true church consisting only of committed disciples who share all things in common; and (5) dualistic ideological frameworks, which ranged from ethical to metaphysical (antithesis of light and darkness, godly and ungodly, everything associated with the body and the inner spirit). With such ontological antitheses, "Müntzer's spiritualism, originating in

4. Engels, *Peasant War*, 18, quoting Luther's letter to Ulrich von Hutten that the reformer related to Spalatin in a letter dated January 16, 1521.

5. Hillerbrand, "Radicalism," 36. Hillerbrand observes that research has shifted from a "monogenetic" origin in Zurich to a "polygenetic" theory of Anabaptist movements (citing the work of James M. Stayer).

6. Following G. H. Williams, Estep, *Anabaptist Story* identifies three groups: Anabaptist, Inspirationist, and Rationalist. See also Roth and Stayer, *Companion*. I suggest below that this classification breaks down and that instead we see a spectrum reflecting the usual trend of radical mysticism leading to rationalism.

7. Verduin, *Reformers*, 156.

8. We encounter these epithets below.

his attack on such external authorities as the Bible, the church, and the state," says Gritsch, "ended in the establishment of a new and dangerous source of authority; namely, that of man with all his physical, emotional, and spiritual instability so well illustrated in Müntzer's own life."[9]

Close in age, Luther, Müntzer, and Paracelsus came from reasonably affluent families associated with a mining culture where alchemy was particularly at home.[10] Luther's father managed mines and smelting operations, serving on the Mansfeld town council.[11] "I very much like the science of alchemy which is, indeed, the philosophy of the ancients," the reformer said. "I like it not only because, by melting metals, and decocting, preparing, extracting, and distilling herbs and roots, it produces profits: but also because of its allegorical and secret meaning."[12] He went on to say that it was an allegory of the final judgment at the end of history.[13] For Müntzer and Paracelsus, however, it was the secret meaning of events unfolding in the present through their agency that caused them to adopt alchemy allegorically: a "smelting" of the ungodly from the elect in the sociopolitical sphere. Like the authors of the ancient Hermetic texts, Paracelsus saw such transmutation as simultaneously spiritual and physical, inward and outward, transforming an age of lead into an age of gold.

All three figures had a keen sense of their extraordinary role in history, but Luther's agenda was radically different. As B. Rosenstock observes,

9. Gritsch, "Thomas Muentzer," 180–81.

10. Focusing on the courts of German princes, Tara Nummedel's detailed study "from below" explains the integral relationship between mining and alchemy. See Nummedel, *Alchemy and Authority*, 8–20.

11. Brecht, *Martin Luther*, 1:3–5.

12. Quoted in Maxwell-Stuart, *Chemical Choir*, 85. Maxwell-Stuart points out, "On the Catholic side, Pope Leo X's known tolerance of alchemy led to at least two books being dedicated to him." Luther himself was less enthusiastic than Melanchthon concerning astrology (WA TR 1:566, no. 1149). Melanchthon taught astrology and astronomy as well as theology at Wittenberg. In fact, Lutherans played a significant role in advancing Hermetic ideas and practices throughout the early modern period. The following chapters exhibit Lutheran mediation of alchemy. See also Montgomery, *Cross, Constellation, and Crucible*; Montgomery, *Cross and Crucible*.

13. The quote continues, "This is quite excellent and touches upon the resurrection of the dead at the Last Day. For, just as in a furnace the fire extracts and separates the various parts of a substance, and carries upward its spirit, life, sap and strength, leaving behind at the bottom the unclean matter, the dregs, like a dead, worthless corpse; so God, at the Day of Judgement, will separate everything with fire, the righteous from the unrighteous" (Maxwell-Stuart, *Chemical Choir*, 85).

> Luther himself resists the revolutionary Gnosticism that would attempt to install a new heaven and earth by force of arms, the path followed by Thomas Müntzer. Müntzer inherited the Gnostic radicalism that not merely opposes the transcendent heaven and the present earth but seeks to reduce the earth to nothingness in order that a new creation can take place. . . . The alchemist is responsible for creating the link between earth and heaven because no such link is "naturally" present. . . . We also see how the radicalism of Gnosticism has been "smoothed" down to accommodate itself to a progressive view of the self-transformation of the spirit.[14]

The energy within "heretical Christianity," he adds, was marked by a "Marcion-Gnostic-Joachimite repudiation of the present world order and all its institutions."[15] Müntzer sought a sweeping political revolution, and Paracelsus embodied the *magus* who combined all knowledge into a single system for healing the world. As Andrew Weeks puts it, "Paracelsus and Agrippa were men who would know all things; Luther was the man who would know the one necessary thing."[16] However, all three figures were indebted deeply to the German mysticism represented by the *Theologia Germanica*, which was composed, according to the preface, by a cleric from Frankfurt.[17]

Spiritual Alchemy and the *German Theology*

The message of the *German Theology* (TG) is drawn from the fourteenth-century Dominican mystic Meister Eckhart. "Basic to an understanding of Eckhart," says Werner Packull, is "his explanation of the Trinity in terms of a Neoplatonic emanation theory of creation."[18] Similar to Eriugena, Eckhart correlated the generation of the Son with the rupture of absolute unity into difference while the Spirit returns the emanation to unity. This threefold process could be mapped easily onto the three stages of alchemy: the dark abyss (*nigredo*), separation (*albedo*), and union of opposites producing a third thing (*rubedo*), called the "child of the work." The process leads ultimately back to unity with the One. "For only in total detachment

14. Rosenstock, "Jacob Taubes," 388. Rosenstock observes that sixteenth-century alchemy and science share a common Copernican worldview in this respect (viz., that nature itself does not offer links to the heavenly world).

15. Rosenstock, "Jacob Taubes," 391.

16. Weeks, *German Mysticism*, 133.

17. On the provenance of the work see Peters, "Theologische Deutsch," 258–62.

18. Packull, *Mysticism*, 22.

(*Gelassenheit*) from all creatureliness could the 'inner Word' be apprehended," notes Packull, "teaching us that we are *the same Son*."[19] The contrast between inner and outer realities extends in Eckhart's reflections to the inner Word that the Spirit breathes in the soul and the outer Word of scripture and preaching, comments that would be frequently quoted by radical mystics and Enlightenment rationalists alike.[20]

Everything bodily is creaturely and therefore cursed, while souls are divine sparks of the One and therefore sinless. Packull notes that "the Neoplatonic matter-spirit dichotomy forced the conclusion that all preoccupation with externals and material things hindered man's communion with the Divine."[21] According to Tauler, the soul falls from the One and returns, from unity to diversity and back to unity.[22]

Henry Suso, the most popular preacher of the fourteenth century, knew Eckhart and Tauler.[23] After Eckhart's posthumous condemnation in 1329, Tauler and Suso continued to spread their fellow Dominican's teaching from their base in Strasbourg.[24] Their teaching and practice drew charges of antinomianism, but it was actually a pantheistic perfectionism: by surrendering the will entirely, one was united to God to such an extent that he wills through them and they no longer sin.[25]

19. Packull, *Mysticism*, 22, emphasis added. Notice that there is no distinction here between the divine nature of the Son and the sonship of human beings by adoption. This would lose the intrinsic and ontological *syntērēsis* between God and the soul.

20. Thomas Müntzer wrote, "When St. Paul told Timothy to 'Preach the Word,' he did not mean that word that merely beats the air, but the secret, inborn Word." See Müntzer's "Sermon to the Princes" in Baylor, *Radical Reformation*, 11–31. Eckhart was also a personal favorite of Hegel's. Ernst Benz observes that the continuity between German medieval mysticism and German idealistic philosophy has been thoroughly recognized at least since Wilhelm Dilthey (Benz, *Mystical Sources*, 2). For this connection especially between Hegel and Eckhart (as well as ancient Gnosticism), see also O'Regan, *Heterodox Hegel*.

21. Packull, *Mysticism*, 23.

22. Packull, *Mysticism*, 21.

23. McGinn, *Harvest*, 198.

24. Two of his most famous works were *The Clock of Wisdom* and *Little Book of Truth*. See Rozenski, "Henry Suso."

25. G. Lerner, *Feminist Consciousness*, 79–82. The informal community of the Brethren of the Free Spirit as well as the Beguines (women) and Behards (men) were affected deeply by Eckhart. An example is the Beguine writer Mechtild of Magdeburg. In *The Mirror of Simple Souls* she says that "a soul annihilated in the love of the creator could, and should, grant to nature all that it desires." Quoted in G. Lerner, *Feminist Consciousness*, 79–80. See also Field, *Beguine*. However, Lerner explains, "At the fourth stage the soul is at a level of contemplation in which it is free of all obedience to external authority and laws. In the seventh stage, the soul arrives at

Reading the *Theologia Germanica*

The *Theologia Germanica* (hereafter *TG*) celebrates the "birth of God in the soul."[26] The work opens with Christ's soul having two eyes, inner and outer: "Thus the inner man of Christ, according to the right eye of his soul, stood in perfect enjoyment of his divine nature, in perfect bliss, joy and eternal peace. But the outward man and the left eye of Christ's soul stood in perfect suffering, in all tribulation, affliction, and travail."[27] Eckhart reprises the traditional monastic path from purgation to illumination to ecstatic union.[28] However, the trajectory from Eriugena to Eckhart, Tauler, and Nicholas of Cusa was more voluntaristic. This is interesting for two reasons. First, Eckhart and Tauler were Dominicans. Traditionally, Franciscans were voluntarists, identifying the will as the chief faculty, while Dominicans, following Aquinas, gave primacy to the intellect. Second, some scholars today treat medieval voluntarism (or nominalism) as the opposite of Neoplatonism.[29] Yet nominalism and Neoplatonism are interwoven in German mysticism. Nominalists placed an emphasis on God's absolute power (*potentia Dei absoluta*) according to which God may suspend his ordained power (*potentia Dei ordinata*). Thus, God *could* impose the Ten Commandments at one time and suspend them at another, or even damn the elect if he so chose. This emphasis on God's arbitrary freedom suffuses the *TG*. The human will is similarly limitless. The highest part of the soul is the will, not the intellect, so a fusion of wills is the goal of deification. Even in this life, God's willing and our willing may become one and the same act.[30] It was

a level of 'glorification' in which 'all the works of virtue are enclosed in the soul and obey her without contradiction.' Porete goes on to argue that in this stage the soul need not concern itself with masses, penance, sermons, fasts or prayer. This belief, bordering on Antinomianism, was of itself offensive to the orthodox. . . . Like Joan of Arc and much later the Quaker Mary Dyer, she remained silent during her trial and refused to cooperate with Church or state authority" (70–80). See also McGinn, *Harvest*, 198. The Beghard leader, Guiard of Cressonessart, supported his spiritual sister, appealing often to the writings of Joachim of Fiore. Both were burned at the stake in 1310. Following the papal bull (*Ad nostrum qui*), the Council of Vienne (1312) condemned Beguines and Beghards along with similar groups. Suso was not condemned, but the Dominicans withdrew his teaching position. Suso was beatified by the Roman Catholic Church in 1831.

26. Translations from Petry, *Late Medieval Mysticism*, 327–51.

27. Translations from Petry, *Late Medieval Mysticism*, 327.

28. Translations from Petry, *Late Medieval Mysticism*, 336.

29. According to the narrative of John Milbank and radical orthodoxy, Franciscans (e.g., Scotus to Ockham) are the progenitors of radical voluntarism and nominalism leading to secularism. While recognizing the importance of nominalism in shaping modernity, I am simply pointing to other sources that, ironically (and despite being declared heretical by the church), Milbank regards as defenders of "radical orthodoxy" ("Reformation 500," 607–29).

30. Packull, *Mysticism*, 25–26.

this line of radical mysticism that found in the God of absolute power a direct immediacy and spontaneous freedom that did not depend on the ordained power mediated through the church and its external ministry.

Western mystics such as John of the Cross and Teresa of Ávila are closer to Origen than to Dionysius, Andrew Louth argues. Dionysius believed that the intellect is essential in the mystical ascent, even though it is transcended by union. But in the context of late medieval and Counter Reformation mysticism "the teaching of Denys's *Mystical Theology* takes on a different light: the insistence that the intellect must be transcended is interpreted as a rejection of the intellect in favour of the will or feeling. So we find in the *Cloud of Unknowing*, which is a good example of the influence of Denys on medieval mysticism, the dictum: 'by love he can be gotten and holden, but by thought never.'"[31] Grasping God "by love . . . but by thought never" surely leads to a separation of faith and reason that is more extreme than one finds in Ockham. This more voluntaristic approach characterizes Eckhart and the Rhineland mystics who shaped the *TG*.

On the one hand, the *TG* emphasizes complete passivity: the creature must no longer exist, so that the divine spark may lose its identity in the Godhead.[32] In practice, though, this surrendering or serenity (*Gelassenheit*) was the most difficult work of all. "And even as in truth all essences are one in essence in the perfect Essence," the treatise argues, "and all goods are one in the One, and cannot exist without that One; so likewise shall all wills be one in the one perfect Will, and there shall be no will without that One . . . for I-hood and selfhood must depart."[33] This is not an existential union, but an essential one: "For God is the One and must be the One, and God is All and must be All. For, verily, All is One and One is All in God."[34] Indeed, "the Will in the creature, which we call a created will, is as truly God's as the eternal Will, and is not a property of the creature. . . . For God himself would will in him, and not the man, and that Will would be one with the eternal Will, and have flowed out into it."[35] Even heaven and hell are subjectivized as states of mind

31. Louth, *Origins of Christian Mysticism*, 177–78. Thus, many of the central theses of nominalism appear already in the radical Neoplatonism distinctive of Western mysticism. Identifying explicitly with this tradition (e.g., Eriugena, Eckhart, Cusanus), John Milbank nevertheless fails to recognize the protonominalist voluntarism that is woven into late medieval and Renaissance Neoplatonism.

32. See Petry, *Late Medieval Mysticism*, 330.

33. Translation from Petry, *Late Medieval Mysticism*, 337.

34. Translation from Petry, *Late Medieval Mysticism*, 338–39.

35. Translation from Petry, *Late Medieval Mysticism*, 343.

dependent on states of will, so that one who is in the Spirit "can be as safe in hell as in heaven."[36]

Eckhart's teaching was carried by the Rhine to the Low Countries and found a champion in Jan van Ruusbroec, with Jean Gerson, chancellor of the university of Paris, as his chief opponent.[37] As in all expressions of Orphic piety, the ascent of the soul—its union or marriage with the One—easily merges into pantheism. And this was the problem highlighted by Gerson, who linked Ruusbroec's *The Spiritual Espousals* with the "free-spirit" Beghards and Beguines condemned at the Council of Vienne in 1312.[38] Aquinas was eager to point out that participation does not include identity.[39] However, Ruusbroec could say not only that created being depends on the eternal being, but that "this eternal being is one with it in its essential subsistence."[40]

Luther and the *Theologia Germanica*

Werner Packull summarizes well the heart of the Eckhartian theology of the *TG*:

> Through the higher powers lodged in the soul, man was directly connected with the Divinity. In fact, some of Eckhardt's bolder statements suggest that the "nobler (rational) powers of the soul" were identical with the indwelling logos. *The problem for man was to recognize the divine in him.* This could be achieved *only by turning inward.* The senses communicated only external and, therefore, secondary reality, but reason, the noblest power of the soul, could clasp *naked divinity.*[41]

All three of the theses I have italicized in the above quote were attacked sharply by Luther. His Heidelberg Disputation (1518) railed against ladders of ascent to clasp the naked God (*Deus nudus*). Apart from Christ, as he is clothed in the external gospel, Luther states that any purported union with God is actually made with the devil, since he "disguises himself as an angel of light" (2 Cor 11:14). According to "theologians of glory," the soul uses three ladders for its ascent: mysticism,

36. Translation from Petry, *Late Medieval Mysticism*, 334.

37. See Gerson, *De mystica.*

38. Turner, "Dionysius," 124–25. Milbank mentions the Beghards and Beguines as precursors of his radical orthodoxy (Milbank, "Reformation 500," 609–27).

39. See *Summa theologia* II-II, q. 123, a. 2, arg. 1, ad 1.

40. Ruusbroec, *Spiritual Espousals*, quoted in Turner, "Dionysius," 130–31.

41. Packull, *Mysticism*, 21, emphasis added.

speculation, and merit. According to the theology of the cross, however, one receives God as he has descended to us, clothed in our flesh and his gospel.[42] The one lies within the pale of a disincarnational Orphic spirituality with Origen as a fountainhead, while the other follows an Irenaean emphasis.[43]

However, in 1516 Luther had written a marginal note in his copy of Tauler's works: "I have found more solid and true theology in him, even though all written in the German vernacular, than is found in all the scholastic teachers of all the universities—or than could be found in their opinions."[44] And only four months after the Heidelberg Disputation, Luther published his edition of the *Theologia Germanica* with a glowing preface, hailing it as "next to the Bible and St. Augustine."[45] He adds, the work is "not only in line with the Bible and St. Augustine, but it is also a perfect anticipation of the Wittenberg theology."[46]

Upon receiving news of Luther's *TG* in May of 1519, Zwingli dashed off an excited note to Beatus Rhenanus. He announced that the press of Adam Petri "is about to print some new treatises of Luther's German," including "a *German Theology*, compared with which the subtle theology of Scotus appears gross and dull; and other books of this sort." He presses Rhenanus, "If you publicly commend these to the people, that is, persuade them to buy them, the work upon which you are engaged will succeed in accordance with your most ardent desires." A month later he informs Rhenanus, "I shall buy a considerable quantity."[47] Such correspondence shows that the early Zwingli and Luther shared a common German-speaking spirituality in the *TG*.

How do we square the Luther who hailed the *TG* with the Luther of the Heidelberg Disputation? Perhaps he was taken initially by the emphasis on passivity (i.e., surrendering to God) as an antithesis to outward works. Luther always had a sense of the existential dimension that the *TG* emphasizes: hell and heaven residing in his own heart and the passionate desire for intimacy with God over worrying

42. See von Loewenich, *Luther's Theology*.

43. Another shibboleth Charles Taylor imputes to the Reformation is that it is "excarnational" (614). Acknowledging that the Reformation followed the polemic of the Hebrew prophets (who for non-Platonic reasons rejected idolatry) Taylor says, "Among Protestants, the central ritual of the Mass was abolished as itself an example of illicit 'magic'" (*Secular Age*, 614). This has nothing to do with being "excarnational" but substitutes *the* incarnation (and its mediation now through preaching and sacrament) with "illicit 'magic.'"

44. See Luther, "Marginalia on Tauler's Sermons" (WA 9:95.20–23).

45. See the preface to *The German Theology* in *LW* 31:71–76.

46. Ozment, *Mysticism and Dissent*, 20.

47. Zwingli, quoted in Jackson, *Zwingli*, 139–43. Rhenanus studied under Jacques Lefèvre d'Étaples at the Collège du Cardinal Lemoine and was a close friend of both reformers as well as with Farel and Erasmus.

about penance and pilgrimages.[48] "There is the emphasis on the 'bitterness' of the true Christian life for a selfish human nature," notes Ozment, "and for reason, which shuns the way of suffering." His experience of *Anfechtungen* (spiritual terrors) as the precursor to *Gelassenheit* (serenity) of union with God bears the marks of this work. "Finally, there are various motifs which stress humility and self-denial, such as the description of the perfect man as always groaning over the persistence of sin, willing to suffer even eternal damnation if that be God's will, and always striving to suppress his selfishness by the hard way of the cross."[49]

In fact, there were enduring influences of the *TG* in Luther's thought that some of his students would take to an extreme.[50] Luther retains an inner-outer distinction that verges sometimes on contrast. Much depends on the target: Rome or the Anabaptists. Over against reliance on outward works and ceremonies he emphasizes, "Christ is a spiritual, internal priest."[51] Also, even in 1526 Luther extrapolates Athanasius's formula of God becoming human so that humans may become gods in terms familiar to German mystics, as Zwingli does in his Sixty-Seven Articles.[52] Perhaps most importantly, the cosmic Christ of Eckhartian mysticism remains influential in Luther's Christology. He never surrendered the idea that Christ, according to his human nature, was omnipresent—even in a bowl of cabbage

48. Translation from Petry, *Late Medieval Mysticism*, 334.

49. Ozment, *Mysticism and Dissent,* 21–22.

50. The *TG* continues to hold a prominent position in the Lutheran movement. As Ozment points out, even Matthias Flacius Illyricus included it in *Catalogus testium veritatis* (1562), "thereby bestowing the blessing of Lutheran orthodoxy" as late as 1562, sixteen years after the reformer's death (Ozment, *Mysticism and Dissent,* 16).

51. "Christ is a spiritual, internal priest; for he is seated in heaven and intercedes for us as a priest; he teaches internally, in the heart" (*LW* 39:80). The emphasis on the "inner teacher" is simply Augustinian (though referred ordinarily to the Holy Spirit). Yet for Luther the inner–outer dichotomy is more pronounced throughout his thinking than it is in other magisterial reformers—with the exception, ironically, of Zwingli.

52. In a 1526 sermon he is still preaching that "God pours out Christ His dear Son over us and pours Himself into us, so that He becomes completely humanified [*venenschet*] and we become completely deified [*gantz und gar vergottet*, lit. "Godded-through"] and everything is altogether one thing, God, Christ, and you." See Luther, *WA* 20:229–30, quoted in Elert, *Structure,* 175–76, with a literal rendering by Marquart, "Luther and Theosis," 185–86. Zwingli said much the same in his Sixty-Seven Articles (1523): "That a person is drawn to God by God's Spirit and deified [*in Gott verwandeln*: transfigured into God] becomes quite clear from scripture." The aim of God's Spirit is not only to justify a "wretched soul" but "wholly to transform it into itself" (*ac prosus in se transformare*). See Zwingli, "The Sixty-Seven Articles" (1523) in Jackson, *Zwingli,* Art. 13. Deification as the goal of salvation (indeed, of creation) is taught by all of the magisterial reformers, but with the usual patristic qualifications that are lacking in these early formulations.

soup, as he taunted Zwingli. Seizing on such ideas, some Anabaptist spiritualists advocated docetic views that Luther rejected sharply.

The strong voluntarist current of the *TG* preserved quasi-pantheistic emphases. Regardless of what Luther himself was thinking as he found himself breaking away from many of his late medieval assumptions, it is clear from his subsequent theological development that he had left Meister Eckhart behind along with "the scholastics" (mainly his nominalist and semi-Pelagian teachers indebted to Gabriel Biel). As Ozment observes, "Luther would not sympathize with an anthropology that endows man with a soteriologically significant 'eye' that can look into eternity," much less one that issues "the call for man to do the best that is in him if he hopes to achieve union with God. Even in the subtle mystical form of passive resignation—a 'doing' which is a 'doing nothing'—this is still allied to that semi-Pelagian *facere quod in se est*, which Luther overcame theologically in his first lectures on the Psalms (1513–16) and attacked explicitly in writings against the nominalists in 1516–17)."[53]

The *TG* distinguishes sharply between the hidden God (*Gottheit*) and revealed God (*Gott*), which is a corollary of the absolute-ordained contrast. Luther appropriated this distinction in the *Bondage of the Will* (1525). However, the mystics wanted to get behind the revealed God known in Christ according to the gospel to the hidden and naked Godhead. Ozment says, "By pointing to a God who is, so to speak, beyond the revealed God, this distinction, so basic to German mysticism, makes possible an appeal to an authority higher than that to which established Christendom in any age pays homage. In religious matters the depths are never fully plumbed by what is revealed."[54] Luther warned that trying to rise above the revealed God to his hidden essence would lead to damnation rather than salvation. This represents a decisive break from the nominalistic mysticism of the *TG*. Calvin repeated the same warnings, exhorting readers to remain on the safe path of God's revealed will rather than to try to probe his hidden will. Criticizing the nominalist view sharply, Calvin said "we do not advocate the fiction of 'absolute might'; because this is profane, it ought rightly to be hateful to us. We fancy no lawless God who is a law unto himself . . . the will of God is not only free of all fault but is the highest rule of perfection, and even the law of all laws."[55]

R. Scott Clark demonstrates that for Luther there was no "evangelical breakthrough" but rather a gradual process between 1513 and 1521, while being assisted

53. Ozment, *Mysticism and Dissent*, 24.

54. Ozment, *Mysticism and Dissent*, 41.

55. Calvin, *Institutes* 3.23.3.

by Melanchthon, from a "Christ in me" to a "Christ for me" orientation. The controversy around Andreas Osiander also galvanized Luther and his followers, including Calvin, against an Eckhartian notion of justification by an indwelling Christ.[56] "I did not learn my theology all at once," Luther later recalled, "but had to search deeper for it, where my temptations took me."[57] As he lectured through the Psalms, Romans, and Galatians, Luther came to see justification as imputed and instantaneous rather than infused and progressive.[58] This shifted his whole emphasis from looking within to looking outside of ourselves to Christ who justifies the ungodly through faith, which is given by the Spirit through external and physical means. At the very time that Luther was setting sail from the harbor of German mysticism, some of his followers were dropping anchor.

Increasingly, Luther was only too happy to distance himself from the elan of the *TG*, which was noticed by Anabaptist spiritualists. His former student Caspar Schwenckfeld was flummoxed. "At first Luther commended the Taulerum [*TG*], now he despises him," he complained.[59] As Ozment relates, "Luther had already begun to turn against the German Theology in 1521–25, regarding it as a source of 'Schwärmerei.'"[60] Keller also credits Luther with "an approving preface to Johannes Kimeus's 1537 attack on the ideas of the *German Theology*."[61]

Indeed, the editions of the *TG* that followed were composed by the most prominent spiritualists (Denck, Franck, Castellio, Weigel) and pietists (Arndt, with Spener's endorsement, and Gottfried Arnold). In his initial Reformed phase, before he became an Anabaptist leader, Franck's first work was a treatise against Anabaptism (Strasbourg, 1529). Introducing his edition, Sebastian Franck said that "the Christian church fell with the death of the original apostles" and he dismissed "the magisterial church fathers (Ambrose, Augustine, Jerome, and Gregory) as 'apes of the apostles and antichrists.'"[62] But the *TG* is inspired, "descended upon us from heaven."[63] According to Ozment:

56. Osiander's views on justification (as an absorption of the soul into Christ's divinity rather than the imputation of righteousness) were condemned by Lutherans. In fact, Calvin added a sustained rebuttal to his final edition of the *Institutes* (3.2).

57. Quoted in Rupp, *Luther's Progress*, 38.

58. Clark, "Iustitia," especially 288–310.

59. Ozment, *Mysticism and Dissent*, 16 n. 8, quoting Keller, *Die Reformation*, 472: "Luther hat am ersten Taulerum commendiert, jetzt veracht er ihn."

60. Ozment, *Mysticism and Dissent*, 16.

61. Ozment, *Mysticism and Dissent*, 16.

62. Ozment, *Mysticism and Dissent*, 32.

63. Ozment, *Mysticism and Dissent*, 34.

> Sebastian Franck, the most uncompromising spiritualist of the sixteenth century, authored an extensive Latin paraphrase of it. Sebastian Castellio . . . translated it into Latin and French. Valentin Weigel, whose posthumously published works attacked the very foundations of Lutheran orthodoxy, made it the model for his first writings. It is further distinguished by the fact that John Calvin condemned it as the poison of the devil, and Pope Paul V placed it on the Index of Forbidden Books where, somewhat ironically, it still remains today.[64]

Every time Luther saw his endorsement of German mysticism invoked for a more extreme program, he became more critical. And Anabaptist groups appeared suddenly in various places with different complexions.[65]

At the same time that Luther faced the "fanatics" in Wittenberg, Zwingli was opposing the Anabaptists in Zurich. Their erstwhile pupils and admirers were now forming dissenting groups, and the *TG* found a prominent place among Swiss Anabaptists as well.[66] Luther's preface to the *TG* highlighted the fact that it was a *German* theology. With Sebastian Franck, there is no question that patriotism played an important role:

> The Germans, having once been raised up in hope, are even more uplifted [to learn] that that highest Good which is God now as always has been a god of the Germans, a God who in this one German theologian (as in those lights to the world, Thomas à Kempis and Johannes Tauler, whom I mention in passing) imparted as much to his church as has ever been communicated to it by any theologian from the ranks of the Hebrews, Latins, or Greeks.[67]

Sebastian Castellio (1515–1563), whom Calvin made the head of his new academy, became enamored of the *TG* and made his own edition. Castellio is a good example of a non-Anabaptist who nevertheless embraced the radical mysticism of the *TG*. He especially emphasized the role of faith not as trust in the person and work of Christ but as a tool, a sort of spiritual technology, in human hands.

64. Ozment, *Mysticism and Dissent*, 16–17.

65. The diversity of these paths is documented well in Burnett, *Debating the Sacraments*. Challenging compartmentalizing approaches, Burnett shows that pamphlets and books in the controversy cannot be grouped easily even around so-called "titans" as Luther and Zwingli.

66. It was "a basic and widely used document for [Swiss] Anabaptist theology and ethics," says Ozment. However, Thomas Müntzer, Hans Denck, and Valentin Weigel used Luther's edition (1516, 1518) of the *TG* "more as a declaration of dissent than as a guide to peaceful meditation and ethical sanctification" (Ozment, *Mysticism and Dissent*, 15).

67. Sebastian Franck, quoted in Ozment, *Mysticism and Dissent*, 34.

If we had enough faith, we could be "omnipotent," Castellio told his friend Nikolaus Zurkinden, secretary of the Basel city council, promising to send him a copy of the *TG*.[68] Zurkinden shared Castellio's growing antipathy to Calvin, but even he was shocked that Castellio should recommend such a ridiculous and unscriptural book. Ozment writes that Zurkinden in response to Castellio "even questions Luther's ever having supported it—the preface, he concludes, must be a 'pseudo-Lutheran preface'—and warns Castellio not to associate his name with it in his forthcoming translation."[69] Instead, Castellio defended the *TG* to Zurkinden: "Who, he asks, could today disseminate the opening words of the sixth chapter of Hebrews, where one is admonished to 'leave the elementary doctrines of Christ and go on to maturity,' or Christ's words that those who believe in him will do even greater works than he himself did—without being accused of blasphemy?"[70] Castellio told his friend that he was, like so many others, given to "dogmatic quibbling."[71] In Ozment's words, "As in the *Hauptreden* of Denck, Castellio highlights 'abandonment' of one's own will and subjugation to its 'opposite': 'For the remedies of things are always through their opposites, and the will of man is the opposite of the will of God.'"[72] Against Calvin, Castellio sees faith not so much as trust but as "best defined in terms of power.... 'Faith produces virtue [*vertu*], that is, the force and power to make what we believe become reality.'"[73]

Similarities between some of the earliest and most formative Anabaptists and what we know of the thirteenth-century Brethren of the Free Spirit associated with Eckhart are striking.[74] They also absorbed Joachim's millennialism and threefold scheme and sought to establish secretive communes in preparation for the age of the Spirit, which they believed to be dawning in their movement. Generally speaking, German Anabaptists looked to the Old Testament theocracy as their model, while the Swiss Anabaptists envisioned a restoration of the church of the book of Acts.

68. Ozment, *Mysticism and Dissent*, 40.

69. Ozment, *Mysticism and Dissent*, 40–41.

70. Ozment, *Mysticism and Dissent*, 40–41.

71. Ozment, *Mysticism and Dissent*, 43.

72. Ozment, *Mysticism and Dissent*, 44.

73. Ozment, *Mysticism and Dissent*, 45.

74. For a helpful survey of the history and basic ideas of this movement see R. Lerner, *Heresy of the Free Spirit*.

A Spiritual Commonwealth: Brethren of the Common Life

A broader tradition of lay spirituality can be found in the Brethren of the Common Life or *devotio moderna*. Founded in the fourteenth century by Gerard Groote, the Brethren was a voluntary association of laymen meeting regularly for prayer, Bible study, and stimulation to personal discipleship. The movement also started schools to inculcate such piety among children. Similar to the *TG*, the Brethren emphasized surrendering the will to Christ, that is, the priority of the internal over the external, and therefore the downplaying of doctrine and ritual to holiness of heart. However, they were no more fastidious in their mysticism than they were in doctrine and liturgy. More than merging with Christ, the Brethren emphasized "the imitation of Christ," the title of the devotional bestseller written by member Thomas à Kempis. Besides Luther, Erasmus, and Heinrich Bullinger, its distinguished alumni included cardinals and the only Dutch pontiff (Pope Adrian), the nominalist Gabriel Biel, Anabaptist leaders like Balthasar Hubmaier and Hans Denck, and the founder of the Jesuits, Ignatius of Loyola. Thus, it fostered a type of northern pietistic humanism that was influential across the entire landscape of sixteenth-century piety.

Erasmus is probably the best exemplar of this heritage. "The corruption of the Church, the degeneracy of the Holy See, are universally admitted," Erasmus declared. "Reform has been loudly asked for, and I doubt whether in the whole history of Christianity the heads of the Church have been so grossly worldly as at the present moment."[75] His *philosophia Christi* was a call to spiritual and ethical reform that would lead to a rebirth of a Christian society as in the Acts of the Apostles. Frustrated with doctrinal debates, Erasmus nevertheless sparked one of the liveliest with his treatise on free will, which elicited Luther's *Bondage of the Will.* He also appealed to Origen, whose teachings had been anathematized, although they made a comeback in the Platonic renaissance.[76] Yet Erasmus was not a magician. One of the most entertaining specimens of his unusually gifted wit was "The Alchemy Scam" from *The Colloquies*.[77]

The pattern in Acts, according to Erasmus, is sharing all things in common, meeting regularly for spiritual edification, and building a truly Christian society. This was not just a charismatic episode in apostolic history, but it should characterize the present. Erasmus's vision of Christendom as a vast monastery with a

75. Froude, *Erasmus*, 284.

76. Price, *Acts and Council*, 2:70–81. Price notes that the Third Council of Constantinople explicitly mentions this condemnation.

77. Erasmus, *Praise of Folly*, 175–81.

simplified doctrine and ritual, sharing all things in common, and living in peace, echoes Joachim's ideal. Erasmus saw the spiritual crisis of his day chiefly as an ethical one, focusing on abuses in the church. Luther came to see Erasmus as promoting another version of works righteousness, with Christ as more of a moral example than a redeemer. Erasmus's main critique of the late medieval church was that external observances had come to replace inward piety.[78]

The Dutch scholar's New Testament editions (1516, 1519, 1522) and various editions of his *Annotations* had a profound impact on the Magisterial Reformation, but even more so on the early Anabaptists. In the 1522 edition he inserts his idea of a possible rebaptism.[79] In the preface he observes that the taking of monastic vows had been called "a second baptism." Why not a "second baptism" for all who desire sincerely to follow Christ?[80] Without entirely rejecting infant baptism, Erasmus concluded that a "second baptism" upon adult conversion was of greater importance.[81] To Calvin, this was at bottom Zwingli's view as well, which he suspected of being an evasion.[82] This was not quite fair, since Zwingli did develop a covenantal approach that linked circumcision in the old covenant to baptism in the new along the lines of the one Abrahamic covenant of grace. Nevertheless, Zwingli did place the emphasis on baptism as an act of human will, enrolling in Christ's army, just as Erasmus had done.

In Erasmus, Swiss and Dutch Anabaptists discovered an emphasis on the inner versus the outer, a symbolic view of sacraments, pacifism, and an "egalitarian view of a Christian society."[83] As early as 1501, Erasmus saw all believers as Christian

78. *Enchiridion*, 55; Friesen, *Erasmus*.

79. Friesen, *Erasmus*, 44–45.

80. Erasmus, *Praise of Folly*, 136–37: "There are many fifty-year-olds who have no idea what vows they undertook in the baptism ceremony, who never even dreamed of what the articles of faith demand of them, what Sunday prayers mean, or what the sacraments of the church imply." It seems that for Erasmus "infant baptism had—objectively speaking—accomplished nothing." It was only the renewal of those vows that mattered, requiring another public ceremony in which as adults they "would dedicate themselves to Jesus Christ [as so many] new recruits pledging loyalty to his cause." · See also Erasmus, *Praise of Folly*, 27, and Friesen, *Erasmus*, 93–95.

81. Friesen, *Erasmus*, 44, 50–75. In his response to such exegesis of the Great Commission, Calvin later wrote that confirmation or public profession was *not* a "second baptism" but a confirmation of God's fulfillment of his promise in the one and only baptism.

82. See Calvin, *Commentary on Acts*, 2:209–10: "Some take baptism for a new institution or instruction [Zwingli], of whose mind I am not, because, as their exposition is too much racked, as it smelleth of a starting-hold [evasion]."

83. Anabaptists appealed to Erasmus's *Paraphrases* for the community of goods. Friesen, *Erasmus*, 40–41. See Erasmus's "Complaint of Peace," in *Praise of Folly*, 88–116.

knights, donning the spiritual armor for battling Satan and worldly lusts.[84] He was first to advance the idea that the evangelical counsels (i.e., chastity, poverty, obedience) pertain to all Christians.[85] According to Erasmus, Christ teaches us "to regard the entire Christian world as a household, as a single monastery."[86] Is this not exactly what Joachim of Fiore predicted of the age of the Spirit? Tongues, prophecy, and healing disappeared from the church, says Erasmus, "since our love has grown cold," and in their place "congregational singing, the Scripture lesson, and the sermon later appeared."[87] Adopting these views, says Friesen, "sixteenth-century Anabaptists were called 'new monks' by the Reformers." Erasmus's Dominican critic, Ambrose Pelargus, pressed similarly, "Is there not danger in those words of yours that the Anabaptists may also find support for their falsehoods?"[88]

Erasmus's arguments against infant baptism were formative for Anabaptists. Zwingli became settled in his opposition to his Anabaptist students by the time he wrote his *Commentary on True and False Religion* (1524). Whereas Erasmus opposed "make disciples" and "baptizing," Zwingli viewed the latter as the means of carrying out the former.[89] While the *TG* was influential across all Anabaptist groups, the spiritual élan of the Brethren of the Common Life was mostly restricted to the Dutch and Swiss, who were inspired by the Erasmian vision of a peaceful Christian commonwealth based on the book of Acts. For the most part, Dutch and Swiss Anabaptists shared the biblicism of Erasmus and Zwingli, while Müntzerites appropriated the Old Testament holy wars that had been appealed to in the Crusades and questioned the validity of scripture, preaching, and sacraments. At this point, however, there was considerable overlap and cross-pollination. It was only after the catastrophic defeat on the battlefield and at Münster that pacifism became more characteristic.

At least initially, Anabaptism was a phenomenon within the German-speaking world. Along with Farel and Viret, Calvin's roots were in the northern French Renaissance associated with Jacques Lefèvre d'Étaples. Peter Martyr Vermigli and Jerome Zanchi were shaped by the Italian Renaissance, especially the Aristotle

84. Erasmus, *Enchiridion militis Christiani* (Handbook of a Christian knight).

85. Erasmus, *Epistola de contemptione mundi* (1523), noted by Kohls, *Theologie*, 19–34. See also Friesen, *Erasmus*, 27.

86. Quoted in Friesen, *Erasmus*, 30; cf. Allen, *Opus epistolarum*, 1:566. Thus, Max Weber's characterization of Calvinism as "this-worldly asceticism" is actually Erasmian.

87. Erasmus, "Letter to Eberhard von der Mark" (1519), quoted in Friesen, *Erasmus*, 30; cf. Allen, *Opus epistolarum*, 3:482.

88. Friesen, *Erasmus*, 27.

89. Bromiley, *Zwingli*, 141–44; cf. Friesen, 81–82.

revival at the University of Padua. None of these figures passed from a stage of fascination with the *TG* or the Brethren of the Common Life. Either unaware of Luther's *TG* edition or disinclined to associate him with it, Farel conjectured that the original Latin version was "Anabaptist delirium" composed by David Joris.[90] Whoever wrote it, Calvin judged that the *TG* was "conceived by Satan's cunning" and could only "poison the church."[91]

"Against the Enthusiasts"

Adam and Eve were the first "enthusiasts," Luther said. "They were not satisfied with the divinity that had been revealed in the knowledge of which they were blessed, but they wanted to penetrate to the depth of the divinity." In other words, they desired to have access to the hidden God rather than to the God who reveals himself in Christ as he is preached externally.[92] Mysticism, merit, a supposedly omnipotent will, and philosophical speculation represented false ladders the Old Adam climbs to God. Luther dubbed this approach a "theology of glory," "seeking God outside the way," that is, beyond the incarnate Word proclaimed in the gospel. Calvin uses the same phrase of disapproval; indeed, the whole Book 2 of his 1559 *Institutes* was to show that the God who is vaguely known in nature and reason is revealed only in the person of the Mediator, Jesus Christ. The French reformer compared the Romanists with the Protestant radicals in his reply to Cardinal Sadoleto: "We are assailed by two sects: the pope and the Anabaptists." Both claimed an ongoing apostolic office, boasting in continuing revelations. "In this way, both separate the Word from the Spirit and bury the Word of God in order to make room for their falsehood."[93]

Anabaptists followed Joachim's vision of a final tribulation before the Age of the Spirit could dawn. "It is almost evening," prophesied Joachim of Fiore. "Now is the time for the elect to weep over the imminent destruction of that youngest Babylon lest perchance we share in her sins and be forced to partake of her punishments."[94] Even the wording is similar to the Schleitheim Confession (1527) of the Anabaptists:

90. Ozment, *Mysticism and Dissent*, 16: "delirium anabaptisticum," from a letter to Bullinger from Calvin (July 1557).

91. Calvin, quoted in Hoffman, *Theologia Germanica*, 26.

92. Luther, *LW* 5:42. See Loewenich, *Luther's Theology of the Cross*; cf. Paulson, "Luther," 363.

93. Cf. "Reply by John Calvin to Cardinal Sadoleto," in Beveridge and Bonnet, *Selected Works of John Calvin*, 1:36.

94. Joachim of Fiore, "Selection B: Letter to the Abbot of Valdona," in McGinn, *Apocalyptic Spirituality*, 118.

> Now there is nothing else in the world and all creation than good or evil, believing and unbelieving, darkness and light, the world and those who are [come] out of the world . . . and none will have part with the other. . . . Furthermore, [God] admonishes us therefore to *go out from Babylon* and from the earthly Egypt *that we may not be partakers of their torment and suffering*, which the Lord will bring upon them.[95]

The Manichaean antithesis between holy believers and the godless world, light and darkness, is as absolute as it is unambiguous. There is nothing of Augustine's "mixed body" of elect and reprobate, with even the elect still corrupted by sin, much less of Luther's paradox of the believer being simultaneously justified and sinful. The more "gnostic" the utopianism, the greater is the sense of urgency in ushering in the age of the Spirit.[96]

It is easy to discern the influence of Erasmus on Zwingli and the Swiss Anabaptists. Nevertheless, notes Scott, "it is also difficult to show when Müntzer became attracted to mystical ideas or to the *devotio moderna* and to the spiritual burdens of lay people. One could surmise that Luther's endorsement of John Tauler, whom he regarded as the author of the *Theologia Germanica*, which he edited in 1518, introduced Müntzer to German mysticism."[97] If Melanchthon helped Luther to understand the forensic character of justification, Müntzer's growing radicalism provoked him to refine his view of baptism and the wider metaphysical framework of Neoplatonic mysticism.[98]

As Müntzer's vehemence broadened, Luther withdrew his support, and this had a decisive impact.[99] By 1520, just a few years after Luther's edition of the *TG*, Müntzer was immersing himself in the work of Tauler and Henry Suso.[100] In fact, according to Jones, "Müntzer read Tauler's sermons from his youth up; in his own copy of these sermons, preserved in the library at Gera, a marginal note says that he read them almost continually, and that here he learned of a divine interior

95. Yoder, *Schleitheim Confession of Faith*, 8–12, emphasis added. There is an absolute antithesis between the world (hence, the visible church) and the elect who have "separated from the world." Those who have not left the fallen churches (Roman Catholic and Protestant) "are a great abomination before God and nothing else can or really will grow or spring forth from them but abominable things" (8).

96. See Kaminsky, *Hussite Revolution*.

97. Gritsch, "Müntzer and Luther," 79.

98. Scott, *Theology and Revolution*, 24.

99. Gritsch, "Müntzer and Luther," 62–63.

100. Gritsch, "Müntzer and Luther," 79–80.

Teaching."[101] The Russian historian M. M. Smirin said that Müntzer was already challenging Luther in Zwickau at this point "under the influence of Joachim of Fiore, late medieval mysticism, and Taborite eschatology."[102]

As Luther was distancing himself from German mysticism he was also coming to his mature view of the sacraments. Meanwhile, Karlstadt and the Zwickau prophets were appealing to Luther's earlier writings and sermons. In 1519, the year he assisted Karlstadt in his debate with Eck, Luther struck Erasmian notes on baptism—for example, as an oath taken by a soldier. In fact, he says in the *Babylonian Captivity* that apart from faith, baptism is an obstacle.[103] The efficacy of baptism lies "in faith, and not in anything that is done."[104] And on Mark 16:16, "Here he points out that, in the sacrament, faith is necessary to such a degree that it can save even apart from the sacrament; that is why He did not add, after, 'He who disbelieveth,' the words 'and is not baptized.'"[105] In 1523 Luther placed more emphasis on the outward sign as God's pledge, while still teaching that apart from faith baptism is "worth nothing . . . only seals upon a letter of blank paper."[106] Over against what he considered the rococo philosophical systems of the scholastics, Luther formed much of his theology in reaction to what he as a pastor was hearing on the ground.

Disturbed by the reports of growing radicalism, Luther returned to Wittenberg and the following March preached his *Invocavit* sermons, calling Christians to peace and denouncing insurrection. Soon, the Zwickau Prophets were driven out and order was restored. By 1523 Karlstadt rejected infant baptism, and the next year he gave up his position as archdeacon and announced that the true gospel was not preached in Wittenberg.[107]

While claiming loyalty to Luther, Müntzer began to appeal to continuing revelations with revolutionary implications, and he became enamored of the Zwickau

101. Jones, *Spiritual Reformers*, 19.

102. Gritsch, "Müntzer and Luther," 55.

103. Woolf, *Reformation Writings*, 1:255; Friesen, *Erasmus*, 85–86. "There was 'no loftier, better, greater oath than the oath taken at baptism,' he argued [WA 2:736]. In the *Babylonian Captivity of the Church* (1520) he dealt with the subject more fully and in the context of Christ's Great Commission, but as given in Mark 16:16: 'He that believeth and is baptized shall be saved.' It is significant that Luther does not, as had Erasmus, set this command to baptize into the larger context of the Commission. For he began by asserting that 'Unless faith is present, or comes to life in baptism, the ceremony is of no avail; indeed, it is a stumbling block not only at the moment we receive baptism but for all our life thereafter.'"

104. Luther, *LW* 1:261; cf. Friesen, *Erasmus*, 86.

105. Friesen, *Erasmus*, 86, quoting *WA* 1:265.

106. Lenker, *Sermons*, 2:203.

107. Looß, "Radical Views," 49.

Prophets.[108] The most recent studies of Müntzer focus on his Joachite eschatology as a primary driver of his revolution.[109] At this point, "Luther was, at best, an early ally." His main inspiration came "by his reading of the mystic John Tauler (whom Luther praised) and by the charismatic Zwickau leader of a conventicle, Nicholas Storch, who claimed to have 'gifts of the Holy Spirit' and favored millennial notions." Yet he still professed loyalty to the reformation that Luther had begun.[110] The only question was whether the age of the Spirit was to be awaited patiently or inaugurated by the elect through violence, and Müntzer became convinced of the latter view.

The chronology makes it clear that Müntzer regrets his submissive attitude. Much in the spirit of Paracelsus, he is no subordinate actor in anyone else's reformation but the genius of his own. In a last-ditch effort, he wrote a letter (July 9, 1523) pretending that he had no relation to the Zwickau Prophets, even though he believed in continuing revelation.[111] Luther responded by advising the Alsteadt pastors to withdraw support and "accused Müntzer of shunning debate and of abusing Scripture," whereupon Müntzer composed a "blast against Christendom," including infant baptism.[112] Thomas Finger's conclusion is clear enough from these examples, that "Müntzer proclaimed a kingdom of the Spirit that no longer relied on the external Word or church."[113] Going beyond Origen, Müntzer's outlook is closer to the ancient gnostics. While the pope binds the Spirit to its sacramental operations, says Calvin, Anabaptists deny that the Spirit freely binds himself to work through them.

By the winter, Luther had produced a resounding riposte, directed mainly at Karlstadt, *Against the Heavenly Prophets*. "God has determined to give the inward to no one except through the outward. For He wants to give no one the Spirit or faith outside of the outward word and sign instituted by Him. . . .With all his mouthing of the words, 'Spirit, Spirit, Spirit,' he tears down the bridge, the path, the way, the ladder, all the means by which the Spirit might come to you."[114]

Müntzer moved his operation to Zwickau in 1520 and 1521. He was expelled again, but had "sown dragons," said Luther of the Müntzerites who were fomenting violence. Embraced in Prague (June to December of 1521), Müntzer wrote

108. Reeves, *Joachim of Fiore*, 142.
109. Gritsch, "Müntzer and Luther," 55–56. Cf. Bräuer and Goertz, "Müntzer," 347.
110. Gritsch, "Müntzer and Luther," 55, 64. See also Gritsch, *Reformer*, 27–38.
111. Gritsch, "Müntzer and Luther," 68.
112. Gritsch, "Müntzer and Luther," 68–69.
113. Finger, "Sources," 37.
114. Luther, *WA* 18:136.16–18; 18:137.12–14; *LW* 40:146–47.

the *Prague Manifesto* in which he presented himself as the new Jan Hus with no mention of Luther. This manifesto sounds many of Joachim's themes and even features of his exegesis, particularly "a seven-fold outpouring of the Spirit, superseding all previous religious authority."[115] Packull goes even further, arguing that "Müntzer's own apocalypticism drew both on Taborite chiliasm and on the medieval Joachimite tradition, rather than upon Luther directly."[116] He was also, like Eckhart, fond of Trinitarian speculations in his phenomenology of history.[117] The age of the Spirit was about to begin. He grew more radical, even questioning the resurrection. His entire focus is on the present moment as the final battle that will usher in the age of the Spirit.[118]

Claiming Prague as the New Jerusalem, Müntzer denounced the "hell-based parsons" as "damned people, who have already been long condemned."[119] The external Word merely testifies to "the living speech of God . . . in the hearts of people." Only direct revelations lead to divine truth. "Therefore it is these damned parsons who take away the true key and say that such a way is fantastic and fool-headed, and that it is the most impossible thing. These are the ones already condemned, with skin and hair, to eternal damnation."[120] They merely "gobble whole the dead words of Scripture and then spit out the letter. . . . The office of the true shepherd is simply that the sheep should all be led to revelations and revived by the living voice of God" and not by "their inexperienced Bible. . . . What kind of assurance of faith is this which comes from books? Perhaps [the authors of Scripture] have lied in what they have written? How can one know whether it is true."[121] Müntzer concludes his Prague Protest: "The time of the harvest is at hand! Thus God himself has appointed me for his harvest. I have made my sickle sharp, for my thoughts are zealous for the truth and my lips, skin, hands, hair, soul, body, and my life all damn the unbelievers." Echoing Savonarola, he declares, "For the new apostolic church will arise first in your land, and afterward everywhere. . . .

115. Reeves, *Joachim of Fiore*, 141–42.

116. Packull, *Mysticism*, 32. He was especially fond of the pseudo-Joachimite *Super Hieremiam*.

117. Packull, *Mysticism*, 33.

118. "In the *Manifesto* Müntzer used the language and categories of medieval mysticism to make his point." He and the common people will be the agent of God for "the final renewal at the end of time." Expelled from Prague in December of 1521, he grew more radical still, even criticizing the doctrine of the resurrection. "In a marginal note in his copy of Tertullian's work on the resurrection, Müntzer noted his disagreement with Tertullian and 'the monk Martin Luther' with regard to the second coming of Christ. He apparently agreed with Taborite eschatology, which predicted the imminent end of the world." See Gritsch, "Müntzer and Luther," 67.

119. Müntzer, "Prague Protest," 2–3.

120. Müntzer, "Prague Protest," 4–5.

121. Müntzer, "Prague Protest," 6–7.

After this raging conflagration, the true Antichrist will personally reign, the radical opposite of Christ. And shortly after this, Christ will give to his elect the kingdom of this world for all eternity."[122]

After being expelled from Prague, he wrote a letter to Melanchthon (dated March 27, 1522) describing the Wittenbergers as "gentle scribes" who follow the "dead letter," urging immediate purification and openness to new revelations before it was too late.[123]

At the same time Luther was coming to a forensic understanding of justification, he was becoming convinced that Müntzer had a different gospel. Luther still underscored the inward piety of German mysticism and the Brethren of the Common Life, but his mature view of justification had turned his spiritual vision outward to the historical Jesus—focused on Christ *for* us rather than Christ *in* us. Müntzer was convinced the doctrine of justification through faith alone was a false teaching that undermined the ethical struggle.[124] Not the "justification of the ungodly," but rather "'the Christification of the world' (*Verchristlichung der Welt*)" was his aim.[125]

After failure in Prague, Müntzer flees to Allsteadt (1523–1524) from which he writes his "Sermon to the Princes." Proclaiming himself the new Daniel, prophesying the final kingdom of the Spirit, he casts the Saxon princes as the mighty warriors of Israel. "Beloved ones, do not offer us any stale posturing about how the power of God should do it without your application of the sword."[126] He urges the princes that "godless rulers, especially the priests and monks, should be killed. . . . For the godless have no right to life except that which the elect decide to grant them."[127]

With growing opposition, Müntzer turned from calling on the Lutheran princes to lead the battle to informing them that they were no longer Davidic rulers. The prophets must oppose the kings of Israel. In various letters, Müntzer reveals his belief that nothing short of a "cleansing slaughter" would usher in the third age.[128] "I tell you truly that the time has come for bloodshed to fall upon this impenitent world for its unbelief. . . . Those who have thirsted for blood will

122. Müntzer, "Prague Protest," 10.

123. Yet he still attends a colloquy with Melanchthon and John Bugenhagen in Wittenberg (April 1522), related to the Zwickau prophets (Gritsch, "Müntzer and Luther," 67).

124. Ozment, *Mysticism and Dissent*, 81.

125. Ozment, *Mysticism and Dissent*, 91.

126. Müntzer, "Sermon to the Princes," 28.

127. Müntzer, "Sermon to the Princes," 31.

128. Ozment, *Mysticism and Dissent*, 77.

drink blood." The local regents must be "strangled as dogs."[129] Such explicit intentions are rarely part of the Anabaptist story in modernity, in comparison with the weight (and criticism) given to Luther's subsequent tract, *Against the Murderous and Thieving Hordes*. Luther advised the princes, "Let them preach against whomever they wish as confidently and boldly as they are able. . . . But when they want to do more than fight with the Word, and begin to use force and to destroy, then your Graces must intervene—whether it be ourselves or they who are guilty—and banish them from the country."[130]

Occupying the town hall of Frankenhausen and storming the castle of the Counts of Schwarzburg, Müntzer's forces were defeated by Philip of Hesse and George of Saxony. Müntzer was captured, tortured, and executed on May 27, 1525. By the time it was all over, as many as seventy-five thousand peasants lay dead. Having survived the slaughter, Hans Hut picked up Müntzer's torch, shaping the South German and Austrian Anabaptism marked by "healings, glossolalia, contortions and other manifestations of a camp-meeting revival."[131] Convinced that the Joachite Armageddon would occur in 1528, Hut declared, "Murder all the authorities, for the opportune time has arrived."[132] But he was burned as a traitor to the empire in December 1527.[133] In *On the Mystery of Baptism* and *A Christian Instruction on How Divine Scripture Should Be Compared and Judged*, both written in 1527, Hut displayed his debt to Müntzer and Denck. "Since we have now reached the last and most dangerous period of this world," he says, "we must prepare for the last battle."[134]

Münster and the Reign of the Spirit

A lay preacher named Melchior Hoffman (1495–1543) was one of the first to be influenced by Müntzer's vision. Reeves notes that he "developed the three-fold pattern in terms of Church history," with the age of the Spirit being ushered in by

129. Quoted in Ozment, *Mysticism and Dissent*, 78.

130. Luther, *WA* 15:218.19–20; 219.5–7; *LW* 40:57.

131. Williams, *Radical Reformation*, 8, 667.

132. Quoted by Williams, *Radical Reformation*, 168.

133. Anabaptists themselves appealed to political leaders. Hubmaier in fact convinced the counts of Lichtenstein to imprison Hut for teaching that Christ was merely a prophet, "that when a man is possessed by a good angel he can do only good, and when possessed by a bad angel only evil," and "that with Scripture one receives lies as well as the truth." Interestingly, these charges he brought before the counts of Lichtenstein included, "That Christians wish to rule the world" and "that power should be taken from the government and given to Christians." Ozment, *Mysticism and Dissent*, 101–2.

134. Ozment, *Mysticism and Dissent*, 103.

Jan Hus and "the Letter transformed into the Spirit." He saw himself and his group "as the Woman clothed with the Sun in the Apocalypse fleeing, as the bride of Christ, into the wilderness." Melchiorite Anabaptists predicted the vengeance on the godless before Easter 1534, giving rise to the new Jerusalem in Münster.[135]

At this stage even Swiss Anabaptists sympathized with armed revolution. Hillerbrand notes that "far from being committed to a policy of withdrawal, the first Swiss Anabaptists strove for a 'territorial base.'"[136] From Montanism's Phrygia to Columbus's New World, millennial visions require a beachhead for the spread of utopia. Hoffman's prophetic predictions exercised a broad influence on the Anabaptist movement. [137]

The scene was being set for Münster as the true city of God. Philip of Hesse protected the city from its Catholic prince-bishop overlord. However, "The Reformation in Münster turned out to be a hothouse made to order for the expansion of Melchiorite Anabaptism."[138] Lutheran pastor Bernhard Rothmann had come under the influence of Sebastian Franck and had formed a peaceful Anabaptist community in the city, claiming that "for fourteen hundred years there have been no Christians on Earth."[139] History for Rothmann is "a succession of apostasy and restitution." Like the ancient shaman, he held the concept of "three worlds." Yet he had gone through the Joachite transition to historical consciousness, with each world representing an age rather than sphere of ascent.[140] He challenged the traditional belief that Christ will return to judge: "vengeance is a prior task of the servants of God," he preached. "We have to be his tools and must attack the godless on the days that the Lord will determine." To make Christ's congregation perfect, it must be conformed to the model of the patriarchs in the Old Testament.[141]

The German Peasants' War (1524–1525) and the later Münster experiment filled all of Europe with dread and provoked the Magisterial Reformers to persecute the Protestant radicals without equivocation. In 1531 Hoffman wrote to his disciple John Campanus: "I believe that the outward church of Christ, including all its gifts and sacraments, because of the breaking in and laying waste by Antichrist right

135. Reeves, *Joachim of Fiore*, 143.

136. Hillerbrand, "Radicalism," 38–39.

137. Stayer, "Anabaptist Münster," 118.

138. Stayer, "Anabaptist Münster," 119.

139. Kirchhoff, *Täufer*; Kirchhoff, "Täufergemeinde in Münster," 7–21, with English translation by Bender, "Peaceful Anabaptist Congregation," 357–70. The quotation is from Jakob of Osnabrück in Stayer, "Anabaptist Münster," 117. On the influence of Franck, see Stayer, "Anabaptist Münster," 127.

140. Vogler, "Anabaptist Kingdom," 106.

141. Quoted in Vogler, "Anabaptist Kingdom," 107.

after the death of the apostles, went up into heaven and lies concealed in the Spirit and in truth."[142] Associated with the insurrection, Hoffman was put in prison in 1539, where he died just a few years later.[143]

Pamphlets circulated widely with thrilling propaganda of the revolution's progress in Münster. Apocalyptic visions were catching on and fretful meetings of rulers in the empire demonstrated the serious threat the spread of Münsterite ideology was in the surrounding areas.[144] Stayer says, "The Anabaptists of Münster believed that God had miraculously revealed that they were given the sword for an apocalyptic crusade through which the world would be punished and their kingdom made universal." Jan van Leiden, a Dutch tailor, abolished the constitution in favor of the civil laws of Israel. "Also, polygamous matrimony was introduced during this phase. After the repulsion of the second attack on the town on August 31, 1534, the constitution of the elders was abolished and replaced by the kingdom of Jan van Leiden."[145] The cathedral area was renamed "Mount Zion," and Jan van Leiden assumed the title of "king over the whole world," with all the appropriate regalia and ceremonial retinue. Ironically, Romans 13 was read aloud, calling Christians under Nero to obey the authorities, even after the radicals had slain the existing authorities.[146] Stayer relates that in his *Restitution*, Rothmann had written of "the abolition of 'buying and selling,' working for money, and indebtedness and usury." Money is "unclean," they said. The *Restitution* bears comparing with More's *Utopia* (1518).[147]

The Old Testament's holy wars had been adopted as the model for Christendom's crusades for centuries, but now it was set in a Joachite frame.[148] Yet, apocalyptic visions are rarely as useful in ruling as they are in revolution. The metaphorical Canaanites had been driven out and the inheritance divided by God between the twelve tribes. The new Israel anticipated great things from its philosopher-king, the new Moses and Davidic king. Stayer says of Jan van Leiden, "He played Niccolo Machiavelli's ultimate political role—that of the giver of laws and shaper of institutions, not once but twice, in creating the regime of the Twelve Elders and his own kingship."[149] Vogler relates, "He had twelve dukes elected in May 1535 to

142. Melchior Hoffman, "A Letter to John Campanus" in Williams and Mergal, *Spiritual and Anabaptist Writers*, 149.

143. Stayer, "Anabaptist Münster," 120–24.

144. Vogler, "Anabaptist Kingdom," 113.

145. Stayer, *Anabaptists*, 239, quoted in Vogler, "Anabaptist Kingdom," 114.

146. Vogler, "Anabaptist Kingdom," 108.

147. Stayer, "Anabaptist Münster," 129–30.

148. Vogler, "Anabaptist Kingdom," 110.

149. Stayer, "Anabaptist Münster," 131.

whom were assigned several territories of the Empire. This measure was obviously aimed at preparing the rule over these territories after an Anabaptist victory. . . . The universal claim announced in Jan van Leiden's coat of arms—a globe pierced by two swords and crowned by the cross—remained beyond reality, even though it expressed consistent reflection in terms of the scriptural motivation."[150]

Although Jan van Leiden's court was lavishly appointed, all property—and even their wives—were held in common. Jan himself took as many as sixteen, beheading one wife for insubordination.[151] Though limited to Münster, it was its own world within and opposed to the world, a theocracy that mirrored the secular political order, including currency whose coins bore Jan van Leiden's image and the Anabaptist message of new birth.[152] Scanning primary accounts, Stayer concludes, "In the apocalyptic moment there were to be no rich or poor, no men or women; but in the provisional haven in Münster it appears that men with money were at a premium!"[153] Women and the poor were among the most hopeful yet ultimately the most oppressed members of the Münsterite kingdom.[154]

John van Leiden's reign lasted from February 1534 to June 1535, when the imperial estates gathered an army sufficient to crush the regime.[155] It was only after the shock from the successive defeats culminating in Münster that the pacifist voices in the movement gained credibility. Regathering at a conference at Bocholt in August of 1536, Anabaptist leaders agreed that either it was not yet the time for a militant overthrow of the ungodly, or that this would be achieved without violence by the withdrawal of the perfect from the world.[156] Committed steadfastly to armed revolution, the Müntzer wing was represented by Hut, Franck, and Denck. On the side of the pacifist stance of the Swiss Brethren (especially Grebel) stood Menno Simons and Pilgram Marpeck. David Joris, a Dutch disciple of Hoffman, charted a middle path: the time to take up arms was not quite yet.[157] "In fact," Ozment documents, "his spiritualized version of the Joachite vision of history—Joris speaks of three stages of growth in the Spirit modeled on the progression from boyhood through adolescence to manhood—appears almost verbatim in Castellio's discussion of the working of the Spirit in the faithful."[158]

150. Vogler, "Anabaptist Kingdom," 109.
151. For a good full-length monograph see Arthur, *Tailor-King*.
152. Vogler, "Anabaptist Kingdom," 109.
153. Stayer, "Anabaptist Münster," 128.
154. Stayer, "Anabaptist Münster," 129.
155. Vogler, "Anabaptist Kingdom," 114–15.
156. Stayer, "Anabaptist Münster," 125.
157. Williams, *Radical Reformation*, 582.
158. Ozment, *Mysticism and Dissent*, 199.

Valentin Weigel (1533–1588) takes these various strands—a sharp letter and Spirit dualism, a "heavenly flesh" Christology, Eckhartian *henōsis*, and Paracelsian natural philosophy—and weaves them together with a Joachite eschatology partitioned into "three ages of the world."[159] In the third age, says Weigel, "The external Jerusalem is internalized. . . . Then all monasteries, cloisters, temples are to be torn down, so that not one stone stands upon another. . . . The outer will be brought into the inner. . . . Then one will have no need for ordained preachers or other teachers, for each will be taught by God."[160] Weigel expected this state to appear here and now. According to Ozment, "As in the *Postille*, Weigel's case in the *Dialogue* comes to a halt with a proleptic dethronement of the imperfect, visible ecclesia militans by an ideal, invisible church of true believers." Yet, his new Jerusalem was not a geopolitical realm, but one that existed within each individual. In fact, "Criticism is turned on the 'extra nos': 'The kingdom of God or God is not found in any place outside us, only in the Spirit within ourselves.' And it is said of those who look to the historical Christ: 'The Antichrist clings to the external merit, death, and passion of Christ.'"[161]

Conclusion

Where others like Savonarola had failed, Müntzer felt he was chosen by God to initiate the age of the Spirit. The visible order in both church and state had fallen. They must be abolished, not repaired. In fact, he argued, the church fell away as early as the death of the apostles. Ozment explains that, for Müntzer, "the devastating of the people's 'temple' by the clergy is engineered by the twin theological concepts of the religious establishment: the doctrines that Scripture is the sole authority in the church (*sola scriptura*) and that saving faith comes through hearing the Scripture preached (*fides ex auditu*). These are skillfully crafted tools for the exploitation of the poor and the aggrandizement of the powerful."[162] In Müntzer's own words: "So they poison the Holy Spirit with the Holy Scripture."[163]

When Paul says that "faith comes by hearing the word of God" (Rom 10:8), says Müntzer, "he speaks there of the inner word to be heard in the abyss of the soul

159. Ozment, *Mysticism and Dissent*, 234.

160. Quoted in Ozment, *Mysticism and Dissent*, 235. Ozment comments, "This tendency to overlap the two ages is not surprising given Weigel's concept of Christ's bodily presence in believers."

161. Ozment, *Mysticism and Dissent*, 241.

162. Quoted in Ozment, *Mysticism and Dissent*, 84.

163. Ozment, *Mysticism and Dissent*, 87.

through the revelation of God."[164] The patriarchs and apostles attained visions "in painful tribulation," he adds. "Therefore it is no wonder that Brother Fattened-swine and Brother Soft-life [Luther] rejects visions." Such visions are necessary in order to bring about "the transformation of the world."[165] As Goertz observes, "the battle fought psychologically in the 'inner order' of the soul must also be fought physically in the 'outer order' of sociopolitical power."[166] In this pregnant statement we find the analogy with alchemy played out on a sociopolitical scale.

Ozment notes, "Scripture, as will be echoed by every sixteenth-century dissenter, gives only a witness and not the very experience of faith. It describes the truly faithful, but does not create true faith." All of this to support the idea of "direct, unmediated communion between God and man. . . . Applied to society, the theology of the heart becomes a truly revolutionary ideology."[167] Under Müntzer the angelic pope, the true saints will take into their own hands the final judgment of sheep and goats. Eric Voegelin describes this idea well: "The saint is a Gnostic who will not leave the transfiguration of the world to the grace of God beyond history but will do the work of God himself, right here and now, in history."[168]

It is quite misleading to call this movement the Radical Reformation. Far from representing an extreme version of Luther's teachings, it dropped anchor in the Eckhartian harbor just as Luther was sailing away from it at full tilt. However, Müntzer rather than Luther would have the most enduring historical impact. Despite its anachronistic portrait, the description of Müntzer by Karl Marx's collaborator, Friedrich Engels, brings into sharp focus the revolutionary utopianism at the heart of modernity:

> His philosophico-theological doctrine attacked all the main points not only of Catholicism, but of Christianity generally. In the form of Christianity he preached a kind of pantheism, which curiously resembled modern speculative contemplation and at times even approached atheism. He repudiated the Bible both as the only and as the infallible revelation. The real and living revelation, he said, was reason, a revelation that has existed at all times and still exists among all peoples. To hold up the Bible against reason, he maintained, was to kill the spirit with the letter, for the Holy Spirit of which the Bible speaks is not something that exists outside us—the Holy Spirit is our reason. Faith is

164. Müntzer, "Sermon to the Princes," 20.

165. Müntzer, "Sermon to the Princes," 23–24.

166. Ozment, *Mysticism and Dissent*, 91.

167. Ozment, *Mysticism and Dissent*, 87, 91. Glenn Alexander Magee is correct that "Marx, not Hegel, is the true modern disciple of Joachim." See Magee, *Hegel*, 247.

168. Voegelin, *New Science*, 147.

> nothing but reason come alive in man, and pagans could therefore also have faith. Through this faith, through reason come to life, man became godlike and blessed. Heaven is, therefore, nothing of another world and is to be sought in this life. It is the mission of believers to establish this Heaven, the kingdom of God, here on earth. Just as there is no Heaven in the beyond, there is also no Hell and no damnation. Similarly, there is no devil but man's evil lusts and greed.[169]

These beliefs seem remarkably contemporary, but they were not antireligious. On the contrary, Müntzer believed he was more spiritual than the preachers and teachers who, in his view, lacked the Spirit. Every radical mystic and revolutionary after him would sympathize with this outlook.

169. Engels, *Peasant War*, 23.

4

Gnostic Revival
The Divine Self in the Age of the Spirit

Religious experience of the shamanistic type is individual, not collective.

—E. R. Dodds[1]

Historic Anabaptists, however, often overplayed Spirit and downgraded matter. I attribute this largely to the (conceptual) ontological barrier that prevented the two from interacting. . . . Total personal renewal, where "all creaturely desires are rooted out and smashed," was a significant theme in such preaching. . . . This grace divinized people so fully that they passed beyond "the creaturely."

—Thomas N. Finger[2]

Hence I am the creator of both my eternal and my temporal being. I am born into a temporal being, but because of my eternal birth I can never die. According to my eternal birth, I have always been, am now, and shall always be. My temporal being shall pass away and come to nought, for it is meant only for a time and must pass with time. All things were brought forth in my birth. I was the cause of myself and of all things. Indeed, had I so wished, I and all things would not yet be. Were I not, God would not be.

—Valentin Weigel[3]

1. Dodds, *Greeks and the Irrational*, 141–42.
2. Finger, *Anabaptist Theology*, 563, 474–75.
3. Quoted in Ozment, *Mysticism and Dissent*, 52.

I have argued that Anabaptism is not a radical wing of the Reformation but a different movement arising from late medieval mysticism and the Orphic Renaissance. If such groups were radical, it was in relation to Eckhartian and Erasmian traditions from which Luther distanced himself.[4] Contemporary Anabaptist historians have highlighted this connection. Werner O. Packull observes that, following Eckhart, "the mystics affirmed that God and man share a common nature and are really connected."[5] Whether accurately or not, they were identified by Roman Catholics and Protestants alike with the medieval gnostics as "Catharers."[6] In many respects, the main historical lines pursued thus far—namely, of Gnosticism, Hermeticism, mystical enthusiasm, and Joachite eschatology—intersect in early Anabaptism. As I have suggested, not all spiritualists were Anabaptists and not all Anabaptists took spiritualism to the same degree. Yet there are sufficient family resemblances in comparison to official church teaching, whether Protestant or Roman Catholic. The type of spiritualism outlined in the previous chapter is foundational to later developments that I have chosen to dedicate a chapter to elucidating from primary sources the specific character of its dualism.

There is no group in the sixteenth century that perfected the tradition of the "divine self" I am considering in this project. Their enthusiastic embrace of Joachite prophecy along with Alexandrian gnosis (Neoplatonism, Hermeticism, and Gnosticism) justifies comparisons with shamanism.[7] The shaman soared between three worlds, from hell to earth and to highest heaven. Indeed, advocates of the "perennial philosophy" such as Huxley place Anabaptist spiritualists in this stream of "spiritual religion" exhibited by "the devout contemplatives of India, the Sufis of Islam, the Catholic mystics of the later Middle Ages, Denck, Sebastian Franck and Castellio, as Everard and John Smith and the first Quakers and William Law."[8] This is a generalization, to be sure, but I think he is generally right.

The type of Platonism we find in the *Symposium* directs us to see the shadows

4. This is one of the main lines of argumentation in Packull, *Mysticism*. Steven Ozment refers to the thesis of Alfred Hegler in 1892: "The 'radicals' from Thomas Müntzer to the Antitrinitarians (Socinians), he maintained, were inaccurately portrayed as those who simply exaggerated Protestant ideas. Rather, 'they turn back to medieval ideas. . . . For what has most determined the theories of the radicals in a positive way is mystical soteriology in the form it received in Germany mysticism during the fourteenth and fifteenth centuries'" (Ozment, *Mysticism and Dissent*, 14, from Hegler, *Geist und Schrift*, 13).

5. Packull, *Mysticism*, 20.

6. Verduin, *Reformers*, 95–131.

7. I have in mind particularly the Origenist stream from Evagrius. At least from what we know especially from Athanasius's biography, the "father of monks" Anthony the Great (ca. 251–356) was an ascetic, not a philosopher.

8. Huxley, *Philosophy*, 1–34.

of beauty itself in beautiful things. For Ficino, however, who opposed the corporeal and incorporeal, the soul in the middle could "marry the world" through natural magic. As the opening quote from the Hermetic Asclepius cited in Pico's *Oration* attests, the "Dignity of Man" rests on having an indeterminate nature so that individuals can choose a divine or beastly nature for themselves. With its rational soul, humanity stands midway in the hierarchy, "the *vinculum* or link between the earthly and the divine."[9]

However, the Orphic concept of the divine self is never more evident than in its most extreme versions. Plotinus may have been "ashamed to be in a body," as Porphyry reported (*Vita Plotini* 1–2), but even Plotinus wrote a treatise against the gnostics. At the same time, he acknowledged that their hatred of the corporeal was an unnuanced reading of Plato.[10] While the Anabaptists lacked the flamboyant myths, they were essentially in sync with the gnostic outlook. The evil creator mentioned in ancient gnostic writings may be absent from Anabaptist texts, but it is difficult to avoid the same conclusion when human nature as such is described as utterly evil and irredeemable. A Manichaean choice must be made between adopting a divine nature or a satanic nature in these Anabaptist writings, and this sharp dualism drives all the way down on the same points that we have seen in ancient gnostic texts.

Nature and Grace

In Platonism, the main dichotomy is between nature and grace, while in Christianity, the main antithesis is between sin and grace. Orthodox theologian Andrew Louth explains well that Platonism conceives of the soul's search for God "as a return, an ascent to God; for the soul properly belongs with God, and in its ascent is but realizing its own true nature. Christianity, on the other hand, speaks of the Incarnation of God, of his descent into the world that he might give to man the possibility of communion with God that is not open to him by nature."[11]

The Platonic nature-grace dualism pervades early Anabaptist writings, but it is pushed into gnostic territory. As Plotinus argued, *everything* emanates from the One; the rays of its goodness reach even to bodies, and he upbraids the gnostics for attributing physical nature to an evil deity. An *inferior* world, to be sure, yet

9. Celenza, "Revival," 88.

10. Porphyry, *Life of Plotinus* 1, in Plotinus, *Enneads*, trans. Armstrong, 1:3; cf. Plotinus, *Enneads*, 291 (2.9.17).

11. Louth, *Origins of Christian Mysticism*, viii.

visible nature is nevertheless a faint image of reality.[12] For gnostics, however, the body and the visible world are not shadowy images but dangerous illusions. "As [a] created being, man is himself the forbidden tree in the garden of Eden," according to Weigel. Body and spirit are created from matter and the celestial quintessence, but the soul is an immediate and indestructible spark of God.[13] From Sebastian Franck and Caspar Schwenckfeld especially, Weigel mediated this dichotomy to the radical pietists.

As captured in the epitaph above from contemporary Anabaptist theologian Thomas N. Finger, not only sinful desires but everything creaturely was to be eradicated. Grace was seen not merely as a supplement to nature, as Aquinas taught, but also as an aid to transcending it. Spiritualists spoke of the "new self" being a different spirit that replaces the "old self" in the new birth. According to the Schleitheim Confession (1527), the wicked have a satanic spirit and are therefore "a great abomination" from whom "only abominable things" can come.[14]

The matter-spirit rift extends broadly across Anabaptist theology. On one side is the *reality*: the invisible divine essence (*Gottheit*), Christ's omnipresent spiritual body, the inner Christ, inner sacraments, and the perfect invisible church.[15] On the other side is the *appearance*: the visible incarnate God and his saving acts in history, the external word and sacraments, and the visible church as a mixed body. At the spiritual level all is one; only in appearance are things divided by corporeality.

The Magisterial Reformers considered this entire ontology Manichaean. In contrast, they held that the whole person, in body and soul, is created in God's image, fallen, redeemed, and finally raised. Any notion of passing beyond the creaturely was regarded as violating God's aseity as well as God's goodness in creating human nature. The Reformers even challenged fundamental assumptions of medieval theology about the relation of nature and grace. The problem is not that reason needs assistance in governing the lower self, Luther countered, but that the

12. Plotinus, *Enneads*, trans. Armstrong, 2:235–45 (2.9.4–6).

13. Ozment, *Mysticism and Dissent,* 212–13. Ozment says, "Man, we learn, consists of body, spirit, and soul. The first two proceed from the physical creation. The body originates in the elements of the earth, the spirit in the firmament of the stars. . . . The soul, on the other hand, is a 'spirit from God.' It proceeds 'ex spiraculo vitae,' from the very mouth of God, and is absolutely indestructible. This threefold anthropology is also expressed in terms of man's having 'two bodies' (visible and invisible) and 'two spirits' (from nature and from God). The second 'body' is but a comprehensive way of saying that spirit and soul comprise an (invisible) individual entity distinct from the body proper" (213).

14. The Schleitheim Confession (1527), translation by Yoder, *Schleitheim*, 12.

15. I explain these gnostic dichotomies in *Shaman and Sage*, 293–99.

intellect itself is the citadel from which the soul leads the body into rebellion.[16] The whole self is like a majestic castle in ruins.[17]

Despite his devotion to Augustine, Calvin rejected even his notion of a gracious gift added to nature (*donum superadditum*) but lost in the fall.[18] Adam and Eve had free will originally, but Adam willingly bound human nature to sin and death. "For the depravity and malice both of man and of the devil, or the sins that arise therefrom," says Calvin, "do not spring from nature, but rather from the corruption of nature."[19] Calvin rejected the position represented by Aquinas that the body and its desires tend inherently toward vice: "For not only did a lower appetite seduce [Adam], but unspeakable impiety occupied his mind, and pride penetrated to the depths of his heart. Thus it is pointless and foolish to restrict the corruption that arises thence only to what are called the impulses of the senses; or to call it the 'kindling wood' that attracts, arouses, and drags into sin only that part which they term 'sensuality.'"[20] Such a "Manichaean error" would bring reproach on God the creator.[21]

Yet even after the fall, the divine image was not destroyed.[22] Grace is given

16. Luther on Psalm 51 in *LW* 12.351.

17. Luther, "Lectures on Romans: Glosses and Scholia," in *LW* 25:299. Calvin writes, "Hence the great obscurity faced by the philosophers, for they were seeking in a ruin for a building. . . . They held this principle, that man would not be a rational animal unless he possessed free choice of good and evil; also it entered their minds that the distinction between virtues and vices would be obliterated if man did not order his life by his own planning. Well reasoned so far—if there had been no change in man. But since this was hidden from them, it is no wonder they mix up heaven and earth!" (*Institutes* 1.15.8).

18. Calvin says that Adam fell "by his own free will," adding, "Here it would be out of place to raise the question of God's secret predestination because our present subject is not what can happen or not, but what man's nature was like. Therefore Adam could have stood if he wished, seeing that he fell solely by his own will" (*Institutes* 1.15.8; cf. 2.3.5).

19. Calvin, *Institutes* 1.14.3.

20. Calvin, *Institutes* 2.1.9–10.

21. Calvin, *Institutes* 1.15.1.

22. There did remain in Luther and particularly Mathias Flacius Illyricus a tendency to see the fall as annihilating nature. See Luther, "Lectures on Galatians Chapters 1–5," in *LW* 1:63–64. Luther held that with the fall "the image of God was lost" and it is only "the Gospel [that] brings it about that we are formed once more according to that familiar and indeed better image, because we are born again into eternal life" (*LW* 1:63–64). Instead, Calvin spoke of the image being "effaced," "corrupted," existing now in a condition of "deformity," but "not totally annihilated and destroyed" (*Institutes* 1.15.4). See Horton, "Shattered Vase," 151–63. Once more, some statements in Luther and his associates reflect lingering influences of the *TG*. Yet while Anabaptists took this view further, Lutherans devoted considerable space in their confession to refuting "the doctrine of the Manicheans" by denying that there is any mingling of satanic substance with human nature. "For the chief articles of our Christian faith forcibly and emphatically testify

not to liberate the soul from the body but to liberate the whole person from the guilt and corruption of sin. Following Irenaeus, Calvin emphasizes that the goal of deifying grace is not to make us less human but more fully so. "Therefore, relying on this pledge, we trust that we are sons of God, for God's natural Son fashioned for himself a body from our body, flesh from our flesh, bones from our bones, that he might be one with us. Ungrudgingly, he took our nature upon himself to impart to us what was his, and to become both Son of God and Son of man in common with us."[23] There is no part of our nature that is completely eliminated, accounting for civic virtue, but none that is not corrupted.[24] For the Reformer, the qualitative distinction is drawn between God and creation, not between invisible and visible. There is no divine self, a spark of divinity. The whole self is created, fallen, and redeemed.[25]

Nevertheless, looking backward to Eckhart and anticipating the radical pietist Jakob Böhme, Denck adds in his *Hauptreden*, "For the cause of all disunity, wherever it occurs, is dissimilarity of wills (*ungleiche der willen*). God, being one and desiring unity, is unalterably opposed to all that is 'two.'"[26] Unity is not only a mere appearance of reality, as in Platonism, but it is totally opposed to diversity as the ancient Gnostics taught. Denck tells us that the "One" is "the being and 'Is' of all creatures (*aller creature wesen und Ist*)."[27] This is the view expressed by Amaury de Bène and his followers who were charged with reviving the gnostic heresy at the University of Paris. Ficino backed away from Amaury's formula explicitly. "Further," Denck stipulates, "the One undertakes nothing without the creature.... In order that the seed or image may return to its origin, the One is prepared to welcome back everything that has been separated from him."[28] Thus in treating the superiority of the secret and immediate revelation of the divine Spirit to the human spirit over the external word, Denck reveals the deeper ontological dualism that grounds it.

Precisely because of their commitment to the inner Christ over the historical Jesus, most Anabaptists rejected Luther's mature teaching, not to mention Chalcedonian christology. In Augsburg, Denck wrote more treatises against Luther,

---

why a distinction should and must be maintained between man's nature or substance, which is corrupted by sin, and the sin, with which and by which man is corrupted." See article 1 on original sin in the Book of Concord.

23. Calvin, *Institutes* 2.12.1–2.

24. Ozment, *Mysticism and Dissent*, 183–84.

25. Calvin, *Institutes* 2.2.15; cf. 1.1.1–2, 1.13.26, and 2.12.1.

26. Ozment, *Mysticism and Dissent*, 28.

27. Quoted in Ozment, *Mysticism and Dissent*, 29–30.

28. Quoted in Ozment, *Mysticism and Dissent*, 29–30.

especially on free will and predestination, than against Rome.[29] Ozment notes, "Together, these treatises form a frontal assault on the three Lutheran solae: sola scriptura as authoritative revelation; solus Christus incarnate as the agent of salvation; and sola fides ex auditu verbi as the narrow gate to Christian life. Denck's manifest concern . . . is to dehistoricize and deinstitutionalize 'Truth' absolutely."[30] The disincarnate Logos is central, Ozment points out: "This testimony is in all people, and it preaches to every single one, especially according to how one listens to it. . . . Scripture speaks of a tranquility, which is the means of coming to God, that is, Christ himself, not to be regarded physically, but rather spiritually, as he himself also proclaimed before he came in the flesh." The incarnation appears to be necessary merely as a witness to this spiritual deification.[31] "Those who pay heed more to the 'witness' (the historical Christ of Scripture) than to the 'Truth itself' (the disincarnate, omnipresent Christ of the heart) pervert Christian faith."[32]

In short, Denck manifests clearly the mystical rationalism of philosophical religion that flourishes in the Enlightenment and has become, generally speaking, the presupposition of liberal Protestantism. Spread out on the ground are many religions with their own historical claims, authoritative canon, dogmas, and rites. Yet, with spiritual insight one rises (simultaneously descending into oneself) to discover the Truth itself. Once spirituality is shorn of religion, all people are united in the divine Spirit. This anticipates Kant's dichotomy between universal "pure religion" and particular "ecclesiastical faiths," which is basically the contrast between spirituality and religion. Everything physical and historical lies under condemnation. Augustine's conception of the church as a mixed body is a particular target. As Denck puts it, Luther has "mixed with the Midianites instead of going on into the promised Canaan."[33]

The only true church consists of pure disciples. Outward preaching, baptism, and the Eucharist are in vain. "As fast as the new comes ceremonies and sacraments vanish and fall away. They do not belong to a religion of the Spirit; they are for the infant race and for those who have not outgrown the picture-book. . . . 'When the Kingdom of God with its joy and love has come in us we do not much care for those things which can only happen outside us.'"[34] Anticipating Jakob

29. These treatises are part of Denck's work, *What Scripture Means When It Says That God Is the Cause of Good and Evil* and *On the Law of God: How the Law Is Abolished and Yet Still Must Be Fulfilled.*

30. Ozment, *Mysticism and Dissent*, 125–26.

31. Ozment, *Mysticism and Dissent*, 126–27.

32. Ozment, *Mysticism and Dissent*, 127–28.

33. Quoted in Jones, *Spiritual Reformers*, 37–38.

34. Quoted in Jones, *Spiritual Reformers*, 39.

Böhme, who figures prominently later in this story, Moravian Anabaptist and Denck disciple Christian Entfelder (1526–1544) says, "The visible and invisible creation, in all its degrees and stages, is the outgoing and unfolding of God, who in His Essence and Godhead is one, indivisible and incomprehensible . . . goes out of Unity into differentiation and multiplicity; but the entire spiritual movement of the universe is back again toward the fundamental Unity, for Divine Unity is both the Alpha and Omega of the deeper inner world."[35] Laid on top of Eriugena's Trinitarian metaphysics of emanation, Joachim's three ages form the template for such Christology, notes Packull:

> There are, he says, three well-marked stages of revelation: (1) The stage of the law, when God, the Father, was making Himself known through His external creation and by outward forms of training and discipline; (2) the stage of self-revelation through the Son, that men might see in Him and His personal activity the actual character and heart of God; and (3) the stage of the Holy Spirit which fills all deeps and heights, flows into all lives, and is the One God revealed in His essential nature of active Goodness—Goodness at work in the world. Externals of every type—law, ceremonies, rewards and punishments, historical happenings, written Scriptures, even the historical doings and sufferings of Christ—are only pointers and suggestion-material to bring the soul to the living Word within, "to the Lord Himself who is never absent," and who will be spiritually born within man.[36]

Spirit versus Letter

In 2 Corinthians 3, Paul contrasts the letter with the Spirit. The reformers understood the "letter" to refer to the law without the gospel: the law only condemns apart from the regenerating work of the Holy Spirit. In this manner, the apostle announces the new covenant, as prophesied especially in Jeremiah 31. In contrast, ancient gnostics as well as Origen interpreted this contrast in a Platonic manner: the body, scripture's natural historical sense, and the external word and sacraments versus the spirit, the allegorical meaning, and the inner self. At most, says Erasmus, sacraments are "signs and supports of piety."[37] As with Origen, reflective of Orphic pedagogy, he says they might be necessary "for children in Christ," perhaps until they become more mature. And so even those "more advanced in perfection"

35. Jones, *Spiritual Reformers*, 40–41.

36. Packull, *Mysticism*, 52.

37. Erasmus, *Enchiridion*, in Dolan, *Essential Erasmus*, 68.

should not scorn them, "lest their scorn work great harm among the simple and uninstructed." "My approval," Erasmus continued, "rests on the assumption that they are steps, gradations, that lead to more appropriate means of salvation."[38]

This was the way most Anabaptist writers understood the apostle's contrast of the law and the gospel.[39] Some pushed the contrast further than Erasmus. Karlstadt declared, "All visible and external acts of worship are useless. God esteems only the spirit."[40] The soul that would "receive the noble work of God . . . must be emptied of all creaturely clothing or images, i.e. the heart must become circumcised if it wants to receive divine love."[41] We are reminded of the gnostic trope of stripping off the tunic of flesh. Karlstadt may not have gone as far as others, but it is not surprising that being "emptied of all creaturely clothing" would extend to the incarnation.

Among the first to carry the Reformation to Silesia in Central Europe, Caspar Schwenckfeld (1490–1561) came under the influence of Müntzer and Karlstadt.[42] According to Schwenckfeld, a Christ without true human flesh saved souls without bodies through a word without preaching, a baptism without water, and a Last Supper without bread and wine. Schwenckfeld also tended to elide any distinction between the Holy Spirit and the believer's spirit.[43] "The Scriptures cannot bring to the soul that of which they speak," he said. "This must be sought directly from God Himself."[44] As McLaughlin puts it, "In a sense there was only one inner sacrament, one inner event: spiritual rebirth."[45] Regarding Schwenckfeld's understanding of baptism, Quaker historian Rufus Jones relates that "Christian baptism is therefore

38. Erasmus, *Enchiridion*, 68.

39. See Goertz, *Anabaptists*, 49.

40. Quoted in Sider, *Andreas Bodenstein*, 151.

41. Quoted in Sider, *Andreas Bodenstein*, 219.

42. See McLaughlin, *Schwenckfeld*.

43. McLaughlin, *Schwenckfeld*, 103.

44. Quoted in Jones, *Spiritual Reformers*, 72.

45. McLaughlin, *Schwenckfeld*, 137. Schwenckfeld rejected Luther's conception of the spoken word as a vehicle for the spirit" (see 96; cf. 97). According to McLaughlin, Schwenckfeld held that salvation depends on God's immediate activity, as in Paul's conversion, "'and not upon these letters or external promises' of Scripture. . . . For Schwenckfeld, these two orders were mutually exclusive; the spiritual did not work through the physical. . . . Christ's spiritual flesh shared with believers made Christians participants in his glorified humanity." It was therefore the inner word, the inner baptism, and the inner Eucharist alone that mattered (98, 102–3). As Rufus Jones explains, the believer—quite apart from the Last Supper—receives "something from that spiritualized and glorified nature of Christ" as "the actual food of man's spirit, so that through it he partakes of the same nature as that of the God-Man." It is a continual experience (Jones, *Spiritual Reformers*, 82).

not with water, but with Christ," his "spiritual presence." Hence, Schwenckfeld did not endorse rebaptism, since baptism itself did not matter.[46]

Like Müntzer, Schwenckfeld was another erstwhile follower of Luther who nevertheless remained in the orbit of the *German Theology*. Luther's reform was one merely of the letter, but this is not the kingdom, he concluded. Schwenckfeld said, "The fullness thereof would be achieved in the second stage, the Reformation of the spirit, which was now at hand."[47] Hans Denck disagreed with Luther's identification of Scripture and God's word:

> The Holy Scriptures I consider above every human treasure, but not so high as the Word of God which is living, powerful, and eternal, for it is God Himself, Spirit and no letter, written without pen or paper so that it can never be destroyed. For that reason, salvation is not bound up with the Scriptures, however necessary and good they may be for their purpose, because it is impossible for the Scriptures to make good a bad heart, even though it may be a learned one. A good heart, however, with a Divine Spark in it is improved by everything, and to such the Scriptures will bring blessedness and goodness.[48]

Denck emphasized "an inner religion, grounded on the inherent nature of the soul, and guided by the inner Word." [49] He dispenses with original sin, the bondage of the will, and dependence on divine grace in election, emphasizing instead "a potentially Divine nature" within every individual.[50]

In shifting from external authority (childhood) to inner autonomy (maturity), Anabaptist spiritualists were the first modern biblical critics. Expanding on

46. See Jones, *Spiritual Reformers*, 80–83. Interestingly, Scottish Presbyterian Samuel Rutherford linked Quakers to Schwenckfeld in *A Survey of the Spiritual Antichrist* (1648; ch. 5).

47. Quoted in McLaughlin, *Schwenckfeld*, 109.

48. Quoted in Jones, *Spiritual Reformers*, 29.

49. Jones, *Spiritual Reformers*, 20. Initially a friend and student of Oecolampadius, Denck was recommended by the humanist and reformer to a post as a schoolmaster in Lutheran Nuremberg, but he soon came under the influence of Müntzer. Banished, he wandered until his death, at first organizing a sizable group in Augsburg, where in 1527 the disparate movement came to sufficient agreement to produce the Schleitheim Confession. In Martin Bucer's Strasbourg as well he gained followers. As in Luther's Wittenberg, Bucer was open to public debate as a way of resolving disagreement. However, Anabaptists usually ignored such invitations, eschewing any consensus with "Babylon." Yet Denck conceded. After being granted a public disputation, Denck lost and "was ordered to leave the city forthwith." After a brief stay in Worms, hunted from place to place, he found his final shelter with his old friend Oecolampadius in Basel, where at a mere thirty-two years of age he died of the plague in November 1527. See Jones, *Spiritual Reformers*, 21.

50. Jones, *Spiritual Reformers*, 22–23.

Humbaier's list, Denck's *Hauptreden* offers forty "antitheses" (i.e., contradictions) in scripture.[51] With Denck, the distinction between mystic and rationalist becomes indiscernible, since the inner light is identical with God, who is reason or mind. Jan J. Kiwiet notes that Denck and other South German Anabaptists "protested against the authority of the Book and asserted that a personal relation with God never could be achieved nor mediated by a book consisting of paper and ink."[52] In *The Law of God* (1526) Denck identifies the "letter" not only with the literal sense but with the Bible itself.[53] Even in his *Recantation* (1528) he confessed, "I hold the Scriptures dear above all of man's treasures, but not as high as the Word of God which is living, strong, eternal and free of all elements of this world." The Spirit speaks in one's inner spirit, apart from external means.[54] Similarly, in his *Two Hundred and Eighty Paradoxes*, "Franck argues that 'God needs no external means to perform his inner work,' and he brings forth half a page of quotations from Tauler as proof. Paradox 44 again marshals support from Tauler to maintain that God 'teaches (one who is *gelassen*) more in a flashing moment than all external words, sermons, and Scripture until the end of time.'"[55] The secret, implanted and inborn word, "Christ born in us," is contrasted with "the written and spoken word of God, which he says is but its 'image, shadow . . . and echo.'"[56] For such ideas he appeals again to Tauler and Eckhart.[57] "As little as the inner man can be fed with external bread . . . so little can he be taught by the external word."[58] Franck declares, "'To substitute Scripture for the self-revealing Spirit is to put the dead letter in the place of the living Word.'"[59]

These writers are not atheists but spiritualists—or as Plato said: "a true mystic . . . by which I mean, a philosopher" (*Ep. 335a*; *Phaedo* 69d). The Enlightenment was merely the full flowering of this idea that humanity must escape the bonds of authority to arrive at autonomy. The chief features of "axiality" are on display in this trend: self-discovery, leading to criticism, distanciation, and disembedding. "Spiritual but not religious" fits well with the dichotomy of inner and outer, spirit

51. Packull, *Mysticism*, 27.

52. Kiwiet, "Hans Denck," 1.

53. Furcha and Battles, *Selected Writings*, 63.

54. Furcha and Battles, *Selected Writings*, 123–24. See also Packull, *Mysticism*, 54–55; Ozment, *Mysticism and Dissent*, 106–13, 154, 160, 163.

55. Ozment, *Mysticism and Dissent*, 154.

56. Ozment, *Mysticism and Dissent*, 160.

57. Ozment, *Mysticism and Dissent*, 163.

58. Quoted in Ozment, *Mysticism and Dissent*, 164.

59. Quoted in Jones, *Spiritual Reformers*, 60.

and letter, the supposed orthodoxy of a fallen church versus the gnosis of the divine self within. Franck exhorts his followers to unlearn everything they learned "from our youth up" not only from the papists but "from Luther and Zwingli." The external church is vanishing, yielding to "the inward enlightenment by the Spirit . . . without external means." [60]

Anticipating Gottfried Arnold's church history, Franck wrote *A Universal Chronicle of the World's History from the Earliest Times to the Present* (1531) in which the villains are the so-called orthodox, whom he designates "heretics of the letter."[61] Franck wrote, "Theology is more a matter of experience than of knowledge, and the secret of all theology is therefore more a matter of rebirth than something which can be communicated by any words." Reflecting the program of philosophical religion described by Carlos Fraenkel, Franck here proposes a process of maturity from heteronomy to autonomy. Scripture is needed by children, he says,

> until, as adults and those advanced in Christ, we can turn our backs on everything external, understanding no one and knowing nothing according to the flesh, but being already carried over into the Spirit, we have the Holy Spirit as the living Book of God, and are instructed of God by the one true teacher of the godly. . . . The solid food of the perfect does not come from Scripture. For Scripture is only a witness or testimony to truth for those who are taught by the Spirit.[62]

Valentin Weigel (1533–1588), an important mediator between Anabaptism and pietism, owed much of his thinking to the Hermetic writer Paracelsus. After soaking in Eckhart, the *TG*, Schwenckfeld, and Franck, Weigel embraced Paracelsus's sweeping vision of natural-supernatural philosophy.[63] Weigel expresses "the epistemological primacy of the individual mind over against so-called objective

60. Franck's 1530 *Chronica und Beschreibung der Türkey*, quoted in Jones, *Spiritual Reformers*, 48–49; the last quote is taken from Franck's 1530 *Chronica und Beschreibung der Türkey*.

61. Jones, *Spiritual Reformers*, 50, from *Chronica und Beschreibung der Türkey*.

62. Quoted in Ozment, *Mysticism and Dissent*, 36.

63. Ozment, *Mysticism and Dissent*, 209. Ozment quotes Eduard Zeller: "'In place of a simple mysticism come a point of view schooled in the natural philosophy of Paracelsus and a sharp critique of the church.' The transition, according to Zeller, is marked by the closely interrelated concepts of the 'heavenly flesh of Christ' . . . and the necessity of man's 'bodily' renewal or new birth in Christ." Ozment agrees with the broad lines, but thinks that the third stage is as rooted in medieval mysticism as in Paracelsus.

reality." That is, knowledge comes from the "inner eye" of the knower and not from the object known. He also emphasizes "the soteriological primacy of the depths of the soul over against the institutional loci of divine knowledge and presence (Scripture, creeds, and sacraments)."[64] Like Müntzer, Denck, and Schwenckfeld, Weigel insisted that when the apostle said faith comes by hearing the word (Rom 10:17), he meant the internal word. Scripture and preaching have their place as witnesses. However, "he who hath the inward Schoolmaster loseth nothing of his Salvation although all preachers should be dead and all books burned." The true "measuring line" is not scripture but "the inward Word, the Spirit of Christ, within the believer."[65]

Castellio is another representative of this outlook, influenced by David Joris as well as his own edition of the *TG*.[66] When Beza criticized his biblical translation work, Castellio replied, "The word of God is neither Hebrew, Greek, nor Latin, only spiritual."[67] However, Castellio tended to identify reason rather than the will as point of union with God. He represents the emerging trend of identifying the inner word with inner reason that we see consummated later in this story. Rationalism and mysticism are perfectly compatible in Castellio's thinking. According to Ozment.

> It is not surprising that Castellio finds no ambiguity whatsoever in Holy Scripture when it is searched on the really essential matters such as the existence and nature of God, the duty of love and worship, flight from sin, and the pursuit of virtue. In obscure and disputed matters, however, like baptism, the Lord's Supper, justification, predestination, and the like, Scripture is unclear. In such cases as these, what is one to do? One is to adhere to *the prophet*, to the surest guide, to what Castellio alternatively refers to either as sensory experience and commonsense judgment or, simply, reason. . . . The eternal and *subjective voice of reason* is lauded as more authoritative than "writings and ceremonies," i.e. historical tradition. Being the "more ancient and certain," reason claims absolute precedence, the very Son of God bowing to it. . . . *Reason, I say, is a certain eternal word of God.*[68]

64. Ozment, *Mysticism and Dissent*, 210.

65. Weigel, *On the Life of Christ* (part 1, chapters 4–6), quoted in Jones, *Spiritual Reformers*, 145–47.

66. Ozment, *Mysticism and Dissent*, 198.

67. Quoted in Ozment, *Mysticism and Dissent*, 181.

68. Ozment, *Mysticism and Dissent*, 191, 196, emphasis added.

Jesus of History versus Christ of Faith

G. H. Williams notes, "With the overriding conviction that they were living at the opening of a new age, the Radical Reformers began to alter their conception of the redemptive role of Christ."[69] "As the outer word of the Bible must be purified and interpreted by those who experience the Spirit in the 'depth of the soul,'" Eric Gritsch observes when describing Müntzer's Christology, "so too does the historical, external Jesus become the real Christ only through his spiritual resurrection in the believer. Thus Müntzer's rejection of biblical authority goes hand in hand with a 'dehistorizing' of traditional Christology."[70]

In the thought of the Magisterial Reformers, Christ assumed human nature to redeem it. According to ancient gnostics and sixteenth-century Anabaptists, Christ clothed himself with spiritual flesh to save trapped souls from everything creaturely so that they may return to the hidden depths of the Godhead. The God revealed through external creatures is not the truth but, at best, a semblance or picture of the truth. The reality is the One emanating into diverse appearances and returning to unity.

As part of this restoration, Denck taught that all souls will finally be saved, the same doctrine we have met in Origen and Eriugena: the so-called *apokatastasis*, or final return of all souls.[71] In Augsburg the Lutheran leader Urbanus Rhegius confronted Denck with these rumors and, finding them true, set out to show from scripture the error of universal salvation. "Denck is said to have brought forth 'a fantasy' about 'how God was one, and that in that same oneness all disunited things must be united.'"[72] Denck's disciple Hans Hut followed him on this point.[73]

Arguing that the passages adduced against universal restoration were not to be taken literally, Denck and Hut reverted to an allegorical interpretation. Franck, too, believes, "All that is told in the Genesis account is told of what goes on in the mysterious realm within us. It is told as though it were an external happening, it is in reality an internal affair. . . . Heaven and hell are there."[74] Above all showing their affinity with Origen, they insisted that God's punishment is always remedial and not retributive, and this should trump all literalistic exegesis.[75] As Packull

69. Williams, *Radical Reformation*, 75–84.
70. Gritsch, "Thomas Muentzer," 180–81.
71. Seymour, *Theodicy*, 30.
72. Packull, *Mysticism*, 41.
73. Packull, *Mysticism*, 41.
74. Jones, *Spiritual Reformers*, 57.
75. Packull, *Mysticism*, 42.

observes, "Denck's universalism rested on assumptions which in the final analysis grew from Neoplatonic mystical and humanistic roots." Evil and sin "were a necessary by-product of the creation process, resulting from the Neoplatonic spirit-matter dichotomy and the nature of physical existence *per se*."[76] Heaven and hell were existential states of mind for Denck; one need not remain in remedial punishment.[77] Packull also points out that Denck was drawn to kabbalah, writing that, "just as the mystical assumptions of reunion inspired by Neoplatonism provided a key for his belief in universal redemption, so they provided a stimulus for his ecumenical interests."[78] Cheerfully, Jones says,

> They seem to have wiped their slate clean of the long line of Augustinian contributions, and to have begun afresh with the life and message of Jesus Christ . . . by the experience of the earlier German mystics who helped them to interpret their own simple and sincere experiences. . . . They reject all the scholastic accounts of Christ's metaphysical nature, they will not use the term Trinity, nor will they admit that it is right to employ any words which imply that God is divided into multiform personalities.[79]

It is therefore this cosmotheological process rather than the historical events reported in scripture that are constitutive of Anabaptist Christologies.

Moralism and dualism are fused in Anabaptist Christologies of the sixteenth century, albeit in different degrees. A Manichaean ontology is combined with a practically Pelagian anthropology, rendering Jesus a supreme example of a fully surrendered soul. Anticipating Schleiermacher by two centuries, Denck says that Christ was so united to the will of God that his decisions and acts were God's decisions and acts. "Not that it would be possible for human nature to make anybody saved, but God was so completely identified in Love with Him that all the Will of God was the will of this Person, and the sufferings of this Person were counted as the sufferings of God Himself."[80] The voluntarism of the mystical tradition is in full view—it is not the hypostatic union of natures but the fusion of wills. Jesus is the great example of one who by his own free will surrendered his personality to God.

76. Packull, *Mysticism*, 32, 43–44.

77. Packull, *Mysticism*, 44. As Sebastian Franck, one of his sympathetic contemporaries, explained: "The hell into which the godless are placed he [Denck] holds to be the torment of the conscience which will not be outside man but within him, and which begins when man is shown his sin and unbelief. . . . Not that he has to remain there and that there is no grace in hell."

78. Packull, *Mysticism*, 45–46.

79. Jones, *Spiritual Reformers*, 42–44.

80. Denck, *Von der wahren Liebe*, as quoted in Jones, *Spiritual Reformers*, 25.

This same fusion of wills must occur among Christ's followers. "He insists that no one can be 'called righteous' or be 'counted righteous' until he actually *is* righteous. Nothing can be 'imputed' to a man which is not ethically and morally present as a living feature of his character and conduct."[81] Union with God, according to Denck, is attained through the divine Christ within, not the historical Jesus.[82]

Following Denck, Johann Bünderlin views Christ as God's greatest picture of a soul truly surrendered to God. "But no one must content himself with Christ after the flesh, Christ historically known," he cautions. "That is to make an idol of Him."

> We can be saved through Him only when by His help we discover the essential nature of God and when He moves us to go to living in the spirit and power as Christ Himself lived. His death as an outward, historical fact does not save us; it is the supreme expression of His limitless love and the complete dedication of His spirit in self-giving, and it is effective for our salvation only when it draws us into a similar way of living, unites us in spirit with Him and makes us in reality partakers of His blood spiritually apprehended. . . . Every step of human progress and of spiritual advance is marked by a passage from the dominion of the external to the sway and power of inward experience.[83]

Once again, the paideia of philosophical religion is evident within a Joachite eschatological frame: "God is training us for a time when images, figures, and picture-book methods will no longer be needed, but all men will live by the inward Word."[84]

Franck's Christology was similar to Denck's, according to McLaughlin. "Since creation the inner word, Christ, was present in all men from birth, he taught. The historical Christ had served merely as an outward manifestation or recapitulation of the birth, suffering, and glorification which Christ endured in all men's souls. The historical Jesus lost almost all significance for Franck."[85] For Denck, the whole purpose of the incarnation is to provide an example of morality. Denck wrote that Jesus "fulfilled the Law, not that He wanted to exempt us from it, but because He wanted to give us an example to follow Him."[86] Obviously this Pelagian view of Christ's work tended toward an Arian Christology. As Packull writes, "Unlike

81. Jones, *Spiritual Reformers*, 26.
82. Jones, *Spiritual Reformers*, 56; cf. Packull, *Mysticism*, 48–49.
83. Quoted in Jones, *Spiritual Reformers*, 35, 37–38.
84. Jones, *Spiritual Reformers*, 37–38, quoting Bünderlin, *Ein gemayne Berechnung*.
85. McLaughlin, *Schwenckfeld*, 205.
86. Quoted in Packull, *Mysticism*, 49.

the average person, Christ had lived in harmony and consciousness of the divine presence in Him. . . . Christ was unique inasmuch as He never left union with the Divine." Packull adds that some of his disciples (including Hut, according to Hubmaier) took that next step, denying Christ's unique divinity and consequently the Trinity.[87]

The goal, as in earlier mysticism, is "resignation" or "complete surrender" (*Gelassenheit*). Jesus helps us to reestablish this unity of will with God, the will in both cases constituting the essence. "It is for this reason that the Father sent him forth."[88] Upon reading such sentiments, it is not surprising that two centuries later Friedrich Schleiermacher would call himself "a Moravian of a higher order."[89] In fact, citing various scholars, Packull observes, "Hans Denck has been variously rediscovered as the 'Schleiermacher of the Reformation,' a 'rationalist and Pietist in one person,' and therefore 'neither one nor the other,' a forerunner of an 'undogmatic Christianity,' or 'ethical moral action Christianity,' and as a typical product of the German *Volksgeist*."[90] That moderns of various stripes can see their reflection in Denck attests to his remarkable originality as a forerunner of modern Protestantism. For Denck, Jesus was the most perfect model of humanity, but not divine.[91]

The absorption of creaturely identity into divinity reflects the broader metaphysics of the *TG*. The contrast is not between sin and grace but between the creaturely and the divine. Thus, Schwenckfeld denied that Christ's humanity is creaturely, like ours. McLaughlin summarizes, "During Christ's life, passion, and death this sinless flesh was spiritualized, bereft of its earthly qualities, and divinized."[92] Further, according to Richard Cross, he argued that "the deification of Christ's human nature, achieved at the Exaltation, involves its 'equalization (*Gleichwerdung*)' with the essence—becoming 'equal' to the divine essence, or having no essence (*Wesen*) other than God's essence."[93] Schwenckfeld's associate Valentin Crautwald argued that during Christ's earthly life and death he "gradually was deified."[94] Schwenckfeld could never say that God himself assumed natural humanity in order to recapitulate Adam's trial and redeem it from Adam's curse.

87. Packull, *Mysticism*, 49–50.

88. Ozment, *Mysticism and Dissent*, 30–31.

89. Schleiermacher, "Letter to George Reimer" (1802), quoted by Waring, introduction to Friedrich Schleiermacher, *On Religion: Speeches to Its Cultured Despisers*, x.

90. Packull, *Mysticism*, 35.

91. Seymour, *Theodicy*, 30.

92. McLaughlin, *Schwenckfeld*, 204.

93. Cross, *Communicatio Idiomatum*, 117.

94. McLaughlin, *Schwenckfeld*, 203.

The "old man" is, for Schwenckfeld, simply human nature as such, which must be obliterated.[95]

Schwenckfeld loved to quote Luther's *Christmas Postills* (1522). "Though Luther was later to repudiate these statements for their failure to give due credit to Christ's humanity," McLaughlin argues, "there continued to be real similarities between Schwenckfeld's theology and Luther's."[96] Luther seems to have criticized Schwenckfeld's Christology directly in only one place.[97] In that critique Luther,

> while explicitly rejecting Schwenckfeld's position, came quite close to its substance. Because Luther was ignorant of Schwenckfeld's latest Christological statements concerning Christ's noncreaturely status, he argued against Schwenckfeld's earlier formulation which limited the issue to the glorified Christ. Luther forthrightly asserted that Christ was a creature according to his humanity, and that God was the father of his divinity alone. His humanity was assumed, not begotten.[98]

McLaughlin adds, "Schwenckfeld's Christology was not Lutheran, but then neither was it drastically different. On the continuum which stretched from Nestorianism to Monophysitism Schwenckfeld stood between Luther and Melchior Hoffman, between Luther and Servetus, toward the latter end of the scale."[99] McLaughlin continues what I find to be a plausible and important argument: "For Luther, Zwingli and many of the Anabaptists, Christ's humanity is almost a vessel, instrument or medium of the divine Son's activity. It is closer to Apollinarianism, actually, than Monophysitism, which is why Luther and Zwingli can be seen as more allied in substance at least on this point than either is with Bucer or Calvin. Luther says that the divinity works through the humanity."[100]

Likewise, the true union of God with humanity is as impossible in Weigel's thinking as it was for the ancient gnostics. The Christ of faith must remain always separate from the Jesus of history.[101] For Weigel, says Jones, "always in the last

95. McLaughlin, *Schwenckfeld*, 213–14.

96. McLaughlin, *Schwenckfeld*, 216. He cites Luther's critical remarks on his 1552 *Postills* on 216 n. 91 from Siggins, *Luther's Doctrine*, 219.

97. Luther, "Disputatio de divinitate et humanitate Christi" (February 28, 1540) in *WA* 39.2:92–121.

98. McLaughlin, *Schwenckfeld*, 217.

99. McLaughlin, *Schwenckfeld*, 218.

100. McLaughlin, *Schwenckfeld*, 219–20; cf. Siggins, *Luther's Doctrine*, 166, 169, 197; Jones, *Spiritual Reformers*, 144, quoting from Weigel, *On the Life of Christ*, chapters 3 and 4 of part 2.

101. Ozment, *Mysticism and Dissent*, 233.

analysis it is Christ in us that saves us, but it was Christ in the flesh, the Christ of Galilee and Golgotha, that revealed to men the way to apprehend the inward and eternal Christ of God." Jones continues to observe that Weigel's Christ "is Man not in the crass, crude and earthly form: He is not composed of mortal and earthly substance as our 'Adamical bodies' are. He is wholly and absolutely composed of heavenly, spiritual, divine substance. . . . But that divine, spiritual, heavenly nature, which appeared in Him, is the true, original, consummate nature of Man."[102] Under the rubric of Adam and Christ, Weigel "proceeds to show two radically diverse natures, the traits and characteristics of which he arranges in opposing pairs, in two parallel columns" under the nature of Christ and the nature of Adam.[103]

In the fall of 1538, Schwenckfeld wrote his treatise *On the Incarnation of Christ*, arguing that Jesus did not assume flesh from the Virgin Mary but a heavenly flesh.[104] In March 1540, Lutheran leaders gathered at Smalkald condemned Schwenckfeld's Christology as beyond the pale of the ecumenical creeds. It was drafted by Melanchthon and signed by Bucer and other Reformed leaders as well.[105] In the same year Luther had him expelled from ministry in Silesia. A year later, in 1541, Schwenckfeld published his *Great Confession on the Glory of Christ*, arguing for his "heavenly flesh" doctrine along with the belief that Jesus became progressively more divine especially in his exaltation.[106] In Strasbourg, Schwenckfeld joined Sebastian Franck in emphasizing that the invisible church had replaced the visible church. Franck's *Universal Chronicle* was the first church history to sympathize with ancient heretics, particularly the gnostics. If comparisons with ancient Gnosticism seem too partisan, we have the trail of spiritualist church histories from Franck's *Universal Chronicle* to Arnold's *Impartial Church History* that welcome the association.[107]

Concluding that Schwenckfeld had not gone far enough, Melchior Hoffman posited that Jesus never had been fully human in the first place: "Christ drew nothing from Mary."[108] Schwenckfeld didn't agree entirely at this point, but thought

102. Jones, *Spiritual Reformers*, 142.

103. Jones, *Spiritual Reformers*, 142–43.

104. McLaughlin, *Schwenckfeld*, 211, emphasis added.

105. McLaughlin, *Schwenckfeld*, 222.

106. McLaughlin, *Schwenckfeld*, 202.

107. Ozment points out, "In the preface to his history of heretics, a subsection within the history of the church, Franck points out that he would canonize many whom Rome has anathematized, for 'they have more of the Spirit in one of their fingers than Antichrist in all his sects'" (*Mysticism and Dissent*, 143).

108. McLaughlin, *Schwenckfeld*, 204.

it was better than the Catholic view defended by Martin Bucer.[109] During the summer of 1531, Schwenckfeld engaged in discussions with Michael Servetus before both were exiled from Strasbourg. Besides denying the Trinity, Servetus had written that in the resurrection Christ's human nature was "laid aside just as if it were an accidental thing. There is nothing now in Christ which is animal. He has returned to the original state of the word, and is then God, and is in God, as before.... It was only the divinity that saved."[110] After his interaction with Servetus in the summer of 1531 Schwenckfeld's position was clear.[111]

From Hoffman the "heavenly flesh" Christology was passed to Denck, Menno Simons, and Dirk Philips. Opinions concerning the Trinity ranged from affirmation to rejection, the latter especially among Polish and Italian Anabaptists. For many early Anabaptist leaders, it was another nonessential dogma imposed by the church and state. But significant debate erupted over the incarnation. Hoffman and Simons held that human nature was evil, even demonic. Thus, Simons argued, the eternal Son could not have assumed it. He did not receive his humanity from the Virgin Mary, therefore, but from heaven; a spiritual body that he had from all eternity.[112] Calvin learned of Simons's view mainly through the Polish Reformed leader Jan Łaski (John à Lasco) and included a rebuttal in his *Institutes*, accusing Simons of being a Manichaean.[113] They teach that the eternal Son took flesh from heaven rather than from the Virgin Mary and that whenever he appeared visibly it was because angels attended him. I do not think it was an off-hand comparison when Calvin said in a sermon, "What madness it is to make *such an alchemy*, to frame a body for the Son of God! What shall we do with that passage which saith, 'He took not on him the nature of angels, but he took on him the seed of Abraham' [Heb. 2:16–17]?" Calvin continues:

> It is said. He took upon Him our flesh, and became our brother. Yea, and that He was made like unto us, that He might have pity upon us, and help our infirmities. He was made the seed of David, that He might be known as the Redeemer that was promised, whom the fathers looked for from all ages. Let us remember that it is written, the Son of God appeared in the flesh; that is.

109. McLaughlin, *Schwenckfeld*, 204.

110. Servetus's *Dialogue on the Trinity*, quoted in McLaughlin, *Schwenckfeld*, 207–9.

111. McLaughlin, *Schwenckfeld*, 208.

112. Against the Reformed leader John à Lasko, Menno Simons wrote in "The Incarnation of Our Lord" that "there is no letter to be found in all the Scriptures that the Word assumed our flesh... or that the divine nature miraculously united itself with our human nature." See Wenger, *Menno Simon*, 829. See also Verduin, *Reformers*, 230–53.

113. See Schmidt-Biggemann, *Philosophia Perennis*, 173–80, on "heavenly flesh" Christology.

> He became very man, and made us one with Himself; so that we may now call God our Father. And why so? Because we are of the body of His only Son. But how are we of His body? Because He was pleased to join Himself to us, that we might be partakers of His substance.

This is not "vain speculation," Calvin adds, but essential to our faith. He repeats, "These are *marvellous alchymists*, to make so many new natures of Jesus Christ."

> Thus the devil raised up such dreamers in old times to trouble the faith of the church; who are now renewed in our time. Therefore, let us mark well what St. Paul teaches us in this place; for he gives us good armor, that we may defend ourselves against such errors. If we would behold Jesus Christ in His true character, let us view in Him this heavenly glory, which He had from everlasting: and then let us come to His manhood, which has been described heretofore; that we may distinguish His two natures. This is necessary to nourish our faith.[114]

McLaughlin concludes regarding Calvin's christological critique:

> These differences will, of course, shape as well as reveal the wider and deeper metaphysical assumptions of the West going forward. Luther believes that Christ works through worldly reality in such a way that the latter actually becomes the former; Zwingli separates the reality of Christ from the world except by spiritual recollection and anticipation. Calvin believes that God is active in the world through creaturely means precisely because the latter remain tangible, earthly, and creaturely even in the process of being God's means of revelation and saving grace. Even more radically than Zwingli, the Anabaptists cannot find Christ or his activity anywhere in this world except in the inner recesses of the heart and the gathered hearts of a pure community.[115]

Nominalism contributed in its own significant way to the emptying of this world of divine presence, but both paths of Platonism have played an underappreciated role in the "disenchantment of the world." According to the first path, the creaturely sign is valuable only because it becomes the spiritual reality. This is what I have been calling natural supernaturalism. According to the second path, the sign is not valuable but distracting, as was evident especially in its most extreme version—a form of Gnosticism where divine goodness is withdrawn from

114. From a sermon on 1 Timothy 3:16 in Calvin, *Sermons*, 30.
115. McLaughlin, *Schwenckfeld*, 215–19.

this world entirely. McLaughlin's description of Calvin's view is supported across the Reformer's writings. Precisely *as* natural—never transformed into the reality nor separated from it but bound to it inseparably by the Spirit—certain physical signs and actions appointed by Christ become means of grace. Because they are purely natural, they are tangibly accessible; because they are consecrated, they are no longer just dead symbols.

Reformation versus Restoration

The union of gnosis and millennialism inspired the revolutionary ideal, with the goal of passing from an external church and state to an inward enlightenment. Luther, Calvin, and other evangelicals were Reformers, not revolutionaries. Luther had no attraction to millennialism and rebuffed those who, like Ulrich von Hutten, said he was the angelic pope driving out his wicked double. There is suffering now and has been ever since Christ's ascension, but the antichrist is now restrained, and at Christ's return he will be destroyed.[116] Even Luther's identification of the papacy with the antichrist was based not on Joachite speculations but on his conviction that Pope Leo X and his ilk had hijacked the church and fulfilled Paul's prophecy concerning the antichrist.[117] However, as Pelikan notes, "Although the pope was the Antichrist 'seated in the temple of God,' the church in which he was seated was still the temple of God."[118] Calvin also spoke of the church having fallen into "general deformity" in doctrine but acknowledged that there were true churches among the papists.[119]

The mark of the true church for Rome was the majesty of its outward form of organization, while Anabaptists located it in the will and piety of its members. However, Calvin says with Luther that the marks of the true church are "the pure preaching of God's Word and the lawful administration of the sacraments."[120] Whether considering individuals or the church corporately, Calvin counsels,

> In bearing with imperfections of life we ought to be far more considerate. For here the descent is very slippery and Satan ambushes us with no ordinary devices. For there have always been those who, imbued with a false conviction of their own perfect sanctity, as if they had already become a sort of airy spirits, spurned

116. *LW* 35:378, 405–8.
117. *LW* 26:180.
118. Pelikan, *Christian Tradition*, 173.
119. Calvin, *Institutes* 4.2.12.
120. See Calvin's prefatory address to King Francis I in Calvin, *Institutes*.

> association with all men in whom they discern any remnant of human nature. The Cathari of old were of this sort, as well as the Donatists, who approached them in foolishness. Such today are some of the Anabaptists who wish to appear advanced beyond other men. There are others who sin more out of ill-advised zeal for righteousness than out of that insane pride. When they do not see a quality of life corresponding to the doctrine of the gospel among those to whom it is announced, they immediately judge that no church exists in that place.[121]

"It is not for us to purify the church, although we have to long for its purity," Calvin elsewhere states when commenting on Psalm 22:26. "The church however must wait 'until the heavenly judge separates the rejected from the elect.' (Ps 79:6). . . . As long as the doctrine and the liturgy remain pure, the unity of the church may not be broken due to sins committed by members of the church."[122] Following this Augustinian ecclesiology, John Knox in his treatise *Against the Anabaptists* asked how the apostle Paul could "salute and acknowledge the congregations at Corinth, Galatia, and Thessalonica, for the true Churches of Christ Jesus, in which none the less were crimes most grievous: fornication, adultery, incest, strife, debate, contention, and envy."[123]

Anabaptists saw the entire visible body of the church, whether Protestant or Roman Catholic, as creaturely rather than divine. All that mattered was the invisible church. By the late 1520s, Schwenckfeld and his followers had replaced the Roman Catholic and Lutheran services with their own meeting. Yet, still unsatisfied with the community's level of apostolic perfection, they suspended the celebration of the Last Supper. Schwenckfeld never again communed.[124]

Sebastian Franck also completely spiritualized the church. A purely spiritual Christ within replaces the historical Jesus and his church. Rufus Jones says, "The Invisible Church forms the central loyalty of Franck's fervent soul. . . . 'It is a Fellowship, seen with the spiritual eye and by the inner man. . . . Love is the one mark and badge of Fellowship in it.'"[125] In the age of the Spirit there will be no visible churches, sermons, or sacraments.[126] Christ, who is in his very nature God, "is not limited to the historical Person who lived in Galilee and Judea." "He is an eternal Logos, a living Word, coming to expression, in some degree, in all times and lands, revealing His Light through the dim lantern of many human lives—a Christ reborn

121. Calvin, *Institutes* 4.1.13.
122. Selderhuis, *Calvin*, 230.
123. Knox, *Warning*, 26.
124. McLaughlin, *Schwenckfeld*, 75–76.
125. Jones, *Spiritual Reformers*, 58–59, quoting Franck's *Paradoxa*, sections 8–9.
126. Jones, *Spiritual Reformers*, 59.

in many souls, raised again in many victorious lives, and endlessly spreading His Kingdom through the ever-widening membership of the Invisible Church."[127]

This spiritualization was carried forward by Valentin Weigel, who mediated it to the pietists. Weigel taught that, like the inner word, heaven and hell are within us.[128] "All real knowledge is in the knower. Both external world and written scriptures are in themselves *shadows* until the inward spirit interprets them, and through them comes to the Word of God which they suggest and symbolize." Yet, as a devoted Hermeticist, Weigel appropriated Paracelsus, who had already been involved in Müntzer's revolution. And, as Jones notes, "He was himself, in turn, a most important influence in the development of the religious ideas of Jacob Boehme."[129]

In *Astrology Theologized*, Weigel says each person's "star" is "in his own breast. It lies in his own power to 'theologize his astrologie,' to turn his universe into spiritual forces."[130] According to Ozment, "His defense of the subjective character of knowledge . . . earned Weigel the reputation of being, not only among the first to pose the 'basic problem of modern philosophy,' but also of materially anticipating the critical philosophy of Immanuel Kant." Be that as it may, though, Ozment does not see him as a harbinger as much as a carrier of the medieval past into modernity.[131] For Weigel, after the incarnation, Adam is "no more."[132] "This 'becoming God,' this existentialized incarnation, as it were, is what Weigel has in mind when he speaks more traditionally about 'new birth,' 'new man,' 'conversion,' 'true obedience,' or 'repentance.'"[133] Ozment continues:

> As the *German Theology* has it: "God does not want it [the new birth] to happen without man, and man does not want it to happen without God." . . . In the logic of German mysticism, man cooperates in the attainment of salvation by simply freely doing nothing (i.e., *Gelassenheit*). Weigel dismisses the synergistic controversy with a mystically influenced reciprocity of divine and human activity—a reciprocity . . . which springs from the most basic presuppositions of his theological thinking.[134]

In his *Short Account and Introduction to the German Theology* (1571), Weigel comments on the opening words of the *TG*, which quote 1 Corinthians 13:10: "When

127. Jones, *Spiritual Reformers*, 61.
128. Jones, *Spiritual Reformers*, 147–48.
129. Jones, *Spiritual Reformers*, 148.
130. Jones, *Spiritual Reformers*, 150.
131. Ozment, *Mysticism and Dissent*, 211.
132. Ozment, *Mysticism and Dissent*, 46.
133. Ozment, *Mysticism and Dissent*, 46.
134. Ozment, *Mysticism and Dissent*, 47.

the perfect is come, the imperfect will pass away." Ozment says, "It is significant, if coincidental, that this biblical verse was also of fundamental importance for Joachim of Fiore (d. 1202). Weigel and the *German Theology*, unlike Joachim, give the verse an exclusively anthropological rather than institutional interpretation. Joachim expected the papal church to be transformed (around 1260) by a new, monastically modeled societal reform."[135] This is a great point, but wholly explicable when we see that Joachim's monastic ideal itself is a condition of universal and unmediated gnosis. As Ozment has observed, the coming perfection according to the *TG* is "God's ruling presence in the soul of the individual rather than in a democratized church of the Spirit."[136] Only with Joachim's eschatological vision of an age of the Spirit does Eckhartian mysticism acquire a world-historical significance. In any case, Ozment is exactly right in his assessment of Weigel's influence:

> The shift from institutional to anthropological structures, under way in Weigel from his earliest writings, entails a shift in the horizon of religious authority from historically mediated and interpreted tradition to experiences interior to the individual soul. . . . Neither the Bible nor the German Theology bears an intrinsically clear and authoritative mandate. . . . The "pure eye" of the soul must make the authoritative assessment. "It is not sufficient to have read, and take at face value useful and good books—not even the Bible. One must have an absolutely pure eye if one is to take up and read divine writings. There are many who are so deluded as to think the Bible an open book which anyone who picks it up can read. But the Bible is a book closed with seven seals, which no one can open save he who has the key of David. The same is true of this little book called the *Theologia Germanica*, which, like the Bible, also requires a pure heart in order to be understood."[137]

Weigel exerted considerable influence on Johann Arndt, Gottfried Arnold, and Gottfried Leibniz. Like all these figures, he believed that the inner "spiritual church" was superior to any external church or scripture. "Weigel's basic (and hardly original) position," Ozment adds, "is that baptism with physical water is simply a prefiguring of baptism with inward, heavenly water—the renewal and purification of the Holy Spirit. . . . Weigel has, in effect, released the new birth from its traditional mooring in priestly activity and sacramental power and made it a reciprocal act between the individual and his God."[138] Weigel himself said, "He who has this new birth within, be he husband or wife, young or old, Jew or

135. Ozment, *Mysticism and Dissent*, 53.
136. Ozment, *Mysticism and Dissent*, 54.
137. Ozment, *Mysticism and Dissent*, 55.
138. Ozment, *Mysticism and Dissent*, 48.

heathen, Christian or Turk, is already saved, even if he is not physically baptized with water."[139] Ozment writes:

> His comments on the role of priestly mediation and sacramental efficacy ended with a witness to religious universalism. Weigel now unites this reciprocity and universalism as he comments critically on still another contemporary theological preoccupation—the doctrine of Original Sin. In so doing, he makes manifest the presuppositions behind his belief in the reciprocity of divine and human activity and the equidistance of the Spirit from every soul. A transition is made from history to ontology as anthropological structures replace institutional structures as the authoritative locus of the spirit of God.[140]

Not the visible church but rather the soul "is the definitive locus of the divine Spirit" and, Weigel says, "the Spirit of God illumine[s] each man equally." He adds, "As the child becomes a man and reaches the age of reason, he finds himself in the middle. If he lives according to the spirit, he remains in God's grace. If he lives according to the flesh, he falls away from [spiritual] baptism." What he calls the "true inward covenant" is set over against a historical, visible covenant, a point that Weigel defends with appeals to Eckhart.[141]

Conclusion

The attitude of Anabaptists toward the central concerns of the Magisterial Reformers—particularly the doctrine of justification—varied from indifference to contempt.[142] Anabaptists insisted that faith is obedience.[143] Anabaptists did not take Luther's doctrine of justification further but rejected it entirely. In fact, they pressed further into Pelagian and Manichaean territory than did Roman Catholic

139. Quoted in Ozment, *Mysticism and Dissent*, 49.

140. Ozment, *Mysticism and Dissent*, 49.

141. Quoted in Ozment, *Mysticism and Dissent*, 52.

142. Finger, *Anabaptist Theology*, 109. Finger further observes, "Robert Friedmann found 'A forensic view of grace, in which the sinner is . . . undeservedly justified . . . simply unacceptable' to Anabaptists. A more nuanced scholar like Arnold Snyder can assert that historic Anabaptists 'never talked about being justified by faith.'" Finger believes that Anabaptist soteriological emphases (especially on divinization) can bring greater unity. especially between marginalized Protestant groups (Pentecostals and Quakers) and Orthodox and Roman Catholic theologies of salvation (110). Finger observes that recent Anabaptist reflection is no more marked in its interest in this topic than its antecedents, with discipleship ("following Jesus") and the inner transformation of the believer as central (132–33).

143. Fallmann, *Hans Denck*, 89; cf. Brewer, *Handbook*, 87.

theologians. "We may label these dissenting reformers 'radical,'" notes Hillerbrand, "even though they were theologically closer, in some respects, to Catholic thought than were either Luther or Zwingli."[144] To be sure, the Radical Reformation exhibited a passion to *complete* the Reformation, as Hillerbrand argues.[145] "Luther, wrote the Hutterite *Chronicle*, broke the pope's pitcher but kept the pieces in his hands."[146] Yet, I have argued that Anabaptist leaders, many of whom had been followers of Luther and Zwingli, continued to engage early emphases that these Reformers came to question and even reject.

Radicalizing the monastic ideal of seclusion from the world, Anabaptists separated entirely from the reprobate, including the fallen church. Ozment explains:

> According to Eckhart and Tauler, true self-realization entails the suspension of normal rational and volitional activities, a shutting down of the regular processes of the soul. . . . With the collapse of the normal activities of the soul follows as surely as the night the day the irrelevance of everything the visible world has to offer. . . . In the mystical traditions, quietism is no less negative a judgment on established power than violent revolution. Mystical salvation is the discovery of the final power and authority of the Self within one's own self.[147]

"In the most literal sense of the words," notes Ozment, "the mystical enterprise is transrational and transinstitutional. And because it is such, it bears a potential *anti*-intellectual and *anti*-institutional stance, which can be adopted for the critical purposes of dissent, reform, and even revolution."[148]

> How can men embrace the routine of the church after they have been in the very mind of God? A recent study has convincingly shown how, beneath the historical and sacramental relation between God and man transacted by the church, Eckhart constructed a more fundamental nature and involuntary (non voluntate, sed naturaliter) arrangement played out in the depths of the individual soul. A "natural covenant" of more basic soteriological significance than God's historical covenants can also be extrapolated from the writings of Tauler.[149]

144. Hillerbrand, "Radicalism," 29.
145. Hillerbrand, "Radicalism," 37–41.
146. Hillerbrand, "Radicalism," 36–37.
147. Ozment, *Mysticism and Dissent*, 12.
148. Ozment, *Mysticism and Dissent*, 8–9.
149. Ozment, *Mysticism and Dissent*, 11–12.

And, as in the Orphic tradition, the way of ascent to the divine One is the way of descent into the inmost self. No one emphasized this trope more than Eckhart, with natural comparisons to Zen Buddhism.[150]

Our focus has been on the Anabaptists, but Roman Catholic piety during this period reflects the same sources, trends, and awkward negotiations with mystical currents. Markus Friedrich points out that Ignatius of Loyola's *Exercises* "may be taken as representative of two extremes of early modern Catholic piety: a workmanlike piety of small steps, based on the fulfillment of religious duty and the virtuous practice of spiritual habits (ascesis); and a piety that aspired to obtain direct, immediate access to God, for example, in a vision or an ecstatic state of grace (mysticism)."[151] I have suggested, broadly speaking, that these two approaches are evident in the Swiss and German wings of Anabaptism, respectively. Stock phrases of the latter included "'self-annihilation,' 'the innermost depths of the soul,' 'contemplation and unification with God,'" and so forth. As Friedrich puts it, "The inner world of man, where encounters with God supposedly took place, was crucial. But there was always at least the latent threat that mystics might devalue and thus set themselves above external authorities—the church, the sacraments, even the Bible."[152]

Among Jesuits, he adds, the "legacy of mysticism . . . began with Ignatius himself, whose spirituality was heavily influenced by contemporary trends that were on the margins or even went beyond accepted forms of Catholic devotion. His various interrogations and trials before the most diverse ecclesiastical tribunals may not have resulted in conviction, but he was hardly untouched by the new forms of intensive devotional mysticism." His autobiography stresses "intense 'illumination' (*iluminiación*); that is, the experience of a clarity transmitted directly from God (*entendimiento*)." Friedrich expands:

> Ignatius was so unshakably certain of these moments of illumination that he placed them even over the Bible. . . . The product of this certainty was a kind of independence from the established liturgical and sacramental forms of devotion—the *Exercises*, for example, largely do without the sacraments. . . . Instead of adhering strictly to established rules, he considered it legitimate to 'search about and make many kinds of experiments' to attain spiritual perfection. . . . Hence he believed from the start that he was entitled and able to override the established rules of Catholic devotion and to speak and preach

150. Shizuteru and Heisis, "Ascent and Descent," 52–73.
151. Friedrich, *Jesuits*, 84.
152. Friedrich, *Jesuits*, 85.

> about matters of the faith without theological training. In the eyes of many contemporaries, these aspects of his faith brought him dangerously close to the controversial *alumbrados*, a group of devout laymen and clergy who had been declared heterodox and persecuted by the church for the direct relationship with God they claimed.[153]

In fact, Friedrich notes, "The very first book produced by a Jesuit (namely, by Peter Canisius) was an edition of sermons by the controversial Rhenish mystic Johannes Tauler in 1543."[154] The College of Gandía was enthralled by the *TG*. "Even the fiercely contested messianic thinking of Joachim of Fiore from the twelfth century could be found in Gandía." Moreover, the Order's third superior general, Francisco de Borja, not only supported these trends but "was declared the 'Angelic Pope,' a key figure in Joachim's thought."[155]

These mystical trends faced opposition from the church. Jean-Joseph Surin "drew a sharp distinction between the accomplishments of theologians, on the one hand, and mystics, on the other—the anti-intellectual overtones can hardly be missed. . . . The label *mysticus* was rarely intended as a compliment." The fourth superior, Everard Mercurian (1514–1580), prohibited Tauler, the *TG*, and similar mystical writings. Some religious left in frustration. "Jean de Labadie (1610–74), for example, turned his back on the order in 1639 and supported the Huguenots in southern France and Calvinist pietists in the Netherlands before ending up as a separatist millenarian in Altona."[156] Miguel de Molinos, founder of quietism, was condemned by the Holy Office to life in prison for advocating gnostic and antinomian ideas in his widely read *Spiritual Guide* and for practicing them by sexual misconduct.[157] Nevertheless, "Despite all their prohibitions, the medieval classics and major contemporary authors continued to be widely read in the Society of Jesus."[158]

Going forward into the seventeenth century, it seemed to many that the choice was less between Rome and the Reformation than between a divided Christendom and private inspiration, whether identified with visions or reason. The choice was between the traditions of the past and new revelations, authority and autonomy, public and private, religion and spirituality. Shaped by German mysticism,

153. Friedrich, *Jesuits*, 86–87. See also Hamilton, *Heresy and Mysticism*.

154. Friedrich, *Jesuits*, 87.

155. Friedrich, *Jesuits*, 87–89. Friedrich points out that other Jesuits "wanted nothing to do with Joachimite messianism."

156. Friedrich, *Jesuits*, 91–92.

157. See Baird and McGinn, introduction to de Molinos, *Spiritual Guide*, 21–39.

158. Friedrich, *Jesuits*, 93.

the movement produced some of the most sensitive intellects of the period, whose influence—and emphasis on the divine self—continued into the Enlightenment and Romantic era. It seems to be the very essence of what is meant today by being "spiritual but not religious."

5

Magical Medicine

Shamans of the North

> Therefore no commandment shall stand nor exist among people that is to serve [to bring] blessedness [except]: Believe only that the Holy Spirit baptizes you. Then every human being is his own prince, his own king and master, to command himself . . . the entire world is a church.
>
> —Paracelsus[1]

Just as Apollo traveled to the northernmost steppes of the legendary Hyperborea, Hermes Trismegistus received a warm welcome among the peripatetic shamans of the northern Renaissance. Indeed, alchemy and astrology survived longer in German-speaking lands than anywhere else, even among pioneers of the Scientific Revolution. The Renaissance alchemist, explains Peter Marshall, "prays on his knees in front of a tabernacle."

> The Latin word *Laboratorium* is inscribed above the mantelpiece, combining the two essential aspects of the alchemist's endeavour: *Labor* (work) and *Oratorium* (prayer). The alchemist cannot hope to discover the Philosopher's Stone or attain divine wisdom without the two. It is the process which brings together the traditional distinction between inner and outer alchemy: success in the laboratory is not possible without the spiritual illumination of the soul.[2]

1. Paracelsus, *Sämtliche Werke*, 2.2:159.
2. P. Marshall, *Theatre of the World*, 137.

While we might refer to such individuals as eccentrics, these adepts were far from being intellectual dilettantes. They were "polymaths." Early in the sixteenth century, many of these alchemists were monks and even abbots, and some of them are presently considered founders of niche fields of modern studies. Though steeped in philosophical and practical literature, they were early modern legatees of what Burkert called "craftsmen of the sacred."[3]

Magic of course had an auspicious history in Europe long before the Renaissance, but writers like Ficino wedded it to the idea of reviving a golden age of Orphic mysteries from the distant past. As the sixteenth century unfolded, translations of the Corpus Hermeticum multiplied and gained a growing following.[4] After Ficino, important writers like Agostino Steuco (1496–1549), the Vatican librarian, continued the search for a pure ore of wisdom in his work *On Perennial Philosophy*.[5] Ploughed by Rhineland mysticism, Germany offered fertile soil for Hermetic philosophy.[6] Yet it was also more practically oriented, part and parcel of German mining culture. Many magicians were priests, but adepts could be found not only among natural philosophers and mathematicians but also at the the forge among blacksmiths and among treasury officials and physicians. The most successful of these figures were snapped up by princes to compete for the office of court alchemist.

German Magi

While there are antecedents in ancient Alexandrian gnosis, what Yates calls the "Hermetic-Cabalist" tradition was the invention of the Renaissance.[7] The Corpus Hermeticum embodied a syncretistic collection of Platonism, Aristotelianism, and Stoicism attributed to the Egyptian philosopher-lawgiver Hermes Trismegistus, but astrology and alchemy remained separate disciplines. As Newman and

3. Burkert, referring to ancient sages in *Orientalizing Revolution*, 9–33.

4. Faivre, "Renaissance Hermeticism," 114.

5. Celenza, "Revival," 91.

6. See the foreword by Assmann in Ebeling, *Secret History*, vii. See also Ebeling, *Secret History*, 60. The mining culture also provided a natural environment for alchemical ideas. Two key Hermetic texts, the Asclepius and the Tabula Smaragdina (Emerald Tablet), had been in Latin translation from Arabic texts at least three centuries before Ficino. However, the natural magic of the former dominated the Italian Renaissance, while the alchemy-centered Tabula was more central in northern Hermeticism. Consequently, says Kristeller, the latter "viewed itself as a practical, alchemical-medical science." See Kristeller, *Renaissance Thought*, 52–53.

7. Francis Yates, *Giordano Bruno*. Some specialists criticize Yates for conflating Hermeticism and kabbalism, but for the period she studies it is justified.

Grafton explain, "Astrology was a form of divination . . . whereas alchemy was an artisanal pursuit concerned with the technologies of minerals and metals. The fundamental practices of the two fields were vastly different."[8]

In the Renaissance not only were astrology and alchemy fused but so were kabbalism and Joachite millennialism. As usual, all these diverse ingredients were stirred into a stew with a Neoplatonic stock. Simple categories such as atheist, deist, and theist do not illuminate a great deal where the Neoplatonist-Hermetic worldview is concerned. The basic opposition is between natural supernaturalism and supernaturalism, pantheism/panentheism and theism. According to Orphic emanationism, everything visible is an unfolding appearance. Like a play, it is not the reality but a "moving picture of eternity" (Plato, *Timaeus* 37d). Yet, as in image, it participates in the divine reality above. Everything in nature possesses a soul that shares in the World Soul. Jones notes that these ideas received fresh interest in the Renaissance rediscovery of "Stoic, Neo-Platonic, and Neo-Pythagorean ideas," mixed with "medieval mysticism, Persian astrology, Arabian philosophy, and the Jewish Cabala." Pico and Johann Reuchlin had especially introduced kaballah into Christian interpretation. According to kabbalistic thinking, notes Jones,

> It would be blasphemous to suppose that God the infinitely perfect, God the absolutely immutable One, by direct act made a world of matter or created a realm of existence marked with evil as this lower realm of ours is. Instead of supposing a creative act, therefore, the Cabala supposes a series of emanations, or overflows of divine splendour, arranged in three groups of threes, called *Sephiroth*, which reveal all that is revealable in God, and by means of which invisible and visible worlds come into being.[9]

Along these lines, kabbalistic thinking maintained the existence of three realms: intelligible ideas, spiritual forms (including incorporeal beings, such as angels and souls, and astral substance), and the natural world. Jones notes that according to Agrippa, "man unites all the worlds in himself, and in his unfallen state as Adam-Cadmon combined all men in one ideal, undifferentiated Man." Hidden within and behind the outer appearance of things is the inner realm of the World Soul. Through such "Occult Philosophy" we can decode the signs and perform wondrous operations of a natural kind because of the operation of these higher

8. Newman and Grafton, *Secrets of Nature*, 15–16.
9. Jones, *Spiritual Reformers*, 136.

worlds on this one.[10] When man the microcosm establishes harmony between all these worlds within himself,

> through his highest essence he can win the secrets of the lower worlds—the astral and the material. . . . To accomplish *that* is to be spiritual, to become like Adam, a paradisaical Man, or like Christ the new Adam. Even the lowest world is penetrated with the spiritual "seed" or "element." The very basic substances of which it composed—sulphur, mercury, and salt—are in essence spiritual principles, and the lower world is written over, like a palimpsest, with 'signatures' of the divine world to which it belongs.[11]

Kabbalism endowed alchemy with a deeper cosmotheological meaning, while alchemy made kabbalism more concrete. Both understood reality (including God) as a process of becoming through the coincidence of opposites. Joachite eschatology added a historical frame for this process. This threefold process—at once psychological, cosmological, and historical—was represented in the familiar trope of a marriage restoring primordial unity (the alchemical wedding). For Plato, the truth in the *Symposium* allegory was that androgyny was the original condition of perfect humans before they were separated into sexes. It is the body that is responsible for this separation, and in the soul's return this nonsexed condition is restored: the end is like the beginning. Philo, gnostics, and Origen taught the same, as did Eriugena.[12]

However, for serious alchemists, this was no mere metaphor. An important example of a kabbalist who took Plato's allegory literally is Leone Ebreo (also known as Judah Leon Abravanel), a Portuguese Jewish refugee in Naples who became an advisor to the king of Naples. He was also a friend of Pico and of Pico's teacher, Elia del Medigo. In his *Dialoghi di Amore* (Dialogues of love), Ebreo tried to reconcile Plato's myth in the *Symposium* and *Timaeus* of androgynous humans being divided into sexes and the urge to restore this primal unity through Eros.[13] After all, he wondered, didn't Moses teach that Eve was taken from Adam's side? Gilles Quispel explains:

> In the *Zohar*, allegedly written by Moses, God, or rather his personified Glory, Adam Qadmon, was born both male and female and even had male and fe-

10. Jones, *Spiritual Reformers*, 135–36.
11. Jones, *Spiritual Reformers*, 138–39.
12. Van der Lugt, "Sex Difference," 101–21.
13. Quispel, "Reincarnation," 226.

> male sexual organs. From this Leone Ebreo concluded that Plato had derived his ideal of androgyny from Moses: Plato and revealed religion agreed. . . . All Pansophists followed Leone Ebreo and aimed at androgyny as *the* ideal of their lives. . . . It is the basic idea of the *Gospel of Thomas*, found near Nag Hammadi in 1945 and for that reason unknown to Leone Ebreo. Its author had Christianized androgynous Adam who had also been proclaimed by the Jewish philosopher Philo of Alexandria.[14]

The true fall, according to the gnostic Gospel of Thomas, was "the split between the two halves of Adam. Christ came to make the two whole again, as is said in logion 22: 'If you make the male and the female one and the same, so that the male is no longer male and the female is no longer female, . . . then you will enter the Kingdom of God.' These Pansophists were gnostics, but they did not know it."[15] The survival of this basic gnostic idea, even centuries before the Nag Hammadi discovery, is remarkable.

From Pico, the mantle of Renaissance kabbalism fell to Johannes Reuchlin (1455–1522), the greatest Hebrew and Greek scholar prior to Erasmus. The same year that Luther posted his Ninety-Five Theses, Reuchlin published his *De arte cabalistica* (1517), promoting a form of angel magic that was adopted by Trithemius and Cornelius Agrippa.[16]

Johannes Trithemius (1462–1516) was a Benedictine abbot and magician. According to Peter French, Trithemius's *Steganographia* (placed on the index in 1609) "gives the procedure for summoning the angels who govern the parts of the earth; the second section deals with those who govern time; and the last part of the work is primarily concerned with summoning a higher order of angels who rule the planets, and particularly Saturn." For example, the head angel of Saturn is Orfiel.[17] Gnostics and Hermeticists shared the Ptolemaic cosmology in which the "governors of the seven planets" are powerful daemons

14. Quispel, "Reincarnation," 227.

15. Quispel, "Reincarnation," 226–27.

16. Yates, *Giordano Bruno*, 102.

17. French, *John Dee*, 36. The first to mention the historical figure Johann Georg Faust, Trithemius himself was regarded as a necromancer. In a letter to his student Cornelius Agrippa, Trithemius mentions Dr. Faustus of Knittlingen as one who sought dangerously to go beyond the bound allowed by the church to obtain secret knowledge. Luther refers in passing to the account of Trithemius conjuring Alexander the Great. Communicating secret knowledge over distances through spirits became the basis for Trithemius's invention of cryptography. See Brann, *Trithemius*, 165. Brann also notes that Luther refers to a person whom most scholars consider to be Trithemius in his *Tischreden* (*Table Talk*).

capable of opposition or assistance. Their visible bodies are animated by a divine soul that may harass the human soul and impede its return to the One. French explains that within this system "time is also astrologized: the thirty-six decans, originally Egyptian sidereal gods [fixed stars], rule over the sections of the zodiac according to a ten-degree division."[18] Trithemius's pupils Heinrich Cornelius Agrippa von Nettesheim (1486–1535) and Paracelsus likewise carried this astrological work forward.

Impelled by restless brilliance, Agrippa was a physician, legal expert, theologian, alchemist, and soldier best known today for his highly influential *Three Books of Occult Philosophy* (1531–1533). Reminiscent of Pico's final work, his conclusion to the third book offers a recantation of his occult pursuits as damnable arts in the ignoble line of Simon Magus.[19] Regardless, this third book of Agrippa is the first useful survey of Renaissance magic.[20] It had a considerable influence on Hermeticism's proliferation, particularly in the thought of Giordano Bruno, who figures prominently later in the story.

Bringing together Neoplatonism, kabbalah, and alchemy, Agrippa poached Gianfrancesco Pico's title for his own *Declamation Attacking the Uncertainty and Vanity of the Sciences and the Arts* (1526), a work that later influenced Montaigne, Bayle, Descartes, and Goethe. As Hanegraaff explains, Agrippa held that faith and reason were totally separate, such that we place our hope in the one and philosophize about the other. Yet for Agrippa faith corresponded to "a hermetic doctrine of gnosis strongly influenced by Lodovico Lazzarelli."[21] In short, skepticism could be used effectively by any school, pouring acids of doubt on all rival views to the end of defending one single and indubitable truth.

Agrippa divided his cosmos into the three worlds, a schema that we have met numerous times before: elemental, celestial, and intellectual (corresponding to body, soul, and spirit). The lowest part of the science is a world that is purely natural, mechanical, and of interest to budding cryptographers, chymists, mechanicians, explorers, and so forth. Following Proclus, Agrippa maintains, "Each world receives influences from the one above it, so that the virtue of the Creator descends through the angels in the intellectual world, to the stars in the celestial world, and thence to the elements and to all things composed of them in the elemental world, animals, plants, metals, stones, and so on. Magicians think that

18. French, *John Dee*, 70.

19. Agrippa, *Three Books*, 706.

20. Yates, *Giordano Bruno*, 130.

21. Hanegraaff, *Esoterism and the Academy*, 84 and 84 n. 26.

we can make use of the same progress upwards, and draw the virtues of the upper world down to us by manipulating the lower ones."[22]

As Yates observes regarding this three-world structure, "What Orpheus called gods . . . the Cabalists call numerations (that is the Sephiroth). . . . We next have more on the Hebrew divine names, a magical arrangement of Abracadabra and pictures of talismans inscribed with names in Hebrew. . . . The vaguely Trinitarian character of the religion of the Magus is maintained by the numerological 'three' groupings."[23] The whole tradition of Christian Neoplatonism assimilates so much of paganism as *praeparatio evangelica* because of its abstraction. More than basing philosophy on the Christian Trinity, it is a "principle of Threeness pervading the cosmos." Yet Agrippa's system is presented in terms of "Pseudo-Dionysian angelic hierarchies, and thus becomes a Christian magic."[24]

In *De la démonomanie des sorciers* (1580), the chancellor of the University of Paris, Jean Bodin, identified Zoroaster as the bad seed, Socrates as admittedly demon possessed, and Plotinus, Iamblichus, and other Neoplatonists as satanic. But Agrippa, he said, was "the grand doctor of the Diabolical art."[25] As Yates observes:

> Agrippa is going much further than Pico, for it is evident that the magic in the third or intellectual world which is now going to be discussed is really priestly magic, religious magic, involving the performance of religious miracles. He next outlines a true divinely magical religion, based on faith, and a superstitious religion, based on credulity. . . . The magician must know the true God, but also secondary divinities and with what cults they must be served, particularly Jupiter whom Orpheus described as the universe.[26]

Despite ecclesiastical censures, Agrippa appealed to the everyday experience of late medieval people. Everyone believed that certain prayers, attended by statues and various ritualistic acts of theurgy, attracted angels, saints, and even the Blessed Virgin to come to their aid. Why then exclude other beneficial acts that attract the sympathies of the planets and cure the physical and psychological ills

22. Yates, *Giordano Bruno*, 131.

23. Yates, *Giordano Bruno*, 139 and 139 n. 1.

24. Yates, *Giordano Bruno*, 140.

25. Quoted in Hanegraaff, *Esoterism and the Academy*, 87. He includes Peter of Abano, Roger Bacon, Ramon Llull, Geber (author of the *Picatrix*), al-Kindi, George Ripley, Girolamo Cardano, Giovanni Baptista della Porta, and Pietro Pomponazzi.

26. Yates, *Giordano Bruno*, 138–39.

of people as well as metals?[27] Reminiscent of the shaman, "The Agrippan Magus aims at mounting up through all three worlds . . . and beyond even that [intellectual world] to the Creator himself whose divine creative power he will obtain." Yates adds, "The door into the forbidden which Ficino had left only slightly ajar is now fully opened. . . . Agrippa gives lists of names, attributes, powers of the planets to be used in invocation to them, above all the Sun is to be called upon by 'whoever wishes to do a marvelous work in this lower world.'"[28] Secrecy is a key element in Agrippa's magic, solemnized in such ceremonies with pupils as the laying on of hands.[29]

Hermeticists did not simply want to understand the world; they wanted to change it. This is true especially of Renaissance magi, who interpreted androgyny as an allegory for a true process of separation and union that created a third thing, a higher type of being than either of its opposing "parents." This "child of the work" comes into existence simultaneously on three levels: the material (transmutation in the lab), the psychological (the operator herself), and the world (social, religious, and political history).

Paracelsus and the "Universal Reformation"

With Paracelsus, we are in touch with an important transitional figure from the medieval to the modern age. Goodrick-Clarke observes, "His ideas concerning the cosmic life, the spiritualization of matter, and the divine nature of virtue and energy have emerged in the philosophies of science of Vitalism and Holism, and in the archetypes of Jungian psychoanalysis."[30]

Influenced by Agrippa, his much older classmate under Trithemius, the historical figure known to us as Paracelsus helped to mediate the Spiritualist tradition to German pietism. In his own words, "Therefore no commandment shall stand nor exist among people that is to serve [to bring] blessedness [except]: Believe only that the Holy Spirit baptizes you. Then every human being is his own prince, his own king and master, to command himself . . . the entire world is a church."[31] The Holy Spirit, identified with the inner spirit of each individual, was viewed by Paracelsus as the autonomous source of truth. Pentecostal enthusiasm and

27. Yates, *Giordano Bruno*, 133.
28. Yates, *Giordano Bruno*, 136.
29. Yates, *Giordano Bruno*, 138–39.
30. Goodrick-Clarke, *Paracelsus*, 36–37.
31. Paracelsus, *Sämtliche Werke*, 2.2:159.

a distinctly modern individualism are fused together in Paracelsus's vision. For him, the decadence of healing is due to the "deceitful Jews in medicine," followed blindly by Catholics and Protestants alike. He settled in Nuremberg at the time when Anabaptists were being expelled, and although he never officially left the Roman Catholic fold, he joined Müntzer's uprisings. Weeks observes, "Hans Denck and the so-called 'godless painters,' doctrinally unorthodox apprentices of Durer, had already been banished; and the prolific Sebastian Franck, a Spiritualist and Humanist who was still in the city when Paracelsus arrived, would soon be forced into exile."[32] Yet he is also considered the founder of toxicology, identifying disease with germs rather than humors in the blood.

If there is no greater miracle than man, as the "Thrice-Greatest" Hermes exults in the Asclepius and Pico repeats at the beginning of his "Oration," then the one who transforms man into someone or something higher still is surely divine. Such a promethean vision required Dr. Frankenstein-like personalities: eccentric, bold, and even megalomaniacal. On that score the German Swiss polymath Phillipus von Hoenheim does not disappoint.[33] "I am different," he said, "let this not upset you."[34] Keeping with the fashion of the day, he adopted the Latin name Theophrastus Bombastus Paracelsus. Most likely, Paracelsus ("beyond Celsus") is his chosen Latin name, while his family name was Bombastus (origin of "bombastic"). His claim to noble lineage is suspect, as his father was a physician, and wilder visions of grandeur contributed to his reputation among some of being a charlatan. Among his followers, however, he was a pioneer of Hermetic medicine.

At the moment when Luther was confronting the "Enthusiasts," Paracelsus was styling himself "Philosopher of the Monarchia, Prince of Spagyrists, Chief Astronomer, Surpassing Physician, and Trismegistus of Mechanical Arcana." In the emerging spirit of modernity, Paracelsus conceived of himself as the fulfillment of the perennial philosophy. Though defamed as wandering Swiss ignoramus, he said, he was in truth the "Prince of Spagyrists [i.e., alchemists] and how my posterity in this age of grace will imitate me." The author invites readers to compare him with Hermes Trismegistus and his heirs, to see how clearly he furthers their basic ideas while surpassing them in intelligence. The "Sophists" (i.e., Aristotelian scholastics), he asserted, are stupid in comparison.[35]

"Follow after me, Avicenna, Galen, Rhasis, Montagnana, Mesue, etc.," Para-

32. Weeks, *Paracelsus*, 133.

33. Paracelsus, *Das Buch Paragranum*, 5.5 (1529–1530), in Goodrick-Clarke, *Paracelsus*, 73. See Moran, *Distilling Knowledge*, ch. 3.

34. Quoted in Ball, *Devil's Doctor*, 3.

35. The full title of Paracelsus's work is *Book Concerning the Tincture of the Philosophers Written against Those Sophists Born since the Deluge, in the Age of Our Lord Jesus Christ, the Son*

celsus boasted. "Follow me, and not I after you, you from Paris, you from Montpellier. . . . Not one of you will survive, even in the most distant corner, where even the dogs will not piss. I shall be monarch and mine will be the monarchy."[36] Indignant at comparisons with Luther, Paracelsus asserted his uniqueness on the stage of history:

> I am Theophrastus and more so than him to whom you compare me. . . . I will let Luther justify his own affairs, and I will account for mine, and will rise above the charges which you level against me: the arcana will raise me up to that height. Who are Luther's foes? The very rabble that hates me. And what you wish him you wish me—to the fire with us both. . . . I will not defend my monarchy with empty talk but with arcana. . . . Let me tell you this, the stubble on my chin knows more than you and all your scribes, my shoebuckles are more learned than your Galen and Avicenna, and my beard has more experience than all your high colleges.[37]

Luther wanted to reform the church, particularly its doctrine of justification, but Paracelsus called for a universal reformation that incorporated all knowledge, which he called the "new medicine." Its "four pillars" are philosophy, astrology, alchemy, ethics, and iatrochemistry.[38] Echoing Ficino, he said, "One must understand that medicine is grounded in the stars and the stars are the means for healing . . . a doctor should be trained in such a way that medicine operates through the heavens just as do prophecy and other celestial events."[39] Further, doctors must be trained in actual medical practice. In his day, surgeries were performed often by barbers and other artisans, while physicians pored over ancient texts. Paracelsus wanted to unite academic and artisanal medicine.[40] Despite these enmities he caused with important physicians and apothecaries in Basel, the city council allowed him to lecture on a narrowly specified list of topics, which he gave in German rather than the usual Latin.[41]

---

of God. Quotations in this paragraph from Waite, *Hermetic and Alchemical Writings*, 1:19–30, here at 19–20.

36. Paracelsus, *Das Buch Paragranum*, 5.5 (1529–1530), in Goodrick-Clarke, *Paracelsus*, 73.

37. Paracelsus, *Das Buch Paragranum*, 5.6, in Goodrick-Clarke, *Paracelsus*, 74–75.

38. Rossi, *Francis Bacon*, 140.

39. Rossi, quoting Paracelsus in *Francis Bacon*, 140–41.

40. Goodrick-Clarke, *Paracelsus*, 15–16.

41. Goodrick-Clarke, *Paracelsus*, 17–18.

Paracelsus and Renaissance Cosmotheism

Paracelsus's first writings from 1524 and 1525 were on scriptural criticism, the Trinity, and Mary, all with a running anticlerical emphasis. The sharp dualism between inner and outer, incorporeal and corporeal, invisible and visible runs through Paracelsus's entire system as it did in ancient gnostic treatises.

Following the trend from Plotinus to Eckhart and Nicholas of Cusa, Agrippa thought that the third and highest stage of knowledge was, as Steiner puts it, "plunging deep into itself," where the soul perceives immediately "the spiritual, the Root-Being of the world." The same was true of Paracelsus, "only in a more perfected form."[42] Steiner explains, "The first factor in humanity's nature Paracelsus calls the 'elementary body'; the second, the ethereal-heavenly, or 'astral body' and the third he names 'the Soul.'"[43] Only when at the level of the "spiritual soul" does the human arrive at that knowledge "of which Eckhart spoke when he felt no longer that *he* was speaking within himself, but that in him the Root-Being was uttering Itself. The condition has come about in which the All-Spirit in man beholds Itself. Paracelsus has stamped the feeling of this condition with the simple words: 'And that is a great thing whereon to dwell: there is naught in heaven or upon earth that is not in Man. And God who dwelleth in Heaven, He also is in Man.'"[44] In his early writings, German Marian devotion was adapted to the gnostic idea of Sophia. Just as Christ was a cipher for the divine Intellect, Mary was a cipher for the World Soul or Sophia that mediated between supernatural and natural realms.[45] It is not book learning but direct experience that reveals the truth. Paracelsus invokes the familiar imagery of gnosis as an immediate inner revelation, like a flash of lightning.[46]

Antoine Faivre notes that Paracelsus "developed a chemical—or rather, alchemical—vision of the world that encompassed the theory and practice of medicine and astrology."[47] For Paracelsus, medical healing is part of soteriology. The stars do not exercise a causal effect that would take away from divine providence, but "remain as indicators of the inner human ones" like a picture.[48] In the "spiritual sense," all visible things are "signatures" of the real. Where Luther highlighted the literal sense, "Paracelsus can be said to have inherited the ruins of the spiritual

42. Steiner, *Mystics*, 196.
43. Steiner, *Mystics*, 204.
44. Steiner, *Mystics*, 208–9.
45. Gantenbein, "Virgin Mary," 4–37.
46. Weeks, *Paracelsus*, 122–23.
47. Faivre, "Renaissance Hermeticism," 115.
48. Weeks, *Paracelsus*, 120.

meanings, when these were dislocated by his radical iconoclasm and reapplied to his nature, shored up by a now all the more literal historical sense. The meanings purged from ceremonies and churches were reallocated to nature. For, as he put it: 'the entire world is a church' (*die ganz Welt ist ein Kirche*)."[49]

Weeks explains Paracelsus's basic outlook:

> Just as creation was a divine revelation, Christ on earth was God become visible. But now Christ is invisible in another form—just as the great world is invisible within the human being—a form "which is not what it is." The form is the Eucharist, which is and is not the bread and wine in containing the invisible Christ concealed beneath it. The argument takes flight from the phenomenal realm. . . . Knowing that Christ is invisibly present beneath the material makes it possible to accept that the cosmos is invisibly present in the human organism.[50]

There is little here that Schwenckfeld's Christology had not already articulated. Paracelsus explains,

> There are two creatures within the human being: a mortal one created from Adam and an eternal one created from Christ, two bodies: the one is from the Father (who is invisible, but whose works have been made visible in creation), the other from the Son (who was made visible in Christ, but whose works are invisible). And both bodies must be fed: the former requires the nourishment that is transformed into flesh and blood by the *archeus*, the alchemist in the stomach; the latter feeds on the bread and wine which are transformed into the invisible spiritual body.[51]

The false teachers in theology and in medicine look for the visible to instruct them in the invisible, Paracelsus complains. Just as the exegete of scripture looks for the invisible (spiritual sense) in the letter, the physician seeks the inner source of things from visible appearances.[52] However, in true science one looks to the invisible to explain the visible. As Weeks summarizes, "The heathens who recognize the visible things of nature as divine works live by the 'letter'; the [true]

49. Weeks, *Paracelsus*, 128.

50. Weeks, *Paracelsus*, 122.

51. Weeks, *Paracelsus*, 142. Paracelsus, *Das Mahl des Herrn*, 1523–1534, dedicated to Pope Clement VII.

52. Weeks, *Paracelsus*, 144.

Christians, who are taught by the Holy Spirit to recognize the invisible things of God, live by the invisible spirits—the 'virtues' which they recognize in the letters of the world."[53]

To the absorption of Christ's humanity in divinity Paracelsus's Schwenckfeldian Christology adds the absorption of humanity in Christ's now wholly invisible nature. With acute anticipations of Hegel, Paracelsus writes,

> Thus, Christ, whom no one recognized as the second person of the Trinity, was considered by everyone a man, because *what He actually was remained invisible*. . . . For man is the revealer of that which is hidden in all things. . . . We too should make manifest that which He has put in us, to the end that the unbelievers may see what God can achieve through man.[54]

By this time, Luther himself had abandoned his spiritualizing tendencies of the 1520s and his followers ensured a Christology that was more conformable to the Definition of Chalcedon: no separation or mingling of natures. But Schwenckfeld only deepened his commitments to the Christology of the *TG*, and Paracelsus followed.[55]

However, as usual in Christian Neoplatonism (and especially alchemy), everything comes in threes, so that dualism is resolved into a higher unity. There is not only the opposition of Father and Son, but the unifying love of the Spirit. The opposites (viz., the mortal body we receive from the Father and the eternal one created from Christ's essence) require a third stage, under the unifying auspices of the Spirit. Paracelsus's book on the Trinity (1524), written in Salzburg, advances the view of a divine family that corresponds to tripartite anthropology (body, soul, spirit) and the three elements (fluid mercury, solid salt, and combustible sulfur) from which all nature springs. Goodrick-Clarke notes, "Paracelsus quoted Hermes Trismegistus, who stated that all seven metals, 'the tinctures' (generating principles), and the Philosopher's Stone all derive from three substances, namely spirit, soul, and body."[56]

So, the three elements are "mothers" of all combinations that we see in the natural world. According to Weeks, "in the evolving projection of the Salzburg trinity, the heavens or macrocosm correspond to the trinitarian father. The domain of alchemy, instructed in its art by the heavens, corresponds to the trinitarian son,

53. Weeks, *Paracelsus*, 141.
54. Paracelsus, *Astronomia Magna*, 9.21, in Goodrick-Clarke, *Paracelsus*, 119, emphasis added.
55. Weeks, *Paracelsus*, 143.
56. Goodrick-Clarke, *Paracelsus*, 33–34.

since the alchemist exercises a Christ-like office of redeeming and transforming substances. The virtues in all things, as well as the *spiritus vitae* as a whole, correspond to the third trinitarian person."[57] Everything is in process, including the Trinity and its human image.[58]

The process of digestion is a microcosm of this Trinitarian process.[59] As Weeks points out, for Paracelsus the linking of the Trinity to the macrocosmic and microcosmic process was not analogous but identical:

> The process of digestion in the human being is the same as the work of the alchemist in transforming substances. But Christian doctrine stands against the materialistic or pantheistic tendency in which the human being is made after the image of God: namely, as body, soul, and spirit. Wilhelm Kammerer has documented the two tendencies of Paracelsus toward the dualism of body and soul and toward the trichotomy, including spirit. With this inclusion, the body can also be spiritualized through the arcane forces and virtues, and the soul spiritualized in the creative imagination which corresponds to the creative power of the *spiritus creator* that hovered above the dark waters in the creation according to the Book of Genesis. As Regin Prenter has observed, Luther was similarly taken with the real connection between spiritual rebirth and the creation of the cosmos.[60]

Paracelsus says, "The *world machine* is made of two parts—one tangible and perceptible, and the other invisible and imperceptible. The tangible part is the body, the invisible is the stars. The tangible part is in turn composed of three parts—Sulphur, Mercury, and Salt; the invisible also consists of three parts—feeling, wisdom, and art."[61] For example, he explains, "Take a piece of wood. It is a body. Now burn it. The flammable part is the Sulphur, the smoke is the Mercury, and the ash is the Salt." Then there are the three tastes: "sweet, sour, and bitter."[62]

Besides the three substances, Paracelsus posits four elements. "It is the four elements which can break down and transform Sulphur. They are the artists which transmute Sulphur and cause it to generate disease in four types: cold, hot, moist,

57. Weeks, *Paracelsus*, 126–27.

58. Weeks, *Paracelsus*, 115–16.

59. Weeks, *Paracelsus*, 124–27.

60. Weeks, *Paracelsus*, 115–16.

61. Paracelsus, *Opus Paramirum*, 9.6 (1530–1531), in Goodrick-Clarke, *Paracelsus*, 112–13, emphasis added.

62. Paracelsus, *Opus Paramirum*, 6.4–5, in Goodrick-Clarke, *Paracelsus*, 78.

and dry."[63] Thus, health is dependent on balancing not humors in the blood but these elements, which depend on the right balance of earth, wind, fire, and air. However, of chief importance is the quintessence—a fifth essence beyond earth, wind, fire, and air. In *Astronomia Magna* (1537–1538) he asserts that God in creation "took each of the four elements and also extracted the essence of wisdom, art, and reason from the stars." He explains later in the same section:

> And then he combined both natures, the elemental and the astral, with a massa which is known as the limus terrae [clay] in the Scriptures. Thus two bodies have arisen from this mass, the sidereal [astral] and the elemental. And this is called the fifth essence [quintessence] according to the light of Nature; that is to say, the massa is extracted and both the firmament and the elements have been combined into one. Thus it follows: what has been extracted from the four [elements] makes the fifth, so that the four are like a mother to the fifth. And moreover, the fifth essence is the whole basis and core of all essences and properties of the whole world; the hand of God held all Nature, virtues, and properties and essences in the upper and lower regions and formed man out of these in His image.[64]

The combination of elements is akin to the kabbalist's goal of repeating God's original act of creation through the combination of Hebrew letters. The fifth element conjectured by Aristotle is raised to the level of the philosopher's stone. Paracelsus's "clay" (*limus terrae*) in which elemental and astral are combined is reminiscent of the Golem (clay statue) that Jewish kabbalists enlivened by various secret incantations.[65] Paracelsus saw himself as the revealer of "the Kabbalah of the spiritual, astral, and material worlds."[66] For him, Rossi observes, "Chemistry was the key to unlocking the structure of the world and creation was a divine chemical 'separation.' First the four elements were separated from one another, then Fire was separated from the Firmament, Air from the spirits, Water from marine flora, and Earth from wood, stone, land flora, and animals until individual objects and creatures remained."[67]

Paracelsus identified prime matter with the Logos, understood not in New Testament terms but as found in the Corpus Hermeticum and kabbalism. Be-

63. Paracelsus, *Opus Paramirum*, 6.18, in Goodrick-Clarke, *Paracelsus*, 87.

64. Paracelsus, *Astronomia Magna*, 9.15 (1537–1538), quoted from Goodrick-Clarke, *Paracelsus*, 116–17.

65. See Idel, *Golem*.

66. Quoted by Waite, *Hermetic and Alchemical Writings*, 1:xi.

67. Rossi, *Francis Bacon*, 141.

sides these sources, Yates notes, "It can be said with certainty that Paracelsus was much influenced by Ficino and the Ficinian magic, his *De vita longa* having been inspired by the *De vita coelitus comparanda*."[68] Plato's *forms* become Paracelsus's *essences*, all of which derive from the ultimate essence and humankind is the microcosm of the macrocosm. Paracelsus explains,

> That is to say, man receives heavenly wisdom, reason, and art and such from the stars, and flesh and blood from the elements. Therefore man is the fifth essence, the microcosm and the son of the whole world, because he has been created as an extract of all creation by the hand of God. . . . Thus man beats like the stars and also like the elements, from which he is made. Just as he has all her properties within himself, so the Great World nourishes and feeds him in wisdom, reason, food, and drink as her own flesh and blood so wonderfully born of her.[69]

Paracelsus was also influenced by an important figure in medieval philosophy and poetry, Solomon Ibn Gabirol (1020–1070), known to the West as Avicebron.[70] Though he was thought during the Middle Ages to have been a Christian, Avicebron was a Jewish Neoplatonist philosopher and kabbalist. He was said to have created a Golem—a female to do his house chores.[71] Avicebron's *Fons Vitae* argued that all of creaturely reality, both spiritual and physical, consists of matter and form. Obviously this excluded God, John Francis Quinn observes, but intellects and angels were considered to be composed of at least a "spiritual" (rather than "corporeal") matter.[72]

In addition to this notion of universal hylomorphism, Avicebron emphasized the role of the will, which mediated between divine and natural reality.[73] Although criticized on these points by Aquinas, Avicebron had a significant impact on Franciscan metaphysics, including the thought of Bonaventure and Duns Scotus.

It is worth mentioning this twelfth-century thinker not only because of his medieval influence and his impact on Paracelsus but also because the trend toward the materialization of nature and voluntarism is so much a part of emergent modernity. Teaching a similar view, David of Dinant had been condemned for pantheistic heresy in the twelfth century. Goodrick-Clarke observes,

68. Yates, *Giordano Bruno*, 150, referring to Pagel, "Prime Matter," 119.
69. Paracelsus, *Astronomia Magna*, 9.16, in Goodrick-Clarke, *Paracelsus*, 117.
70. Goodrick-Clarke, *Paracelsus*, 35.
71. Bokser, *From the World*, 57.
72. Quinn, *St. Bonaventure's Philosophy*, 141–45, 314–16.
73. See Loewe, *Ibn Gabriol.*

> David of Dinant (d. 1290) adapted Avicebron's doctrine of prime matter to denote the Godhead which originates, sustains, and exists in all things. The emanationist implications of David's popular preaching reached and influenced many mystical anarchist and millenarian movements in the late Middle Ages, including the Waldensians, the Brethren of the Free Spirit, the Amaurians, the Behards and the Beguines, the Bohemian Adamites, and the Anabaptists. . . . It is therefore possible to see Paracelsus as an heir of the same popular pantheism which inspired sectarian revolutionaries.[74]

In spite of (or perhaps because of) this speculative and unorthodox tendency, Paracelsus professed to be opposed to church dogmas of any stripe.[75] There are obvious gnostic influences. The Neoplatonic striving to free one's true inner self from bodily shackles in Paracelsus's writings takes the form not of the philosopher's or monk's contemplation but in the active separation of opposites that yields a higher synthesis:

> The strength of this mystery of Nature is hindered by the bodily structure, just as if one were bound in a prison with chains and fetters. . . . Since, then, hindrance arises from this source, one has to see how to get free from it. For such freedom being secured, this art of separation can only be compared to the art of apothecaries, as light is compared to darkness. . . . And let no one wonder at the school of our learning. Though it be contrary to the courses and methods of the ancients, still it is firmly based on experience, which is mistress of all things, and by which all arts should be proved.[76]

Consistent with gnostic treatises, Gilly notes, "The famous Swiss physician Paracelsus (1493–1541) distinguished between a highest Saviour-God and lower Archons who had created the world."[77] In fact, Gilly highlights other gnostic elements in Paracelsus's system:

- The pessimistic appraisal of the material world of elements and creatures as something base and excrementitious (*plērōma tēs kakias*, hell);
- The distinction between the Highest God of redemption from the lower powers

74. Goodrick-Clarke, *Paracelsus*, 35.
75. Goodrick-Clarke, *Paracelsus*, 35.
76. Paracelsus, *Neuen Bücher Archidoxis*, 4.1, in Goodrick-Clarke, *Paracelsus*, 64–70.
77. Pagel, *Paracelsus*, 367–68, quoted by Gilly, "Bekenntnis zur Gnosis," 391.

of astral *demiurges* (*archontes*, administrators, *dioikētai*) who are responsible for creation;

- *Separatio* in matter uncreated, in contrast, to creation *de novo* from nothing;
- The role of water as universal matter, the seat of Behemot or devil;
- Creation of Adam from eight parts, the eight astronomies and philosophies, the eight mothers, the dark fire, the middle body, the planets as blacksmiths, the ineptitude of the lower creators such as *vulcani* and *demiurges*.[78]

Many modern scientists such as Albert Einstein have found this pantheistic outlook appealing. Even some intellectuals today who are regarded widely as atheists, such as Carl Sagan and Sam Harris, embrace Spinozist pantheism. We cannot reduce this phenomenon to Paracelsian influences, to be sure, but we also cannot understand it apart from its roots in this type of Hermeticism. For Paracelsus, notes Steiner, it would be a categorical mistake to seek for the divine as a personal being outside of us. "Paracelsus therefore does not seek for God or for spirit in Nature; but Nature, just as it comes before his eyes, is for him wholly, immediately divine. . . . This Spirit does not create Nature, but develops itself out of Nature."[79]

However, in Paracelsus's version of natural supernaturalism, faith-healing is a higher art than medical healing. In his 1520 book on medicine, Paracelsus likewise argues that "we should seek their treatment in religious faith and not in Nature, as the fifth book will show. Thus you should know that you should seek the whole basis of healing in the fifth book, where the true medicine is demonstrated. All health and disease comes from God and not from man. The diseases of man must be divided into two groups: the natural and the purgatorial. . . . For every disease is a chastisement, therefore no physician can heal it, until this chastisement is ended by God."[80] At the same time,

> God will do nothing without men. If he works a miracle, he does it through men, namely through physicians. But since there are two kinds of physicians, those who heal miraculously and those who heal through medicine, understand above all that he who believes works miracles. But because faith is not so strong in all men, and yet the hour of chastisement comes to an end, the physician accomplishes that which God would have done miraculously had there been faith in the sick man.[81]

78. Gilly, "Bekenntnis zur Gnosis," 391. See Pagel, *Paracelsus*, 367–68.
79. Steiner, *Mystics*, 210–11.
80. Paracelsus, *Volumen medicinae paramirum*, 2.20–21, in Goodrick-Clarke, *Paracelsus*, 56.
81. Paracelsus, *Volumen medicinae paramirum*, 2.22, in Goodrick-Clarke, *Paracelsus*, 57.

"The difference between a saint and a magus," he adds, "is that the saint works through God, the magus through Nature."[82]

Once more we see the confluence of Neoplatonism and an extreme voluntarism at the heart of the Renaissance. Humankind is free because unlike insensible creatures that carry their seeds in their natures, according to Paracelsus, "Man is free without the embedded seeds and does not procreate as other creatures."[83] Indeed, here Paracelsus virtually repeats Pico's *Oration*:

> God created all things, but man alone He placed in the light of Nature to be free and independent. Because of the eternal in man, God took away his seeds and his instinct. . . . He created man and woman and gave neither seeds, in order that lust might not lead them out of the light of Nature. But in order that they could procreate He gave them free will to decide whether they wanted to or not and thus he planted the seed in their imagination.[84]

Further, Paracelsus holds that "God placed the seed in the speculation and gave free will to the speculation, to decide whether it had desire or not." It is thus the will that determines even whether it will have a desire for an object. "Thus God left the seed to the free decision of man, and the decision depends upon man's will." The same is true for the woman. "It will happen according to the decision of their will. Thus is the propagation of the seed."[85]

Humankind is therefore the one creature, ranged between divinity and the filthy world of matter, who can *improve* nature with its own inherent resources. Where does one find all the things in nature necessary for improvement? Paracelsus answers as follows:

> This lack compels the use of magic. Thus, Nature will put into words, *gamaheu*, and images virtues like those which inhere in herbs and roots. . . . Cabbala also uses such magical forces. . . . [W]hatever the elemental body can achieve, the spiritual body can far surpass it by means of cabbalism. . . . One should not be astonished by this, for the Scriptures say "Ye are Gods"; we are much more like stars, only more powerful than them.[86]

82. Paracelsus, *Astronomia Magna*, 9.29, in Goodrick-Clarke, *Paracelsus*, 144.
83. Paracelsus, *Das Buch*, 3.1, in Goodrick-Clarke, *Paracelsus*, 58.
84. Paracelsus, *Das Buch*, 3.1–2, in Goodrick-Clarke, *Paracelsus*, 58–59.
85. Paracelsus, *Das Buch*, 3.2, in Goodrick-Clarke, *Paracelsus*, 58–59.
86. Paracelsus, *Astronomia Magna*, 9.28, in Goodrick-Clarke, *Paracelsus*, 144.

As in Pico's *Oration*, what distinguishes humans from animals in Paracelsus's thought is not a rational soul but rather the free will to choose. In his own words: "He who lives according to the image of God will conquer the stars."[87]

Indeed, Paracelsus knew no bounds. His sense of inner divinity led him to argue in his *De Natura Rerum* that a person can be born without a natural womb. "Let the semen of a man putrefy by itself in a sealed cucurbite with the highest putrefaction of the *venter equinus* for forty days, or until it begins at last to live, move, and be agitated, which can be easily seen." Then feed it "with the Arcanum of human blood," kept for forty weeks "in the perpetual and equal heat of a *venter equinus*." Then at last "it becomes, thenceforth, a true and living infant, having all the members of a child that is born from a woman, but much smaller." He continues:

> This we call a homunculus; and it should be afterwards educated with the greatest care and zeal, until it grows up and begins to display intelligence. Now, this is one of the greatest secrets which God has revealed to mortal and fallible man. It is a miracle and marvel of God, an arcanum above all arcana, and deserves to be kept secret until the last times, when there shall be nothing hidden, but all things shall be made manifest.[88]

On the one hand, then, human beings in Paracelsus's view are part of nature and ineluctably follow the patterns of the stars. On the other hand, they share with God a will that can transcend the rest of creation. Avicebron had at least excluded God from his universal hylomorphism, but that line becomes blurry in Paracelsus. Goodrick-Clarke judges, "In his religious ideas Paracelsus remained committed to theological individualism and popular pantheism."[89] Ball describes his system as "alchemical materialism."[90] While these positions may at first appear to be polar opposites, they are perfectly synonymous in the Hermetic worldview, which we have seen to be a Stoicized Platonism. Rather than assimilating God to nature, Paracelsus assimilates nature to God. The *invisible* is the reality that is not to be found in the *visible*.

Given this panentheistic vitalism, it hardly makes sense to speak anymore of miracles as transcending natural causes. If all of nature is a miracle, then all miracles are natural. In terms that we are not used to meeting in historical surveys before Spinoza, Paracelsus offers a clear précis for natural supernaturalism:

87. Paracelsus, *Astronomia Magna*, 9.17, in Goodrick-Clarke, *Paracelsus*, 117.
88. Paracelsus, *De natura rerum*, 14.2 (1537), quoted from Goodrick-Clarke, *Paracelsus*, 175.
89. Goodrick-Clarke, *Paracelsus*, 35.
90. Ball, *Devil's Doctor*, 88.

> If one was to regard such events as Christ's resurrection [and the wonders of the Saints] as natural phenomena and signs, then Christ's words "there will be great signs" would be confirmed. But ignorance caused man to see these events as supernatural, just as the first practitioners of medicine were revered as gods by the common folk. The same thing occurs in the case of these bodies [of Christ and the Saints] because one did not know that virtues inhered in them. The unglorified body is nothing but a natural object. Coloquinth [a viney plant] purges and all arcana for that matter act in heathens as well as Christians. Nature is simply following its own inherent order and command.[91]

It is difficult to resist comparisons with Spinoza a century later.

Despite his connections with Anabaptists (especially in the 1520s and 1530s) and his emphasis on the individual's rights and socioeconomic equity, he was not willing to take up arms against secular rulers.[92] Paracelsus thrived on controversy, and he provoked some writers to enter the lists against Hermeticism. The Reformed and Lutheran orthodox theologians such as Erastus and Hippius attacked Paracelsianism as both theological and scientific heresy. The erstwhile apprentice of Agrippa, Dutch physician Johann Weyer, traced Hermeticism from the fallen angels to Ham and his son, Zoroaster, from whom the Egyptians, Babylonians, and Persians descended. Pythagoras, Democritus, and Plato did, in fact, pick up these vile heresies in their travels to the East.[93]

The cautious attraction of humanists to Hermeticism is evident in Erasmus. He did not show much interest in Hermetic magic or kabbalah. In fact, he has a delightful parody, "The Alchemy Scam," in *The Colloquies*.[94] But as a thoroughgoing Neoplatonist, he was open-minded toward his close friend Reuchlin, a devoted kabbalist. And as a reader more appreciative of Origen than Augustine, he was not completely ill-disposed to Hermes Trismegistus.[95] In fact, during his Basel sojourn, Paracelsus lived in the house of Basel publisher Johann Froben along with Erasmus. Froben had fallen ill, but Paracelsus seemed to have fanned him

91. Paracelsus, *Opus paramirum*, 6.40; quoted from Goodrick-Clarke, *Paracelsus*, 90.

92. Goodrick-Clarke, *Paracelsus*, 35–36.

93. Hanegraaff, *Esoterism and the Academy*, 85.

94. Erasmus, *The Colloquies*, in *Praise of Folly*, 175–81.

95. Yates, *Giordano Bruno*, 164. He did question the authenticity of the Dionysian writings, Yates notes: "Moreover, even the Christian basis of the synthesis of the Christian *magus* is shaken when Erasmus in his New Testament Paraphrases, throws doubt on Dionysius the Areopagite as the author of the *Hierarchies*. This critical impiety, in which Erasmus was following the bold Valla, greatly shocked the English Carthusians and must also, one would think, have alarmed his friend John Colet, an ardent Dionysian" (165).

back to health. "It is not incongruous to wish continued spiritual health to the medical man through whom God gives us physical health," he praised. "You have resurrected Froben, that is, my other half: if you restore me also, you will have restored both of us by treating each of us singly. May we have the good fortune to keep you in Basel!"[96]

Erasmus convinced the university to make him a professor of medicine at Basel. With the assistance of the Reformed leader Oecolampadius, Paracelsus received an appointment to teach medicine in March of 1527 but immediately set about to attack academics and burn the books of ancient medical writers.[97] In addition, Froben died before the end of the year.[98] And after a further series of battles, in February of 1528 Paracelsus left Basel.[99]

His reputation, pro and con, followed him to Nuremberg in 1529. But here he antagonized not only the physicians but also the pastors, "for he believed in an extreme formulation of the independence of free will and was an advocate of the common people."[100] Paracelsus kept moving around, writing treatises based on his theory of three principles: sulfur, salt, and mercury.[101] Wandering as a poor lay preacher, he settled in a monastery where he wrote a work on spa-based healing, establishing "his reputation as the founder of balneology." From the Black Forest monastery he moved north in Bavaria, arriving at Ulm early 1536. There he wrote a work on surgery and his *Prognostication for the Next Twenty-Four Years*, "a book of political and religious predictions."[102]

We find him next in Bohemia, where he wrote *Astronomia Magna or the whole Philosophia Sagax of the Great and Little World* (1537–1538). As briefly observed earlier in this chapter, this work presented a systematic account of Paracelsus's scientific worldview based on the macrocosm-microcosm correspondence of Renaissance Neoplatonism, including his classification of nine members (branches of knowledge) in each of the four varieties of astronomy, which he understood as the study of the totality of the heavens and the earth.[103] In 1540 the bishop suffragan, Ernst von Wittelsbach, invited him to stay in Salzburg, but soon after, Paracelsus had a stroke and died on September 24, 1541.[104]

96. Erasmus, "To Theophrastus Paracelsus" (1527), in Huizinga, *Erasmus*, 242–43.
97. Rossi, *Francis Bacon*, 140.
98. Huizinga, *Erasmus*, 243 n. 1.
99. Goodrick-Clarke, *Paracelsus*, 18.
100. Goodrick-Clarke, *Paracelsus*, 18–19.
101. Goodrick-Clarke, *Paracelsus*, 19.
102. Goodrick-Clarke, *Paracelsus*, 21.
103. Goodrick-Clarke, *Paracelsus*, 21.
104. Goodrick-Clarke, *Paracelsus*, 22.

Nevertheless, Paracelsian ideas were infused into early modernity. As Goodrick-Clarke writes:

> At the beginning of the seventeenth century Paracelsus gave an important impetus to the Rosicrucian movement and strongly influenced Michael Maier (1568–1622) and the famous Christian mystic Jakob Boehme. Other Continental and English Paracelsists included Oswald Croll, John Dee, Francis Anthony, and Robert Fludd. . . . But Paracelsus' ideas were rediscovered by Goethe, Novalis, Schelling, and other Romantic thinkers at the close of the eighteenth century. His name and works were popularized by H. P. Blavansky, Franz Hartmann and Rudolf Steiner in the modern occult revival at the end of the nineteenth century.[105]

Paracelsus's vision for reforming medicine was carried forward by many, including Joachim Tancke (1557–1609), professor of surgery and anatomy at Leipzig, who "interpreted alchemy as part of biblical *heilsgeschichte* (salvation history)." Thus, he identified the rise of alchemy in the sons of Cain in Genesis 4.[106] Aristotelianism represents a decline. It was content simply to examine outward things via the senses and the unity from which all particular things emerge—the reality behind appearances.[107]

Several Anabaptist leaders we have encountered earlier were instrumental links between nature mysticism and the rediscovery of Hermeticism and kabbalistic thought, as attested in the writings of Paracelsus. Florian Ebeling points out that Sebastian Franck was "a remarkable exponent of Hermeticism."[108]

For Franck, Hermes Trismegistus was "beyond all measure an enlightened philosopher, an excellent priest, and a noble, apparently serene king," Ebeling relates.[109] In fact, Franck, who composed his own edition of the *TG*, made the first translation of the Corpus Hermeticum into German, although it was never published.[110] Franck learned about Hermes "largely from Ficino," though he ascribed to the Egyptian *magus* an even earlier date, saying he was "a contemporary of Abraham and thus clearly antedated Moses." According to Ebeling: "Franck's interpretation of Hermeticism was far more radical, however, in that he consid-

105. Goodrick-Clarke, *Paracelsus*, 36. He adds, "The collected editions of his works were first published by Johannes Huser of Waldkirch (Baden) in 1589–91, 1603, and 1605."

106. Ebeling, *Secret History*, 72.

107. Ebeling, *Secret History*, 74.

108. Ebeling, *Secret History*, 82.

109. Ebeling, *Secret History*, 83.

110. Ebeling, *Secret History*, 84.

ered the Hermetic writings to be a pagan replacement for Christianity and for Judeo-Christian revelation." He continues, quoting Franck,

> The *Pimander* contained "all that is necessary for a Christian to know." This text was in no way a primitive, early stage of a truth that finally reached its explicit perfection in the Bible. This Hermetic theology was "as masterfully written as by Moses or any prophet" and thus must be put on a level with theirs. Franck goes even further and sees in Hermes a clearer herald of God than Moses was. Moses, as part of his mission, "was not to speak out half as lucidly, in order to give the people, who were accustomed to thinking figuratively, everything covered in figures, so that this mystery would be revealed only through Christ." Hermes, however, had been able to express himself more clearly. . . . He assumed that every people had its prophets. As Moses had taught the Hebrews the essence of God, so Plato had taught the Greeks, and Hermes Trismegistus the Egyptians: "Thus this Egyptian Moses instructed and enlightened the Egyptians in Egypt, just as Plato, the Greek Moses, enlightened the Greeks, and Moses the Hebrews."[111]

And yet, Ebeling argues that Franck inflects this perennial tradition in a distinctly modern fashion. Though superior to Moses in enlightenment, Hermes Trismegistus was not the fountainhead of a universal perennial tradition in Franck's view but only of Egypt's. Every culture has its own philosophical religion, a program of education leading from immaturity (needing authority) to adulthood (autonomy). Christianity is not the consummation of the perennial tradition, according to Franck, but is merely a necessary version or historical vessel for a particular culture.[112] God favors no one, Franck says, "but those who do right among all peoples and fear God so that he benefits them." This God is also "the god of the heathens and has always been he who has enlightened, informed, inmirrored the Heathens with this light, word, grace and Christianity."[113] In this vein, Franck anticipates the distinction between "pure religion" (absolute, inward, and intuitive morality) and "ecclesiastical faiths" (particular religions) that we will meet much later in Kant.

I have noted Luther's enthusiasm for alchemy as an allegory of salvation and damnation: leading out the gold, as it were.[114] However, the German Reformer

111. Ebeling, *Secret History*, 83.

112. Ebeling, *Secret History*, 84.

113. Quoted in Ebeling, *Secret History*, 84.

114. There are similarities here with the fifteenth-century German Franciscan, Father Ull-

rejected judicial astrology, as did most early Reformers, who were as opposed to Stoic determinism as much as they were to the "Epicurean" philosophy of humanists like Erasmus.[115] According to Newton and Grafton:

> Luther mocked the genitures that Italian astrologers had put into circulation and that connected his birthday with celestial portents like the great conjunction of 1484. After all, he pointed out, the date of his own birth was uncertain even to him. Luther showed himself even more intolerant when a conjunction in the sign of Pisces, which took place in 1524, led many astrologers to predict that a second universal flood would take place, but none of them foresaw the Peasants' Revolt of 1525.[116]

When, through the influence of Heironomus Wolf, Philipp Melanchthon embraced astrology, an embarrassed Luther averred that it was no more than a private therapy, "as I take a drink of strong beer when I am troubled with grievous thoughts."[117] Nevertheless, "Melanchthon taught astrology, Joachim Camarius edited astrological classics, and Caspar Peucer argued that even the devils and angels who sat on the shoulders of every Christian used astrology to unlock the secrets of their characters and lead them more effectively to salvation or damnation."[118]

Anna Maria Zieglerin and the "Lion's Blood"

The goal of alchemy was to create the "third thing," the "child of the work"—in other words, the philosopher's stone. But this threefold alchemical *magnum opus* had now been folded into the Joachite three ages. This great work was viewed not only as an inner transformation with external results for the individual but also as a cosmic reality that unfolds in history. With roots all the way back in Hellenistic antiquity, the first-century philosopher Zosimus of Panopolis adduced three stages in alchemy. In the first, known as *nigredo* (blackening), the operator would

mann, whose *Buch der heiligen Dreifaltigkeit* (Book of the Holy Trinity) interpreted Christ's passion and resurrection in elaborate alchemical correspondences with metals and the operation of torture (*nigredo*) leading to the philosopher's stone. Ralph Bauer describes Ullmann's work in *Alchemy of Conquest*, 84.

115. Calvin's opposition to Stoicism as well is pertinent here. A superb account is found in Torrance Kirby, "Stoic *and* Epicurean?," 309–22.

116. Newman and Grafton, *Secrets of Nature*, 4.

117. Luther, *Table Talk* 1.17, in *LW*, vol. 54.

118. Newman and Grafton, *Secrets of Nature*, 13–14.

be confronted with a confused mass subjected to blackening by rotting, burning, or fermentation. In the middle stage, *albedo* (whitening), opposites would be separated in a process of purification. In the reddening or *rubedo* phase, the opposites would be united to form a third thing, superior to the "parents" and often called "the child of the work."[119] Violent separation was essential for a union that would produce the philosophers' stone. The cosmology of kabbalism is similar. When combined with Joachim's three ages, this complex of gnostic influences holds significant potential for revolutionary violence as the ineluctable route to the union that gives birth to the new age. Like the pains of childbirth, the cosmos and its political manifestation must emerge from travail into the birth of the child, who is superior to the opposites. Revolutionary gnostics cannot live in this world as it is, and they must either transmute flesh into spirit through force or retreat into a pure society of spirit.

The intersection of all these triads is evident in a tragic episode. The career of Anna Maria Zieglerin displays vividly not only the combination of Joachite prophecy and Hermetic magic but, more importantly, its political potency. Zieglerin represents in microcosm the radical Anabaptist movement's revolutionary spirit and the crushing defeat it met when it threatened the preservers of public order. In this, Zieglerin reminds us of the boundary-defying shaman.

Prior to her arrest, Anna Maria Zieglerin had been an alchemist attached to the courts of German princes, especially Duke Julius of Braunschweig-Lüneburg (northern Germany). According to Tara Nummedel:

> Julius was drawn to Anna's recipes for a golden oil she called the lion's blood, which was said to possess the extraordinary ability to stimulate the growth of plants, make gemstones, and even transform lead into the coveted philosophers' stone, a precious secret in its own right that could transmute metals and promote health. Equally intriguing was the way Anna framed her alchemy as a tool for addressing a matter that weighed heavily on the minds of pious Christians in sixteenth-century Europe: the rapidly approaching end of time. Anna claimed that she and an enigmatic adept named Count Carl von Oettingen were to fulfill a prophecy, using the lion's blood to conceive children whose alchemical bodies would help prepare the world for its end. Anna and those close to her drew parallels to the Virgin Mary, likening Anna's extraordinary generation of life, as well as its profound implications for sacred history, with the virgin birth of Christ. The real promise of the lion's blood was not simply

119. See Bogdan, *Esotericism*, 197.

gold and gemstones, but nothing less than the redemption of the world in its final moments.[120]

Angels, appearing as "little men," dictated to Zieglerin not only secret recipes but political policy, advocating war against the Holy Roman Emperor Ferdinand I. Given her following, this was taken with utmost seriousness by imperial authorities.[121] According to Zieglerin, only after the "four lords" (three German dukes joined by King Erik XIV of Sweden) conquered the godless would the Last World Emperor (Duke Johann Friedrich II) initiate the millennium.[122] "In medieval central Europe," notes Nummedal, "the Last World Emperor came to be identified with the messianic German emperor, a 'third Friedrich.'"[123]

Encouraged by Zieglerin 's prophecies, Johann Friedrich II moved against not only Roman Catholics but also Lutherans who, in his view, had failed to shed the graveclothes of the fallen church.[124] Julius also adopted this policy in his realm, as guided by Zieglerin's visions. Following Paracelsus, Zieglerin believed that menstrual blood—far from being a taboo—was essential to the alchemical search. As Nummedel notes, menstrual blood "was central to the Paracelsian desire to create artificial human life in the form of the homunculus, a kind of pure, artificial human that embodied the alchemists' loftiest aims."[125]

Like Paracelsus, "Anna, too, shared the ambitious desire to extend alchemy's powers into the creation of human life." Attempting to repeat something like Christ's virgin birth, the Joachite new age would produce a human simultaneously artificial and more divine.[126] In the end, Anna confessed to "a mix of medicine, magic, and poison, both demonic and natural, and all designed to kill, cripple, manipulate affections, and even strengthen one's resolve not to confess evil deeds." She admitted to using black magic to dupe Julius's credulous wife into suicide.[127] She also confessed to mixing a love potion so that Julius would embrace her.[128] In February of 1575, Anna Maria Zieglerin was torn with tongs of hot iron and strapped into an iron chair that was lowered into the flames.[129]

120. Nummedel, *Alchemy and Authority*, 2–3.
121. Nummedel, *Alchemy and Authority*, 17.
122. Nummedel, *Alchemy and Authority*, 21.
123. Nummedal, *Alchemy and Authority*, 22.
124. Nummedel, *Alchemy and Authority*, 26.
125. Nummedel, *Alchemy and Authority*, 115.
126. Nummedel, *Alchemy and Authority*, 116–17.
127. Nummedel, *Alchemy and Authority*, 170.
128. Nummedel, *Alchemy and Authority*, 173.
129. Nummedel, *Alchemy and Authority*, 1.

Hermes without Magic

Beyond German lands, the "Egyptian" Hermes Trismegistus cast his spell on Elizabethan England, the Valois and Bourbon courts of France, and the Prague of Holy Roman Emperor Rudolph II. The English humanist John Colet returned from the Continent a student of Savonarola and Ficino, corresponding regularly with the latter. As Kristeller observes, Neoplatonism was not just "an offshoot of the humanistic movement," but was a major force across all camps.[130] Renaissance Aristotelians were also enthralled by Plato and Ficino.

One notable example at the center of the French Renaissance was Jacques Lefèvre d'Étaples (ca. 1450–1536). Initial reception of Hermeticism in France is described as "Hermes without magic." Already steeped in Plato as well as Aristotle, Lefèvre visited Ficino and Pico in Florence and returned to France as an ardent admirer of their work. Surprisingly perhaps, his own edition based on Ficino's Latin version of the Corpus Hermeticum's first treatise, *Poimander*, was published in 1494 by the University of Paris. However, d'Étaples toned down not only the magic of the Ascelpius but also the *prisca theologia* of Ficino. A decade later, Lefèvre published the first single-volume edition of Ficino's version of the *Poimander* and the Asclepius and added his own commentary with a warning against the "bad magic" and "idol-making passages of the Asclepius."[131] As Yates notes, Lefèvre's new edition of Ficino's writings "was dedicated to a famous French bishop, Guillaume Briçonnet, thus inaugurating the ecclesiastical career of Hermeticism without magic in France."[132] It was in the circle of Briçonnet that the French Renaissance flowered, including the reformist pupils around Lefèvre like Guillaume Farel and John Calvin.

Lefèvre's interest in reviving a pristine Aristotle displays the breadth of his influences, although gradually his attention turned toward biblical commentary

130. Kristeller, *Renaissance Thought*, 57–60. He adds, "On the other hand, we note that certain Aristotelian philosophers like Nifo, who wanted to defend the immortality of the soul, made use of the arguments given in Plato's *Phaedo* or in Ficino's *Platonic Theology,* and that even the more 'naturalistic' among the Renaissance Aristotelians, like Pomponazzi or Cremonini, were willing to accept certain specific Platonist doctrines" (60).

131. Yates, *Giordano Bruno*, 170. Until recently this work was thought to have been written by Ficino. Yates indicates, "We have no commentary by Ficino on the Asclepius, for the commentary supposedly by him which is printed with the Asclepius, in his collected works is now known to have been not by Ficino, but by Lefèvre d'Étaples. In that commentary Lefèvre d'Étaples expresses strong disapproval of the 'god-making' passage" (40).

132. Yates, *Giordano Bruno*, 171–72; see also Walker, *Studies*, 70–71.

and theology, arriving at the doctrine of justification through faith alone and the sufficiency of scripture a decade before Luther. Symphorien Champier (1471–1539), a famous physician, also imbibed the Neoplatonism of the Hermetic treatises but was staunchly opposed to the occult.[133] The "learned magic" of the Florentines was held in high suspicion by French Renaissance thinkers who nevertheless showed interest in the philosophical idea of the Hermetica.[134]

Yet with each generation there was growing fascination in France with the magical side of Ficino's project. The early modern amalgamation of astrology and alchemy, often with kabbalistic mysticism, was either accepted or rejected *in toto*. Consigning all occult pursuits to vain superstition, Calvin devoted an entire treatise to opposing judicial astrology, and he mentions it critically in twenty-one passages in his commentaries.[135] In his treatise against judicial astrology in 1549, Calvin warns:

> There has been for a long time a foolish curiosity which consists of judging by the stars all that should happen to men, and of inquiring of them what course to take. . . . Rejected in the past as pernicious to the human race this phenomenon is in full revival today, with the result that many people who believe themselves to be of sound mind and who indeed have the reputation of being so are almost bewitched.[136]

Significantly, though, across Northern Europe magical Hermeticism reached its apogee in the late sixteenth century and especially in the seventeenth century. As Yates argues:

> There seems to be a tendency by which the holier and more Christian Hermes Trismegistus becomes, the more his date is pushed back, now to before Moses. François de Foix de Candale, Bishop of Aire, reaches new heights of ecstatic religious Hermeticism. In 1574 he published another edition of the Greek text of the *Hermetica*, based on that of Turnebus with emendations suggested by Scaliger and others. He thinks that Hermes attained to a knowledge of divine

133. He wrote in 1532 an *Epistola campegiana de tranmutatione metallorum contra alchimistas*. This trend spread to Maruice Scève (1501–1564), Joachim du Bellay (ca. 1522–1560), and Pierre de Ronsard (1524–1585).

134. Hanegraaff, *Esoterism and the Academy*, 83.

135. Probes, "Calvin," 25.

136. See Calvin, "Avertissement contre l'astrologie judiciaire," in Calvin, *Opera*, 7:515–16. Quoted and translated by Probes, "Calvin," 24.

> things surpassing that of the Hebrew prophets and equaling that of the Apostles and Evangelists. He lived at an earlier date than Moses and must have been divinely inspired. The bad passages in the *Asclepius* were put in by Apuleius. In 1579, Foix published a French translation of the *Hermetica*, in the preface to which he repeats these statements and seems almost to elevate the works of Hermes Trismegistus to the level of canonical scriptures.[137]

By this time, Yates observes that "the magical current was also pretty strong in France."[138] In fact, Pontus de Tyard, Bishop of Châlons, called it the "holy Egyptian school."[139] Catherine de' Medici, the queen consort, belonged to the Italian banking family that had supported Ficino and Pico. Yates relates, "Catherine was notorious for her interest in talismans and her encouragement of magicians and astrologers, and it would be difficult to believe that there was not also something of a magical intention behind her festivals. When in the *Ballet comique de la reine* of 1581, the product of the festival tradition which she founded, Catherine saw Jupiter and Mercury descending from heaven in response to the incantatory music and singing, it is doubtful, great artist though she was, whether she saw this as a purely artistic representation."[140]

Yet Lefèvre's rendering of Hermetic thought as "Hermes without magic" continued through the humanist and Huguenot theologian Philippe du Plessis Mornay (1549–1623), who drew heavily on Hermeticism in his *De la vérité de la religion chrétienne*, which was dedicated to the Reformed king of Navarre. Yates notes that he speaks of "the world as a 'shadow of the splendour of God.' Mornay is an example of how men were turning to the Hermetic religion of the world to take them above these conflicts, and as a possible way of escape from the agonies inflicted by fanatical use of force by both sides."[141] Case in point, Mornay drew directly on the Corpus Hermeticum and on Pico's mystical meditations along with kabbalah. In Yates's words:

> Mornay is making the familiar synthesis between Hermeticism and Cabala, but it is *emphatically not Magia and practical Cabala* of which he is speaking. The synthesis is entirely mystical and theological. He states most emphatically later on that Cabala is not magic, that Moses was not a magician, and that all

137. Yates, *Giordano Bruno*, 173.
138. Yates, *Giordano Bruno*, 173.
139. Yates, *Giordano Bruno*, 174.
140. Yates, *Giordano Bruno*, 175–76.
141. Yates, *Giordano Bruno*, 176.

magic is wrong and vain. Mornay's work reflects the situation at Antwerp in 1581 where William of Orange was trying to establish the Southern Netherlands, now temporarily freed from Philip II of Spain, as a state in which religious toleration should be practiced.[142]

However, among other Reformed scholars there was a concerted deconstruction of Hermeticism at its philological heart. Joseph Scaliger, Matthieu Berodale, and Isaac Casaubon proved that the Corpus Hermeticum was forged in the second or third century.[143] Then, in 1603, the repentant alchemist Nicholas Guibert "took aim at the authenticity of even the *Tabula* [Emerald Tablet], noting that identifying gold and silver with the names of planets finds its source in Proclus's commentary on the *Timaeus*."[144] Authorities mattered most, and the more Reformed philologists followed Lorenzo Valla's deconstruction of textual myths the greater the divide between philosophical Neoplatonists and practical magicians. In France at least, the reception of the Hermetic tradition was divided rather sharply. Evangelicals drew on its philosophical ideas while, according to Eugene Lefrance, thirty thousand astrologists, alchemists, and sorcerers lived in Catherine de' Medici's Paris.[145]

Meanwhile, Jesuits were working overtime to establish a link between the perennial philosophy and Christianity. The German Jesuit Athanasius Kircher's *Oedipus Aegyptiacus* (The Egyptian Oedipus, 1652–1654) is a prime example of this. Ignoring Casaubon's devastating critique, Kircher "assumes that Hermes Trismegistus is a composite of several historical personalities."[146]

The situation changed fundamentally, however, in the mid-seventeenth century. In 1648 Herman Conring, an orthodox Lutheran theologian, legal scholar, and professor of medicine at Helmstedt University, published a work entitled *De hermetica Aegyptiorum vetere et nova Paracelsicorum medicina liber unus.*[147] Building on the Calvinist critiques, he argued that Hermes Trismegistus never lived, Egyptian medicine was pure superstition and inferior to Greek, and the alchemical texts are also forgeries. Further, Conring also asserted, according to Ebeling, that the Hermetic writings were "magic, irreconcilable with either Christian belief or general custom. The Paracelsists were harming, not helping, their patients. Nev-

142. Yates, *Giordano Bruno*, 177, emphasis added.
143. Ebeling, *Secret History*, 95; cf. Grafton, "Protestant versus Prophet," 154.
144. Ebeling, *Secret History*, 96.
145. Defrance, *Catherine de Medicis*, 15.
146. Ebeling, *Secret History*, 97.
147. Ebeling, *Secret History*, 97.

ertheless, as Conring acknowledged, Hermeticism enjoyed an uninterruptedly good reputation."[148]

In spite of his independent spirit, Paracelsus insisted that his magic was of the "white" variety. "I have written as a Christian and am no heathen," he avowed, "I am a German."[149] In this vein, Philip Ball demonstrates that Paracelsus's interest in the Bible and theology was far greater than is usually recognized.[150] Although critical of the papacy, Paracelsus never met Luther and insisted against any comparison with the German Reformer. Rather, he interpreted the dissent in apocalyptic terms as a judgment.[151]

Conclusion

From the preceding summary, one could classify Paracelsus as "spiritual, not religious." He was as peripatetic in crossing confessional boundaries as he was in his geographical wanderings. Building on the Renaissance individualism inherent in the rediscovery of the divine self, Paracelsus's motto was *Alterius non sit qui suus esse potest*: "Let no man belong to another who can belong to himself."[152] Though he never left the Roman Catholic fold, Paracelsus's sympathies lay with the Anabaptists, notes Goodrick-Clarke: "His ethical speculations were in line with those of the Brethren of the Free Spirit, the Anabaptists, and other sectarian exponents of radicalism and popular pantheism in the Middle Ages and on the eve of the Reformation. At Salzburg in 1525 Paracelsus supported the cause of rebellious peasants, was arrested, and only narrowly escaped the death penalty."[153]

A stanza from Robert Browning's *Paracelsus* summarizes this synthesis well, along with the development of the spiritual-versus-religious outlook:

> Truth is within ourselves; it takes no rise
> From outward things, whate'er you may believe.
> There is an inmost centre in us all,
> Where truth abides in fulness; and around,
> Wall upon wall, the gross flesh hems it in,

148. Ebeling, *Secret History*, 97.

149. Paracelsus, *Opus Paramirum*, 9.3, quoted from Goodrick-Clarke, *Paracelsus*, 112.

150. Ball, *Devil's Doctor*, especially 106–7, but throughout the work there are engagements with figures like Erasmus and Luther.

151. Goodrick-Clarke, *Paracelsus*, 20.

152. Paracelsus, *Das Buch Paragranum*, 5.5, quoted from Goodrick-Clarke, *Paracelsus*, 73.

153. Goodrick-Clarke, *Paracelsus*, 16.

This perfect, clear perception—which is truth,
A baffling and perverting carnal mesh
Binds it, and makes all error: and to KNOW,
Rather consists in opening out a way
Whence the imprisoned splendour may escape,
Than in effecting entry for a light
Supposed to be without.[154]

154. Browning, *Paracelsus*, 36.

6

Utopia
New Worlds of the New Age

> With respect and good cause, I state, most magnificent rulers, that greater things are in store for you, for we read that Joachim, abbot of Calabria, predicted that someone from Spain would recover the wealth of Zion.
>
> —Christopher Columbus[1]

The dogma of the divine self is so familiar that it is easy to forget that it is a contingent historical tradition, with fresh esoteric lava reshaping the exoteric landscape. The widely agreed-on features of axiality are self-discovery, disembedding, individualism, and criticism of constraints to the autonomous self. But this utopian flight from a locative outlook inspired outer as well as inner voyages across the seas.

We have seen that Joachim of Fiore placed the ladder of purgation, contemplation, and union on its side, such that the vertical ascent becomes a historical one leading to the age of the Spirit. Whether it is Savonarola in Florence, Columbus in the Americas, Müntzer's followers in Münster, or John Dee in London and Prague, the divine self is impatient with the status quo, critical of traditional boundaries, longing to build a new Jerusalem in one's heart and also somewhere in this world. This chapter explores key Renaissance utopias that sought to provide a blueprint for the new age presided over by the shaman-sage who can unite the worlds above, below, and within.

1. Columbus, *Book of Prophecies*, 221, p. 317.

New World

I read Plato's *Republic* as an allegory for the truth that no *civitas* on earth is capable of leading the masses out of the cave into light of being. The best philosophy can do is save the few it can. Some, however, have read it as a blueprint for an actual state. Plotinus negotiated with the emperor to purchase land for the erection of "Platonopolis." As the medieval period Arabic Hermetic text *Picatrix* tells it, Adocentyn was a city of magic built by Hermes Trismegistus himself, "who placed around the circumference of the city 'engraved images and ordered them in such a manner that by their virtue the inhabitants were made virtuous and withdrawn from all wickedness and harm.'"[2] Whatever other sources for the Renaissance imagination, surely Adocentyn loomed large. One might also note Plethon's blueprint for a pagan Platonic republic in his native Mistra as well.

However, Joachim of Fiore's interpretation of the book of Revelation shifted hopes from a sectarian republic of philosopher-mystics to an era of history. His work was not only a commentary on biblical prophecy but a new way of viewing history that shaped the early modern imagination of Europeans.[3] The third era, the age of the Spirit, was not just a stage above in the ascent of the alone to the Alone for Joachim, but rather one that would be realized as a universal state in the historical ascent of the human race.[4] Already in the fourteenth century the Italian scholar Petrarch directly employed the age of the Spirit in the service of Renaissance humanism, coining the term "Dark Ages" and anticipating an epoch in which there would be no popes, dogmas, scriptures, or sacraments separating people. It would be the triumph of spirit over flesh, of the inward and direct over the external and hierarchical.

In his openly pantheistic scheme, Petrarch was the champion of the universal World Spirit. It was a new age, and one that sought earnestly for a new canvas—a new world—on which to paint its hopes and dreams. In many ways, Savonarola, steeped in Joachim's prophetic visions, represented this acute sense of history's climax, for woe and for well, that dominated the Florentine populace. It was in Renaissance Florence that Joachite prophecy and Ficinian Orphism first congealed. These distinct, sometimes opposing, utopian narratives became combined especially in Catholic humanism and Paracelsian natural philosophy. A literal po-

2. Quoted in Yates, *Giordano Bruno*, 232.

3. Along with many others, Henri de Lubac has traced many of the prominent lines of Joachite influence to the present day in de Lubac, *Posterité spirituelle*.

4. Van Cleve, *Frederick II*, 13–16. Again, my interest is less in whether such accounts are legendary but whether they were disseminated widely enough to contribute to the effective history of Joachite prophecy.

litical interpretation of the *Republic* and an allegorical interpretation of biblical prophecy could fire the imaginations of those dissatisfied with the present order. Luca Signorelli's painting *The Preaching of the Antichrist* (1500) favors Ficino's final evaluation of Savonarola.[5]

Yet, as Joachim had his spiritual *fraticelli*, Savonarola continued to have followers in Florence called the *Piagnoni* (weepers), among whom Gianfrancesco Pico della Mirandola was the most reputed. McGinn notes, "The attacks of Ficino and Signorelli can be contrasted with the extravagant praise of Giovanni Nesi whose *Oracle of the New World* of 1497 saw the Dominican as a messianic initiator of the millennial age of history."[6] Nesi composed his famous *Oracle* at the peak of tensions between his two close friends, Savonarola and Ficino. Reeves's reflection on this confluence is insightful:

> The most eloquent spokesman of the Platonist *Piagnoni* was Giovanni Nesi who, in his *Oracolo de nova saeculo*, gathered together a strange mixture of Neoplatonism, occult mysteries and Christian prophecy. It is addressed to the younger Pico and calls him to participate in this latest banquet of the *novum saeculum* or golden age. Here Savonarola appears surrounded by hermetical and astrological symbols. Nesi was seeking to blend the Neoplatonism of Ficino's Academy with the prophetic tradition of Joachimism, as derived from the Bible. In his union of philosophy and Christianity he envisages the eagle of philosophy nesting with Christ, the phoenix. The nest is Florence and from this union will spring the "new race" of fledglings which will spread throughout the world.[7]

In fact, Marjorie Reeves states that "Nesi's vision of the new city is as much the new Jerusalem as the Platonic Republic."[8] Nesi was totally committed to Savonarola's prediction that the age of the Spirit will begin in 1517.[9] This was the same year that Luther's Ninety-Five Theses sparked the Reformation, so it is not surprising that the Reformer had to rebuff some followers who claimed for him the mantle of "angelic pope."

In 1481 Giovanni Annio of Viterbo had argued that the pope would be the universal monarch. Under him there would be twelve regions, "each ruled by a

5. Riess, *Luca Signorelli*. This fresco inspired much of Michelangelo's Sistine Chapel.

6. McGinn, *Apocalyptic Spirituality*, 183. See also Celenza, *Piety and Pythagoras*. The first part is a superb introduction to Nesi and his world of thought, in dependence on Ficino and Savonarola, while the second is the unedited translation of Nesi's *Oracle of the New World*.

7. Reeves, *Joachim of Fiore*, 90. See also Lodone, "Nesi."

8. Reeves, *Joachim of Fiore*, 91.

9. Reeves, *Joachim of Fiore*, 93.

patriarch, a king and a '*custos angelus*.' This would indeed be the New Jerusalem, embodying a new heaven, that is, a new state of the Church, and a new earth, a new state of the laity." He even called it the *tercius status* (third age).[10] We have seen the same template employed during Jan van Leiden's regime in Müntzer in chapter 3. But while some expected the *renovatio* to occur in Europe, others turned to the New World as the theater of prophetic fulfillment.

The age of exploration was bound up, at least in part, with the age of the Spirit. Christendom was finished. The New World was the next phase in God's plan. Scholarios, one of Plethon's opponents, fell under Joachim's spell. As the first Patriarch of Constantinople under Ottoman rule, he drew on the biblical year of Jubilee (Lev 25; Isa 61:1–5; Luke 4:18–19) to declare in 1492—the year of Columbus's famous first exploration—"the year of our Lord's favor."[11] The same rhetoric was employed across Europe. In fact, as Djelal Kadir says, "Europe's new-worlding tradition is of a conscious weave, tightly knit with skeins of prophetic apocalypticism that bind Novatian zeal, Joachimite arithmetic, orthodox eschatology, Reformationist enthusiasm, and Humanist expectation."[12]

Amerigo Vespucci, Florentine banker and explorer, led voyages on behalf of Spain and Portugal around the same time as Columbus. One of his letters, dated from 1502, included the words *Mundus novus*, and the phrase "New World" became as established in the European imagination as "America," named after Amerigo Vespucci.[13] As Allison Brown notes regarding Vespucci's letter, "Among the novelties of the native inhabitants that he commented on—including their nude, beautiful, and 'most libidinous (*libidinosissime*) women'—was the fact that they had no churches, no laws, nor were they idolatrous. 'What more can I say? They live according to nature and can be called Epicureans rather than Stoics.'"[14]

Against such an Epicurean natural theology thriving in the New World, the spirit of Savonarola raised its confidence in Joachite prophecy. Writing to his patrons, King Ferdinand of Aragon and Queen Isabella of Castile, Christopher Columbus declared, "I have already said that for the voyage to the Indies neither intelligence nor mathematics nor world maps were of any use to me; it was the fulfillment of Isaiah's prophecy. . . . With respect and good cause, I state, most magnificent rulers, that greater things are in store for you, for we read that Joachim,

10. Reeves, *Joachim of Fiore*, 124–25. Citing Giovanni Annio of Viterbo, *Glosa super Apocalypsim* (1481).

11. Kadir, *Columbus*, 153.

12. Kadir, *Columbus*, 42.

13. Brown, *Return of Lucretius*, 89.

14. Brown, *Return of Lucretius*, 89–90.

abbot of Calabria, predicted that someone from Spain would recover the wealth of Zion."[15] John L. Phelan explains:

> During the Joachimite third age of the Holy Ghost all men would have an angelic nature, and they would live in apostolic poverty. Everyone would have full knowledge of all the mysteries, just as the vague prophecies of the Old Testament were obscure until the coming of Christ clarified them. The full meaning of the sacraments, the allegories, and the symbols of the "Papal Church" would become clear to all men during the third age of the "Spiritual Church" of the friars. Joachimism is the ancestor of the modern idea of progress, for the doctrine of the three ages implied that man would grow more nearly perfect as historical time unfolded. It is also one of the sources of inspiration out of which grew not only the bucolic and utopian ideas of the Renaissance but also the terrestrial paradise of the Age of Discovery.[16]

Rusconi relates that Columbus relied on Pierre d'Ailly to deduce a universal chronology in his *Book of Prophecies*, "leaving only 155 years until the time 'when the world must end.'"[17] Phelan observes the influence of the Spiritual Franciscan and alchemist Johannis de Rupescissa, but also points out places in the *Book of Prophecies*—an incomplete collection of apocalyptic revelations compiled by Columbus toward the end of his life—in which the Italian explorer displays more direct knowledge of Joachim's writings.[18] John of Rupescissa was a pioneer of this vision for converting Asia. Phelan explains, "Like many of similar temperament in that period, Rupescissa was deeply influenced by the abbot Joachim of Fiore. . . . This fourteenth-century Catalan Franciscan must be considered as a precursor to Christopher Columbus. For the discoverer was the first to see the possibility of converting all the races of the world as an apocalyptic and Messianic vision."[19]

Among the pseudo-Joachite writings was the prediction that the Last World Emperor would come from Spain (not France or Germany, as Joachim actually taught). In a 1301 treatise, the Catalonian physician and theologian Arnald of Villanova wrote, "The earth will be destitute, until the new David comes to restore the arch of Zion," and he would wear the Spanish crown.[20] We have seen Savonarola

15. Columbus, *Book of Prophecies*, 011, pp. 71–75, and 221, p. 317.

16. Phelan, *Millennial Kingdom*, 59–60.

17. Rusconi, introduction to Columbus, *Book of Prophecies*, 19.

18. West and Zimdars-Swartz, *Joachim of Fiore*, 108.

19. Phelan, *Millennial Kingdom*, 18–19.

20. Rusconi, introduction to Columbus, *Book of Prophecies*, 31, referring to Villanova's *Tractatus de mysterio cymbalorum*, 1301.

congratulating Charles of France as the Last World Emperor, but the Spaniards would have nothing of it. Franciscans in Spain, not surprisingly, were especially drawn to Villanova's prediction, and it quickly attained political significance in the reign of Ferdinand and Isabella.[21]

West and Zimdars-Swartz conclude, "It was Columbus's plan, and one which he promoted to the Spanish monarchs, to utilize the gold expected to be taken from the New World in order to capture the Holy Sepulcher and to rebuild Jerusalem in preparation for the Lord's Second Coming. On this he 'quotes' Joachim of Fiore twice that Zion must be rebuilt by a man from Spain."[22] In fact, notes Reeves, Columbus says, "The Calabrian Abbot Joachim says that from Spain will spring the one who must rebuild the House of Sion."[23] He refers to this prophecy in a letter to Ferdinand and Isabella from Jamaica while on his fourth voyage (July 7, 1503). His thinking was clearly influenced by "the broad tradition of apocalyptic eschatology in the Franciscan circles" that was especially acute at the opening of the sixteenth century.[24]

Phelan, however, goes too far in suggesting that Columbus thought of himself as a "Joachite Messiah."[25] Columbus clearly saw himself as a key prophetic figure, but not as the Last World Emperor or angelic pope, much less the messiah. Instead, he saw himself as a new Elijah. Joachim saw in this prophet's career a host of portents, as Reeves notes:

> In general he typifies the Holy Spirit. His sojourn by the brook Cherith and with the widow at Zarepath signify that two peoples, the Greek and the Latin, will receive the Spirit when the Jews reject it. Even the food offered first by ravens and then by the widow has a special meaning . . . the baking of the cake by the widow typifies the Host and the two iron plates within which this is made, the two Testaments. Elijah's raising of the widow's son signifies the rise of St. Benedict.[26]

Converting the heathen and rebuilding the temple in Jerusalem were the twin objectives of Columbus's mission, as he describes them in the *Libro*.[27]

21. Rusconi, introduction to Columbus, *Book of Prophecies*, 17; cf. Columbus, *Book of Prophecies*, 001, pp. 67–69.

22. West and Zimdars-Swartz, *Joachim of Fiore*, 109.

23. Reeves, *Joachim of Fiore*, 129; cf. Rusconi, introduction to Columbus, *Book of Prophecies*, 32–33.

24. Rusconi, introduction to Columbus, *Book of Prophecies*, 33.

25. Phelan, *Millennial Kingdom*, 24–25.

26. Reeves, *Joachim of Fiore*, 11.

27. West and Kling, *The "Libro de las Profecías,"* 29.

The capstone of Joachim's eschatology—with crucial import for Franciscan missions—was that the Last World Emperor "will assemble the exiles of Israel."[28] Rebuilding the temple was one thing, but what would Columbus's mission have to do with regathering the exiles? Like many of his day, Columbus believed that the natives of the Americas were descendants of the lost tribes of Israel.[29] The "divine primitive" will be the angelic race, at first subordinated to the Europeans, that will exhibit the new age of holy monasticism.[30] The "savages" would become the marvel of all Europe as the pure race of Israel's diaspora.[31] Spain viewed itself as God's holy nation. Missions evangelized gentiles while crusades and inquisitions exterminated heretics.[32]

It is not an exaggeration to refer to Columbus's apocalyptic interests as a "frenzied preoccupation with . . . bizarre millenarianism."[33] Studying prophecies was not for Columbus a curious hobby but a serious vocation that gripped him and the missionaries who followed in his wake. He believed that he was a key instrument of God in the third age, and by this time Joachim's millennial scheme was assumed not only by Spiritual Franciscans but by Franciscans more broadly and indeed by much of Europe.

In the Wake of Columbus

Francesco de Meleto had spent the 1470s in Constantinople looking for prophetic material. With Savonarola and Patriarch Scholarios, he was convinced that the age of the Spirit would commence in 1517. After a reformation of the church, the whole world will be governed by one shepherd as one flock. In his *Quadrivium temporum prophetarum* that he presented to Pope Leo X, Meleto argued that the "universal reformation" would be completed in 1530. "But although the humanists secured him an interview, the authorities were now growing alarmed by the radical reformers."[34] In fact, one of his followers, Pietro Bernardino, founded his true church of the "Anointed" (*Uni*) in 1496. The conflicted loyalties in Florence reflect a wider sense of confusion over whether Joachite "prophets" like Savona-

28. Columbus, *Book of Prophecies*, 114, p. 177; cf. Phelan, *Millennial Kingdom*, 17–26; Kadir, *Columbus*, 138–49.

29. Phelan, *Millennial Kingdom*, 24.

30. Kadir, *Columbus*, 138–92.

31. Kadir, *Columbus*, 105–37.

32. Graziano, *Millennial Kingdom*, 22; cf. Kadir, *Columbus*, 20.

33. Sale, *Christopher Columbus*, 28.

34. Reeves, *Joachim of Fiore*, 93–94.

rola were harbingers of the new age or precursors of the antichrist. According to Reeves, "By 1498 [Meleto] had become the *Papa Angelica* of his sect, preaching a new outpouring of the Holy Spirit and a prophetic programme which echoed Savonarola closely."[35]

Even the great reforming humanist Cardinal Contarini "admitted to believing in the future *renovatio* and defended Savonarola whilst seeking to dissociate his reputation from the radical prophets."[36] According to Joachite millennialism, the kingdom would arrive only when the gospel had been preached to all nations, the temple in Jerusalem had been rebuilt, and the Israelites had returned to the land. Phelan relates, "When Friar Francisco de los Angeles, minister-general of the Franciscan order, bade farewell to the twelve friars who were leaving to undertake the conversion of the recently conquered Aztecs, he referred to their mission as the beginning of the last preaching of the gospel on the eve of the end of the world."[37]

Phelan emphasizes that there were "three main axes" for interpretations of the conquest of the New World by Spaniards of the day. He observes that "part of the drama of the spiritual conquest of the New World comes to light when these three different exegeses of the parable of Luke 14 are placed in juxtaposition." In Luke 14, Jesus tells of a king who sends messengers to invite the proper guests to his wedding feast, but they all offer excuses. After three attempts, the king sends the heralds to bring in guests from the alleys and streets.

The first interpretation, represented by Juan Ginés de Sepúlveda, stressed a purely this-worldly glory for Spain and its conquistadors. "He suggested that the servant's first invitation—*introduc eos*—corresponded to the Primitive Apostolic Church" (i.e., the church before Constantine), when coercion was not employed. "The servant's third invitation—*compelle eos*—corresponded to the Church after Constantine."[38] In the current era, the guests must be compelled. In Sepúlveda's view, though, "Compulsion was increased in proportion to the distance that separated the Jews, the Moslems, and the Gentiles from the Holy Land."[39]

The second line of interpretation was taken by Bartholomé de Las Casas, the enthusiastic companion and biographer who attended Columbus on his voyages.[40] Interpreting Columbus more in a "great man" tradition of Roman biography, Las Casas could understand his tale as a glorious rise from obscurity to greatness that

35. Reeves, *Joachim of Fiore*, 94.
36. Reeves, *Joachim of Fiore*, 94.
37. Phelan, *Millennial Kingdom*, 23.
38. Phelan, *Millennial Kingdom*, 9.
39. Phelan, *Millennial Kingdom*, 10–11.
40. See Sullivan, *Indian Freedom*, 70.

nevertheless ended in failure with his oppression of natives. He adds, "Unclean is the offering sacrificed by an oppressor. Such mockeries of the unjust are not pleasing to God. The Lord is pleased by those who keep to the way of truth and justice. . . . The one whose sacrifice comes from the goods of the poor is like one who kills his neighbor. The one who sheds blood and the one who defrauds the laborer are kin and kind (Ecclesiasticus 34:18ff.)."[41] Citing Matthew 10:14, Las Casas insisted that judgment would be reserved for Christ himself on the last day. Jesus authorized no other ground for missionary growth than "peaceful and rational persuasion, employing no coercion whatsoever."[42]

Representing a third line of interpretation is Gerónimo de Mendieta. "Mendieta was responsible for formulating what must be considered the mystical interpretation of the conquest."[43] According to Phelan, Mendieta believed that "the Papal Church would be resurrected as the Spiritual Church in which all men would lead the contemplative life, practice apostolic poverty, and enjoy angelic natures." Phelan also notes that "Apocalyptic mysticism with a Joachimite tinge enjoyed a revival in Spain during the reign of Ferdinand and Isabella when Cardinal Francisco Ximénez de Cisneros, a Franciscan Observant himself, undertook a highly successful reformation of the regular clergy." In that manner, Mendieta's "mysticism is permeated with a Joachimite spirit."[44]

Mendieta read Jesus's parable in Luke 14 as a vision of the Last World Emperor of Joachite prophecy who would send messengers far and wide to fill his palace with guests for the wedding feast after the invited guests declined. Instead of Jesus, though, the king in Mendieta's reading of the parable is the end-times, universal monarchy of the Spanish Habsburgs, and the three groups of invitees who reject him are Jews, Muslims, and heretics. These groups required compulsion. Jews were considered "perfidious," Muslims were "false," and gentiles were "blind." And heretics were fit for nothing but the Inquisition.[45] Mendieta insisted that Ferdinand and Isabella must cleanse not only Spain but also the New World of wickedness and spread the true religion before Christ would return.

Shrouded in the aura of being lost tribes of Israel, natives encountered by Franciscan missionaries were regarded as a spiritual race: a *genus Angelicum*.[46] Concerning Mendieta's view of these natives, Phelan writes:

41. Sullivan, *Indian Freedom*, 4.

42. Phelan, *Millennial Kingdom*, 9.

43. Phelan, *Millennial Kingdom*, 6.

44. Phelan, *Millennial Kingdom*, 16. Phelan's primary source for Mandieta is the *Historia eclesiastica indiana* (1595).

45. Phelan, *Millennial Kingdom*, 13–15.

46. Phelan, *Millennial Kingdom*, 59–68.

> There are many audible echoes of these Joachimite doctrines in Mendieta's idea of the personality of the Indians. They were reasonable and capable of receiving grace, but lacked the passions that led Europeans into sin. They were so pure that if it were not revealed that all have descended from Adam and Eve he would think they were of another species. Confessors have little work to do, as the natives search ardently for the smallest sin to justify absolution.[47]

The conflict between strict Franciscans and the pope was being played out in the Americas. While Pope John XXII was not fond of Franciscans generally, he declared Spiritual Franciscans (i.e., strict observers of apostolic poverty and Joachite prophecy) heretical. According to Phelan, they believed that "during the Joachimite third age of the Holy Ghost, in which the 'spiritual' Church of the friars would replace the 'carnal' Church of the popes, all men would live in apostolic poverty." Mainstream Franciscans "continued to be influenced by a moderate Joachimite spirit without endangering their orthodoxy."[48] Phelan adds:

> The followers of Joachim of Fiore prophesied that all men would attain quasi-angelic perfection during the third age of the Holy Ghost. The ideals of apostolic poverty and Adam-like simplicity implied the liquidation of the whole development of the Church since its recognition by the Emperor Constantine. The papal monarchy of Gregory VII, Innocent III, and Boniface VIII, the political hierarchy of the Church and its organization, the predominance of jurisprudence during the later Middle Ages, and Scholasticism institutionalized in the new universities were all thus repudiated. These mystical currents sometimes overflowed into heresy, for in this period both mysticism and heresy were subjective in approach. Sometimes the mysticism of poverty allied itself with antisacramentalism, as in the movement of Peter Waldo. Innocent III realized the need and the advantage of incorporating a part of the cult of poverty into the magic circle of the Roman Church. It was this realization which prompted him to act as the cautious cofounder of both the Franciscan and Dominican orders.[49]

For this reason, Spaniards and natives could never live together in a common society with the same laws and courts. Natives are so meek, says Mendieta, that "they would never harm a fly. Consequently one must always assume in case of doubt

47. Phelan, *Millennial Kingdom*, 59–60.
48. Phelan, *Millennial Kingdom*, 45.
49. Phelan, *Millennial Kingdom*, 44–45.

that the Spaniard is the offender and the Indian is the victim." Mendieta is clear that natives are not constituted to be teachers but only pupils, parishioners but not priests. Nevertheless, "for this they are the best in the world." In this manner, Mendieta conceived of New Spain as one large monastery.[50] What was still needed was a viceroy, preferably of royal blood. Based on the theories of Duns Scotus, he believed that this supreme governor must have absolute power, but the crown would not grant such authority to a single man.[51]

If Mendieta glorified the American natives as an angelic race that must be "protected" from sinful Spaniards, the sixteenth-century humanist Juan Ginés de Sepúlveda (drawing on Aristotle) regarded them as a lower form of life destined to be ruled by the superior race. Like Dante, who thought that the Romans were destined to rule the world, Sepúlveda believed that this was true in particular of the Spaniards.[52] The Spaniard was to elevate his ward, to Hispanize as well as Christianize, but the native would always be a serf if not a slave. "Both Las Casas and Mendieta rejected Sepúlveda's attempt to apply the Aristotelian doctrine of natural slavery to the Indians."[53] In fact, argued Las Casas (drawing on Aquinas), it cannot be applied to any race. Although he shared Sepúlveda's view of the inferiority of natives in purely this-worldly terms, Mendieta insisted that Aristotle was irrelevant after Paul's declaration that all believers are equal in Christ (Gal 3:28). In fact, the natural simplicity of natives was an asset, not (as Sepúlveda thought) a liability. In their Christian piety natives were superior to Spaniards. As Phelan writes, "Mendieta's idea of the Indian can be summed up as the Christian noble savage. . . . In fact, the genesis of the noble savage is to be found in the traditional Franciscan image of human nature, which developed around the cults of apostolic poverty, primitive simplicity, and Joachimite mysticism."[54] The natives are childlike, innocent, meek, angelic—like Adam before the fall.[55]

The King of Spain and Holy Roman Emperor Charles V (1516–1556) placed episcopal jurisdiction under the mendicants, but his successor Philip II reversed this, and by the late sixteenth century secular clergy dominated the friars.[56] How could the friars inculcate a society of evangelical poverty and simplicity once the natives had witnessed the opulence of episcopal courts? This is one reason why Mendieta liked Hernán Cortés, the first governor of New Spain, for he "had asked

50. Phelan, *Millennial Kingdom*, 61.
51. Phelan, *Millennial Kingdom*, 64.
52. Phelan, *Millennial Kingdom*, 65.
53. Phelan, *Millennial Kingdom*, 66–67.
54. Phelan, *Millennial Kingdom*, 67.
55. Phelan, *Millennial Kingdom*, 66–67.
56. Phelan, *Millennial Kingdom*, 54.

Charles V to send poor friars and not greedy priests to convert the Indians."[57] The antipathy of Franciscan monks to the secular priests was almost equivalent to that of the Anabaptists on the Continent. Sharing everything in common, separating from the pseudo-Christians of Europe, and expressing the age of the Spirit were common themes. *Christianitas*, according to the mendicant missionaries, was the opposite of *hispanitas*. The Spaniards boast in outward circumcision, whereas the natives evidence the circumcision of the heart.[58]

Mendieta came to see the reign of Philip II as a time of tribulation before the millennium to begin sometime in the future "somewhere in the Indies—a magic island vision of an innocent paradise," with a new messianic king of Spain to take the lead.[59] If the Spanish monarchy did not stop the slaughter, Franciscans like Mendieta concluded, God would judge them.[60]

The Dominican friar Francisco de la Cruz was burned by the Inquisition in Lima in 1578 for his prophecies and visions of Spain's destruction by God for its treatment of the native populations.[61] In Phelan's words, "Mendieta's description of the condition of the Indian in colonial society influenced the ideology of the independence movement in Mexico in the early nineteenth century. . . . Mendieta did not surrender to a mood of apocalyptic gloom until the epidemic of 1596 occurred. The demographic crisis of the 1590s seemed fresh evidence to some of the mendicant chroniclers that the New World was in fact the End of the World."[62]

The reliance on Joachim of Fiore and his commentators was full of tension. In reliance on Joachim, Dante also wrote of an angelic pope and enlightened Last World Emperor. According to Phelan:

> The highest end of man in More's *Utopia* is self-improvement; that is, Dante's ideal of terrestrial salvation through the human intellect. The highest end of man in Mendieta's terrestrial paradise is to sing the praises of God; that is, Dante's ideal of celestial salvation through faith. In spite of the almost overwhelmingly otherworldly stress, there is, nevertheless, a this-worldly note in Mendieta's thinking. . . . The yearning to bring heaven down to earth is equivalent to sanctifying and hallowing not only this world but also—and this is decisive—a particular region of this earth, that is, the Indies.[63]

57. Phelan, *Millennial Kingdom*, 56.
58. Phelan, *Millennial Kingdom*, 88–89.
59. Reeves, *Joachim of Fiore*, 131.
60. Phelan, *Millennial Kingdom*, 106.
61. Phelan, *Millennial Kingdom*, 75.
62. Phelan, *Millennial Kingdom*, 90, 96.
63. Phelan, *Millennial Kingdom*, 71–72.

Joachim's eschatology already placed the mystical ladder on its side. Instead of a monk rising rung by rung toward perfection, history itself was now unfolding toward a universal beatific vision. Thus, the otherworldly direction of Platonic ascent became an immanent goal within history. The garden of Eden may even have been located in the New World, some argued. "The first man to place the beginnings of the human race in the New World was, of course, Christopher Columbus," notes Phelan. "In his third voyage he identified the mouth of the Orinoco River with one of the four rivers flowing out of the Garden of Eden."[64] Dismissing this theory, Mendieta "did not look back to the past. He looked forward to the future when the friars and the Indians could create the millennial kingdom of the Apocalypse." [65]

> What merits careful scrutiny is to what extent Mendieta may be considered a social revolutionary.... From the first crusade in the eleventh century until the Anabaptists in the sixteenth century revolutionary chiliast movements periodically erupted in western Europe. Revolutionary chiliasm was not only the protest of the poor against the privileged. These outbreaks often combined the Messianic and apocalyptic vision of the millennial kingdom on earth, to which the Joachimites had made such a significant contribution, with the active demands of oppressed strata of society for a more equitable distribution of temporal goods... Mendieta was certainly not a revolutionary chiliast. Yet his ideas are not totally immune from some germs of social revolution.... Mendieta wanted the leadership to come from the top—from the Messiah—the World Ruler who would be aided by the friars.... Yet his notion that the Messiah was to break the chains of economic exploitation of a particular group in society, so that the Indians might achieve "the most perfect and healthy Christianity that the world has ever known," was one step but only one step in the direction of revolutionary chiliasm.[66]

The real difference, then, between missionaries like Mendieta and secular conquerors like Sepúlveda was whether natives would be singing from the Psalms or working in the fields. Mystics sought to spiritualize nature, others sought to naturalize spiritual goals, but both represent visions of a new garden of Eden in this world. For Christian Hermeticists, these goals were not mutually exclusive but intimately related. The following utopian blueprints highlight the "divine self" at the turn of the seventeenth century.

64. Phelan, *Millennial Kingdom*, 72.
65. Phelan, *Millennial Kingdom*, 73.
66. Phelan, quoting Mendieta in *Millennial Kingdom*, 73–74.

More's *Utopia*

Thomas More (1478–1535) was a deputy sheriff in London when he wrote *Utopia*, published in 1516, and a year later he accepted the invitation of Henry VIII to become a royal councilor.[67] In this capacity, and at the king's behest, he wrote treatises against Luther.[68] Yet, More was a complex figure trying to survive the gauntlet of royal politics. Preferring the secular life as a lawyer and member of parliament in 1504, he nevertheless wore a hairshirt and occasionally engaged in self-flagellation. He was a humanist who wrote spiritual poems and satirical essays and translated the *Life of Pico* by Gianfrancesco. As his *Utopia* reflects, More identified with Erasmus's Christian humanism, yet he seems to have relished torturing Protestants, even children.[69] In many ways, More seems to be working out his own demons, hoping for a future beyond the bloodshed to which he had contributed.

Typical of the era's utopian writings, More begins by draping the bleak backdrop on the real world he knows too well. As in the piety of Erasmus and the Anabaptists, More envisioned a society holding all things in common. More's interlocutor Raphael is taken with Plato's ideal of the philosopher-king, but More tries to teach him about the *Realpolitik* that Raphael must master if he intends a public career. Book 2 of *Utopia* turns to the world he imagines.[70] It is set somewhere in the New World and places Raphael among the twenty-four men who

67. Copenhaver and Schmitt, *Renaissance Philosophy*, 277.

68. As secretary and chief advisor, he assisted in King Henry VIII's *Assertio* against Luther, for which the pope gave Henry the title "Defender of the Faith." At the king's behest, More also pelted Luther with excremental insults in *Responsio ad Lutherum* in 1523. See Ackroyd, *Thomas More*, 230, who notes that, according to More, Luther was an "ape, an arse, a drunkard, a lousy little friar, a piece of scurf, a pestilential buffoon, and a dishonest liar." The rest of More's epithets cited by Ackroyd descend, quite literally, to the toilet. He was convinced that Luther was nothing less than the harbinger of the antichrist in the last days. See also Ackroyd, *Thomas More*, 310.

69. He personally led raids on homes suspected of harboring Lutheran contraband. In an otherwise sympathetic gloss on Peter Ackroyd's positive treatment of More, James Wood refers to his caning of Protestant youths and burning other Protestants at the stake. See also Schuster et al., *Thomas More*, 8:20; Marius, *Thomas More*, 386–406.

70. For defenses of various interpretations, see the introduction of the editors to this edition of Logan and Adams, *Utopia*, ix–xi. While warning against facile resolutions, Logan and Adams point out the various Greek puns in the work. First, utopia actually means "no-place," although when spoken in English it sounds like *eutopia*, meaning "good place." Second, Raphael's last name is Hythloday, meaning "nonsense-peddler," and he is the protagonist as well as reporter of this fabulous island. The island's great river is Anydrus, "no-water," and other countries are called Anchora, "no-lands." Perhaps, like Plato's *Republic*, More's *Utopia* is intended to show that the good city cannot be found below.

were left by Amerigo Vespucci in Brazil. (Note that twenty-four equals the number of the twelve tribes, apostles, and elders doubled.) Afterward, Raphael comes finally to the magical island, taking account of the natives for five years. It's a small island, only "two hundred miles across," he says. The political design is perfectly proportioned: fifty-four cities, divided into quarters, with the capital Amaurot in the middle.[71]

What is perhaps most interesting about this communalistic utopia is that there are several religions on the island. Some worship the moon or the sun, others are devoted to ancestor worship, and some are monotheists. Yet there is complete tolerance, and doctrinal disputes are frowned upon. Utopians cherish health and believe that virtue is the best path to happiness. Most believe in the immortality of the soul and rewards and punishment. In fact, public office is denied to those who deny the afterlife and divine providence.[72]

Becoming a missionary, Raphael reports that he has been able to begin to make some gains in Utopia even for Christianity. All Utopians pray a nonsectarian prayer, and if one converts to Christianity, bigotry toward other religions is punished severely, even with banishment. In sharp contrast with his own political activities, More's Utopians observe the separation of church and state. No royal decree could be lawful for everyone in the matter of religion.[73] Copenhaver and Schmitt summarize as follows:

> Reason and natural virtue have made them better morally than Europeans who are Christian in name only, and Utopians are therefore quick to accept the Gospel as soon as they understand it. In some respects, the studious and regimented collectivism of Utopia recalls the medieval monastic ideal, but the sources of More's perfect society, the Stoic-Epicurean ethics and Platonic politics, are squarely in the humanist tradition, and the purpose of his book was to advance the Erasmian project of social and moral change, using irony and polemic to shame Europeans into becoming better Christians. In matters of religion, Utopians are more open-minded than Christians, certainly more tolerant than More in the *Dialogue Concerning Heresies* of 1529, and they practise the relentless educational regimen that Erasmus preached, thus brightening More's darker view of the human condition corrupted by pride and other sins.[74]

71. Each city consists of six thousand households of ten to sixteen adults. For every thirty families there is a political body that elects a leader or "phylarchus." Each ten of these elect a ruler, and the two hundred elected leaders of each city elect a lifetime prince (barring misconduct).

72. Burnet, *Utopia*, 96, 144–45.

73. Yates, *Giordano Bruno*, 186. See Burnet, *Utopia*, 101–2.

74. Copenhaver and Schmitt, *Renaissance Philosophy*, 274–75.

In fact, More sees pride as the root of all evil. For this reason, Utopians do not allow private property; they trade houses every decade, and people take whatever they need from communal warehouses, making locks unnecessary. Everyone eats together in shifts at various dining halls, with various households taking their turn in the cooking and distribution. There are no taverns or other places for private dining and socializing, since everyone's conduct must be open to public scrutiny. Healthcare is free, euthanasia is permitted, and even priests may marry and divorce. However, sexual intercourse outside marriage is punishable by enslavement.

Given the perfection of the laws, there is no need for lawyers (an interesting dream coming from England's chief lawyer). The primary occupation is farming, women having the same work as men—some even becoming priests. There are other occupations, but everyone must spend a couple of years in agriculture and everyone must work, although the workday is only six hours long. The same simple clothes are worn by everyone. Only children wear jewelry, which they do until they reach adulthood. Despite its communism, on average every household has two slaves, either nonnatives or criminals who must win back their freedom. And they are decidedly antimilitaristic.

More's *Utopia* not only stands in deliberate contrast with the European societies of his day but also with his own policies. Nevertheless, in the wake of Columbus's expeditions, it offered a blueprint for missionaries (and some governors) in New Spain. The convergence of Joachite eschatology with More's visionary plan is evident especially in what is now Mexico.[75] "Friar Martín de Valencia, the leader of the 'Twelve Apostles' of Mexico, was explicitly inspired by Joachimite-apocalyptic ideals" and experienced several visions of his own.[76] But it was the Spanish jurist Vasco de Quiroga (1470–1565) who interwove Joachite prophecy with the Erasmian *philosophia Christi* and a close reading of More's *Utopia*. The first Archbishop of Mexico (Michoacán) and a judge of New Spain's supreme court, Quiroga blended Joachite eschatology with his organization of the native population into hospital towns—what he called *republicas de Indios*.[77] Though as paternalistic as any other colonial regime, Quiroga's utopian republics were, for the most part, welcomed by the native population.[78]

75. Phelan, *Millennial Kingdom*, 45.

76. Phelan, *Millennial Kingdom*, 46–47. The same is true of the mission to Venezuela in 1516.

77. Phelan, *Millennial Kingdom*, 46–47. Quiroga became the chief justice in the Second Audencia, which replaced the brutally oppressive First Audencia.

78. See Zavala, *Sir Thomas More* and more recently, Verastique, *Michoacán and Eden*. According to Zavala, it was after reading More's *Utopia* that Quiroga dedicated himself to implementing its program by organizing the region's native population into hospital towns—what he called

Postel's Universal Monarchy

While there are touches of northern Hermeticism in More's *Utopia*, its most conspicuous influence is Erasmus. A thoroughgoing Joachite mysticism is evident in the work of the philologist, kabbalist, and mystic Guillaume Postel (1510–1581). A professor at the University of Paris, he called his project "panthenosia," which meant a unification of all ideas and religions—or rather, their conclusion—in one Joachite stream of consciousness. This played a significant role in his appropriation of Joachite prophecy.[79] "The strange history of Guillaume Postel," notes Reeves, "brings together the themes of World Emperor, Angelic Pope and New Men. . . . He met some of the Jesuits in Paris before 1535 and seized on this new order as one of the principal agencies of the eschatological programme."[80] He even "sought an interview with Francis I in order to proclaim the stupendous choice before him: if the King would reform Church and State he would become monarch of the universe, if not, evils worse than any previous would come upon him." But by 1545 doubts were being raised as to his "extravagant fantasies." He submitted to discipline but could not control himself.[81] Finally, though they admired him, the Jesuits expelled him from the Order.[82]

Following his expulsion, Postel explained "that by divine illumination it had been revealed to him that the Gallic King must be the reformer of the Church and the whole world." According to Reeves:

> He bombarded French kings and people with appeals to realize their great destiny and, when Henry II and Francis II in turn were deaf, he threatened them with the fates of Moses and Saul. After another vision c. 1551 he drifted into a mystical state in which he came to believe that he had been reborn as the Holy Spirit and that it was his own mission to bring in the Age of the Spirit. He plunged into a frenzy of linguistic and cabbalistic studies and sought to work out his world religion through contacts with Ethiopians, Arabs, Jews and others.[83]

---

republicas de Indios. He began with Santa Fe (Mexico City), using his own money to finance it. After one failed attempt, he succeeded in sailing to the Old World for some sessions of the Council of Trent, attended by several natives. See Zavala, *Sir Thomas More*, 225.

79. Reeves, *Joachim of Fiore*, 352–59.

80. Reeves, *Joachim of Fiore*, 121.

81. Reeves, *Joachim of Fiore*, 121.

82. Reeves, *Joachim of Fiore*, 122.

83. Reeves, *Joachim of Fiore*, 122.

Finally, in the absence of French interest, Postel turned to proclaiming Ferdinand the Last World Emperor. Already reigning as Holy Roman Emperor, Ferdinand not only displayed considerable interest in his missionary plans but gave Postel a chair at the University of Vienna. "So Postel sketched out an imperial version of the future: Rome was to be the temporal capital of the world, Jerusalem the spiritual; there would be a general reformation, the earthly paradise would be restored, and the purpose of the world would have been fulfilled. But he was at heart a Gallican and, returning to his true allegiance, was proclaiming a French version of the approaching millennium as late as 1579."[84]

Utopia's Sun-King: Giordano Bruno and Pagan Enthusiasm

Joachite prophecy and Hermeticism were fused in fifteenth-century Florence with Savonarola, Ficino, and Pico. McGinn observes, "The prevalence of such ideas in Renaissance Italy should come as no surprise—the optimistic side of late medieval apocalypticism could blend quite well with Humanist hopes for a returning Golden Age, and the darker side of the Renaissance world with its concern for magic, astrology, and demonic forces could thrill with delicious terror at rumors of the Antichrist."[85]

One example of an Italian humanist who turned to "the darker side of the Renaissance" is Giordano Bruno (1548–1600). He was influenced by Avicebron, but his debts were many. Like Savonarola (and later Campanella), Bruno was a Dominican who was eventually defrocked and condemned to death for heresy. In fact, Bruno's first rebuke from his brothers came when they discovered that he was reading Erasmus's works held by the monastery's library.[86] Bruno envisioned a new city, worldwide in its circumference, where peace and the natural religion of sun worship displaced confessional strife. Unlike More's vision and that of others who associated utopia with the New World, Bruno's was more of a universal age than a secluded paradise beyond the sea. It was the age of the Spirit, to be sure, but unlike Joachim's third person of the Trinity, Bruno's "Spirit" was the World Spirit of Neoplatonism.[87] While Ficino had evangelized Hermes Trismegistus, Bruno's program was closer to Plethon's.

84. Reeves, *Joachim of Fiore*, 122.

85. McGinn, *Apocalyptic Spirituality*, 186.

86. De Leon-Jones, foreword to Bruno, *Expulsion of the Triumphant Beast*, vi.

87. Yates, *Giordano Bruno*, 350: As Yates notes, "His view of the Third Person as the *anima mundi* or the Virgilian '*spiritus intus alit*' was an interpretation frequently made in the Renaissance."

Although Adocentyn, the city built by Hermes Trismegistus, was on Bruno's mind, there are striking similarities between his ideal in the *Expulsion of the Triumphant Beast* and Thomas More's *Utopia*.[88] Even the nature of the religious rites is essentially that of theurgic Neoplatonism, part of the daily routine of Ficino and his fellow magi across Europe. The remarkable religious diversity, including sun worship, is affirmed even as true natural religion preparing them for Raphael's evangelization. Nevertheless, where More has at least some Utopians embracing Christianity as a fuller truth, Bruno can see it only as a corruption.[89]

Bruno's fascinating and fractious career offers a particularly good window for viewing the excitement of a more pagan form of Renaissance humanism as it spread, especially through his influence, throughout Europe. In Paris Bruno's public lectures on theology "attracted the attention of the king, Henri III. And here he published two books on the art of memory which reveal him as a magician."[90] Lactantius had interpreted the Hermetic Lament of Egypt as prophesying Christ's advent, but Bruno "takes it to mean that the Christian suppressors ('*Mercurios quosdam*') legislated against the true Egyptian solar religion which, beyond the sensible sun, penetrated to the divine *mens*. In spite of the suppression, that true religion did not cease and Bruno is reviving it."[91] "And now," Yates adds, "into this world where Catholic Christian Hermeticism was flourishing in French ecclesiastical circles, and perhaps in the Capucin movement around Henry III, there erupts Giordano Bruno proclaiming a deeply magical Hermeticism, rejoicing in the magic of the *Asclepius*, carrying Ficinian magic to lengths of which Ficino never dreamed."[92] In short, Bruno was at least in his own self-understanding not merely a Neoplatonist who, like Iamblichus and Proclus, was captivated by Egyptian religion; he thought that the Corpus Hermeticum and later tracts attributed to Hermes offered an unobstructed path back to the dark side of Alexandria.[93]

Ficino's mission had been nothing less than to restore "the magical religion of the pseudo-Egyptians of the Asclepius."[94] Yet Bruno goes even further in his *Expulsion of the Triumphant Beast* (*Spaccio della bestia triofane*, 1584), part of a trilogy with the *Cabala of the Pegasean Horse* and *The Heroic Furors*, all of them with an underlying theme of what Karen Silvia de Leon-Jones calls "the ethics of

88. Yates, *Giordano Bruno*, 233.

89. Yates, *Giordano Bruno*, 160–61. While indebted to Yates, I demur somewhat from some of her overly sharp distinctions—in this case, between humanism and Hermeticism.

90. Yates, *Giordano Bruno*, 190.

91. Yates, *Giordano Bruno*, 194 n. 1.

92. Yates, *Giordano Bruno*, 203.

93. Yates, *Giordano Bruno*, 197.

94. Yates, *Giordano Bruno*, 211.

mutation."[95] Arthur D. Imerti, the translator of the English version, points out that Bruno's dialogues "are concerned with each individual's obligation to accept being governed by the religion of reason."[96] In his Neoplatonic context, notes de Leon-Jones, that meant opposition to ignorance (*synderesis*), linking up to "the Archetypal Idea . . . which is to say that although Bruno can be superficially interpreted as a rationalist, he is not a man of the eighteenth century or of the Age of Reason." He moves from the recognition of ignorance ("All I know is that I know nothing") to the ascent of reason.[97]

As far as the religion of the Egyptians is concerned, says Bruno in the *Expulsion*, they worship "God in all things." This is why the religion of the Egyptians is superior to all others, he continues. They did not worship animals themselves but the divinity in them. "You see, then," says Bruno, "how one simple divinity which is in all things, one fecund nature, mother and preserver of the universe, shines forth in diverse subjects, and takes diverse names, according as it communicates itself diversely." For Bruno, then, the names given to various gods are actually diverse shinings of the One.[98]

Throughout this provocative work, Bruno argues that the outer husk of religions is always changing, while the kernel of eternal truth that unites them all remains the same. The old gods wear out and are replaced. For him the pre-Christian religions of the Chaldeans, Egyptians, and Greeks at least were unified in worshiping the sun—the One of Neoplatonism. Bruno draws extensively on the Hermetic text known as the Kore Kosmou, a dialogue between Isis and her son Horus with a gnostic orientation. In this work, God begins creation by arranging the celestial images, but the lower world proves to be an unsatisfactory copy. So, he creates man by having each planetary god contributing its gifts. After this also fails, God expunges the ignorance and pollution and fills the cosmos with another emanation of his nature. Yates observes, "The treatise ends with the praises of Isis and Osiris; who have put an end to slaughter and have restored justice; who having learned from Hermes that things below must be kept in sympathy with things above have instituted on earth the sacred functions vertically linked with the mysteries of heaven."[99]

First published in 1591 and grouped with the other Hermetic writings along with a Latin translation by Patrizi, in Bruno's hands Kore Kosmou became a mani-

95. De Leon-Jones, foreword to Bruno, *Expulsion of the Triumphant Beast*, vi.

96. Imerti, introduction to Bruno, *Expulsion of the Triumphant Beast*, 26.

97. De Leon-Jones, foreword to Bruno, *Expulsion of the Triumphant Beast*, vii.

98. Quoted by Yates, *Giordano Bruno*, 213–14.

99. Yates, *Giordano Bruno*, 216. Kore Kosmou is a little-known treatise (not in the Corpus Hermeticum) preserved by the fifth-century compiler of Greek fragments, Strobaeus.

festo for the triumph of the long-suppressed Egyptian religion in his *Expulsion*.[100] Even in its title, Yates argues, Bruno's *The Expulsion of the Triumphant Beast* reveals a double meaning: "The beast is expelled on one level and triumphs on another. One wonders whether Pope Alexander VI thought along these extremely difficult lines at Apis. . . . The Appartamento Borgia frescoes, showing the Greek cow, Io, turning into Isis in Egypt, perhaps move within a similar frame of reference, though they are orthodox in showing the Egyptian bulls worshipping the Virgin and saints, like proper *prisci theologi*."[101] The Jews, he says, are "the excrements of Egypt." Rather than trying to make Moses the father of Egyptian religion, Bruno candidly attacks Judaism as a corruption of it."[102]Bruno's *Cabala of Pegasus*, printed in England in 1585, elaborates the argument in his *Expulsion*. However, his kabbalah is not medieval Jewish kabbalah, as he emphasizes, but goes back to Egypt. In contrast with Ficino, there are no Jewish or Christian restraints on Bruno's full embrace of demonic magic. "Bruno *wants* to reach the demons; it is essential for his magic to do so; nor are there any Christian angels within call in his scheme to keep them in check."[103]

While Ficino avoided censors by grafting the perennial tradition onto biblical history, Bruno followed Plethon's neo-pagan enterprise. He is precisely, as Yates describes, "the direct and logical result of the Renaissance glorification of Man as the great Miracle, man who is divine in his origin and can again become divine, with divine Powers residing in him. He is, in short, the result of the Renaissance Hermeticism. If man can obtain such powers through Hermetic experiences, why should not this have been the way in which Christ obtained his powers? Pico della Mirandola thought to prove the divinity of Christ through Magia and Cabala. Bruno interpreted the possibilities of Renaissance Magic in another way."[104]

Bruno stood on the side of Copernicus, but only because the new cosmology jibed with his mysticism. Copernicus himself made much of his system being a revival of Pythagorean teaching. Bruno's relation to Copernicus is similar to his praise of Fabrizio Mordente's new compass, followed by criticism that Mordente failed to appreciate the mystical significance of his own invention. Whereas Galileo's views were based on math, Yates observes, Bruno's were "the religion of the world. . . . Thus, the legend that Bruno was prosecuted as a philosophical thinker, was burned for his daring views on innumerable worlds or on the movement

100. Yates, *Giordano Bruno*, 216.
101. Yates, *Giordano Bruno*, 222–23.
102. Yates, *Giordano Bruno*, 223, quoting from Bruno, *Expulsion* dialogue 3.
103. Yates, *Giordano Bruno*, 264–65.
104. Yates, *Giordano Bruno*, 266.

of the earth, can no longer stand."[105] Bruno is Shakespeare's Prospero, the ideal *magus* trying to create the ideal state.[106] If Bruno had succeeded in his delirium, Europe would have been like Plethon's Mistra.

For the most part, magical Hermeticism was a Roman Catholic phenomenon.[107] When Bruno came to Oxford, boldly announcing himself in the third person as "the Nolan" who brings enlightenment to the world, the dons were not impressed. Following Bruno's report too closely, Yates chalks up his reception to Oxford's hostility to Hermetic discussions.[108] However, the research of Mordechai Feingold shows conclusively that the famous university was not run by "pedants."[109] On the contrary, Oxford and Cambridge, though dedicated to the Reformed religion, were quite liberal in their studies. George Abbot, future Archbishop of Canterbury, snuck out of Bruno's lecture to fetch his copy of Ficino and returned to confront the so-called Nolan publicly with his plagiarism. Thus, they were quite familiar with Renaissance philosophy but were quite unimpressed with Bruno. Moreover, Copernicus had not been rejected at Oxford. Not even Abbot's comment suggests this. Rather, Bruno himself was considered ill-prepared to discuss such matters.[110]

Having found no home in Geneva or Oxford, Bruno tried Wittenberg, where he received a warm welcome and apparently some followers for a while, until he was driven from that city as well. Returning to Italy, Bruno now announced that the pope would lead the new reformation with the Nolan's assistance. "There is little doubt that Bruno thought of himself as a Messiah," Yates observes, "an illusion not uncommon in the Renaissance. . . . Hermeticism, with its belief in a 'divinising' experience, is conducive to religious mania of this kind."[111] However, Bruno was put in the prisons of the Holy Office on May 26, 1592. After abjuring his heresies,

105. Yates, *Giordano Bruno*, 355.

106. Yates, *Giordano Bruno*, 357.

107. Yates, *Giordano Bruno*, 187.

108. Yates illustrates her point by referring to Anthony Wood's report of a 1550 removal of Hermetic books from Oxford's library. Wood reported, "Sure I am that such books wherein appeared Angels or Mathematical Diagrams, were thought sufficient to be destroyed because accounted Popish, or diabolical, or both." Yates says, "The humanist dislike of metaphysical and mathematical studies has turned into Reformation hatred of the past and fear of its magic." Yates, *Giordano Bruno*, 167, referring to A. Wood, *Oxford*, 2:107.

109. Feingold, *Mathematician's Apprenticeship*. For a fuller study of English academia in the sixteenth century, see the collection of essays in Feingold, *History of Universities*.

110. Yates, *Giordano Bruno*, 168: "Madly impossible in a Protestant country which had been through the Erasmian reform, Bruno's philosophy also brought him to the stake in Counter Reformation Rome." However, contra Yates, they denounced Bruno as a charlatan, not as a heretic.

111. Yates, *Giordano Bruno*, 339.

Bruno later withdrew his retractions and was handed over to the secular authorities for punishment.[112] On February 17, 1600, after eight years of imprisonment and torture, Bruno was burned on the Camp de' Fiori in Rome.[113]

Campanella's *City of the Sun*

It is less important that Hermetic magic was rationalized and Joachite prophecy was secularized than that both opened new vistas. Besides More's *Utopia*, the *City of the Sun* by Tomasso Campanella (1568–1639) provided a concrete blueprint for hypothetical dreams—the "what if's" that would drive revolutionary experiments.

Campanella was an important catalyst in the evangelization and colonialization of New Spain.[114] According to Yates, "the faith which Campanella wanted to propagate throughout the whole world was, of course, the Catholicised natural religion."[115] This was true of More's *Utopia* as well. D. P. Walker argues that Campanella's magical assistance to the astrologically sensitive Pope Urban VIII was an attempt to gain support for such plans. "If he could convince the Pope of the sun's slow approach and the events this portended, then missionaries, trained by Campanella, would go forth from Rome to convert the whole world to a reformed, 'natural' Catholicism, which would introduce the millennium, the universal City of the Sun."[116] Yates concurs, judging, "And it does seem that for a time, and through the favour of Urban VIII, Campanella was exercising some influence on policy in Rome."[117]

Like Joachim of Fiore, Campanella hailed from Calabria in southern Italy. As Daniel J. Donno summarizes: "He saw himself as the bearer of a message, the designer of a program for mankind involving nothing less than a thorough reform of virtually all human institutions, both secular and spiritual. . . . He was only twenty-four when he entered the first of several prisons he would occupy during his life, and he was not completely free until he was sixty-one. He was a great survivor."[118] Baptized Giovanni Domenico Campanella, he joined the Dominicans at

112. Yates, *Giordano Bruno*, 349.
113. Yates, *Giordano Bruno*, 349.
114. Reeves, *Joachim of Fiore*, 127.
115. Yates, *Giordano Bruno*, 388.
116. Walker, "*Prisca Theologia* in France," 208.
117. Yates, *Giordano Bruno*, 388.
118. See Donno, introduction to *Città del Sole*, 1.

fourteen, taking the name Tomasso in honor of Aquinas.[119] Devouring books on a wide range of topics, at twenty years of age he discovered a copy of *De rerum natura* (1570) edited by fellow Calabrian, bishop of Cosenza, and pioneer of the scientific method Bernardino Telesio.[120] From reading Telesio, Campanella acquired the humanist disdain for Aristotelian scholasticism, a view of nature as a coincidence of opposites, and an empiricist epistemology.[121]

Welcomed into various humanist circles from 1589 to 1591, he became friends with the highly reputed magician-scientist Giambattista Della Porta.[122] Building on the interests that Campanella had already acquired from Telesio, Della Porta convinced his friend to pursue magic.[123] During this period Campanella wrote *De investigatione rerum* and *De sensu rerum*, which were seized by the Inquisition soon after they fell from the press. Acknowledging that Aquinas said that we cannot know the Trinity from nature, Campanella replied, "But St. Thomas 'had not read the Platonists nor Trismegistus, whose works in his time had not been translated into Latin.'"[124] Campanella was not alone in this regard; even Cardinal Cajetan in his 1570 edition of Aquinas's works accepted talismans.[125]

Like Ficino (and unlike Bruno), Campanella sought to harmonize Christianity as much as possible with his Hermetic vision. By the time he was thirty, Campanella had gone back and forth between dungeons. He was sent to the same prison where, several years before, Bruno was incarcerated before being taken to the stake in 1600. After repeated torture, he was condemned as a heretic. "This time he yielded, just as Galileo was to do thirty-eight years later. Then, as part of his sentence, he took up obligatory residence in the monastery

119. See Donno, introduction to *Città del Sole*, 4.

120. See Donno, introduction to *Città del Sole*, 5. Tomasso was determined to discuss the arguments of the work with its author, but he arrived to find the old bishop and astronomer's body "lying in state in the cathedral."

121. See Donno, introduction to *Città del Sole*, 5. "'*Non ratione*,' he declared, '*sed sensu*.'"

122. Although he wrote plays and essays, Della Porta's greatest success was in the natural sciences. He was writing his demonstration of the telescope when he died, and Galileo completed his invention. He also invented a sympathetic telegraph and conducted groundbreaking research in astronomy, physiology, physiognomy, and pharmacology. He was also a famous *magus*, the author of *Magiae naturalis* (Natural magic), which was published in 1558, and the founder of the *Academia secretorum naturae*. For his occultic activities he was summoned before Pope Paul V. It is a rather odd detail, since the same pope would also summon Campanella for assistance.

123. See Donno, introduction to *Città del Sole*, 6.

124. Yates, *Giordano Bruno*, 379.

125. Yates, *Giordano Bruno*, 379.

of S. Sabina on the Aventine. There he wrote on physics, as well as on poetics, and a *Dialogue against Lutherans, Calvinists and Other Heretics*."[126] Announcing 1600 as the year of astrological significance, he took it upon himself after his release to lead a revolution in Calabria.[127] He was transferred to the Inquisition's dungeon in Rome at the end of 1594 for (among other charges) teaching the heretical doctrine of a World Soul. Unfazed, he presented a plan to the pope for the pontiff's universal monarchy.[128] Upon release, Campanella was rounded up with 150 accomplices, many of them Dominicans, charged with insurrection. Tortured and transported to Naples in chains, Campanella wrote *City of the Sun* (*La Città del Sole*) in 1602.

Campanella informs us that his *Città del Sole* is "divided into seven large circuits, named after the seven planets. Passage from one to the other is provided by four avenues and four gates facing the four points of the compass."[129] The city is enclosed by walls decorated with all sorts of images from which the precocious children glean an early knowledge of every science.

But the heart of the city is its astonishing temple.[130] The walls of the temple reveal secrets that are even deeper than those truths inculcated on the statues, images, and inscriptions on the walls encompassing the city.[131] Campanella relates, "Nothing rests on the altar but a huge celestial globe, upon which all the heavens are described, with a terrestrial globe beside it. On the vault of the dome overhead appear all the larger stars with their names and the influences they each have upon earthly things set down in three verses." For the first time in one place, the exact correspondence of things above and things below will be documented

126. See Donno, introduction to *Città del Sole*, 7.

127. See Donno, introduction to *Città del Sole*, 8–9.

128. Yates, *Giordano Bruno*, 363.

129. Campanella, *Città del Sole*, 27.

130. Campanella, *Città del Sole*, 31.

131. Campanella, *Città del Sole*, 33. The inner wall displays mathematical figures and on the outer wall "there is a map of the entire world with charts for each country setting forth their rites, customs, and laws; and the alphabet of each is inscribed above the native one. On the inner wall of the second circuit there are both samples and pictures of all minerals, metals, and stones." On its outer wall "all kinds of lakes, seas, rivers, wines, oils, and other liquids are shown with their sources of origin, their powers, and their qualities indicated. There are also carafes full of diverse liquids, a hundred and even three hundred years old, with which nearly all infirmities are cured." See Campanella, *La Città del Sole*, 33–35. Another wall displays all manner of sea creatures, birds, reptiles, insects; on another, "all the mechanical arts . . . with their inventors" (37). There is a wall honoring "Moses, Osiris, Jupiter, Mercury, Muhammad, and many others there. In place of special honor I saw Jesus Christ and the twelve Apostles, whom they hold in great regard" (37).

and rendered common knowledge.[132] Essentially, the whole city is nothing other than a modern research university.

The religion of the Solarians in the *City of the Sun* is a Hermetic natural theology. "They have a Prince Prelate among them whom they call Sun, but in our language he would be called Metaphysician."[133] Of course, this is none other than Campanella himself. "He is both their spiritual and their temporal chief, and all decisions terminate with him. There are also three collateral princes: Pon, Sin, and Mor, that is to say Power, Wisdom, and Love."[134] "Power has charge of war and peace" while "Wisdom has charge of all the sciences." Besides these, there are an official astrologer, a cosmographer, a geometer, a logician, a rhetorician, a grammarian, a physician, a physical scientist, a politician, and a moralist. "Wisdom has but one book in which all the sciences are treated and which is taught to all the people after the manner of the Pythagoreans."[135]

Campanella goes on to describe how "Love has charge of breeding and sees to the coupling of males and females who will produce healthy offspring." Teachers are able to discern sexual maturity by watching the boys and girls wrestling, naked as in ancient Greece, and can pair couples according to the proper matching of sexual organs. Then, after bathing, they are paired off for intercourse. The astrologer and the physician determine the proper time for this mass intercourse, "when Mercury and Venus are oriental to the Sun in a benefic house and are seen by Jupiter, Saturn, and Mars with benefic aspect."[136] All of this is overseen by the council on procreation, and the metaphysician chooses their names based on some characteristic.[137] But make no mistake about it: "The Metaphysician [Prince Prelate or Sun] governs all matters through these three officers. Without him nothing is done."[138] Notably absent from the list of learned rulers is the theologian, of course, but this is perfectly consistent with Campanella's natural religion.

The hospitaler asks his host, "Do they have a republic, a monarchy, or an oligarchy?" and receives the following response, presupposing the standard *philosophia perennis* narrative: "This is a people that came from India, many of them being philosophers, who fled before depredations of the Tartars and other plunderers and tyrants, and they resolved to live in a philosophic community." They share everything in common, including wives.

132. Campanella, *Città del Sole*, 31.
133. Campanella, *Città del Sole*, 31.
134. Campanella, *Città del Sole*, 31–33.
135. Campanella, *Città del Sole*, 33.
136. Campanella, *Città del Sole*, 55.
137. Campanella, *Città del Sole*, 59.
138. Campanella, *Città del Sole*, 37.

> They claim that property comes into existence when men have separate homes with their children and wives. From this self-love is born; for in order to increase the wealth and dignity of his offspring or leave him heir to his goods, every man becomes publicly rapacious if he is strong and fearless, or avaricious, deceitful, and hypocritical if he is weak. When self-love is destroyed, only concern for the community remains.[139]

Similarly, men and women dress alike, "in a manner suitable for combat."[140] They change their uniforms four times each year, "when the sun enters Cancer, Capricorn, Aries, and Libra."[141]

Although the author assures us that it is a happy state, it is hardly a liberal one. In fact, rather ironically for an author who spent most of his life in dungeons because of informers to the Inquisition, his utopia (like More's) is essentially a police state. "All are well supervised, and there are informers who report to the state about everything."[142] Continuing the usual Hermetic genealogy, he tells us that the Solarians "are descended from Pythagorean Brahmans," although—perhaps displaying Campanella's more Christian sympathies—he says that "they do not believe in the transmigration of souls, except possibly through some act of Divine judgment."[143] Campanella's Solarians are simultaneously Ficinian in their cosmotheology and Joachite in their eschatology.[144]

In sharp contrast with More's *Utopia*, Campanella's *City of the Sun* is decidedly militaristic. The Solarians have no reservations about "wounding enemies who are rebels to reason and, as such, do not deserve to be called men." There are daily lessons in war and military exercises.[145] Not only are the sciences treasures of the city worth defending, it also appears that warfare is a driving force of new technologies. There are even "baggage trains" and advanced weapons transported on wagons.[146]

> The conquered cities and those surrendered to the victors immediately change over to the system of communal ownership of goods. They receive Solarian officials and a garrison from the City of the Sun and proceed to model their

139. Campanella, *Città del Sole*, 39.
140. Campanella, *Città del Sole*, 41.
141. Campanella, *Città del Sole*, 51.
142. Campanella, *Città del Sole*, 67.
143. Campanella, *Città del Sole*, 69.
144. Yates, *Giordano Bruno*, 372.
145. Campanella, *Città del Sole*, 69.
146. Campanella, *Città del Sole*, 73.

> institutions after those of that city, which is henceforth their guide. They also send their children to study in the City of the Sun and pay nothing for their maintenance.[147]

They are masters at spying and all manner of intelligence gathering.[148] "They have treaties with the Chinese and with other people of the islands and of the continent—with Siam, Cochin-China, Calcutta—solely to explore them. They also know great secrets about how to produce artificial fires for use in naval and land warfare."[149] Only Solarian men over fifty years old may drink wine undiluted by water.[150] They are fit and healthy because they live consistently with the stars and know the secrets of alchemy.

If we accept Campanella's identification of true piety with natural theology, the everyday life of Solarians is infused with spirituality. They, for instance, believe in other worlds.

> Their metaphysical principles are being, which is God, and nothingness, which is absence of being. . . . It will surprise you to know that they worship God in the Trinity, saying that God is supreme Power, whence proceeds supreme Wisdom, and that from these two comes supreme Love. But they do not distinguish and name the three persons as we do because they are not in possession of revelation.[151]

On an appointed day, the Sun (the high priest and metaphysician) requires a human sacrifice chosen by the people. It is merely a show. "After twenty or thirty days, God's wrath having been appeased, he is brought down outside the temple. He may then become a priest."[152] Solarians believe in immortality but "are not so sure about" heaven and hell and "are also very curious to know whether or not punishment is everlasting."[153] They acknowledge that "so much disorder came about through Adam's sin," but they attribute evil chiefly to astral determinations as well as "breeding and education."[154]

147. Campanella, *Città del Sole*, 77.
148. Campanella, *Città del Sole*, 79.
149. Campanella, *Città del Sole*, 87.
150. Campanella, *Città del Sole*, 89.
151. Campanella, *Città del Sole*, 115.
152. Campanella, *Città del Sole*, 103.
153. Campanella, *Città del Sole*, 113.
154. Campanella, *Città del Sole*, 119.

> If these people who follow only the law of nature are so near to Christianity, which adds nothing but the sacraments to the law of nature, I conclude from your report that Christianity is the true law and that, once its abuses have been corrected, it will become mistress of the world. I also conclude that for this reason the Spaniards discovered the rest of the world so as to unite it all under one law, even though Columbus, your fellow Genoese, was its first discoverer. These philosophers you speak of must be elected by God to be witnesses for the truth. . . . [T]here will be a great new monarchy, reformation of laws and of arts, new prophets, and a general renewal. They say that all this will be of great benefit to the Christians, but first the world will be uprooted and cleansed, and then it will be replanted and rebuilt. . . . Know this: they have discovered the art of flying, the only art the world lacks, and they expect to discover a glass in which to see the hidden stars and a device by which to hear the music of the spheres.[155]

Campanella also attributes the spread of Luther's heresies to the conjunction of planets.[156]

Transferred from a horrible Neapolitan prison (calling it a "burial" place in a letter to Galileo), Campanella was sent to Rome to answer charges of heresy. "By then his many books had won him powerful supporters," Donno relates. "Pope Urban VIII, on whose behalf he had employed his skill in astrology and magic, had assigned him a pension, and there were even rumors that he was to be invested with a cardinal's hat."[157] However, he did not know how to proceed with moderation; he was on a mission. When Galileo was forced to publicly recant and was placed under permanent house arrest, Campanella spent his considerable capital with the pope in the astronomer's defense.[158] Released in 1626, only a few weeks later the papal *nuncio* had Campanella arrested again and sent to Rome in chains in disguise to avert attempts by the secular authorities to release him yet again without Inquisition approval.[159]

The failure of the Calabrian revolt turned Campanella's eye toward opportunism. In *Monarichia di Spagna* (1620), he argues now that the city of the sun would be built by the Spanish! "This universal monarchy will be Catholic with the Pope as its spiritual head . . . all religions would be converted into one, and there would be a world-wide religious and political unity."[160] But then he goes to

155. Campanella, *Città del Sole*, 123.
156. Campanella, *Città del Sole*, 125, 127.
157. See Donno, introduction to *Città del Sole*, 3.
158. See Donno, introduction to *Città del Sole*, 4.
159. See Donno, introduction to *Città del Sole*, 12–13.
160. Yates, *Giordano Bruno*, 385.

France announcing that its king is the Last World Emperor.[161] Finally, he settled on Calabria as the capital of the age of the Spirit.[162] Following yet another plot of his followers to overthrow Spanish rule, "Campanella was to be extradited to Naples, but the pope and the French ambassador hatched a plot to let him slip away in disguise to France, where he was welcomed by Louis XIII and Cardinal Richelieu."[163] He spent his last years in the French court, with sufficient peace to write polemical tracts to try to convert French Calvinists. (There are reports of him having success with some English visitors as well.) In fact, this now became central to his universal mission. He even tried to convince Cardinal Richelieu to relax views on transubstantiation to encourage greater success.[164]

Richelieu favored Campanella's magic, and Campanella implored him to build the solar city.[165] "Spain now represented the end of the Fourth Monarchy of Daniel," Reeves writes, "but a Fifth Monarchy was arising, that of the Most Christian King whose destiny was to aid the Pope in bringing in the old promise of one fold and one shepherd."[166] As we will see, this "Fifth Monarchy" was interpreted by Cromwell's New Model Army with a quite different outcome. Unlike Bruno, Campanella lived to see the dauphin's birth, notes Yates, "who was afterwards to reign as Louis XIV, as destined to be the Sun King in a reformed world."[167] Having survived the Inquisition, Campanella could not stave off death much longer. As Donno reports, "Early in 1639, foreseeing his imminent death in the stars, he sought to nullify their malefic influence by resorting to propitiatory rites he had found apparently efficacious in 1626 when he had applied them on behalf of Urban VIII in similar circumstances; but he died on May 21 of that year in the Dominican monastery in Rue St. Honoré."[168] For a time, Bruno and Campanella occupied the same dungeon, apparently without knowing each other. Yet Bruno was burned at the stake as a heresiarch, while Campanella's funeral was an assembly of France's noblest and most learned individuals.[169]

161. Yates, *Giordano Bruno*, 385–86.

162. Yates, *Giordano Bruno*, 386. When we look at the propaganda for the Calabrian revolt, we find that it is full of mystical imperialism and of prophecy of the return of an imperial golden age, such as the one Lactantius and the Sibyls speak of, combined with apocalyptic prophecy, Joachimism, and the like. Campanella believed from the portents that the hour had struck for such a renewal of the age; the Calabrians and the Dominicans were to prepare for it by establishing the ideal city in Calabria, whence it was to spread to the rest of the world.

163. See Donno, introduction to *Città del Sole*, 13.

164. Yates, *Giordano Bruno*, 390.

165. Yates, *Giordano Bruno*, 376.

166. Reeves, *Joachim of Fiore*, 128.

167. Yates, *Giordano Bruno*, 361.

168. See Donno, introduction to *Città del Sole*, 14.

169. Yates, *Giordano Bruno*, 391.

Conclusion

In many respects, the vision of Anabaptist spiritualists was carried with full force by leading humanists into the seventeenth century and beyond. For the eighteenth-century *philosophes*, attention for New World utopianism turned to the British Colonies as the new promised land. Indeed, the eighteenth-century French philosopher and politician Marquis de Condorcet argued that the education of the human race would achieve its goal in the new United States, the first nation to emerge from the doctrine of the universal and natural rights of humankind.[170]

The *City of the Sun* concludes with an impatient Genoese, namely Campanella himself, needing to return to the business of the city. "Wait, wait!," exclaims the hospitaler, receiving the reply, "I can't, I can't."[171] One may imagine this brief and concluding dialogue as the epitaph not only for Campanella but for the new utopian age.

170. Phelan, *Millennial Kingdom*, 77.
171. Campanella, *Città del Sole*, 127.

7

Jakob Böhme

Christian Shamanism

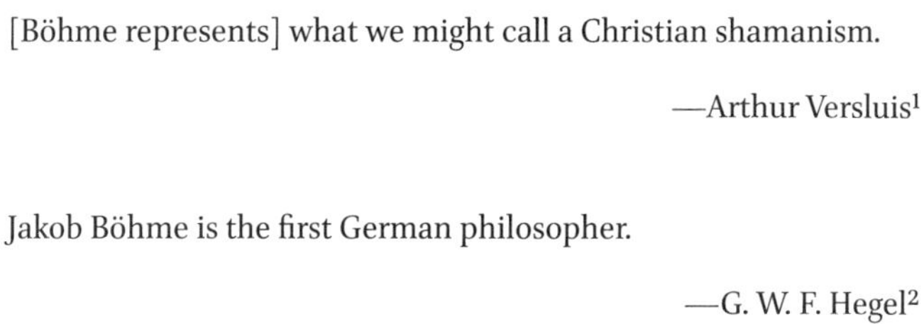

[Böhme represents] what we might call a Christian shamanism.

—Arthur Versluis[1]

Jakob Böhme is the first German philosopher.

—G. W. F. Hegel[2]

In the year 1600, just before the outbreak of the Thirty Years' War, Jakob Böhme (1575–1624) experienced a crisis. How could a good God allow such misery? He claimed to have had a vision in which the whole structure of the cosmos was revealed through a single beam of light reflected in a pewter bowl:

> In one quarter of an hour I saw and knew more than if I had been many years together at an University. . . . I saw it as in a great deep in the internal; for I had a thorough view of the Universe, as a complex moving fulness wherein all things are couched and wrapped up; but it was impossible for me to explain the same. . . . It was with me for the space of twelve years, and was, as it were, breeding.[3]

1. Versluis, "Christian Theosophical Literature," 219.

2. Hegel, *The Encyclopedia*, 133. He says similar things in other places, especially *Lectures on the History of Philosophy*, 3:188–219. See also Muratori, *First German Philosopher*.

3. Quotations of Böhme's *Confessions* taken from W. Palmer, *Confessions*, 41–42.

Böhme often speaks of a "flash" in the moment of revelation but also in a moment in the life of the Godhead as part of the cosmological process.

This idea of a mystical gnosis beyond all reasoning characterizes the whole Orphic tradition but is especially marked in the ancient gnostic texts that call this immediate vision a "flash." Yet it happens through a surrender of self-will. "He must make his will as it were dead," he says.[4] Walsh summarizes this as follows:

> The first that can be isolated is the wrestling of faith in which the resolve of the will is purified; then the breakthrough of light in the rebirth of Christ within the soul; the recognition of the universal process of light emerging from and being manifested only in darkness; and, finally, the vision of the process of overcoming as a process within God himself, the birth of the divine self-revelation. . . . At the center of Boehme's experience is the flash (*Blitz*) in which the divine light breaks through the darkness of self-will and the soul sees in a glance (*Blick*) that all reality is constituted by the same struggle to give birth to the light of divine revelation.[5]

Only when the dark fire of self-will surrenders to divine love, and the light unites with darkness, can the "flash" occur, in which "the dark fire loses its anger and begins to burn with a light or love-fire."[6] As Böhme says, "When you move silently, then you are that which God was before nature and creature, out of which He created your nature and creature."[7]

To us, such a complex speculative scheme may seem to have been remote from the concrete life of the average person in Germany at the dawn of the seventeenth century, but in fact it was bound up with current events. Living on the Bohemian border on the verge of the Thirty Years' War, Böhme's pessimism regarding the political and religious state of affairs fueled his *Sturm und Drang* theogony. Could hatred and love be grounded in God's own being? If so, could the overcoming of wrath by love within God be the ground of the same in nature and history?

Joachite eschatology gave Böhme's system a view of history in which tribulation leads to triumph in the Age of the Spirit. "In the prevailing atmosphere of political and religious tension and spiritual malaise," notes McIntosh, "many people turned, in their dismay, to the old millenarian dream of a new age."[8] In

4. W. Palmer, *Confessions*, 155.
5. Walsh, *Innerworldly Fulfillment*, 41–50.
6. Walsh, *Innerworldly Fulfillment*, 53.
7. Böhme, *Way to Christ*, 171.
8. McIntosh, *Rose Cross*, 23.

fact, "there was a wide expectation in Germany that the new age would begin in the early years of the seventeenth century. These millenarian expectations went hand in hand with an esoteric viewpoint that drew on a variety of sources including Gnosticism, Neoplatonism, the Hermetic tradition, kabbalah, and alchemy."[9] Böhme was a major figure in mediating Anabaptist spiritualism and utopianism to modernity.

Hegel began his lectures on the history of modern philosophy by introducing Francis Bacon and Böhme as contrasting figures with enduring impact. They had different objects of inquiry. "This domain in Bacon is the finite, natural world; in Boehme it is the inward, mystical, godly Christian life and existence; for the former starts from experience and induction, the latter from God and the pantheism of the Trinity."[10] The center is spiritual rebirth, and Böhme coined the term "theosophy" for his system. Versluis explains, "Theosophy represents a paradigm with certain common elements that reappear even if various groups are wholly unaware of one another, including (1) the focus upon Wisdom or Sophia, (2) an insistence upon direct spiritual experience, (3) reading Nature as a spiritual book, and (4) a spiritual leader who guides his or her spiritual circle through letters and oral advice."[11] It represents "what we might call a Christian shamanism." In fact, theosophy is "a synthesis of the main European esoteric traditions under the special genius of Böhme."[12] We should take Hegel seriously when he calls Böhme "the first German philosopher." What the cobbler from Görlitz saw in a pewter bowl had a profound impact on European thought.

The Making of a Christian Shaman

Although Böhme represents his whole system as a revelation received in a sudden flash, his thoughts had been shaped in a small circle of radical pietists. His chief direct influence was Martin Möller, a Lutheran pastor in Görlitz, "a remarkable man of broad learning and mystical leanings," says McLean, "who organized within his parish a small group, 'The Conventicle of God's Real Servants,' which had Boehme as a member."[13] One member, Abraham Behem was a correspondent with the

9. McIntosh, *Rose Cross*, 24.

10. *Lectures on the History of Philosophy*, 3:170.

11. Versluis, "Christian Theosophical Literature," 221.

12. Versluis, "Christian Theosophical Literature," 219, 233.

13. McLean, introduction to *"Key" of Jakob Boehme*, 8. Pietist conventicles were "a church within the church," that is, places where it was felt the true Christians gathered apart from the weekly assembly of Christians to discern and express a deeper experience of Christ within.

Anabaptist mystic Valentin Weigel.[14] Böhme's main debt is to Schwenckfeld and Weigel. He pored over Weigel's edition of the *Theologia Germanica* (*TG*) and his writings on Paracelsus.

Like most radical pietists, Böhme was a Lutheran who nevertheless adopted the basic outlook of Anabaptist spiritualists, including their rejection of justification through faith alone. Indeed, there was little connecting him theologically to confessional Lutheranism. Only repentance and rebirth justify, Böhme preached: "Not as Babel teacheth. There must be an entire and sincere earnestness, and not only a comforting and applying promise of consolation, but we must with Abraham obey God, and then we put on Christ's suffering and death . . . else Christ's death is not at all profitable to any."[15] One must be hungry, banish self-will, and become obedient, "else no comfort of satisfaction and merit will help thee."[16] Böhme was convinced that Protestants as well as Roman Catholics had closed off their inner spirit to live merely in the realm of historical facts, doctrines, and liturgies.

In 1612 he published his first book. Writing it originally for himself with the title *Die Morgenröte im Aufgang* (The rising of dawn, but more commonly rendered as *Aurora*), Böhme says, "I saw it as in a great deep in the internal; but it was impossible for me to explain the same. . . . It was with me for the space of twelve years, and was, as it were, breeding."[17] Möller was replaced as chief pastor by Gregorius Richter, into whose hands the manuscript fell, and who judged the work to be heretical. After several warnings, the city council banished Böhme temporarily on March 26, 1624. Leaving his wife and three children, Böhme came to Dresden, where he was welcomed by nobles and clergy.

In the meantime, *Aurora* circulated among Böhme's friends, some of whom had traveled widely and imbibed new ideas from the East as well as kabbalah. Key among these was Balthasar Walther, physician and alchemist to various dukes of the Holy Roman Empire, whose meanderings centered on publicizing Paracelsian ideas.[18] After traveling to Egypt, Palestine, and Syria "in search of Kabbalah, magic, and alchemy," Walther became friends with Böhme in 1612. The two seem to have influenced each other.[19] Along with the chiliast Paul Nagel, Walther and Johann

14. Weeks, *Boehme*, 30.

15. Böhme, *Mysterium Magnum*, 2:451.

16. Böhme, *Mysterium Magnum*, 2:706. See also Böhme, *Mysterium Magnum*, 2:421.

17. W. Palmer, *Confessions*, 41–42.

18. McLean, introduction to *"Key" of Jakob Boehme*, 9.

19. Schmidt-Biggemann, *Philosophia Perennis*, 117.

Huset (editor of Paracelsus's works) became propagandists for Böhme's views.[20] Theosophy would transcend the opposites of rival confessions.[21]

Though he was influenced by the tradition of German mysticism, "Jacob Böhme is a special case," Quispel explains:

> In the year 1600 this uneducated and gifted shoemaker went through an overwhelming experience of peace in the contrarieties of life: light and darkness, ire and love, good and evil, male and female, all originate in God. . . . God and his spouse Sophia are the prototype of the human being, who should realize his female features (or the reverse) and become one again. As Joseph Ritman has discovered, Böhme's noble and learned friends, who also supported him, were fully aware of the fact that Böhme was a gnostic, an avatar of the ancient Christian Gnostic Valentinus (ca. 150).[22]

The connection with ancient Gnosticism was made explicitly by friend and foe alike. In his 1699 church history, the pietist writer Gottfried Arnold included an anonymous text comparing the ideas of Paracelsus and Valentinus, commending both as good Christians. It turns out that it had been written by Böhme's friend, patron, and biographer, Abraham von Franckenberg.[23]

Inward Principles Manifesting Themselves Outwardly: Theology as Cosmology

The Magisterial Reformers focused on Christ for us, outside of us, in history. They viewed this good news as being brought to us by preaching and scripture and confirmed through visible sacraments of baptism and Eucharist. The whole person is changed by these measures, but from the outside in—that which arrives outwardly is embraced inwardly. The fundamental event for spiritualists, however, was the experience of Christ within—that which happens within a person is expressed outwardly.[24] For these figures, scripture was merely a witness to the truth of Christ in our hearts. The subjective and psychological take precedence over the

20. Versluis, "Christian Theosophical Literature," 218.

21. Weeks, *Boehme*, 56.

22. Quispel, "Reincarnation," 227–28.

23. Quispel, "Reincarnation," 228.

24. George Lindbeck applies to liberal theology the label "experiential-expressivism" in Lindbeck, *Nature of Doctrine*. As a main source of Protestant liberalism, pietism could just as easily be so described.

objective and historical. Echoing the traditional Orphic ascent through purgation, contemplation, and union, the anxious stages of pietist conversion are for Böhme the microcosm of a cosmological alchemy that begins within God himself through the dialectic of anger and love. As Böhme wrote, "Heaven is *in* a holy man."[25]

Cosmic Alchemy

Böhme's second book, *The Three Principles of the Divine Essence* (1618–1619) must be read together with its sequel, *The Threefold Life in Man* (1620). This is because the emanation of the cosmos is simultaneously in God, in us, and in history. Whatever happens in the inner world occurs in the outer world, above and below, macrocosm and microcosm, and always in three stages. As Underhill summarizes, "The universe in its essence consists of three worlds, which are 'none other than God Himself in His wonderful works.'" Beyond nature is the "Abyss," the Plotinian One, the Father of wrath and love. "The three worlds are the trinity of emanations through which the transcendent Unity achieves self-expression." Fire world, light world, and dark world "are not mutually exclusive spheres, but aspects of a whole. . . . From the primal fire or fount of generation in its fierceness are born the pair of opposites through which the Divine energy is manifested: the 'dark-world' of conflict, evil, and wrath which is Eternal Nature in itself, and the 'light-world' of wisdom and love, which is Eternal Spirit in itself—the Platonic *Nous*, the Son of Christian theology."[26]

God in Himself

One feature that distinguishes Böhme from Valentinus and other gnostics is that he believes that good and evil, love and wrath, exist in an unseparated fashion in the original moment, or person, of the Father—*Ein Sof* in kabbalah, the Infinite or Abyss. Gnostics considered such a notion blasphemous; instead, they attributed creation and therefore evil to a petty spawn of Sophia's broken contemplation. For Böhme, God and the world are necessary and interdependent realities. Everything *inside* (both God and world) is an incorporeal whole (i.e., reality). Everything *outside* (both God and the world) is a corporeal whole (i.e., appearance). Along

25. Quoted in Versluis, "Christian Theosophical Literature," 220.

26. See Evelyn Underhill's introduction in W. Palmer, *Confessions*, 26–28. In the following summary I am drawing mostly from "The Key," because it is Böhme's most lucid and laconic summary of both these works.

these lines, he is reconciling opposites at all four coordinates: God and world, inner and outer.

The Father is the *Urgrund*, equivalent to Eckhart's divinity (*Gottheit*) above God (*Gott*), but he is not aware of his own existence until he emanates the Son. As in Eriugena, the Father for Böhme represents the moment of utter simplicity, pure nothingness, unknowable even to himself.[27] To emerge from the abyss of divinity to a divine person, the Father requires a Son. Yet, as tinctured by Eckhart and the *TG*, this abyss is Pure Will more than Pure Mind. In its simplicity, this divinity has will but not *a* will, showing the extent of his voluntarism: to be *a* person is to exercise *a* will. The Father is, in himself, "a consuming fire," that is, anger and powerful force. From this single fire come both good and evil, wrath and love. Böhme writes:

> This ground is called *Mysterium Magnum*, or a *Chaos*, because good and evil arise out of it, namely Light and Darkness, Life and Death, Joy and Grief, Salvation and Damnation. For it is the ground of Souls and Angels, and of all Eternal Creatures, as well evil as good; it is a ground of Heaven and Hell, also of the visible world, and all that is therein. . . . Yet we cannot say that the spiritual world has had any beginning, but has been manifested from Eternity out of that *Chaos*.[28]

Another deity is Sophia. Paracelsus identified Sophia with the Virgin Mary, and it is reasonable to think that Böhme has a similar idea. Clearly, she has the characteristics of the Pythagorean Dyad and the Sophia of gnostic myths: virtuous but the source of duality. "She is the true Divine Chaos, wherein all things lie," says Böhme, "namely a Divine Imagination, in which the *Ideas* of Angels and Souls have been seen from Eternity, in a Divine Type and Resemblance."[29] "In relation to God," he teaches, "Wisdom has a female form, because in her the ungrounded will has brought forth the essences and wonders contained within itself. She is the partner of God in the work of creation and revelation, since she contains the ideas of all things which the Spirit forms into separate realities."[30] The divine Sophia, explains Weeks, is the "third thing"—in which God, Christ, the first Adam, and all of the reborn are united. "Since she embodies the magic process by which

27. Schmidt-Biggemann, *Philosophia Perennis*, 118–19.

28. Translation of Jakob Böhme's *Key* is from Law, *Key*, 25, emphasis original.

29. Law, *Key*, 23. Böhme adds, "She is the breathing of the Divine Power . . . for the Wisdom is the Passive, and the Spirit of God is the Active, or Life in her, as the Soul in the body."

30. Walsh, *Innerworldly Fulfillment*, 75.

the principle of darkness is reflected as light her role is a more striking one in Boehme's writings than that of the historical Christ."[31]

Being—which includes God as the Being of beings—is in becoming, but this becoming is not a calm process of eternal emanation for Böhme. Rather, it is a struggle within God himself, between opposing attributes.[32] "Starting from this border [of absolute beginning], the next step is divine self-contemplation and definition of the Father and the Son."[33] From the "desire of attraction" there is a direction of the Father toward the Son.[34]

There is a violent "flash" when the Father bursts forth from calm immutability, "anxious about its own existence" and trying to "maintain the will in its original state." The attraction of the wrathful Father to the loving Son provokes an inner conflict. This attraction, at the heart of life—indeed, at the heart of the One—is "like a raging madness" and "a horrible anguish."[35] As Böhme describes it, "The second substance [the Son] is the separable will"—the first will that unites into one will. This is the "Love-Fire, or Light."

> And in this place of working God calleth himself a loving, merciful God, according to the sharpened fiery burning Love of the unity; and an Angry Jealous God, according to the fiery Ground, according to the Eternal Nature. The *Mysterium Magnum* is that *Chaos*, out of which Light and Darkness, that is, the foundation of Heaven and Hell, is flown from Eternity, and made manifest; for that foundation which we now call Hell, being a Principle of itself, is the ground and cause of the Fire in the Eternal Nature; which fire, in God, is only a burning Love; and where God is not manifested in a thing, according to the unity, there is an anguishing, painful, burning fire.[36]

In the intra-Trinitarian life, the Spirit is the *magus* who unites opposites. Instead of annihilating all that has become separate from God, the creation (like its archetype, the Son) is followed by a sweet convergence by the Holy Spirit that is something different from, indeed more beautiful than, the original state of immutable self-contemplation and independence.[37]

31. Weeks, *Boehme*, 150.
32. Schmidt-Biggemann, *Philosophia Perennis*, 121.
33. Schmidt-Biggemann, *Philosophia Perennis*, 118–19.
34. Schmidt-Biggemann, *Philosophia Perennis*, 121.
35. Schmidt-Biggemann, *Philosophia Perennis*, 124–25.
36. Law, *Key*, 24.
37. Schmidt-Biggemann, *Philosophia Perennis*, 126.

Emanation of the World

When Böhme wrote *The Threefold Life of Man* in 1620, he rejected all external authorities. The natives in the New World are more godly than Christians, he says.[38] Christendom represents the age of the Son, which is now ruled by an antichrist (encompassing both Roman Catholic and Protestant communions). "History unfolds as the growth and division within the One Will: it 'grows' from unity to conflict and then back to unity."[39] The Spirit (Sophia) is the unifier of opposites in the Godhead, in the self, in nature, and in history. Creation (not *ex nihilo* but from the essence of God), Fall (self-will), and Rebirth (divine unity) are correlative of this trinitarian process. But this is not a "historical faith," Böhme emphasizes. Faith is directed not to Christ outside us in the past but by "going into ourselves [*unserm Selbst-Eingehen*]."[40]

Böhme adopted from Pico and Paracelsus the view of humanity as the intersection of natural, astral, and divine orders, with the ability of each person to choose his or her affinity.[41] Again, this was not just abstract theorizing. It is a theodicy-driven cosmology. Self-will, the result of remaining with the opposition of hatred and love, was what Böhme saw in the world around him.

In summary thus far, Böhme's threefold pattern is wholly integrative. His private experience unfolded in stages that mirrored the stages of the world's emergence from God: Father, Son, Spirit; *nigredo* (darkness), *albedo* (separation into opposites), and *rubedo* (a third thing); thesis, antithesis, and synthesis; contraction, expansion, and unity. Weeks observes,

> *The Threefold Life of Man* makes increasing use of Gnostic symbols and images to depict earthly alienation. The Christian is a pilgrim wandering in search of the lost Paradise of his true Fatherland. We are not at home in the external world, the author declares at the outset. . . . The soul is therefore like a prisoner condemned to death. . . . Human life manifests itself as desire and will, as the ineluctable tormenting freedom which cannot escape from nature (III 61–62/4.5–8). This is the sense of the "fire will," the "fire of life," "the fire-wheel," and "flaming worl" (*die feurende Welt*). . . . The eternally self-spoken Word and

38. Böhme, *Threefold Life*, III 13/7.8; III 228/11.92.

39. Weeks, *Boehme*, 150.

40. Weeks, *Boehme*, 150, quoting *The Threefold Life*, IV 88/1.11.8.

41. See Evelyn Underhill's introduction in W. Palmer, *Confessions*, 24–25. R. J. W. Evans adds that "especially true in German lands, where the Renaissance magical tradition of Trithemius, Agrippa, and Paracelsus was steeped in Neoplatonism and intimately linked with the mystical experience of men like Valentine Weigel" (Evans, *Rudolf II*, 197).

the self-made God coincide with "the divinity within us."— "God appears to us in the will" (III 29/2.51).[42]

The Bible's historical fall is ontologized and allegorized in Böhme's writing. Instead of being something that happened, it encapsulates what happens everywhere and always. The separation or fall from unity of spirit into diversity of bodies is a necessary tragedy, the opening stage of the One's self-manifestation. Like Eriugena, Böhme sees the Father as coming to self-consciousness by emanating the Son and the Spirit as the unifier. In Böhme's system, the individual soul also becomes conscious of itself as an individual, distinct from God, as a primarily willing agent: "I will; therefore, I am," one might say. Yet this is but a moment on the way to the third act, namely, reconciliation. This reunification occurs within the Godhead through the Holy Spirit and within nature through Sophia, but it is all part of a single process.

Self-will (*die Eigenwilligkeit*), Böhme says, is the refusal of the soul to go on to the third stage of merging with God in a "unified union [*in die einige Einigung*]."[43] Only when one's soul is united to God by an act of willing surrender does her will (and thus mind and soul) become identical with God's, like a flame reuniting voluntarily with its fire. Consequently, in this "flash," the subject is dissolved in the object. Böhme says, "Not I, the I that I am, know these things; but God knows them in me."[44] This is correlative to the Father knowing himself and all things through the Son.

Reflecting a common Orphic inheritance, all these circles had at their core a cosmotheological myth divided in three stages. Gilles Quispel is exactly right: "For every gnostic myth begins in heaven, unfolds on earth and returns to heaven."[45] The soul ascends by three steps: purification, contemplation, and union. Hermetic alchemy also follows three stages: *nigredo* (darkness), *albedo* (separation into opposites), and *rubedo* (the production of the philosopher's stone).[46] In the Lurianic kabbalism that Böhme imbibed there is the threefold pattern of stillness, contraction, and expansion. The *Ein Sof* (Infinite) transcends all duality, containing the potential for good and evil, but then withdraws into its own center to make room for creation through a combination of opposites and, finally, comes

42. Weeks, *Boehme*, 144–45, quoting *The Threefold Life*.

43. Böhme, "Mystical Points," in *Sämtliche Schriften*, 4:89–90, quoted in Bach, "Jakob Böhme," 265.

44. Böhme, *The first apologie to Balthazar Tylcken*.

45. Quispel, "Reincarnation," 228.

46. Bogdan, *Esotericism*, 197.

to self-awareness through humanity, through whom good conquers evil. The union of opposites occurs within God.[47]

Adopting this view, Böhme maintains that just as thoughts must flow out of the mind into the body to be self-realized, so "selfhood" is realized in God and in ourselves by encountering otherness.[48] God needs the world, as he needs the Son, in order to become conscious of himself—indeed, even, to complete himself. Böhme describes this alterity in violent terms as opposites separate and are united in a flash (*Blitz*). As McLean notes, "He deals with the existence of polarities, the Thesis-Antithesis-Synthesis, which lies at the foundation of a Hermetic-alchemical view of the world; the Three Principles, Salt, Mercury, and Sulphur, and their manifestation as archetypes in various realms; and the Seven Properties, which connect with the Planetary archetypes, which also bear within them polarity and the three principles."[49]

Correlative to the threefold mystical ascent, Joachite eschatology has its three ages from the childhood of authority to enlightened autonomy. As Weeks observes, in Böhme's thinking millennialism is combined with a Copernican cosmology:

> His vision of the world in time is rounded out by the chiliastic belief in a final age: an age coinciding with the restoration of an ancient knowledge which would clarify the letter of the Gospel and resolve all conflicts over its meaning. . . . It revealed the latent omnipresence of the hidden divinity within a fallen world. . . . Liberated from the mechanical spheres, the celestial bodies were now guided through a fluid and continuous space by spirit forces, by the planetary "souls" of Gilbert, or the *animae motrices* of Kepler. . . . Kepler upheld the Copernican model of the world as an image of the Trinity—and as a reconfirmation of the ancient wisdom of the Sidonians, Chaldeans, Persians, and Platonists. He affirmed that "most rightly is the sun held to be the heart of the world and the seat of reason and life, and the principal one among three members of the world."[50]

In fact, as Weeks also states, "The heliocentric world is arrayed around the likeness of Christ, as the light of the world, the power by virtue of which the life of nature is continually reborn in the dead element of the earth. . . . Heliocentrism, as we can see, had its distinct advantages: it provided a natural symbol for the God within,

47. Walsh, *Innerworldly Fulfillment*, 54–55.
48. Walsh, *Innerworldly Fulfillment*, 58.
49. McLean, introduction to *"Key" of Jakob Boehme*, 12.
50. Weeks, *Boehme*, 57.

it reconfirmed the ubiquitous presence of the triune deity, and opened the door to a new understanding of the relations of human microcosm and natural macrocosm."[51] In short, whatever happens on the psychological dimension happens on the ontological and historical ones as well, simultaneously.

In its logical order the intellectual world emanates first, then expresses itself in the material realm. Just as the Father (Divine Will) shuts itself up in its center and then generates the Trinity by separations (the Son as delight and the Spirit as life), Böhme writes that the same occurs in "the second Separation, that is, of Nature, and in that expression wherein the Natural Will separates itself in its Center, into a preconception, the Separation out of the fiery Science [Understanding] is understood; for thence comes the Soul and all Angelical Spirits. The third Separation is according to the outward Nature of the expressed formed Word, wherein the Beastial Science lies."[52] Platonism is inherently Romantic, with the self-awareness and then expression of an Absolute Self manifesting itself in visible images. In God's self-contemplation the world emerges.[53] This is natural supernaturalism in a nutshell.

For Aristotle, the quintessence was the rarified substance above the sphere of the moon, which Hermeticists like Ficino sought to bring down to earth for medicinal healing. Similarly, Böhme insists that this spiritual essence makes itself visible in the corporeal world. Yet humanity, like the Son, contains quintessence of the Godhead above God. The eternal begetting of the Son is also the emanation of the world. There is a "moment" in which the One "suddenly reaches a breaking point and explodes. Following this archetype, every separation has this moment of fright and explosion, occurring in a single instant. Different from the soft, tamed fire of life as it exists in the holy trinity, this fiery force expresses itself as a flash in its separation from the divine loving fire. This is the emergence of the difference between good/light and evil/darkness."[54] This separation and union, in both "worlds," is the *mysterium magnum*. Böhme asserts, "Nature, in its first ground, consists in seven Properties, and these seven divide themselves into

51. Weeks, *Boehme*, 70.

52. Law, *Key*, 53.

53. Schmidt-Biggemann, *Philosophia Perennis*, 118–19. Underhill suggests that the Holy Spirit is "assigned a position very close to the Plotinian *Psyche*, or 'soul of the world.'" See Underhill's introduction in W. Palmer, *Confessions*, 29–30. However, Böhme is clear that the World Soul falls on the side of nature. He says, "The *Spiritus Mundi* is hidden in the four Elements, as the Soul is in the body, and is nothing else but an Effluence and working Power proceeding from the Sun and Stars; its dwelling wherein it works is spiritual, encompassed with the four Elements." See Law, *Key*, 45.

54. Schmidt-Biggemann, *Philosophia Perennis*, 125.

infinity."[55] Otherness is an essential part of the cosmotheological drama, yet it is painful. Self-will begins with the Father, who does not want to desire another and yet cannot come to self-consciousness without him.

Elaborating the character of these seven properties, Böhme compares the first (desire) to a magnet. Almost like a contemporary psychoanalyst, he says:

> The will desires to be something, and yet it has nothing of which it may make something to itself; and therefore it brings itself into a Reception of itself, and compresses itself to something; and that something is nothing but a Magnetical Hunger, a harshness, like a hardness, whence even hardness, cold, and substance arise. This compression or attraction overshadows itself, and makes itself a Darkness: At the beginning of the world, salt, stones, and bones, and all such things were produced by this sharpness.[56]

He adds that the motion of desire divides and separates "into Forms and Images; between these two Properties arises the bitter woe, that is, the string of Perception and Feeling."[57] The desire was expressed when God said, "Let there be."[58]

There follows an intricate Paracelsian kabbalistic scheme of various properties of the divine nature manifesting themselves in nature. For example, anguish, the third property of the eternal nature, is the ground of both mind and senses "and the true foundation of Hell."[59] Sulfur, mercury, and salt correspond to these divine properties. The upshot: "Thus an Heavenly always lies hidden in the Earthly, for the invisible spiritual world came from, with, and in the Creation."[60] Böhme's system is more Hermetic than gnostic. The dualistic opposition may even be more pronounced than in Gnosticism (if that is possible), but the third entity (a person of the Godhead or a stage) *reconciles* opposites.

For spiritual alchemists like Böhme as well, the goal of the process—whether

55. Law, *Key*, 26–27. The properties are: (1) Desire, the cause of "harshness, sharpness, hardness, cold, and substance"; (2) Attraction, "stinging, breaking, and dividing the hardness; it cuts asunder the attracted desire, and brings it into multiplicity and variety; it is a ground of the bitter pain, and also the true Root of Life; it is the *Vulcan* that strikes fire"; (3) Anguish, manifested as "a Fire or Light, namely a flash, or shining" and "in these three first Properties consists the Foundation of Anger, and of Hell, and of all that is wrathful"; (4) Fire or "burning Love"; (5) Light; (6) Voice, "wherein the five senses work spiritually, that is, in an understanding Natural Life"; and finally, (7) Ground or Place of Nature, "the Subject, or the Contents of the other Six Properties."

56. Law, *Key*, 29.

57. Law, *Key*, 29.

58. Law, *Key*, 30.

59. Law, *Key*, 31.

60. Law, *Key*, 32.

in the "outer" laboratory, the "inner" laboratory of the self, the Trinity, or the cosmos—is to "lead out" the gold from its base matter. The quintessence is the eternal and spiritual gold. Aristotle thought it was a rarified substance beyond the moon that held everything together, but Hermeticists believed it may be distilled from large quantities of raw materials in which it is especially concentrated (e.g., wine, dew, and human secretions). Böhme dwells on these points especially in *The Signature of All Things* (1621).

By itself, the emphasis on all invisible and spiritual realities expressing themselves visibly in the material realm might seem to valorize corporeality. However, as with all forms of idealism since Parmenides, the corporeal world falls on the side of appearance rather than reality. On the one hand, God needs the world for the self-manifestation essential to his own inner transmutation. Thus, the world is nothing but God's appearing. On the other hand, matter is transmuted into spirit, creation into creator. In contrast with the doctrine of *ex nihilo* creation, where the world has a dependent but distinct existence, nature in Böhme's conception is, literally, spiritualized out of existence. He takes Luther's doctrine of the ubiquity of Christ's humanity to its extreme, says Weeks: "The Formula of Concord put it quite simply: 'the right hand of God is everywhere.' It would be left to Boehme to develop fully the *mystical* implications of the bitterly contested doctrine of [Christ's human] omnipresence. One finds innumerable affirmations of the divine ubiquity in Boehme's writings. . . . Boehme's ubiquitous divinity is seen and experienced by the inner spirit, not by the outer eye of the body."[61]

Böhme then unfolds this process of creation by appealing to the days of Genesis 1. On the second day "arose the Male and Female kind, in the Spirit of the outworld world; that is, the Male in the fiery *Mercury*, and the Female in the watery."[62] The myth of a perfect race of androgynous humans being separated violently into sexes first appears in Orphic texts (and their Eastern equivalents). It is found in Plato's *Timaeus* myth and in the *Symposium* (189c–193e), and it was a principal motif in Gnosticism, Hermeticism, and theurgic Neoplatonism. All the way back to Philo of Alexandria, the Primal Man—ideal Adam prior to bodily incarceration—unites microcosm and macrocosm. Originally androgynous, this cosmic human underwent a violent separation into male and female sexes but will one day restore its unity: the anthropological version of the wider cosmic pattern of emanation into division and plurality ("femaleness") and return to unity ("maleness"). Regardless of whether Aristophanes's speech in the *Symposium* is a serious statement of Plato's own view, Hermeticists—particularly in the Renais-

61. Weeks, *Boehme*, 38.
62. Law, *Key*, 42.

sance—took it quite literally and were committed to enacting it. Images abound from medieval times symbolizing this process from androgyny (i.e., inchoate substance) to violent separation and, finally, union (the "chymical wedding"). The whole point is that the *magus* is a creator like God himself, except he or she is bringing a new thing into being through that which exists already. Böhme picks up on this theme with considerable imagination.

On the fifth day of creation, says Böhme, "the *Spiritus Mundi*, that is, the soul of the great world, opened itself in the fifth Essence (we mean the Life of the fiery and water *Mercury*); therein God created all beasts, fishes, fowls, and worms; every one from its peculiar property of the divided *Mercury*." The "divided Mercury," which constitutes the prized quintessence (or philosopher's stone), was revealed above as the division of mercury into male (fiery) and female (watery). "Here we see how the Eternal Principles have moved themselves according to Evil and Good, as to all the seven Properties, and their Effluence and Mixture; for there are evil and good Creatures created, every thing as the *Mercury* (that is, the Separator) has figured and framed himself into an *Ens*, as may be seen in the evil and good Creatures."[63] Steiner explains, "As the light is only able to shine when it pierces the darkness, so the good can bring itself to life only when it permeates its opposite. From out of the 'fathomless abyss' of darkness there streams forth the light; from the 'groundlessness' of the indifferent there is brought to birth the Good."[64] Salt is this dark astringency, Böhme says, following Paracelsus. "By swallowing up its opposite, the first nature-form passes over into the form of the second; the astringent, the motionless, takes on movement; Power and Life enter into it. Quicksilver (Mercury) is the symbol for this second form. In the struggle of Rest and Motion, of Death with life, the third form of Nature unveils itself (Sulphur)."[65]

Böhme often draws on the alchemical concept of a tincture, which is an extract made by soaking herbs or other plants in alcohol so that their active ingredients become a concentrated liquid. On the "Seventh Day," he says, "The Tincture pierced through the Earth, and through all Elements, and tinctured All; and then Paradise was on Earth, and in Man; for evil was hidden: as the Night is hidden in the Day, so the wrath of Nature was also hidden in the first Principle, till the fall of Man. . . . For the wrath rose aloft, and got the predominancy, and that is the curse."[66]

Just as the Father keeps his wrath hidden until the separation and then the

63. Law, *Key*, 43.

64. Steiner, *Mystics*, 239.

65. Steiner, *Mystics*, 241–42.

66. Law, *Key*, 44.

Spirit extracts the light from the fire, the same is true of nature until the fall. The curse was neither a moment in time nor a direct act of God. Rather, the wrath was always present within nature, though not manifested apart from human self-will. Originally, sulfur, mercury, and salt were "only one thing. . . . But when Mercurius, viz., the sound of the formed Word, doth move itself in the Principle, viz., in its first original by an opposition or contrary aspect, then he is terrified in himself: that is, the motion stirreth the original of the heat and cold, viz., the original of the first Principle according to the cold and hot fire; which is the beginning of the contrariety and horror." For example, he continues, fire and brimstone did not actually fall upon Sodom and Gomorrah from heaven, "but the wrath came forth from the inward into the outward [Principle], so that the outward, in the might of the inward, did impress and enkindle itself out of the properties of the inward. And this is a real type of the inward dark world," with God as a "consuming fire."[67]

Thus far we may discern striking commonalities with Valentinian gnosis. Böhme polemicizes sharply against creation *ex nihilo* and the creator-creature distinction it entails. "The Simple says, God made all things out of nothing; but he knows not God, neither does he know what he himself is. When he beholds the earth together with the deep above the earth, he thinks verily all this is *not* God; or else he thinks God is *not there*." This is what is found in "the books and writings of Doctors."[68] Rather, "The universal God is *that one only body*. But sin is the cause that thou does not wholly see and know him. With and by sin thou, within this great divine body, liest shut up in the mortal flesh. . . . But if thou in the spirit breakest through the death of the flesh, then thou seest the hidden God."[69]

Böhme's Christology is also frankly docetic. According to his own confession, the ascended Christ "is no more in the hard palpability, but in the divine palpability, of nature, like the angels. Our bodies also at the resurrection will have no more such hard flesh and bones, but be like the angels; and though indeed all forms and powers shall be therein, yet we shall not have the hard palpability. . . . So during the forty days after his resurrection he did not always walk visibly among the disciples, but invisibly, according to his heavenly and angelical property."[70]

However, what distinguishes Böhme's system from ancient Gnostics is the Hermetic *reconciliation* of opposites. Theodicy is cosmology for Böhme, and in the existential angst of his day a number of important figures were convinced that he had finally resolved the problem of evil. Far from being a hidden mystery, God's

67. Böhme, *Mysterium Magnum*, 2:414.
68. W. Palmer, *Confessions*, 78.
69. W. Palmer, *Confessions*, 81, emphasis added.
70. W. Palmer, *Confessions*, 74–76.

predestination is manifested in the necessary unfolding of history from God's own inner tension. In the moment of separation, dark hatred momentarily gains the upper hand, but it is absorbed into love. Instead of annihilating all that has become separate from God, the creation (like its archetype, the Son) is followed by a sweet convergence that is something different from, indeed more beautiful than, the original state of immutable self-contemplation and independence.[71]

For Böhme, the inward world is the true one, expressing itself outwardly in something like a stage play. "Were we not in the beginning made out of God's substantiality?"[72] And yet, only spiritual substance can emanate from spiritual substance. So it is not the materialistic pantheism that we find in the Stoics and Spinoza, but the idealist pantheism that treats divinity as descending quantitatively down the scale of being. The real is intelligible, not sensible. Standing closer to the Parmenidean tradition, Böhme considers the world a mirror in which God discovers himself rather than a distinct (and botched) creation. He says, "God is himself the Being of all beings; and we are as Gods in him, through whom he revealeth himself."[73] So too Böhme claims:

> We cannot say that the outward world is God, or the speaking Word; or that the outward man is God. That is only the expressed Word, which has stiffened itself in union with the elements. I say, the inward world is the heaven where God dwells; and the outward world is expressed out of the inward, through the moving of the eternal speaking Word, and enclosed between a beginning and an end. The inward world abides in the eternal speaking Word.[74]

Having suggested above that Böhme's system is panentheistic, I confess that at times I cannot distinguish this view from pantheism. The Trinity does not transcend the cosmological process; in fact, the Father himself is the *Urgrund* from which the dramaturgy evolves. As in the entire Orphic, Pythagorean-Platonic tradition, the divine unity of all things is purely spiritual. If humanity is called divine, it is in virtue of the soul; if the cosmos is a god, it is because of the World Soul that permeates it. In this mutual awakening of powers to each other we find the "immeasurable and abyssmal being of the One which is All," he teaches.[75] Similar to

71. Schmidt-Biggemann, *Philosophia Perennis*, 126.
72. W. Palmer, *Confessions*, 142.
73. W. Palmer, *Confessions*, 116.
74. W. Palmer, *Confessions*, 158.
75. W. Palmer, *Confessions*, 160.

Eckhart, Böhme asserts, "We know nothing *of* God; he, God himself, *is* our knowing and seeing; we are nothing that he may be all in us."[76] As he writes elsewhere:

> I declare unto you that the eternal Being, and also this world, is like man. Eternity bringeth to birth nothing but that which is like itself; as you find man to be, just so is eternity. Consider man in body and soul, in good and evil, in joy and sorrow, in light and darkness, in power and weakness, in life and death: *all is in man, both heaven and the earth, stars, and elements; also the threefold God.* O man! seek thyself and thou shalt find thyself. Open the eyes of thy inward man and see rightly. This is the noble precious stone, the philosopher's stone, which wise men find.... For heaven is in hell and hell is in heaven, and yet the one is not manifest to the other.[77]

The inner light shines, but the devil "hides it often with the outward and fleshly moving, so that the natural is in anxiety and in a strait, as if it were imprisoned... for wrath abides in the fleshly moving.... If wrath should be wholly taken away from the astral, then in that he would be like God and know all things as God himself does."[78] Later Böhme divulges:

> Indeed all is as it were one body, the outermost and the innermost moving together with the firmament of heaven, as also the astral moving therein, in and with which the wrath of God unfolds; but yet they are one to another as the government, frame or constitution in man. The flesh marks the outward moving, which is the house of death. The second moving in man is the astral, in which the life stands, and wherein love and wrath wrestle with one another.... The third moving is generated between the astral and the outermost, and is called the animated or soulish moving, or the soul, and is as great as the whole man.[79]

Only the outer flesh obscures the immediate gnosis of divinity. The earth hungers for the influence of the stars and the *Spiritus mundi*, Böhme argues in the *Key*, but the inner spirit hungers for union with God, from whom it has never been truly alienated except to separate the lead from the gold. Man should "not run headlong in such blindness, seeking his Native Country afar off from himself, when it is within himself.... Now when the strife of the Elements ceases, by the

76. W. Palmer, *Confessions*, 149, emphasis added.
77. W. Palmer, *Confessions*, 126, emphasis added.
78. W. Palmer, *Confessions*, 66–67.
79. W. Palmer, *Confessions*, 70–71.

Death of the gross body, then the Spiritual Man will be made manifest. . . . For the outward visible Man is not now the Image of God, it is nothing but an Image of the *Archaeus*, that is, a house [or husk] of the Spiritual Man, in which the Spiritual Man grows, as Gold does in the gross Stone."[80] There is no question whether he believes that the same body that has died will be raised in a glorious condition. In terms reminiscent of Origen, he writes:

> The outward gross Body of the four Elements shall not inherit the kingdom of God, but that which is born out of that one Element, namely out of the Divine Manifestation and Working. For this Body of the Flesh and of the Will of Man is not it, but that which is wrought by the heavenly *Archaeus* in this gross Body, unto which this gross [Body] is a house, a tool, and instrument. But when the Crust is taken away, then it shall appear why we have been called Men.[81]

The four elements of this world will be destroyed, "together with the Starry Heaven, and the Earthly Creatures, namely the outward gross life of all things." However, "the Inward Power and Virtue of every substance remains Eternally." Once the outward manifestation is fulfilled, the corporeal world is no longer needed. Thus, "The place of the Eternal Paradise is hidden in this World, in the Inward Ground; but manifests in the Inward Man, in which God's Power and Virtue works."[82] In his *Confessions*, Böhme adds:

> The outward spirit, which is from the stars and elements, is not thus disturbed and perplexed; because it liveth in its own matrix from which it had its birth. But the poor soul is entered into a strange lodging, into the spirit of this world, which is not its proper home. Whereby that fair creature is obscured and defaced, and is also held captive therein, as in a dark dungeon. The soul is in its first being a magical fire-source from God's nature.[83]

According to Böhme, when his "will-spirit" is finally one with God's, "Paradise shall be in me. . . . I shall be the manifestation of the divine and spiritual world and an instrument of God's Spirit, wherein he makes melody with himself, with this voice which I myself am."[84]

80. Law, *Key*, 48.
81. Law, *Key*, 49.
82. Law, *Key*, 51.
83. W. Palmer, *Confessions*, 175.
84. W. Palmer, *Confessions*, 163–64; cf. Law, *Key*, 46.

Neither God and the angels nor Satan and his demons exist somewhere outside this world according to Böhme. Rather, they live within us, so that we are in heaven or in hell depending on whether we surrender our will to God or not. As Underhill observes, "All lies in the direction of the will: 'What we make of ourselves, that we are.'" This is the hypervoluntarism that we have seen not only in German mysticism but also in the Florentine ideal of the magus (e.g., Pico's *Oration*). Salvation—the goal of life—comes from the "bringing of the Light out of its fiery origin—spiritual beauty out of the raw stuff energetic nature."[85] We have all three worlds within us, so all of us can do this. "'When I see a right man,' says Boehme, 'there I see three worlds standing.'"[86] Heaven and hell are present wherever the will turns its sails either toward God's will or its own.[87] If we surrender wholly to God, our will and his will become identical, and we know him (more importantly, *will* him) as he is in himself.

The bodies of the stars are not their virtue, just as the soul is distinct from the body and the spirit of scripture is different from the letter. In his *Confessions*, Böhme says, "For man is made out of all the powers of God, out of all the seven spirits of God, as the angels also are . . . yet it is incomprehensible to the corrupted nature. For the Holy Ghost will not be held in the sinful flesh, but rises up like a lightning-flash, as fire sparkles and flashes out of a stone when a man strikes it."[88] Later on he adds, "And suddenly in that light my will was set on by a mighty impulse to describe the Being of God." Böhme distinguishes his "reason" and his "exact understanding thereof," which he received twelve years later. In other words, the "flash" of gnosis is a reason-transcending mystical experience, while the articulation of this immediate vision required considerable labor.

Böhme is not naive; he knows that such views will not pass muster in orthodox circles, but, similar to Thomas Müntzer's Sermon to the Princes, Böhme declares, "O ye theologists, the spirit here opens a door and gate for you! If you will not now see and feed your sheep and lambs on a green meadow, instead of a dry, parched heath, you must be accountable for it before the severe, earnest and wrathful judgement of God; therefore look to it."[89] Böhme teaches that we must "go with Christ out from this world, out from the stars and elements, and enter into God; for in the will of earthly reason we are children of the stars and elements, and the spirit of this world ruleth over us. But if we go out from the will of this world

85. See Underhill's introduction in W. Palmer, *Confessions*, 29–30.
86. See Underhill's introduction in W. Palmer, *Confessions*, 30–31.
87. See Underhill's introduction in W. Palmer, *Confessions*, 32–33.
88. W. Palmer, *Confessions*, 46.
89. W. Palmer, *Confessions*, 73–74.

and enter into God, then the spirit of God ruleth in us and establisheth us for his children."[90] Scriptures, creeds, and confessions are superfluous and even injurious to this enterprise. "The Spirit of God suffers not itself to be tied or bound up, as outward reason supposes, with decrees, canons and councils, whereby always one chain of Antichrist is linked to another. . . . God has made one covenant with us in Christ; that is enough for eternity, he makes no more."[91]

Böhme's Legacy

Ironically, Böhme's corpus was edited by the son of his nemesis, Gregorius Richter, who succeeded as chief pastor in Görlitz. Radical pietism spread Böhme's ideas throughout Germany, and Gottfried Arnold's *Unpartheyische Kirchen- und Ketzer-Historie* (1699) transmitted the mystic's legacy to later generations from Russia to England. After his death in 1624, Böhme's many works were translated into Dutch. In Holland, the influence of Böhme refreshed the native springs of Rhineland mysticism from which the Collegiants emerged, who were formative influences on such thinkers as Spinoza.

English translations of Böhme's work by John Sparrow appeared at the same time as the German edition. Sparrow was associated with the Hartlib Circle, including Henry Oldenberg, secretary of the Royal Society, who promoted Böhme's vision of a universal reformation.[92] Even Charles I is said to have regarded Böhme's work highly and to have financed the translation and publication from the royal treasury, though most of the German mystic's volumes appeared throughout the Civil War.[93] Böhme's speculations were popular across a wide swath of society, including figures like the poet John Milton. Walsh notes:

> In England, the speculative dimension of Boehme's illumination was more fully appreciated because of its reception by circles that were already heavily influenced by the Renaissance hermetic tradition. This is certainly true of men like Samuel Hartlib, Johann Comenius, and John Dury, and especially the translator John Sparrow, who produced an English edition of Boehme's works between 1645 and 1647. It was undoubtedly through such groups that John Milton became acquainted with the ideas of Boehme, although the extent of their direct

90. W. Palmer, *Confessions*, 122.
91. W. Palmer, *Confessions*, 153–54.
92. See Hessayon, "John Sparrow," 329–57.
93. Joling-van der Sar, *Samuel Richardson*, 145.

influence remains open to dispute. In the same way, the Cambridge Platonists formed a sympathetic audience for Boehme's theosophical speculation, and Henry More, while largely disagreeing with him, did much to maintain a context for the serious consideration of his thought.[94]

Early in the century John Pordage, a Church of England minister, alchemist, and astrologist, founded the Behmenist Society. Influenced by Elias Ashmole, Pordage was convicted of heresy (specifically "mystical pantheism"), but was acquitted in 1651. He was then charged again by the Presbyterian-led Parliament in 1654. Ejected as "ignorant and very insufficient for the work of the ministry," Pordage was again reinstated at the Restoration.[95] During the time of his ejection he formed a small monastic commune. Versluis reports that "Richard Baxter, a contemporary of Pordage's, wrote of him in *Reliquiae Baxterianae* while discussing those in England who followed the inward light: the 'Behmenists,' he observes, 'seem to have attained to greater Meekness and conquest of the Passions than any of the rest. . . . The chiefest of these in England are Dr. Pordage and his Family, who live together in Community, and pretend to hold visible and sensible Communion with Angels.'"[96] Despite the meekness of the sect, he said, "Boehme took his views neither from Scripture nor from angels but from that 'drunken conjuror' Paracelsus," a new gnostic who paved the way for "Quakerism."[97] Gisbertus Voetius, Christian Beckman, and other Reformed theologians on the Continent shared Baxter's judgment, which Gregorius Richter had first declared. There is little doubt that this theological critique paved the way for the wider verdicts against Hermeticism by Bacon, Boyle, Mersenne, and Gassendi.

After Pordage's death, his colleague Jane Lead became the leader of the theosophical circle. Lead's mystical writings, in which she claimed to have received visions of Sophia, emphasized the divinity of the soul as a spark of the One. Undergirded by various visions, she defended Origen's doctrine of universal restoration, appealing to various Anabaptist writers. Lead renamed the Behmenist group the Philadelphia Society and launched its journal, *Theosophic Transactions*, as she maintained close associations with the French quietists and millennialists. Drawing on Hindu and Buddhist diagrams of the chakras in the human body, the group made illustrations "to show us how to go from the 'No' of the dark or wrathful world of fallen man to the 'Yes' of divinely regenerated man."[98]

94. Walsh, *Innerworldly Fulfillment*, 25.
95. Versluis, "Christian Theosophical Literature," 222.
96. Versluis, "Christian Theosophical Literature," 222.
97. Hessayon, "Jacob Boehme's Writings," 81.
98. Versluis, "Christian Theosophical Literature," 224.

Influenced by Robert Fludd and associated with the Familist sect, John Everard (1584–1641) made the first English translations of the *TG*, Tauler, Böhme, Franck, Nicholas of Cusa, and the Corpus Hermeticum. The English mystic William Law (1686–1761) made a new translation and edition of Böhme's works.[99] "[Law's] *The Spirit of Love* (1752/54) bears the unmistakable influence of theosophy," notes Versluis.[100] The influence on William Blake, particularly with his gnostic and alchemical cosmology, is obvious.[101] Isaac Newton's "library held several volumes of Boehme that had evidently been read and annotated with considerable care," and the Quakers were particularly interested in Böhme's writings.[102] A trail of mystics kept his spiritual system in circulation, but it flooded the imagination of Romantic and idealist writers (as I point out in my third volume).

Renaissance naturalism was not atheistic but pantheistic. "They believed with Giordano Bruno in the 'God in things.'" There is a convergence of ideas here,

> making possible the elaboration of the cosmic hierarchy through which divine influences are transmitted, as in hermetism; or the dissolving and compacting, material and formative forces that constitute the divine 'signature' in all things, as in alchemy; or the extrapolation of opposing active and passive forces into the very divinity itself, as in the kabbalah; or, finally, the comprehension of the essential pattern of history and its fulfillment, as in radical chiliastic speculation. Recognition of the necessity that determines all things is the pivotal step. It is reached in the discovery of the essential structure of all manifestation, which, since even God is not free to disregard it, provides the fundamental key to why all things are the way they are on every level of existence.[103]

Casaubon's Discovery: Philology over Philosophy

In a long trail of Renaissance and Reformation debunking (e.g., the Donation of Constantine, Dionysius the Areopagite), the Corpus Hermeticum itself was subjected to historical criticism. Viewed by many contemporaries as the leading Greek and patristics scholar of his day, Isaac Casaubon (1559–1614) was a professor at Geneva. Despite his Reformed convictions, he was called by Henri IV of France to the post of royal

99. See McLean's introduction in Law, *Key*, 10–11. A dedicated opponent of stage entertainments, Law wrote numerous works. Two of them made an especially great impression on John Wesley: *A Practical Treatise Upon Christian Perfection* (1726) and *A Serious Call to a Devout and Holy Life* (1729).

100. Versluis, "Christian Theosophical Literature," 227.

101. See McLean's introduction to *"Key" of Jakob Boehme*, 11.

102. Walsh, *Innerworldly Fulfillment*, 26.

103. Walsh, *Innerworldly Fulfillment*, 12.

librarian. Through Francis Bacon, James I successfully recruited Casaubon to England. The king is said to have ordered, "I will have him paid before my wife and myself."[104]

Casaubon had been working on a critique of the twelve-volume church history (*Annales Ecclesiastici*) by Cesar Baronius. An unusually critical scholar for his position as Vatican librarian, Baronius rejected the Donation of Constantine. However, he defended the Corpus Hermeticum as the work of Hermes Trismegistus testifying as a gentile prophet to the coming of Christ and the authority of the papacy.[105] Casaubon proved in 1614 that *the Corpus Hermeticum* dates to no earlier than the third and fourth centuries.[106] As Hanegraaff notes, "Today we know that Casaubon's work was, rather, the culmination of a process of historical criticism that had begun already in the 1560s . . . not only the hermetic writings were robbed of their ancient origins and turned out to be from the first centuries CE, but so were the *Chaldaean Oracles* and the *Orphic Hymns*."[107]

Casaubon's devastating textual criticism came at a time when Hermeticism was at the peak of its historical career. Casaubon was hardly alone, as Ebeling notes:

> Also skeptical was the Calvinist Matthieu Berodale, who suggested that the writings were forged. In 1575 Berodale wrote: "Some claim that Hermes is older than Pharaoh, as Suidas said. It is clear from the work called Paemander that it is ascribed to him that this view is false. For it mentions the Sibyls, who were many centuries after Pharaoh. Also, the Aesculapius to whom Hermes is writing mentions Phidias, who lived in the time of Pericles. It is thus clear that the book of Mercurius Trismegistus is forged."[108]

In the same vein, Nicholas Guibert (1547–1620) took aim at the authenticity of even the Hermetic Tabula, noting that identifying gold and silver with the names of planets finds its source in Proclus's commentary on the *Timaeus*.[109]

104. Pattison, *Isaac Casaubon*, 442–43.

105. Grafton, *Defenders*, 144–45.

106. Among other telling features, Casaubon notes how its original language was Greek and not a translation from the Egyptian, otherwise it could not contain Greek puns. The Greek, moreover, was not early but late, for it was pocked with technical terms derived from Greek philosophy and Christian theology. The author also mentions the Greek sculptor Phidias, who had lived long after the Egyptian Hermes. And the author knew more about Christian theology than any pagan (or Jewish) prophet who had lived before the birth of Christ. Such a text could not come from the chronological niche to which tradition assigned it. Grafton tells this story well in Grafton, *Defenders*, 174.

107. Hanegraaff, *Esotericism and the Academy*, 75.

108. Ebeling, *Secret History*, 95.

109. Ebeling, *Secret History*, 96.

Nevertheless, Casaubon's discovery did not disenchant true believers. After all, Lorenzo Valla's demonstration that the Donation of Constantine was a forgery came after it had already been invoked frequently by popes for secular power. The Dionysian corpus, too, had impressed itself on the medieval imagination, regardless of authorship. We see different sensibilities at work. For the heirs of the Magisterial Reformers, authenticity was determined by the production of certain texts within the circle of the apostles. Canonicity depended on strict historical-critical evaluation. In medieval theology, however, authenticity was discerned by its truth, as ascertained by the magisterium. Eco notes, "Thomas [Aquinas] repeatedly uses the term *authenticus*, but for him (and for the Middle Ages in general) the term signifies, not 'original,' but 'true.'"[110] Jan Assmann notes that

> the most important element in Hermetic tradition is the motif of revelation. The various Hermetic discourses do not draw their authority from the persuasive power of their arguments but from their appeal to a higher revelation that lies beyond mundane reason. They set this revelation on a par with that of the Bible, and if the Hermeticists can show that the Bible and the texts they ascribe to Hermes Trismegistus agree in the essential points of their theology and cosmology, then clearly both stem from the same divine source of revelation. Hermetic discourse is revelatory discourse. . . . Truth was more a matter of antiquity and origin than of coherence and evidence, a principle that has characterized Hermetic traditions down to their contemporary, postmodern manifestations. These reasons proved to be the undoing of Hermes Trismegistus, when his pseudepigraphic character was convincingly exposed by Isaac Casaubon in the year 1614.[111]

In this way, nonbiblical texts attained a quasi-canonical status simply because they could be seen as enriching, confirming, and supplementing the Christian scriptures. It is not surprising, then, that Casaubon's evidence against the dating of the Corpus Hermeticum was not only disputed but disregarded by many. Casaubon was assuming an approach that Valla, Erasmus, and his mentor at the Genevan Academy, Joseph Scaliger, helped to make standard among humanists. They were more sensitive to the view that ideas, like texts, have histories. Tradition is easier to absolutize in an age when its historical foundations are assumed. Hermeticism was a well-established tradition; philosophy trumped philology. In an age of criticism, however, the question arises: Are the texts that mediate this

110. Eco, *Labyrinth*, 234.
111. See Assmann's foreword to Ebeling, *Secret History*, ix.

tradition to us today early, with plentiful copies for comparison, and are they accurately translated? If we go back to the sources, do we find that we are heirs to a golden age, or have sources been corrupted and fakes been incorporated over intervening centuries?

Rebuttals were offered, and not only by Roman Catholics. Cambridge Platonists like Ralph Cudworth felt obliged to accept that some of the Corpus Hermeticum's text was late, but he still clung to the notion that the doctrines of the Hermetic treatises—and the perennial tradition they supported—remained unscathed. Cudworth and his associates insisted that the Asclepius was authentic and that Hermes Trismegistus was a historical figure in the distant past.[112] Cudworth still thought there was an initiation of Moses into this perennial tradition.[113] Cudworth's unflagging zeal for Hermes even after Casaubon's decisive criticism reminds us that this priority of philosophy over philology endured well into the seventeenth century. Prominent writers—including natural scientists, philosophers, and mathematicians—would continue to defend what they saw as a core of truth in spite of historical origins. This was the case all the way up to Isaac Newton.

What good can come from denying the testimony of the Sibyls and Trismegistus to the coming of Christ, asked the learned James Howell. The question was not philological or historical, but doctrinal. Why would they "'prefer John Calvin or a Casaubon' to such venerable antiques?"[114] In any case, the thrill of an oral tradition from ancient sages trumped a written canon. The very name kabbalah (tradition) attests to the wide appeal of this notion for conveying superior gnosis. On philological grounds, kabbalistic texts are no older than the late Middle Ages, but according to adherents the truth they contained was eternal. From Pythagoras onward, secrecy is essential to shield the Orphic tradition—its doctrines and legends—from historical investigation. In fact, Eco explains, "apokryphos originally meant occult and secrecy," like the apocryphal gospels. "Hence, 'apocryphal' came to signify 'excluded from the canon.'"[115] In short, the drive toward including Hermetic, gnostic, and Origenist literature was not motivated by historical examination but by agreement with whoever was including them.

Much like the contributors to the Corpus Hermeticum, Renaissance Hermeticists ranged between strict Platonism (even some with gnostic tendencies) to a Stoicized Platonism that emphasized the labor of the *magus* in uniting both

112. Ebeling, *Secret History*, 94.

113. Ebeling, *Secret History*, 93.

114. Grafton, "Protestant versus Prophet," 91. This essay remains exceptional as a documentation of Casaubon's method and argument as well as reactions.

115. Eco, *Labyrinth*, 225.

worlds. The goal of this philosophy was to discover the divine essence within oneself through a gnostic rebirth. According to the Hermetic tractate Poimander, Nous gives birth to man (image of the Father), with whom he fell in love, and handed over his creation. Then man also was permitted by the Father to imitate him by creating his own work, and each of the seven rulers contributed its own power. Nature united with man and the result was a "third thing": "astonishing offspring," seven humans, male and female, corresponding to the nature of the seven governors.[116]

As Peter French notes, "How different in origin from the man created out of dust in Genesis!" Soon, however, the body assumed by man to consummate the loving act for nature became seen by many early moderns as a burden, and the bond was broken. Bondage to the body led only to sorrow and forgetfulness. "But man can rejuvenate his divinity through intellect," French says of John Dee's view, since 'it is light and life that constitute the father of all things and man was born of him.'"[117] French continues,

> Primordial Hermetic man was identical with astral man; the true man, in the eyes of Hermeticists like Paracelsus, Agrippa, Dee and his English follower [Robert] Fludd, remained the star-demon within. On the surface, this notion seems rather innocent, but it implies a new and daring view of the universal structure, and it prepared the way for the most monumental intervention in the divine order that man had ever attempted. Through his intellect man could perform marvellous feats—it was no longer man *under* God, but God *and* man. Pico's previously quoted description of man's role in the universe fits perfectly into the Hermetic context, and so does John Dee's *Monas Hieroglyphica.* Much of the arrogant self-esteem that inspired Dee's claims about revealing universal knowledge, and strangely contrasts with his deep Christian humility, comes from this source.[118]

Conclusion

Though limping along, Hermes Trismegistus survived in learned circles where the Renaissance blending of pagan and Christian imaginations held strong. The Jesuit Egyptologist Athanasius Kircher in his *Oedipus Aegyptiacus* (1652–1654) argued that the gold of the ancients was mined, not produced by alchemy. According to

116. French, *John Dee,* 76.
117. French, *John Dee,* 73.
118. French, *John Dee,* 76.

Ebeling, "He saw the *Tabula* as nothing more than the expression of a 'One-and-All' doctrine that was already to be found in Plato's *Parmenides* and in the Hermetic Asclepius. . . . Kircher entirely overlooks Casaubon's critique of the *Corpus Hermeticum*, but he assumes that Hermes Trismegistus is a composite of several historical personalities."[119] In fact, "The Tabula Smaragdina and the Hermetic texts of alchemical content do not seem, at first, to have been affected by Casaubon's critique. The situation changed fundamentally, however, in the mid-seventeenth century. In 1648 Herman Conring, an orthodox Lutheran theologian, legal scholar, and Professor of Medicine at Helmstedt University, published a work entitled *De hermetica Aegyptiorum vetere et nova Paracelsicorum medicina liber unus*."[120]

By this time, it was revealed that Hermes Trismegistus never lived, Egyptian medicine was pure superstition and inferior to Greek medicine, and the alchemical texts were also revealed to be forgeries. Further, as Ebeling notes, "it was magic, irreconcilable with either Christian belief or general custom. The Paracelsists were harming, not helping, their patients. Nevertheless, Hermeticism enjoyed, Hermann Conring acknowledged, an uninterruptedly good reputation."[121] Paracelsus and his followers "knew absolutely nothing of the ancient Egyptian Hermetic doctrines," says Conring, but simply exploited the name of Hermes Trismegistus for their own speculations.[122]

Regardless, Böhme accepted the label *Philosophus Teutonicus*, which was supported by German Romanticism. Weeks writes that "the Protestant Peip honored him in 1860 as *der deutsche Philosoph*, but . . . wrote that, whereas Luther had 'cleansed' what he had received from German mysticism, Boehme had not."[123] "Relatively late in his life," says Versluis, "Boehme produces a corpus of work that was to inspire virtually the whole of subsequent theosophy, so much so that many later theosophers held that their spiritual lives really began only with their discovery of Bohme's vast body of writings, and even today scientists, philosophers, and literati find inspiration there."[124]

119. Ebeling, *Secret History*, 97.
120. Ebeling, *Secret History*, 97.
121. Ebeling, *Secret History*, 97.
122. Quoted in Ebeling, *Secret History*, 98.
123. Weeks, *Boehme*, 129.
124. Versluis, "Christian Theosophical Literature," 218.

8

Christianopolis

Evangelical Utopias and the "Universal Reformation"

> I launched out once more upon the Academic Sea, though the latter had very often been hurtful to me. . . . I left the port together with many others and exposed my life and person to a thousand dangers that go with a desire for knowledge.
>
> —Johann Valentin Andreae[1]

> "The End of our Foundation is the Knowledge of Causes, and secret motions of things; and the enlarging of the bounds of Human Empire, to the effecting of all things possible."
>
> —Francis Bacon's character the governor of Bensalem in *The New Atlantis*[2]

Contrasting vividly with Pico's Promethean *Oration on the Dignity of Man*, John Donne's *Anatomy of the World* encapsulates the ennui some felt at the transition from a locative to a utopian outlook:

> We seem ambitious, God's whole work t'undo; . . .
> With new diseases on our selves we war,
> And with new physic, a worse engine far.

1. Translation from Held, *Christianopolis*, 142.
2. Bacon, *New Atlantis*, 98–99.

"Thus man, this world's vice-emperor," dares to rise to the sovereign throne though God "did down to man descend."

> This man, so great, that all that is, is his,
> Oh what a trifle, and poor thing he is!
> If man were anything, he's nothing now; . . .
> And freely men confess that this world's spent,
> When in the planets, and the firmament
> They seek so many new; they see that this
> Is crumbled out again to his atomies.
> 'Tis all in pieces, all coherence gone,
> All just supply, and all relation;
> Prince, subject, father, son, are things forgot,
> For every man alone thinks he hath got
> To be a phoenix, and that then can be
> None of that kind, of which he is, but he.[3]

Donne here decries the disintegration of the feudal order and a fresh transition to the divine self. With references to "a true religious alchemy," "microcosm" and "atoms," Donne's poem gives us a window into the setting of the utopias considered in this chapter.

Right at the birth pangs of the Scientific Revolution, Hermeticism and millennialism were at their peak. Alchemy was not merely a thriving enterprise but a root metaphor with many cultural resonances. Exploration, conquest, and experimentation became commonly expressed in the alchemical language of the great work (*magnum opus*).[4] Uncharted worlds above and below, abroad and within, had to be conquered and blackened (*nigredo*). After this "dark night of the soul" followed the *albedo* (whitening or illuminating) stage—the sacred wedding between opposites, while the reddening (*rubedo*) stage signaled success in achieving the "third thing" (the child of the work). These stages echoed the mystic's ascent from purgation to contemplation to union and were correlated frequently with Joachim's three ages, the age of the Spirit being equated with the golden age. Court magi not only cast horoscopes but counseled their sovereign on state matters. By 1630, the millennialism that had been condemned as the fruit of Anabaptist

3. John Donne, "The Anatomy of the World," in *Complete English Poems*, 275–76.
4. Ralph Bauer explores the myriad facets of this phenomenon in Bauer, *Alchemy of Conquest*.

sectarianism was embraced eagerly by philosophers, statesmen, and pioneers of the Scientific Revolution.[5]

New maps of these inner and outer worlds were called for, and the charts themselves fostered a new sense of one's place in the cosmos. In every sphere of life, a utopian outlook was erasing the locative horizon. Wealth was no longer determined merely by vicissitudes of birth or land but could be carried from place to place. With self-discovery came the realization that there are options, that is, different paths toward the experience of fullness. As F. E. Held observes, the turning from syllogisms to practical affairs of life, "and especially the discovery of the western world, all tended to give man and society a new impetus—a swelling, crowding, longing desire for a fuller, freer, larger life. . . . A feeling developed that civilization could be redeemed only by stripping it of all useless and vain conventionalities; and in order that this might be done, primitive man would have to furnish the model."[6]

The hope of returning to the childlike innocence of humankind in paradise before the fall was held up by reports of discovered peoples that encouraged fictional accounts of natives whose piety put European Christianity to shame. Despite the official proscription of chiliastic eschatology by Protestant and Roman Catholic churches, expectation of an imminent dawning of the age of the Spirit spread rapidly in the last two decades of the sixteenth century. This chapter focuses on utopias envisioned in Protestant circles that had a powerful effect on the scientific age.

The Fairie Queene, the Magician, and the British Empire

For Protestants at least, Queen Elizabeth I was the harbinger of good days ahead. As Francis Yates points out, "The atmosphere of imperialist mysticism surrounding Elizabeth I" was thick with the symbolism of Astraea, who according to Greek mythology was "the just virgin of the golden age."[7] An astrologically appropriate date for Elizabeth's coronation was chosen by John Dee (1527–1608/1609), a mathematician, philosopher, alchemist, astrologer, and pioneering cartographer whose volume on navigation was essential for the voyages of exploration. Like many court astrologists, Dee was a close political advisor to the monarch and privy council. Backing Francis Drake's expeditions, he also developed a foreign policy

5. Barnes, *Prophecy and Gnosis*, 239.

6. Held, *Christianopolis*, 4–5.

7. Yates, *Giordano Bruno*, 392. For an overview, see Yates, *Occult Philosophy*.

that drew upon Arthurian legend, Joachite prophecy, and Trithemius's linking of the seven angels of the Apocalypse to the seven planets that governed the globe.[8] From England, a Reformed (and decidedly Hermetic) Christendom would spread both at home and abroad. At the queen's request, Dee wrote up a foreign policy in which he coined the name "British Empire."

While professing fidelity to "our Reformed Church," Dee was indicted regularly for practicing magic. He is a consummate example of the magician and mechanic inhabiting the same person without any sense of tension. Besides making crystal balls for communicating with angels, he created in 1543 one of the first robots: a wooden beetle that flew above the crowd during a play at Cambridge. Was this magic or mechanics? Opting for the former explanation, the university authorities prosecuted Dee for sorcery. As Yates notes, "'In those dark times,' the seventeenth-century historian John Aubrey wrote of Dee's era, 'astrologer, mathematician and conjuror were accounted the same things.'"[9] Dee is Shakespeare's Prospero and Marlowe's Doctor Faust, as picked up later by Goethe.

On the Continent, Dee and his colleague Edward Kelley laid foundations for an invisible network of collaborators for his universal reformation. In 1584, they were received by Emperor Rudolf II in Prague and King Stefan of Poland—courts steeped in Hermetic projects. Besides adopting a communal lifestyle, they "engaged in having and recording conversations with spirits who appeared to Kelley, the sensitive, in a ball or mirror, and had their messages and instructions relayed to Dee who sat in a corner of the room and wrote them down." They only performed these celestial communications after prayer and fasting, and Dee claimed that the angels had dictated several of his works, including *Monas Hieroglyphica* (Hieroglyphic monad, 1564) and *On the Mystical Rule of the Seven Planets* (1582). Apparently, they had formed a close relationship, especially with the archangels Michael and Gabriel, and Kelly convinced Dee that the angel Uriel had commanded them to share not only their possessions but also wives in common.[10]

Based on the Emerald Tablet, it was held by many Hermeticists that alchemy was inferior to astrology.[11] Clulee observes, "The problem for the alchemist was

8. In a private paper he drew up for Elizabeth at her request, entitled *The Limits of the British Empire* (1593), he sought to convince the queen that she was the prophesied Last World Emperor and that there were in fact no limits to her realm. In 1493, Pope Alexander VI had "donated" the Americas, divided between Spain and Portugal, based on their "discovery." However, Dee argued that a proper claim depended not merely on discovery but settlement, which was lacking especially in North America. See G. A. Williams, *When Was Wales?*, 124.

9. Yates, *Giordano Bruno*, 24.

10. Maxwell-Stuart, *Chemical Choir*, 98–99.

11. Clulee, "*Astronomia inferior*," 173.

how to imitate the natural process and speed up nature in its production of gold. In most views this involved the creation of an elixer or the 'philosophers' stone,' which had the power to rapidly transform large quantities of imperfect metals by rectifying their imperfect composition."[12] Yet this operation symbolized a broader process through which the *magus* brought order out of disorder, harmony out of dissonance, unity out of opposition, on psychological, cosmic, and sociopolitical and religious levels simultaneously. The divinity within the *magus* was the divinity above him and below him in the hidden recesses of corrupt matter. In Renaissance Hermeticism, we have seen how astrology, alchemy, kabbalah, and Joachite prophecy were often blended. Reconciling opposites, Protestants and Catholics, as well as matter and spirit, nature and grace, cold and hot, contrary substances, male and female, was an ordinary day in Rudolf's court.

Dee believed that numbers were the language of creation. To know these numbers in various combinations gave the *magus* power as a co-creator. "Cabalism," notes Fanning, "provided a technique for preparing invocations that could summon spirits and influence events, as prayers were supposed to do, but formulated according to systematic, almost scientific principles. Unlike prayers, such incantations would work whether one were Jewish, Catholic, or Protestant."[13] Once again we see the tendency of natural supernaturalism to subordinate, if not eliminate, God's providence and especially miraculous intervention in nature and history. Like any mechanical invention or operation, the proper spiritual technology obtained the desired results without relying directly on God's hidden will. In short, while the average believer supplicates, the *magus* operates.

At the heart of Dee's interest was that the angels would reveal the universal language, which he called "Enochian," that had been lost since the time of Adam but was nevertheless crucial to the unification of humanity. Dee calls it "real cabala." Whereas the original (literal) message is studied by scholars, Dee says his art reveals the real meaning of the words "emanating by nature or art from God himself."[14] Clulee writes, "At the root of this [Dee's] reform is the claim that the new writing of the monas reforms the basic cosmological framework in which all specific disciplines operate: Dee's uniquely modified symbol of Mercury is the 'rebuilder and restorer of all astronomy.'"[15] The third age was to time what the New World was to space: a spreading out of the imagination to new possibilities.

12. Clulee, "*Astronomia inferior*," 184.

13. Fanning, *Isaac Newton*, 18.

14. Dee, *Monas Hieroglyphica*, 124–25.

15. Clulee, "*Astronomia inferior*," 177, quoting from Dee, *Monas Hieroglyphica*, 122–23; cf. Burtt, *Metaphysical Foundations*, 60–61.

Kelley stayed on in Prague as the court astrologer and alchemist when Dee returned to England in 1605 to find his library destroyed and a new monarch on the throne. James I included warnings against magic in his own work, *On Demonology*, and the king informed Dee that his services were no longer required. His hopes of being at the helm of a magical empire faded, and the Elizabethan *magus* died in poverty. His son Arthur, who attended him in his various alchemical and astrological projects, carried on his work, which was published by Elias Ashmole.[16]

Lion of the North

The Reformed theologian Johann Heinrich Alsted (1588–1638) is considered the father of the encyclopedia and indeed his scholarly interests were wide-ranging, publishing the first Protestant treatises on metaphysics and natural theology as well as works on constitutional law, physics, and history. Alsted was also the first Reformed theologian to embrace a millennial, even Joachite, eschatology. His influence was immense.

At first, Alsted assumed a traditional Protestant nonmillennial position, anticipating the return of Christ, the last judgment, and the saints reigning with Christ in everlasting peace. Even so, he drew upon Hermetic sources, especially astrology, to make his own calculations for Christ's return. He thought the millennial age lasted from Constantine until around 1300. According to Hotson:

> As Alsted summarized the doctrine, "it is well-established from the annals of history that a great conjunction never appears without some extraordinary mutation of polity or church." . . . In Alsted's age, moreover, the theory of the great conjunctions was of more than merely historical interest; for such a conjunction had occurred in 1603, and it had coincided closely with a second great astronomical abnormality: the new star which appeared in Serpentarius, directly between Saturn and Jupiter, in early 1604, just a few months after the conjunction.[17]

Galileo likewise observed the same phenomenon as bearing apocalyptic import.[18] Hotson also reports that

16. Maxwell-Stuart, *Chemical Choir*, 103.
17. Hotson, *Alsted*, 187.
18. Maxwell-Stuart, *Chemical Choir*, 106.

> Johannes Kepler was so impressed by the intimate coincidence in both space and time of these two extraordinary events that he compared it to the coincidence of the Star of Bethlehem with the great conjunction before the First Advent of Christ and digressed from his astronomical studies to write a series of chronological treatises relating these new events to the Second Advent. Campanella believed that these extraordinary astrological events would establish the ideal conditions for realizing his utopian "City of the Sun." Retrospectively, 1604 was identified as the year in which the tomb of Christian Rosencreutz was supposedly discovered, and the new star featured prominently in Rosicrucian literature including the *Confessio fraternitatis*.[19]

In his second defense of the Rosicrucians, Robert Fludd also treated this coincidence in apocalyptic terms.[20]

Gradually, Alsted began to move in a more millennialist direction.[21] The optimism that marks Alsted's mature writing is certainly not based on his Augustinian anthropology. Hotson observes that "what is clear is that the source of Alsted's most acutely optimistic expectation for the immediate future is an astrologically based prophecy of a final period of gnostic illumination deriving from a Silesian mystical numerologist." His more millennial perspective is evident in the *Diatribe de mille annis apocalypticis* (1627). Further, Alsted embraced the Joachite ideas of Paracelsus and Michael Sendivogius concerning a northern lion, as identified with the fourth monarchy in Daniel's prophecy.[22]

The Bavarian Eustachius Poyssel is one of many examples of the growing tension between Lutheran orthodoxy and pietist chiliasm. As Barnes points out, "In his 1609 *Magic Proof* of prophetic truth, Eustachius Poyssel cited with seeming approval the opinion of 'Schwenckfeld, Osiander, Franck, and others' that 'Luther and Melanchthon established an Aristotelian theology that smacks more of the flesh than of the Spirit.'"[23] Penman adds:

> From the late 1580s he authored a series of books and pamphlets that predicted the fall of the papacy and the dawning of a golden age in 1623. . . . He was convinced that there existed a magical "key of David" that could unlock the secrets of the world in the Last Days. Paracelsus's influence may well have been crucial:

19. Hotson, *Alsted*, 187.
20. Hotson, *Alsted*, 189.
21. Hotson, *Alsted*, 190.
22. Hotson, *Alsted*, 193–97, 203.
23. Barnes, *Prophecy and Gnosis*, 238.

in 1609 Poyssel declared that a Protestant Messiah would soon arrive to lead the required "universal reformation" in the lead up to the crucial date of 1623.[24]

Another Lutheran, Johann Valentin Andreae (1586–1654), envisioned an invisible society of "Rosy Cross Brothers." The fictional Rosy Cross Order appeared with two manifestos: the *Fama Fraternitatis* (1614) and the *Confessio* (1616).[25] Grandson of the Lutheran reformer Jakob Andreae, he lived in the Duchy of Württemberg, which adjoined the Reformed Palatinate on its southern border.[26] The *Fama Fraternitatis* (News of the brotherhood) narrates the order's fictitious origins from "our Christian Father" after he toured the Middle East in search of arcane wisdom—among them, a Sufi Islamic master. Yet only now was the world ready for the mature secrets of the order to be revealed. The symbolic figure Christian Rosenkreutz ("Rosy Cross") was born in 1378, living to the age of 106, and had been lying in his tomb for 120 years. His tomb was discovered, along with his Hermetic secrets, in 1604.[27]

Dee is mentioned explicitly in the *Fama*, along with quotations and symbols from his *Hieroglyphic Monad.* Further, "A Brief Consideration of More Secret Philosophy," appended to the *Confessio*, "is based on John Dee's *Monas hieroglyphica*, much of it being word for word quotation from the *Monas*."[28] The "short reply sent by Herr Haselmayer," entitled *Answer to the Praiseworthy Brotherhood of Theosophers of Rozenkreuz*, brings the *Fama* closer still to Dee. Adam Haselmeyer, a devoted Paracelsian, was notary public to Archduke Maximillian. He lived with

24. Penman, *Hope and Heresy*, 14.

25. Authorship of the *Fama Fraternitatis* and the *Confessio* has been debated. Yates observes that Joachim Jungius, "the noted mathematician admired by Leibniz," has been put forward as author of the manifestos as early at 1698 by classical scholar and bibliographer J. A. Fabricius. "The problem is that with the destruction of the Palatinate by Ferdinand's army, and the spoiling or removal of the vast holdings of the Palatine Library, little evidence is available to us" (Yates, *Rosicrucian Enlightenment*, 127). It is generally recognized today that Andreae is the author of the manifestos and the *Chymical Wedding.* See McIntosh, *Rose Cross*, 26–27; cf. the introduction by McLean in Godwin, *Chemical Wedding*, 8–9. Donald R. Dickson points out that his father was an alchemist and his mother was an apothecary. In addition, he uses similar vocabulary and images to the *Confessio* in his *Theca gladii spiritus* (1616), and the translator of the *Fama*'s preface was Andreae's close friend, Christoph Besold. See Dickson, *Tessera of Antilia*, 18, 22, 63–66.

26. Yates, *Rosicrucian Enlightenment*, 1–23, 39, 44.

27. Relying on legend, Maurice Magre and Reginald R. Merton argue that this figure was the only member of his family who survived the Inquisition's slaughter of the Albigensian gnostics and was raised in a monastery dominated by this sect (Magre, *Return*, 114–15). Throughout this work, the authors carry a brief for Albigensianism.

28. See the commentary by McLean in Godwin, *Chemical Wedding*, 154; cf. Yates, *Rosicrucian Enlightenment*, 54–55.

Karl Widemann, secretary to Dee's partner Edward Kelley, in Prague and collected Dee's manuscripts. He was the first to describe the Rosicrucian circle from a manuscript of the *Fama* he possessed in 1610. When this manifesto for a "Universal and General Reformation of the Whole Wide World" was published four years later, his commendation was appended.[29]

Faivre notes, "The anonymous authors of the manifestos claim to be on the verge of revealing the Adamic language, which will make it possible to understand the hidden meanings of the Bible, and they quote Paracelsus as one of their principal sources of inspiration."[30] They shared "Haselmayer's belief that the Rosicrucian brotherhood had come into existence in order to fulfill certain prophecies related to the purging of Europe by Antichrist and the start of a 'Third Age,' the Age of the Spirit, and to spread the teaching of Paracelsus whose effect upon Protestant occult writers in particular was growing ever more powerful, especially as he had predicted the appearance of a kind of prophet or interpreter called Elias who would emerge 58 years after his (Paracelsus's) death."[31]

Furthermore, by using the appellation "Theosophers," Haselmayer displays some connection to Böhme, who coined the term "theosophy" soon before the *Fama* appeared. Similarities are not surprising, since Böhme's writings were appearing at this time and "Görlitz, in Lusatia on the border with Bohemia, would have made it very unlikely that someone like Böhme would not have been familiar with Dee, Kelley, Croll and Rudolph's magical court and the complete disaster of 1620 with Frederick's downfall."[32]

There is a more direct link to Böhme through Andreae's prefatory note in *Christianopolis.* He begins by saluting "our hero Doctor Luther." Luther's reforms ignited the flame, he acknowledges.

> But the secret snares of the Devil give us trouble, as a result of which our rejoicing is made less firm, and a mere name without the substance is left us. For though all our doings should be patterned after Christ, whose name we bear

29. The full title in English reads, "Universal and General Reformation of the Whole Wide World: Together with the *Fama Fraternitatis*, News of the Laudable Brotherhood of the Rosy Cross, Written to All the Erudite and the Leaders of Europe; Also a Short Reply Sent by Herr Haselmayer, for Which Reason He Was Held Prisoner by the Jesuits and Chained on a Galley. Now Put into Print and Communicated to All Loyal Hearts" (Maxwell-Stuart, *Chemical Choir*, 107). For a more recent treatment, departing from Yates at certain points, see Gilly, *Adam Haslmayr*, 106.

30. Faivre, "Renaissance Hermeticism," 116.

31. Maxwell-Stuart, *Chemical Choir*, 107.

32. Yates, *Rosicrucian Enlightenment*, 135.

> and confess, yet it happens on account of our weak indulgence that Christians differ in no respect from men of the world. . . . And yet that impostor does not deceive all, and least of all those who have a higher light within. . . . From their number I will mention only Doctor John Gerhard, Doctor John Arndt, and Doctor Mart.[33]

Of the three who "have a higher light within," only Gerhard received a doctorate. "Doctor Mart" is Martin Möller, the self-taught mystical poet and preacher in whose circle Jakob Böhme was a devoted follower. "Möller," he adds, is "especially deserving of it [viz., praise] of me, most upright theological scholars, although [he] is a little disturbed on the subject of the Lord's Supper."[34] Andreae's sympathy for these figures centered on their concern for piety over doctrine. The *Confession* followed in 1616, which Lutheran and Reformed churches could only have seen as an alternative to their own confessions. As McLean puts the matter, "Rosicrucianism seems to have arisen as an antithesis to the development of the codified Protestantism of Luther and Calvin."[35] The Latin manifestos circulated widely in the international intellectual network known as the Republic of Letters and were very soon translated into other languages.[36]

In 1604, Simon Studion published an apocalyptic and prophetic work, entitled *Naometria*, interpreting immediate events in the light of biblical prophecy, numerology, and the measurements of Solomon's Temple.[37] Among his provocative predictions was that Islam and the papacy would fall, and the pope would be crucified in 1604. Playing with Joachim's date of 1260, Studion was convinced that the age of the Spirit would dawn in 1620.[38] Studion links these predictions with "those of the Abbot Joachim, St. Brigid, Lichtenberg, Paracelsus, Postel, and other *illuminati*."[39] McLean argues that the dates surrounding the fictional Christian Rosenkreutz—entombed for 120 years—"corresponds to the cycle of 120 years which Simon Studion . . . indicated in his *Naometria* manuscript as being the basis for the unfolding of spiritual impulses in time. Studion also identified the year 1604 as central to his thesis and undoubtedly his work provides the basis for Rosicrucian chronology." Thus, it is plausible to conclude that the whole story

33. Held, *Christianopolis*, 134–35.

34. Held, *Christianopolis*, 134–35.

35. See the commentary by McLean in Godwin, *Chemical Wedding*, 155.

36. The *Fama Fraternitatis* (1614) soon appeared in Dutch (1615), French (1616), Italian (1617) and eventually in English (1652). See Held, *Christianopolis*, 11 n. 1.

37. Yates, *Rosicrucian Enlightenment*, 43.

38. Ákerman, "Rosicrucians," 4–5.

39. Yates, *Rosicrucian Enlightenment*, 46–47. Cf. Waite, *Brotherhood*, 641.

of Father Rosenkreutz is a deliberate fiction to give veiled support to Studion's Joachite prophecies.[40]

Suffused with millennial and Hermetic influences, Württemberg—especially its seminary, the Tübinger Stift—was a center of pietism.[41] Also, Andreae's father was an alchemist and his mother was an apothecary, so he knew how to host a "chymical wedding." The explicit mention of Dee along with symbols and paraphrases of his *Hieroglyphic Monad* are not surprising in this context. At the Stift, Andreae became a friend of Kepler, whose mystical Trinitarianism is also similar to Böhme's.[42] Andreae and Kepler kept up continual correspondence until the latter's death.[43] Andreae also came under the influence of Studion's millennialism through the Paracelsian physician Tobias Hess and the jurist Christoph Besold. That Andreae and Hess worked collaboratively is demonstrated from their references to each other's works.[44] Andreae himself mentioned the *Naometria* in his *Turris Babel* (1619). It was just such prophecies that encouraged the rash move of some to pin all hopes on the Elector Palatine and the Bohemian crown.

In short, Andreae's original circle of Rosy Cross Brothers consisted of Paracelsians with a strong interest in Studion's version of Joachite prophecy. Yates correctly perceives that "Simon Studion's *Naometria* and the 'Militia Evangelica' which it describes, is a basic source for the Rosicrucian movement."[45] From Müntzer, Franck, Weigel, and Böhme, there was an unbroken chain to Andreae and his friends. "The key to their universal reformation, which aimed at completing the Lutheran Reformation, should therefore be found in religious Hermeticism." It was nothing less than "The Harmonious Fellowship of the Eternal Sons."[46] This unification would come through a universal reform beyond the Reformation.

40. See McLean's commentary in Godwin, *Chemical Wedding*, 154.

41. A native of radical pietism's seedbed in Württemberg, Andreae studied at its University of Tübingen and became a major advocate of the Tübinger Stift, the evangelical seminary established by Duke Ulrich, whose alumni would include Kepler, Bengel, Oetinger, Hölderlin, Hegel, Schelling, D. F. Strauss, F. C. Oetinger, and F. C. Bauer. Nietzsche would quip, "One need merely say, 'Tübinger Stift' to understand what German philosophy is at bottom—an insidious theology" (Nietzsche, *Twilight and Anti-Christ*, 133).

42. Alexandr Koyré sees a close affinity with the Rosicrucians in Koyré, *Philosophie*, 34, 42.

43. Held, *Christianopolis*, 12.

44. Andreae commemorated Hess's work by drawing together his manuscripts as *Theca gladii spiritus* (1616), which included many references to Andreae's work from 1612. See Dickson, *Tessera of Antilia*, 762.

45. Yates, *Rosicrucian Enlightenment*, 46–47. Cf. Waite, *Brotherhood*, 641.

46. Edighoffer, "Hermeticism," 213.

The Rosicrucian manifestos called the merely "formal" Christians to rebirth, which reconciles man with nature.[47]

Without the appearance of the *Chymical Wedding*, the secret and seemingly imaginary Rosy Cross society may have passed into oblivion, McLean argues. Here the order possesses "a great mystery indeed, the mystery of inner transformation."[48] Like the manifestos, this strange work is laden with symbols taken from Dee's *Hieroglyphic Monad*. It begins with a woman appearing in a vision, inviting the narrator to a wedding. Her "exceedingly aged son" announces the imminent fulfillment of the prophecy "when all men shall be equals, and no one will be rich or poor. . . . From all this I concluded that I was invited by God to attend this secret and occult wedding."[49] As the author traces each of the seven days of his angelic visitation, he presents attendance at the wedding as a reward for strenuous cleansing of body and soul—each prisoner, including himself, being weighed in the scales by the virgin bride. Being found worthy, the author is set free with great ceremony and allowed to choose one prisoner to free, and he becomes an advisor to the rest.[50]

On the fourth day, the narrator is led to a fountain, where a lion holds a tablet bearing the worn inscription, "Prince Hermes. After so many injuries done to the human race, by God's counsel, and by the aid of art, here I flow, made a healing medicine. Drink from me who can; wash who wishes; stir who dares; drink, brethren, and live."[51] On this day the narrator also makes bold to ask the virgin her name, which she reveals in the form of a riddle, which, as Leibniz was the first to decipher, is "ALCHYMIA."[52] The old queen in the allegory is probably theology. "These two are the complementary facets of Sophia," McLean suggests.[53] After washing, the narrator and his companions are led up the 365 steps to the wedding hall where the king and queen preside in splendor, with musicians inspired by Orpheus.[54] A sumptuous feast is enjoyed, and afterward a comedy is staged, with a bewildering blend of biblical and pagan imagery. Like Hamlet's play within a play, the comedy presents *in nuce* the allegory's meaning.[55]

47. Edighoffer, "Hermeticism," 197.
48. See McLean's introduction in Godwin, *Chemical Wedding*, 9.
49. Godwin, *Chemical Wedding*, 20–21.
50. Godwin, *Chemical Wedding*, 40–41.
51. Godwin, *Chemical Wedding*, 60.
52. See McLean's commentary in Godwin, *Chemical Wedding*, 125.
53. See McLean's commentary in Godwin, *Chemical Wedding*, 127.
54. Godwin, *Chemical Wedding*, 60–62.
55. Godwin, *Chemical Wedding*, 63–68, 97–102.

From "a great white egg" a naked bird is hatched that becomes transformed through various plumages (black, white, then multicolored) by consuming the blood of the king and queen. These colors were well known as the alchemical stages of *nigredo*, *albedo*, and *rubedo*.[56] However, the false companions are engaged in a merely natural work of transmuting metals; Rosenkreutz's alchemy is higher, bringing resurrection and new birth. The king and queen, whose true spiritual essence is symbolized by the bird, become transformed through this alchemical process.[57] The crisis introduced by opposition and its resolution in a "third thing" (synthesis) is typical of alchemy's operation, producing the "child of the work." This descent into death (crisis of antitheses), if successful, leads to new birth, which McLean takes to be the central point of the allegory:

> [It] is subtly hinted at in the opening sentence which shows that the events begin on Easter Eve, the Saturday evening upon which symbolically the Christ or divine spiritual impulse died and descended into the earth in order to be resurrected and reborn. . . . If we center the process on the young King or Bridegroom, we see that he has to die on the Fourth Day, and in order for this act to take place he must have gathered to himself a group of adepts whom he can make responsible for his resurrection.[58]

The imaginary author has ascended through three domains. "In the outer world, Christian Rosenkreutz is a Brother of the Red-Rosie Cross, while in the domain of the Castle he becomes a Knight of the Golden Fleece, and later, after the successful ascent of the Tower, he is made a Knight of the Golden Stone." On the seventh day, the bridegroom king is reborn, calling Christian Rosenkreutz his "father."[59] There is nothing distinctively Christian, much less evangelical, in this fascinating work. As McLean observes, "The events unfold like an ancient Greek or Egyptian initiation ritual rather than incorporating definitive Christian elements, such as atonement and redemption through the suffering of a Christ figure for the sins of the world." Indeed, none of the characters can be seen legitimately as Christ figures.[60]

56. See McLean's commentary in Godwin, *Chemical Wedding*, 143.
57. See McLean's commentary in Godwin, *Chemical Wedding*, 144, 147.
58. See McLean's commentary in Godwin, *Chemical Wedding*, 119–20.
59. See McLean's commentary in Godwin, *Chemical Wedding*, 122, 124.
60. See McLean's commentary in Godwin, *Chemical Wedding*, 154.

Christianopolis

With his fictional utopia *Christianopolis* (1618), Andreae is more explicit in his description of an ideal evangelical society.[61] However, it is milder in its Hermetic chiliasm. In this story, Europeans on a ship called Phantasy are driven by a storm to Caphar Salama, "City of Peace."[62] After they land, a guide approaches the sailors with its leader interrogating the crew.

> He asked me, in most pleasant terms it is true, to what extent I had learned to control myself and to be of service to my brother; to fight off the world, to bring harmony with death, to follow the Spirit; what progress I had made in the observation of the heavens and the earth, in the close examination of nature, in instruments of the arts, in the history and origin of languages, the harmony of all the world; what relation I bore toward the society of the church, toward a compendium of the Scriptures, the kingdom of heaven, the school of the Spirit, the brotherhood of Christ, the household of God.[63]

If we use F. Ernest Stoeffler's categories, Andreae is a churchly rather than radical pietist, as the guide's question about his relation to "the society of the church" implies.[64] In the beginning he was on the more radical end of the spectrum but by the time he writes *Christianopolis* he had become more conservative, as I explain below. "It is a fascinating mixture of the mystical and the practical," Yates notes, "with a large temple and officials bearing angel's names (Uriel, Gabriel, etc.)." There is a college at the center. The religion is intensely pietistic, and the culture just as intensely scientific, especially mechanics and mechanical arts, chemistry, alchemy, and medicine, with natural history painted on the walls, tools, and all of these crowned by mystical mathematics.[65]

Christianopolis prefers aristocracy to monarchy. Leaders reach common consent in decisions and are themselves elected without any care for lineage but only

61. Held, *Christianopolis*, 140–41. Held quotes here a poignant evaluation by Johann Herder in 1782: "All that Andreae writes takes the form of the fable—the expression in clever garb (*Einkleidung*); he speaks truths to which we hardly venture to give utterance now, after a hundred years' advancement. He speaks them with as much love and honesty, as brevity and sagacity; so that even yet he stands new and fresh in this quarreling, heretical century, and blooms in delicate fragrance like a rose among thorns."

62. Held, *Christianopolis*, 145.

63. Held, *Christianopolis*, 148.

64. Stoeffler, *Evangelical Pietism*.

65. Yates, *Rosicrucian Enlightenment*, 189.

virtuous education and godly living.[66] They have order without domination. In contrast, he laments the incompleteness of the Reformation at home: "And now because the church has renounced these principles, she has become richer and more formidable, but not at all holier, she who could not be influenced even in her last cleansing to lay aside arrogance and harshness and persuade her curators to use a more sensible government. And so the Christian grieves and is kept in the midst of Christianity, neither giving orders nor yet sufficiently obeying."[67]

Eschewing vows of poverty and conspicuous wealth, these Christians embrace moderation.[68] "No one owns a private house," he says, but people live in healthy and bright homes with modest furniture and a balcony.[69] The armory is located far away from the citizens, who despise war but distribute weapons to each family for self-defense against invaders.[70]

The narrator is led finally to the college.[71] "All the children of citizens in general, children of both sexes, are taken into training. When they have completed their sixth year, the parents give them over to the state, not without prayers and pious vows.... Moreover, they can visit their children, even unseen by them, as often as they have leisure."[72] Women no less than men are expected to be educated.[73]

With respect to religion, says Andreae, "Looking all things over, I might have suspected this place of being some fanatical city, since, in the world whatever seeks the skies is heretical. But a double plate on which stood the sum of their confession and profession inscribed in letters of gold soon freed me from error. The words of the tablet, as I wrote them down, have the following import." In contrast with the natural religion of More and Campanella, this tablet includes the Nicene Creed with evangelical interpretations.[74]

66. Held, *Christianopolis*, 174 and 165.

67. Held, *Christianopolis*, 168–69.

68. Held, *Christianopolis*, 239.

69. Held, *Christianopolis*, 169–70.

70. Held, *Christianopolis*, 192.

71. Held, *Christianopolis*, 173.

72. Held, *Christianopolis*, 208.

73. Held, *Christianopolis*, 210.

74. Held, *Christianopolis*, 176–77. It includes belief in creation *ex nihilo*, with nature as originally good but fallen into sin. Moreover,

> We believe that by His life, suffering, and death He has given satisfaction to the justice of God, that mercy has been merited, the same has been brought to us through the Gospels, given over to our faith, entrusted to the purity of life, and that thence the dominion of sin was crucified, destroyed, and buried.... We believe in a holy universal church, purified by the water of baptism from infancy, and fed by the communion of the Eucharist, thus guarded with the seals of the new covenant, taught in

The library is filled with books from every continent, read assiduously by all citizens. Nevertheless, "The highest authority among them is that of sacred literature, that is, of the Divine Book; and this is the prize which they recognize as conceded by divine gift to men and of inexhaustible mysteries."[75] At every point along the way, the leader of the visitors is introduced to a Christ-centered piety that governs all arts and sciences. There are laboratories and hands-on classrooms, even distinct schools of astrology, numerology, prophecy, metaphysics, theology, and theosophy.

Astrology and alchemy are valued, but citizens are taught to distinguish genuine practitioners from "peddlers and quacks." In fact, Andreae distances himself from an earlier connection with such charlatans.[76] As usual, Andreae concludes each scene by contrasting it with the status quo: "How easily bought is the human race which has sold its Christian liberty to Antichrist, its natural liberty to tyranny, and its human liberty to sophistry; and has surrendered its wretched efforts for the cheapest return: superstition, servitude, and ignorance!"[77]

Despite the antischolastic polemic, Andreae's utopian education takes students through the stages of grammar, dialectic, and rhetoric.[78] The purpose of logic is "to learn to apply the instruments of method to every variety of human affairs, to classify whatever is necessarily true, what is possible, and where some fallacy of judgment lurks." However, the dialectical wrangling of the "sophists" is discouraged.[79]

The guide explains, "This same hall serves also for the study of something still higher, and this is theosophy, a science which does not recognize any human invention or research, but which owes its whole existence to God." Here, God reveals himself not through reason but "in a moment."[80] Arithmetic and geometry, in-

---

> the ministry of the Word, disciplined with the cross, ready to serve in prayers, active in charity, generous in communion, powerful in excommunication, which though distributed over the earth, the unity of faith joins, the diversity of gifts strengthens, Christ, the Bridegroom and Head, renders invincible, and which the standing of the different classes and the purity of marriage embellish.

The confession concludes, "We believe in a free forgiveness of sins through the ministry of the Word, and in the obligation of our gratitude and obedience on account of this," and in heaven and hell.

75. Held, *Christianopolis*, 191.
76. Held, *Christianopolis*, 197.
77. Held, *Christianopolis*, 196.
78. Held, *Christianopolis*, 213–14.
79. Held, *Christianopolis*, 215–16.
80. Held, *Christianopolis*, 217–18.

cluding mystical numerology, are also important.[81] Music, the fourth department, eschews the songs of "Venus and Bacchus" for the Psalms.[82]

Astronomy is the fifth department of the Christian republic. On the one hand, Andreae's citizens reject the idea of astral determinism as contrary to divine sovereignty and human liberty.[83] But those who think the stars have no governing effect in the sublunar realm are foolish. It is by faith in Christ that they triumph over whatever influence the stars may have over their lives.[84] They break free from their horoscope by the victory of Christ over the celestial powers.[85] At the same time, "let us not excuse the stupidity of those who . . . foolishly scorn the very sky. . . . For he who does not know the value of astrology in human affairs, or who foolishly denies it, I would wish that he would have to dig in the earth, cultivate and work the fields, for as long a time as possible, in unfavorable weather."[86] It is because of their piety toward God that the people of this republic devote so much energy to natural science, the sixth department. "He who recognizes Christian liberality will never subject himself to the base servitude of creatures."[87] This, as we will see, becomes a major feature of Bacon's *New Atlantis* and *Instauration.* Natural supernaturalism has placed humans under the determinism of purely natural bodies. Christ has freed us from this fear.

There is a school of prophecy in Christianopolis, treating contemporary claims with neither excessive suspicion nor credulity.[88] The eighth and final school "is devoted to theology, the queen of all that human beings possess, and the mistress of philosophy."[89] Despite a higher appreciation for theology, Andreae shares the broader pietist criticism of academic debates: "This they call scholastic theology." Instead, "they do tend toward preparing one for accomplishing something."[90] Their theology is for living, not disputing.[91]

The last sections of *Christianopolis* describe the lavish gardens, some for medicinal research and applications, others simply for their beauty. "Let us lament the lost paradise and long for its restoration. For though we look upon natural

81. Held, *Christianopolis*, 221–22.
82. Held, *Christianopolis*, 223–24.
83. Held, *Christianopolis*, 227–28.
84. Held, *Christianopolis*, 229.
85. Held, *Christianopolis*, 229.
86. Held, *Christianopolis*, 229.
87. Held, *Christianopolis*, 231–32.
88. Held, *Christianopolis*, 243–44.
89. Held, *Christianopolis*, 240–41.
90. Held, *Christianopolis*, 240–41.
91. Held, *Christianopolis*, 242–43.

objects now with faulty vision, when our sight has been restored through the cross, we will behold all things not on the surface, but in their inmost depths."[92] There are no hotels in Christianopolis because people take foreigners into their homes.[93] "God forbid that I should ever suffer myself to be separated from this republic!"[94] But the chancellor discourages Andreae's visitor from regarding Christianopolis as a utopia. "As all human beings are imperfect," he says, "we have not been able to show you anything beyond our mortal lot; but we have lessened the burdens of our mortality, we trust, and according to the pattern which we have shown you."[95]

Andreae Considers Rosicrucianism a Joke

The Rosicrucian manifestos are stamped by the radical pietism in which millennialism, Hermetic magic, and the kabbalistic philosophies of Paracelsus and Böhme were fused. However, things changed in 1610. Andreae was considered too radical and was driven out of the community, whereupon he reconsidered his orientation.[96] In the same year, Andreae visited Geneva.[97] His description of Geneva's flourishing educational institutions, diaconal system, and generosity to strangers—suffused throughout by simple piety—served as a model for Christianopolis.

Returning to study theology at the Tübinger Stift, he acquired a more moderate, though still quite millennial, pietism. He was interested in the Renaissance Hermeticism of More and Campanella.[98] However, he was now focused on a distinctively Christian pietism that did not marginalize the visible church or the distinctive truths of the faith. Already in 1617 (in his *Christian Mythology*) he had called it a "lampoon" (*ludibrium*), like one of the comic stage plays that he enjoyed. In *Christianopolis* and *Turris Babel,* both published in 1619, Andreae disowns the "Rosy Cross" fiction.[99] Andreae still gave an important place in *Christianopolis* to

92. Held, *Christianopolis*, 268–69.

93. Held, *Christianopolis*, 272–73.

94. Held, *Christianopolis*, 278.

95. Held, *Christianopolis*, 278.

96. Dickson, "Utopian Brotherhoods," 769–70.

97. Andreae, *Vita*, 24, quoted in Held, *Christianopolis*, 13.

98. Andreae was familiar also with Campanella's *City of the Sun* and even translated several of his sonnets in 1619. Held adds that Andreae speaks of him as "the talented, untiring, heroic champion against the heathen Aristotle and against all hypocrites, sophists, and tyrants" (Held, *Christianopolis*, 20–21).

99. Held, *Christianopolis*, 137.

theosophy, astrology, alchemy, kabbalah, and number mysticism, but with significant qualifications and with an explicitly evangelical gloss.[100] In 1617 and 1618 he was still building his *Christliche gottliebende Gesellschaft* (Christian God-loving society) in Calw. Although his Christian Society was destroyed in the war, as late as 1628 he still planned a *unio Christiana*. Kepler showed interest in it, and Leibniz sought later to revive its embers.

A further reason for Andreae's sudden distancing from the Rosicrucian fiction is the tempest it caused when the legatee of John Dee, Robert Fludd, published two treatises defending the Brotherhood right on the heels of the manifestos' publication. Appropriating the invisible society for advancing his own extreme version of Paracelsian Hermeticism, Fludd provoked a controversy that involved the pioneers of modern science. Andreae now called the whole Rosy Cross fiction a joke or stage play of his youth, distancing himself from both the extremism that attracted Fludd and the controversy that ensued. Instead of peace and brotherhood, the whole episode brought strife and disputation.

One final reason for Andreae's withdrawal from the fiction is the fate of Frederick V, Elector of the Palatinate and head of the Protestant Union of princes. The Reformed nobility of Bohemia managed to crown Frederick and his wife Elizabeth Stuart (daughter of King James of England) king and queen in Prague. But Protestant hopes were soon dashed. Simultaneous with Böhme's works, Andreae's writings appeared as Catholic and Protestant forces were taking battle positions. The cheerful optimism of the Rosy Cross tracts, especially the *Chymical Wedding*, was darkened on November 8, 1620, at the Battle of White Mountain, which effectively launched the Thirty Years' War. Leading a combined army of twenty-three thousand against the Protestant princes, the Habsburg emperor took the Bohemian crown, assumed Frederick's lands in the Palatinate, decimated Heidelberg, and carried off to Rome its famous library, the Biblioteca Palatina.[101] At the same time, Robert Fludd's defense of the Rosicrucians served to substantiate the fear that there was a real-life order of secret mystics infiltrating European cities.

Bacon's *New Atlantis*

Although Francis Bacon (1561–1626) was twenty-five years older than Andreae, his *New Atlantis* appeared eight years after *Christianopolis*, and the *Fama Fraternitatis* and *Confessio* had been circulating widely for a decade. There are close parallels

100. Held, *Christianopolis*, 197.
101. Yates, *Rosicrucian Enlightenment*, 40.

between these utopian works, but Andreae's came first. Bacon's *New Atlantis* was an untitled and undated manuscript attached to Bacon's 1626 *Sylva Sylvarum, or a Natural History in Ten Centuries*. Written in English around 1623, *The New Atlantis* was translated into Latin and published in 1627, a year after his death. He names his utopia Bensalem, "offspring of peace," which he identifies as a Pacific island somewhere west of Peru.[102] While Bacon's *Great Instauration* was the programmatic essay of experimental philosophy, his *New Atlantis* reveals a concrete picture of such a society.

In his opening address to King James, who appointed him Lord Verulam, an aged Bacon begs the monarch to continue the philosopher's "example in taking order for the collecting and perfecting of a Natural and Experimental History, true and severe (unencumbered with literature and book-learning), such as philosophy may be built upon." He explains in his preface to the reader his judgment that people overrate their tools while underrating their strength. They rely on "endless repetitions of the same thing, varying in the method of treatment, but not new in substance." The Renaissance has recovered ancient texts, but this has led merely to modern imitators and epigones, competing schools that never advance forward.

> And for its value and utility it must be plainly avowed that wisdom which we have derived principally from the Greeks is but like the boyhood of knowledge, and has the characteristic property of boys: it can talk, but it cannot generate; for it is fruitful of controversies but barren of works . . . barking disputations . . . and all the tradition and succession of schools is still a succession of masters and scholars, not of inventors and those who bring to further perfection the things invented. In the mechanical arts we do not find it so.[103]

The making of machines advances by building on previous inventions, while natural philosophy returns to age-old disputes.[104] Bacon is famous not for any invention of his own but for sounding a clarion call for nothing less than the independence of what we call science from natural philosophy.

Impatient with this state of affairs, Lord Verulam supplements programmatic essays with an exercise of imagination. Sailing from Peru "for China and Japan, by the South Sea," the ship is tossed by "strong and great winds from the south."[105]

102. Bacon's "Atlantis" is what remains of North America after a cataclysm.

103. Bacon, *New Atlantis*, 8–9.

104. Bacon, *New Atlantis*, 10.

105. Bacon, *New Atlantis*, 63–65.

Shipwrecked, they row toward an unknown island. As they approach the shore, the leader stands up in the boat "and with a loud voice in Spanish, asked, 'Are ye Christians?'"[106]

The visitors are treated to a hearty dinner and ask who first brought Christianity to the island, given its remoteness "from the land where our Saviour walked on earth." The governor explains that about twenty years after Christ's ascension "a great pillar of light" descended with "a large cross of light" at the top. "One of the wise men of the society of Salomon's House, which house or college is the very eye of this kingdom," dared to approach the shining column of light. He prayed, acknowledging God's grace in giving the inhabitants a knowledge of nature and of grace "and to discern (as far as appertaineth to the generation of men) between divine miracles, works of nature, works of art, and impostures and illusions of all sorts." Suspicious of false miracles, the wise man of Salomon's House testified that "the thing which we now see before our eyes is thy Finger and a true Miracle." The column of light disappeared but revealed a chest in which was found a complete Bible, even the parts of the New Testament that had not yet been written. There was also a letter from St. Bartholomew, relating how an angel told him to put this ark to sea.[107]

The visitors next ask why the citizens of Bensalem are not known by others, even though they know so much about every other people and land. The spokesman assures the governor "that we were apt enough to think there was somewhat supernatural in this island; but yet rather as angelical than magical." This statement reveals Bacon's distance from natural supernaturalism: miracles are not magic.[108] The ancient ruler ordained that "every twelve years there should be set forth out of this kingdom two ships, appointed to several voyages," always attended by "a mission of three of the Fellows or Brethren of Salomon's House; whose errand was only to give us knowledge of the affairs and state of those countries to which they were designed, and especially of the sciences, arts, manufactures, and inventions of the world; and withal to bring unto us books, instruments, and patterns in every kind."[109] Aside from any Rosy Cross Order, there were plenty of Protestant courtiers shuttling between European capitals who could be described in this way.[110]

Later, the leader of the visitors meets Joabin, part of a Jewish community that

106. Bacon, *New Atlantis*, 66.
107. Bacon, *New Atlantis*, 69–76.
108. Bacon, *New Atlantis*, 78–82.
109. Bacon, *New Atlantis*, 84–86.
110. Bacon, *New Atlantis*, 84–86.

resided in Bensalem since pre-Christian times. Unlike Jews elsewhere, those in Bensalem accept Christ's virgin birth and that he was more than human, but they do not accept him as the divine Son of God.[111] Suddenly news is brought of the surprising arrival of one of the fathers of Salomon's House, who has learned of these visitors, and Joabin promises a private audience with this "Father" who blessed him and divulged the secret order's mission: "The End of our Foundation is the Knowledge of Causes, and secret motions of things; and the enlarging of the bounds of Human Empire, to the effecting of all things possible." This is exactly Bacon's program. The father divulges the massive caves under mountains, reaching three miles deep, and the high towers rising three miles above-ground. The former are used for mining as well as for "coagulations, indurations [hardenings], refrigerations, and conservations of bodies." Some hermits live there as voluntary subjects for tests on the prolongation of life. From the high towers are observed meteors and other astronomical phenomena.[112]

A host of experiments are conducted on the island, including transforming salt to fresh lakes, grafting trees to create new growths, and various animals into new ones. The guide continues, "We make a number of kinds of serpents, worms, flies, fishes, of putrefaction [decaying matter], whereof some are advanced (in effect) to be perfect creatures, like beasts or birds, and have sexes and do propagate. Neither do we this by chance, but we know beforehand of what matter and commixture what kind of those creatures will arise."[113]

There are also many medicine shops—these include "dispensaries," "furnaces of great diversities . . . whereby we produce admirable effects," and "perspective-houses" that multiply differently colored lights "which we carry to great distance" and from which they devise microscopes.[114] The people make metals and gems, including "loadstones of prodigious virtue, both natural and artificial." There are "sound-houses"—like audio studios—and "engine-houses, where are prepared engines and instruments for all sorts of motions," and even cannons that far exceed anything known in Europe.[115]

Significantly, the guide adds, "We have also houses of deceits of the senses; where we represent all manner of feats as juggling, false apparitions, impostures, and illusions, and their fallacies." They could easily be adduced as miracles to the superstitious. "But we do hate all impostures and lies." Twelve fellows of the

111. Bacon, *New Atlantis*, 91–92.
112. Bacon, *New Atlantis*, 98–99.
113. Bacon, *New Atlantis*, 101–3.
114. Bacon, *New Atlantis*, 104–5.
115. Bacon, *New Atlantis*, 106–7.

Society "sail into foreign countries under the names of other nations (for our own we conceal) who bring us the books, and abstracts, and patterns of experiments of all other parts. These we call Merchants of Light." There are other divisions into threes who follow upon these reports: "Mystery-Men" who collect the experiments, "Compilers," and the "Benefactors" who examine the experiments to discern their usefulness. There are also three individuals who "direct new experiments, of a higher light, more penetrating into nature than the former."[116]

The Andreae and Bacon Connection

Frances Yates draws a line of Hermetic kabbalistic magi from John Dee to Giordano Bruno and Tommaso Campanella via the Hermetic court of Frederick V as leader of the Protestant Union, which led to the Scientific Revolution. The whole aura of the work anticipates Freemasonry, she says:

> By the diffusion of a philosophy, or a theosophy, or a Pansophia, which they hoped might be accepted by all religious parties, the members of this movement perhaps hoped to establish a non-sectarian basis for a kind of freemasonry—I use this word here only for its general meaning and without necessarily implying a secret society—which would allow persons of differing religious views to live together peaceably. The common basis would be a common Christianity, interpreted mystically, and a philosophy of Nature which sought the divine meaning of the hieroglyphic characters written by God in the universe, and interpreted microcosm and microcosm through mathematical-magical systems of universal harmony.[117]

While this is an accurate description of Freemasonry, it fails to recognize the distinguishing character of what we may call the evangelical enlightenment. Yates makes a number of educated hunches linking Dee, Bruno, and Campanella with Bacon and Andreae.[118] She draws occult connections also to the court

116. Bacon, *New Atlantis*, 108–9.

117. Yates, *Rosicrucian Enlightenment*, 134–35.

118. For example, Yates locates the castle of the *Chymical Wedding* in "Heidelberg castle owned by the Palatine Lion." The prayer books in the room where guests knelt for prayer "might refer to Elizabeth's plain, Puritan oratory, to her English prayer books, and to the divine significance of her wedding—that wedding which had been celebrated with such pomp and circumstance in London as a wedding 'for religion'" (*Rosicrucian Enlightenment*, 94).

of Frederick V.[119] However, Carlos Gilly and Didier Kahn have shown that such Reformed centers were decidedly anti-Hermetic; Calvinists identified Rosicrucians with Anabaptist spiritualists.[120] Calvinists on the Continent held the same suspicions of Hermetic theories as Dee's English critics.[121] As an Anglican Calvinist, Bacon's Bensalem would never have had schools of theosophy, astrology, and prophecy. Nor would it have entertained mystical numerology and other features found in Christianopolis. However, Andreae hedges these practices with qualifications and emphasizes, as does Bacon, that the close study of nature makes it possible to distinguish truth from falsehood.[122]

Bacon was very familiar with More's *Utopia*, of course, and he acknowledged his acquaintance with Campanella's ideas.[123] A common influence across all these utopias is Erasmus's *philosophia Christi* and the ideal of a Christian commonwealth as a vast monastery (which could fit well with Joachite visions of the third age). They were united by humanist antipathy to scholasticism and contrasted their utopias with a Christendom riven by factions, pride, and vice.

However, the natural religion of Utopians and Solarians in More's work con-

119. Yates states that Christian I of Anhalt "was an enthusiastic Calvinist, but like so many other German Protestant princes at this time he was deeply involved in mystical and Paracelsist movements." How do we know this? "He was the patron of Oswald Croll, Cabalist, Paracelsist, and alchemist. And his Bohemian connections were of a similar character" (*Rosicrucian Enlightenment*, 47–49). Croll certainly was as Yates describes him. His *Basilica Chymica* (Chemical Cathedral) of 1609 may have influenced Andreae's 1616 *Chymical Wedding*. Closely connected to the Bohemian occult network, Croll praises Hermes Trismegistus as the father of true science (69–71). Nevertheless, Croll was merely Christian's physician, and the prince's personal engagement with Hermetic practices is unknown. Furthermore, Bruno's cold receptions in Geneva and Oxford deprive him of any formative role in this narrative. Although it is possible that Bruno left behind some followers in Wittenberg, there is insufficient evidence that they were part of Andreae's circle.

120. See Kahn, "Rosicrucian Hoax," 242. "As for the court of Heidelberg," says Kahn, "it was scarcely, if at all, interested in the Rosicrucian movement, and when it became interested, it was not to support it, but to condemn it as a whole. It is moreover in the reformed University of Marburg and on the order of the Calvinist landgrave Moritz von Hessen-Kassel that in 1619–20, the first trial for Weigelianism, Rosicrucianism and other 'errors' stemming from the 'Theophrastic move' [Paracelsus] took place." Gilly's groundbreaking work on Adam Haslmayr demonstrates the same conclusion. See Gilly, *Adam Haslmayr*.

121. See Kahn, "Rosicrucian Hoax," 241. Moreover, Andreae's Lutheran commitment is evident in the Rosicrucian writings. It was not Frederick but the Lutheran princes of Württemberg and Anhalt whom Tobias Hess designated as the Last World Emperor in 1605, "and Adam Haslmayr in 1611 endeavored to set up as political leaders of the future universal reform" (Kahn, "Rosicrucian Hoax," 241–42).

122. Held, *Christianopolis*, 218.

123. Held, *Christianopolis*, 47.

trasts sharply with the frankly evangelical character of Andreae's Christianopolis and Bacon's Bensalem. Unlike the utopias of More, Bruno, and Campanella as well as those of Anabaptist spiritualists and radical pietists, the utopias of Andreae and Bacon eschew natural supernaturalism. While Christian supernaturalism permeates these writings, God and the world are distinguished qualitatively. They express a belief in miracles but not magic, such that miracles are God's extraordinary acts beyond his ordinary providence. And not until after Bacon's death did millennialism spread rapidly in England.

Bacon was indirectly dependent on Andreae's *Christianopolis*.[124] In both utopias the college is "the very eye of their kingdom" (Bacon) and "the innermost shrine of the city" (Andreae). Andreae's state is called Caphar Salama, "City of Peace," and Bacon's Bensalem means "Son of Peace." Andreae introduces his journey as launching out "once more upon the Academic Sea, though the latter had very often been hurtful to me. . . . I left the port together with many others and exposed my life and person to a thousand dangers that go with a desire for knowledge."[125] Similarly, Bacon's preface to the reader is essentially a diatribe against the academic philosophy of his day.[126] Citizens of both utopias share a practical orientation rather than the wrangling of the schools. For both societies, education and scientific knowledge are not ends in themselves but serve the greater goal of alleviating human suffering. Craft is valued over syllogisms. In terms very similar to Bacon's, the narrator in *Christianopolis* explains, "Here in truth you see a testing of nature herself; everything that the earth contains in her bowels is subjected to the laws and instruments of science."[127] As in the *New Atlantis*, the craftsman—especially the engineer of machines—is highly prized in Andreae's utopia: "In walking around the city, I could easily notice what the distribution of the craftsman was."[128] There are "clock-makers and organ-makers, cabinet-makers,

124. Like most of his kinsmen, especially Puritans, Bacon would not include schools of theosophy, mystic numbers, astrology and prophecies. He is so focused on the "instauration" (foundation) of experimental science that, in comparison with Andreae, he has very little to say about advancing the arts and literature. Bensalem is more of a research university in physical sciences. In addition, Held observes, "The idea of freedom, so oft recurring and so much emphasized in the *Christianopolis*, does not play so important a part in the *New Atlantis*." Held, *Christianopolis*, 73.

125. Held, *Christianopolis*, 142.

126. Bacon, *New Atlantis*, 12: "Men of this kind, therefore, amend some things, but advance little; and improve the condition of knowledge, but do not extend its range . . . since their aim has been not to extend philosophy and the arts in substance and value, but only to change the doctrines and transfer the kingdom of opinions to themselves."

127. Held, *Christianopolis*, 154–55.

128. Held, *Christianopolis*, 156.

sculptors, and masons on the same basis. Their feature, moreover, is entirely peculiar to them, namely, that their artisans are almost entirely educated men."[129]

An unmistakable connection appears in Bacon's description of the governor wearing a white turban "with a small red cross on the top," and he says, "by vocation I am a Christian priest." The only reward he sought for his services "was our brotherly love and the good of our souls and bodies."[130] He presents a scroll written in ancient Hebrew, Greek, and Latin, "signed with a stamp of cherubim wings, not spread but hanging downwards, and by them a cross." This is the distinctive symbol stamped on the Rosicrucian manifestos. Moreover, the crew tried to offer gold coins to the servant and crimson velvet to the officer, "but the servant took them not, nor would scarce look upon them," since they would not offer mercy for money.[131] Bacon's benefactors are none other than Rosy Cross Brothers. These "Mystery-Men" voyage from the Salomon House society, bringing back intelligence from their undercover missions, refusing any reward for their humanitarian services.[132]

In Christianopolis "they want everything written down very plainly, and they confess all their doings, even their faults, frankly in order that posterity may know the events of the past without disguise."[133] Similarly, Bacon complains about the dearth of reliable chronicles of successes and failures in natural investigations "so neither the births nor the miscarriages of Time are entered in our records."[134]

In Bacon's narrative, the Jewish scholar Joabin stoutly defends the distinctive chastity of Bensalem and its defense of marriage in contrast with European standards, focusing on the deleterious nature of dowries.[135] "Yet it is nowhere safer to get married than here," Andreae says of Christianopolis. "For as the unusualness of the dowry and the uncertainty of daily bread are lacking, it remains only that the value of virtues and sometimes of beauty be made. . . . There is no dowry at all except the promises of Christ, the example of parents, the knowledge acquired by both, and the joy of peace."[136]

One more comparison may be indulged. Gradually, a magical worldview of Renaissance Neoplatonism was yielding to a mechanical natural philosophy. Significantly, Andreae praises Martin Möller, but his writings lack the speculative

129. Held, *Christianopolis*, 157.
130. Bacon, *New Atlantis*, 71–74.
131. Bacon, *New Atlantis*, 63–65.
132. Bacon, *New Atlantis*, 75–76.
133. Held, *Christianopolis*, 232.
134. Bacon, *New Atlantis*, 10–11.
135. Bacon, *New Atlantis*, 93–94.
136. Held, *Christianopolis*, 258–59.

visions of Möller's most famous pupil, Jakob Böhme. Mystic numbers are still studied to "note down the Messiah present in all things." However, "In this *cabala* it is advisable to be rather circumspect . . . since God has reserved the future for Himself, revealing it to a very limited number of individuals and then only at the greatest intervals."[137] Astrology is still being taught in the same hall as astronomy. Yet "they emphasize rather this, as to how they may rule the stars, and by faith shake off the yoke if any exists. . . . The most fortunate horoscope is that of adoption into the ranks of sons of God."[138] There is a "school of prophecy," but it is used to distinguish truth from "soothsaying which deceives so many."[139] Bensalem, too, is founded on a miracle that gave the ancestors the New Testament. However, its university fellows are also adept at distinguishing false miracles from true ones.[140]

Besides a mutual fondness for Geneva, Bacon and Andreae shared common friends.[141] A direct connection is Georg Rodolf Weckherlin, the Duke of Württemberg's private secretary.[142] He and Andreae were friends since their college days at the Tübinger Stift, and Bacon's friendship with Weckherlin began when the latter was part of a German delegation in London from 1607 to 1610. After marrying an English noblewoman, Weckherlin moved permanently to England, where he became an undersecretary of state and sided with Parliament in the civil wars. In 1644 he was even made "secretary of foreign tongues."[143] Another common friend of Andreae and Bacon was the historian and poet Edmund Bolton.[144]

137. Held, *Christianopolis*, 222.

138. Held, *Christianopolis*, 228–29.

139. Held, *Christianopolis*, 243.

140. Yates, *Rosicrucian Enlightenment*, 163–64.

141. One example is Jacques Auguste de Thou, who used his office as president of the Parlement of Paris to negotiate the Edict of Nantes, and in the name of the Gallican church he opposed the adoption of the Council of Trent's decrees. After Henry IV was assassinated, the queen regent Marie de' Medici demoted de Thou to a member of the council of finance. His *History* was put on the index, and enemies considered him a crypto-Protestant. With [King] James, Casaubon was very intimate. As Held observes, "The latter spent hours in conversation with him and supported him with a considerable pension. The Bishop of Ely and the Dean of St. Paul's were his closest friends, and he also spent much time at Oxford and Cambridge. . . . He had become acquainted with some of Bacon's writings and had written to Sir George Cary, expressing appreciation of them. Bacon took advantage of this fact to open a correspondence with him, and this was at least partly responsible for the call which Casaubon received from James the following year. This letter expresses the desire for friendship and cooperation in the great work of scientific research." Held, *Christianopolis*, 50–52.

142. Held, *Christianopolis*, 52.

143. Held, *Christianopolis*, 51–52.

144. Held, *Christianopolis*, 53 n. 1.

As I've said, millennialism spread rapidly after Bacon's death. "It is a remarkable fact that seventeenth-century England produced a number of utopias," says Held, encouraged perhaps by "widely spread chiliastic hopes of the religious sects."[145] Through Comenius and the Hartlib Circle, Alsted's millennial views spread. Joining Samuel Hartlib, they formed the circle of émigrés that mediated the idea of a "universal reformation" to what would become the Royal Society.[146] Another important utopian work appeared in 1648, titled *Nova Solyma: The Ideal City, or Jerusalem Regained.* It is now known that the author was the Presbyterian Samuel Gott, a member of Parliament in the Hartlib Circle.[147] Gott was a warm admirer of Comenius and corresponded with Andreae himself.[148] Bacon's reference to "these Jewish dreams" of a literal millennium "when the Messiah should come and sit on his throne in Jerusalem" is identical to the eschatology of *Nova Solyma.* As in Bacon's *New Atlantis*, a Jewish sage appears. Yet there is a more extreme mysticism in Gott's version: "'Inner light,' 'inner feeling,' and 'revelation' are expressions often used. 'Flashes of light,' 'Excess of heavenly light,' 'Dark places made plain as it were by the light of heaven,' 'true renewed life of the soul, and a lively exercise and warm experience of faith.'"[149]

In summary, these formative utopias reflect the convergence of Hermeticism, evangelical piety, and experimental philosophy at a critical point in European history. Steeped in Paracelsian mysticism and Joachite millennialism, Andreae became increasingly critical of radical pietism. Theosophy, alchemy, astrology, and numerology were still present in his ideal curriculum, but they were interpreted in a more orthodox way. The controversy with Fludd distanced other pietists like Kepler, Andreae's lifelong friend, from Hermetic metaphysics and cosmology, while the famous scientist nevertheless remained enthralled by Pythagorean ideas and practiced astrology. Even Bacon still wanted to include alchemy—including the transmutation of base metals into gold—in the Scientific Revolution and saw the Rosy Cross Brotherhood as a noble fiction. Even when Apollo presides at Delphi, Dionysus lies furtively in his tomb until he is awakened by votaries, eager to be stung again by his divine madness.

145. Held, *Christianopolis*, 76.

146. Popkin, *History of Skepticism*, 64–65.

147. When the entire work appeared in English in 1902, the editor, the Rev. Walter Begley, concluded that Milton was the author, but it is now known that the author is Samuel Gott. See Popkin, *History of Skepticism*, 77–78. Gott also wrote *The Divine History of the Genesis of the World*, published in London in 1670.

148. Held, *Christianopolis*, 80–81.

149. Held, *Christianopolis*, 92–93.

9

Invisible Made Visible

The Royal Society

> The body is a prison, and the desires of the world are empty and destructive of the mind. I long to be a mirror of myself whereby I may contemplate what I am.
>
> —Robert Fludd[1]

> Whether for better or for worse, it is no longer possible for historians interested in the "scientific revolution" to regard the movement solely in terms of the victory of true and rational scientific ideas over the scholastic and magical modes of thought circulating in the sixteenth and seventeenth centuries.
>
> —Mordechai Feingold[2]

The invisible One manifests itself visibly in a multitude of appearances. Utopias imagined became real social spaces for further exploration and invention beyond the tumultuous debates in church and state. Some formerly suppressed sects emerged visibly enough to be identified as a threat to both public institutions. United by a pantheistic tendency and a millennial utopianism, these groups represent the extreme end of the divine self's appearance on the stage of early modern history. Another trajectory is represented by Robert Fludd and the Cambridge Platonists, with early Freemasonry as a social space. Finally, at the more conservative end is the "universal reformation" proposed by Andreae and Comenius, leading to

1. Fludd, *Apologia Compendiaria* in Huffman, *Fludd*, 56.
2. Feingold, "Occult Tradition," 73.

the founding of the Royal Society. Most founding members of the Royal Society were, as philosopher Robert Boyle reported, "Orthodox Christian Naturalists."[3] In fact, the divine self is confronted with a deep and broad critique by experimental philosophers on both theological and scientific grounds. However, throughout the seventeenth century these were overlapping forces. The fate of the divine self in the modern world is at stake in the intersection of these vigorous streams.

"Smoke from the Bottomlesse Pit": Pantheistic Sectarianism

During the 1960s and 1970s, so-called hippies were largely dismissed or harassed by those in power. It is only in hindsight that we see the revolutionary impact of this generation, particularly as many of its voices eventually became cultural elites themselves.[4] Similarly, radical mystics, millennialists, and magicians tend to be buried in footnotes or ignored altogether by modern historians. However, their utopianism and radical egalitarianism, not to mention a fondness for "New Age" spiritualities over against institutional religion, bears comparison with our own time. The seventeenth century belonged not only to the familiar pioneers of the Scientific Revolution but to radical sectarians whose influence was deeper and broader than is often assumed.

The invisible was becoming sufficiently visible already in 1553 when Archbishop Thomas Cranmer drafted the Forty-Two Articles (precursor of the Thirty-Nine Articles) for the established church. These articles concluded with several condemnations of "Anabaptist" errors: a merely spiritual resurrection; freedom from the moral law; that the soul sleeps or is annihilated or merges with God; that there is a literal millennium; and that all will be saved. Burns observes, "It is possible to trace to the reign of Edward VI a group of enthusiasts so unworldly, so spiritual, so dedicated to achieving unheard of perfection in their lives in this world through a mystical union with the deity that many of them refused to believe in a personal immortality for man either as soul alone or as soul in a resurrected body."[5]

"Epicurus turned Enthusiast"

The group called the "Family of Love" (or "Familists") became a popular movement under whose canopy diverse sects found shade. Familists conformed outwardly to the established church while drawing their inner nourishment in private gath-

3. Hunter, *Boyle*, 136.
4. See Trueman, *Rise and Triumph*.
5. Burns, *Christian Mortalism*, 45.

erings. Burns observes that they "sought the way to a direct knowledge of God through the mystical experience," although, ironically, "newcomers to this 'Family of Love' were given the guidance of the sect's books and spiritual counselors."[6] The Family of Love seems to have flourished during Mary's reign, and "the sect also had adherents in Queen Elizabeth's household and in the court of James I." However, in 1580 Elizabeth issued *A Proclamation against the Sectaries of the Family of Love.*[7]

The founder of the Family of Love was Hendrik Nicholis (also known as Henry Nichleas), born in Münster in 1501 or 1502. A disciple of Anabaptist leader David Joris, he was imprisoned in Amsterdam on the charge of participating in the Münster rebellion. Signing his letters "H. N.," the initials for *Homo Novus*, he emigrated to England and founded the Family of Love (Familists), the era's most notable sect. As Paul Lim explains, "This movement had the Neoplatonist tinge and was indebted to Meister Eckhart, the Jewish kabbalah, *Theologia Germanica*, Pseudo-Dionysius, and Nicholas of Cusa."[8] The leader of the Cambridge Platonists, Henry More, denounced Nicholis as "*Epicurus* turned *Enthusiast*," although we will see below striking similarities with More's circle.[9] The sharp inner-outer contrast pervades Nicholis's teaching. One of his favorite phrases was being "Godded with God," an Eckhartian expression that Anabaptist spiritualists like Valentin Weigel used frequently. According to Ronald Knox, "perhaps the leading characteristic of seventeenth-century English enthusiasm was the distinction . . . between the Christ of history and the Christ of experience."[10]

Seventeenth-century historian John Strype provides a concise summary of the group's complexion:

> The sectaries of the *family of the mount* held all things in common, and lived in contemplation altogether; denying all prayers, and the resurrection of the body. They questioned, whether there were an heaven or an hell, but what is in this life. And they said, that what the scriptures spake of, was begun and ended in men's bodies here, as they do live. As heaven was, when they do laugh and are merry, and hell, when they are in sorrow, grief, or pain. And lastly, they believed that all things came by nature.[11]

6. Burns, *Christian Mortalism*, 45.

7. Burns, *Christian Mortalism*, 59–60.

8. Lim, *Mystery Unveiled*, 102.

9. Joseph Downing notes: "Henry More, in his *An Explanation of the Grand Mystery of Godliness*, denounced Nicholas as but '*Epicurus* turned *Enthusiast*' because he detected a certain equivocation in Nicholas's books whenever he dealt with scriptural passages usually thought to support belief in the immortality of the soul" (55, in More, *Theological Works*, 185–88).

10. Burns, *Christian Mortalism*, 48–49.

11. Strype, *Annals*, 2.1:563.

From Strype's summary, Henry More's clever designation for Nicholis, "Epicurus turned Enthusiast," is close to the mark. The last feature, "all things came by nature," refers to their denial of divine providence.

However, the Familists were not simply antinomian Epicureans but drank deeply from the well of German mysticism. Paul Lim observes, "The Familists were assuredly nontrinitarians, but not because of their explicit denial of the Nicene doctrine of the Trinity." Rather, the Trinity was eclipsed by the absorption of the self into God. In short, "the doctrine became, more or less, superfluous."[12] Lim adds:

> Writing with a perfect hindsight of the post-Restoration critique of "enthusiasm," John Turner's *A Phisico-Theological Discourse* (1698) surveyed the tendency of the "*Weigelians* and *Familists*," whose shibboleths included the "Magnificent Language of being Godded with God, and Christed with Christ." This frightening tendency, of persons attaining such a degree of union with God that it results in "Conjunction of Substance with the Deity," had been taught in varying degrees by "*Plotinus*, *Porphirius*, *Iamblicus*, and *Proclus*."[13]

John Turner also mentions "the '*Arabian* Philosophers'" and of course Origen in this hall of shame.[14] Samuel Rutherford's *A Survey of the Spirituall Antichrist* (1647) drew a line from "Caspar Schwenckfeld, Thomas Müntzer, Hendrik Nicholis, and the Familists," with the *TG* as a common feature. They not only collapsed the distinction between creator and creature but between the already and the not yet. "For Rutherford," Lim writes, "this overrealized eschatology was why these Familists and others ended up denying the pro-Nicene theology."[15]

Like Epicureans, Familists believed in a divinity that was not involved in worldly affairs. Catherine Wilson reminds us, "No one is destined for the fiery pits of hell, Lucretius assured his readers. The ceremonies of religion were far worse than empty superstition in the eyes of the Epicureans. They were indoctrination into a fiction, as one of Cicero's Epicurean characters remarks, 'invented by wise men in the interest of the state, to the end that those whom reason was powerless to control might be led in the path of duty by religion.'"[16]

Much of this critique applies across the board to many of the radical sects of

12. Lim, *Mystery Unveiled*, 104.
13. Lim, *Mystery Unveiled*, 96.
14. Lim, *Mystery Unveiled*, 96.
15. Lim, *Mystery Unveiled*, 97.
16. Wilson, *Epicureanism*, 6, from Cicero, *De natura deorum*, 1.42 (Rackham, LCL).

the seventeenth century, including those with whom Hobbes and Spinoza were associated.[17] The early members of the Royal Society stood squarely against this trajectory, as we see in the inclusion of Hobbes with the sects in the critique by Seth Ward and John Wallis.[18] Among some of the radical sects of the seventeenth century, Epicureanism blended with Gnosticism. Since all souls are sparks of divinity and the body is a mere shadow, there is no immortality. Rather, personal identity is absorbed back into the unity of the Absolute. Resurrection is spiritual, not bodily. The inner Christ, not the Jesus of history, is what ultimately counts. Everything external is to be rejected and even ridiculed, including traditional morality.

Some soldiers in Cromwell's New Model Army thought the revolution did not go far enough. This included the communalist Levellers and the Ranters as well as the Fifth Monarchists. The notion of the Fifth Monarchists stems from the book of Daniel, which prophesies that after four monarchies, the fifth would be an everlasting kingdom. Traditionally, Christians have interpreted this as having been fulfilled in Christ's reign, first now in weakness and then in glory at Christ's second advent. Fifth Monarchists, first in Europe and then in England, instead took it to refer to a utopian age before Christ's return. There was a significant group of Fifth Monarchists in Cromwell's New Model Army. Another attempt was made by this group, led by Thomas Venner, at the Restoration. The attempted coup of January 1661 was foiled, and Charles II had Venner and other leaders executed. However, the Fifth Monarchist insurrection allowed the regime to crack down even further, "forbidding all private meetings and assemblies of the Fanaticks and Sectaries," naming "Anabaptists, Quakers, and Fifth-monarchy men, or some such-like appelation."[19]

Dissolving Parliament, Cromwell's New Model Army ejected the Presbyterian members and began a military rule that nevertheless instituted greater freedom of religion. The radical elements grew in numbers and influence during the Interregnum, particularly within the Army itself. Anabaptists, Familists, Quakers, Fifth Monarchy Men, Levellers, Diggers, Ranters, and others were viewed as a many headed monster of enthusiasm threatening church and state. The Scottish commissioner to the Westminster Assembly, Robert Baillie, included independency as springing from the Anabaptist fountain.[20] Millennialism was viewed with suspicion by Presbyterians, but they were alarmed especially by the pantheism of the

17. Osler, *Reconfiguring the World*, 90. I discuss Spinoza's relation to the Collegiants at the beginning of volume 3.

18. As detailed in Lomas, *Invisible College*, 9.

19. Shapin and Schaffer, *Leviathan*, 287.

20. See Baillie, *Dissuasive*; Baillie, *Anabaptism*.

sects, as exhibited in Thomas Edwards's 1646 *Gangrena* and his 1647 *A Catalogue of the Several Sects and Opinions in England and Other Nations*.

Such alarms were not unjustified. The age of the Father, identified with the order of the married, was overtaken by the age of the Son, the order of the clergy, but the age of the Spirit recognized neither order. The sharing of property, including wives and even orgies beyond heterosexual activity, were viewed as sacramental unions. Laurence Clarkson joined the Ranters in 1649. Though he turned away from Anabaptism, he remained a radical Neoplatonist. His most important work, *A Single Eye* (1650), adumbrates Eckhartian pantheism: "No matter what Scripture, Saints, or Churches say, if that within thee do not condemn thee, thou shalt not be condemned."[21] Lim relates:

> Clarkson unequivocally maintained these statements were true, namely, God is light; God's "Being and Essence . . . admits not of the plural but singular"; darkness was a "seeming reality" that pertained to creatures alone, thus was none other than "imagined Darknesse," and most worryingly, "there is no act whatsoever, that is impure in God, or sinful with or before God," and sin has "conception only in the imagination" . . . the complete absorption of the person's selfhood in God.[22]

Clarkson's *A Single Eye* begins with a poem strikingly similar to John Lennon's popular song "Imagine":

> Look not above the skies
> For God, or Heaven; for here your Treasure lies
> Even in these Forms, Eternall Will will reigne,
> Through him are all things, onely One, not Twain:
> Sure he's the Fountain from which every thing
> Both good and ill (so term'd) appears to spring.[23]

The last line displays the connection between pantheistic mysticism and antinomianism. According to Ranters like Clarkson, "good and ill (so term'd)" represent a duality that ultimately does not exist. That which we consider sin, God views as good; "that the devil and [God] are one, that the devil is but a part of Gods back sides, which terrifies because of the curtain, that he sports and feasts himself in swearing, drinking, whoring, as when he is holy, just and good: that the holiness of

21. Smith, *Ranter Writings*, 115–16.
22. Lim, *Mystery Unveiled*, 109–10.
23. Laurence Clarkson, "A Single Eye," in Smith, *Ranter Writings*, 115.

man and unholiness of man are both one to him."[24] The male becomes female and vice versa.[25] Ranters played out Böhme's cosmic alchemy in real life in antinomian defiance of what the unspiritual consider truth and goodness.

The resurrection is only spiritual when one realizes identity with God, Winstanley declares:

> But, poor Creatures, you are deceived; this expectation of glory without [outside] you, will vanish, you shall never see it; this outward heaven is not the durable Heaven; this is a fancy which your false Teachers put into your heads to please you with, while they pick your purses, and betray your Christ into the hands of flesh, and hold *Jacob* under to be a servant still to Lord *Esau*. . . . But when the second *Adam* rises up in the heart, he makes a man to see Heaven within himself, and to judge all things that are below him, who is the power of righteousnesse that rules therein: And this is Heaven that will not fail us. . . . This Christ is within you, your everlasting rest and glory.[26]

According to Abiezer Coppe in his 1649 treatise *Some Sweet Sips, of Some Spiritual Wine*: "The knowing of men after the Flesh, and of Christ (himselfe) after the Flesh, out of date. . . . Flesh must be crucified and dye, and the eternall Spirit—dwell in the Saints everlastingly."[27] As in similar sects, everything external, including the scriptures and the historical Jesus, belongs to "the Flesh. . . . The formall, externall, or outward" is opposed to "the powerful, glorious, and inward Death and Resurrection of Christ . . . the death of Christ at Jerusalem, and the Resurrection out of Josephs Tombe without us, is nothing to the dying of the Lord in us; and the Resurrection of the Day-star in our hearts."[28]

"John Holland's *The Smoke of the Bottomlesse Pit* (1651) captured succinctly the gist of what the Ranters were propounding, both in London and in the countryside," says Lim:

> "God is essentially in every creature, and that there is as much of . . . the essence of God . . . in the Ivie leaf, as in the most glorious Angel. . . . They all say there is no other God but what is in them, and also in the whole Creation, and that men ought to pray and seek to [*sic*] no other God but what was in them." . . .

24. Anonymous, "Justification of the Mad Crew," in Smith, *Ranter Writings*, 142.
25. Coppe, "Some Sweet Sips," in Smith, *Ranter Writings*, 38.
26. Winstanley, "New Law of Righteousness," 97.
27. Coppe, "Some Sweet Sips," in Smith, *Ranter Writings*, 39.
28. Coppe, "Some Sweet Sips," in Smith, *Ranter Writings*, 38.

> In the Ranter-Quaker denial of the crucial nature of Christ's historical death, the inexorable consequence was that they were "no more to eye or mind Christ that died in *Jerusalem*, but we are to mind Christ in our selves," thereby giving greater credence to the Christ of one's heart than to the Christ of history. . . . The rest of the "doctrine of Ranters" included a radical rejection of Scripture as mere "Tale," "dead Letter," and "a bundle of contradictions"; affirmation of polygamy, for monogamy was a "fruit of the curse"; and labeling of *all* commandments of God as fruits of the same curse, thereby providing the basis for antinomianism.[29]

Nigel Smith informs us, "After his time as a Ranter, Clarkson practised as an astrologer and physician in Cambridgeshire and Essex, using 'magical' manuscripts to help him divine the whereabouts of stolen goods, 'to raise spirits, and fetch treasure out of the earth.'"[30]

Combined with Joachite millennialism, this pantheistic emphasis led to radical autonomy. Burns explains, "Those sectarians who believed they were living under the Third Dispensation, the Age of the Spirit, recognized no earthly authority in spiritual matters; scrutinized by their spiritual eye, the Holy Scripture became a source of a great variety of revolutionary ideas, and those who opposed their interpretations on traditional grounds they dismissed as 'legalists.' They refused to be intimidated by the learning of their orthodox opponents."[31] They knew the hidden meaning of the letter by direct revelation of the Spirit within, so there was no arguing about exegesis.

"A Son of God in a Deep Sleep"

Even among Cambridge Platonists one heard similar language. In a sermon before the House of Commons in 1647, Ralph Cudworth said, "Every true Saint, carrieth his Heaven about with him, in his own heart, and Hell that is without him, can have no power over him."[32] His language is similar to that of the English enthusiasts generally, Burns observes:

29. Lim, *Mystery Unveiled*, 86–87.

30. Smith, "Atheism," 138.

31. Lim, *Mystery Unveiled*, 99.

32. Cudworth, *A Sermon Preached before the Honourable House of Commons at Westminster, March 31, 1647*. Quoted in Burns, *Christian Mortalism*, 39.

> The birth, Crucifixion, and Resurrection of Christ that took place inwardly in each regenerate man put him in a state that was not just *like* heaven, but one that was the *actual* heaven promised in the Gospel. Those who were in bondage to the "outward Law" and the "dead and killing Letter" of Scripture were in hell, and in thrall to sin, knowing not the liberty of the Spirit; heaping their sins on a Christ by whose historical sacrifice they shall be reckoned righteous, these carnal men expect their reward after death and therefore miss the only resurrection and heaven the Gospel promises.[33]

As the names given to them suggest, the Ranters and Quakers were seen as the archetypal example of irrationality. Mulligan observes, "Winstanley the social and religious radical, Vaughan the hermetic, and Henry More the academic Platonist were all haunted by the specter of Ranterish epistemology, which allowed complete liberation from the moral constraints of the Scriptures understood through right reason."[34]

A rather extreme example among the Cambridge Platonists is Peter Sterry. An early member and student of Benjamin Whichcote and John Smith, Sterry wrote, "Everything that *IS* beareth written upon it this Name of God, *I AM*."[35] Eckhart's "two eyes," spiritual and fleshly, are frequent images in his writings.[36] "He will bring forth yet divine Birth in your Soule, which is himself in a spark of Glory. . . . Such a spark as will never die, but spread it self into a spirituall flame, as large as heaven and Earth, comprehending ye live, Beauties, Loves, and joys of all Eternall Spirits in it self."[37] Spirit is higher than soul for Sterry, and in mystical union the soul empties itself not only of all images of sense but of reason itself: "The soule shuts up the windowes of sense, when she would have the room fill'd with the light of Reason. Reason's self must first be cast into a deep sleep and die, before she can rise again in the brightnesse of the Spirit."[38] This inner light is the "candle of the Lord."[39]

Sterry's grasp of ancient Greek and Roman literature was remarkable even for his time, notes Vivian de Sola Pinto. Plato, Plotinus, Clement and Origen of

33. Burns, *Christian Mortalism*, 39.

34. Mulligan, "Reason," 396.

35. See Sterry's "An Universal Being," in Pinto, *Peter Sterry*, 145.

36. For example, Sterry, "Living in a Divine Principle," in Pinto, *Peter Sterry*, 179.

37. See Sterry's "The Spark and the Flame," in Pinto, *Peter Sterry*, 182.

38. Pinto, *Peter Sterry*, 17, quoting Sterry.

39. Sterry asserts: "The Candle of God hath been upon thy head: God hath look'd sweetly forth from the top of thy Spirit, through the Principles of Nature, and this hath been thy light" (quoted in Pinto, *Peter Sterry*, 184).

Alexandria, Eriugena, Ficino, Campanella, kabbalists, Cusa, and Böhme appear on the list of his library. "Like his masters, Plotinus, Origen and Nicholas of Cusa, Sterry is a strict monist," judges Pinto.[40] Sterry saw Christ as "The True Orpheus."[41] "This shadowy figure is that, which we call this world, & the body," he says.[42] There are intimations that the resurrection is bodily, but they are buried in allegorical references to the new birth, and paradise is within.[43]

The "inner light" doctrine itself was considered by many to be a confusion of the believer's spirit with Christ. Regardless, the inner light produced external spectacles heated by millennial fervor. On Palm Sunday in 1656, James Naylor, the Quaker leader of the missionaries called the "Valiant Sixty," made an underwhelming yet provocative triumphal entry into Bristol as the Messiah.[44] While Peter Sterry was leading the service at Whitehall as chaplain to the council of state, a naked woman entered the church announcing herself as the resurrection. Sterry himself said the Messiah would come "in the year 1656 or thereabouts."[45] His excessive eulogy of Oliver Cromwell as a mediator like Christ in heaven alarmed even Richard Cromwell and the rest of the family.[46] Though he disputed these reports, Pinto notes that "such an expression would not seem in the least blasphemous to one who wrote, 'Every man in his Natural state is a divine Spirit, an Immortal Soul, and Image of God, a Son of God in a deep Sleep.'"[47]

Richard Baxter expressed concern over "a method of theologie . . . lately revived . . . by some deep students who are verst in ye Platonke Philosophie, & thinke yt Reason must know more of the Divine Being than Scripture." It was, he considered,

40. Pinto, *Peter Sterry*, 89.

41. See "The True Orpheus" and "Orpheus and Christ," in Pinto, *Peter Sterry*, 157 and 181.

42. See Sterry, "Narcissus," in Pinto, *Peter Sterry*, 161–62.

43. He writes, "so Christ at his Coming shall say to our Spiritual Man, which hath been so long imprison'd in this Flesh: Go forth" (Sterry, "As at the Entrance of Kings," in Pinto, *Peter Sterry*, 186). In "Thou Art in Heaven," Sterry relates, "A believer is ever in Heaven, and hath Heaven in himself . . . thou indeed art in Heaven: All Things are as the Angels of God, as Divine Emanations, Divine Figures, and Divine Splendors circling thee in on every side, and God himself as a Foundatin of Glories in the midst of them" (in Pinto, *Peter Sterry*, 95). See also "A Paradise Within," 192, and "Thou Hast All," 193, both in Pinto, *Peter Sterry*.

44. He was not executed, but authorities bored his tongue and sentenced him to two years of labor. See Barrow, *Mirror*, 2:1070.

45. Sterry, *Resurrection Revealed.*

46. This was reported, however, by the Restoration churchman and Archbishop of Canterbury John Tillotson. See Pinto, *Peter Sterry*, 35, who writes: "He reports that 'Sterry, praying for Richard, used those indecent words next to blasphemy, *Make him the brightest of the father's glory, and the express image of his person.*'"

47. Pinto, *Peter Sterry*, 33, quoting Sterry, *The Rise, Race and Royalty* (1683), 497.

"a mixture of Platonisme, Orgenisme & Arianisme not having all of any of these, but somewhat of all." Among those he names in this connection is "an excellent pious wit Peter Sterry."[48]

A close friend of Oliver Cromwell, Sterry was made chaplain to the council of state and resided with John Milton at Whitehall Palace. A Calvinist and a Platonist, Sterry was also a fierce independent who expressed the latitudinarian spirit of the Cambridge Platonists toward all but the Presbyterians. In thanksgiving for the victory in 1651 against Charles II and the Scottish army, he preached a sermon before Parliament titled, "England's Deliverance from the Northern Presbytery compared with its Deliverance from the Roman Papacy." Actually, the papacy came out better than the Presbyterians in this comparison. At least Rome has preserved, according to Sterry, "mysticall divinity," but the Presbyterians "contemn the Spirit, and its Impressions upon the heart when they are set up for Pillars of fire to go before us in this dark night of flesh, as *Enthusiasmes*." They also reject "the openings of the glory of Christ, the mutual interviews, walkes, embraces, kisses between God and the Soul, in the Spirit, as *Whimsicall*. . . . So both these, the Romish-Papacy, the Scottish-Presbytery, as it hath been formerly stated by me, appear like the Witch of Endor, the fleshly principle dressed up in the forme of Christianity."[49] Rome and Presbyterians alike, notes Pinto, "are said to agree in setting up 'the *Scriptures*, the *Word of God outwardly exprest* as the *Letter* of [the] Law,' but without 'the *Light of Revelation*' granted to 'a Living Member of *Jesus Christ*,' and hence as a mere 'breathlesse Carkasse, or a Dead Letter.' They agree in setting up a human authority as the sole interpreter of scripture, the Pope or a Council in the case of the Romanists, a National or Ecumenical Assembly in the case of the Presbyterians. . . . Both lay stress on '*outward Formalities*,' '*Ceremonious Observations* of outward Rites.'" And both raise the church above the state.[50] "O England! London!," Sperry cries, "Remember Hierusalem. . . . Christ hath been preach'd among you: but as in the Flesh, clouded with carnall rites and ceremonies."[51]

To Presbyterians like the Scottish Commissioner to the Westminster Assembly Robert Baillie, Sterry and other Cambridge Platonists were basically one with the Anabaptist, Familist, and Ranter and Quaker sects.[52] Henry More felt obliged to distance the school from the "enthusiasts," just as Quakers like George Fox

48. Pinto, *Peter Sterry*, 87. Baxter himself came under fire for his doctrine of justification. After Sterry's death, Baxter read Sterry's treatise on free will and changed his impression. See Baxter, *Catholick Theologie*, Part II, 107.

49. See Sterry, "Catholics and Presbyterians," in Pinto, *Peter Sterry*, 170–71.

50. Pinto, *Peter Sterry*, 23.

51. See Sterry, "Remember Hierusalem," in Pinto, *Peter Sterry*, 172.

52. See Pinto, *Peter Sterry*, 36.

reproved Naylor for fanaticism. And since radical sectarians equated the inner light with reason (the "candle of the Lord"), the precise line between irrational and rational was a contested boundary. Epithets such as Puritan, Romish, Rationalist and Enthusiast were lobbed by enemies, but the actual situation was more fluid.

The Presbyterian Parliament, particularly the Westminster Divines, were aligned with the position expressed in the Edwardian Articles. Reformed theologians in Britain and on the Continent considered such enthusiasm to embody "the spirit of antichrist" as much as, if not more than, the papal church. They taught that believers will be glorified but will never pass from the creaturely rank to be absorbed in the One. Lim observes that Edward Leigh's *Systeme or Body of Divinity* (1654) "acknowledges that this idea of *theosis* (or deification) was an orthodox theme pushed to the extreme."[53] Lim relates that "John Everard, a friend of Robert Fludd, fueled such extremism by translating the *Theologia Germanica* and other writings by Tauler along with Sebastian Franck's *On the Tree of Knowledge of Good and Evil*, Cusa's *On Learned Ignorance* and *De Visione Dei*, and the *Corpus Hermeticum*."[54] Everard preached this message of the Christ born within and "crucified, dead and buried Within You."[55] According to Burns, Everard was "harassed by the bishops and, in 1636, charged before High Commission with Familism, antinomianism, and anabaptism."[56] The proximity of Cambridge Platonists and Everard to the center of intellectual life in England exhibits the breadth of attraction to natural supernaturalism.

As we have seen among gnostic groups, the divine self seeks either to escape the iron cage of this world or to remake it according to its utopian pattern. Levellers, Diggers, and Fifth Monarchists represent the latter, more political, wing. For them, the age of the Spirit meant casting off the bonds of private property, just as the utopian writings envisioned and the Anabaptists had attempted. Gerrard Winstanley (1609–1660) represents this position well.[57] His treatise, *The New Law of Righteousness*, advanced his "True Leveller or Digger" position that all things should be held in common and that the soul is a spark of divinity. As Burns notes, "The Holy Scripture, for Winstanley, is not the direct Word of God, but a record of

53. Lim, *Mystery Unveiled*, 89.

54. Lim, *Mystery Unveiled*, 102. Lim also notes here that Everard "translated Pseudo-Dionysius's *On the Name of God* and had a hand in Cusanus's *De Visione Dei*, even though the published version owed its final translational touch to Giles Randall, another London radical, as it was printed in 1646 as *The Single Eye*."

55. Quoted in Burns, *Christian Mortalism*, 48–49.

56. Burns, *Christian Mortalism*, 49.

57. Burns, *Christian Mortalism*, 43–44.

the religious experiences of inspired men, and true understanding of the record requires a repetition of those experiences in one's own soul and a readiness to transmit new messages from the Father."[58] One of the most important of these messages was communalism. "In the beginning of Time, the great Creator Reason, made the Earth to be a Common Treasury to preserve. . . . Man," Winstanley said in 1649. "This work to make the Earth a Common Treasury was shewed to us by Voice in Trance, and out of Trance, which words were these, 'Work together, Eate Bread together, Declare this all abroad': which Voice was heard three times."[59]

Historians generally classify Winstanley as a "pantheistic rationalist."[60] All of these sects shared a common horizon of Hermeticism and a radical Anabaptist and pietist influence poised to repeat the Münster revolution. Winstanley is representative of a wider trajectory of sectarians who embraced the doctrine that the soul is annihilated by being absorbed into the One. Burns notes that "during and following the Interregnum the doctrine was more boldly preached as part of a thoroughly pantheistic message that incorporated the idea of universal restoration and even, in at least one instance, introduced the possibility that the soul will be purified in a series of incarnations."[61]

What Happens to the Soul?

While pantheism was a common factor among the radical sects, some were materialists while others were spiritualists. Smith explains, "While the Seekers, Ranters, and Quakers were extreme spiritualists, regarding only the spiritual world as having any absolute reality, the Muggletonians (like Overton, 'soul-sleepers') gave bodies to supernatural entities. . . . To the extent that both the spiritualists and the materialists made all reality into a higher nature, then all of them are nominalists as opposed to realists."[62] The Leveller Richard Overton and the Ranter Laurence Clarkson represent the materialists. Nigel Smith explains:

> While maintaining that the soul is really part of the body, Overton does not deny God, but, like Clarkson, he tends to reduce the concept of a deity, as with that of death, to a metaphysical and cosmological abstract that in itself is materialistic. The sun, for instance, becomes literally a veil between man and

58. Burns, *Christian Mortalism*, 47.

59. Mulligan, "Reason," 375. See Ratiansi, "Paracelsus," 24–32; cf. Ratiansi, "Evaluations," 148–66.

60. Mulligan, "Reason," 392–93.

61. Burns, *Christian Mortalism*, 61.

62. N. Smith, "Atheism," 140–41.

> God, a shadow and reflector of his glory, while hell is either "*outer darknesse*," or "Earth reduced to its *prima materia* or *created matter*, which he saith cannot be consumed." Although Overton's mortalism cannot be connected with pantheism or deism, he was none the less absolutely certain of the fictionality of the soul. . . . What both groups are doing is making the distance between the human and the divine much smaller than before, a not uncommon habit of seventeenth-century idealists. By a kind of paradox, the Ranters and Quakers placed the Godhead within the individual, while the Muggletonians realized divine bodies in human terms.[63]

Levellers especially drew from humanist skepticism, in particular the Pyrrhonic skepticism of Sextus Empiricus and Montaigne.[64] "In the writings of extreme religious radicals like Clarkson, Overton, Muggleton, and Reeve," Smith observes, "forms of speculation were developed concerning the organization of existence that located the divine and the hitherto transcendental in the natural world, or that construed the divine in terms of very basic human identities and processes."[65]

John Calvin's earliest treatise, *Psychopannychia*, was also the first critique of "soul-sleep," a doctrine taught by some Anabaptists. Written in Latin in 1534, it was published in 1542. Calvin appeals to Irenaeus (*Against Heresies* 5), who "wishes us, however, to learn that by nature we are mortal and God alone immortal." Nevertheless, Calvin maintained that God has granted souls immortality.[66] We have also seen above that Cranmer's Forty-Two Articles also rejected such teaching. Interestingly, Bullinger in his Second Helvetic Confession (1566) targets three divergent views as part of a combined threat: "We condemn all those who mock at, or by subtle disputations call into doubt, the immortality of the soul, or say that the soul sleeps, or that it is part of God."[67]

All three of these illicit views were promoted vigorously in England. Mortalism, the belief that the soul dies with the body, was a broad label that encompassed different positions. As Norman T. Burns explains, the broadest distinction can be drawn between Sleepers and Annihilationists. The former held that the soul sleeps until the resurrection, while the latter were called "Sadducees" because they denied the resurrection.

63. N. Smith, "Atheism," 140–41.
64. N. Smith, "Atheism," 143–44.
65. N. Smith, "Atheism," 158.
66. Calvin, "Psychopannychia" (1542) in Beveridge, *Tracts*, 3:478.
67. Schaff, *Creeds*, 3:842.

> The annihilationists were part of a group of enthusiasts, most often called "Libertines" or "Familists" by their contemporaries, that was often accused of denying the resurrection of the body. . . . It must suffice at this point to say that many of these enthusiasts became pantheists who envisioned immortality only for the "divine essence" in man, an impersonal eternal existence as an undifferentiated part of God. For them the Gospel message of resurrection referred only to the spiritual rising from the bonds of sin in this life; at death the immortal essence of the soul was dissolved in God while the body and personality, by which man had been individualized, underwent complete and final annihilation.[68]

Sleepers were further divided between thnetopsychists, who believed the soul dies with the body, and psychopannychists, such as John Milton, who held that the soul sleeps until the resurrection.[69]

The radical sects represented an extreme expression of a broader natural supernaturalism that experimentalists like Bacon and Boyle opposed. In fact, Robert Boyle discovered that his opponents, both Epicurean and Neoplatonic, were indebted to the Anabaptist sects of his age. He shared the view expressed in the title of a treatise by Robert Baillie: *Anabaptism, the Trve Fovntaine of Independency, Brownism, Antinomy,* [and] *Familism* (1647).[70] In fact, "in 1648 the conservative majority in Parliament recognized the danger and prescribed the death penalty for those who obstinately denied the General Resurrection or a day of Judgment after death."[71] Burns observes:

> The chiliasts were alienated from the orthodox majority by the millennial heresy itself; soul sleeping added little to their burden. Although belief in the millennial Kingdom had been condemned by the Council of Ephesus (431) and, during the English Reformation, by the Edwardine Articles of 1553, it persisted in popular religion, ready for a resurgence in times of social upheaval. . . . The annihiliationist enthusiasts were commonly called "Epicureans" by their enemies, and the epithet was not completely off the mark.[72]

68. Burns, *Christian Mortalism*, 14.

69. Burns, *Christian Mortalism*, 18.

70. However, it should be noted that under Cromwell, Oxford's vice-chancellor John Owen and Thomas Goodwin, president of Magdalen College, were staunch opponents of "Quakerism" and "atheism," sweeping categories that in their day encompassed Anabaptist enthusiasts along with Arminians, Socinians, Cartesians and Hobbesians.

71. Burns, *Christian Mortalism*, 15.

72. Burns, *Christian Mortalism*, 35–36.

However, "They were tutored not by pagan philosophy but, more likely, by that German mysticism that has never been far from the surface of Protestant piety, a mysticism that had thoroughly assimilated Neoplatonic concepts and transmuted a pagan into a Christian tradition."[73] In short, belief in the soul's annihilation was, for many sectarians, another way of saying that upon death personal identity surrenders to *henōsis,* that is, absolute absorption into the Unity embracing all souls. We shall see the influence of these sects on Thomas Hobbes, particularly his heterodox view of the Trinity, his materialistic pantheism (similar to Overton and Clarkson), and his mortalism. Millennialism also was a common factor in anti-Trinitarianism from Socinus to Newton.[74]

Basically, Luther's confrontation with the "Enthusiasts" was being repeated in England. Maxwell-Stuart summarizes this well:

> Royalists, Puritans, Levellers, sectarians of all kinds alike, then, were prepared to steep themselves in the crapulent brew which a mixture of alchemy and millenarianism offered because alchemy was, in Mendelssohn's words, "an especially powerful metaphor for the problem of uncertainty and its resolution, because alchemy's history was in such a large part the history of its contested credibility," and the establishment of an English republic coincided, not altogether by accident perhaps, with widespread active interest on all sides of the religious and political divide in the possibility of transmutation, however that was to be interpreted. So when Charles II was restored to his English throne in 1662, we should not be surprised to find that he happily brought with him Nicholas le Fèvre, a French alchemist, who now effectively became a royal alchemist-in-residence and set up his laboratory in St. James's Palace. With Böhme, Vaughan and Charles II's French alchemist, we begin to catch a glimpse of those international circles of scholars and practitioners of various sciences, which had characterized intellectual exchange at the beginning of the seventeenth century and continued to do so even after the disastrous Thirty Years' War.[75]

Fludd's Defense and Rosicrucian Hysteria

The ink of the Latin Rosy Cross manifestos had barely dried before sharp denunciations appeared. Robert Fludd's *Apologia* for the Rosicrucianism fraternity was published the same year. He wrote another in 1617, and it is not coincidental that

73. Burns, *Christian Mortalism,* 35–36.
74. Hotson, "Arianism and Millenarianism," 9–35.
75. Maxwell-Stuart, *Chemical Choir,* 127.

Andreae wrote his *Christianopolis* the following year, though it was published in 1619. Fludd was becoming the real-life ambassador of the Rosicrucians, but he was the more thoroughgoing Paracelsian than Andreae was before 1619.

Fludd was born in 1574, the son of Sir Thomas Fludd, a member of Parliament and Elizabeth's war treasurer. Like Dee, whom he admired, Robert Fludd was a respected mathematician. At St. John's College, Oxford, he developed an interest in Neoplatonism and astrology under his tutor John Perrin.[76] Dropping out of university, Fludd traveled to the Continent in search of occult wisdom. He claimed to have studied theurgy with Jesuits in the Pyrenees.[77] For six years he met with dignitaries of the Republic of Letters and tutored princes in Hermeticism.[78] In 1604 he enrolled in medical programs at Oxford and began practicing in London. But his vehement exchanges with peers over traditional medicine barred his membership in the College of Physicians until 1609. At the same time, Michael Maier, a Paracelsist physician of the Holy Roman Emperor Rudolf II, joined the list of Rosicrucians, and Maier became an important link between Fludd and Continental Hermeticism.[79]

The first salvos against Fludd came from the Zurich theologian and physician Thomas Erastus and the orthodox Lutheran Andreas Libavius. Already in 1572 Erastus wrote a treatise against "new Paracelsian medicine," targeting Paracelsus's vitalistic monism (i.e., natural supernaturalism). Libavius's claim to fame was his 1597 chemistry textbook, entitled *Alchemia*, the first of its kind. At this stage, the terms *alchemia* or *chymistry* referred to the same field. Nevertheless, on grounds both theological and scientific Libavius also opposed Paracelsus's macrocosm-microcosm

76. Huffman, *Fludd*, 16. This counts against Bruno's characterization of Oxford, which Yates and others follow. Mordechai Feingold's detailed study provides conclusive proof that there was a wide range of intellectual interest at Oxford during this period. See Feingold, *Mathematician's Apprenticeship*.

77. Szulakowska, *Alchemy of Light*, 168.

78. Huffman, *Fludd*, 17. During this period, Fludd taught the Papal Vice Legate for whom he wrote a treatise on a method of divination called geomancy. He also wrote an astrology text for Reginaud of Avignon and tracts for the Marquis d'Orizon and instructed the Duke of Guise and his brother François in mathematics, macrocosm history and astrology, geometry, and "secret military arts." From France he went to Rome, Venice, Augsburg, and the learned courts of the Elector Palatine in Heidelberg and Moritz the Learned, Landgrave of Hesse.

79. Yates, *Rosicrucian Enlightenment*, 97–98. Yates notes, "The huge tomes of Robert Fludd's *History of the Macrocosm and the Microcosm* were published by Johann Theodor de Bry at Oppenheim from 1617 to 1619. Michael Maier's *Atlanta fugiens*, a book of emblems in which spiritual alchemy reached a high point of artistic expression, was also published by de Bry at Oppenheim in 1618." While these facts are right, they do not justify the Hermetic-Cabalistic character of the Heidelberg court on which this work bases its general argument.

doctrines along with his use of magic, astrology, and kabbalah. In a 1616 treatise Libavius accused the Rosicrucians of being Paracelsian pantheists and pseudo-scientific quacks.[80] According to Kirsteller, Libavius claimed that "the Cabala is a falsehood and a deceit," and he also "attacked the magia and cabala for elevating the use of rhetorical figures (*tropologia*) to the point where it could transform God into man, man into God, in metamorphoses more marvelous and more dangerous than anything in Ovid."[81] Libavius even criticized the German physician Daniel Sennert (1572–1637), who was a transitional figure between alchemy to chemistry and an important influence on Robert Boyle.[82] Bacon reserved his sharpest invective for the "idolatry" of Paracelsus's macrocosm-microcosm scheme.[83] Besides confusing the creator-creature relationship, Bacon held that such Hermeticism elided any distinction between creatures. It was bad theology and bad science.[84]

The first volume of Fludd's *History of the Microcosm and Macrocosm* appeared in 1617.[85] Fludd provides one of the most eloquent statements of the chain of being, from the "bright soul" in vegetables to the "supernatural light" of the first day of creation.[86] Fludd rhapsodizes in his second volume, "The light itself which

80. Benbow, "Theory and Action," 135–39.

81. Kristeller, *Philosophy*, 136–37.

82. Kristeller, *Philosophy*, 138. Sennert offers no proof, just assertions, Libavius charges. Libavius also challenges Sennert's goal of producing a human being without parents. "As for their invisible Elements we shall believe it when they prove any such hidden things under these: for their affirmations only cannot create new beings" (quoted in Kristeller, *Philosophy*, 138).

83. Kristeller, *Philosophy*, 132–33. See Bacon's *Advancement of Learning* 3.370 and 4.379–80, in Vickers, *Francis Bacon*.

84. Kristeller, *Philosophy*, 134.

85. Huffman, *Fludd*, 25.

86. See Fludd, "The History of the Macrocosm," in Huffman, *Fludd*, 64–65:

> In men it is the process of clear reasoning, in the other animals it is the hidden fire that evidently governs the actions of their life and senses; in vegetables it is a sort of bright soul, that hides round their central parts and causes them to grow and multiply endlessly; in minerals it is the spark of brilliance impelling them to their goal of perfection. The macrocosms of the skies [heavens], and also the differences between the bodies that exist in them, arise from that supernatural light created on the first day; for one finds, indeed, that the highest heaven differs from the lowest, and the lowest from the middle according to the excess or deficiency of this essence in them, and that any element of each sky [heaven] is pushed or raised up by its absence or presence, for the further Matter is from nobleness of Natural Pattern, the grosser, more impure, darker and less worthy it is. Hence, indeed, arises the diversity of created objects and substances, hence too their perfection and imperfection, their rawness and ripeness, volatility and fixity, thickness and rarefaction, darkness and brilliance, weight and lightness, and the proportions that distinguish one thing from another.

is in every soul" is no less than "the Jews' Great Jehovah, Elohim, Adonay, their Hochma or wisdom. It is the Christians' Messiah." He continues with a delirious mixture of kabbalism and alchemy.[87]

With echoes of Böhme, Fludd pairs heat and cold with soul, their "marriage" resulting in the process of rarefaction and compression that gives birth to "pure and simple elements or qualities," wetness and dryness.[88] In brief, there are two primary substances (fire and primal matter), two primary elements (heat and cold), and two other systems (wetness and dryness). Fire and heat are active; matter and cold are passive. With further similarity to Böhme's application of dualism to the divine attributes (paired with wet/dry, sweet/sour, etc.), Fludd speculates that some angels are watery, others airy, and others fiery.[89] He applies the same cosmic alchemy to the stars and planets.[90]

Far from offering an alternative to biblical revelation, the perennial philosophy is a sublime witness to it, says Fludd:

> It is clear from the opinions of these pagan Philosophers that even they did not stray far from the true knowledge of the divine mind: among whom I can never sufficiently praise nor admire that sacred revelation of Hermes Trismegistus, and his profundity concerning the divine mysteries, since his *Pymander*, of divine and superhuman derivation, bares the hidden secrets of God and his whole creation to us. We reckon that Plato was the next man who knew most about the divine, because, contrary to the assertions of the Peripatetics, he constantly maintained that the world and all that is therein, whether visible or invisible, is made from the innate and essential first principle or material.[91]

Like Ficino, Pico, and Patrizi, Fludd thinks he can demonstrate the Trinity as part of the *prisca theologia*. Descending from Orpheus and Hermes Trismegistus to the Pythagoreans and Plato, Fludd writes that this divine philosophy teaches that the

87. Huffman, *Fludd*, 162–63.

88. See Fludd, "The History of the Macrocosm," in Huffman, *Fludd*, 66.

89. See Fludd, "The History of the Macrocosm," in Huffman, *Fludd*, 68.

90. Fludd then applies his cosmic alchemy to astrology, with hot and dry bodies that are "fiery" (Mars, the sun, and the constellations Aries and Leo); warm and wet natures that are "airy" (Jupiter and Venus; Gemini and Libra); "earthy" and "melancholic" bodies (Saturn and Capricorn); and "watery" ones (Luna; Cancer and Pisces). "Finally, no one, not even an ignoramus, can be unaware that the lowest space in the universe is occupied by elements and things created from elements; but here they are more impure, grosser, and more subject to our senses, and more liable to decay, and they are far less noble and less pure and simple than in the other higher regions." See Fludd, "The History of the Macrocosm," in Huffman, *Fludd*, 69.

91. See Fludd, "The History of the Macrocosm," in Huffman, *Fludd*, 60.

"indivisible Trinity" is "infinite nature, which is boundless Spirit," beyond being and knowing, "the unity of all creatures ... the divine mind, free and separate from mortal matter."[92] The whole system is a farrago of kabbalism, alchemy and astrology with Pythagorean theology and number mysticism proving the Trinity (with a heterodox formulation). To this mix he adds Nicholas of Cusa's panentheistic picture of God as center and circumference with the World Soul in the middle of the three heavens. So just as there is a Trinity of the divine essence, there is a trinity in creation with a primal matter and fiery or spiritual power.[93]

We need not repeat what has become a familiar pattern of Neoplatonic Hermeticism. Fludd's *History of the Macrocosm* and *History of the Two Worlds* are dependent on Paracelsus. He adds his own touches in identifying the Neoplatonic World Soul, the Hermetic *Spiritus Avis*, and the Holy Spirit of the Christian Trinity.[94] Moreover, Fludd tried to synthesize his kabbalistic and Hermetic ideas with Bacon's plan for experimental philosophy.[95]

Fludd's scheme goes far beyond even the Rosicrucian manifestos, much less Andreae's later views. His first defense of the Rosy Cross Brothers goes to "the heart of the matter," as he calls it, offering "A Philosophical Key." The Rosicrucians are "learned and famous Theosophists and Philosophers" like "the most high Prophet and prime Theosopher Moses."[96] Fludd's magic is steeped in medieval sources such as Roger Bacon.[97] Yet he was able to combine this with Bacon, who after all "hoped to restore to man the knowledge which Adam had before the Fall," even though Fludd's tract focuses especially on Dee's type of vision.[98]

Upon his coronation, King James had summarily dismissed Dee. A Scottish Presbyterian by upbringing, James had little patience for anything savoring of magic, and in fact placed great stock in Casaubon for proving the inauthentic claims of

92. See Fludd, "The History of the Macrocosm," in Huffman, *Fludd*, 58–59.

93. See "The History of the Macrocosm," in Huffman, *Fludd*, 60–61.

94. See "The History of the Macrocosm," in Huffman, *Fludd*, 76.

95. Yates, *Rosicrucian Enlightenment*, 107.

96. See Fludd, "The History of the Macrocosm," in Huffman, *Fludd*, 101–3. Cf. Fludd in "*A Nosce te ipsum*: To the Malicious Detractor or, the Calumniators Vision" in Huffman, *Fludd*, 109–10.

97. Fludd says, "Roger Bacon in his *Mirror of Alchemy* admonishes us to make election of such a matter as has in it a pure, clear, white and red *argentum vivum* or quick silver which is not as yet produced to perfection, but remains in his natural compositions equally and proportionably mingled, that is, by just measure with pure sulphur of his like nature, and congealed into a solid mass, that by our wit and discretion, and by the help of our artificial fire, we may reduce him to his complete purity and make him such a thing as after his complement may be a thousand times stronger and more perfect than those simple bodies that are only concocted by natural heat" (Huffman, *Fludd*, 168).

98. Yates, *Rosicrucian Enlightenment*, 132–33.

the Corpus Hermeticum. The king called Fludd to appear before him to respond to charges of magic. Fludd then published his "Brief Declaration to James I," assuring him of the orthodoxy of his defense of the Rosy Cross Brothers:

> Therefore, in the first place, Your Majesty, it [*Tractatus Apologeticus*] does not deal with religious innovation, nor does it share even an iota of any heresy, inasmuch as I, the author of that work, have steadfastly adhered to this Reformed religion (which is now the custom among us) from infancy, and indeed almost from the time I lay at the breast of my nurse in England at the very beginning of my life and right up to this day. . . . Besides, even the Brothers themselves confirm in their Confession that they profess the Reformed religion of Germany.[99]

He argued that such explorations were useful to the kingdom: "We are able to show certain modest truths and things that are useful to our country by which its various illnesses can be cured. These truths are not to be divulged in a common manner which is uncertain and inconstant, but in a new way, unknown to the world, which is most certain and infallible."[100]

This contrast between "uncertain and inconstant" knowledge that is public and "divulged in a common manner" and arcane knowledge that is "infallible" marks the red line between Hermeticism and the experimental method. Fludd tried to convince the king that the secret wisdom he divulged descended from Orpheus, Hermes Trismegistus, and "the Magi or wise men of Babylonia, Persia and India" as well as Empedocles, Pythagoras, and Plato.[101] "In this number," he says, "Plato and Hermes are counted in particular."[102] For his brief to the king, Fludd solicited a note from a "Philosopher and Doctor of Medicine at Anhalt," Matthias Engelhart, which reads:

> Your writings on the arcane philosophy are very much approved of by their most profound followers. Your works therefore will also constitute additional things which pertain to the Macrocosm and Microcosm, and lead to the very centre of things. For undoubtedly you will give an opportunity to other more

99. See Fludd, "The History of the Macrocosm," in Huffman, *Fludd*, 83–84. It is difficult to imagine that Fludd did not know that Andreae and the so-called Rosy Cross Brothers were Lutherans. Perhaps he, like some English Calvinists, considered Lutheranism equivalent to "the Reformed religion of Germany." However, James and Fludd were well aware that there were Reformed churches in Germany.

100. See Fludd, "The History of the Macrocosm," in Huffman, *Fludd*, 85.

101. See Fludd, "The History of the Macrocosm," in Huffman, *Fludd*, 85.

102. See Fludd, "The History of the Macrocosm," in Huffman, *Fludd*, 86.

> occult philosophers to come forward into the public forum, so that at least when these strengths are thus joined together, in this Saturnine age, it will be possible for us, the inquirers, to investigate, with open eyes, the heaven and earth as well as *all of Nature disrobed of her garment*, etc.[103]

What Fludd professes to reveal, Engelhart says, are "the secrets of nature which have been concealed or hidden by the ancient Philosophers under the guise of allegorical riddles and enigmas."[104] The assumption of course is that Fludd and his associates are now decoding them. Disrobing nature of her garment is the sort of trope that we would expect from Bacon and the mechanical philosophers, yet it originated in the Hermetic tradition. However, there are completely different methods and metaphysical assumptions at work here. As we see below, even scientists who practiced occult arts were beginning to distinguish more clearly between mathematics and mysticism, physics and magic.

Whether because of sheer disinterest or out of persuasion, James I seemed sufficiently placated. With a nod from the king and the Privy Council, Fludd was given a patent to make steel. Huffman observes that "his alchemical laboratory graduated to the point where he employed technicians to make better steel than had been previously known in England; and the Privy council agreed that his steel was to be preferred above that made by the prior patentees."[105] Still, though, he aroused suspicion among the College of Physicians.[106] His animism undergirded such ideas as the "weapon-salve," a special preparation that brought healing to a victim when applied to the weapon that caused the injury.[107]

Rumors of the presence of Rosy Cross Brothers aroused considerable interest and alarm across Europe.[108] "Rosicrucianism" became a shibboleth for whatever mystical extremism was being sparked across Europe.[109] Fludd was taking the "Christian Rosenkreutz" myth seriously, along with the Neoplatonic Hermeticism, while Andreae was becoming increasingly critical of the entire "joke." But the Rosy

103. See Fludd, "The History of the Macrocosm," in Huffman, *Fludd*, 90, emphasis added.

104. See Fludd, "The History of the Macrocosm," in Huffman, *Fludd*, 92.

105. Huffman, *Fludd*, 31.

106. Huffman, *Fludd*, 25–26.

107. Fludd appeals to Sir Nicholas Gilbourne, who apparently related to Fludd a story that Lady Raleigh allegedly related to him that her late husband, Sir Walter Raleigh, "would suddenly stop the bleeding of any person (albeit he were far and remote from the party) if he had a handkirchers, or some other piece of linen dipped in some of the blood of the party sent to him." This could hardly have been the work of Satan, Fludd argues (Huffman, *Fludd*, 206).

108. McIntosh, *Rose Cross*, 27.

109. Kahn, "Rosicrucian Hoax," 246–71.

Cross Society was no laughing matter to Father Marin Mersenne (1588–1648), who was especially worried upon receiving reports in 1620 that they had infiltrated Paris. An excellent mathematician and physicist in his own right, Mersenne was France's unofficial secretary of scientific correspondence. Yates writes, "The Rosicrucian scare affected Mersenne, and Fludd seemed to make the invisible brothers visible."[110] Kahn explains, "During the summer of 1623, posters were put up at the crossroads and upon the church doors of Paris, proclaiming the presence of some 'representatives of the Principal College of the Brothers of the Rose-Cross' endowed with marvelous powers and desirous of saving their fellow men from 'error and death.'"[111]

Descartes's search for the Rosy Cross Brothers expressed his longing for a humanitarian Christianity. Like other twenty-two-year olds, Descartes left France and in 1618 enlisted in the Dutch army to see the world. Switching sides in 1619, he joined the Duke of Bavaria's troops in their victory over Elector Frederick in Bohemia, after which he sought a place of solitude for the rest of the winter warmed by a stove in a cabin on the Danube. Yates relates that Descartes found

> some contacts with persons from whom he heard about a society established in Germany under the name of the Brothers of the Rose Cross, who promised a new wisdom and a "veritable science." These rumours chimed in so well with his own thoughts and efforts that he tried to find these Brothers, but without success. One of their rules was to wear no distinguishing dress, so it was naturally very difficult to find them. But a great stir was being made by the numbers of publications which these Brothers were producing. On the night of 10 November 1619, he had dreams, which seem to have been a most important experience, leading him towards the conviction that mathematics were the sole key to the understanding of nature.[112]

Moving on to Ulm for the summer, Descartes met Johann Faulhaber, a mathematician who collaborated with Kepler. Faulhaber had been embroiled in controversy for arguing in his 1619 *Fama syderea nova* that the Great Comet of 1618 prophesied the beginning of the Thirty Years' War.[113] And Faulhaber was "one of the first persons to publish a work addressed to the R. C. Brothers."[114]

110. Yates, *Rosicrucian Enlightenment*, 148–49.
111. Kahn, "Rosicrucian Hoax," 235.
112. Yates, *Rosicrucian Enlightenment*, 151–52.
113. Schneider, "Between Rosicrucians and Cabbala," 311–30.
114. Yates, *Rosicrucian Enlightenment*, 153–54.

After wandering through Moravia, Germany, and Belgium, Descartes returned to Paris finally in 1623, discovering anxious gossip about him becoming a Rosicrucian. Yates relates, "Here he met the full force of the Rosicrucian scare."[115] He had to work convincingly to bring his Parisian colleagues to realize that he was not of their number. Remarkably, then, Descartes had experienced the whole history of this movement up close: in Germany, where the Rosy Cross Brothers achieved fame, in Prague where his army brought defeat to the Protestants, and back in Paris where the scare was in full swing.[116] Descartes's cross-confessional meanderings worried Jesuits in Paris, but Mersenne's greatest concern was whether the brightest thinker of his generation had returned infected by the Hermetic virus. And Descartes was not the only intellectual figure susceptible to the Rosicrucian scare. Soon after the manifestos appeared, a number of prominent scholars searched far and wide to join the Rosy Cross Society.[117]

Fludd's published defenses of Rosicrucianism brought the debate to a fine point, with Mersenne piling on to Erastus's attacks. Kahn says:

> Now all of Paracelsus's conceptions found themselves questioned, and the *mysterium magnum* was in the front line. In the course of these attacks in which, as we know, Mersenne advocated that the alchemists be thrown into the sea with a millstone attached to their necks, the Minim scarcely restrained himself from using violent invectives against Paracelsus, calling him on the occasion of the passage on the *homunculus*, "the Germanic monsters."[118]

Mersenne focused on Genesis (*Quaestiones in Genesim*, 1623), also drawing upon Casaubon's work to bury Hermes Trismegistus once and for all.[119] The Catholic priest and French philosopher Pierre Gassendi likewise published a critique of Fludd's views in 1630. Unlike Mersenne, he considered him "a learned and Christian gentleman," charging him nevertheless with reckless biblical exegesis and with placing scripture, Neoplatonic philosophy, and kabbalah on the same level.[120] Kepler also criticized Fludd in *Harmonices mundi* (1619).[121] Mersenne in-

115. Yates, *Rosicrucian Enlightenment*, 152.

116. Yates, *Rosicrucian Enlightenment*, 153–54.

117. J. T. Young mentions examples in Young, *Johann Moriaen*, 7, 16–21, 156–57.

118. Quote from Mersenne, *Quaestiones celeberrimae in Genesim*, column 651, from Kahn, "Rosicrucian Hoax," 283.

119. Yates, *Rosicrucian Enlightenment*, 148–49.

120. Huffman, *Fludd*, 33. The title of Gassendi's critique is *Examen philosophiae Fluddanae* (1630).

121. Copenhaver, "Occultist Tradition," 464–65.

sisted that "the Renaissance ways of thinking must be eliminated, root and branch, Renaissance animist philosophy must be destroyed, and Renaissance magic, in its modern or Fluddian manifestations, severely repressed." He argued this case not on the basis of an atheistic naturalism, but as a Christian who considered Fludd's interpretation deleterious to both theology and science. "It is one of the more profound ironies of the history of thought that the growth of mechanical science, through which arose the idea of mechanism as a possible philosophy of nature, was itself an outcome of the Renaissance magical tradition. Mechanism divested of magic became the philosophy which was to oust Renaissance animism and to replace the 'conjuror' by the mechanical philosopher."[122]

Meanwhile, in England there was nothing like a Rosy Cross scare. Though "disowned by James I," the Rosy Cross Brothers gained remarkable traction among the leading lights in Stuart society.[123] It was not until 1652 that Vaughan's English translation of the manifestos appeared, but the Latin originals had enjoyed a broad readership, and Fludd gained a high standing as an interpreter of the Rosicrucian aims. It is fascinating to see how little Casaubon's *tour de force* regarding Hermeticism's origins affected thinkers from Fludd to the Cambridge Platonists and Newton.

Eventually, the same College of Physicians that had once barred Fludd made him a censor, supported by good friends such as William Harvey, Richard Andrewes, and the royal physician Sir William Paddy, to whom he dedicated his *Catholic Medicine* in 1629.[124] Huffman points out that there were three overlapping circles of Fludd's London medical community: London physicians like Harvey and Paddy, alchemists like the Bishop of Worcester John Thornborough who were in touch with the so-called Rosicrucians, and a circle around Sir Robert Bruce Cotton "and his renowned library, which . . . included the remains of John Dee's library."[125] Fludd was also among the first to support Harvey's theory of the circulation of blood.[126] In 1629 Charles I gave Fludd and his heirs a grant "for some service performed for the Crown."[127] That service is unknown (perhaps success at steelmaking), but it illustrates how mainstream Fludd was in his day, especially when rewarded by a monarch who yawned at petitions for a royal society of natural philosophers.[128]

Andreae was not Fludd. While he included alchemy and astrology in the curriculum of his *Christianopolis*, Andreae saw his mission as reconciling opposites

122. Yates, *Rosicrucian Enlightenment*, 150, adding, "This fact is not yet generally understood."
123. Yates, *Rosicrucian Enlightenment*, xiii–xiv.
124. Debus, *Chemical Philosophy*, 208.
125. Huffman, *Fludd*, 20.
126. Huffman, *Fludd*, 20.
127. Huffman, *Fludd*, 33.
128. Huffman, *Fludd*, 36–37.

in church and society but most of all within the human heart.[129] Fludd was a direct legatee of Paracelsus and Dee, with a good deal of Böhme running in his veins. While Andreae's *Confessio* and *Chymical Wedding* drew directly from Dee's *Monas hieroglyphica*, these were for Andreae allegorical symbols and rhetorical embellishments. In contrast, Fludd relied on Dee's work for the substance of his system. Andreae and his ilk—including Bacon and Comenius—knew when they were writing fiction. But it was not fiction any longer. Fludd and his critics alike took the whole affair very seriously. There was a growing cleft between those who treated Hermetic ideas as allegorical symbols or analogies and those who saw the relation of macrocosm and microcosm in terms of identity.

This helps to explain why Andreae hesitated to identify himself with the Rosy Cross Order, preferring to speak simply of a Christian society, whose values he tried to implement on the ground. The "false Rosy Cross Brothers," he says in his 1616 comedy *Turbo*, engage in "an art without art, . . . whose truths are to tell tall stories," and whose life is to wander begging for money until they finally get put on a cross.[130] We are reminded of Plato's criticism of pretended Orphic magi who carry their books and spells from town to town knocking on doors to make a sale.

In my view, Andreae's term for his fiction—*ludibrium*, which refers to a farcical stage play—possesses twofold meaning. First, he actually did intend his fiction to serve as a playful experiment, albeit one with a keen genius for allegory and allusion. The Christian Rosenkreutz legend was a deliberate fabrication, not meant to be taken seriously as a historical narrative. He said in fact that he had written *Chymical Wedding* when he was only nineteen, a decade before it was published. Second, after Fludd and his critics had turned the whole thing into, as he says, "the unworthy mockery [*ludibrium*] of the fiction of the Rosicrucian Fraternity," Andreae threw up his hands. He calls "false Rosicrucians" mere "impostors" (in fact, posting a guard to bar their entrance to Christianopolis).[131] This suggests both that there was a real Rosy Cross fraternity and that it was hijacked. According to Yates, "About 1629 Andreae made an attempt to restart it at Nuremberg and, through this branch, Leibniz came into contact with Rosicrucian ideas and seems to have joined a Rosicrucian Society there in 1666."[132] In fact, "the rules for Leibniz's proposed Order of Charity are practically quotations from the *Fama*."[133]

129. The "great mystery" possessed by the Order of the Rosy Cross in the *Chymical Wedding* is "the mystery of inner transformation." See McLean's introduction in Godwin, *Chemical Wedding*, 8.

130. The full title is *Turbo, sive moleste et frustra per cuncta divagans ingenium* (Turbo, or a spirit wandering badly and vainly everywhere). See Maxwell-Stuart, *Chemical Choir*, 116–17.

131. Quoted in Dickson, *Tessera of Antilia*, 41.

132. Yates, *Rosicrucian Enlightenment*, 197.

133. Yates, *Rosicrucian Enlightenment*, 198.

Comenius and the Royal Society: World-Transforming Mission

Jan Amos Comenius (1592–1670), regarded as the father of modern education, represents a direct link between Andreae and English Puritans who tried to create during the pro-Presbyterian Long Parliament, a "further reformation" not only of the church but also of society. "If his thought has 'utopian characteristics,'" writes Jan Milíč Lochman, "it is this very world-transforming utopia of hope that takes seriously God in his promises and precisely for this reason hesitates to abandon the world in its status quo."[134] As late as 1656 Comenius said, "from [Andreae] I obtained almost the very elements of my pansophic thoughts." Despite his humility, Held judges that this relationship between Comenius and Andreae was "in all probability to a considerable extent a mutual one."[135] The principles in Comenius's *Theophilus* are those of Andreae's *Christianopolis*.[136] And the curriculum described in these works is identical, including instruction in astrology and mystical numbers.[137]

In fact, a disheartened Andreae wrote a letter to Comenius, giving the frankest explanation for what happened in the aftermath of the *Fama* and *Confessio* and his hope that Comenius would carry the work forward:

> We were a few men of good standing, who came together after the mockery [*ludibrium*] of the vain report [*Fama*] about eight years before, and there were more still in arms. But the unrest in Germany surprised and nearly destroyed us. Many, drawn to a better country, deserted us: hence some mourned, some were involved in the uproar, others despaired—I shortened the sails. Only we few have remained, more panting for a happy outcome, than sufficient to clean the Augean stables. And so we hand the tables of our shipwreck to be read by you and improved, if it pleases: it would be blessing enough if we shall not have failed altogether in our great enterprise.[138]

134. Lochman, preface to *John Comenius*, 5.

135. Held, *Christianopolis*, 103–4.

136. Held, *Christianopolis*, 104–5.

137. Held notes that Comenius followed Andreae's belief that schools require "large, roomy, and pleasant halls and apartments for the pupils." Further, "Comenius accepts Andreae's views on astronomy, astrology, and mystic numbers directly. . . . Finally and most important of all is Andreae's scheme for the organization of a college, that is, a body of men, educated, equipped and desirous of improving human affairs, 'working together' to fulfill a common purpose" (Held, *Christianopolis*, 106).

138. See the letter of Andreae to Comenius, dated September 15, 1629 (*Opera didactica omnia*, 2:284), quoted in Dickson, *Tessera of Antilia*, 163–64.

Comenius developed an ambitious program he called "pansophia": the knowledge of all things for all people. It was a major influence on the Hartlib Circle, the intellectual network established by Samuel Hartlib, which was the "forerunner in fact of the Royal Society," Maxwell-Stuart notes. Alchemy, health and extending life, and "millenarian speculations and prophecies" fueled "the great reforms and improvements they had in mind for society."[139]

In 1631, Comenius's first major work appeared, entitled *Janua linguarum reserata*. Its expansive vision for educational reform attracted a wide readership across Europe in many languages.[140] This work argued that language is better taught to children through natural objects and pictures than by rote memorization—exactly as in Andreae's *Christianopolis*.[141]

In July of 1627, the Habsburgs gave Protestants six months to either convert or leave the lands of the Holy Roman Empire.[142] Comenius led the Brethren to Leszno, Poland. Here he began his correspondence with Andreae and wrote *The Great Didactic*, which laid out the goals of his educational reform. Boys and girls were to be educated together and "taught in a spontaneous and natural manner" rather than in austere and windowless classrooms under strict teachers. "All of life was a school designed to prepare humanity for eternity" according to Comenius, and nature offered the best analogies for abstract ideas. According to Louthan and Sterk, "He argued that failure to learn was an indication that the instructor, not the student, was at fault. True learning was a pleasant and stimulating experience. To this day, Comenius's groundbreaking work is widely respected by child psychologists and educators alike."[143]

Comenius was convinced that only a Christ-centered education could lead youth to true understanding of all things. Louthan and Sterk observe, "Education, therefore, is a form of repentance. . . . For Comenius, education was in essence a pastoral calling. It was the process by which people could be trained to see beyond the apparent chaos of the world and discover the underlying unity." In Comenius's own words, "I have written, not as a pedagogue, but as a theologian."[144] Comenius's pansophia turns toward the world of concrete particulars, awakening the senses and leading inevitably to a greater use of the inductive method. However, like Bacon, he acknowledges that the senses as well as reason sometimes deceive, requiring humility and self-criticism.

139. Maxwell-Stuart, *Chemical Choir*, 127.
140. Louthan and Sterk, *John Comenius*, 18; cf. Held, *Christianopolis*, 101.
141. Louthan and Sterk, *John Comenius*, 21.
142. Louthan and Sterk, *John Comenius*, 13–14.
143. Louthan and Sterk, *John Comenius*, 13–14.
144. Louthan and Sterk, *John Comenius*, 27.

With *The Great Didactic*, Comenius became a European celebrity. "Cardinal Richelieu invited him to France, and John Winthrop may have hoped he would accept a position as the first president of Harvard College."[145] Comenius corresponded with Samuel Hartlib, who published his *Christian Pansophy* in 1637 and invited him to establish a "pansophic college" in London.[146] Instead, Comenius accepted the invitation of Louis de Geer to reform Sweden's schools. On his way to Sweden, he had a long meeting with René Descartes but "Descartes's division between mind and matter was unacceptable to Comenius."[147]

Comenius was invited by Prince Sigismund of Transylvania in 1640 to establish a school in Sarospatak, where he wrote his first picture book and renewed his friendship with a circle of prophets whom he held in high regard. "He eagerly listened to their predictions concerning the imminent collapse of Habsburg rule in Bohemia," Louthan and Sterk relate. "In 1657 Comenius published *Light in Darkness*, a voluminous tome containing the prophecies of his three colleagues. Even in his own time, Comenius's credulous attachment to Drabík's circle damaged his reputation."[148] Based on their visions, Comenius set 1672 as the year of the millennium's dawn, and believed that Cromwell, the Swedish king Gustavus Adolphus, and the Prince of Transylvania would overthrow the papal church. To that end he tried, in vain of course, to persuade even the French monarch Louis XIV to join the cause.

Comenius had lived through decades of persecution, losing his family, being hounded by Roman Catholic authorities who burned his house and library filled with precious manuscripts, and leading the Brethren to Poland due to persecution. At age sixty-four, while exiled in Holland, he completed a seven-volume "blueprint for the unification of all knowledge and a universal system of education." In his final years, according to Louthan and Sterk:

> He argued that education in turn would lead to both an ecumenical religious settlement and worldwide peace.... A new war between England and the Netherlands had broken out in 1665. Urging a cessation of hostilities between the

145. Spinka, *Comenius*, xi, quoting Cotton Mather: "That brave old man, Johannes Amos Comenius, the fame of whose worth hath been trumpeted as far as more than three languages (whereof everyone is indebted unto his *Janua*) could carry it, was indeed agreed withal, by our Mr. Winthrop in his travels through the low countries, to come over into New England and illuminate this College [i.e., Harvard] and country in the quality of a President. But the solicitations of the Swedish Ambassador, diverting him another way, that incomparable Moravian became not an American citizen."

146. Held, *Christianopolis*, 101.

147. Louthan and Sterk, *John Comenius*, 14–15.

148. Louthan and Sterk, *John Comenius*, 15.

two Protestant countries, Comenius himself attended the peace conference at Breda in May 1667. For this occasion he wrote the *Angel of Peace*, an indictment of these two commercial rivals. Three years later he was dead.[149]

The *Labyrinth* of Comenius

Common Renaissance tropes, including the labyrinth, the human mind as an idol factory, and the need for new spectacles that are strung together particularly by John Calvin are also evident in the writings of Bacon and Comenius. Regarding Comenius in particular, Louthan and Sterk explain:

> According to Comenius, God has provided humanity with three tools to learn wisdom: the five senses to discover the secrets of the natural world; reason and intelligence to increase their knowledge; and faith, for it is only with this spiritual gift that God's children may hear his voice through Scripture, meditation, or prayer. These three bases of Comenius's pedagogical reforms are central components of the *Labyrinth*.[150]

Opening with a familiar shipwreck scene, Comenius's book *Labyrinth of the World and Paradise of the Heart* sends its pilgrim on a tour not of an imagined utopian society but of the dystopian maze of a society in which he actually lives.[151] Similar to Bacon's description of "Idols," the pilgrim in the *Labyrinth* is faced with "the bridle of curiosity" and the "spectacles of delusion." The Queen of Worldly Wisdom appoints deceitful guides—Delusion and Searchall Ubiquitous—who endeavor to convince the pilgrim that he should settle for the illusions of happiness. He is shown the working class, fighting over materials and disagreeing over their useless tasks, and then encounters the educated, who believe they are immortal.[152]

After trying each department of the city that the guides show him, the pilgrim is dissatisfied with them all, even astrology and alchemy. He observes sympathetically that some called astrologists "astro-liars."[153] Comenius (like Bacon) charges

149. Louthan and Sterk, *John Comenius*, 16. The seven-volume work is titled, *De rerum humanarum emendatione consultatio catholica*.

150. Louthan and Sterk, *John Comenius*, 25. They add that Comenius outlined his educational principles in the *Panaugia* (Universal dawn), the second volume of his magnum opus, the *Consultatio*.

151. Louthan and Sterk, *John Comenius*, 92.

152. Louthan and Sterk, *John Comenius*, 100.

153. Louthan and Sterk, *John Comenius*, 110.

these alchemists with performing useless experiments.[154] Finally, the pilgrim encounters the Rosicrucians.[155] He does not doubt their many accomplishments; on the contrary, the Rosicrucians receive the most favorable descriptions thus far. Yet, the noisy clamor is vanity. "Should I wait for this," the pilgrim asks, "since I have not seen a single example of success among so many thousands of people more learned than I? I do not want to gawk at this any longer. Let us leave this place."[156] Coming to the physicians, the pilgrim sees them cutting, chopping, cauterizing, heating, and cooling, although "meanwhile patients were dying in their arms."[157]

The bottom line is that everyone encountered by the pilgrim is working, but none of them are doing so for any purpose—they are doing more harm than good. The fault is not that these vocations are evil in themselves. The point is rather that "human reason and sensory perception have their limits. With them, the pilgrim is only able to discover the deception and chaos of the world. The harmony and unity underlying this confusion can only be discerned through revelation. When the pilgrim meets Christ, he is given a new pair of spectacles. The Word of God and the Holy Spirit replace the lens of Assumption and rim of Habit."[158] Turning from the illusions, the pilgrim finally sees the harmony of God's universe.[159]

Comenius's *One Thing Necessary*

"When John Heydon adapted the *New Atlantis* in his *Holy Guide* (1662)," Yates informs us, "the governor of the House of Strangers announces himself as 'of the Order of the Rosie Cross.'"[160] Bacon's Bensalem "is intensely Christian in spirit, though not doctrinal, interpreting the Christian spirit in terms of practical benevolence, like the R. C. [Rosy Cross] Brothers." Yates continues,

> It is profoundly influenced by Hebraic-Christian mysticism, as in Christian Cabala. The inhabitants of New Atlantis respect the Jews; they call their college after Solomon and seek for God in nature. The Hermetic-Cabalist tradition has borne fruit in their great college devoted to scientific enquiry. . . . The inhabi-

154. Louthan and Sterk, *John Comenius*, 113–14.
155. Louthan and Sterk, *John Comenius*, 114–15.
156. Louthan and Sterk, *John Comenius*, 117–18.
157. Louthan and Sterk, *John Comenius*, 119.
158. Louthan and Sterk, *John Comenius*, 25–26.
159. Louthan and Sterk, *John Comenius*, 26.
160. Yates, *Rosicrucian Enlightenment*, 167, quoting from John Heydon, *The Holy Guide* (1662).

> tants of New Atlantis would appear to have achieved the great instauration of learning and have therefore returned to the state of Adam in Paradise before the Fall—the objective of advancement both for Bacon and for the authors of the Rosicrucian manifestos.[161]

Yates's description, "intensely Christian in spirit, though not doctrinal," highlights the difference between the pansophic and Puritan outlooks. Though both were broadly Reformed, the one was oriented toward a universal reformation of society, while the other was oriented toward a further reformation of the church. Both were attracted to an "experimental Calvinism" that integrated doctrine with feeling and practical action. However, those whom we usually identify as Puritans were steeped in scholastic theology, and most were ardent Calvinists, as was the Church of England generally until Archbishop Laud.

Having experienced heavy personal losses from the forces of the Catholic League, Comenius and his colleagues—Samuel Hartlib, John Dury, Johann Moriaen, Henry Oldenberg and others—were devoted to evangelical unity. All of these figures were influenced by Johann Heinrich Alsted. Despite being an important figure in Reformed orthodoxy, he nevertheless came gradually to embrace millennialism. He also sought reunion with Lutheranism in an effort to form a united evangelical church against Rome.

Arminianism was rejected as a heresy after the Synod of Dort in 1618–1619, which included delegates from the Church of England. However, members of the Hartlib Circle formed friendships with Remonstrants and other individuals disenfranchised from the Dutch Reformed Church in an effort to secure a pan-Protestant alliance against the Church of Rome. Loyalty to the Book of Concord or the Reformed confessions was secondary to an anti-Roman program. The Presbyterian-dominated Long Parliament was seen by the Hartlib Circle as the greatest opportunity for the pansophic reformation to flourish, but millennialism was excluded from the Westminster Confession and Catechisms along with Arminianism and other perceived dangers. The worry among pansophists was that instead of being a catalyst for universal knowledge and reformation, the established church was falling into the same "scholastic wrangling" that Andreae and others decried in Lutheran orthodoxy.

Near his death, Comenius wrote *Unum Necessarium* (One thing necessary, 1668), taken from the contrast in Luke 10:42 between Martha's busyness with Mary's sitting at Jesus's feet as "the one thing needful." Dedicating the work to Prince Rupert, son of Elector Frederick V, Comenius examined the condition of

161. Yates, *Rosicrucian Enlightenment*, 168–69.

his day in terms of "Daedalean Labyrinths, Sisyphean Exhaustions, and Tantalean Illusions." In laws and politics, "the one thing necessary" was summarized by Jesus as loving God and neighbor. By rejecting this command, we multiply laws, courts, and penalties. Philosophers multiply schools, warring over unimportant questions, and even modern thinkers like Descartes wander in labyrinths while genuine expansion of natural knowledge languishes.[162] Not only in religion but in all of life, "the one thing necessary" is Christ, but we wander in scholastic labyrinths and divide into sects.[163] There is a somewhat naive utopianism here that assumes that rebirth in Christ would eliminate the proliferation of laws, jails, synods, and detailed doctrinal systems. A mild enthusiasm pervades Comenius's thinking, as he compares the age of the prophets and apostles with the present day. If Christ's ministers knew the nearness of the end, they would exercise their spiritual gifts as contemporary prophets with fresh visions and revelations.[164]

Millennium Dawning and the Regathering of Jews

Despite the fact that the Book of Concord rejected millennialism, by the dawn of the seventeenth century it was being taught by Lutheran theologian Eustachius Poyssel, who influenced Johann Valentin Andreae. And, as we have seen, millennialism was advanced by the Reformed theologian Alsted, who taught Comenius, Hartlib, and Dury.

Central to these interpretations was the regathering of the Jewish people to their ancient homeland, the rebuilding of the temple, and the thousand-year kingdom under Christ or the Holy Spirit. For Comenius, Dury, and Hartlib (and indeed most founding members of the Royal Society), it meant the readmission of Jews to England through the mediation of the rabbi of Amsterdam, Menasseh ben Israel. For nearly two years Menasseh had lived in London for the duration of the Whitehall Conference that considered readmission of Jews. Menasseh encouraged the view that the "angelic" natives in the New World were descendants of the lost tribes of Israel. His writings were eagerly translated and read, especially his *Hope of Israel*, and he spent a lot of time with the Hartlib Circle, Cambridge Platonists, and more radical prophets. "They especially valued him as the Jewish expositor of a common Messianic vision," notes Nadler, "wherein the worldly empires will

162. Comenius, *Unum Necessarium*, 18.
163. Comenius, *Unum Necessarium*, 19.
164. Comenius, *Unum Necessarium*, 77.

be swept away by a 'Fifth Kingdom' ruled by a savior sent by God."[165] A devoted kabbalist, Menasseh also developed a Jewish interpretation of reincarnation. On a side note, while Menasseh was in London, his student Baruch Spinoza was excommunicated from his Amsterdam synagogue.

During the same period, the writings of the British scholar Joseph Mede became widely influential. After reading Sextus Empiricus as an undergraduate, Mede fell into a skeptical crisis and in his search for certainty discovered biblical prophecy.[166] A fellow of Christ's College, Cambridge, he was an Egyptologist, Hebraist, and lecturer in Greek. Based on his prophetic interpretation of Revelation, Mede maintained that the end would come in 1716. Considered fanaticism at the beginning of the century, Mede's interpretation of biblical prophecy later became mainstream. After his death in 1639, his tracts circulated widely, including his *Key of Revelation Searched and Demonstrated* (English translation, 1643). Even William Twisse, prolocutor of the Westminster Assembly, praised this work.[167]

A complete edition of Mede's works was published by Cambridge Platonist John Worthington in 1665. Educated in the Puritan bastion of Emmanuel College, Worthington was made vice chancellor of Cambridge and was the intermediary between Hartlib and More. Though he was not a philosopher, Worthington was in the Hartlib Circle and wrote on devotional subjects, including an unpublished work on Jakob Böhme. According to Haykin, "The ecumenist Scotsman John Dury, the German scientist Samuel Hartlib, and the Czech educationalist Comenius had each been profoundly influenced by the millenarianism of Alsted and Mede, and seem to have seriously entertained the idea that London was the centre from which human knowledge and divine rule would spread."[168] Not only in content but in practical action, members of the Hartlib Circle exhibited the passion of the divine self to break free from the oppressive system of a locative order and reconfigure society along utopian lines.

Invisible College to the Royal Society

By now we can see several streams converging. Yet, Christian monotheism was also reasserting itself against natural supernaturalism, with considerable implications for the experimental revolution. The ideals expressed in the Rosicrucian

165. Nadler, *Menasseh ben Israel*, 3.
166. Popkin, *History of Skepticism*, 64–65. See Jue, *Joseph Mede*, 7–16.
167. Haykin, "Separatists," 126. See also Jue, *Joseph Mede*.
168. Haykin, "Separatists," 126.

manifestos, including their "invisible college," was kept alive in England especially by Bohemian and German refugees as well as those who had been close to Samuel Hartlib, including Boyle and Newton. Despite their personal losses in the Stuart Restoration, most founders of the Royal Society were Puritans.[169] Founded in 1584 as a Puritan seminary, Emmanuel College, Cambridge became the nursery of Cambridge Platonism by 1630.[170]

Called "the Intelligencer of Europe," Hartlib played a role in England analogous to that of Marin Mersenne in France. Like those of Comenius, Dury's educational views were fostered by Andreae's *Christianopolis.* "Hence in 1640 definite plans were undertaken to make the theory a reality," notes Held. "Comenius was asked to map out the details for a society of scholars and finally urgently invited to come to England and describe the whole in assembly."[171] Hartlib was also involved with the German utopian Society of Antilia.[172] His idea of an English colony in Virginia for the society was another grand scheme that was interrupted by the civil war.[173] Hartlib was convinced that, like the Jews, natives in the Americas needed Protestant intervention against their Spanish oppressors.[174] Hartlib's correspondence with Comenius began around 1635, when Hartlib translated and published some of his writings. With the opening of the Long Parliament in 1640, they joined together to write a plea for an institution based on Bacon's principles. And once more, it was in the form of a fictional utopia, *A Description of the Famous Kingdom of Macaria,* with its thriving "College of Experience" for natural philosophy. But the Irish Rebellion (1641) consumed the king's attention, and Comenius went to Sweden.[175]

Refugees from a Continent riven by wars pressed the interest of the Hartlib group in a constitutional republic with close ties to Sweden and the Netherlands. Wide-ranging in its interests, the Hartlib Circle was fired by Bacon's vision fused with

169. Yates, *Rosicrucian Enlightenment,* 248.

170. Similarly to Sidney Sussex College in 1596, Emmanuel College was founded in 1584 by Elizabeth's exchequer, Sir Walter Mildmay, as a Puritan seminary. Preston's fame as a preacher and a theologian attracted many students, including some who would become key figures in the Massachusetts Bay Colony (e.g., John Cotton and John Harvard) and the founder of the Connecticut Colony, John Davenant. King James, fond especially of his anti-Arminian arguments, made him chaplain to Prince Charles. After succeeding John Donne briefly as preacher at Lincoln's Inn, he became master at Emmanuel. See Gordon, "Preston."

171. Held, *Christianopolis,* 109–10, 112.

172. Dickson, *Tessera of Antilia,* 114. This group was led by Johann Abraham Pömer and Heinrich Hein.

173. Dickson, *Tessera of Antilia,* 124.

174. Fradkin, "Protestant Unity," 273–94.

175. Dickson, *Tessera of Antilia,* 171.

millennial hopes that the rise of a Presbyterian Parliament might procure a lasting peace, the overthrow of tyranny, and the beginning of genuine science. Held points out, "The fact that parliament appointed [Hartlib]—a foreign-born man—as 'agent for the advancement of universal learning' shows in what esteem he was held by his contemporaries. He introduced the writings of Comenius into England. In 1644 Milton addressed to him his *Tractate on Education*."[176] The college he envisioned was not merely focused on experimental science but on experimental learning in all areas. "It was to be fundamentally a 'universal science' containing a resumé of all human knowledge, both resting upon a religious basis and leading toward a religious enlightenment."[177] The "invisible college" envisioned in the Rosicrucian manifestos and in the utopias of Andreae and Bacon was destined to become a reality.

While less committed to Hermetic dogmatism than figures like Fludd, the Hartlib Circle was sympathetic to alchemy.[178] They passed this interest on to Robert Boyle and other young members of the circle. Dutch German alchemist and clergyman Johann Moriaen (1591–1668) is an extreme example in this regard.[179] A recruiter for the group, his path was similar to others. After studies at Heidelberg, he became a Reformed minister and formed connections with the Dutch Collegiant leader, Adam Boreel. Attracted to Boreel's pantheistic natural theology, Moriaen eventually renounced his ordination, reflecting his "apparent indifference to doctrinal issues."[180] Instead, he embraced alchemy full throttle. Whatever theological problems Comenius had with Boreel, for Moriaen the pansophia project was everything.[181] Like Renaissance Hermeticism in general, alchemy was a natural theology that could absorb the doctrines of Christianity through allegorical interpretation.

The Hartlib Circle included also George Starkey and Robert Boyle, both of whom were alchemists.[182] Maxwell-Stuart relates that Starkey created a "separate existence" as "Eirenaeus Philalethes," linking himself to the original Rosicrucians:

> It is all part of the millenarianist psychology of the period. The Golden Age will be preceded by the Age of Antichrist, when the harbinger of the New Jerusalem is persecuted. Real gold—and the art of transmutation which produces it—is

176. Held, *Christianopolis*, 107.
177. Held, *Christianopolis*, 108.
178. Young, *Johann Moriaen*, 51.
179. On Moriaen see Young, *Johann Moriaen*.
180. Young, *Johann Moriaen*, 86.
181. Young, *Johann Moriaen*, 80–89.
182. Young, *Johann Moriaen*, 49–59, 184–86, 218–49.

> ultimately valueless, and humankind must be brought to understand this. Only a purging and renewal of the world will transform the age of (moral) dross into the age of genuine gold, and those who realize this will be granted, by God's favour, the secrets of Nature which not only reveal to humankind some of the intimate workings of God's mind, but also present in concrete metaphors the transmutation which God intends for His creation.[183]

Starkey's outlook, in the words of Maxwell-Stuart, "owes much to Paracelsus and his particular followers."[184] As we will see, he became a friend and important collaborator with Boyle, who represents a striking example of the complicated relationship between alchemy and mechanical philosophy.

In correspondence, first with his tutor Marcombes in Geneva and then with Francis Tallents, Boyle mentions "the invisible college" several times in 1646 and 1647.[185] The initial meeting took place in 1645 in rooms at Gresham College in London, whose faculty focused on scientific matters. It was led by Theodore Haack, another German Reformed refugee.[186] Christopher Wren taught astronomy and Robert Hooke geometry. Sir Robert Moray, a staunch Royalist, was also welcomed among their number. Another important figure was John Wallis, the Savillian Professor of Geometry at Oxford in 1659 and inventor of infinitesimal calculus. Also, the cleric John Wilkins was involved in the Gresham meetings, as was the polymath Sir William Petty. Petty, a friend of Fludd, had an interest in mechanics from his youth and studied in Leiden where he focused on medicine.[187] Finally, Henry Oldenburg, a Calvinist refugee from Bremen, came to England in 1640 and became the first secretary of the Royal Society.[188]

The civil war and the plague interfered with the meetings. Otherwise, as Held observes, "the Royal Society might well have been founded nearly two decades earlier than it was." According to Held, "The moving factors of this second attempt, Boyle, Haacke, and others, were also acquainted with and inspired by the Andreae-Comenius system."[189] Nor was Andreae more interested in Hermetic matters than many of the Society's founders. Held says, "In speaking of Andreae, the criticism is

183. Maxwell-Stuart, *Chemical Choir*, 130–31.

184. Maxwell-Stuart, *Chemical Choir*, 130–31.

185. Held, *Christianopolis*, 115.

186. John Wallis recalled, "A German of the Palatinate and then resident in London, who, I think gave the first occasion, and first suggested these meetings." Quoted in Held, *Christianopolis*, 115.

187. Held, *Christianopolis*, 116 n. 1.

188. Held, *Christianopolis*, 114 n. 2.

189. Held, *Christianopolis*, 124–25.

often made that he leaned too strongly toward astrology, alchemy, and the supernatural." However, the Society leaned further. The items of the plan "border on the alchemistic and supernatural as well: 'What river turns wood into stone,' 'Turning water into earth,' 'growth of pebbles in water,' 'Springs that petrify,' 'gold into silver,' 'feeding of a carp in air,' 'making insects of cheese and sack,' 'As to whether spiders are enchanted by a circle of unicorns' horns or Irish earth roundabout them.' It might be noted here that Boyle had some faith in transmutation and alchemy, for he was instrumental in repealing the statute against 'multiplying gold.' And even Bacon was at times, especially early in his career, not quite ready to give up all contentions in favor of the magical."[190] Indeed, most of these marvels appear in the *New Atlantis*.

Thomas Vaughan's translation of the Rosicrucian manifestos in 1652 was read widely and critically, as were his own magico-theosophical works. Henry More initiated a protracted and heated exchange. John Wilkins and Seth Ward dismissed the tracts as silly or perhaps heretical.[191] Ben Johnson's *The Alchemist* mocks them as "a pretty kind of game, Somewhat like tricks 'o the cards, to cheat a man."[192] Yet other founders of the Royal Society were enthusiastic, particularly the Royalists Elias Ashmole and Sir Robert Moray, who became Vaughan's patrons and were instrumental in early Freemasonry.

If anything, the Rosicrucian fraternity became more popular in the Stuart Restoration, as opportunistic advocates switched loyalties to Charles II.[193] The critics of the Rosicrucians satirized the Royal Society, sometimes in the same breath. Samuel Butler alleged that Rosicrucians were involved in witchcraft and the founders of the Royal Society pore over "subjects fit for sport of Boys, and Rabble-wit."[194] In particular, as he said elsewhere, "The Fraternity of the Rosy-Crucians is very like the Sect of the ancient Gnostici who call'd themselves so, from the excellent Learning they pretend to, although they were really the most ridiculous Sots of all Mankind."[195]

Return of Hermes Trismegistus

Sir Thomas Browne's *Religio Medici* (1643) brought the phrase "Hermetic Tradition" into common use: "Now besides these particular and divided Spirits, there may be (for aught I know) a universal and common Spirit to the whole world. It was the

190. Held, *Christianopolis*, 121.
191. Willard, "*De furore Britannico*," 61.
192. Quoted in Maxwell-Stuart, *Chemical Choir*, 116–17.
193. Schuchard, *Temple of Vision*, 595.
194. Bembridge, "Rosicrucian Resurgence," 225.
195. Gilly, "Bekenntnis zur Gnosis," 422.

opinion of Plato, and is yet of the Hermeticall Philosophers."[196] Of course, it was the view also of the Cambridge Platonists as well, which is one of the reasons why Henry More was particularly eager to denounce magi like Vaughan. John Everard, a disciple of Robert Fludd and close friend of many founders of the Royal Society, exhibits this connection. As noted earlier, Everard produced the first English translations of the *TG* alongside the works of Tauler, Böhme, Sebastian Franck, Nicholas of Cusa, and the Corpus Hermeticum. The Court of High Commission convicted him of "Familism, Antinomianism, Anabaptism," imposing a heavy fine. Convicted again in 1640, he recanted his spiritualist beliefs.[197]

What is clear in Bacon, as in Campanella, is that natural philosophy must shed its theoretical speculations by rolling up its sleeves to do real work. Pansophists shared with Hermeticists a passion to unite all knowledge in a universal system and were generally open to alchemy, astrology, numerology, and the like. However, while pansophia was a collaborative effort of wide exchange throughout Europe and sought to change the world, Hermeticists worked alone. Pansophists prized induction and submitted their investigations to peer review, while Hermeticists gave free rein to speculative theories and bristled at criticism. Pansophists, from Andreae to the Hartlib Circle and the founders of the Royal Society, stood midway between Hermeticism and science. The scientist, like the magician, gets his hands dirty and sometimes scorched. Engineers of machines are more valuable for this extension of human empire than are monkish scholars poring over ancient texts and whispering arcane secrets. The craftsman ascends in the seventeenth century to a nobility that had been denied him in previous ages.

Freemasonry, in its very name, displays this connection. Although its founders were mostly academics, the lodges established the lore of an unbroken fellowship from Hermes Trismegistus. As Margaret Jacob observes:

> Seventeenth-century masonic manuscripts from the operative guilds stress this "ancient" history and as late as the 1690s make mention of a secret mathematical wisdom descended from Hermes. In this tradition, possibly rooted in popular culture and artisan craft, as well as in the scientific literature of the Renaissance, we once again encounter a version of the Hermetic tradition. Freemasonry provides one link between Renaissance Hermetism, with its strongly naturalistic tendencies, and the early stages of the Enlightenment in England. Gradually the Hermetic lore would be replaced by the "magic" of Newtonian science, just as the artisans would be displaced from this 'specu-

196. *Religio Medici* 1:32 in Browne, *Religio Medici*, 57.

197. Versluis, *Theosophia*, 228.

> lative' institution. Yet both would leave their mark, in a mysticism that could easily lend itself to the worship of nature, in a dedication to the study of mathematics, and of course in ceremonies and rituals for the installation of grand masters and the initiation of apprentices, in aprons and emblems such as the square and the compass—all of which hearkened back to a world of mechanics and craftsmen.[198]

Importantly, Jacobs reminds us, "For these practical men of affairs the Hermetic tradition supplied a universalist ideology based upon the glorification of ancient learning which was vaguely mystical in the telling but immensely practical in application."[199] This is an important point, since elsewhere in this century the focus would turn toward new discoveries. In some sense the church represented a connection to a long tradition, but Freemason lodges claimed one reaching back long before the birth of Christ. One did not feel obliged to give up one for the other, but the explicit rule against religious debates created a new social space in which educated men could avoid them in favor of alternative doctrines and rituals. We recall the paradox of popes and cardinals finding fullness in their Hermetic gardens while still conducting their duties in the public religion.

Freemasonry seems to have grown out of these influences of Renaissance esoterism—"spirituality without religion," giving Hermeticism an "invisible church" that one could join without renouncing membership in the established church. Medieval masonry was based on the guild; it was only in the late seventeenth and especially eighteenth century that Freemasons devised elaborate levels and ceremonies. As Jacob tells us:

> The earliest lodges date from the 1640s and significantly for this story concern two important practitioners of science and magic, Sir Robert Moray and Elias Ashmole. With strong interests in alchemy, Moray became a devoted Mason in 1641 and eventually master of his lodge in Edinburgh. At the time, Moray was general quartermaster to the Scottish army and in the service of Charles I. One of the earliest references to speculative Masonry in European literature comes from a mid-seventeenth-century Scottish poem praising both Masons and the Stuarts: "For we be brethren of the rosi-cross; / We have the mason-word and second sight, / Things for to come we can foretell allright. . . . But for King Charles, his honour we are bold."[200]

198. Jacob, *Radical Enlightenment*, 85.
199. Jacob, *Radical Enlightenment*, 86.
200. Jacob, *Radical Enlightenment*, 90.

Elias Ashmole (1617–1692) was an alchemist, astrologer, and antiquary.[201] The Ashmolean Museum in Oxford was built to contain his vast collections. He considered the Hermeticist William Backhouse his spiritual father who "intytled me to some small part of grand sire Hermes wealth."[202] He attended Brasenose College, Oxford, "specifically to study the science of astrology."[203] His interest in astrology and alchemy is evident in his *Fasciculus Chemicus* (1650) and especially the *Theatrum Chemicum Britannicum* (1652), which preserved the works of John Dee. His work entitled *The Way to Bliss* (1658) is a combination of mystical spirituality and cures of various illnesses. Ashmole was considered by many to be a member of the Rosicrucian order. He not only copied the *Fama* and *Confessio* painstakingly in his own hand but wrote a public address asking to be admitted to their fraternity.[204] Ashmole was influenced by the Paracelsian physician Michael Maier and published John Dee's works.[205] Even as late as Newton, it appeared that natural magic could coexist with mechanistic physical philosophy.[206]

Ashmole was admitted to a lodge at Warrington, Lancashire, in 1646.[207] Later he joined the Masons Hall London, and in the Restoration he was favored with various posts. In many ways Moray and especially Ashmole are transitional figures in the Scientific Revolution, both being Royalists. Ashmole believed that alchemy might provide the foundations for a universal and practical learning. Yet, like Fludd, he was inspired also by Bacon. In 1691 Christopher Wren, professor of astronomy at Gresham, was inducted into a London lodge. Charles II forgave his flirtations with the Cromwell family and gave him the position of which he deprived Seth Ward: the Savillian Professorship of Astronomy at Oxford.

In his purge of the universities at the Stuart Restoration, the king overlooked Gresham, which had a number of professorships in natural philosophy held mostly by Presbyterians, and some of their Oxbridge colleagues held a chair *in absentia* at Gresham that they were able to fall back on when deprived of their university positions.[208] Here were Parliamentarians, recently deprived of their

201. Yates, *Rosicrucian Enlightenment*, 247.

202. See Josten, "Backhouse," 1–33.

203. Lomas, *Invisible College*, 57.

204. Yates, *Rosicrucian Enlightenment*, 249. Yates does not think that he actually believed there was a group that might entertain such a notion, but that he offered it as a pious association.

205. Yates, *Rosicrucian Enlightenment*, 250, 253.

206. According to Yates, Newton owned Vaughn's translation of the *Fama* and *Confessio* (*Rosicrucian Enlightenment*, 255).

207. His diary entry for October 16, 1646, reads in part: "I was made a Free Mason at Warrington in Lancashire, with Coll: Henry Mainwaring of Karincham [Kermincham] in Cheshire." Josten, *Elias Ashmole*, 2:395–96.

208. Hill, *Intellectual Origins*, 105: "Your *Imago Societatis* with a great deal of delight I have

positions and livings, joined with those who had taken their place. The makeup of the founding members reflects the seriousness with which the group excluded the debates that roiled their contemporary world.

John Wilkins, Oliver Cromwell's brother-in-law, was warden of Wadham College, Oxford, and later, master of Trinity College, Cambridge. Deprived of his academic posts at the Restoration, he lived with his friend Seth Ward. Nevertheless, Wilkins was appointed the first chairman of the Royal Society. He advocated for a universal language and something close to the metric system. In ecclesiastical matters, he advocated for comprehension of Presbyterians "and toleration for the rest." And why was Hartlib not involved in the Gresham meetings? He was old, dying in 1662, but he still could have been at least an honorary member, given his prominent role. Boyle expressed delight at reading Andreae's writings that Hartlib sent him in 1647.[209] Hartlib may have conceived the Royal Society, but Charles II gave it birth. It would have been surprising if such a central pro-Parliamentarian figure had been invited to the celebration. Instead, the king appointed his loyal supporter Viscount William Bouncker as the first president. Moreover, Wilkins still carried a grudge against anything connected with "Rosicrucianism" ever since his paper war with John Webster, an English cleric, alchemist, and astrologist who moved eventually toward the Quakers. Webster's *Academiarum Examen* castigated the traditional curriculum at the universities in favor of a pansophic reformation. In his defense of the curriculum, Wilkins accused Webster of corrupting Baconian induction with "the mysticall way of the *Cabala*."[210]

Conclusion

Puritans generally were suspicious of Hermetic metaphysics as well as magic. However, while disapproving of Fludd's system and of astrology, some held favorable opinions of alchemy. Not only Hermeticists like Moray, Ashmole, and Wren,

perused. . . . The epistle prefixed to the *Imago* is both pithy and to the purpose. . . . Campanella's *Civitas Solis*, and that same *Respublica Christianopolitana* . . . will both of them deserve to be taught in our language. Of the *Utopia* he is modeling, though I cannot judge, before it sees the light, yet my expectations will be none of the smallest, if I proportion them to the ingenuity of the author."

209. See Birch, *Works*, xxxviii.

210. Ward and Wilkins, *Vindiciae academiarum*. Wilkins added in a comment of great portent for the emerging dissonance: "There are not two waies in the whole World more opposite, then those of the L. *Verulam* [Bacon] and D. *Fludd*, the one founded upon experiement, the other upon mysticall Ideal reasons; even now he was for him, now he is for this, and all this in the twinkling of an eye, O the celerity of the change and motion of the Wind." Quoted in Burnham, "More-Vauhan Controversy," 44.

but virtually every member of the founding group was engaged in alchemical pursuits. Even Bacon had encouraged the project of transmuting lead into gold, and Boyle was also an ardent alchemist. The Presbyterian Long Parliament had abolished the Court of High Commission, but Anabaptist, Familist, and millennial sects were subjected to a barrage of print artillery. Comenius may have had this in mind when referring in the *Labyrinth* to heated battles not with swords but leather. Although some Puritan writers expressed a remarkably irenic approach, in general they lumped together claims to new revelations and visions and millennial prophecy with the hydra of Familist fanaticism. They would have no schools of theosophy, astrology, prophecy, or numerology.[211]

Pietists like Andreae and Comenius, along with Dury and Hartlib, were outside the mainstream on these points. Nevertheless, Puritans sympathized with many of the goals of the pansophic reformation, especially related to education and experimental science. Four of the twelve founders had been Royalists while the remaining eight had sided with the Presbyterian Long Parliament, and some even supported Cromwell's protectorate. Soon, a list of invitees for membership was drawn up that included others who had been involved in the Hartlib Circle.

As the seventeenth century unfolded, Paracelsian millennialism found eager advocates across confessional and geographical lines. "The point is not simply that religious ideas and events had an important influence on the philosophical thought of the period," says Popkin. "Rather, these religious issues were deeply intertwined with philosophical conceptions of knowledge, revelation, the importance of scientific inquiry, human nature, and what it is to be reasonable."[212]

What we are seeing is not a receding of magic and orthodox religion and a wave of rational science, but rather a lively interaction between these influences. Millennialism, continuing revelations, and other characteristics of what was dubbed Anabaptism in the sixteenth century had by this point become widespread. Even Descartes, while searching for the Rosy Cross Brothers, had visions that convinced him to develop a mathematical system of the world. What is at stake for the divine self in this growing tension between magicians and Baconians? What role will each play in the development of the modern self?

211. Puritans did have "prophesying" meetings, but these were informal gatherings of ministers to hear each other's sermons.

212. Popkin, "Religious Background," 393.

10

"A Semi-Divinity Called Nature"
Refuting Natural Supernaturalism

By mixing the divine with the natural, the profane with the sacred, heresies with mythology, you have corrupted, O you sacrilegious impostor, both human and religious truth. The light of nature, whose holy name is ever on your lips, you have not merely hidden, like the Sophists, but extinguished.

—Francis Bacon[1]

But whoever wants to nourish his mind on the mystical philosophy . . . will not find in my book what he is looking for.

—Johannes Kepler[2]

The vulgar notion of Nature [as a "semi-deity"] seems both injurious to the Glory of God, and a great Impediment to the useful Discovery of his Works.

—Robert Boyle[3]

The now common view of the relation of science and religion—the so-called conflict thesis—was championed by the American historian and politician Andrew Dickson White in his *History of the Warfare of Science with Theology in*

1. See Bacon's *The Masculine Birth of Time*, in Farrington, *Francis Bacon*, 66.
2. Quoted in Rosen, "Kepler's Attitude," 269, and Walker, *Studies*, 53–55.
3. See Boyle's *The Christian Virtuoso* in Boulton, *Theological Works*, 2:80–81.

Christendom (1896). According to this whiggish metanarrative, the steady march of history toward enlightenment required a decisive victory of enlightened science over dogmatic theology, which happened in the seventeenth century. This thesis has been abandoned by historians of science.[4] However, it remains a widespread assumption in popular culture, as illustrated succinctly in the following account:

> With their stumbling, excited experiments, Europe's "natural philosophers" had begun their challenge to religious orthodoxy. With increasing success, they now strove to provide materialist explanations of the natural world. Though most were repaid with hostility and persecution, and some even with death, no Church, and no state, could stop them. The great march of empirical science had begun, and all ears, willing and unwilling, heard the beat of its tremendous drum.[5]

Thus, the pioneering scientists of the seventeenth century are viewed as deists, leaving orthodoxy behind yet straining toward naturalism. In point of fact, however, the scientific leap in the seventeenth century was simultaneously the highest point of Hermeticism as well as Protestant orthodoxy, and it was chiefly the latter that challenged the former. There simply was no science-religion war until scholars like White invented it.

One of the casualties of the conflict thesis is an accurate understanding of what was happening on the ground in the seventeenth century. We recall that what we designate science today was called natural philosophy. The conflict was among natural philosophers, not between them and theologians. In somewhat exaggerated terms, we can say that it was between views inspired by the Orphic tradition and orthodox Christianity: emanationism versus creation *ex nihilo*. Harrison observes,

> The idea that the world had been created out of nothing (*ex nihilo*) by a benevolent Deity contrasts with the Aristotelian doctrine of the eternity of the world, with Platonic and Gnostic teachings about the inferiority of the material world, and with the Neoplatonic idea of the world as an emanation from the

4. As Davis puts it, "Today, all historians of science reject the 'Conflict' thesis as woefully unreliable, ideologically motivated garbage that tells us far more about White and Sarton as historical actors themselves than about the history they purported to relate." See Davis, "Robert Boyle," 2. George Sarton founded the prestigious journal *Isis* and employed A. D. White as his editor.

5. Buckley, *Queen of Sweden*, 8.

> divine. Christians, moreover, had the additional resource of scripture to assist with their version of the quest for redemption.[6]

Some sort of divine voluntarism lies at the heart of biblical faith, which cannot be assimilated to any scheme of necessary emanation. In contrast with the One that shines and flows without any deliberation, Yahweh executes the plans of his eternal counsels. The dominant analogy for God's interaction with the world is that of a wise and mighty ruler accomplishing his will by royal decree.[7] Contingency, mutability, embodiment, and finitude do not represent an ontological fall from an original divine status but are features of human nature as such. The ontological divide is not between visible and invisible, earthly and heavenly, but Creator and creature: "For by him [Christ] all things were created, in heaven and on earth, visible and invisible" (Col 1:16).

Actually, the first noteworthy critique of Aristotelian metaphysics on both Christian and scientific grounds was made by John Philoponus in the sixth century CE. The position of scholiarch (headmaster) of the Alexandrian academy was denied him not only because of his Christian conviction but also because of his provocative tomes against Aristotle and John's mentor Proclus on the eternity of the world.[8] All natural bodies, in the heavens and on earth, are moved not by a divine soul but by "a 'motive force' imparted by God at the moment of creation," notes Harrison.

> In his view, all natural motion was thus imparted, and he may, on this account, be credited with having supposed a unified theory of dynamics. His conception of impetus subsequently influenced Galileo. But setting aside for now the apparent prescience of Philoponus, we can say that the Christian cosmos is not inhabited by deities. Yet, as a divine creation it does bear deep theological significance. . . . In fact much of that critique was directed against astrology, divination, the worship of deified heroes, and belief in the divinity of the celestial bodies, which is to say, against "superstition."[9]

Nebelsick elaborates, "For Philoponos, the concept of God as Creator, who created the world *ex nihilo*, was hardly compatible with either the implicit identification

6. Harrison, *Territories*, 56.

7. For example: "By the word of the Lord the heavens were made, and by the breath of his mouth all their host. . . . For he spoke, and it came to be; he commanded, and it stood firm" (Ps 33:6, 9). So too: "By faith we understand that the universe was created by the word of God, so that what is seen was not made out of things that are visible" (Heb 11:3).

8. For his critique of his mentor, see Share, *Philoponus*; Wilberding, *Philoponus*.

9. Harrison, *Territories*, 52–54.

of God with the deified uppermost heavens implicit in Aristotle's thinking or with the consequent Aristotelian insistence on a differentiation in substance between that of heaven and that of earth." First on theological grounds, and then through physical arguments, "Philoponos was convinced that the cosmos as a whole was composed of the *same kind of matter* and was subject to the *same laws*."

> Further, especially in contrast to the neoplatonism of his day, Philoponos insisted that nature could not be understood as the finite representation of infinite reality but as real in itself. To understand reality one must make deductions based on observation. In contrast especially to Aristotle, he maintained that reality could not be apprehended by making deductions from *known principles*. . . . Thus, whereas in Aristotelian cosmology the planets were described as moving in perfect circles around a common point, observation dictated to Philoponos that the orbits deviated from concentricity. "The stars each have their own specific movements along their spheres and around their own centers, not homocentric with the universe."[10]

Since the world is not divine even in its uppermost regions, there is no reason to seek metaphysical reasons for things when physical explanations are at hand.

This was not a debate between religion and science but between alternative worldviews in which religion and science were not separate domains. The Greeks did not want to understand nature on its own terms but wanted to do so part and parcel with their contemplation of the higher truths beneath, above, and behind nature. This is why science was stillborn in the Greek world. This whole outlook is rejected by Bacon:

> For as all works do shew forth the power and skill of the workman, and not his image; so it is of the works of God; which do shew the omnipotency and wisdom of the maker, but not his image: and therefore therein the heathen opinion differeth from the sacred truth; for they supposed the world to be the image of God, and man to be an extract or compendious image of the world; but the Scriptures never vouchsafe to attribute to the world that honour, as to be the image of God, but only "the work of his hands"; neither do they speak of any other image of God, but man.[11]

10. Nebelsick, *Renaissance*, 12.

11. See Bacon's *Advancement of Learning*, book 2, in Vickers, *Francis Bacon*, 191. This edition is based on the standard, fifteen-volume Victorian translation by James Spedding, R. L. Ellis, and D. D. Heath, *Works of Francis Bacon*.

We are reminded of Calvin's statement, "In the meantime, we dismiss the reverie of Plato, who ascribes reason and intelligence to the stars."[12] Bacon expressed the same view in opposition to Origen and to contemporary expressions of the emblematic worldview "inspired by Platonic hermeticism."[13] From Bacon to Boyle, human beings are endowed with immortal souls, with an innate final cause directed at glorifying and enjoying God forever. However, the rest of nature is a context, a created habitat of humankind, not innately divine or disposed *in its very essence* to final causes. Immortality is not an intrinsic property of souls but is a gift of grace granted to human bodies as well. Harrison adds:

> Bacon's denial of the symbolic transparency of the natural world is accompanied by his recommendation of a new method for revealing "the true signatures and marks set upon the works of creation" as opposed to what he calls the "idols of the mind" and "empty dogmas" of traditional natural philosophy. It is important to understand that Bacon, like many advocates of the "new philosophy," did not imagine himself to be stripping the universe of its religious significance. Rather he presents himself as offering a genuinely Christian approach to nature over against paganism.[14]

If the world is not divine and is not animated by divine souls but is created *ex nihilo* by God, then we do not have to get behind or above natural phenomena to discover what things really are in their essence. For Kepler and Galileo as well, these "signatures" are drawn in the language of mathematics and geometry.[15] Theology and natural philosophy have their own proper domain, distinct from each other, just as God is qualitatively distinguished from the world and yet involved in it through providential and sometimes miraculous actions. The experimental philosophers advocated a distinction between the natural and the supernatural that they had learned from their Protestant scholastic textbooks.

Bacon's screeds against Aristotelianism and scholasticism were aimed at natural philosophy. There are three kinds of imposture, says Bacon. The first is complicating truth by pretense and art: "hence issueth the cobwebs and clatterings of the Schoolmen." The second is spinning myths and legends "and infinite fabulous inventions and dreams of the ancient heretics." The third kind is "of them who fill men's ears with mysteries, high parables, allegories, and illusions: which mystical

12. Calvin, *Commentary on the First Book of Moses*, 1:87.
13. Harrison, *Territories*, 76.
14. Harrison, *Territories*, 77.
15. Harrison, *Territories*, 77.

and gnostic form many heretics have also made choice of."[16] Bacon then continues, "So hath Plato intermingled his philosophy with theology, and Aristotle with logic, and the second school of Plato, Proclus and the rest, with the mathematics. . . . So have the alchemists made a philosophy out of a few experiments of the furnace."[17] Throughout his *Advancement of Learning* Bacon displays a humanist's command of ancient literature. He does not reject scholastic method in other fields, but he is totally convinced that in natural science it has proved disastrous. Knowledge of nature is not like knowing the chief end of man or the nature of life and how we should live it. But the problem is not simply that science is conflated with philosophy but that creation is conflated with the creator in the reigning scholastic and humanist approaches.

Bacon was an Anglican Calvinist who studied, along with his brother, under the Reformed scholastic Lambert Daneua (Danaeus).[18] As Spedding observes, for Bacon "the entire scheme of Christian theology—creation, temptation, fall, mediation, election, reprobation, redemption—is constantly in his thoughts; underlies everything; defines for him the limits of the province of human speculation."[19] First printed in 1641, his personal "Confession of Faith" bears the subtitle, "Penned by an Orthodox man of the reformed Religion."[20] Bearing on our topic, he begins, "I BELIEVE that nothing is without beginning but God; no nature, no matter, no spirit, but one only and the same God" who is "eternally Father, Son, and Spirit, in persons."[21] He confesses that "the matter of heaven and earth was created *without forms*." God's providence is over all things "great and small," and when he performs miracles they are not to correct his creation (viz., natural laws) but are in service to redemption.[22] Along with other forms of enthusiasm, he says in an essay that

16. Bacon, "Of the Several Kinds of Imposture," in Vickers, *Francis Bacon*, 94–95. The Spedding edition, on which this text is based, reads "a kind . . . mystical and profound," but the original reads *genus mysticum et gnosticum*, and so I have rendered it here.

17. Bacon, *Advancement of Learning*, book 1, in Vickers, *Francis Bacon*, 146.

18. See the note in Vickers, *Francis Bacon*, 562. His mother was a patron of Reformed churches abroad, and his brother lodged with Beza in Geneva, Vickers adds. See also Vickers, *Francis Bacon*, xxxvi–xxxvii.

19. Spedding et al., *Works*, 7:21. Quoted in Vickers, *Francis Bacon*, xxxvi–xxxvii. Vickers calls it is "a digest of Calvinist thought, at times drawing closely on Calvin's *Christianae Religionis Institutio*" (xl).

20. Vickers, *Francis Bacon*, xxxvi–xxxvii. Throughout the confession he emphasizes Christ as the mediator within the rubric of covenant (federal) theology: "so in the person of the Mediator the true ladder might be fixed whereby God might descend to his creatures and his creatures might ascend to God" (Bacon, "Confession of Faith," in Vickers, *Francis Bacon*, 107).

21. Bacon, "Confession of Faith," in Vickers, *Francis Bacon*, 107.

22. Bacon, "Confession of Faith," in Vickers, *Francis Bacon*, 108–9.

atheism is another "frenzy of mind . . . as may appear in Lucretius the Epicure. . . . [T]his I dare affirm in knowledge of nature, that a little natural philosophy, and the first entrance into it, doth dispose the opinion to atheism. But on the other side, much natural philosophy and wading deep into it, will bring men's minds to religion. Wherefore atheism every way seems to be joined and combined with folly and ignorance, seeing that nothing can be more justly allotted to be the saying of fools than this, 'there is no God.'"[23]

Arrayed against Hermeticism on the same theological grounds is a formidable phalanx that in addition to Bacon, Mersenne, and Gassendi includes Galileo, Kepler, Libavius, Erastus, and Beeckman. Far from being the nemesis of the Scientific Revolution, Christian orthodoxy provided the inspiration, categories, and justification for finally treating nature *as* nature.

Bacon's Idols of the Mind and the Two Books

Bacon was the enemy of revolution, in either church or state, although he allowed that modest reforms may still be made. In natural philosophy, however, there was no such history of development. Tradition conveyed by books, according to Bacon, will just continue to travel around the cul-de-sac of old errors. "Those who become practically versed in nature are, the mechanic, the mathematician, the physician, the alchemist, and the magician, but all (as matters now stand) with faint efforts and meagre success."[24] Like children playing hide-and-seek, great minds come within an inch of discovery only to pass their target, distracted by the sounds of other players. This is very similar to the polemic of Andreae and Comenius. Moreover, it has something to do with Paracelsus's earlier complaint that academic medicine was divorced from artisanal practice. Bacon is not using hyperbole when he calls for the instauration (i.e., foundation) of serious science, which cannot be a mere augmentation or reformation but something that has not yet been attempted.

Typically, Bacon is seen as the paragon of Promethean anthropocentrism. Yet this is precisely what he rejects. Repeatedly, Bacon underscores the fact that nature is in the driver's seat. Humans gravitate toward confirmation bias (idols of the tribe) as well as individual perspectives that mistake the truth for illusions (idols of the cave), and they are confused by the vulgar use of words (idols of the marketplace). Humans engage in abstract theorizing, creating schools and speculative

23. Bacon, "Of Atheism," in Vickers, *Francis Bacon*, 96.
24. Bacon, *Novum Organum*, Book 1, Aphorism 5.

systems, and presume even to dictate to science (idols of the theater). He encourages greater humility, even distrust of ourselves, if we want to understand nature on her own terms, "for the glory of the Creator and the relief of man's estate."[25]

Rossi challenges the caricature of Bacon as "the spiritual father of a 'neutral technicalism' that lies at the heart of processes of alienation and commercialization so typical of modernity. The exact opposite is true." As early as 1609, Bacon had expressed disdain for Daedalus of Greek myth, "a clever but detestable man, best known for 'illicit inventions' such as the machine that allowed Pasiphae to mate with a bull and give birth to the Minotaur who devoured youths, and the Labyrinth he designed in which to hide the Minotaur and 'protect evil with evil.'"[26] Bacon warns against misusing technology for evil ends, with the magician as the primary exhibit of Faustian megalomania. He does not see human beings as gods but as stewards of nature who respect its integrity as God's creation. At the same time, he wants to understand nature in order to discover medicinal cures and to make mechanical inventions that improve human life in an age of plagues and wars.

Actually, it is the Hermetic *magus* who claimed to possess the spiritual technology to control and manipulate nature. Paracelsus claimed to have created a system that reveals everything above and below. It was not Bacon's *New Organon* but Pico's *Oration on the Dignity of Man* that singled out humans as uniquely capable of choosing their own nature for themselves.[27] Voluntarism was bound up with Neoplatonic thinking ever since Nicholas of Cusa, but Pico's *Oration* is truly the Magna Carta of modernity. It is a bold expression of the "divine self" we have been exploring in this book. However, as Rossi points out, this theory "never took a substantial hold on Bacon."

> For him man's powers were not infinite but always subject to the laws of nature (*obsessus legibus naturae*) and he cannot break or loosen the causal ties that govern it. Man's portion is neither to praise his infinite freedom nor to preserve his essential unity with the whole, but to realise that, in order to consolidate his limited power he must adapt himself to nature, submit to its commands and assist in developing its operations. Only thus can he achieve the true mastery of nature, because to dominate nature man must be its servant and interpreter.[28]

25. Bacon, *Advancement of Learning*, book 2, in Vickers, *Francis Bacon*, 148.
26. Rossi, *Birth of Modern Science*, 40.
27. Rossi, *Francis Bacon*, 18.
28. Rossi, *Birth of Modern Science*, 18.

Despite Paracelsus's criticisms of Aristotelianism, for Bacon both systems fall under his category "idols of the theater," that is, abstract theories from which conclusions in natural studies are deduced. His problem is with an uncritical rationalism (and empiricism, it should be noted) that substitutes confirmation bias for actual investigation. His central argument in *New Organon* is that people are not sufficiently self-critical.[29] Bacon wanted human beings to recover their original calling to guard, protect, and extend their dominion as God's viceroys, "to work the ground" and make it fruitful (Gen 2:5). Instead, either because of worshiping nature or the laziness and distractions of "idols of the mind," people have resigned this office. The Greeks want to contemplate nature, and the magi want to operate upon nature, but Bacon wants people to investigate nature with a practical purpose.[30] Scripture, therefore, addresses the "why" questions (i.e., God's purposes in nature and history), while science treats the "how" questions (i.e., secondary causes). The observation of nature reveals God's power, while scripture reveals God's wisdom. This is diametrically opposed to the natural supernaturalism from Plato to Paracelsus, which regards empirical facts as allegories of deeper metaphysics.

The trope of the two books, scripture and nature, goes all the way back to patristic sources. However, as Kenneth J. Howell explains in detail, it became particularly important in Protestant Northern Europe as a way of distinguishing general and special revelation without setting them in opposition.[31] Reference to the "two books" appears in the second article of the Belgic Confession (1561). Based on the book of Romans, Lutheran and Reformed confessions from this period teach that the "light of nature" reveals God's existence, love, power, wisdom, and moral will (law) but does not reveal the mysteries of the faith, such as the Trinity or God's saving will in Christ (gospel).[32]

Experimental philosophers during this time still held the classical Greek and ancient Christian view that God is higher than his works and that theology is the highest science. In fact, no group believed that natural philosophy led to the

29. Bacon, *Novum Organum*, Book 1, Aphorism 1.

30. Bacon, *Advancement of Learning*, book 1, in Vickers, *Francis Bacon*, 123.

31. Howell, *God's Two Books*.

32. Belgic Confession, article 2: "We know [God] by two means: First, by the creation, preservation, and government of the universe; which is before our eyes as a most beautiful book [Ps 19:1–8] wherein all creatures, great and small, are as so many letters leading us to perceive clearly the invisible things of God, namely, His eternal power and deity, as the apostle Paul says [Rom 1:20]. All these things are sufficient to convict men and leave them without excuse. Second, He makes Himself more clearly and fully known to us by His holy and divine Word [1 Cor 1:18–21] as far as is necessary for us in this life, to His glory and our salvation."

contemplation of God more than seventeenth-century experimentalists. Most of these early scientists wrote on theological and devotional topics. Yet scriptural references are rare in their natural studies, even in those of theologians like Melanchthon, since they were careful to acknowledge the different object and methods of each discipline. Creation reveals God's invisible attributes and the moral law, but only scripture reveals God's purposes for humankind and the salvation that is found in Christ.[33]

Following Luther, Calvin emphasized that just as the body is distinct from the soul without being at variance, so earthly and heavenly matters are distinguished without being opposed. Believers are "under a two-fold government," he says, "so that we do not (as commonly happens) *unwisely mingle these two*, which have a completely different nature."[34] Similarly, Bacon counsels, "Let no man upon a weak conceit of sobriety or an ill-applied moderation think or maintain that a man can search too far, or be too well studied in the book of God's word, or in the book of God's works, divinity or philosophy [science]; but rather let men endeavor an endless progress or proficiency in both; only let men beware . . . that they do not *unwisely mingle or confound these two*."[35]

Faith and reason, scripture and sense experience, theology and natural philosophy cannot be set in opposition because special and general revelation come from the same source. Yet they follow their own distinct way of knowing (*scientia*). Conflating them leads to heresy in theology and blind superstition in natural philosophy. "This likewise I humbly pray," Bacon adds, "that things human may not interfere with things divine, and that from the opening of the ways of sense and the increase of natural light there may arise in our minds no incredulity or darkness with regard to the divine mysteries; but rather that the understanding being thereby purified and purged of fancies and vanity, and yet not the less subject and entirely submissive to the divine oracles, may give to faith that which is faith's."[36]

As noted at the beginning of this chapter, in 1896 Andrew Dickson White introduced the fiction that, through its promotion by Bertrand Russell and many other prominent thinkers, has proved influential. White says, "Calvin took the lead (against Copernicanism) in his Commentary on Genesis, by condemning all who asserted that the earth is not at the centre of the universe. He clinched the matter by the usual reference to the first verse of the ninety-third psalm, and asked, 'Who

33. Martin Luther, "Heidelberg Disputation," in *LW* 31:39–58 (thesis 29). One does note here that Luther's rejection of Aristotle might not be absolute: one must *first* become foolish in Christ (cf. the analogy of marriage in thesis 30).

34. Calvin, *Institutes* 4.20.1–2, emphasis added.

35. Bacon, *Advancement of Learning* 1.1.3, emphasis added. See Davis, "Word and the Works," 38.

36. Bacon, *New Atlantis and the Great Instauration*, 16.

will venture to place the authority of Copernicus above that of the Holy Spirit?'"[37] However, Calvin never mentions Copernicus, here or anywhere else, and he does not condemn heliocentrists. As Osler notes, "Few astronomers adopted Copernican astronomy during the first fifty years following the publication of *De revolutionibus*."[38] This included Bacon, of course, so it would not be surprising if Calvin was not even aware of Copernicus. More egregious is White's spurious quotation, put into circulation by F. W. Farrar a decade earlier and, through White, passed on by Bertrand Russell and many others.[39]

Instead, what Calvin says is that scripture is accommodated discourse. Regarding Genesis 1 he cautioned, "The Holy Spirit had no intention to teach astronomy." Calvin goes on to proclaim:

> It must be remembered that Moses does not speak with philosophical acuteness on occult mysteries, but relates those things which are everywhere observed, even by the uncultivated, and which are in common use. . . . Therefore, in order to apprehend the meaning of Moses, it is to no purpose to soar above the heavens; let us only open our eyes to behold this light which God enkindles for us in the earth. By this method (as I have before observed), the dishonesty of those men is sufficiently rebuked, who censure Moses for not speaking with greater exactness. For as it became a theologian, he had rather respect to *us* rather than to the *stars*.[40]

"His exegetical task," says Howell, "was not to debate issues of cosmology but to expound the meaning of the text *in the language* of the text."[41] God created the sun to rule the day and the moon to rule the night (Gen 1:14–16). As Calvin explains it:

> Moses makes two great luminaries; but astronomers prove, by conclusive reasons, that the star of Saturn, which, on account of its great distance appears the least of all, is greater than the moon. Here lies the difference; Moses wrote in a popular style things which, without instruction, all ordinary persons endued with common sense are able to understand; but astronomers investigate with great labour whatever the sagacity of the human mind can comprehend. Nevertheless,

37. White, *History of the Warfare*, 1:27.

38. Osler, *Reconfiguring the World*, 51–52.

39. Hooykaas, *Religion*, 121 observes that this alleged quotation was first circulated by Farrar, *History of Interpretation*, xviii. See also Howell, *God's Two Books*, 142–43.

40. Calvin, *Commentary on the First Book of Moses*, 1:84–85.

41. Howell, *God's Two Books*, 142.

> this study [astronomy] is not to be reprobated, nor this science to be condemned, because some frantic persons are wont boldly to reject whatever is unknown to them. For astronomy is not only pleasant, but also very useful to be known: it cannot be denied that this art unfolds the admirable wisdom of God.[42]

Calvin is far from treating Genesis as a myth or limiting scripture's reliability to matters of salvation rather than science. In fact, in theology as well God "lisps" in speaking to us, as nurses commonly do with infants. "Thus such forms of speaking do not so much express clearly what God is like as accommodate the knowledge of him to our slight capacity. To do so he must descend far beneath his loftiness."[43] In his loving urge to communicate with mortals, God draws on familiar analogies from ordinary experience, not only on descriptions of nature but of himself.

Given how slowly natural philosophers came to embrace Copernicanism, it is interesting to observe its warm welcome in Protestant circles early on with the familiar appeal to divine accommodation. Despite notable exceptions such as Gisbertus Voetius and John Owen, many leading Reformed theologians and pastors embraced Copernican theory, such as the influential Leiden theologian André Rivet (1572–1651). According to Hooykaas, "The Reformed minister Philips van Lansbergen (1561–1632), a strict Calvinist, and a famous astronomer, was the most zealous propagator of Copernicanism in the Netherlands." He emphasized the distinction between God's accommodated discourse in scripture and the mathematical language of nature.[44] Van Lansbergen's friend Isaac Beeckman has been called "the virtual father of modern atomism," and Descartes learned much of his physical theory from him during his Dutch sojourn.[45] Hooykaas also relates that Daniel Heinsius, secretary of the Synod of Dort, "wrote laudatory poems on Lansbergen's defence of Copernicanism."[46] Beeckman "set the stage for the strong separation arguments of natural philosophers offered by Calvinists later in the century."[47]

Beginning with Robert K. Merton's justly celebrated 1938 monograph, it has been shown that the Puritan majority among founders of the Royal Society is not

42. Calvin, *Commentary on the First Book of Moses*, 1:86–87.

43. Calvin, *Commentary on the First Book of Moses*, 1:86–87. On accommodation generally, see *Institutes* 1.13.1.

44. Hooykaas, *Religion*, 123. The full title of van Lansbergen's work is *Bedenckingen op den Dagelijckshen, ende Iaerlijkschen loop van den Aerdt-kloot* (Considerations on the diurnal and annual motion of the earth). See also Howell, *God's Two Books*, 139.

45. Cook, "New Philosophy," 127–29. See also Berkel, *Isaac Beeckman*.

46. In fact, "In strictly orthodox Zeeland, the States granted a pension to Lansbergen so that he could devote all his time to his astronomical studies." Hooykaas, *Religion*, 131–32.

47. Howell, *God's Two Books*, 139.

a coincidence. From Bacon onward, a Calvinistic theological orientation informed and inspired natural investigation.[48] Hooykaas notes that "among the group of ten scientists who during the Commonwealth formed the nucleus of the body that was to become the Royal Society, seven were strongly Puritan, even after the Restoration."[49] Reformed members "far outnumbered the Roman Catholics" even in the Académie de Sciences in Paris, and in Belgium, where Calvinists were also the minority.[50] In fact, many of the textbooks for physics, mathematics, astronomy, and related subjects were written by theologians. Clergymen were disproportionately represented in these scientific societies, but lay members were unusually well read in theology.[51]

Rather than offer speculative theories from the outside, it is more illuminating

48. Merton, *Science*, 136, adds: "Puritanism, and ascetic Protestantism generally, emerges as an emotionally consistent system of beliefs, sentiments and action which played no small part in arousing a sustained interest in science." Specifically, "The Puritan complex of a scarcely disguised utilitarianism, of intramundane interests; methodical, unremitting action; thorough-going empiricism; of the right and even the duty of *libre examen*; of anti-traditionalism—all this was congenial to the same values in science"; Merton, "Motive Forces," 117–18. This is a reprint from his initial essay, Merton, "Science, Technology, and Society," 360–632. Nevertheless, Merton's explanation of the data is too dependent on Max Weber's influential thesis that Calvinism bred a this-worldly asceticism; see Merton, "Motive Forces," 120, 130. Merton carries over Weber's flawed thesis regarding the relationship of Calvinism and capitalism to science. In addition, specialists acknowledge that "Puritanism" is a contested category, some even disputing its usefulness. "Calvinism" is not a distinguishing factor, since the Thirty-Nine Articles expresses such theology, as did all of the archbishops of Canterbury since Cranmer until Laud. Nonconformity also fails as a marker, since most of the leaders of Elizabethan "Puritanism" were conforming ministers. William Perkins, called the father of Elizabethan Puritanism, refused this moniker. The godly cannot be called pure, he said, so Puritan is "a vile name." Perkins, *Works*, 1:342. Cf. Breward, *William Perkins*, 22.

49. Hooykaas, *Religion*, 99.

50. Hooykaas, *Religion*, 98–99: "A. de Candolle (1885) found that among the foreign members of the Academie des Sciences in Paris, from 1666 to 1883, the Protestants by far outnumbered the Roman Catholics. . . . Prof. J. Pelseneer, the Belgian historian of science, found that in the Southern Netherlands (Belgium) in the sixteenth century the Protestants formed but a small minority (perhaps 100,000 people), yet Protestant scientists were far more numerous than those of the Roman Catholic faith." And Robert Merton's study in 1938 showed that "among the group of ten scientists who during the Commonwealth formed the nucleus of the body that was to become the Royal Society, seven were strongly Puritan. Sixty-two percent of the members of the Royal Society in 1663 were clearly Puritan by origin, a percentage that is the more striking because the Puritans constituted a minority of the population."

51. For instance, notes Charles Webster, "Boyle, though he never took [holy] orders, was deeply religious: not only did he devote large sums for the translation of the Bible and establish the Boyle lectures in theology, but he learned Greek, Hebrew, Syriac and Chaldee that he might read the Scriptures in the original. For similar reason did Nehemiah Grew, the estimable botanist, study Hebrew, as he states in his *Cosmologia Sacra*." Webster, "Origins," 106. Merton, "Motive Forces," 128.

to discern the rationale for natural studies from these figures themselves. First, the Reformers held the study of nature in high esteem, as we see especially in Melanchthon and Calvin. Melanchthon taught astronomy as well as theology in Wittenberg.[52] In both arts and sciences, Calvin emphasized that human curiosity should explore that "to which the finger can point" instead of soaring in high-flown speculation.[53] Second, Luther's doctrine of vocation gave spiritual validation to common callings. The baker and the milkmaid become "masks" that God wears in answering our petition for daily sustenance.[54] Contemplation serves the active life in the world, which in turn arouses contemplation of God. Third, Protestants enjoyed a new sense of freedom from extrabiblical authority, whether the pope or Aristotle, both of whom were on the receiving end of Luther's thunderbolts. This by no means made them revolutionaries, but it did free natural philosophers from having to accommodate theories to ancient and medieval commentators.

Yet, perhaps the most important incitement of Reformed theologians toward the new philosophy was the opportunity to defeat, once and for all, the nature mysticism of Greek cosmotheology. Creation *ex nihilo* treats the world as good but not divine, and thus something that can be studied without recourse to speculative and even magical theories.[55] With these theologians, according to Levitin, "Bacon drew on the second tradition when he criticized Aristotle and Plato for mixing the metaphysical (i.e., understood as 'natural theological') study of final causes with natural philosophy."[56]

Whatever criticisms one may make of Bacon and his heirs, their turn outward—away from a supposedly divine self within—was a turning point from contemplation to action. A similar set of beliefs characterizes Galileo. According to a familiar narrative, Galileo serves alongside Patrizi, Bruno, Campanella, and Pucci as a symbol of the church's persecution of science. However, Patrizi was not a Copernican, and he demanded that the entire academic curriculum be rewritten according to his radical Neoplatonism. Bruno was less concealed in his pantheism; his adoption of a heliocentric cosmology owed more to his program of replacing Christianity with neo-pagan cosmotheology than to astronomy or mathematics.[57] As for Campanella, a supporter of Bruno and Galileo, his *Athe-*

52. Osler, *Reconfiguring the World*, 37.

53. Calvin, *Institutes* 2.2.15.

54. A superb survey is Wingren, *Luther*

55. Calvin, *Commentary on the First Book of Moses*, 1:87.

56. Levitin, *Ancient Wisdom*, 242.

57. Rossi, *Birth of Modern Science*, 109–10. As Rossi notes, "The animate universe that Bruno described has even been termed astrobiology. . . . Bruno believed that the laws governing celestial motion had to do with the individual stars and planets that had 'souls of their own' that

ism Conquered shows that he was hardly a religious skeptic. Yet, he also favored an astrological natural religion and, inspired by Joachim's prophetic writings, fomented revolution in Calabria. Pucci was condemned as a "Pelagian" and his plan for a secret society, entitled *Forma di una republica catholica*, envisioned toleration only for those of his persuasion.[58] Cremonini, like Pompanazzi, was a Renaissance Aristotelian (i.e., Averroist) who insisted on dogmatic grounds that heavenly bodies are spherical and smooth. Even when Galileo invited Cremonini to look through his telescope to see the moon's peaks, valleys, and craters, the philosopher refused. Although Galileo had considered him a friend, Cremonini offered evidence to the Inquisition against the astronomer. Here we have a pious Catholic being denounced to the Holy Office as a heretic by a philosopher who denied the existence of God along with angels and souls.[59] From these examples alone, any tidy division between science and religion disappears. It was a contest between two opposing natural philosophies full of theological import, and the progenitors of genuine post-Copernican science were Christian theists. In contrast with these other figures, Copernicus, Kepler, Tycho, and Galileo held to an ordered universe, with each part making up a whole world.[60]

It did not occur to these pioneers of the Scientific Revolution that the Bible, properly interpreted, was contradicted by science. However, as Osler notes,

> Many Renaissance philosophers in the Neoplatonic, Hermetic, and Paracelsian traditions portrayed a highly animistic world characterized by sympathies and antipathies, which act at a distance and endow the material world with its own innate activity. The mechanical philosophers rejected the activity of matter because they thought that active matter, insofar as it is self-moving, seemed capable of explaining phenomena without any reference to God.[61]

The orthodox Christians who paved the way for modern science did so on both theological and scientific grounds.

---

guided them through the heavens: 'Motion is intrinsic to the very nature, soul, and intelligence of these racing objects.'"

58. See the intriguing essay by Tarrant, "Concord and Toleration," 983–1003.

59. Leibniz, *Theodicy*, 81.

60. Rossi, *Birth of Modern Science*, 109–10.

61. Osler, *Reconfiguring the World*, 89.

Boyle's War

Robert Boyle was writing during the highest pitch of sectarian pantheism, the Cambridge Platonists, and Hobbes's Epicurean-Stoic system. Engaged in alchemical experiments throughout his life, he inserted these goals into the charter of the Royal Society. Considered the founder of modern chemistry, Boyle's contributions are nevertheless wider.[62] He was greatly influenced by his lengthy stay in Geneva, where partaking of the Eucharist led him to genuine faith.[63] He also learned Hebrew from a rabbi and wrote "one million words on biblical and theological topics," and was passionately involved in missions and apologetics.[64]

The years 1655–1658 represent the development of Boyle's mature program. It began with focused criticism of Aristotle and Paracelsus.[65] In 1662, Boyle let his valuable assistant Robert Hooke leave his employ to become Curator of Experiments for the Royal Society.[66] As the Great Plague ravaged London, the royal court and the Society resided in Oxford, and during this time—just outside of Oxford—Boyle wrote treatises on *The Excellency of Theology, Compar'd with Natural Philosophy*. Though not opposed, the "two books" mentioned in his title are different, and the knowledge that comes from theology transcends natural philosophy.[67]

During this period Boyle formulated a focused critique of natural supernaturalism. Bacon had argued that the dogma of the sacredness of nature is an affront to God but also an obstacle to understanding nature. The central question in the transition from the Renaissance to experimental science was whether nature is divine, which Bacon rejected at the very beginning of his personal confession of faith.[68] The distinction between theology and natural philosophy, the gospel and the laws of nature, primary and secondary causes, and the two books ultimately derives from the qualitative distinction between God and the world. Other natural philosophers were emerging from a Hermetic cocoon, such as Kepler after his debate with Fludd, but Boyle was particularly eager to dismantle the whole microcosm-macrocosm theosophy.

Boyle's *A Free Enquiry into the Vulgarly Received Notion of Nature* (1686) has

62. Davis, "Robert Boyle," 1.

63. De Mornay, *Worke*.

64. Davis, "Robert Boyle," 3.

65. Hunter, *Boyle*, 104.

66. Hunter, *Boyle*, 144.

67. Hunter, *Boyle*, 148. "From manuscript evidence it seems clear that Boyle was working at much the same time on a companion volume, *Some Considerations about the Reconcileableness of Reason and Religion*, published in 1675."

68. Bacon, "Confession of Faith," in Montagu, *Francis Bacon*, 2:407–9.

been called "one of the key texts of the Scientific Revolution."[69] His major argument in this regard is that nature is *not* supernatural but is designed cosmos. As Boyle writes, Plato, Aristotle, and their followers consider the world to be an eternal god, and the latter did "openly deny God the production of the world, so by ascribing the admirable works of God to what he calls nature, he tacitly denies him the government of the world."[70] It is not only Hermeticism but also the whole of Greek philosophy that Boyle puts on trial, especially in light of Christian revelation.[71]

Worried that Hobbes's materialism and Descartes's version of mechanical philosophy, especially the latter's stark dualism, threatened belief in God's involvement in nature and history, Cambridge Platonists fell back on the World Soul as a medium of God's providence. "Like Descartes's God," says Funkenstein, the God conceived by Cambridge Platonists like Henry More represented a "Spirit-in-Chief," such that "all other spirits or forces depend on him. Some spirits lack reflection and purposefulness, such as the (Stoic) *anima mundi*; some have it; God is the vertex in the hierarchy of spirits (or ideas)." God is infinitely extended spirit, "space itself." Funkenstein adds regarding More in particular, "Now, this forces us to deny of God what More ascribed to spirits—namely spissitude [density or thickness]. God cannot expand or contract. He, like space, is always the same." Furthermore, according to Funkenstein:

> More's is an emanational theology, not unlike the Kabbalistic speculations he admired: God is veritably the *en sof* (*infinitum*), both identical with and different from the powers (*sefirot*) of which he is the source. . . . More's concept of the divine amounts to the concept of a harmonious sum total of all mechanical and purposive forces in the universe. Such a God could not but be reasonable. He is the very embodiment of *pronoia*, as much as was the Stoic Pneuma. He contrasts again with Descartes's God, in whom will had primacy over reason.[72]

The Cambridge Platonists, reluctant to accept the philological conclusion of Casaubon, remained devotees to Hermes Trismegistus and the perennial philosophy.

Boyle was opposed to Descartes's extreme dualism, the resurgent natural supernaturalism of Cambridge Platonists, and the Stoic and Epicurean materialism of Hobbes. Like Calvin and Bacon, he rejected the "heathen" idea that the whole

69. Davis and Hunter, "Making," 204.

70. Section 1.10, 13 in Boyle, *Free Enquiry*.

71. Boyle, *Free Enquiry*, 1.10, 13.

72. Funkenstein, *Theology and the Scientific Imagination*, 79–80.

creation is the image of God, endowed with intellect and will.[73] Aristotelian and Hermetic nature mysticism was, for Boyle, not merely a different account of natural philosophy but an alternative worldview to Christian theism. As such, he countered any notion of "Nature" as a "semi-deity."[74] As Davis and Hunter observe, "By denying 'Nature' any wisdom of its own, the mechanical conception of nature located purpose where Boyle believed it belonged: over and behind nature, in the mind of a personal God, rather than in an impersonal semi-deity immanent within the world."[75] In other words, the world becomes a craft, not an emanation, of God.[76]

Identity to Analogy

A popular theory in contemporary scholarship holds that the seed of secularization is the notion of a "univocity of being," and that it was sown by Duns Scotus and his nominalist heirs. My narrative agrees with the first clause, but Scotus cannot bear all the blame. The tradition that originates in Orphic philosophy and is mediated by Plato, Aristotle, and the Stoics, passing through the Renaissance to the modern world, ranges from panentheism to pantheism. If nominalism renders God a being among beings, natural supernaturalism renders God the being of all beings. The whole cosmos is merely a mirror; it is not real, but God cannot do without it. Everything emanates from God, cascading into lower pools of being. Yet that *being* is divine. The difference from God is therefore quantitative, not qualitative. This version of the univocity of being has had a much longer and influential course than that of nominalism. We have seen that Eckhart and Nicholas of Cusa, both Neoplatonists *and* nominalists, had an enormous impact on early modern movements.

According to this perspective, which I have been calling natural supernaturalism, the creator is viewed less as acting *in* nature than as the active principle *of* nature itself. Everything is related in sympathy and correspondence in nature (e.g., the seven planets and the seven metals) and also in the human body. Collecting a sufficient quantity of dew, wine, and bodily secretions (where the quintessence is especially concentrated), one could obtain the quintessence.[77] On this basis,

73. Boyle, "The Christian Virtuoso," in Boulton, *Theological Works*, 2:82.
74. Boyle, "The Christian Virtuoso," in Boulton, *Theological Works*, 2:80–81.
75. Davis and Hunter, introduction to *Free Enquiry*, x.
76. See Boyle's preface in *Free Enquiry*, 4.
77. McIntosh, *Rose Cross*, 85.

the highest science is that which endeavors to discover the spiritual quintessence within natural objects that will provide medicine for universal healing, both physical and spiritual.

Following the biblical prophets, early Christians rejected any identification of creatures with the creator. Instead of profiting from God's universal self-revelation through "the things he has made," the corrupt heart turns to these creatures themselves as objects of worship (Rom 1:19–25). Affirming God's incomprehensibility, Lutheran and Reformed orthodoxy repeated frequently the Cappadocian formula that God is known only in his works, not in his essence, and affirmed Thomas Aquinas's doctrine of analogy over against Scotist univocity.[78] Because human beings are created according to the image and likeness of God, they can know God and God's works in their own finite manner. Yet, just as there is no point of identity (univocity) between God and creatures in terms of ontology, there is no intersection of divine and human knowledge. Such knowledge is formal, not essential, analogical rather than univocal, and ectypal rather than archetypal.[79] If God and creatures are qualitatively distinct, there can be no identity at any point. Strictly speaking, pantheism and atheism embrace a univocity of being, while nominalism advocates an equivocal perspective. We have seen that *ex nihilo* creation commits Christianity to some type of voluntarism: God alone is necessary and all else is a contingent creation that God called into being of his own free will. In rejecting emanation, however, Reformed scholastics upheld the doctrine of analogy, rejecting the radical voluntarism found in Duns Scotus and William of Ockham (but also in Eckhart and Nicholas of Cusa). And, following patristic precedent along with Aquinas, they stipulated that even though God is not related to the world (which would compromise his aseity), God freely relates the world to himself.[80]

The impact of this rejection of natural supernaturalism is broad and deep. For one thing, natural phenomena are not an allegory whose occult meanings are deciphered by the magi.[81] Thus, from multiple angles, the idea of getting beneath or above nature's outer shell to contemplate its inner divinity was being

78. Behind only Luther and Martin Chemnitz in formative influence on confessional Lutheranism, Johann Gerhard (1582–1637) clearly affirms Thomist analogy over Scotist univocity in his *Theological Commonplaces*, 92. The same Reformed consensus is summarized clearly by Turretin, *Institutes*, 1:190. Cf. Muller, "Not Scotist."

79. Expanding on the scholastic doctrine of analogy, the distinction between archetypal and ectypal theology coined by Reformed theologian Franciscus Junius the Elder (1545–1602) became standard also in Lutheran systems.

80. See Muller, "Not Scotist," 242.

81. Harrison, *Territories*, 63.

cast aside. The occult meaning of things was becoming subjected to actual observation, showing how far the reality was from the traditional picture.[82] Again, this is because creation is the result of God's free determination, not a necessary emanation. Thus, we should expect the artifact to display the attributes of the artist but in its own way as distinct production.[83]

Miracles

Natural supernaturalism encourages magic but not miracles. Plato's metaphorical pilot who sometimes has to intervene to keep the ship from being scuttled on the swells of matter is not the triune God whose providence governs everything visible and invisible. Christianity presupposes a personal God who created everything *ex nihilo* and directs it according to a plan. Sometimes miracles are needed, not because nature is flawed but because human beings steer history away from God and therefore their own good. In the supreme miracle of Christian revelation, the "pilot" assumes humanity, bears the sins of the world, and rises bodily on the third day. In either providence or miracle, God alone is the eternal, necessary, and incorporeal agent who is at work within nature to accomplish his ends. The Aristotelian concept of nature did not require either creation or providence, since every material thing is animated by its own soul.

For the mechanical philosophers, the world is radically contingent and not filled with necessary essences.[84] However, it would be just as erroneous to maintain that miracles are impossible violations of physical laws as to assert that everything is miraculous. Like Aquinas and Protestant scholastics, Boyle rejected this common conflation in his important work *Miracles and Things Contrary to the Laws of Nature* (1681). These terms ought to be distinguished, Boyle says, since "there are diverse Miraculous Operations recorded in the holy scripture, that are rather *Preternatural* or *Supernatural* than (if I may so speak) *Contra-natural*." The miracles recorded in scripture were neither of nature nor against it, but above it. With Bacon, Boyle maintains that miracles are not meant to correct nature and its laws but to redeem the world from the curse of sin and death.[85] God did not merely design creation with self-sufficient laws. Nor does this show merely his

82. Ebeling, *Secret History*, 107–8.

83. Galileo, "History and Demonstrations Concerning Sunspots" (1613), in Finnocchiaro, *Galileo*, 101.

84. Davis, "Robert Boyle," 9.

85. Davis, "Robert Boyle," 6.

omnipotence but "his boundless Wisdom; and consequently [he] did nothing without weighty reasons." Thus, God's work is free but not arbitrary.[86] Mechanical philosophers like Boyle appealed to a Christian understanding of divine agency. In opposition to Epicurean atomism, regularity and diversity are accounted by Boyle in a Christian doctrine of providence. This is not the clockmaker deity of Descartes. In fact, Calvin's view of providence was motivated by a concern to uphold against the "new Epicureans" God's presence in the world. The regularity and order of the cosmos as a whole and in every part is due to God's constant and caring presence.[87]

It was secondary or natural causes to which experimental philosophers sought to restrict their investigation. After all, natural causes are explained by natural philosophers, not by theologians. Bacon insisted that, for natural philosophy at least, the secrets of nature were *revealed* by empirical observation, whereas Neoplatonists believed these natural secrets were *concealed* by material appearances.[88] For the latter, it was the *magus* who accomplished this feat, cracking open the husk. Instead of bringing down the power of the heavens and sharing with God in a continual creation, the experimentalist was content to explore the work of creation: "For my part I am emphatically of the opinion that man's wits require not the addition of feathers and wings, but of leaden weights."[89] And precisely by limiting his domain, he expanded the practical usefulness of experimental research.[90]

Philosophers such as Bacon and Boyle did not reduce all knowledge to the experimental type, but they demanded that it should be accorded full weight in considering natural matters of fact.[91] For them, when natural philosophers went beyond matters of fact to matters of cause, they left the realm of science to take up metaphysics and theology. Boyle was a wide reader beyond the Hartlib Circle, and his assistant Robert Hooke helped him understand Descartes. He was happy to see

86. Davis, "Robert Boyle," 10.

87. Calvin, *Institutes* 1.17.9.

88. Citing an anonymous eighteenth-century tract, Ebeling notes that all of the important alchemical texts conceive the "mystery of nature" as an ontological property of nature itself. "The point was to lift this mystery of nature so as to reveal the causes of natural processes, causes that were hidden from the senses. This notion was almost a maxim of Hermetic research: 'Hermetic wisdom deals, in particular, with nature and its works; it investigates the mysteries that lie hidden within it'" (Ebeling, *Secret History*, 104).

89. Rossi, *Francis Bacon*, 33.

90. Boyle, "Origin of Forms and Qualities," in Stewart, *Philosophical Papers*, 14.

91. Boyle, "Origin of Forms and Qualities," in Stewart, *Philosophical Papers*, 14.

that the great philosopher had not reduced God to matter. The Oxford group was alarmed by the political as well as philosophical and religious implications of the materialistic monism Thomas Hobbes articulated in *Leviathan* (1651). However, in *The Usefulness of Natural Philosophy* Boyle took issue also at some length with "those who would exclude the Deity from intermeddling with Matter."[92] So Boyle is seen to be ranged against Aristotelians, Paracelsians, and "Epicureans" like Hobbes as well as the pioneer of mechanical philosophy, Descartes.[93]

Conclusion

By distinguishing a real supernaturalism of God in creation and miracle from providence, Bacon acknowledges the likely criticism that he has not offered his own epistemology to ground the experimental method. True, he replies, but that is the point: "For we are founding a real model of the world in understanding, such as it is found to be, not such as man's reason has distorted. Now this cannot be done without dissecting and anatomizing the world most diligently; but we declare it necessary to destroy completely the vain, little and, as it were, apish imitations of the world, which have been formed in various systems of philosophy by men's fancies." It is not a godless universe, but it is also not an idolatrous one:

> Let men learn (as we have said above) the difference that exists between the idols of the human mind and the ideas of the divine mind. The former are mere arbitrary abstractions; the latter the true marks of the Creator on his creatures, as they are imprinted on, and defined in matter, by true and exquisite touches. Truth, therefore, and utility, are here perfectly identical, and the effects are of more value as pledges of truth than from the benefit they confer on men.[94]

When Bacon says that truth and utility are the same thing in scientific matters, he means that, unlike knowledge of other things, knowledge of natural phenomena need not be justified by deeper occult meanings. For example, Bacon believed the Old Testament sacrificial system anticipated in "figures" the truth realized in

92. Hunter, *Boyle*, 110.

93. Hunter, *Boyle*, 111.

94. Bacon, *Novum Organum*, Book 1, Aphorism 124. The Latin reads: *Itaque ipsissimae sunt (in hoc genere) veritas et utilitas.*

Christ, "the Lamb of God who takes away the sins of the world."[95] But Bacon also held that the study of nature was different than this. It does not speak in enigmas that disclose a higher truth. The gold lies on the surface, as it were. The air is either light or heavy. The upshot is captured well in Thomas Shadwell's play *The Virtuoso* (1676): "'But to what end do you weigh this Air, Sir?' 'To what end shou'd I? To know what it weighs. O knowledge is a fine thing.'"[96]

95. Bacon, "A Confession of Faith," in Vickers, *Francis Bacon*, 109–10.
96. Quoted in Hunter, *Boyle*, 155.

11

The Mortal God

Hobbes's Hermetic Leviathan

> When I wrote my Treatise about our System, I had an Eye upon such Principles as might work with considering Men, for the Belief in a Deity.
>
> —Isaac Newton[1]

> All of them are my enemies.
>
> —Thomas Hobbes, referring to the founders of the Royal Society[2]

One front of Robert Boyle's war was "natural supernaturalism," while the other was the Epicurean-Lucretian philosophy of nature represented by Thomas Hobbes (1588–1679). In fact, when Boyle founded his apologetics lectures to refute "atheism, materialism, and mortalism," he had Hobbes in view. If Henry More could describe the founder of the Familists as "Epicurus turned Enthusiast," perhaps Hobbes could be characterized as "Enthusiast turned Epicurus." However, Hobbes's ontology is Stoic: the cosmos is the one body of the immortal God, and the state is the one body of the mortal God, Leviathan. His work *Leviathan* presents a secularized theology: the fear of God is transferred to the fear of the sov-

1. Newton, *Philosophiae Principia*, 942–43, quoted in Osler, *Reconfiguring the World*, 163.

2. Hobbes, *Dialogus physicus*, quoted in Shapin and Schaffer, *Leviathan*, 112. Shapin and Schaffer note that "All of them are my enemies" was added in the *Opera philosophica* in 1668, showing "that Hobbes' view of the Royal Society and the experimental programme had, if anything, hardened as a result of his exchanges with Boyle" (112 n. 7).

ereign. Hobbes was reacting against the ecclesiastical disputes of his day, but his main invective was directed toward the Long Parliament and what he regarded as the Presbyterian conspiracy against him.[3]

Hobbes's *Leviathan*

Although Hobbes's system bears closer comparison to Stoic ontology, there is an Epicurean moment in it, something like the "swerve" of atoms wherein free will is possible. This for Hobbes is the state of nature, in which every person exercises absolute free will. But this leads to chaos, the war of all against all. Consequently, individuals enter into a contract with each other, surrendering their absolute freedom in exchange for security and autonomy in exchange for protection. While retaining their natural freedom in the realm of private conscience, citizens conform outwardly in behavior and speech to the sovereign political power that embodies this single entity.

Importantly, Boyle and other pioneers of the Scientific Revolution embraced Epicurean atomism to conceive the mechanics of nature while nevertheless affirming God's supernatural agency in creation, providence, and miracles as well as the human being uniquely as created in God's image and likeness and the survival of the soul. Nature consists of miniscule bits of matter (called corpuscles) flying through space. If space were completely filled, as held by *plenists* (e.g., Stoics, Neoplatonists, and Aristotelians), then these atoms could not actually move through it. Thus, the mechanical philosophers like Boyle affirmed *vacuism*: space as an empty void or vacuum. Hobbes dogmatically opposed this theory, both in natural philosophy and politics. In fact, his metaphysics was driven by political theory since a void for free movement of atoms in nature invites its political corollary. Shapin and Schaffer observe, "During the Civil War and Interregnum 'enthusiasts,' hermeticists and sectaries threatened to bring about a radical individualism in knowledge: a situation in which 'private judgment' eroded any existing authority and the credibility of any existing institutionalized conventions for generating valid knowledge." The philosophers, too, were at war, school against school.[4]

For Hobbes, the problem of "seeing double" begins with a distinction between incorporeal and corporeal substance.[5] This underwrote the distinction between the church and the state. Augustine wrote of the two cities in his *City of God*, and

3. See dialogue 1 in Hobbes, *Behemoth*, 14–15.

4. Shapin and Schaffer, *Leviathan*, 73.

5. Gorham, "Embodied God."

medieval canonists similarly referred to the two swords. Luther referred to God's two kingdoms, charging the pope and the Anabaptists with being enthusiasts who wanted to conflate them. In opposing the "contrived empire" of Christendom, Calvin says that we must recognize that we are "under a two-fold government . . . so that we do not (as commonly happens) unwisely mingle these two, which have a completely different nature." Just as the body and spirit are distinct without being intrinsically opposed, "Christ's spiritual kingdom and the civil jurisdiction are things completely distinct. . . . Yet this distinction does not lead us to consider the whole nature of government a thing polluted, which has nothing to do with Christian men." These two kingdoms are "distinct," yet "they are not at variance."[6] This entire worldview "makes men see double," Hobbes argues.[7]

In the Hebrew Scriptures, Leviathan and Behemoth (e.g., Ps 74:14; 104:26; Isa 27:1) most likely refer figuratively to Israel's historical nemeses: pharaonic Egypt and the Assyrian Empire. But in Hobbes's interpretation Behemoth stands for the religious chaos of mid-century England in contrast with the security that Leviathan would bring. We are probably on the wrong track in searching for Hobbes's understanding of Leviathan in the book of Job (chapter 41) or in other references that prophesy its destruction. On the contrary, Leviathan is the only monster capable of securing our safety from Behemoth, as we see below.

There is little question that, despite Hobbes's dismissals of Hermes Trismegistus, the Hermetic Asclepius provides the imaginative frame for Hobbes's *Leviathan*, just as it had for Pico and Paracelsus. In the Asclepius, Hermes Trismegistus explains to his son that God is an immortal man in heaven, and man is a mortal God on earth. According to the Chaldean Oracles and Iamblichus's *Mysteries of Egypt*, statues were constructed out of materials considered to have sympathetic attractions for the gods they represented. This "art of making of gods," the Asclepius tells us, brings down the appropriate deity for giving oracles and spells for releasing fearful souls from oppressive daimons.[8] Significantly, Hobbes draws directly on this reference, although his "mortal God" on earth is the divine sovereign, which is fabricated by the will of the people in the social contract—cooperation based on mutual self-interest.[9] "The multitude so united in one person is called a Commonwealth, in Latin *Civitas*," says Hobbes. "This is the generation of that great Leviathan, or rather (so to speak more reverently) of that Mortal God,

6. Calvin, *Institutes* 4.20.1–2.

7. Hobbes, *Leviathan*, chapter 39. Unless otherwise noted, I am citing from the Macpherson edition.

8. See Horton, *Shaman and Sage*, 266–84.

9. Hobbes, *Leviathan*, chapter 17. See Paganini, "Hobbes's 'Mortal God,'" 7–28.

to which we owe under the Immortal God, our peace and defence."[10] Thus the Commonwealth is like a fabricated statue that embodies God's absolute power (*potentia absoluta*). In humanity's current condition, only covenants based on fear (self-maledictory oaths) are obligatory.[11] Karl Schumann argues persuasively that Hobbes drew on the Hermetic corpus for the idea that the human being is always in motion and able to fly anywhere at will.[12] Yet, through the social contract, this freedom is surrendered. The allusion to the mortal God as Leviathan is therefore two-toned: only fear will drive self-interested individuals to coalesce into a single society, and this mortal God is the enlivened statue representing the *potentia absoluta* of the Immortal God.

Hobbes treated the sects roughly in the final book of *Leviathan*, entitled "The Kingdom of Darkness." However, unlike a host of his Puritan contemporaries, Hobbes's critique is guided not by a concern for doctrinal purity but by a fear of the pluralism that sectarianism posed to a Christian society. In my view, Hobbes is best understood in the context of radical sectarianism.

First, much of Hobbes's *Leviathan* is devoted to an idiosyncratic interpretation of biblical history, with distinct echoes of Joachim's three ages: a state of nature, a commonwealth, and the millennial kingdom of Christ at his second advent. Stranger still is Hobbes's identification of God the Father with Moses, the Son with Jesus, and the Holy Spirit with the apostles and their successors. It is true that for him there is no king or kingdom other than the civil one—for now. Patricia Springborg notes, "Hobbes's doctrine of ecclesiastical power follows from one central assertion: that the church is not the Kingdom of God."[13] Israel was a true commonwealth or kingdom, but it rejected the king, Jesus. The kingdom left the earth with its king and will appear, in more glorious form, when Christ returns as "God's lieutenant."[14] To a large extent, Hobbes is simply amplifying the view of Marsilio of Padua and the Zurich theologian Thomas Erastus that places the church's outward form and structure in the hands of the temporal rulers. This was the tradition, after all, since Henry VIII assumed the role of temporal head of the church. However, Hobbes's view is not only more radical in this regard but is driven by an anticlericalism that owes as much to the sects as to Lucretius.

Hobbes emphasizes with Joachim of Fiore the absence of priests. However, it is not because every individual knows God immediately but just the opposite:

10. Hobbes, *Leviathan*, chapter 17.
11. Hobbes, *Leviathan*, chapter 14.
12. Schumann, "Rapidità," 203–27.
13. Springborg, "Hobbes on Religion," 355; see Hobbes, *Leviathan*, chapter 44.
14. Springborg, "Hobbes on Religion," 355.

Only the general will of Leviathan knows God immediately. The rest of us must accept its interpretations. Right now clerics answer only to this mortal God. If the present age is a church without a kingdom, the future age is a kingdom without a church. But before the eschaton, the only kingdom of God on earth is the civil realm embodied in the sovereign. Hobbes's friend and biographer John Aubrey recounts that on his deathbed he refused the ministrations of any priest with the threat, "Let me alone, or else I will detect all your cheates from Aaron to yourselves."[15] At the same time, Hobbes protested often that he was not an atheist. Understandably, this apparent contradiction has given rise to a variety of scholarly conclusions, from viewing Hobbes as an atheist to seeing him as an eccentric Calvinist.[16] Instead, I view him against the backdrop of his sectarian context.

Second, Hobbes employs the sectarian critique of the Reformation as not going far enough in departing from Rome. Springborg says, "He was dismayed to see that national religions of the Reformed Church still retained theological doctrines which could give Roman Catholicism a foothold in the realm."[17] However, whereas Anabaptist spiritualists were indebted deeply to Neoplatonic mysticism and some even felt a kinship with the ancient Gnostics, Hobbes is closer to the Socinians in regarding the early church councils as infected by Greek philosophy.[18]

This anticlerical narrative served the purpose of rationalizing his own construal of Trinitarian theology mentioned above. If Joachim was charged with dividing the persons of the Godhead (tritheism), Hobbes's view conflated them in one person who represents himself in different ways in different ages (modalism). The Holy Spirit for Hobbes is "*the person of God* born now in the third time. . . . For as Moses, and the High Priests, were Gods Representative in the Old Testament, and our Saviour himself, as man, during his abode on earth: So the Holy Ghost, that is to say, the Apostles and their successors, in the Office of Preaching and Teaching, that had received the Holy Spirit, have Represented him ever since."[19]

In other words, the one *person* of God represents himself through Moses and the priests (age of the Father), then a single individual—Jesus (age of the Son)—and now, by apostles and their successors (age of the Spirit). Besides the hetero-

15. Springborg, "Hobbes on Religion," 346.

16. For the former view, see Skinner, "History and Ideology," 151–78. Other "secularists" include Gauthier and Curley, "How to Read." See also A. E. Taylor, "Ethical Doctrine"; Warrender, *Political Philosophy*; and Hood, *Divine Politics*. For the latter view, see Martinich, *Two Gods*.

17. Springborg, "Hobbes," 555.

18. Adolf von Harnack's thesis that "Catholicism" represents "the acute Hellenization" of the church is a continuation of this polemic. See Harnack, *History of Dogma*, 1:227.

19. Hobbes, *Leviathan*, chapter 42, quoted in Springborg, "Hobbes on Religion," 360, emphasis added.

doxy of this position, it is inconsistent with the three ages expounded above. How can the Holy Spirit represent himself in the persons of the apostles and their successors if the millennial age is beyond all priestly ministrations? Lim notes, "Hobbes's heterodox view of the Trinity was basically a strange concoction of Sabellianism [modalism], but with Moses, Christ, and the Holy Spirit. . . . In his letter to Matthew Wren of October 21, 1651, Henry Hammond called *Leviathan* a 'farrago of all the maddest divinity that ever was read,' with a clear penchant for demolishing the 'Trinity, Heaven, hell' and other cardinal doctrines of the Christian faith in one fell swoop."[20] If Hobbes were merely disguising his atheism by using Trinitarian terminology, why would he have chosen deliberately to adopt *heretical* views of the Trinity?

In the appendix to the Latin *Leviathan*, Hobbes sees the church deviating from the simplicity and scripturalism of the apostolic church with philosophy and the greedy bishops. He does not reject the Trinity per se but relativizes Nicaea.[21] The argument is at once Lucretian and sectarian. It was not freethinkers but dissenters who said, "This Clergy-pride is it that hath set the World on fire, and will not consent that it be quenched."[22] Hobbes argues in his *Historia Ecclesiastica* that the church fathers abandoned the simplicity of the faith for the philosophical verbiage that divided the church. Lim observes,

> By the time one gets down to line 60, the reader is confronted by a Hobbesian riddle: if it is true that one cannot know anything about God, aside from God's "work, sacred laws, and his name to be feared," how could one arrive at the conclusion that Christ is "himself God"? Either fideism, or "theological lying" masquerading as chastened humility before God, or yet an expression of apophatic theology, thereby utterly dependent upon Scripture to reveal further the divine identity? Whatever else might be knowable about God, Hobbes was absolutely certain that "these learned disputes" that focused on semantic differences, not substantial divergence, were the leading causes for the obfuscating of religious truth, thereby shipwrecking the "holy boat" of faith, jettisoning "piety and simplicity" along with it.[23]

20. Lim, *Mystery Unveiled*, 225. Lim observes, "Two major advances in Hobbes studies in the last decade have been the publication of the critical edition of *Historia Ecclesiastica* in 2008 and George Wright's *Religion, Politics and Thomas Hobbes*, particularly the translation of the 1668 appendix to the Latin *Leviathan*, which allows greater access to this key aspect of Hobbes's political theology."

21. Lim, *Mystery Unveiled*, 228–29.

22. Baxter, *Church-History*, 117.

23. Lim, *Mystery Unveiled*, 235.

Hobbes developed this interpretation of church history further after the tumult raised by the *Leviathan.*[24] His *Historical Narrative Concerning Heresy* defends the Nicene Creed, but his *Historia Ecclesiastica* gives "his highly critical account of the proceedings of the first four councils and indictment of Constantine for ever having admitted church doctors to an area of legitimate state power."[25] The conclusions of these councils presented an obstacle to Hobbes's metaphysics. The early church departed from what he called "'the three words of God': reason, science, and prophecy . . . seduced as they were by the philosophy of the Greeks."[26] Nevertheless, the law of the land is whatever the ruler prescribes.[27] Hobbes could not be true to his own convictions about the absolute power of the ruler if he himself joined the radical spirits (atoms moving freely through space) in opposing the established religion. Instead of a direct attack, therefore, Hobbes caricatures the Council of Nicea as dominated by power-hungry clerics.

Hobbes does not argue as a French *philosophe* or freethinker but as a radical Protestant. Had the Protestant Reformers not said that the Mass is more pagan than Christian? Then why should the Trinity be seen any differently? The simplicity of scriptural doctrines had been obscured and even contradicted by sophistry, superstition, and the intercessions of a great crowd of mediators akin to pagan deities. Socinians, Arminians, Familists, and dissenting sects of every kind associated orthodox Christianity with Roman Catholicism. According to Lim, "Their battle cry can be summarized as three *T*s: Tradition, Transubstantiation, and Trinity."[28] Lim notes that "the Ranter and Socinian threats were seen as flip sides of the same destructive coin."[29] In short, the forerunners of modern estrangement from Christian orthodoxy were not atheists but radical mystics.

Third, Hobbes was a mortalist.[30] The materialistic pantheism of the Leveller Richard Overton and Ranter Laurence Clarkson, as well as their mortalism, dominate Hobbes's system. Not even at death is there a separation of the soul from the body. Though it sounds modern, Burns says that many interpretations "fail to see that mortalism had far more support among radical, even fanatic, Christians than among natural philosophers, and that this Reformation attack on a medieval

24. Hobbes, "Narration Concerning Heresy," in Molesworth, *English Works*, 4:388–89. Hobbes also discusses his own religious views in book 4 of the *Leviathan* (1651), *Behometh* (1668), and the appendix to the Latin *Leviathan* (1668).

25. Springborg, "Hobbes on Religion," 350.

26. Springborg, "Hobbes on Religion," 351.

27. Hobbes, *Leviathan*, chapter 42, quoted from Tuck, *Leviathan*, 399.

28. Lim, *Mystery Unveiled*, 12.

29. Lim, *Mystery Unveiled*, 75.

30. Hobbes, *Leviathan*, chapter 44. See Johnston, "Hobbes' Mortalism," 647–63.

concept called not for an advance into the scientific future, but for a return to the apostolic past revealed in Scripture."[31] In endowing his famous lectureship, Boyle's will stipulated that lecturers will defend Christianity against false religions as well as "atheism, materialism, and mortalism."[32]

Fourth, there are similarities between the Münster regime and Hobbes's idea of the sovereign representing the immortal God as a new Moses, the mediator of divine revelation and its proper interpretation. To be sure, Christendom itself was conceived of as a holy empire with an infallible priest, and by the end of the sixteenth century the picture of the monarch as high priest and sacred head of the body was gaining ground. Following Marsilio of Padua, the monarchs of France and England claimed sovereign temporal authority in church and state. Moreover, Hobbes was very familiar with the more republican construal of a "holy commonwealth" on the pattern of the Israelites entering into a solemn covenant with God. However, Hobbes's Leviathan is more like Müntzer or Jan van Leiden than the House of Commons, and such a parallel was drawn by some contemporaries.

Fifth, *Leviathan* is marked by an extreme voluntarism that characterizes the trajectory from Eckhart to antinomian English sects. The individual in the state of nature, God, and the sovereign are outside of law, so it is impossible for them to act unjustly.[33] After the "war of all against all," individuals surrender their freedom to the ruler for security and peace. Like God, the sovereign's will (absolute power) transcends even the laws he himself imposes (ordained power). However, rulers of different civilizations have established their own dogmas and practices. Even in a Christian commonwealth, therefore, it is only the authority of the sovereign that determines the public religion. "Hobbes was merely restating a familiar doctrine, then, when he maintained that ecclesiastical power was an attribute not of the church, but of the king," notes Springborg. "The problem was that Hobbes was not consistent, for he went on to claim for the sovereign sacerdotal powers that violated the very functional demarcation he was concerned to establish. The sovereign takes over the role of supreme pastor as both priest and governor."[34] Just as the election of a mayor is valid only because it is the act ultimately of the sovereign, so too is a congregation's election of a pastor.[35]

Sixth, like the Familists, Hobbes not only defended but also exhibited personally a willingness to conform outwardly to the established church while clinging

31. Burns, *Christian Mortalism*, 190–91.
32. Wilson, *Epicureanism*, 30–31.
33. Hobbes, *Leviathan*, chapter 17.
34. Springborg, "Hobbes on Religion," 358.
35. Hobbes, *Leviathan*, chapter 42.

to his liberty of conscience. One of the most aggravating characteristics of the members of the Family of Love was that they belonged to the Church of England while meeting secretly to exchange individual teachings, experiences, visions, and revelations. There is no evidence that Hobbes belonged to any such group, but his policy is similar. As Springborg observes, "Hobbes both professed official conformity to the doctrines of the Anglican Church and a vehement anticlericalism throughout his long life."[36] She goes on to observe, "It was for this reason that Milton had declared with anticlerical fervor that 'New Presbyter is but old Priest writ large.'"[37] Interestingly, in terms of the church's organization, Hobbes opts for "Independency of the Primitive Christians," partly because it eschews any collective authority or embodiment beyond local assemblies. This may have reflected his initial hope that Cromwell's Protectorate would be Leviathan.[38]

As Hobbes wants to clip the wings of priests, especially theologians, he eliminates natural theology. Thus, Hobbes not only rejects the univocalist tendency of Neoplatonists, who thought they could prove the Trinity from magic, and kabbalah, but he also elides the analogical view of patristic and scholastic theology. Instead, Hobbes adopts equivocity: "Personally, I incline to the view that no proposition about the nature of God can be true save this one: *God* exists, and that no title correctly describes the nature of God other than the word 'being.' Everything else, I say, pertains not to the explanation of philosophical truth, but to proclaiming the states of mind that govern. Our wish is to praise, magnify and honour God. . . . Therefore [the words 'God sees, understands, wishes, acts, bring to pass'] are rather oblations than propositions."[39] Such extreme apophaticism is the pretext for concluding that the sovereign "shall judge what *names* or *appelations* are more, what lesse *honourable* for God, that is to say, what doctrines are to be held and profest concerning the nature of God, and his operations."[40]

Assumed in this equivocal view is that the attributes of God described in scripture are arbitrary. This is consistent with Hobbes's nominalism, which separates faith from reason. It is pure fideism, blind surrender to the dictates of the ruling power. Consequently, philosophy for Hobbes is a purely secular study of *caused* causes, not of the uncaused Cause.[41] Even scripture is relativized. Hobbes believed with Lucretius that scientific explanation will eventually replace religious dogma, and as such he wished that the Bible had never been translated into vernacular

36. Springborg, "Hobbes on Religion," 347.
37. Springborg, "Hobbes on Religion," 366–67.
38. Hobbes, *Leviathan*, chapter 47.
39. Hobbes, *De Mundo*, 434, quoted in Tuck, "Christian Atheism," 115.
40. Hobbes, *De cive*, 15.16, quoted in Tuck, "Christian Atheism," 115.
41. Springborg, "Hobbes on Religion," 367–68.

languages.[42] He writes that, "While the Scriptures have divine approval, falling under the rubric of publicly allowable tales that are independently sanctioned, they do not represent the immediate word of God. Nor were they necessarily written by the authors to whom they are ascribed."[43] The immediate word of God is that of the ruler, as it was in the cases of Moses and Jesus. This ruler may be a parliament, a protector, or a monarch, but "the Civil sovereign (whether one or more) is chief pastor."[44]

It should be clear by now that for Hobbes the truth in the public sphere is whatever the sovereign determines arbitrarily. His radical skepticism is in service to a hyper-Protestant position, resulting in the removal of authority for interpreting God's word from priestly popes, Presbyterian synods, and inner lights to the absolute decree of the sovereign. The civil authority now is in the position of Moses, with the people looking to him for revelations and their interpretation. Springborg observes, "Hobbes followed the formula of the great theocracies in making behavior, and not belief, the test of fidelity. His follower Henry Stubbe correctly intuited that a religion of ritual was better suited to the state than a religion of belief, pondering whether Islam was not preferable, and Falkland declared himself 'not only an anti-Trinitarian but a Turk, whensoever more reason appears to me for that, than for the contrary.'" The Reformation made true doctrine and personal faith and piety the test, which had only introduced myriad sects.

> The strategy was to abandon emphasis on conscience, to withdraw from the individual the right to interpret Scriptures, to disempower priests, and to make conformity of morals and manners the test of the Christian faith. . . . The "power of the Law," he says, "is the Rule of Actions onely," and should not be extended "to the very Thoughts and Consciences of men, by Examination, and Inquisition of what they Hold, notwithstanding the Conformity of their Speech and Actions."[45]

However radical his views may appear, Hobbes was not inventing but radicalizing a Tudor dogma. His policy is not entirely different from that envisioned for the ruler in the utopias of Thomas More and Tomasso Campanella.

However, it was just such a dogma that the Presbyterians and Independents

42. Hobbes, *Leviathan*, chapter 11.

43. Hobbes, *Leviathan*, chapter 33.

44. Hobbes, "Illustrations of the State of the Church," 173, quoted in Tuck, "Christian Atheism," 112–13.

45. Springborg, "Hobbes on Religion," 352, citing Hobbes, *Leviathan*, chapter 46.

opposed. John Owen "read Leviathan attentively, but considered that Hobbes deified 'the magistrate and spyled [spoiled] all by ye Kingdome of Darknesse.'"[46] Hobbes lashed out at Owen in his *Dialogus physicus*.[47] Yet, Hobbes saw John Wallis as his greatest foe next to Boyle, particularly since Wallis's response to Hobbes challenged his knowledge of mathematics and physics. The father of infinitesimal calculus (including the symbol for infinity), the Oxford math professor wrote the first public treatise on the circulation of blood and several theological treatises. He was also a nonvoting scribe of the Westminster Assembly, one of twelve Presbyterian observers at the Savoy Conference, and remained a moderate Presbyterian under the Restoration. "Hobbes now revived charges of Presbyterian conspiracy against him."[48]

Whereas Aristotle regarded human beings as political animals by nature, Hobbes held that one realizes his or her nature only by an act of will, that is, by taking up one's role as a citizen. Thus, relations among human beings are contractual rather than natural. This was far from Boyle's view, or that of the fellows of the Royal Society in general.

Leviathan and the Air Pump

Boyle's career seemed already to be at its peak in 1659. However, with the engineering aid of Robert Hooke, who also helped him to understand Descartes, Boyle produced an experiment where previous attempts had proved insufficient to prove a vacuum.[49] The whole animistic worldview depends on the notion that there are no vacuums in space—that is, places where nothing exists. It has to all be filled up, whether this is interpreted in Platonic, Aristotelian, or Stoic ways. Hobbes, who had no scientific background but was well-versed in the history of Roman politics, presupposed that there could be no vacuum in space *because* that would entail individualism in religion and society.

Boyle published the results of his Oxford experiments in *New Experiments Physico-Mechanical, Touching the Spring of the Air and Its Effects*.[50] His air pump experiment was useful for many practical reasons, but he had also a polemical

46. Shapin and Schafer, *Leviathan*, 309.

47. Shapin and Schafer, *Leviathan*, 309. However, neither Owen nor Barlow was totally committed yet to the experimental model.

48. Shapin and Schafer, *Leviathan*, 311.

49. Hunter, *Boyle*, 106.

50. Hunter, *Boyle*, 124.

intent: to prove the existence of a vacuum.[51] But attacks came in the same year from Thomas Hobbes. In brief, Hobbes pointed out that Boyle violated his own rule by trying to determine causes. Moreover, he had a naive view that matters of fact could be neatly separated from considerations of cause.[52]

Boyle set out immediately to answer these objections with a new edition of his original book. Fortified by new findings, what became known as "Boyle's Law" became more fully established.[53] Boyle's open and associative approach, cooperating with many whom he credited in his work, reflected the Hartlib Circle's sensibility as well as Boyle's own personally. Such sharing of research was a major contribution to the Scientific Revolution. It contrasts with Hermetic secretism and the later career of Newton, as we will see. "The result was one of the most seminal and innovative works of the scientific revolution," Hunter claims.[54] In fact, in his frontispiece for the *History of the Royal Society*, Thomas Sprat depicted the air pump to be a symbol of the Society.[55] Boyle and Hobbes were locked in combat throughout their careers, as witnessed in the quote at the beginning of this chapter.

First, Boyle and Hobbes offered rival ontologies. Hobbes was a univocalist, holding that all things that exist are possessed of quantity, however rarefied. Not even God, angels, or souls transcend dimension and quantity. All being is univocal, even if his religious epistemology embraces equivocity. In contrast, Boyle continued Calvin's conviction that distinction does not mean separation. Boyle held that all reality consists of corporeal *and* incorporeal beings. And, in disagreement with Descartes, he believed that (1) God qualitatively transcended both corporeal and incorporeal creatures; and (2) God was constantly involved in nature and history through providence and sometimes miracles. Although Boyle allowed supporting arguments from natural theology, he shared Bacon's wariness of speculative systems. Natural philosophy discovers the innumerable effects of God's creative, providential, and redeeming work, but the ultimate causes are unknown to us apart from that which God is pleased to reveal in scripture. As with God himself, the essence of things transcends the tools at the experimental philosopher's disposal. What we are seeing, and Boyle is opposing, is the movement toward a univocity of being in which divine and creaturely agency are seen as a competi-

51. Shapin and Schafer, *Leviathan*.

52. *Physical Dialogue, or a Conjecture about the Nature of the Air taken up from the Experiments recently made in London at Gresham College* was written in 1666 and published in 1681.

53. Hunter, *Boyle*, 132–34.

54. Hunter, *Boyle*, 126.

55. Hunter, *Boyle*, 131–32.

tion of arbitrary wills. In Boyle's view, which is to say the perspective of classical Christian theism, God's action enables rather than replaces human agency.

The English Jesuit Franciscus Linus criticized Boyle's vacuist thesis on grounds similar to those of Hobbes: a Nominalist "horror of a vacuum," which would in their view delimit God's (and the ruler's) absolute power. Protestant scholastics followed Thomas Aquinas's view of the analogical relation of creation to the creator. But extreme Scotists like Linus and Hobbes believed that there must be a univocal intersection between God's sovereignty and human agency. In the analogical perspective, many things in nature are above nature but not against it. Boyle defends this view in "Miracles & Things contrary to the Laws of Nature."

"For the voluntarists," notes Osler, "the laws of nature are simply descriptions of regularities observed in nature," which God is free to suspend through miraculous intervention. "The laws of nature simply describe empirical generalizations."[56] These laws do not tell us what *must* be but what ordinarily is the fact. That is because God is completely independent of the world. However, Descartes held that "the laws of nature are necessary truths that follow directly from God's attributes, specifically his immutability," which will inform Spinoza's logic in spite of radical differences. Moral and physical laws, Descartes held, are necessary expressions of God's communicable and incommunicable attributes, respectively.[57]

Both Descartes and Hobbes omitted final causes (chief ends) from their systems. Harrison states, "Bacon thought that 'the final cause rather corrupts than advances the sciences.' Descartes agreed that because human nature is 'very weak and limited whereas the nature of God is immense,' it follows that 'the customary search for final causes [is] totally useless in physics." Characteristically, Hobbes put the matter more crisply, declaring that "there is no such *finis ultimus* (utmost aim), nor *summum bonum* (greatest good), as is spoken of in the books of the old moral philosophers."[58] In Descartes's system the weight is placed on God as efficient cause; final ends drop off entirely. This is due in part to his radical dualism between matter (extension) and mind (thought).

For Boyle, however, final causes remain at every level of nature.[59] There was

56. Osler, *Reconfiguring the World*, 90.

57. Osler, *Reconfiguring the World*, 91.

58. Harrison, *Territories*, 89. See Hobbes, *Leviathan*, chapter 11.

59. Boyle, "The Christian Virtuoso," in Boulton, *Theological Works*, 2:208–9: First, there are "Universal Ends" of the universe as a whole. "*Secondly*, There may be ends in a restrictive Sense in the Number, Fabrick, Situation and Motions of the great Masses of Matter, which make considerable Parts of the Universe." These may be called *Cosmic* or *Systematic Ends*. "*Thirdly*, another sort of Ends respect the Parts of Animals" and their species—"*Animal Ends*." "Fourthly, other Ends which chiefly respect Man, may be called *Human Ends*, which Nature is said to aim at,

no doubt for Boyle that human beings were created for a supernatural goal. Boyle also does not reduce nature's *telos* to human use. Though it is wrong to say that "all the Ends are investigatable by Man," for Boyle it is also "erroneous to say, in the strict sense, that all things in the visible World were made for the use of man."[60] Boyle notes that Cartesians insist that "there is always the same Quantity of Matter in the World. For they suppose, as God is immutable, that when he first put Matter into Motion, he gave it such a Quantity as neither wanted to be augmented nor lessened." It is easier to discern whether something is made for an end than whether it can have only that end, naturally. "And how can a *Cartesian* tell but that amongst the Ends he allows God hath proposed in the Production of his Creatures, one may be that his Intelligent Beings, who are capable of admiring and praising him, should be moved to do so, for the Wisdom and Goodness he hath shewn in the World?"[61] Boyle reasons, "I see not why it may not be as inconsistent with his Immutability to alter his way of acting to produce particular Ends, as to bring his Eternal Decrees to pass though not yet done." The Cartesian allows for the daily creation of rational souls to be united to bodies, so why not ends? Though not *all* ends are decipherable, surely humans cannot have a duty to discover their chief end if they do not have one.[62] Nevertheless, final ends are revealed in scripture rather than by natural philosophy. Experimental sciences cannot prove all these final causes, but this just shows the limits of the discipline. Boyle counsels, "The Naturalist should not suffer the Search or the Discovery of a Final Cause of Nature's Works, to make him undervalue or neglect the studious Indagation of their Efficient Causes."[63] Boyle affirmed God as efficient as well as final cause while rejecting the pantheistic notion of God as formal cause.[64] It is clear by now that Boyle has no trouble appealing to Aristotelian categories for explanations that are beyond experimental observation. Boyle and Hobbes had rival ontologies.

Second, and consequently, Boyle and Hobbes had rival epistemologies. Hobbes was a rationalist. He said, "We cannot from experience conclude . . . any proposition *universal* whatsoever."[65] The whole point of the *Leviathan* was to offer, once and for all, an absolutely certain and universal theory, one applicable in every time

---

when she forms Animals, Vegetables, &c. for the use of Man. And these Ends may be further distinguished into *Mental* . . . and *Corporeal*."

60. Boyle, "The Christian Virtuoso," in Boulton, *Theological Works*, 2:209–10.

61. Boyle, "The Christian Virtuoso," in Boulton, *Theological Works*, 2:210.

62. Boyle, "The Christian Virtuoso," in Boulton, *Theological Works*, 2:211.

63. Boyle, "The Christian Virtuoso," in Boulton, *Theological Works*, 2:176; cf. Boyle, "Origin of Forms and Qualities," in Stewart, *Philosophical Papers*, 70–71.

64. Hunter, *Boyle*, 202–3.

65. Hobbes, "Human Nature," 18, quoted in Shapin and Schaefer, *Leviathan*, 151.

and place. Boyle did not deny universal truths, of course, but in his view, whatever Hobbes's profession was, it could not be called properly natural philosophy (i.e., science). While being a rationalist with regard to nature, Hobbes presents an irrational view of religion as sheer obedience to the arbitrary power of the sovereign as God's mouthpiece. His radical apophaticism deprives the priests and theologians of an occupation, so that the sovereign's will alone is acknowledged. The relation of the creation to God, and thus of scriptural revelation to the truth concerning God, reason and faith, is purely equivocal.

For Boyle, however, the relation is analogical; revelation and reason are distinct but interdependent. Although we cannot know God's transcendent essence, we can know God from his effects through reason and nature and more clearly in scripture. In Boyle's view, competent members of an experimental community (viz., the Royal Society) create machines for performing experiments that will yield assent on *matters of fact*. Matters of *cause* are metaphysical and therefore beyond the scope of proper experimental science. Following on Beeckman's experiments with the air pump, Boyle argued that it does not offer any causal explanation (vacuism versus plenism) but merely presents the fact that a vacuum can be created under experimental conditions in a lab. There is something of the later positivism of fact versus value in this debate. The result was a contrast between forms of life, what counts as truth, and the sort of communities that will yield that truth in scientific matters. The goal can never be absolute certainty, as in geometry, but "moral certainty": a confidence that a reasonable and well-informed person should yield. Common "confession" was the goal, that is, neither private opinion nor absolute and incontestable certainty.[66]

Third, as a result, there had to be a society that actually embodied and facilitated consensus in matters of fact. The freedom of movement for atoms traveling through empty space had epistemological and political implications, as Hobbes was eager to point out in criticism. If the sovereign embodies Hobbes's plenist order, the Royal Society embodies Boyle's vacuist one. While artisans and engineers were prized by experimental philosophers, Hobbes held Plato's view of laborers. "Replication is the set of technologies which transforms what counts as belief into what counts as knowledge," explain Shapin and Shafer.[67] Just as claims to private enthusiasm are excluded from the church's General Assembly, Hermeticists could participate in the Royal Society only if they submitted to the discipline of public experiment. The creed, one might say, was the experimental method. Thus, the Royal Society must exclude both "the knowledge-claims of alchemical 'secretists'

66. Shapin and Schafer, *Leviathan*, 104–5.

67. Shapin and Schafer, *Leviathan*, 225.

and of sectarian 'enthusiasts' who claimed individual and unmediated inspiration from God, or whose solitary 'treading of the Book of Nature' produced unverifiable observational testimony."[68]

Metaphysical dogmatists—whether Peripatetic, Paracelsian or Hobbesian—were excluded. As Shapin and Schafer note, it was a kind of "church discipline," to which a member had to submit himself in trying to prove alchemical transmutation. "In experimental science one way of securing the multiplication of witnesses was to perform experiments in a social space. The experimental 'laboratory' was contrasted with the alchemist's closet precisely in that the former was said to be a public and the latter a private space."[69] Boyle makes it clear in *The Sceptical Chymist* that alchemists should be welcomed into the fold only if they could bend their neck to the yoke of this public process.[70]

Moreover, Boyle disliked the intentional obscurantism of these sects much as Puritans dissuaded students from sophistry in preaching.[71] In *The Sceptical Chymist* there are two Hermeticists in the dialogue, one who accepts the public discipline of the experimental theater, and the other who remains in his attic. If they wish to speak candidly, for the edification of everyone, fine; if they wish to hide secrets, they are wasting people's time. Conclusions cannot be simply adduced or deduced but must be "clearly enough demonstrated both by Reason and Experience."[72] The secretive Newton, for one, refused this compromise of pure alchemy, criticizing Boyle's decision to publish his alchemical research.[73] Boyle emphasized open debate and mutual assent, focusing on issues rather than persons; his ideal setting was a "conference" rather than a Socratic dialogue between a "master" and "pupil."[74] In sharp contrast, Hobbes invoked "Vespasian's Law": don't initiate an attack, but feel free to return one with vitriol.[75]

Boyle saw himself and his cohorts as "priests of nature" and did not shy away from seeing his vocation as serving Christian apologetics. When writing on Restoration politics, he borrowed language from Puritan treatises on casuistry. While Hobbes lamented the day that the Bible was available in the common tongue to every English ploughboy, Boyle paid for the translation and publication of the

68. Shapin and Schafer, *Leviathan*, 39; cf. Hobbes, *Leviathan*, chapter 33, and Springborg, "Hobbes on Religion," 353.

69. Shapin and Schafer, *Leviathan*, 57.

70. Shapin and Schafer, *Leviathan*, 70.

71. Robert Boyle, *Sceptical Chymist*, 6.

72. Robert Boyle, *Sceptical Chymist*, 22.

73. Shapin and Schafer, *Leviathan*, 72–73.

74. Shapin and Schafer, *Leviathan*, 74.

75. Shapin and Schafer, *Leviathan*, 153–54.

Bible into Irish. While Hobbes describes his calling to geometry after reading Euclid one day, Boyle in his autobiography described his "conversion" that he experienced in Geneva at the Eucharist.[76] God's Word, he said, is "less a stockpile of weapons than a grand cathedral to occupy." "As the moon, though darkened with spots, gives us a much greater light than the stars that shine all-luminous," he said, "so do the Scriptures afford more light than the brightest human authors."[77]

So, there was a close parallel between Boyle's vocations as Christian and scientist. According to Shapin and Schafer, "Their functions reinforced each other and Hobbes was their common enemy." Although the "two books" were to be kept distinct, they couldn't be separated. "But for Hobbes any profession that claimed such a segregated area of competence, whether priestly, legal, or natural philosophical, was thereby subverting the authority of the undivided state." This was crucial in the Restoration era.[78]

To summarize thus far: Boyle's cosmos was created and governed by a God whose power was inseparable from his wisdom, goodness, justice, and love. There was nothing in nature that is divine and there was a vacuum in which atoms in space and humans in society have freedom to move. Between body and soul, civil and spiritual kingdoms, there was distinction without separation. For Hobbes, the cosmos was ruled by God's immediate and arbitrary power and society by that of the sovereign with no vacuum. Thus, for Hobbes any distinction between body and soul or two kingdoms constituted "seeing double." The state embodied in the ruler becomes the divine self: the mortal God.

Spirits and Demons

Unlike Hobbes, Boyle was on relatively good terms with Henry More but sharply rejected his "World Spirit" mediating between God and nature. While acknowledging Boyle's success with experiments, More suggested that this animating spirit offered a better interpretation. Hunter observes:

> In 1671 he had the temerity to publish a book setting out such claims in detail, his *Enchiridion metaphysicum* (Manual of Metaphysics), two chapters of which gave a detailed reinterpretation of Boyle's air-pump experiments according to More's principles. This stimulated Boyle to a crushing response in the form of

76. Hunter, *Boyle*, 46–48.
77. Shapin and Schafer, *Leviathan*, 319.
78. Shapin and Schafer, *Leviathan*, 284.

> his "Hydrostatic Discourse," which formed part of the 1672 volume of *Tracts* and in which, through a detailed examination of the experimental data that More had deployed, he proved that the hypothesis of an active spiritual agency in the world was superfluous.[79]

A "semi-divine" spirit, force, soul, or whatever else was the very thing Boyle rejected in *A Free Enquiry into the Vulgarly Received Notion of Nature* (1686). Despite Boyle's influences, Newton adopted a position similar to More's with his notion of an occult force being responsible for gravity and motion.

While Boyle focused on natural experiments as a testimony to God, More's experiments were with individuals who reported some contact with the invisible world, whether good or ill. As Hunter put it, "Sectarian enthusiasts saw spirits everywhere and materialist atheists saw them nowhere."[80] Henry More said that "Hobbists" could be won over by various reports, such as that of "faith-healers Matthew Coker and Valentine Greatrakes." Boyle and Pierre du Moulin said that these stories could never be proven by experimental tests in a lab, but that stories of spirits should be examined by similar criteria: evaluating testimony in the light of moral credibility and public verification.[81]

Not only were experimental philosophers taking up the role of Christian apologetics, but they became arbiters of superstition and sorcery. Bacon noted in his *De augmentis scientiarum*, "Neither am I of opinion in this history of marvels, that superstitious narratives of sorceries, witchcrafts, charms, dreams, divinations, and the like, where there is an assurance and clear evidence of the fact, should be altogether excluded." Not only do we not know all causes, but we also need to have solid criteria for court examinations, and "likewise for further disclosing of the secrets of nature."[82]

Demonology was a legitimate topic in the Royal Society. However, one cannot assume that the craze was stoked by rationalists, as a significant debate demonstrates. In 1677 the secretary of the Royal Society gave its imprimatur to a book by John Webster, *The Displaying of Supposed Witchcraft* (1677), even after it had been denied publication by the ecclesiastical censors.[83] This was the same Webster who

79. Hunter, *Boyle*, 172.

80. Hunter, *Boyle*, 314.

81. Hunter, *Boyle*, 314–15.

82. Quoted in Clark, "Demonology," 355.

83. As Michael Hunter shows, neither the president of the Society, Viscount Brouckner, nor the secretary, Henry Oldenburg, was aware that the vice president, Sir James Moore, had given the book a license even after it was denied one by ecclesiastical authorities. See Hunter, "John Webster," 7–19.

had been a Parliamentary chaplain and then supporter of Cromwell, and whose *Academiarum Examen* had provoked John Wilkins and Seth Ward to fire back in defense of traditional education. A physician and natural philosopher, Webster argued along Helmontian lines against the existence of actual witches. In the process, he called into question the reality of demons and angels.[84]

The opposition to this view came, ironically, from the latitudinarian Cambridge Platonists, Henry More and Joseph Glanvill, the latter being a member of the Royal Society. In short, the *virtuosi* influenced by Cambridge Platonists took witchcraft more seriously than those influenced by Puritanism, especially after the Restoration. Interestingly, the Cambridge Platonists were trying to prove the *reasonableness* of believing in invisible spirits by appealing to the evidence of contemporary wonders that some colleagues classed with *enthusiasm.* Visits from "strangers" was still occurring among Hermetic scientists. Dutch physician Johann Friedrich Schweitzer—also known as "Helvetius" (1630–1709)—received angelic visitors to reveal how to make the philosopher's stone, which he performed successfully according to the mint master of his province. In 1702 Boyle tells of another account in which unimpeachable witnesses confirmed a genuine transmutation, though he had nothing to do with angelic visitors.[85]

Mechanical philosophy did not explain miracles or, as demonic activity was regarded, sorcery. Materialists were just as speculative in their dogmatic rationalism as those who defended natural supernaturalism. However, mechanical philosophers like Boyle denied that science can prove or disprove ultimate causes. Yet they did believe it was within their province to adjudicate matters of fact.

Like the Cambridge Platonists, Boyle emphasized the inactivity of matter, but for the former this required a World Spirit, which Newton carried forward in his postulation of a vague force at the core of his law of gravity. Boyle lost. Increasingly, scientists came to laurel something in nature itself with divine attributes—eternity, immutability, simplicity, and so forth—leaving nothing important to distinguish God from the world.

"Last of the Magicians": Newton's Physico-Theology

Since Isaac Newton is the last of our scheduled stops in this volume, we might expect him to exhibit at last the transition from magician to mechanic. However, we are as surprised as Sir Maynard Keynes after examining a bevy of unpublished

84. Hunter, "John Webster," 7–19.

85. See Maxwell-Stuart, *Chemical Choir*, 124–25.

papers he had purchased at auction in 1936: "Newton was not the first of the age of reason. He was the last of the magicians, the last of the Babylonians and Sumerians, the last great mind which looked out on the visible and intellectual world with the same eyes as those who began to build our intellectual inheritance rather less than 10,000 years ago."[86]

Newton plied the same habits and methods of critical investigation, mathematical exactitude, and speculative imagination to his anti-Trinitarian and prophetic research that he did to physics. It was all of one piece in his attempt to find a comprehensive world picture. It is by now a familiar scene: the same person poring over the Emerald Tablet and Genesis, searching far and wide for recipes to make the philosopher's stone while developing a theory of gravity. It's not merely that he engaged in these activities at the same time but that they were facets of an encyclopedic worldview that thrilled pansophists ever since Andreae.[87]

By 1650, there was a backlash against Cartesianism as well as Hobbes.[88] The link between mind and body remained obscure in Descartes's system, although in his last book, *Les passions de l'Âme* (1649), he argued that the soul was principally situated in (though not completely confined to) the pineal gland. More problematic were "the twin issues of how God could be present in the Cartesian universe, and also how human beings could have free will in a world that functioned (and could be explained) on almost entirely mechanistic lines."[89] John Worthington, ex-master of Jesus College, asked More to write a natural philosophy textbook that countered Cartesian philosophy. According to Iliffe, "It was in these ambivalent contexts that Newton encountered Descartes's works."[90] He turned his guns toward deists, which upends a familiar misunderstanding of Newton as one himself.[91] After an initial fascination with Descartes, Newton joined the criticism. Besides taking much from others without attribution, Newton concluded, according to Iliffe, that "Descartes's entire physics was based on the false idea that body was equivalent to extension, and his metaphysics was 'nothing but a tapestry of assumptions.'"[92] If taken seriously, the Cartesian system would lead to atheism, rendering God unnecessary.[93] The rest of Newton's system is in a large degree an effort to provide an alternative to this conclusion.

86. Keynes, "Newton," 27. Quoted in Dobbs, *Foundation of Newton's Alchemy*, 13.
87. Newman, *Atoms and Alchemy*, 6.
88. Iliffe, *Priest of Nature*, 88–89.
89. Iliffe, *Priest of Nature*, 87–88.
90. Iliffe, *Priest of Nature*, 89.
91. Iliffe, *Priest of Nature*, 21.
92. Iliffe, *Priest of Nature*, 89.
93. Iliffe, *Priest of Nature*, 90–91.

UNIVOCITY AND ABSOLUTE POWER

Despite their shared critique of Aristotelian and Hermetic forms of univocity, Descartes and Hobbes in different (even opposite) ways thought of God as a supreme instance of a being rather than the transcendent creator of being.[94] So did Newton.[95]

The experimentalists have already taken us far from the harbor of scholastic distinctions and discussions. Newton never went through the antischolastic phase that seems by now a rite of passage for experimentalists. In fact, he used Aristotelian categories to transgress crucial distinctions of scholastic theology. "The analogy between the human and the divine would remain at the heart of Newton's theological metaphysics," says Iliffe.[96] However, as we will see, it was not really an analogy. Newton was what we would call a panentheist but of an Arian sort. Only a small group of his closest friends knew that he was committed passionately to disproving Trinitarianism in manuscripts he hoped would be published after his death. With one divine person acting upon the world, he was drawn to a radically voluntaristic picture: a God of absolute power, with More's World Spirit dropped in as a sort of *deus ex machina* to explain gravity and space as the place of God in the universe.

As in ontology so also in epistemology Newton's univocal position led to him to conclude that humans can know God as God knows himself, since they are created in his image.[97] It is not surprising that this rationalistic-univocal view was held by Aëtius and Eunomius in the fourth–fifth centuries, in rejecting the Trinity. Clearly, Newton has no clear conception of God *transcending* the world qualitatively. Newton's rationalistic biblicism contrasts sharply with Owen's embrace of mystery."[98]

Considered in its own integrity, Christianity escapes the absolute monotheism

94. See Descartes, *Principia Philosophia*, Part 1, Article 27.

95. Iliffe, *Priest of Nature*, 91–92.

96. Iliffe, *Priest of Nature*, 120–21.

97. "*Just like God*, the most *supreme* thinking being, minds had to be extended, for otherwise they would be nowhere and the existence of persons a mere fiction. . . . *Mind itself was in nature*, and any plausible metaphysics had to take account of it. It remained to propose and carry out the experiments that would clarify the nature of self-motion and thus provide an inlet into the workings of God" (Iliffe, *Priest of Nature*, 105).

98. Owen, "A Practical Exposition upon Psalm CXXX," in Goold, *Works of John Owen*, 6:622: After a detailed scholastic argument, Owen concludes, "And now I cannot think what I have said, but only have intimated what I adore." Such mysticism—i.e., submission to mysteries—characterizes Calvinism; cf. Junius, *Treatise on True Theology*, 104, 117; Turretin, *Institutes*, 2:57 and 179. Impatience with mystery is the engine of heresy.

on the one hand without rebounding into polytheism or pantheism on the other. God freely created the world, to be sure, but did so not as one person acting upon creation but as the Father, in the Son, and by the Spirit. The Son actually assumed human creatureliness, and the Spirit is at work within creation to direct it to its eschatological *telos*. There is no need for intermediating spirits, souls, forms, or ideas because God himself operates in the world in the Son and by the Spirit. Newton's God, however, is one person acting upon the world. Iliffe summarizes this well:

> God could enact all possible things with perfect freedom, accomplishing everything that was best and that most accorded with reason. By freely governing one's own actions, human beings thus mimicked the boundless dominance of the *pantokrator* (the Almighty) over his own creation. Newton's voluntaristic conception of God's activity, that is, the idea that God created things and values by mere force of his will, became one of the best-known features of his metaphysical theology, and his accounts of God's creative powers, effected by a mere act of will, were often accompanied by statements about analogous powers in humans.[99]

In the place of the Holy Spirit, Newton inserts More's semi-divine mediator, the "Spirit of the World" that Boyle attacked. Mechanical philosophers had argued that matter cannot act at a distance, but Newton endowed matter with innate activity.[100] On this crucial point Newton shows himself to be the heir to More rather than to Boyle.[101] Newton's Hermetic worldview suggests various attractions, sympathies, and forces within nature itself that account for purposeful motion.

However, Newton goes one step further, identifying the World Spirit with God himself. Has Newton rejected both Trinitarian theism and deism only to embrace pantheism?[102] He also identifies God with space, or at least accords to space many of the traditional attributes of God, including eternity, simplicity, immutability, and omnipresence. In fact, Newton describes space as God's *sensorium*. The meaning as well as cogency of the argument in his "Query 28" has been debated ever since Leibniz criticized it. According to Patrick J. Connolly, God's sensorium is simply space as the ambit of God's will.[103] However, a *sensorium* refers to the part of the brain or mind that receives and interprets sense data, not to an act of

99. Iliffe, *Priest of Nature*, 120–21.
100. Osler, *Reconfiguring the World*, 156–57.
101. Osler, *Reconfiguring the World*, 160.
102. Osler, *Reconfiguring the World*, 162.
103. Connolly, "Newton," 185–201.

will. John Henry argues that Newton posited the divine *sensorium* because it was felt that his theory of gravity lacked a cause, so he introduced active principles as secondary causes of gravity.[104] Iliffe explains:

> Newton added that he had shown that the analogy between humans and the divine was much closer than had previously been realised by philosophers. Noting that the Bible testified that we were created in God's image, he concluded that by granting humans the capacity of free will and self-motion, God had simulated his own creative power in human faculties to the same extent that he had his other attributes (such as reason and goodness). Although the power of creating minds and bodies was not available to finite beings, Newton continued, the created mind might—"because it is the image of God"—"eminently" contain body in itself.[105]

However we interpret Newton's divine *sensorium*, it is difficult to see how it does not compromise the creator-creature distinction. In contemporary terms, it is panentheistic: nature (space) is not just a realm God created but is a necessary part of his being. If Descartes's separation of God from the physical world leads to atheism, as Newton thought, the question arises whether Newton himself avoided pantheism.[106] Regardless of where we fall on that issue, the one thing we can surely detect is that he was *not* a deist.

Alchemy and Eschatology

Writing in the 1620s and 1630s, the chiliast Joseph Mede attracted great interest among those who saw themselves as the persecuted godly. John Worthington (1618–1671) was a student of Mede and Wichcote at Emmanuel College, an avid reader of Böhme and the Familists' founder, Hendrik Nicholis, and in close touch with the Hartlib Circle as well as their continental contacts such as Adam Boreel. He was also vice chancellor of Cambridge under Cromwell and a formative figure among the Cambridge Platonists. After the Restoration, Worthington produced various editions of Mede's work, including a biography. One common bond that

104. Henry, "Cause of Gravity," 329–51.

105. Iliffe, *Priest of Nature*, 104–5.

106. Osler judges, "Despite his belief in God's literal omnipresence, Newton did not accept pantheism. He insisted on a strict separation between God and creation" (*Reconfiguring the World*, 162). However, his description of space as the divine *sensorium* makes it difficult to draw this conclusion confidently.

remained after the Restoration was Mede's interpretation of biblical prophecy. "Although Newton thought that Mede had made some mistakes in his *Clavis*," says Iliffe, "he believed that it had laid down the true principles of the field, and he adopted many facets of Mede's authorial identity."[107] Based on Revelation 14:4–5, Newton committed himself to lifelong celibacy, and King Charles II allowed Newton to be one of the few professors who did not take holy orders.[108]

Besides the influence of Mede, the perennial philosophy played a large role in Newton's interpretation of history.[109] Newton concluded that the worship of the sun and fire was an understandable corruption of the original Noachic worship of one God.[110]

> There was no reference to the Ancients in the *Principia* when it appeared in the summer of 1687 but Newton's commitment to various forms of the *prisca* tradition was not kept secret. In early 1692, he told his friend, the Swiss mathematician Fatio de Duillier, that he was about to add classical allusions (the so-called Classical Scholia) to propositions IV–IX of the third book of a proposed second edition of the *Principia.* Fatio told Christiaan Huygens that Newton believed that he had discovered that Plato and Pythagoras possessed all the demonstrations offered in his "System of the World" (Book 3 of the *Principia*) that were founded on the inverse-square law. They made a great mystery out of their learning, Newton claimed, but if the surviving fragments of their writings were properly reconstructed, they would show that the Ancients had the same ideas as those enunciated in the *Principia.*[111]

No one believed more than Newton that the perennial tradition "handed down the sacred philosophy by means of types and enigmas, while the rhetoricians ('orators') wrote down the vulgar version openly and in a popular style."[112] This tradition descended through Noah and his sons to Abraham and Moses. It was a way of representing the heavens.[113]

As with other sectarians, including Hobbes, Newton argued that it was the malign priests who perverted the original worship into superstition and magic

107. Iliffe, *Priest of Nature*, 220.
108. Iliffe, *Priest of Nature*, 17.
109. Iliffe, *Priest of Nature*, 189–90.
110. Iliffe, *Priest of Nature*, 201.
111. Iliffe, *Priest of Nature*, 202.
112. Iliffe, *Priest of Nature*, 208.
113. Iliffe, *Priest of Nature*, 211.

(analogous to the Roman Church).[114] In Newton's perspective, Moses reformed the Egyptian system, purging it of idolatry and necromancy while maintaining all its true doctrines. When this was corrupted by paganism, Christ came, but "Christian depravity would plumb depths that were much lower than those to which the Jews had sunk."[115] Lord Herbert of Cherbury (author of *De veritate*, 1624; *De religione laici*, 1645) and Charles Blount would press this idea. There was an original natural and rational religion corrupted by the priests. But Newton "was no 'deist' insofar as the term denotes support for the idea of a largely absent divinity or an aversion to revelation or religious ceremony. Nor did he make any criticisms of modern clergymen as a group claiming at one point that they were more godly than their forebears."[116]

Newton did push Israel aside in favor of Egypt. As Iliffe writes, "By saying that Christ essentially did nothing more than restore the Noachian religion, Newton implied that nothing much more was required of the true religion than to recognize the divine origins of the cosmos, to believe that Christ was the Messiah who was resurrected on the third day after his death, and to observe the moral obligations of Christianity."[117] Newton took to a new level the sectarian's genealogy of decline from the apostles to the Roman priesthood that continues in the Reformed church.[118]

He kept his heterodox views to himself in unpublished papers, but hoped that after his death they could be published and, according to Iliffe, "would conceivably form part of the great dispersion of the gospel that would precede Christ's Second Coming. . . . If they had been unveiled to the Republic of Letters when he wrote them, and his authorship revealed, he would now be part of an elite pantheon of original thinkers who are lauded as part of a Radical Reformation or Radical Enlightenment. However, like William Whiston, his successor in the Lucasian chair, he would have been immediately expelled from his college."[119]

Newton was not a freethinker but another hyper-Protestant sectarian. One does not need Lucretius for his cynical view of church history as power-hungry priests turning heresy into orthodoxy. It is part and parcel of the anti-orthodox polemic from the so-called Radical Reformation. "Periodically, men like Abraham, Moses, and even Jesus Christ himself had come to restore the truth," Newton argues. According to Iliffe:

114. Iliffe, *Priest of Nature*, 213.
115. Iliffe, *Priest of Nature*, 216.
116. Iliffe, *Priest of Nature*, 217–18.
117. Iliffe, *Priest of Nature*, 218.
118. Iliffe, *Priest of Nature*, 220.
119. Iliffe, *Priest of Nature*, 11.

> There is a strong sense in Newton's writings—though he never stated it explicitly—that he saw himself as the latest in this line of restorers. . . . In so doing, he was consciously working in the *prisca sapientia* tradition. . . . If the world was the temple of God, then those like Newton who properly studied it were priests of nature. It is in this context that one should place his great work of 1687, the *Principia Mathematica*, a text in which he believed that he had resurrected a major component of the *prisca*.[120]

Apocalyptic studies occupied much of Newton's attention between 1675 and 1689. He wanted especially to "reorder the visions of Revelation," turning to the works of Joseph Mede. He then immersed himself in history to discern fulfillments.[121] In addition, he poured himself into alchemy in search of the philosopher's stone. Newton incorporated the whole history of the world as well as his physics into a unified theory of reality. "For Newton, who believed that he was restoring an ancient wisdom (called the *prisca sapientia*)," says Osler, "the ancient methods were superior to those of his contemporaries."[122] She adds, "Newton's growing acquaintance with chymical phenomena—he left at least a million words in manuscript on alchemical subjects—reinforced his perception of specificity and activity in nature. The manuscripts reveal that Newton was deeply immersed in alchemical studies." The whole idea of attraction and repulsion derives from such sources.[123] In addition, Newton added a "General Scholium" to a second edition of *Principia* in which "he argued that existing in a time and place was the 'common affection' of all things."[124] According to Iliffe:

> Now Newton believed that he was one of the remnant who, as the true saints described in Revelation, would be resurrected to rule over mortals in the millennium. At the core of Newton's religion was the idea that Christianity was a simple faith. . . . First, Newton believed that being a Christian was not primarily concerned with holding allegedly correct doctrines, and that the main requirement of a godly life was to live according to the practical moral precepts of Christianity. . . . Technical theological subjects whose resolution was not easily accomplished by empirical research, or by his own understanding, were off limits.[125]

120. Iliffe, *Priest of Nature*, 16.
121. Iliffe, *Priest of Nature*, 132–33.
122. Osler, *Reconfiguring the World*, 151.
123. Osler, *Reconfiguring the World*, 158.
124. Iliffe, *Priest of Nature*, 102–3.
125. Iliffe, *Priest of Nature*, 6–8.

Nor was this obsession with the perennial tradition a mark of Newton's dotage. Iliffe shows in detail that his fascination with biblical and church history, prophecy, alchemy, and the perennial tradition was not as "baroque glosses that were composed simply to make the work more accessible, or to give a superficial aura of authority to the text. They were the tip of an intellectual iceberg in which Newton told the story of the original pristine religion, whose perversion was accompanied by that of the scientific wisdom held by the priesthood."[126] "Indeed," he adds, "in contrast to the great Enlightenment myth that Newton only pursued these studies after his creative powers had dried up, it is clear that his most intensive and innovative religious studies took place early in his career, when he was in the prime of his life for pursuing extended and innovative studies in any field that attracted him."[127] Newton had good reasons not to publish much on these topics. He criticized Boyle's decision to publish on alchemy, lest the secrets fall into the wrong hands, and his anti-Trinitarianism was still a public crime. Unlike the ascendent naturalists and freethinkers, Newton's Neo-Arianism was motivated by a rock-ribbed biblicism and anti-Romanism. Far from anticipating the critical spirit fostered by Spinoza, Newton saw himself as a defender of the true faith against Athanasius and the Nicene-Constantinopolitan Creed.

Conclusion

There are now two Protestant movements in our narrative. The first is self-consciously heir to the Magisterial Reformation and therefore in continuity on many points with the Roman Church. The second is a continuation of the radical reformers.

William Perkins, often called the father of Elizabethan Puritanism, begins his work *The Reformed Catholic* with these words: "By a Reformed Catholic I understand anyone that holds the same necessary heads of religion with the Roman Church, yet so as he pares off and rejects all errors in doctrine whereby the said religion is corrupted. How this may be done I have begun to make some little declaration in this small treatise, the intent whereof is to show how near we may come to the present Church of Rome in sundry points of religion and wherein we must ever dissent."[128] Architects of Reformed and Lutheran orthodoxy exegeted scripture from the original languages and were steeped in patristic and medieval sources,

126. Iliffe, *Priest of Nature*, 201.

127. Iliffe, *Priest of Nature*, 22.

128. William Perkins, "The Reformed Catholic," in Breward, *William Perkins*, 521.

which they used to oppose Anabaptism, enthusiasm, millennialism, and the rising tide of Arminian and Socinian influences. For radical Protestants, the Lutheran and Reformed orthodox remained in the graveclothes of scholastic Romanism.

The doctrinal criticism from heterodox sects was not done in vacuum of disinterested scholarship, much less by atheism or even deism, but in order to shift the focus from God to the self, justification to sanctification, doctrine to morality. Thus, although Hartlib, Dury, Moriaen, and other leaders in the network that would become the Royal Society expressed a greater intensity of anti-Romanism than the Reformers, they showed little interest in the actual doctrines at the heart of the Reformation. They could work with pantheists like Adam Boreel or Socinians to galvanize a last-ditch effort to defeat the Roman antichrist. Then Hobbes advocated this sectarian reading of church history, with the early councils as the fabrication of proto-Roman prelates. Newton drew his inspiration from this milieu.

What is clear is that for Newton physics was inseparable from theological apologetics. As he says in the *Principia*, "When I wrote my Treatise about our System, I had an Eye upon such Principles as might work with considering Men, for the Belief in a Deity."[129] Osler offers a fitting conclusion:

> In 1715 and 1716 a controversy about providence erupted between Leibniz and Newton's spokesman, Samuel Clarke. Leibniz argued that the Newtonian insistence on divine activity implies that God's workmanship is so imperfect that he must constantly intervene in nature and repair his work. . . . Clarke, replying as a Newtonian voluntarist, argued that Leibniz's account implies an unacceptable limitation on God's freedom and power because it assumes that God is subject to principles that exist independently of him. In many ways, this debate between the two towering figures of late-seventeenth-century natural philosophy stands as the culmination of early modern concerns with the relationship between theology and natural philosophy.[130]

129. Newton, *Principia*, 942–43, quoted in Osler, *Reconfiguring the World*, 163.
130. Osler, *Reconfiguring the World*, 164.

CONCLUSION

Immanentizing Transcendence

Triumph of Natural Supernaturalism

> While the preoccupation with increasing material well-being and the pursuit of purely instrumental goods doubtless includes a strong secular component, it now appears that the dynamic underlying forces which motivate and sustain this trend are functionally equivalent to earlier forms of religious enthusiasm. . . . The historical appearance of secular man is intimately related to the correlative epiphany of divinized man.
>
> —David Walsh[1]

I began this project with the transition from the shaman to the sage. Whether one calls it the Axial Age or simply features of axiality in different contexts, there is general agreement that this profound cultural shift represented identifiable characteristics that we often associate with modernity. There is an awakening to the self, the individual, who can ascend through three worlds and behold the truth directly. In fact, this inmost self is a spark of divinity, emanating from and returning to the One after fleshly incarcerations. This is the core dogma of the Orphic consciousness, that is, the Greek inflection of the Axial Age. This self-discovery leads to a distancing from the embodied world of visible institutions and public life, including religion, as a cage that imprisons the autonomous spirit within. Like the body, the external world is seen as an oppressive realm. The divine self seeks to escape the locative, bounded, limited, and finite laws of nature and society. This utopian trend is associated in every time and place with urbanization, rational-

1. Walsh, *Innerworldly Fulfillment*, 9.

ization, and utopianism.[2] The Florentine Renaissance marks a major transition from a locative to a utopian outlook.

One of the broad conclusions I take from my reading of early modernity is that transcendence becomes increasingly immanentized. It is not Nietzsche's much later reversal of Platonism that designates the upper world as imaginary and the lower world as real. Rather, it is the opposite—the sacralizing of the world—that lies at the heart of the secularization process. As we will explore in volume 3, it is this process that "killed God," according to Nietzsche, and his "reversed Platonism" is his response to this condition. The divine self is the major driver of this phenomenon, which means (counterintuitively) that "spirituality" (i.e., enchantment) is the alternative to "religion" (i.e., Christianity and other forms of monotheism). Whether within the inner recesses of the self, the grandeur of nature below and infinite space above, the sublimity of art, autonomous reason, or the power of the state, the transcendent is brought within an immanent horizon. The sacred is identified less with a personal God and the people, places, things, and events that God sanctifies than with a natural divinity.

The Cathedral and the Garden

I referred in this volume's introduction to the ducal palace with an intentionally thin divider between a chapel to the Muses and one to the Triune God. This space symbolizes the return of the repressed and the tensions that ensued from the interaction between Christian and pagan paths to fullness. From the gardens of Renaissance popes and dukes to Newton's alchemical pursuits, there is a search for the sacred, a desire for fullness that is not satisfied by the church's traditional faith and practice. Interestingly, the father of the disenchantment theory, Max Weber, described premodern societies as those in which "the world remains a great enchanted garden."[3] It becomes clear in Weber's vision that "enchantment" is natural supernaturalism and "disenchantment" is Judaic and Christian theism.

The juxtaposition of cathedral and garden works also as an analogy for the intricate fabric of scholastic theology and the organic vitalism of the Neoplatonic-Hermetic imagination. The eye is drawn from nature to the heavens in the former, while the Renaissance *magus* seeks to bring the power of the heavens to earth. As I

2. For example, Peter Harrison points out that the twelfth-century Platonic renaissance was occasioned by "renewed urbanization and the rise of the medieval universities—Bologna (1150), Paris (1200), and Oxford (1220)." Harrison, *Territories*, 67.

3. Weber, *Sociology of Religion*, 270.

have said, these are not airtight compartments but overlapping sensibilities. What the mysticism of innerworldly fulfillment seeks is in a sense some incarnation of the divine in this world. However, it is more "god-within-us" than God with us. The presuppositions of natural supernaturalism do not permit a positive evaluation of the material world, much less the incarnation of God.

Critics accuse and friends celebrate the magisterial Reformation as the seed-bed of modern liberalism, including rationalism, democracy, capitalism and other drivers of secularization. If indirectly, the Reformation fostered modernity by "unintended consequences."[4] However, more than any sixteenth-century movement, Anabaptism promoted features commonly associated with modernity or the "Axial Age": disembedding, distanciation, criticism, spiritualization, rationalization, individualism, and voluntarism.

The Radical Reformation turns out to be a major exhibit of the argument running through my narrative in these three volumes, namely, that rationalism is bound up integrally with mysticism, locating truth within the divine self rather than in external mediation or authority. "That was the project," observes Diarmaid MacCulloch, namely, "to produce a more rational Christianity." He continues:

> It was the agenda of those who had seen the esoteric literature of the hermeticists and the cabbalists as keys to understanding divine purposes both in the physical world and beyond. Such interests coalesced with a renewed Protestant mysticism and personal religion which, to begin with, the "magisterial" Reformation had held at bay. All that too found its way into the Enlightenment and was not antichristian at all: it was able to alter Christianity and open it to ways of reformulating the questions and answers which made up Christian belief.[5]

Very rarely is radical religion given its due in histories of atheism. According to modern rationalists, irrational religious fanatics could hardly have been the forebears of Feuerbach, Marx, Nietzsche, and Freud. However, the early Anabaptists were the first critics of religion and were followed in this endeavor by radical pietists and the various sects of seventeenth-century England. Everything that orthodox Christians consider essential to the faith was regarded by spiritualists as externals: scripture, preaching, sacraments, the historical Jesus, the visible church, the resurrection of the body, and a final judgment. As we have seen, Anabaptist spiritualists were the first critics of the Bible, shifting the locus of authority from

4. This is a central argument in the Radical Orthodoxy narrative and is defended coherently in Gregory, *Unintended Reformation.*

5. MacCulloch, *Reformation,* 698.

external sources to the inner autonomy of the enlightened individual. Lucretius's account of religion as the invention of priests to dominate the masses through fear played its part, but a deeper and more decisive revolt against orthodoxy—of spirituality against religion—was fostered among radical mystics, both Roman Catholic and Protestant.

Radicals also discovered in Sextus Empiricus the extreme skepticism of Pyrrho but employed it in service to rationalism. Dissolving all authorities and beliefs in the acids of doubt and leaving one thing that cannot be doubted was a pattern during this period. For Savonarola, the remaining factor was scripture. For the Jesuits, it was the church. For Anabaptist spiritualists, it was the inner light. For Mede, this remaining element was biblical prophecy. For Descartes, it was self-consciousness. And for Hobbes, it was the unquestionable dictates of the state. Picking up the story in volume 3, we shall also see that Spinoza's criticism of religion and the Bible in particular was shared by the radical pietist group to which he belonged.

By the standard of Christian orthodoxy, virtually all of the radical sectarians were "atheists."[6] Monists like Cambridge Platonist Peter Sterry would be included, along with the Ranter Laurence Clarkson and many others. As Nigel Smith points out, "Pantheism, annihilationism, the internalization of scriptural figures so that heaven and hell are delocalized, and a highly individualized subjectivity are introduced, as the Bible becomes a map of the self's inner life."[7] Laurence Clarkson renounced all scriptures as the fetters of the divine self. In Smith's words, "As a Ranter, he became his own God, as he claimed to be a part of the Godhead, complete with a metaphysic that was part and parcel of his religion of the free spirit and free love."[8]

De-christianizing enchantment, immanentizing transcendence, naturalizing the supernatural are the trend—not of secularists, but of spiritual enthusiasts. Nature is bristling with divinity. Moreover, the modern individual can choose his or her own nature. Mediating between the two worlds, the Neoplatonic *magus* can bring down the powers of the heavens for the Epicurean goals of this-worldly prosperity. I find fullness not by looking outside of myself, but within. Spiritualists and sectarians of various hues confused the Holy Spirit with their inner spirit and revelation. They saw revelation as no longer mediated by scripture and preaching, but as an immanent inner light. This is the meaning of that broad term "enthusiasm" (god-within-ism). Such radical autonomy cannot help but disintegrate reli-

6. N. Smith, "Atheism," 134–35.
7. N. Smith, "Atheism," 136–37.
8. N. Smith, "Atheism," 138.

gious, social, and political institutions.[9] In reaction to this fragmentation, Hobbes completed a process underway well before the *Leviathan* to transfer divinity to the absolute ruler. A god of absolute power becomes incarnated this time not in Jesus Christ, who is conveniently absent at present, but in a monster we create—a mortal God, who requites our fear of its majesty by eliminating the fear of chaos. Absolutism and individualism were responses to the same anxieties provoked by the disintegration of a catholic consensus. In all these ways we meet false incarnations, a contrived immanence, that draws on spent longings for an external redemption by a transcendent God.

Where Do I Find Fullness? The Sacralizing of Nature

Soul or Spirit—something in the middle between the higher and lower worlds—becomes a divine force infusing and animating all living things. It is possible to conceive of nature as self-generating and self-sufficient precisely because it is moved by its own spirits. Like "enchantment," spirituality without religion means a return to pre-Christian philosophical religion (i.e., Orphic spirituality) over against traditional theism.

As I suggested in volume 1, when considering Platonism our modern categories of pantheism and panentheism dissolve. The One manifests itself in the diversity of the visible world. This is the world-affirming moment in the emanative process. Yet this manifestation gathers itself back into unity by evacuating the real (i.e., divine souls) from the material world. Even in Stoicism there is a dualism between active and passive matter. In all these systems we meet a dualism within an ultimate monism. In contrast, Epicurus taught an extreme form of transcendence, with the gods removed from this world in absolute bliss. The Calvinist Reformer Pierre Viret coined the term *deiste* (deist) for this view in 1563.

However, the common thread in all these schools is the idea that nature, whether animated by divine essence or not, is self-sustaining and self-sufficient. If this conclusion is correct, many of our assumptions about the rise of deistic and atheistic naturalism will have to be revised. Physicalist naturalism is not only the offspring of natural supernaturalism but remains inextricably bound to it, as we see in Hobbes. The future would belong to monism, whether idealist or materialist.

David Walsh's description of Böhme's theosophy as "the mysticism of innerworldly fulfillment" is, I think, the best way of summarizing the broader trend in

9. The standard work on this subject is Lim, *Mystery Unveiled.*

early modern spirituality.[10] Is it a search for the sacred, a longing for transcendence? It is, but is so by bringing transcendence under the "immanent frame," as Taylor calls it.[11] The truth is found in the deepest recesses of the self, which is identical with God. We might assume from the mystical aspect of such spirituality that it is a longing for transcendence, and it is, but it is an experience of the divine within oneself. From a Christian perspective, I suggest, enchantment *is* secularization, or at least a contributing factor. Therefore, I think it unwise to accept the Weberian model. Enchantment assumes that nature itself bristles with divine forces, which renders unnecessary a personal God who creates and acts in history. While Christianity is a driver of disenchantment in Weber's sense, it is far more "enchanted" than natural supernaturalism in its narration of a transcendent God freely involving himself in his creation even to the point of the Son assuming to himself a complete human nature. Hence, Boyle's defense of supernaturalism, including miracles, required a deconstruction of natural supernaturalism.

Walsh says that it is in Böhme where we discover "the crucial redirection of salvation-history toward a more innerworldly *telos* was first consistently enunciated."[12] Actually, Böhme was dependent on Joachite eschatology and Anabaptist metaphysics. But Walsh is right about Böhme's significance in this trajectory:

> He absorbed the two great streams of religious thought that had previously existed separately and modified and united them through the unique conjunction that he forged in the fire of his own revelatory experience. The first was the influence of radical pietism that had erupted with the Reformation and had renewed the expectations of medieval apocalypticism, with its uncompromising emphasis on the transformative experience of grace. The other was the range of esoteric religious symbolisms, chiefly hermetism, kabbalah, and alchemy, which had emerged with a new respectability and prominence in the Renaissance as *the* means of experiencing God more tangibly present within the created universe.[13]

Anabaptism was a different reformation, one rooted in late medieval mysticism but also one that has played a more formative role in the formation of modernity than the Magisterial Reform. Our traditional modern periodization favors the "mainstream": the Reformation, the Scientific Revolution, the Enlightenment, and

10. Walsh, *Innerworldly Fulfillment.*
11. Taylor, *Secular Age*, especially 539.
12. Walsh, *Innerworldly Fulfillment*, 10.
13. Walsh, *Innerworldly Fulfillment*, 11.

Romanticism. But while Reformation convictions remained quite deep in the Scientific Revolution, radical Protestant spirituality ended up in the long run to have the greater impact. At least for the history of autonomy—the "divine self"—in Western civilization, Anabaptism proved far more consequential than the Magisterial Reformation.

The project of "inner-worldly fulfillment" could only succeed by altering theology from within Christianity itself. As MacCulloch noted above regarding esoteric Protestantism, "All that too found its way into the Enlightenment and was not antichristian at all: it was able to alter Christianity and open it to ways of reformulating the questions and answers which made up Christian belief."[14] Walsh explains,

> The beginnings of this process may be discerned in a great variety of phenomena emerging from the fifteenth century on, but its definitive appearance must be identified with the establishment of man's new and exalted self-interpretation on a coherent theological foundation. Without an explanation of the divine necessity that required it, the growing emphasis on man's inner-worldly perfection and fulfillment could never be secured against the charge of distorting the traditional relationship between God and man. The evocation of the latter's increasing power and autonomy had to be derived from the earlier symbols of his limitation and dependence. Moreover, it is only if reality itself is a process moving toward an immanent transfiguration that the hitherto unrealized transformation of human nature can be expected to take place. The elaboration of such a new and fundamental symbolism, which subsumed most of the major preceding currents of self-aggrandizement from the Renaissance and provided the basis for their eventual consummation in the secular messianism of the later ideological movements, was the achievement of an obscure Silesian shoemaker named Jacob Boehme.[15]

However, there were other streams of Renaissance natural supernaturalism that made their way into the early Enlightenment. Contributing to the immanentizing of transcendence, Hermeticism remained a major influence all the way to Newton. Through the use of such spiritual and mechanical technology, one could harness these divine powers; what was formerly attributed to God's providential will, unknowable to us, was made available to those who knew the secrets of natural magic. Theists supplicate; magicians operate. According to an anonymous seventeenth-century tract, Ebeling summarizes:

14. MacCulloch, *Reformation*, 698.
15. Walsh, *Innerworldly Fulfillment*, 9–10.

> And when it came to the power of the Philosopher's Stone, the dangers of taking control of the world seemed especially clear. . . . As a medium of universal salvation, it could bestow "all temporal bliss, corporal health, and earthly luck." It seemed to open a path to redemption that was no longer tied to the crucifixion of Christ and to divine autonomy in the act of salvation. . . . Since it was immanent in the world, the medium of redemption, the Stone, had to be hidden.[16]

The Orphic tradition could even incorporate atomism. William R. Newman demonstrates that atomism itself has a long lineage in alchemy.[17] In fact, the divisibility of atoms was essential to the notion that mercury, while retaining its own character, could modify the inner structure of metals, as in the transmutation of lead into gold.

Traditional Christian theism worked as much against magic as it did atheism. Biblical supernaturalism had always been opposed to natural supernaturalism. History and nature were governed ultimately by God alone, not by spirits (good or evil) or supernatural properties in nature itself. God could be invoked but could not be manipulated by spiritual technology. In rare instances, God might act miraculously, but even these events would have a rational purpose that God disclosed to his prophets, usually as signs of judgment and redemption rather than ends in themselves. Moreover, in contrast with the state priests and the soothsayers, the scope of these prophecies pertained not to personal or even national fates. Rather, they announced a universal and apocalyptic transformation in the future. Most of the time, however, God's operations were providential. Simon During puts it well: "Orthodoxy minimized the role of such spirits: God ordered the sublunary world by natural means—that is, providentially—and permitted spirits to intervene in worldly affairs only on extraordinary occasions. The magical tradition, in contrast, regarded spirits as active, if not visible, in most causal chains."[18] The doctrine of God's all-inclusive providence excludes irrationality and randomness but not mystery, opening a wide vista for purely natural explanations. Not knowing the ultimate reasons of God's providential activity, human beings are to concentrate on the effects of God's creative and continuance of the world through the secondary causes, especially natural laws. Furthermore, according to its doctrine of analogy, the contingency of actions performed by creatures (human and nonhuman) is enabled rather than threatened by God's sovereignty. In scripture it often happens that the same event is attributed to God and to humans. In

16. Ebeling, *Secret History*, 105.

17. See Newman, *Atoms and Alchemy*; cf. Klein, "Styles of Experimentation," 247–56.

18. During, *Modern Enchantments*, 13.

short, the qualitative distinction between creator and creation entails the same between God's hidden and revealed purposes, ultimate efficient causality and secondary causes, theological explanations and scientific ones.

Christopher Hill notes, "The victory of Army and Independents over the Presbyterians William Lilly interpreted as a victory for the friends of astrology." Astrology and alchemy were popular among Ranters like Lawrence Clarkson, Socinians, and even founding members of the Royal Society. "For Familists and Behmenists, so influential on Ranters and Quakers, alchemy was an outward symbol of internal regeneration. . . . Chemistry became almost equated with radical theology. . . . So astrology, alchemy and natural magic contributed, together with Biblical prophecy, to the radical outlook."[19]

It was not only Anabaptists and Quakers who relied on visions and angelic communication, but also figures like Dee and Descartes. Isaac Newton thought that soon money would be useless, with base metals being transmuted into gold, and that the defeat of the Roman antichrist was imminent and, with it, the dogma of the Trinity. At the heart of his theory of gravity is an occult "force" that works at great distances. Far from being opposed, mechanical philosophy flourished among the sects, particularly common laborers. In Hill's words, "The radicals ended by advocating not only mechanical preachers but also mechanical doctors, mechanical lawyers, and judges."[20]

Like Ficino, Henry More thought that Plato's doctrine of the soul's preexistence was neither taught nor rejected by scripture or the church, leaving the door wide open to the perennial tradition of gentile sages. More and Cudworth sought to salvage what they could from Casaubon's exposure of the Corpus Hermeticum, convinced that the most important Hermetic doctrines, such as preexistence and the World Soul, were authentic: "In Egypt, that ancient Nurse of all hidden sciences, that this Opinion was in vogue amongst all the wise men there, those fragments of Trismegistus do sufficiently witness." It is the testimony "not only of the Gymnosophists," said More, "but also the Brahmans of India, and the Magi of Babylon and Persia; as you may plainly see by those Oracles that are called either Magical or Chaldaical . . . [and] the abstruse Philosophy of the Jews, which they call their Cabbala . . . and how naturally applicable this Theory is to those three mysterious chapters of Genesis, I have, I hope, with no contemptible success, endeavoured to shew in my Conjectura Cabbalistica."[21] Before he rejected Descartes's mechanistic philosophy, More thought Descartes's mechanistic philosophy was "a

19. Hill, *World Turned Upside Down*, 221–22.

20. Hill, *World Turned Upside Down*, 229.

21. H. More, *Immortality of the Soul*, 246–47.

truth anciently known to Moses and preserved in Cabalist tradition which Descartes had rediscovered by divine inspiration." Ralph Cudworth's *True Intellectual System of the Universe* (1678) argues that these ancient polytheists nevertheless held ultimately to one God. Even if Hermes Trismegistus were to be left out of consideration, the *prisca theologia* is amply revealed by the Sibylline oracles, Hermes, Zoroaster, Orpheus, Iamblichus, Plutarch, and others.[22]

However, as Grafton notes, the Cambridge Platonists "overstated the similarities between classical and Christian professions of monotheism."

> And they lent credence to particular texts, like the Hermetic Corpus and the Sibylline oracles, which had been exposed as fakes. Just after the English revolution ended, more orthodox divines like Theophilus Gale and Stillingfleet attacked what they saw as the Platonists' excessive tolerance in large-scale polemical treatises. Stillingfleet's Origines Sacrae argued that "there is no credibility in any of those Heathen Histories, which pretend to give an account of ancient times"; the Old Testament was the only reliable source, and Jewish writers the only reliable witnesses, to the early history of mankind. The pagans had been foolish men sunk in ignorance, not monotheist sages. . . . They were pale reflections of the biblical history and theology of the Jews, borrowed and corrupted by Greeks and others.

Ralph Cudworth responded to critics with his *True Intellectual System of the Universe* (1678). "Cudworth subtly defended the notorious ancient forgeries, like the Hermetic Corpus," says Grafton, "arguing that they must have contained some genuine elements even if the transmitted texts he knew were late."[23]

The main opponent became Richard Bentley, England's premier classicist as well as a respected clergyman and member of the Royal Society. Grafton relates, "The *True Intellectual System* and its author, however, were not Bentley's only targets. Behind both of them lurked the more disturbing figure of More. He too had argued for the priority and purity of pagan revelations. More had fused Cabalism and the *Orphica*—two branches of literature Bentley found especially detestable—long before Cudworth."[24] Stillingfleet and Bentley "disliked More's dissolution of historical boundaries as much as Spinoza's dissolution of Revelation." Yet, while seeking the civil suppression of enthusiastic sects, "he had also dabbled in learned magic and spiritual healing, encountering spirits in dreams,

22. Yates, *Giordano Bruno*, 426–27.
23. Grafton, *Defenders*, 17–18.
24. Grafton, *Defenders*, 18–20.

and populated the cosmos with rank on rank of angels and daemons. He had popularized and debated with Descartes and helped to create the infinite cosmos of the New Science." In any case, Grafton writes:

> By the 1680s More seemed an enthusiast rather than an enemy of enthusiasm. His cosmos had to be replaced by Newton's, which Bentley would expound so lucidly in his Boyle Lectures. And his party had to be eliminated from the church—or at least clearly distinguished from the party of Stillingfleet, the members of which also insisted on the value of pagan culture and the study of the past. The attack on disorderly and eclectic use of the past thus had a sharp and practical bearing on the present.[25]

Newton saw an occult force as the mediator between the divine and nature, but this force, along with space itself, possesses most of the attributes ascribed traditionally to God alone. Even Galileo adopted a similar view, Wootton observes. "In some of his private correspondence, he drops curious hints of his belief in a weird, quasi-Egyptian, quasi-Neoplatonic 'world soul'—a 'very spiritual, tenuous, and extremely rapid substance that, diffusing itself throughout the universe, penetrates everything without effort, brings warmth, enlivens, and renders fecund all living things' and whose 'principal receptacle' is 'the body of the Sun.'"[26] In nature, therefore, there remains a vital force ("a semi-divinity" in the phrasing of Boyle) that is neither God himself nor a creature. In myriad ways we see a sacralization of nature: natural supernaturalism.

Where Is History Going? The Sacralization of Time

The modern metanarrative of a steady march from an enchanted age of faith to a disenchanted age of enlightenment is a myth that was written mainly by mystics and magicians. On the surface, natural supernaturalism appears to endow everything with sacred meaning, yet at a deeper level it immanentizes and secularizes both nature and history. If God is everything, then there is no God, and if everything is sacred—set apart by God as holy––then nothing is sacred. Böhme's cosmotheology assimilates God to the world and eschatology to the immanent unfolding of history from thesis and antithesis to synthesis.

In a biblical frame, nature as a whole does not mirror God's being but displays his

25. Grafton, *Defenders*, 18–20.

26. Wootton, *Galileo*, 246, quoting Galileo to Piero Dini, March 23, 1614.

creative love, freedom, wisdom, and power. Similarly, time is not a moving picture of eternity but is the register for God's creative, providential, and redemptive operations and creaturely existence. Wherever and whenever God acts in judgment or grace, certain people, places, and times are no longer common but holy. God rested on the Sabbath, rendering it holy, but the rest of the week is common. Such holiness does not arise from anything inherent in nature but from God's purposeful actions in the history of redemption. God appropriates certain analogies from the world he made for his self-revelation, but they are not inherent signatures of the macrocosm. God hallows certain creaturely signs—water, bread, and wine—to be sacred means of grace. If everything is divine, there is no God. If everything is sacred, nothing is sacred. If everything is in a sense miraculous, there can be no miracles in a traditional Christian sense.

The immanentizing of transcendence occurs in history as well as nature. Renaissance humanists and mystics spoke of a renewal of the world (*renovatio mundi*), a consummation of history (*plenitudine temporum*), and the time for restoration (*tempora restitutionis*). These slogans are taken from the Latin New Testament, where in each instance they refer to Jesus as the fulfillment. In Acts 2:17, Peter quotes the prophecy of Joel:

> And it shall come to pass afterward,
> that I will pour out my Spirit on all flesh;
> your sons and your daughters shall prophesy,
> your old men shall dream dreams,
> and your young men shall see visions. (Joel 2:28)

Peter announces in Acts 2 that this prophecy is fulfilled then and there on the day of Pentecost. Later, he speaks of the ascension of Jesus, "whom heaven must receive until the time for restoring all the things [Latin: *tempora restitutionis*] about which God spoke by the mouth of his holy prophets long ago" (Acts 3:21). The whole creation will be liberated from the curse, but for now it groans together with us, awaiting Christ's return in glory. "But if we hope for what we do not see, we wait for it with patience" (Rom 8:18–25). Thus, New Testament eschatology coalesces around Christ's two advents.

In its understanding of both nature and history, natural supernaturalism secularizes the Christian imagination. No longer awaiting the return of Christ to "rend the heavens" and make all things new (Isa 64:1), judgment and salvation are placed in the hands of the saints here and now. Whereas Peter in Acts 2 announced the fulfillment of Joel 2 on the day of Pentecost, Joachim of Fiore believed the prophecy described the age of the Spirit that would dawn in the year 1260. A time of terrible persecution of the true saints will be followed by their victory, led by an angelic pope and last world emperor.

Jesus told Pilate, "My kingdom is not of this world. If my kingdom were of this world, my servants would have been fighting, that I might not be delivered over to the Jews. But my kingdom is not from the world" (John 18:36). Yet, Columbus believed the king of Spain would rebuild the temple in Jerusalem. Millennial expectations held enormous potential for politics, often combined with nationalism.[27] In traditional eschatology, Christians await the return of Christ at the end of this present age. It is an apocalyptic advent—God incarnate now glorified, appearing in judgment and grace. But according to the widely held Joachite scheme, the age of the Spirit dawns in this present age before Christ's return, and it is inaugurated by the triumph of the saints. The irruption of a transcendent God into immanent history is transformed into an immanent movement here and now.

With various permutations, many Roman Catholics and Protestants were convinced that Christ's kingdom was very much of this world. The defeat of the Spanish Armada was viewed broadly in England as a victory over the beast in John's Apocalypse. The victories of Britain, Sweden, and the Netherlands over the Catholic League were described by sober contemporaries as "supernatural."[28] Daniel's fifth and everlasting kingdom was no longer prophesying Christ's reign but that of a temporal monarch here and now. Fifth Monarchists formed a significant movement in Cromwell's Army. Yet this broad sentiment, nourished by writers like Joseph Mede, characterized England across all ecclesiastical and political parties all the way to Isaac Newton. On the one hand, the most sensitive intellects of a whole epoch were fascinated by biblical cosmology (e.g., "physico-theology"), historiography, and prophecy. On the other hand, this turned the Bible into quite a different book, one that did not center on Christ with a plotline leading from creation to the consummation as supranatural events in history. In fact, as the example of Isaac Newton demonstrates, one did not even need the Trinity or other central Christian mysteries for the defense of theism.

Theology to Social Transformation: "The Vanity of Dogmatising"

Another sign of the transmutation of transcendence to immanence is the growing shift from theological discourse to utopian social visions. We have seen a radical voluntarism spreading across early modernity from different directions. One source is the trail from Duns Scotus to William of Ockham. However, along this path we meet Nicholas of Cusa, who was both a nominalist and a Neoplatonist.

27. For example, see Popkin, "Millenarianism," 77–84.

28. Popkin, "Religious Background," 395.

According to Eckhartian mysticism, the soul is absorbed in God not by intellect but by will. As much as in Ockham, we see in Eckhart that the disjunction of God's ordained will from his absolute power entails the separation of scripture from reason, the ordinary means of grace from an arbitrary will. The same idea of arbitrary liberty characterizes human beings and political arrangements. Pico's invitation to choose one's nature was an early manifesto of this modern spirit. It is the will, not the intellect, that is the spark of divinity. More's Utopians are punished if, upon becoming Christians, they criticize other religions on the island, although office holders should affirm the soul's immortality, rewards, and punishments in order to guarantee public morality.

Scripture itself was seen by some spiritualists as an oppressive weight placed upon the divine self. Anabaptists and radical pietists ridiculed book learning and doctrinal precision, even though many of their writings are exceedingly intricate and speculative. Moreover, we have seen a line from Anabaptist spiritualists to radical pietists who wrote church histories in which the heretics are orthodox and the orthodox are heretics. Paradoxically, heterodox sects were as obsessed as their critics with doctrinal controversy, but this served only to push moderates further toward a doctrinal indifference.

The downplaying of orthodoxy in favor of orthopraxy, voluntarism over intellectualism, was a broader Renaissance phenomenon that is evident also in Erasmus. His ideal of a Christian society, on the pattern of a vast monastery where the distinction disappears between clergy and laity, was typical of Anabaptist and pietistic movements. The greater agency given to the saints to usher in the age of the Spirit was a major factor in this shift toward immediate action.

From Andreae and Bacon to Comenius and the Hartlib Circle, the pioneers of the Royal Society envisioned a "universal reformation" that focused more on a renewal of piety and social transformation than on the doctrinal concerns of Luther and Calvin. In the face of wars and political instability, disease and deprivation, it would be educational and social reformers more than theologians who would take the helm. Soon, natural philosophers assumed a leading role in defending the faith, and even clergymen among them concentrated on scientific matters.

Erudition in theology was precisely what was receding, as doctrinal indifference led to increasingly trimmed-down creeds that jibed with people's experience and moral sensibilities. Bacon's clarion call to turn away from scholastic contemplation to experimental action was not a rejection of theology or metaphysics but stressed the independence of natural science as a distinct discipline. However, the experimental method became an all-encompassing outlook that privileged natural philosophy over theology. Overripe attacks on Aristotelian method and scholastic terminology by humanists, Hermeticists, and experimental philosophers served inadvertently to dismantle the scaffolding of Christian theology. Theologians like Voetius and Beza may have overreacted by implying that Christianity stands or falls with Aristotelian method. However, there was some truth in their argument that the form in which theology had been done for so many centuries could not be abandoned surreptitiously without exposing the content to vulnerability. A naive biblicism could not compensate for centuries of biblical exegesis and theological argumentation in the face of ancient heresies that returned with a vengeance in the sixteenth and seventeenth centuries. While Hermetic Neoplatonism presented a significant *alternative* to Christian metaphysics and theology, pietism encouraged a significant *diminution* of the same.

The first casualty was natural philosophy, then natural theology, and, finally, revealed theology. Wallace Marshall documents the interest of Reformed scholastics and Puritans in natural theology. Alsted's *Theologia naturalis* (1614) "seems to have been the first Protestant treatise published under that title. The first English book so titled was the Puritan Matthew Barker's *Natural Theology* (1675)."[29] This was not a creeping modern rationalism. "As the English Puritan Ezekiel Hopkins put it, 'reason itself teaches us, that such a being cannot be God, which may be comprehended by man.'"[30] God does not submit to human reason, but reason submits to its creator. However, these writers shared the belief of medieval scholastics that general as well as special revelation was an object of theological exploration. If metaphysical questions—such as final causes—are impertinent, as some of the mechanical philosophers held, the light of nature is extinguished. If Ficino and his Hermetic tribe went too far in thinking the mysteries of the faith could be proved by magic and kabbalah, the opposite danger was to think that no natural theology could serve as supporting preparation for revealed theology.

Plato and Aristotle would heartily confess the first answer in the Westminster Shorter Catechism: "The chief end of man is to glorify God and to enjoy him forever." The divines who drafted it believed that this final end could be demonstrated from the light of reason in various ways, even though scripture alone revealed the merciful will of this God and how this end could be reached. Increasingly, though, final ends drop out altogether, and this becomes an equivocal assertion that surrenders either to doubt or to dogmatism. The overall trend of the era was toward an antimetaphysical—and thus, to a great extent, antitheological—attitude. It was not anti-Christian but rather anticontroversial. Exhausted by doctrinal conflict, Europeans wanted to know how to be happy, healthy, and holy.

Yates's description of the fictional Rosy Cross Order as "intensely Christian in

29. Marshall, *Puritanism*, 1.
30. Marshall, *Puritanism*, 11.

spirit, though not doctrinal," is becoming a familiar trend.[31] Andreae's citizens of Christianopolis are pious Christians, but they eschew scholastic wrangling and prefer fellowship and good works to doctrinal disputes. The pansophists and pietists insisted that they were criticizing the form of scholastic theology and not the content of the Apostles' Creed. However, they did not recognize the extent to which scholastic method was the framework of orthodox theology—beyond a few fundamental doctrines. For Hermeticists, Anabaptists, pietists, and experimental philosophers alike, "scholasticism" became a shibboleth for arcane debates that had nothing to do with the conversion of individuals and society.

Significantly, Comenius assumed a great deal more than the new birth when speaking of "one thing necessary." But what about the next generation? Assuming Christ as redeemer, Comenius nevertheless wanted more focus to be given to Christ as renovator. But this could (and, in fact, did) lead to Christologies that required a moral example but not necessarily a divine savior. The Rosy Cross fiction became a reality, the invisible visible, in the Royal Society, one of the most important institutions of the early modern world, while Paracelsian Hermeticism and radical millenarianism flourished on its edges. Freemasonry, too, sought to create a social space in which the perennial philosophy from Hermes Trismegistus could provide an adequate basis for fellowship. Even among the more evangelical pansophists, doctrinal consensus was becoming strained, gradually revising what "essentials" of theology might be.

The Westminster Assembly appointed by the mostly Presbyterian Parliament summarized these essentials in a detailed confession and catechisms. However, even those—like the members of the Hartlib Circle—who saw the Long Parliament as a harbinger of the "universal reformation" were less interested in these doctrines than in union of all Protestants for the final expulsion of the antichrist and the new age of enlightenment. Men of action, not contemplation, were needed for this endeavor. There is at least one central dogma that all these diverse groups share: sweeping social, political, moral, educational, and scientific transformation. Contemplation, including theology, must yield to a pansophic vision of world transformation. The pietist emphasis on conversion lies at the heart of this transformationalist emphasis.

As Joachim of Fiore transformed the mystic's ascent into ages, pietists integrated inner and outer alchemy. The search for the true philosopher's stone and the transformation of lead into gold is first and foremost a spiritual and psychological operation. The inner transformation produces external works. Similar to the alchemical stages, conversion followed a strictly defined series of steps from repentance to faith. Anglican and Presbyterian divines expected conversion to take place

31. Yates, *Rosicrucian Enlightenment*, 168–69.

gradually, often imperceptibly, through the ordinary means of grace. However, Independents based church membership on the elders' assessment of someone's conversion narrative. This was true also in German pietism, as Kant's testimony attests.[32] It should not surprise us that the proponents of a radical conversion experience would seek the most radical political transformation as well.

The Bible was perhaps more popular than ever, but its meaning was increasingly found in providing support for the activistic impulse. The millennial reign of the saints emboldened this spirit. A God-centered outlook was gradually being replaced with a more human-centered one. A pared-down theology was needed toward "the end of enlarging of the bounds of Human Empire, to the effecting of all things possible."[33] In its place, this was a noble goal, and it led to the advance of science and the alleviation of suffering. But not long after Bacon and Boyle it became not only a goal for science but also for the all-encompassing frame.

It is also crucial to recognize that attacks on scholasticism went hand in glove with the anti-Romanism of seventeenth-century Protestantism. Especially in England following the Gunpowder Plot (1605), anti-Romanism galvanized Englishmen from radical sects to High Churchmen. The three-year reign of the Roman Catholic King James II only confirmed these fears, all sides cheering the Glorious Revolution with William of Orange ascending the British throne in 1688.

But how far does one take anti-Roman sentiments? Neo-Arians from Socinus to Isaac Newton considered the Trinity and the deity of Christ to be the invention of the antichrist. Against this heresy, Reformed theologians sought to affirm the doctrine of the Trinity, like Franciscus Junius the Elder and his *A Defense of the Catholic Doctrine of the Trinity*. Similarly, William Perkins, the father of Elizabethan Puritanism, set out to show in *The Reformed Catholick* that Calvinists uphold the ecumenical consensus.[34]

Comenius and the Hartlib Circle were generally orthodox, but their vision of a pan-Protestant social reformation, with all of its millennialist accoutrements, encouraged an evangelical latitudinarianism that could (and in fact did) contribute to hyper-Protestant deviations from orthodoxy. The Moravian Brethren motto of "essential, useful, incidental" raises the question regarding what exactly is essential. The "one thing necessary" for Comenius was "Jesus Christ, understood as the eschatological *Christus Renovator*, the Renewer of all things."[35] But what

32. A fascinating social history in this regard is Strom, *German Pietism*.

33. Francis Bacon's character the governor of Bensalem in the *New Atlantis*. See Bacon, *New Atlantis*, 98–99.

34. Perkins himself refused to be identified as a Puritan. The godly cannot be called pure, he said, so puritan is "a vile name" (Perkins, *Works*, 1:342). Cf. Breward, *William Perkins*, 22.

35. Lochman, preface, 4.

about Christ as the justifier of the ungodly? Comenius held staunchly to Christ as the second person of the Trinity, priest as well as king, but his centering on Christ as renovator of all things reflected an important shift in emphasis. Cambridge Platonists tried to carve a latitudinarian lane between Calvinist orthodoxy and enthusiasm. Joseph Glanvill, who came to Henry More's aid in defending the reality of witchcraft, wrote *The Vanity of Dogmatising* in 1661.

Dutch and English Arminians located the Trinity among the nonessentials, while Socinians regarded the doctrine as an invention of the antichrist. There was a growing passion among some writers to identify genuine Protestantism with a purging of Nicene orthodoxy.[36] Case in point, the anti-Trinitarian Anabaptist Edward Whitman was the last person to be burned for heresy in England in 1612. Late in the same century, Isaac Newton poured his energies into private projects attempting to demonstrate that the doctrine of the Trinity was a Romanist fabrication. In Newton's view, to be a true, Bible-believing Protestant was to side with Arius. Paradoxically, scholastic theology held that the most important truths were mysteries transcending finite minds, while antischolastics like Newton thought that the human mind could comprehend even God's essence.

As natural philosophers became the leading apologists, the Christian doctrines to be defended were circumscribed by what could be supported by scientific arguments. The experimentalist disliked enthusiasm. Hunter relates an encounter Menasseh ben Israel shared with Boyle:

> Hearing that in London there were "some new Pretenders to the Gift of Tongues," he went to visit them and asked one of them whether he could speak Hebrew. Receiving an affirmative answer, he desired to hear him utter a few words in that language. But after "the Fanaticke had spoken an Extemporary Gibberish, as little understood by the Hearers as by himself," the rabbi firmly assured him that it was not Hebrew, explaining that he was himself a born Hebrew and spoke the language of Moses and Abraham. To this his interlocutor replied: "my Hebrew is better & Ancienter then Your's, for I speake the Hebrew that Adam spoake in the Garden." Boyle saw this as illustrating "what strange Absurditys the Impudence of some, blusheth not to entitle the Spirit to," thus pointing to a further peril of living in the England of the Commonwealth, in that such men might unwittingly abet the rationalist threat to Christianity which so concerned him and which he now invoked experiment and erudition to overcome.[37]

36. The standard work on this subject is Lim, *Mystery Unveiled*.
37. Hunter, *Boyle*, 85–86.

Hunter adds:

> Yet, ironically, there were aspects of the intellectual ferment in post–Civil War England which struck a chord with Boyle. Thus the English translation of the mystical writings of Hermes Trismegistus which inspired him in "Of the Study of the Booke of Nature" was made by the religious radical John Everard; and equally revealing is Boyle's association in Amsterdam with Adam Boreel, said to be a follower of such spiritualists as Sebastian Franck and Jacob Boehme. At a later date Boyle was to have comparable links with men whom some contemporaries would have dismissed as "enthusiasts," and he seems to have felt considerable sympathy for those who espoused mystical ideas, whom he saw as potential allies in the fight against excessive rationalism. There are even tantalizing hints that Boyle may have been affected by the millenarian expectations common in England at this time; indeed, these constituted one of the reasons for supporting the readmission of the Jews, which was widely seen as a necessary preliminary to the Second Coming.[38]

What are we waiting for? At least for many people in the early modern era, it was not for the return of Christ but the dawn of the age of the Spirit or a millennium in which the starring role would be given to contemporary actors. For these figures, the apocalypse would evolve out of current events rather than a descent of God to bring history from the present age into the age to come. The eschaton became immanentized.

Theology to Apologetics

Finally, the rise of Christian apologetics contributed paradoxically to the immanentizing of divine transcendence. Not only was the content of Christian belief changing but so also was the way of believing it. Everyone could point to the sects for their definition of irrationalism, but leaders of sectarian groups claimed to follow their inner light, which was identical to reason. Anxiety emerged not only over the diversity of beliefs considered reasonable but also over the standards of reason itself. Cambridge Platonists attacked enthusiasts but faced criticisms that they also were too affected by Neoplatonic and Hermetic mysticism.

In the first place, apologists—mostly scientists—assumed much of the vocation previously belonging to theologians. Kepler, Boyle, Hooke, and so many

38. Hunter, *Boyle*, 85–86.

others were now saying that while they wanted to enter the ministry, they could worship and serve God more with their gifts through natural philosophy.[39] As Harrison points out, "Bishop Sprat, in his defense of the activities of the early Royal Society, agreed that natural philosophers were uniquely qualified to judge the authenticity of 'prophetic visions' and 'extraordinary events.'"[40] Nevertheless, the figures Sprat named were respectful of the distinct role of theology, based on scripture, and natural philosophy. Medieval and Protestant scholastics were correct in maintaining that natural theology could not demonstrate the mysteries of the faith, such as the Trinity, the incarnation and atonement, salvation by grace, and the return of Christ. However, much of the theology being defended by the end of the century was in the hands of natural philosophers and thereby restricted to arguments from nature. The essentials of Christianity were what natural philosophers could defend. Increasingly, experimental philosophers became arbiters of miracles versus frauds and demon possession versus self-delusion. Given that churchmen formed a significant portion of the group, this is perhaps unsurprising. Nevertheless, as science grew more independent of theology, its practitioners could use this position to criticize the doctrines that their predecessors defended. Attacks on scholasticism in experimental science had spread to a broader critique that weakened the orthodox systems that employed Aristotelian categories. Natural theologians now had their own vocation, emerging as what Amos Funkenstein calls "secular theologians."[41]

In the second place, apologetics now was setting the agenda for what constituted the fundamental articles of the faith. In the process, doctrine drifted from its goal of union with God in Christ and became an end in itself. From Aristotle onward, *scientia* (Greek: *noēsis*) was a habit or disposition of the soul that strives for its fulfillment by contemplating its *telos*. As we have seen, natural philosophy was merely the first stage of *paideia* preparing for the contemplation of truths (i.e., metaphysics and mathematics), which lead finally to the highest knowledge, theology. Premoderns viewed religion (*religio*) also as a habit: a sense of piety toward God and doctrines served this end. As Harrison observes,

> While Calvin links such [doctrinal] knowledge with what he calls "true religion" (*veram religionem*), tellingly, this was typically translated "*the* true religion." This rendition appears as early as the first English translation of the *Institutes* (1561). The subtle insertion of the definite article signifies an important change

39. Harrison, *Territories*, 111.
40. Harrison, *Territories*, 113.
41. Funkenstein, *Theology and the Scientific Imagination*, 4–10.

> in how religion is conceptualized. For Calvin, the profession of explicit beliefs is directed toward the promotion of an inner quality—"true religion." . . . In English books printed during the first decade of the seventeenth century, the expression "Christian religion" (without the definite article) is used five times more frequently than "*the* Christian religion." By the final decade of the century the latter expression is much more common.[42]

In step with Reformed definitions, Bacon and Boyle viewed faith as informed *trust*. However, according to Harrison, "Locke explicitly repudiated the notion of faith as trust (*fiducia*), because in his view it led to implicit faith and stifled inquiry." *The* true religion is *the* Christian religion, albeit pared down.[43]

Consequently, during this period explicit knowledge of doctrines drifted from its goal of piety or union with God and became simply a set of propositions to defend. First, Roman Catholics and Protestants began to issue confessions and catechisms. Yet, these documents still directed doctrine toward piety, as witnessed in the first question and answer of the Westminster Shorter Catechism: "The chief end of man is to glorify God and enjoy him forever." Moreover, Lutheran and Reformed confessions were structured by the order of the Apostles' Creed and departed from Roman Catholicism only on the issues related to the Reformation debate. Next, various radical movements arose challenging this consensus. Finally, there were challenges to Christian theism itself, eliciting sophisticated apologetic arguments.

No longer a *habitus* driving the soul toward perfection, both religion and science became domains, and the scientist became the apologist. As Harrison observes, "To the extent that Christianity was now understood to be 'a religion' constituted by beliefs that were supported by certain kinds of evidences, it invited a denial of those beliefs and their grounds, and thus of the whole enterprise for which those beliefs had come to stand."[44]

In the third place, the apologist became in some sense the arbiter of a minimal doctrinal confession that the monarch could enforce as temporal head and governor of the church. Theologians had failed to provide adequate grounds for state churches, so the natural philosophers gained greater importance. The latitudinar-

42. Harrison, *Territories*, 92–83.

43. Harrison, *Territories*, 108.

44. Harrison, *Territories*, 115. All of these points are salient, but the broader narrative lacks the important complications of Roman Catholic apologetics, which Harrison completely ignores (e.g., the use of skepticism). The real nominalism is not the Protestant orthodox, who still till in Thomist furrows, but in the blind faith of the Jesuits.

ian religious and political views of Cambridge Platonism characterize Restoration England. After Archbishop Laud, the Calvinist consensus was questioned. The doctrines at the heart of the Reformation were treated increasingly with either indifference or rejection. Doctrines such as election, original sin and the bondage of the will, Christ's substitutionary sacrifice, regeneration, and justification were central to the Reformation and were affirmed in the Thirty-Nine Articles as well as the Book of Concord and the Westminster Confession. So now what are the "fundamental articles" to which one must give assent?

In the Stuart Restoration, the Lord Chancellor imposed his infamous Clarendon Code forbidding public debates on these topics. To be strictly enforced, the doctrinal basis of the established church must be minimal. In doing so, the content of "reasonable religion" was pared down. Case in point, the Cambridge Platonists asserted in the halls of Emmanuel College—the erstwhile nursery of Puritanism—that Augustinian emphases of the Reformers were perhaps true but no longer essential. So too Hobbes, Mede, Cudworth, and Locke were in close contact with Arminian theologians in the Netherlands. For Arminians like Limborch and Episcopius, essential doctrines were only those that were judged conducive to virtue and morality. The main problem was dogmatism, whether Socinian or Catholic. For Locke, the articles to which assent should be yielded were few indeed. Arminians reduced the "fundamentals" to whatever was necessary for practical morality. Though they did not deny the Trinity, they did not consider it essential. According to Hugo Grotius, "the true Religion, which has been common to all Ages" is "built upon four fundamental Principles." These four principles are:

> The *first* is, that *There is a GOD, and but one GOD only*. The *second*, that GOD *is not any of those Things we see, but something more sublime than them*. The *third*, that GOD *takes Care of human Affairs, and judges them with the strictest Equity*. The *fourth*, that *The same God is the Creator of all Things but himself*. . . . And from these speculative Notions follow the practical, as, that *GOD is to be honoured, loved, worshipped, and obeyed*.[45]

Missing from this quasi-creed is practically everything in Christianity. Tuck adds, "And Grotius accompanied this theory with an equally confident assertion that the *civil* magistrate has, in all times and places, had the ultimate responsibility for religious matters, an assertion made most plainly in his *De imperio summarum potestatum circa sacra*, which was not published until 1647 but which circulated

45. Grotius, *Rights*, 442–43.

as a manuscript in England amongst groups with which Hobbes was familiar."[46] Hobbes's *Leviathan* advances "a universalist political theory and minimalist religious doctrine, purported to be true regardless of time and place."[47] Hobbes's "Christian Atheism" proved to be a bridge too far, but only for a while.[48]

As if resigning to the fact that Christianity itself had already been lost, apologists withdrew the line of defense to mere theism based on a slender thread of the design argument. God, whether the Trinity or an Arian deity, was the effectual cause without discussion of God as the final cause. Once belief was reduced to assent, as with Locke, the question arose concerning how much of traditional belief there can be in an increasingly fragmented society. That is, what are the "fundamental articles"? The Hermetic search for the lost language of Adam to reunify humanity was carried forward in earnest all the way to Leibniz. And, as Nicholas of Cusa had argued, it was this philosophical religion that transcended differences in doctrines and rites.

A fourth aspect of this trend among apologists is toward a univocity of being, namely, seeing God as if he were a being among beings. By the 1680s, we are no longer talking about the God who transcends being, unrelated to the world while relating the world to himself analogically. Across the various proposals of seventeenth-century philosophers, there is an assumption that God is the supreme species in a genus of being, whether supreme thought (Descartes), power (Hobbes), or force (Newton).

As Newton's system unfolds, nature acquires much of God's portfolio. Primary attributes belonging to God uniquely are ascribed to space and force. Then there is the eliding of final causes, with all the emphasis being placed on God as the ultimate efficient cause, proved by evidence of design. We have seen that Boyle affirms final ends in detail, both of every part of nature and of human beings in particular.

With all the emphasis falling on efficient causes, however, the danger is that God is seen as an agent within the world who acts upon it. Voluntarism wedded to the univocity of being reaches its intensity with Malebranche's idea that God is the only real cause, and we see bodies through ideas in God's mind. But if one can imagine God, as it were, wiping creation from the canvas, it is possible to conceive of the creature erasing God and asserting his or her own absolute power, as I will observe in volume 3.

46. Tuck, "Christian Atheism," 116–17.

47. Springborg, "Hobbes on Religion," 349.

48. Tuck, "Christian Atheism," 111–30. See especially his excellent treatment of Pierre Charron on 87–110.

At this point, we are not only talking about a subtraction of fundamental articles but also of naturalists upending hard-won struggles since the patristic era to uphold God's qualitative distinction from the world. Indeed, we have seen that Newton accorded incommunicable divine attributes to space. After centuries of ignoring or rejecting the doctrine of analogy, arguments against divine action in the world become more plausible. Amos Funkenstein summarizes this development well:

> The medieval sense of God's symbolic presence in his creation, and the sense of a universe replete with transcendent meanings and hints, had to recede if not give way totally to the postulates of univocation and homogeneity in the seventeenth century. God's relation to the world had to be given a concrete physical meaning. Descartes did so by maintaining the medieval sense of God's utter transcendence; the only relation of God to the world that could thus be rescued was that of causality, a relation that Descartes exploits to the extreme. More, on the other hand, rather translated the panpsychism, or even pantheism, of philosophies of nature in the Renaissance into a "clear and distinct" language. God thus acquired a body of sorts, or at least a *sensorium*. . . . Leibniz avoided both positions by denying bodies and places an absolute ontological status. All of them and most of the others believed that the subjects of theology and science alike can be absolutely de-metaphorized and de-symbolized. It is clear why a God describable in unequivocal terms, or even given physical features and functions, eventually became all the easier to discard. As a scientific hypothesis, he was later shown to be superfluous; as a being, he was shown to be a mere hypostatization of rational, social, or psychological ideals and images. Our story thus comes to a halt. We have seen how and why God lost his body in Christian theology, how and why he regained it in the seventeenth century. Once God regained transparency or even a body, he was all the easier to identify and to kill.[49]

Boyle not only set out to disprove natural supernaturalism but to defend biblical miracles, especially the resurrection. There is one place where God not only entered but took on created nature. As if writing to someone on advice for a friend in doubt, he says:

> First, then, I take it for granted that he does not mean *whether the resurrection is a thing knowable, or directly provable, by the merely light of nature*. For if God had not in the scripture positively revealed his purpose of raising the dead,

49. Funkenstein, *Theology and the Scientific Imagination*, 116.

> I confess I should not have thought of any such thing; neither do I know how to prove that it will be, but by flying not only to the veracity but the power of God, who having declared that he will raise the dead, and being an almighty agent, I have reason to believe that he will not fail to perform what he has foretold. Nor do I (secondly) understand the question to be *whether the resurrection be possible to be effected by merely physical agents and means*. . . . I remember that when our Saviour, treating the resurrection, silenced the Sadducees that denied it . . . [by saying], "You err," says he, "not knowing the scriptures, nor the power of God." And when an angel would assure the blessed virgin that she should bear a child without the intervention of a man . . . he concludes his speech by telling her *that nothing shall prove impossible to God*.[50]

Finally, he takes for granted that in order to be a resurrection, it must "be fit to be reputed the *same* body."[51] Even quite apart from extraordinary considerations, our bodies are always changing, "from a *corpusculum* no bigger than an insect to the full stature of a man," all the way to old age and death. Similarly, metals retain their identity in spite of being transformed by chemical operations.[52] The soul separated from the body is in a state of "widowhood."[53]

With Jesus as our prototype, Boyle continues, "it is necessary that every body should be that [which is] is rejoined to the soul in the resurrection—and yet this *glorified* body had the same qualifications that are promised to the saints in their state of glory, St. Paul informing us that 'our vile bodies' shall be transformed into the likeness of '*his* glorious body,' which the history of the Gospel assures us was endowed with far nobler qualities than before its death." If indeed Jesus was raised, we should not wonder that "this great change of schematism in the saints' bodies will be effected by the irresistible power of Christ . . . for in the twinkling of an eye, an opacous, dark, languid, and stinking smoke loses all its stink, and is changed into a most active, penetrant, and shining body."[54] Boyle's robustly Christian apologetics was in some respects a last stand before the battle lines

50. Robert Boyle, "Some Physico-Theological Considerations about the Possibility of the Resurrection," in Stewart, *Philosophical Papers*, 192–93.

51. "Some Physico-Theological Considerations about the Possibility of the Resurrection," in Stewart, *Philosophical Papers*, 193.

52. Robert Boyle, "Some Physico-Theological Considerations," in Stewart, *Philosophical Papers*, 198–99.

53. Robert Boyle, "Some Physico-Theological Considerations," in Stewart, *Philosophical Papers*, 206.

54. Robert Boyle, "Some Physico-Theological Considerations," in Stewart, *Philosophical Papers*, 208.

shifted to a defense of bare theism hanging by the single thread of the design argument—God as effectual cause but no longer the final cause of creation. In a Hermetic frame, nature includes God or "divinity," an outlook also held by Newton, which he undoubtedly learned from Henry More.

Boyle knew, on traditional Christian grounds, that he could not demonstrate the mysteries of the faith from natural philosophy, but that these beliefs were nuclear to Christianity. He had a clear distinction between the "two books" but saw both as necessary. In contrast, Newton collapsed theology into natural philosophy, assuring that his unified system could prove the unmysterious existence of a non-Trinitarian deity. He was convinced that his mechanical system provided the foundation not only for mathematics but for religious belief.[55] At the same time in New England, Cotton Mather also placed the weight upon science for his premature triumph, "Atheism is now forever chased and hissed out of the World."[56] As apologetics increasingly migrated from the "two books" to one, it was only a matter of time before science uses the power theologians invested in it to pronounce judgment on the other book.

Newton's anti-Trinitarianism was not epiphenomenal to his apologetics. Rather, the God he was defending was different from the Christian God. In Christian theology, all external works of the Godhead extend from the Father, in the Son, and by the Spirit. The Son identifies with our creatureliness to the point of assuming it to himself, and the Spirit is at work within nature and human souls to bring about a corresponding effect to the Father's word. A single divine person acting upon the world with absolute power, mediating this operation by natural forces equivalent to the semi-divine World Soul, is rather different from a relation in which the Holy Spirit, a person of the Trinity, draws creatures willingly to the Son.

Richard Bentley, the first recipient of the honorary Boyle Lectureship, although a Trinitarian, used Newton's physics to refute Hobbes in 1692. The following lecturers defended a robust Christian theology from historical evidences as well as nature. But the 1704 Boyle Lectureship went to Newton's arch-defender Samuel Clarke, a proponent of Arianism, who coined the term "physico-theology." As Michael Buckley shows at length, Roman Catholic and Protestant apologists alike did not seem to think that Christology or pneumatology was essential to the definition of the God they were defending. "Thus, Christianity entered into the defense of

55. Buckley, *Denying and Disclosing God*, 18.

56. Cotton Mather, "The Christian Philosopher," quoted in Buckley, *Denying and Disclosing God*, 40.

the existence of the Christian god without appeal to anything Christian."[57] Newton's Neo-Arianism, though held in relative secrecy, was far from nondogmatic.

Surprisingly perhaps, the century closes not with deism, much less atheism, but with "the last of the magicians": Newton's pantheism or at least panentheism drawn from Cambridge Platonism and Hermeticism. From Newton onward, a vigorous defense of theism could be drawn entirely from science, as "physico-theology" suggests. Ever since Aristotle, there was considerable overlap between natural investigation and theology, the philosopher insisting that they were distinct disciplines with their own object, sources, and methods. "From the twelfth century onward, the demarcation between natural philosophy and theology had been scrupulously upheld," Harrison observes. Ironically, it was the seventeenth-century experimental philosophers who blurred the lines. "The early modern category of 'physico-theology' nicely captures the new overlap of interests, and the very name embodies the idea that physics (or natural philosophy) might profitably be combined with theology."[58] Newton was convinced that his mechanical system was the foundation not only for mathematics but for religious belief.[59] Thus, the Enlightenment emerges not out of rationalistic naturalism but out of natural supernaturalism.

Conclusion

In a strange irony, apologetics helped facilitate the reduction of doctrine to ethics. Recall that Dante had Epicureans in the lowest hell for denying the soul's immortality (book 10 of the *Divine Comedy*). For him, the main criticism was theological. In his world, to deny a providential God was to condemn oneself to eternal damnation. Yet, as broadly Epicurean sentiments spread, apologists move the front line backward. Of course, a convinced Epicurean is not going to be moved by theological arguments, so the attack shifts to moral implications for society. Surely the denial of rewards and punishment in the afterlife would threaten public morality.[60] The vertical dimension—one's relation to God—surrenders to the hor-

57. Buckley, *Origins*, 67.

58. Harrison, *Territories*, 109–10.

59. Buckley, *Denying and Disclosing God*, 18.

60. Alison Brown notes, "Thus, in book 10 of the *Divine Comedy*, Dante has Epicureans in the lowest hell since they alone believed 'that man's soul, when his body does, will die,' and, as Cristoforo Landino explained in his influential 1481 *Commentary* on Dante, 'removes every basis for right living in civil society and for true religion.'" Brown, *Return of Lucretius*, 3.

izontal relationship between human beings in society. But what if nonbelievers could create a just and moral civil society, as Pierre Bayle argued in the 1680s?[61]

As Nietzsche recognized, once the front has been moved to this moral-political argument, the game is over. This apologetic, a staple during the Enlightenment, was itself a secularizing and immanentizing force. Trying to find common ground on which to reason for belief in God, many apologists kept losing the ground they were trying to defend. The new apologists were not theologians but philosophers. By focusing on this argument, apologists made religion subservient to civic morality, which lent support to Lucretius's argument. Eventually, as philosophical and moral arguments became unpersuasive, rulers took matters into their own hands. However tolerant a European state might be with respect to confessional diversity, the disintegration of public norms was indeed a political matter. This gave more power to the state, which in turn placed more emphasis on public decorum than on doctrine and gave Lucretius's critique another victory.

Overall, there is a noticeable shift from a theocentric perspective to an anthropocentric concern with improving and extending life, social reform, and preserving a moral consensus in the face of growing skepticism. Aware of inner powers, the divine self ascends from the iron cage of embodied and embedded givens, forming new institutions based on freely chosen affinities. Theology was left without the defense of metaphysics, and metaphysics without the defense of a natural theology that drew upon but could never be limited to physical arguments.

By the time of Newton, metaphysics and theology had lost their place. Yet, he saw his system as their replacement, stating in the *Principia* (1687), "When I wrote my Treatise about our System, I had an Eye upon such Principles as might work with considering Men, for the Belief in a Deity."[62] But the sort of deity who remains is not the Christian God. What does survive is the divine self, whose new adventures we explore in the next volume.

61. Israel, *Radical Enlightenment*, 330–41.

62. Newton, *Principia*, 942–43, quoted in Osler, *Reconfiguring the World*, 163.

Works Cited

Abrams, M. H. *Naturalistic Supernaturalism: Tradition and Revolution in Romantic Literature.* New York: Norton, 1973.

Ackroyd, Peter. *The Life of Thomas More.* New York: Anchor, 1999.

Agrippa, Cornelius. *Three Books of Occult Philosophy.* Edited and translated by Donald Tyson. Woodbury, MN: Llewellyn, 1992.

Åkerman, S. "The Rosicrucians and the Great Conjunctions." Pages 1–8 in *Continental Millenarians: Protestants, Catholics, Heretics.* Vol. 4 of *Millenarianism and Messianism in Early Modern European Culture.* New York: Springer, 2001.

Allen, Joseph Henry, and Richard Eddy. *A History of the Unitarians and the Universalists in the United States.* New York: Christian Literature Company, 1894.

Allen, P. S., ed. *Opus epistolarum des Erasmi Roterdami.* 12 vols. Oxford: Clarendon, 1906–1958.

Armstrong, Karen. *The Great Transformation: The Beginning of Our Religious Traditions.* New York: Knopf, 2006.

Arthur, Anthony. *The Tailor-King: The Rise and Fall of the Anabaptist Kingdom of Münster.* New York: St. Martin's, 1999.

Assmann, Jan. *Moses the Egyptian: The Memory of Egypt in Western Monotheism.* Cambridge: Harvard University Press, 1998.

———. *The Price of Monotheism.* Stanford: Stanford University Press, 2007.

Baader, Franz von. *Sämtliche Werke.* Vol. 15. Leipzig: Scientia, 1855.

Bach, Jeff. "Jacob Boehme." Pages 265–86 in *Protestants and Mysticism in Reformation Europe.* Edited by R. K. Rittgers and Vincent Evener. Leiden: Brill, 2019.

Bacon, Francis. *New Atlantis and the Great Instauration.* Edited by Jerry Weinberger. 2nd ed. Oxford: Wiley Blackwell, 2017.

———. *Novum Organum.* Whithorn, UK: Anodos Books, 2019.

Baillie, Robert. *Anabaptism, the True Fountaine of Independency, Antinomy, Brownisme, Familisme, and the Most of the Other Errours.* London: 1647.

———. *A Dissuasive from the Errours of the Time.* London, 1645.

Baird, Robert P., and Bernard McGinn. Introduction to *Miguel de Molinos: The Spiritual Guide*. Edited and translated by Robert P. Baird. New York: Paulist, 2010.

Ball, Philip. *The Devil's Doctor: Paracelsus and the World of Renaissance Magic and Science*. New York: Farrar, Straus & Girioux, 2006.

Barnes, Robin Bruce. "Images of Hope and Despair: Western Apocalypticism: ca. 1500–1800." Pages 143–84 in vol. 2 of *The Encyclopedia of Apocalypticism*. Edited by B. McGinn. New York: Continuum, 2000.

———. *Prophecy and Gnosis: Apocalypticism in the Wake of the Lutheran Reformation*. Stanford: Stanford University Press, 1988.

Barrow, John Henry. *The Mirror of Parliament*. Vol. 2. London: Longman, Brown, Green & Longmans, 1840.

Bauer, Ralph. *The Alchemy of Conquest: Science, Religion, and the Secrets of the New World*. Charlottesville: University of Virginia Press, 2019.

Baxter, Richard. *Catholick Theologie*. London, 1675.

———. *Church-History of the Government of Bishops and Their Councils Abbreviated*. London, 1680.

Baylor, Michael G., ed. *The Radical Reformation*. Cambridge: Cambridge University Press, 1991.

Beckwith, Christopher I. *Greek Buddha: Pyrrho's Encounter with Early Buddhism in Central Asia*. Princeton: Princeton University Press, 2015.

Bembridge, Paul. "Rosicrucian Resurgence at the Court of Cromwell." Pages 219–46 in *The Rosicrucian Enlightenment Revisited*. Edited by Ralph White. Hudson, NY: Lindisfarne, 1999.

Benbow, Peter K. "Theory and Action in the Works of Andreas Libavius and Other Alchemists." *Annals of Science* 66.1 (2009): 135–39.

Bender, Elizabeth. "Was There a Peaceful Anabaptist Congregation in Münster in 1534?" *Mennonite Quarterly Review* 44 (1970): 357–70.

Benz, Ernst. *The Mystical Sources of German Romantic Philosophy*. Translated by Blair R. Reynolds and Eunice M. Paul. Allison Park, PA: Pickwick, 1983.

Berkel, Klaas van. *Isaac Beeckman on Matter and Motion: Mechanical Philosophy in the Making*. Translated by Maarten Ultree. Baltimore: Johns Hopkins University Press, 2013.

Bessarion, Jean. *Bessarionis in Calumniatorem Platonis libri IV*. Edited by Ludwig Mohler. Paderborn: Schöningh, 1927.

Beveridge, Henry, and Jules Bonnet, eds. *Selected Works of John Calvin: Tracts and Letters*. 7 vols. Grand Rapids: Baker, 1983.

Birch, Thomas, ed. *The Works of the Honourable Robert Boyle in Six Volumes*. London: Rivington, 1772.

Bogdan, Henrik. *Western Esotericism and Rituals of Initiation.* Albany: SUNY Press, 2007.

Böhme, Jacob. *The first apologie to Balthazar Tylcken being an answer of the authour concerning his book the Aurora, opposed by an enemicitious pasquil or opprobrious libel, this answer written anno 1621; Englished by John Sparrow.* London: Giles Calvert, 1661.

———. *The Key.* Translated by William Law. Grand Rapids: Phanes, 2000.

———. *Mysterium Magnum: An Exposition of the First Book of Moses Called Genesis.* 2 vols. Translated by John Sparrow. London: John M. Watkins, 1924, 1965.

———. *The Threefold Life of Man.* Translated by John Sparrow. Gorlitz, 1620.

———. The Way to Christ. Translated by Peter C. Erb. Rev. ed. New York: Paulist, 1978.

Bokser, Ben Zion. *From the World of the Cabbalah.* Whitefish, MT: Kessinger, 2006.

Boulton, Richard, ed. *The Theological Works of the Honourable Robert Boyle, Esq., Epitomiz'd.* 3 vols. London: Taylor, 1715.

Boyle, Robert. *The Sceptical Chymist.* New York: E. P. Dutton, 1911.

Brann, Noel L. *Trithemius and Magical Theology: A Chapter in the Controversy over Occult Studies in Early Modern Europe.* Albany: SUNY Press, 1999.

Bräuer, Siegfried, and Hans-Jürgen Goertz. "Thomas Müntzer." In *Gestalten der Kirchengeschichte.* Vol. 5 of *Die Reformationszeit.* Edited by Martin Greschat. Stuttgart: Kohlhammer, 1981.

Brecht, Martin. *Martin Luther.* Translated by James L. Schaaf. 3 vols. Philadelphia: Fortress, 1985–1999.

Breward, Ian, ed. *The Work of William Perkins.* Abingdon: Sutton Courtenay, 1970.

Brewer, Brian C. *Handbook of Anabaptism.* London: T&T Clark, 2021.

Bromiley, G. W., ed. *Zwingli and Bullinger.* Philadelphia: Westminster, 1953.

Brown, Alison. *The Return of Lucretius to Renaissance Florence.* Cambridge: Harvard University Press, 2010.

Browne, Thomas. *Religio Medici.* London: Bell & Sons, 1898.

Browning, Robert. *Paracelsus.* London: Effingham Wilson, 1835.

Buckley, Michael J. *At the Origins of Modern Atheism.* New Haven: Yale University Press, 1987.

———. *Denying and Disclosing God: The Ambiguous Progress of Modern Atheism.* New Haven: Yale University Press, 2004.

Buckley, Veronica. *Christina Queen of Sweden: The Restless Life of a European Eccentric.* New York: Harper, 2004.

Burke, John G. "Descartes on the Refraction and the Velocity of Light." *American Journal of Physics* 34 (1966): 390–400.

Burkert, Walter. *Babylon, Memphis, Persepolis.* Cambridge: Harvard University Press, 2007.

———. *The Orientalizing Revolution: Near Eastern Influences in Greek Culture in the Early Archaic Age*. Translated by Margaret E. Pinder. Cambridge: Harvard University Press, 1998.

Burnet, Gilbert, trans. *Utopia: Written in Latin by Sir Thomas More, Chancellor of England.* Dublin, 1737.

Burnett, Amy Nelson. *Debating the Sacraments: Print and Authority in the Early Reformation.* Oxford: Oxford University Press, 2019.

Burnham, Frederic B. "The More-Vaughan Controversy: The Revolt Against Philosophical Enthusiasm." *Journal of the History of Ideas* 35.1 (1975): 33–49.

Burns, Norman T. *Christian Mortalism from Tyndale to Milton.* Cambridge: Harvard University Press, 1972.

Burtt, Edwin Arthur. *The Metaphysical Foundations of Modern Physical Science: A Historical and Critical Essay.* London: Dover, 2003.

Calvin, John. *Commentaries on the First Book of Moses called Genesis*. Edited and translated by John King. 2 vols. London: Banner of Truth Trust, 1965.

———. *Commentary on Acts*. Translated by Henry Beveridge. 2 vols. Grand Rapids: Baker, 1966.

———. *Institutes of the Christian Religion*. Edited and translated by Ford Lewis Battles and John T. McNeill. 2 vols. Philadelphia: Westminster, 1960.

———. *Johannis Calvini opera quae supersunt omnia*. Edited by G. Baum, E. Cunitz, and E. Reuss. 59 vols. Berlin: Brunswick, 1863–1900.

———. *A Selection of the Most Celebrated Sermons of John Calvin, Minister of the Gospel.* New York: Forbes, 1830.

Campanella, Tomasso. *La Città del Sole: Dialogo Poetico. The City of the Sun: A Poetical Dialogue*. Translated with introduction by Daniel J. Donno. Berkeley: University of California Press, 1981.

Cawthorne, Nigel. *The Sex Lives of the Popes.* Totneys: Prion, 1996.

Celenza, Christopher. "Late Antiquity and Florentine Platonism: The 'Post-Plotinian' Ficino." Pages 71–91 in *Marsilio Ficino: His Theology, His Philosophy, His Legacy.* Edited by Michael Allen and Valery Rees. Brill's Studies in Intellectual History 108. Leiden: Brill, 2002.

———. *Piety and Pythagoras in Renaissance Florence: The Symbolum Nesianum*. Studies in the History of Christian Traditions 101. Leiden: Brill, 2001.

———. "Pythagoras in the Renaissance: The Case of Marsilio Ficino." *Renaissance Quarterly* 52.3 (1999): 667–711.

———. "The Revival of Platonic Philosophy." Pages 72–96 in *The Cambridge Companion to Renaissance Philosophy*. Edited by James Hankins. Cambridge: Cambridge University Press, 2007.

Cicero. *On the Nature of the Gods*. Translated by H. Rackham. LCL. Cambridge: Harvard University Press, 1933.

Clark, R. Scott. "Iustitia Imputate Christi." *Concordia Theological Quarterly* 70.3–4 (2005): 269–310.

Clark, Stuart. "The Scientific Status of Demonology." Pages 351–74 in *Occult Scientific Mentalities in the Renaissance*. Edited by Brian Vickers. Cambridge: Cambridge University Press, 2010.

Clausen, Claus-Peter. *Anabaptism: A Social History 1525–1618. Switzerland, Austria, Moravia, South and Central Germany.* Ithaca: Cornell University Press, 1972.

Clulee, N. H. "*Astronomia inferior:* Legacies of Johannes Trithemius and John Dee." Pages 173–234 in *Secrets of Nature: Astrology and Alchemy in Early Modern Europe.* Edited by William R. Newman and Anthony Grafton. Cambridge: MIT Press, 2006.

Cobb, Noel. Foreword to *The Planets Within: The Astrological Psychology of Marsilio Ficino*, by Thomas Moore. Plainsboro, NJ: Associated University Presses, 1982.

Columbus, Chrisopher. *The Book of Prophecies* (Reportorium Columbianum). Edited by Robert Rascine. Translated by Blair Sullivan. Berkeley: University of California Press, 1997.

———. *Select Letters of Christopher Columbus*. Edited by Richard Henry Major. Cambridge: Cambridge University Press, 2010.

Comenius, John Amos. *Unum Necessarium: The One Thing Necessary*. Translated by Vernon H. Nelson. Winston-Salem, NC: Moravian Archives, 2008.

Connolly, Patrick J. "Newton and God's Sensorium." *Intellectual History Review* 24.2 (2014): 185–201.

Cook, Harold J. "The New Philosophy in the Low Countries." Pages 115–49 in *The Scientific Revolution in National Context*. Edited by Roy Porter and Mikuláš Teich. Cambridge: Cambridge University Press, 1992.

Copenhaver, Brian P. "How to Do Magic, and Why: Philosophical Prescriptions." Pages 137–70 in *The Cambridge Companion to Renaissance Philosophy*. Edited by James Hankins. Cambridge: Cambridge University Press, 2007.

———. "The Occultist Tradition and Its Critics." In vol. 1 of *The Cambridge History of Seventeenth-Century Philosophy*. Edited by Daniel Garber and Michael Ayers. Cambridge: Cambridge University Press, 1998.

Copenhaver, Brian P., and Charles B. Schmitt. *Renaissance Philosophy*. Oxford: Oxford University Press, 1992.

Cross, Richard. *Communicatio Idiomatum: Reformation Christological Debates*. Oxford: Oxford University Press, 2019.

Davidson, Nicholas. "Unbelief and Atheism in Italy, 1500–1700." Pages 55–86 in *Atheism from the Reformation to the Enlightenment*. Edited by Michael Hunter and David Wootton. Oxford: Oxford University Press, 1992.

Davis, Edward B. "Robert Boyle, the Bible, and Natural Philosophy." *Religions* 14 (2023): 1–17.

———. "The Word and the Works: Concordism and American Evangelicals." Pages 34–58 in *Perspectives on an Evolving Creation*. Edited by Keith B. Miller. Grand Rapids: Eerdmans, 2003.

Davis, Edward B., and Michael Hunter, eds. *Robert Boyle: A Free Enquiry into the Vulgarly Received Notion of Nature*. Cambridge: Cambridge University Press, 1996.

———. "The Making of Robert Boyle's *A Free Enquiry into the Vulgarly Received Notion of Nature* (1686)." *Early Science and Medicine* 1.2 (1996): 204–68.

DeBolt, Darien C. "George Gemistos Plethon on God: Heterodoxy in Defense of Orthodoxy." Paper presented at the Twentieth World Congress of Philosophy. Boston, MA, August 10–15, 1998.

Debus, Allen G. *The Chemical Philosophy: Paracelsian Science and Medicine in the Sixteenth and Seventeenth Centuries*. 2 vols. New York: Science History, 1977.

Defrance, Eugene. *Catherine de Medicis, ses astrologues et ses Magiciens-envouteurs et les sciences occultes du XVIe siècle*. Paris: Mercure de France, 1911.

Descartes, René. *Discourse on Method and Meditations on First Philosophy*. Translated by Donald A. Cress. 3rd ed. Indianapolis: Hackett, 1993.

———. *Meditations on First Philosophy with Selections from the Objections and Replies*. Translated by Michael Moriarty. Oxford: Oxford University Press, 2008.

Dickson, Donald R. "Johann Valentine Andreae's Utopian Brotherhoods." *Renaissance Quarterly* 49.4 (1996): 760–802.

———. *The Tessera of Antilia: Utopian Brotherhoods and Secret Societies in the Early Seventeenth Century*. Leiden: Brill, 1998.

Dobbs, Betty Jo Teeter. *The Foundations of Newton's Alchemy: Or, 'The Hunting of the Greene Lyon'.* Cambridge: Cambridge University Press, 1975.

Dodds, Eric Robertson. *Greeks and the Irrational*. Berkeley: University of California Press, 2022.

Dolan, John P., ed. and trans. *The Essential Erasmus*. New York: New American Library, 1964.

Donne, John. *The Complete English Poems*. London: Penguin, 2004.

Donno, Daniel J. Introduction to *La Città del Sole: Dialogo Poetico. The City of the Sun: A Poetical Dialogue*, by Tomasso Campanella. Translated by Daniel J. Donno. Berkeley: University of California Press, 1981.

During, Simon. *Modern Enchantments: The Cultural Power of Secular Magic*. Cambridge: Harvard University Press, 2002.

Ebeling, Florian. *The Secret History of Hermes Trismegistus: Hermeticism from An-*

cient to Modern Times. Translated by David Lorton. Ithaca: Cornell University Press, 2007.

Eco, Umberto. *From the Tree to the Labyrinth: Historical Studies on the Sign and Interpretation*. Translated by Anthony Oldcorn. Cambridge: Harvard University Press, 2014.

Edighoffer, Roland. "Hermeticism in Early Rosicrucianism." Pages 197–216 in *Gnosis and Hermeticism from Antiquity to Modern Times*. Edited by Roelof van den Broek and Wouter J. Hanegraaff. Albany: SUNY Press, 1998.

Elert, Werner. *The Structure of Lutheranism*. St. Louis: Concordia, 1962.

Engels, Frederick. *The Peasant War in Germany*. 3rd ed. New York: International Publishers, 2012.

Erasmus, Desiderius. *The Praise of Folly and Other Writings*. Selected, edited, and translated by Robert M. Adams. New York: Norton, 1989.

Ernst, Germana. "'Veritatis amor dulcissimus': Aspects of Cardano's Astrology." Pages 39–68 in *Secrets of Nature: Astrology and Alchemy in Early Modern Europe*. Edited by William R. Newman and Anthony Grafton. Cambridge: MIT Press, 2006.

Estep, William R. *The Anabaptist Story*. Grand Rapids: Eerdmans, 1995.

Evans, R. J. W. *Rudolf II and His World*. Oxford: Oxford University Press, 1973.

Faivre, Antoine. "Renaissance Hermeticism and the Concept of Western Esotericism." Pages 109–24 in *Gnosis and Hermeticism from Antiquity to Modern Times*. Edited by Roelof van den Broek and Wouter J. Hanegraaff. Albany: SUNY Press, 1998.

Fallmann, Walter, ed. and trans. *Selected Works of Hans Denck*. Pittsburgh: Pickwick, 1976.

Fanning, Ashley. *Isaac Newton and the Transmutation of Alchemy*. New York: North Atlantic Books, 2009.

Farmer, S. A. *Syncretism in the West: Pico's 900 Theses (1486). The Evolution of Traditional Religious and Philosophical Systems with Text, Translation and Commentary*. Medieval and Renaissance Text and Studies 167. Tempe: Arizona State University, 2016.

Farrar, Frederic W. *History of Interpretation: Eight Lectures Preached before the University of Oxford in the Year 1885*. London: Macmillan, 1886.

Farrington, Benjamin. *The Philosophy of Francis Bacon: An Essay on Its Development from 1603 to 1609 with New Translations of Fundamental Texts*. Chicago: University of Chicago Press, 1964.

Febvre, Lucien. *The Problem of Unbelief in the Sixteenth Century: The Religion of Rabelais*. Cambridge: Harvard University Press, 1942.

Feingold, Mordechai. *The Mathematician's Apprenticeship: Science, Universities, and Society in England, 1560–1640*. Cambridge: Cambridge University Press, 1984.

———. "The Occult Tradition in the English Universities of the Renaissance: A Reassessment." Pages 73–94 in *Occult & Scientific Mentalities in the Renaissance.* Edited by Brian Vickers. Cambridge: Cambridge University Press, 1984.

Ficino, Marsilio. "Knowledge and Reverence of Oneself Are Best of All." Pages 78–79 in *Meditations on the Soul: Selected Letters of Marsilio Ficino*. Edited by Clement Salaman. Rochester, VT: Inner Traditions, 1997.

———. *Mercurii Trismegistis liber de potestate et sapientia dei.* Florence, 1471.

———. *On Dionysius the Areopagite*. Edited and translated by Michael J. B. Allen. 2 vols. Cambridge: Harvard University Press, 2015.

———. *Platonic Theology*. Edited by James Hankins. Translated by Michael J. B. Allen with John Warden. 3 vols. Cambridge: Harvard University Press, 2001.

———. *Three Books on Life: A Critical Edition and Translation with Introduction and Notes.* Edited by Carol V. Kaske and John R. Clark. Binghamton: Medieval and Renaissance Texts and Studies, 1989.

Field, Sean L. *The Beguine, the Angel and the Inquisitor: The Trials of Marguerite Porete and Guiard of Cressonessart.* Notre Dame: Notre Dame University Press, 2012.

Finger, Thomas N. *A Contemporary Anabaptist Theology: Biblical, Historical, Constructive.* Downers Grove, IL: InterVarsity, 2004.

———. "Sources for Contemporary Spirituality: Anabaptist and Pietist Contributions." *Brethren Life and Thought* 51 (2006): 28–53.

Finnocchiaro, Maurice A., ed. and trans. *The Essential Galileo.* Indianapolis: Hackett, 2008.

Floridi, Luciano. *Sextus Empiricus: The Recovery and Transmission of Pyrrhonism.* Oxford: Oxford University Press, 2002.

Fradkin, Jeremy. "Protestant Unity and Anti-Catholicism: The Irenicism and Philo-Semitism of John Dury in Context." *Journal of British Studies* 56.2 (2017): 273–94.

Fraenkel, Carlos. *Philosophical Religion from Plato to Spinoza: Reason, Religion, and Autonomy.* Cambridge: Cambridge University Press, 2014.

French, Peter. *John Dee: The World of an Elizabethan Magus.* London: Ark, 1984.

Friedrich, Markus. *The Jesuits: A History*. Translated by John Noël Dillon. Princeton: Princeton University Press, 2022.

Friesen, Abraham. *Erasmus, the Anabaptists, and the Great Commission.* Grand Rapids: Eerdmans, 1998.

Froude, J. A. *Life and Letters of Erasmus*. New York: Scribner's Sons, 1896.

Fubini, Riccardo, ed. *Poggius Bracciolini opera omnia*. 4 vols. Turin: Bottega d'Erasmo, 1964–1969.

Funkenstein, Amos. *Theology and the Scientific Imagination: From the Middle Ages to the Seventeenth Century.* Princeton: Princeton University Press, 1986.

Furcha, Edward J., and Ford Lewis Battles. *Selected Writings of Hans Denck. Edited and Translated from the Text Established by Walter Fellmann*. Pittsburgh: Pickwick, 1976.

Gandillac, Maurice de. "Neoplatonism and Christian Thought in the Fifteenth Century (Nicholas of Cusa and Marsilio Ficino)." Pages 143–68 in *Neoplatonism and Christian Thought*. Edited by Dominic J. O'Meara. Studies in Neoplatonism: Ancient and Modern 3. Albany: SUNY Press, 1982.

Gantenbein, Urs Leo. "The Virgin Mary and the Universal Reformation of Paracelsus." *Daphnis* 48.1–2 (2020): 4–37.

Garaudy, Roger. "Faith and Revolution," *Ecumenical Review* 25.1 (1973): 59–79.

Gauthier, David, and Edwin Curley. "'I Durst Not Write So Boldly,' or How to Read Hobbes' *Theological-Political Treatise*." In *Studi su Hobbes e Spinoza*. Edited by Emilia Giancotti, Daniela Bostrenghi, and Cristina Santinelli. Naples: Bibliopolis, 1997.

Gerhard, Johann. *Theological Commonplaces: On the Nature of God and on the Trinity*. Concordia: St. Louis, 1970.

Gerson, Jean. *De mystica theologia*. Edited by Andre Combes. Thesaurus mundi 9. Lugano: In Aedibus Thesauri Mundi, 1958.

Gill, Roger. "Pinturicchio's Frescoes in the Sala dei Santi in the Vatican Palace: Authorship and a New Iconological Interpretation of the 'Egyptian' Theme." PhD diss., Birmingham City University, 2015.

Gilly, Carlos. *Adam Haslmayr. Der erste Verkünder der Manifeste der Rosenkreuzer*. Amsterdam: Bibliotheca Philosophica Hermetica, 1994.

———. "Das Bekenntnis zur Gnosis von Paracelsus bis auf die Schüler Jacob Böhmes." Pages 385–425 in *From Poimandres to Jacob Böhme: Gnosis, Hermeticism and the Christian Tradition*. Edited by Roelof van den Broek and Cis van Heertum. Leiden: Brill, 2000.

Godwin, Joscelyn. *The Chemical Wedding of Christian Rosenkreutz*. Introduction and Commentary by Adam McLean. Magnum Opus Hermetic Sourceworks 18. Grand Rapids: Phanes, 1991.

———. *The Pagan Dream of the Renaissance*. London: Thames & Hudson, 2002.

Goertz, Hans-Jürgen. *The Anabaptists*. Translated by Trevor Johnson. London: Routledge, 1996.

Goodrick-Clarke, Nicholas. *Paracelsus: Essential Readings*. Berkeley: North Atlantic Books, 1999.

Gordon, Alexander. "Preston, John, D. D. (1587–1628)." Pages 308–12 in vol. 46 of *Dictionary of National Biography*. Edited by Sidney Lee. London: Smith, Elder & Company, 1896.

Gorham, Geoffrey. "Hobbes's Embodied God." Pages 171–88 in *Embodiment: A History*. Edited by Justin E. H. Smith. Oxford: Oxford University Press, 2017.

Grafton, Anthony. "The Availability of Ancient Works." Pages 767–91 in *The Cambridge History of Renaissance Philosophy*. Edited by Charles B. Schmitt and Quentin Skinner. Cambridge: Cambridge University Press, 1988.

———. *Defenders of the Text: The Traditions of Scholarship in an Age of Science, 1450–1800*. Cambridge: Harvard University Press, 1991.

———. "Protestant versus Prophet: Isaac Casaubon on Hermes Trismegistus." *Journal of the Warburg and Courtauld Institutes* 46.1 (1983): 78–93.

Grafton, Anthony, and Nancy Siraisi. "Between the Election and My Hopes: Girolamo Cardano and Medical Astrology," Pages 69–132 in *Secrets of Nature: Astrology and Alchemy in Early Modern Europe*. Edited by William R. Newman and Anthony Grafton. Cambridge: MIT Press, 2001.

Graziano, Frank. *The Millennial Kingdom in the New World*. New York: Oxford University Press, 1999.

Gregory, Brad. *The Unintended Reformation: How a Religious Revolution Secularized Society*. Cambridge: Harvard University Press, 2015.

Gritsch, Eric. *Reformer Without a Church: The Life and Thought of Thomas Müntzer, 1488?–1525*. Philadelphia: Fortress, 1967.

———. "Thomas Müntzer and Luther: A Tragedy of Errors." Pages 55–84 in *Radical Tendencies in the Reformation: Divergent Perspectives*. Edited by H. J. Hillerbrand. Sixteenth Century Essays and Studies 9. Kirksville, MO: Sixteenth Century Journal Publishers, 1988.

———. "Thomas Muentzer and the Origins of Protestant Spiritualism." *Mennonite Quarterly Review* 37.3 (1963): 172–94.

Grotius, Hugo. *The Rights of War and Peace*. Edited with introduction by Richard Tuck. 3 vols. Indianapolis: Liberty Fund, 2005.

Grunsky, Hans. *Jakob Böhme*. Stuttgart: Frommann, 1956.

Hames, Harvey J. *Like Angels in Jacob's Ladder: Abraham Abulafia, the Franciscans, and Joachimism*. Albany: SUNY Press, 2009.

Hamilton, Alastair. *Heresy and Mysticism in Sixteenth-Century Spain: The Alumbrados*. Cambridge: Clarke, 1992.

Hanegraaff, Wouter J. *Esotericism and the Academy: Rejected Knowledge in Western Culture*. Cambridge: Cambridge University Press, 2012.

Hankins, James. "Cosimo de' Medici and the 'Platonic Academy.'" *Journal of the Warburg and Courtauld Institutes* 53.1 (1990): 144–62.

———. "Marsilio Ficino and the Religion of the Philosophers." *Rinascimento* 48 (2008): 101–21.

Harnack, A. von. *The History of Dogma*. Translated by Neil Buchanan. New York: Dove Publications, 1961.

Harrison, Peter. *The Territories of Science and Religion*. Chicago: University of Chicago Press, 2015.

Hasse, Dag Nikolaus. "Arabic Philosophy and Averroism." Pages 113–36 in *The Cambridge Companion to Renaissance Philosophy*. Edited by James Hankins. Cambridge: Cambridge University Press, 2007.

Haykin, Michael A. G. "Separatists and Baptists." Pages 113–38 in *The Post-Reformation Era, c. 1559–1689*. Vol. 1 of *The Oxford History of Protestant Dissenting Traditions*. Edited by John Coffey. New York: Oxford University Press, 2020.

Hegel, G. W. F. *Encyclopedia of the Philosophical Sciences in Outline and Critical Writings*. Translated and edited by Ernst Behler. New York: Continuum, 1991.

———. *Lectures on the History of Philosophy*. Volume 3: *Medieval and Modern Philosophy*. Translated by E. S. Haldane and Frances H. Simson. Lincoln: University of Nebraska Press, 1995.

Hegler, Alfred. *Geist und Schrift bei Sebastian Franck: Eine Studie zur Geschichte des Spiritualismus in der Reformationzeit*. Freiburg: Mohr, 1892.

Held, Felix Emil. *Christianopolis: An Ideal State of the Seventeenth Century, Translated from the Latin of Johann Valentin Andreae with an Historical Introduction*. New York: Oxford University Press, 1916.

Henry, John. "Newton, the Sensorium of God, and the Cause of Gravity." *Science in Context* 33.3 (2020): 329–51.

Hessayon, Ariel. "Jacob Boehme's Writings During the English Revolution and Afterwards: Their Publication, Dissemination, and Influence." Pages 77–97 in *An Introduction to Jacob Boehme: Four Centuries of Thought and Reception*. Edited by Ariel Hessayon and Sarah Apetrei. New York: Rutledge, 2014.

———. "Jacob Böhme's Foremost Seventeenth-Century English Translator: John Sparrow (1615–1670) of Essex." Pages 329–57 in *Jakob Böhme and His World*. Edited by Bo Andersson, Lucinda Martin, Leigh Penman, and Andrew Weeks. Leiden: Brill, 2018.

Hessayon, Ariel, and Sarah Apetrei, eds. *An Introduction to Jacob Boehme: Four Centuries of Thought and Reception*. London: Routledge, 2013.

Hill, Charles E. *Regnum Caelorum: Patterns of Millennial Thought in Early Christianity*. 2nd ed. Grand Rapids: Eerdmans, 2001.

Hill, Christopher. *Intellectual Origins of the English Revolution Revisited*. Oxford: Oxford University Press 1997.

———. *The World Turned Upside Down: Radical Ideas during the English Revolution*. Harmondsworth: Penguin, 1975.

Hillerbrand, Hans J. "Radicalism in the Early Reformation." Pages 25–42 in *Radical Tendencies in the Reformation: Divergent Perspectives*. Edited by Hans J. Hillerbrand. Sixteenth Century Essays and Studies 9. Kirksville, MO: Sixteenth Century Journal Publishers, 1988.

Hladký, Vojtěch. *The Philosophy of Gemistos Plethon: Platonism in Late Byzantium, Between Hellenism and Orthodoxy*. Burlington, VT: Ashgate, 2014.

Hobbes, Thomas. *Behemoth; or, The Long Parliament*. Edited by Ferdinand Tönnies. Introduction by Stephen Holmes. Chicago: University of Chicago Press, 1990.

———. *Leviathan*. Edited with introduction by C. B. MacPherson. New York: Penguin, 1985.

———. *Leviathan*. Edited by Richard Tuck. Cambridge: Cambridge University Press, 1996.

———. *Thomas White's* De Mundo *Examined*. Translated by Harold Whitmore Jones. London: Bradford University Press, 1976.

Hoffman, Bengt, ed. *The Theologia Germanica of Martin Luther*. Preface by Bengt Hägglund. New York: Paulist, 1980.

Holmes, George. *The Florentine Enlightenment, 1400–50*. London: Weidenfeld & Nicholson, 1969.

Hood, F. C. *The Divine Politics of Thomas Hobbes: An Interpretation of 'Leviathan'.* Oxford: Clarendon, 1964.

Hooykaas, R. *Religion and the Rise of Modern Science*. Vancouver: Regent College, 1971.

Horton, Michael. "A Shattered Vase: The Tragedy of Sin in Calvin's Thought." Pages 151–63 in *A Theological Guide to Calvin's Institutes: Essays and Analysis*. Edited by David W. Hall and Peter A. Lillback. Phillipsburg, NJ: P&R, 2008.

Hotson, Howard. "Arianism and Millenarianism: The Link Between Two Heresies from Servetus to Socinus." Pages 9–35 in *Continental Millenarians. Protestants, Catholics, Heretics*. Vol. 4 in *Millennialism and Messianism in Early Modern European Culture.* Edited by John Christian Laursen and Richard H. Popkin. New York: Springer, 2001.

———. *Johann Heinrich Alsted (1588–1638): Between Renaissance, Reformation, and Universal Reform.* Oxford: Clarendon, 2000.

Howell, Kenneth J. *God's Two Books: Copernican Cosmology and Biblical Interpretation in Early Modern Science.* Notre Dame: University of Notre Dame Press, 2004.

Howell, James. *Epistolae Ho-Elieae*, IV.43. Edited by J. Jabops. London, 1890.

Huffman, William H., ed. *Robert Fludd: Essential Readings*. Berkeley: North Atlantic Books, 2001.

Huizinga, Johan. *Erasmus and the Age of the Reformation*. Mineola, NY: Dover, 1984.

Hunter, Michael. *Boyle: Between God and Science*. New Haven: Yale University Press, 2010.

———. "John Webster, the Royal Society and *The Displaying of Supposed Witchcraft* (1677)." *Notes and Records of the Royal Society of London* 71 (2017): 7–19.

Hunter, Michael, and Edward B. Davis, eds. *The Works of Robert Boyle*. 14 vols. London: Pickering, 1999–2000.

Huxley, Aldous. *Perennial Philosophy.* New York: Harper Perennial Modern Classics, 2009.

Idel, Moshe. *Golem: Jewish Magic and Mystical Traditions on the Artificial Anthropoid.* Brooklyn, NY: Ktav, 2019.

Iliffe, Rob. *Priest of Nature: The Religious Worlds of Isaac Newton.* Oxford: Oxford University Press, 2017.

Imerti, Arthur D. Introduction to *The Expulsion of the Triumphant Beast*, by Giordano Bruno. Foreword by Karen Silvia de Leon-Jones. Lincoln, NE: Bison, 1992.

Inwood, Brad, and L. P. Gerson, trans. and ed. *The Epicurus Reader: Selected Writings and Testimonia.* Indianapolis: Hackett, 1994.

Israel, Jonathan I. *The Radical Enlightenment: Philosophy and the Making of Modernity 1650–1750.* Oxford: Oxford University Press, 2001.

Jackson, Samuel M. *Huldreich Zwingli: The Reformer of German Switzerland.* Heroes of the Reformation 5. New York: Putnam, 1900.

Jacob, Margaret C. *The Radical Enlightenment.* Lafayette, LA: Harvard Cornerstone Book Publishers, 2006.

Jaspers, Karl. *The Origin and Goal of History*. Translated by Michael Bullock. London: Routledge, 1953.

Johnson, Patricia Cannon. "The Neoplatonists and the Mystery Schools of the Mediterranean." Pages 143–62 in *The Library of Alexandria: Centre of Learning in the Ancient World.* Edited by Roy McLeod. London: I. B. Tauris, 2004.

Johnston, David. "Hobbes' Mortalism." *History of Political Thought* 10.4 (1989): 647–63.

Joling-van der Sar, Gerda J. *The Spiritual Side of Samuel Richardson: Mysticism, Behmenism and Millenarianism in an Eighteenth-Century Novelist.* Leiden: Leiden University Scholarly Publications, 2003.

Jones, Rufus. *Spiritual Reformers in the Sixteenth and Seventeenth Centuries.* London: Macmillan, 1914.

Josten, C. H. ed. *Elias Ashmole (1617–1692): His Autobiographical and Historical Notes, Correspondence, and Contemporary Sources Relating to His Life and Work.* 5 vols. Oxford: Clarendon, 1967.

———. "A Translation of John Dee's *Monas Hieroglyphica* (Antwerp, 1564) with an Introduction and Annotations." *Ambix* 12 (1964): 9–99.

———. "William Backhouse of Swallowfield." *Ambix* 4.1–2 (1949): 1–33.

Jue, Jeffrey K. *Heaven upon Earth: Joseph Mede (1586–1638) and the Legacy of Millenarianism.* International Archives of the History of Ideas 194. Dordrecht: Springer, 2006.

Kadir, Djelal. *Columbus and the Ends of the Earth: Europe's Prophetic Rhetoric as Conquering Ideology*. Berkeley: University of California Press, 1992.

Kahn, Didier. "The Rosicrucian Hoax in France (1623–24)." Pages 235–344 in *Secrets of Nature: Astrology and Alchemy in Early Modern Europe*. Edited by William R. Newman and Anthony Grafton. Cambridge: MIT Press, 2001.

Kaminsky, Howard. *A History of the Hussite Revolution*. Eugene, OR: Wipf & Stock, 2004.

Keller, Ludwig. *Die Reformation und die älteren Reformparteien*. Leipzig: Hirzel, 1885.

Keynes, John Maynard. "Newton, the Man." In *The Royal Society Newton Tercentenary Celebrations, 15–19 July 1946*. Cambridge: Cambridge University Press, 1947.

Kirchhoff, Karl-Heinz. *Die Täufer in Münster 1534/35: Untersuchungen zum Umfang und zur Sozialstruktur der Bewegung*. Münster: Aschendorff, 1973.

———. "Gab es eine friedliche Täufergemeinde in Münster 1534?" *Jahrbuch des Vereins fur westfälische Kirchengeschichte* 55–56 (1963): 7–21.

Kiwiet, Jan J. "The Theology of Hans Denck," *Mennonite Quarterly Review* 32 (1958): 3–27.

Klein, Ursula. "Styles of Experimentation and Alchemical Matter Theory in the Scientific Revolution." *Metascience* 16 (2007): 247–56.

Klutstein, Ilana. *Marsilio Ficino et la théologie ancienne: Oracles chaldaïques, hymnes orphiques—hymnes de Proclus*. Florence: Olschki, 1987.

Knox, John. *A Warning Against the Anabaptists*. Dallas: Presbyterian House, 1984.

Kohls, Ernst-Wilhelm. *Theologie des Erasmus*. 2 vols. Basel: Reinhardt, 1966.

Kopp, Hermann. *Die Alchemie in älterer und neuerer Zeit*. Heidelberg: Winter's Universitätsbuchhandlung, 1886.

Koyré, Alexandre. *La Philosophie de Jakob Böhme*. Paris: Franklin, 1929.

Kristeller, Paul Oskar. "Marsilio Ficino as a Beginning Student of Plato." *Scriptorium* 20.1 (1966): 41–54.

———. *The Philosophy of Marsilio Ficino*. Translated by Virginia Conant. Gloucester, MA: Smith, 1964.

———. *Renaissance Thought and Its Sources*. Edited by Michael Mooney. New York: Columbia University Press, 1979.

Lansing, Carol. *Power and Purity: Cathar Heresy in Medieval Italy*. Oxford: Oxford University Press, 2001.

Law, William, trans. *The "Key" of Jakob Boehme*. Magnum Opus Hermetic Sourceworks 9. Grand Rapids: Phanes, 1981.

Leibniz, G. W. *Theodicy: Essays on the Goodness of God, the Freedom of Man, and the Origin of Evil*. Translated by E. M. Huggard. 5th ed. La Salle, IN: Open Court, 1996.

Lemper, Ernst-Heinz. *Jakob Böhme: Leben und Werk*. Dresden: Union, 1976.

Lenker, John Nicholas, ed. and trans. *Sermons of Martin Luther.* 8 vols. Grand Rapids: Baker, 1983.

Lenoble, Robert. *Mersenne: La Naissance du mécanisme.* Paris: Vrin, 1943.

Leon-Jones, Karen Silvia de. Foreword to *The Expulsion of the Triumphant Beast,* by Giordano Bruno. Translated with introduction by Arthur D. Imerti. Lincoln, NE: Bison, 1992.

Lerner, Gerda. *The Creation of Feminist Consciousness: From the Middle Ages to 1870.* Oxford: Oxford University Press, 1993.

Lerner, Robert. *The Heresy of the Free Spirit in the Later Middle Ages.* Berkeley: University of California Press, 1972.

Lévi-Strauss, Claude. *The Savage Mind.* Chicago: University of Chicago Press, 1966.

Levitin, Dmitri. *Ancient Wisdom in the Age of the New Science: Histories of Philosophy in England, c. 1640–1700.* Cambridge: Cambridge University Press, 2015.

Lim, Paul C. H. *Mystery Unveiled: The Crisis of the Trinity in Early Modern England.* Oxford: Oxford University Press, 2012.

Lindbeck, George. *The Nature of Doctrine: Religion and Theology in a Postliberal Age.* Louisville: Westminster, 1984.

Lochman, Jan Milíč. Preface to *John Comenius: The Labyrinth of the World and the Paradise of the Heart.* Translation and introduction by Howard Louthan and Andrea Sterk. Mahwah, NJ: Paulist, 1998.

Lodone, Michele. "Nesi, Giovanni." Pages 2320–21 in *The Encyclopedia of Renaissance Philosophy.* Edited by Marco Sgarbi. Cham: Springer, 2022.

Loewe, Raphael. *Ibn Gabirol.* Cambridge: Cambridge University Press, 1989.

Loewenich, Walther von. *Luther's Theology of the Cross.* Minneapolis: Augsburg, 1976.

Logan, George M., and Robert M. Adams, eds. *More: Utopia.* 2nd ed. Cambridge: Cambridge University Press, 2002.

Lomas, Robert. *The Invisible College: The Royal Society, Freemasonry and the Birth of Modern Science.* London: Transworld, 2002.

Looß, Sigrid. "Radical Views of the Early Andreas Karlstadt (1520–1525)." Pages 43–54 in *Radical Tendencies in the Reformation: Divergent Perspectives.* Edited by H. J. Hillerbrand. Sixteenth Century Essays and Studies 9. Kirksville, MO: Sixteenth Century Journal Publishers, 1988.

Louth, Andrew. *The Origins of the Christian Mystical Tradition: From Plato to Denys.* Oxford: Clarendon, 1981.

Louthan, Howard, and Andrea Sterk, trans. *John Comenius: The Labyrinth of the World and the Paradise of the Heart.* Mahwah, NJ: Paulist, 1998.

Lubac, Henri de. *La Posterité spirituelle de Joachim de Flore.* Paris: Lethielleux, 1981.

Lugt, Maaike van der. "Sex Difference in Medieval Theology and Canon Law." *Medieval Feminist Forum* 46.1 (2010): 101–21.

MacCulloch, Diarmaid. *Reformation: Europe's House Divided, 1490–1700*. London: Penguin, 2004.

Madonna, Maria Luisa. "Il Genius Loci di Villa d'Este: Mitit e misteri nel Sistema di Pirro Ligorio." Pages 190–213 in *Natura e artificio: L'ordine rustico, le fontane, gli automi nella cultura del Manierismo europeo*. Edited by Marcello Fagiolo. Rome: Officina Edizioni, 1979.

Magee, Glenn Alexander. *Hegel and the Hermetic Tradition*. Ithaca: Cornell University Press, 2001.

Magre, Maurice. *Return of the Magi*. Translated by Reginald R. Merton. London: Philip Allen, 1930. Repr., Whitefish, MT: Kessinger, 2003.

Majercik, Ruth. *The Chaldean Oracles: Text, Translation and Commentary*. Leiden: Brill, 1989.

Marius, Richard. *Thomas More: A Biography*. Cambridge: Harvard University Press, 1999.

Marquart, Kurt E. "Luther and Theosis." *Concordia Theological Quarterly* 64.3 (2000): 182–205.

Marshall, Peter. *The Theatre of the World: Alchemy, Astrology and Magic in Renaissance Prague*. Toronto: McClelland & Stewart, 2006.

Marshall, Wallace W. *Puritanism and Natural Theology*. Eugene, OR: Pickwick, 2016.

Martinich, A. P. *The Two Gods of Leviathan: Thomas Hobbes on Religion and Politics*. Cambridge: Cambridge University Press, 1991.

Maxwell-Stuart, P. G. *The Chemical Choir: A History of Alchemy*. London: Continuum, 2008.

McGinn, Bernard, ed. *Apocalyptic Spirituality: Treatises and Letters of Lactantius, Adso of Montier-en-Der, Joachim of Fiore, the Franciscan Spirituals, Savonarola*. Mahwah, NJ: Paulist, 1979.

———. *The Harvest of Mysticism in Medieval Germany*. London: Herder & Herder, 2005.

———. *Visions of the End: Apocalyptic Traditions in the Middle Ages*. New York: Columbia University Press, 1998.

McIntosh, Christopher. *The Rose Cross and the Age of Reason: Eighteenth-Century Rosicrucianism in Central Europe and Its Relationship to the Enlightenment*. Leiden: Brill, 1992.

McLaughlin, R. Emmet. *Caspar Schwenckfeld: Reluctant Radical*. New Haven: Yale University Press, 1986.

McLean, Adam. Introduction to *The "Key" of Jakob Boehme*. Translated by William Law. Magnum Opus Hermetic Sourceworks 9. Grand Rapids: Phanes, 1981.

Merry, Bruce. "George Gemistos Plethon (c. 1355/60–1452)." Pages 127–30 in *Multicul-*

tural Writers from Antiquity to 1945: A Bio-Bibliographical Sourcebook. Edited by Alba Amoia and Bettina L. Knapp. Westport, CT: Greenwood, 2002.

Merton, Robert K. "Motive Forces of the New Science." In *Puritanism and the Rise of Modern Science: The Merton Thesis*. Edited with introduction by I. Bernard Cohen. New Brunswick: Rutgers University Press, 1990.

———. *Science, Technology and Society in Seventeenth Century England.* New York: Harper, 1970.

———. "Science, Technology, and Society in Seventeenth-Century England." *Osiris* 4 (1938): 360–632.

Milbank, John. "Reformation 500: Any Cause for Celebration?" *Open Theology* 4 (2018): 607–29.

Mirandola, Gianfrancesco. *Examen vanitatis doctrinae gentium et Veritatis Christianae disciplinae*. Mirandola, 1520.

Molesworth, William, ed. *The English Works of Thomas Hobbes*. 11 vols. London: Longman, Brown, Green & Longmans, 1839–1845.

Monfasani, John. *Liber defensionum contra obiectiones in Platonem: Cardinal Bessarion's Own Latin Translation of His Greek Defense of Plato against George of Trebizond.* Byzantinisches Archiv: Series Philosophica 6. Berlin: de Gruyter, 2023.

———. *Vindicatio Aristotelis: Two Works of George of Trebizond in the Plato-Aristotle Controversy of the Fifteenth Century*. Tempe: Arizona Center for Medieval and Renaissance Studies Press, 2021.

Montagu, Basil, ed. *The Works of Francis Bacon, Lord Chancellor of England.* 3 vols. Philadelphia: Carey & Hart, 1842–1859.

Montgomery, John W. *Cross, Constellation, and Crucible: Lutheran Astrology and Alchemy in the Age of the Reformation.* Toronto: Transactions of the Royal Society of Canada, 1963.

———. *Cross and Crucible: Johann Valentin Andreae (1586–1654), Phoenix of the Theologians.* The Hague: Nijhoff, 1974.

Moore, Thomas. *The Planets Within: The Astrological Psychology of Marsilio Ficino.* Plainsboro, NJ: Associated University Presses, 1982.

Moran, Bruce T. *Distilling Knowledge: Alchemy, Chemistry, and the Scientific Revolution.* Cambridge: Harvard University Press, 2005.

More, Henry. *The Immortality of the Soul.* London: Flesher, 1659.

———. *The Theological Works of Henry More according to the author's improvements in his Latin edition.* London, 1708.

Mornay, Philippe Plessis de. *A Worke Concerning the Trewness of the Christian Religion, Written in French: against Atheist, Epicures, Paynims, Iewes, Mahumetists, and Other Infidels. By Philip of Mornay Lord of Plessie Marlie. Begunne to Be Trans-*

lated into English by Sir Philip Sidney Knight, and at His Request Finished by Arthur Golding. London: Cadman, 1587.

Muller, Richard A. "Not Scotist: Understandings of Being, Univocity, and Analogy in Early-Modern Reformed Thought." *Reformation and Renaissance Review* 14 (2012): 127–50.

Mulligan, Lotte. "'Reason,' 'Right Reason,' and 'Revelation' in Midseventeenth-Century England." Pages 375–402 in *Occult and Scientific Mentalities in the Renaissance.* Edited by Brian Vickers. Cambridge: Cambridge University Press, 1984.

Müntzer, Thomas. "The Prague Protest." Page 1–10 in *The Radical Reformation.* Edited by Michael G. Baylor. Cambridge Texts in the History of Political Thought. Cambridge: Cambridge University Press, 1991.

———. "Sermons to the Princes." Pages 11–32 in *The Radical Reformation.* Edited by Michael G. Baylor. Cambridge Texts in the History of Political Thought. Cambridge: Cambridge University Press, 1991.

Muratori, Cecilia. *The First German Philosopher: The Mysticism of Jakob Bohme as Interpreted by Hegel.* New York: Springer, 2015.

Nadler, Steven. *Menasseh ben Israel: Rabbi of Amsterdam.* New Haven: Yale University Press, 2018.

Nebelsick, Harold P. *The Renaissance, the Reformation and the Rise of Science.* Edinburgh: T&T Clark, 1992.

Newman, William R. *Atoms and Alchemy: Chymistry and the Experimental Origins of the Scientific Revolution.* Chicago: University of Chicago Press, 2006.

Newman, William R., and Anthony Grafton, eds. *Secrets of Nature: Astrology and Alchemy in Early Modern Europe.* Cambridge: MIT Press, 2006.

Newton, Isaac. *Philosophiae principia mathematica naturalis.* London: Royal Society, 1687.

Nicoli, Elena. "Ficino, Lucretius and Atomism." *Early Science and Medicine* 23.4 (2018): 330–61.

Nietzsche, Friedrich. *Twilight of Idols, and Anti-Christ.* Translated by R. J. Hollingdale. Introduction by Michael Tanner. London: Penguin, 2003.

Nummedel, Tara. *Anna Zieglerin and the Lion's Blood: Alchemy and Authority in the Holy Roman Empire.* Chicago: University of Chicago Press, 2007.

O'Regan, Cyril. *The Heterodox Hegel.* Albany: SUNY Press, 1994.

Osler, Margaret J. *Reconfiguring the World: Nature, God, and Human Understanding from the Middle Ages to Early Modern Europe.* Baltimore: Johns Hopkins University Press, 2010.

Owen, John. "A Practical Exposition upon Psalm CXXX." In vol. 6 of *The Works of John Owen.* Edited by William Goold. Edinburgh: Banner of Truth Trust, 1991.

Ozment, Steven E. *Mysticism and Dissent: Religious Ideology and Social Protest in the Sixteenth Century*. New Haven: Yale University Press, 1973.

Packull, Werner O. *Mysticism and the Early South German-Austrian Anabaptist Movement, 1525–1531*. Studies in Anabaptist and Mennonite History 19. Scottdale, PA: Herald, 1977.

Paganini, Gianni. "Hobbes's 'Mortal God' and Renaissance Hermeticism." *Hobbes Studies* 23.1 (2010): 7–28.

Pagel, Walter. *Paracelsus. An Introduction to Philosophical Medicine in the Era of Renaissance*. Basel: Karger, 1982.

———. "The Prime Matter of Paracelsus." *Ambix* 9.3 (1961): 117–35.

Palmer, Ada. *Reading Lucretius in the Renaissance*. Cambridge: Harvard University Press, 2014.

Palmer, W. Scott, ed. *The Confessions of Jacob Boehme*. Introduction by Evelyn Underhill. London: Methuen, 1920.

Paracelsus. *Sämtliche Werke I: Medizinische, naturwissenschaftliche und philosophische Schriften*. Edited by Karl Sudhoff. 14 vols. Munich: Oldenbourg, 1922–1923.

———. *Sämtliche Werke II: Theologische und Religionsphilosophische Schriften*. Edited by Kurt Goldammer. 6 vols. Wiesbaden: Steiner, 1955–1986.

Pattison, Mark. *Isaac Casaubon, 1559–1614*. Oxford: Oxford University Press, 1892.

Paulson, Steven D. "Luther on the Hidden God." *Word and World* 19.4 (1999): 363–71.

Pelikan, Jaroslav. *Reformation of Church and Dogma (1300–1700)*. Vol. 4 of *The Christian Tradition: A History of the Development of Doctrine*. Chicago: University of Chicago Press, 1985.

Penman, Leigh T. I. *Hope and Heresy: The Problem of Chiliasm in Lutheran Confessional Culture*. New York: Springer, 2019.

Perkins, William. *The Works of William Perkins*. 10 vols. Edited by J. Stephen Yuille. Grand Rapids, MI: Reformation Heritage Books, 2014.

Peters, Christian. "Theologische Deutsch." Pages 258–62 in *Theologische Realenzyklopädie*, vol. 33 (2002).

Petry, Ray C., ed. *Late Medieval Mysticism*. The Library of Christian Classics. Philadelphia: Westminster, 1957.

Peuckert, Will-Erich. *Das Leben Jakob Böhmes*. Jena: Deiderichs, 1924.

Phelan, John Leddy. *The Millennial Kingdom of the Franciscans in the New World*. Berkeley: University of California Press, 1970.

Pico della Mirandola, Giovanni. *Opera omnia Ioannis Pici*. Basel, 1557.

———. *Oration on the Dignity of Man*. Translated by A. Robert Caponigri. Washington, DC: Regnery, 1956.

Pinto, Vivian de Sola. *Peter Sterry, Platonist and Puritan, 1613–1672*. Cambridge: Cambridge University Press, 1934.

Plotinus. *Enneads*. Edited by A. H. Armstrong. LCL. Cambridge: Harvard University Press, 1969.

Popkin, Richard. *The History of Skepticism: From Savonarola to Bayle*. Oxford: Oxford University Press, 2003.

———. "Millenarianism and Nationalism—a Case Study: Isaac de La Peyrère." Pages 77–84 in *Millennialism and Messianism in Early Modern European Culture*. Edited by John C. Laursen and Richard H. Popkin. Dordrecht: Springer, 2013.

———. "The Religious Background of Seventeenth-Century Philosophy." Pages 393–422 in vol. 1 of *The Cambridge History of Seventeenth-Century Philosophy*. Edited by Daniel Garber and Michael Ayers. Cambridge: Cambridge University Press, 1998.

Price, Richard. *The Acts and Council of Constantinople of 553*. 2 vols. Liverpool: Liverpool University Press, 2009.

Probes, Christine McCall. "Calvin on Astrology." *Westminster Theological Journal* 37.1 (1974): 24–33.

Provan, Iain. *Convenient Myths: The Axial Age, Dark Green Religion, and the World That Never Was*. Waco: Baylor University Press, 2013.

Pulci, Luigi. *Morgante: The Epic Adventures of Orlando and His Giant Friend Morgante*. Translated by Joseph Tusiani. Introduction and Notes by Edoardo Lèbano. Indianapolis: Indiana University Press, 1998.

Quinn, John Francis. *The Historical Constitution of St. Bonaventure's Philosophy*. Studies and Texts 23. Toronto: Pontifical Institute of Medieval Studies, 1973.

Quispel, Gilles. "Hermes Trismegistus and the Origins of Gnosticism." Pages 145–65 in *From 'Poimandres' to Jacob Böhme: Gnosis, Hermetism and the Christian Tradition*. Edited by Roel B. van den Broek and Cis Heertum. Leiden: Brill, 2000.

———. "Reincarnation and Magic in the Asclepius." Pages 167–231 in *From Poimandres to Jacob Böhme: Gnosis, Hermeticism and the Christian Tradition*. Edited by Roelof van den Broek and Cis van Heertum. Leiden: Brill, 2000.

Ratiansi, P. M. "Paracelsus and the Puritan Revolution." *Ambix* 11 (1963): 24–32.

———. "Some Evaluations of Reason in Sixteenth- and Seventeenth-Century Natural Philosophy." Pages 148–66 in *Changing Perspectives in the History of Science*. Edited by Mikuláš Teich and Robert M. Young. London: Heinemann Educational, 1973.

Ratzinger, Joseph. *Principles of Catholic Theology*. San Francisco: Ignatius, 1987.

Reeves, Marjorie. *The Influence of Prophecy in the Later Middle Ages: A Study in Joachimism*. Oxford: Clarendon, 1969.

———. *Joachim of Fiore and the Prophetic Future*. New York: Sutton, 1999.

Rice, Eugene F., Jr. *The Foundations of Early Modern Europe*. New York: Norton, 1995.

Riess, Jonathan B. *Luca Signorelli: The San Brizio Chapel, Orvieto*. New York: George Braziller, 1995.

Rosen, Edward. "Kepler's Attitude Toward Astrology and Mysticism." Pages 253–72 in *Occult and Scientific Mentalities in the Renaissance*. Edited by Brian Vickers. Cambridge: Cambridge University Press, 1984.

———. "Was Copernicus a Hermetist?" *Historical and Philosophical Perspectives of Science* 5 (1970): 163–71.

Rosenstock, Bruce. "Jacob Taubes." Pages 381–98 in *The Palgrave History of Radical Theology*. Edited by Christopher D. Rodkey and Jordan E. Miller. Cham: Springer International Publishing, 2018.

Ross, James Bruce, and Mary Martin McLaughlin, eds. *The Portable Renaissance Reader*. New York: Penguin, 1968.

Rossi, Paolo. *The Birth of Modern Science*. Translated by Cynthia De Nardi Ipsen. Oxford: Blackwell, 2000.

———. *Francis Bacon: From Magic to Science*. Translated by Sacha Rabinovitch. Chicago: University of Chicago Press, 1968.

Roth, James, and James Stayer, eds. *A Companion to Anabaptism and Spiritualism, 1521–1700*. Leiden: Brill, 2007.

Rozenski, Steven. "Henry Suso's *Horologium Sapientiae* in Fifteenth-Century France." *Word and Image* 26.4 (2010): 364–80.

Rupp, Gordon. *Luther's Progress to the Diet of Worms 1521*. London: SCM, 1951.

Sale, Kirkpatrick. *Christopher Columbus and the Conquest of Paradise*. New York: I. B. Tauris, 1990.

Sarton, George. *A History of Science: Hellenistic Science and Culture in the Last Three Centuries B. C.* New York: Norton, 1959.

Savonarola, Girolamo. *Prediche sopra Ruth e Michea*. Edited by Vicenzo Romano. Rome: Belardetti, 1962.

Schaff, Philip, ed. *The Creeds of Christendom: with a History and Critical Notes*. 3 vols. 4th rev. ed. New York: Harper, 1877.

Schmidt-Biggemann, William. *Philosophia Perennis: Historical Outlines of Western Spirituality in Ancient, Medieval and Early Modern Thought*. Archives internationales d'histoire des idées 189. Dordrecht: Springer, 2004.

Schmitt, Charles B. *Gianfrancesco Pico Della Mirandola (1496–1533) and His Critique of Aristotle*. Dordrecht: Springer, 1967.

Schneider, Ivo. "Between Rosicrucians and Cabbala—Johannes Faulhaber's Mathematics of Biblical Numbers." Pages 311–30 in *Mathematics and the Divine: A Historical Study*. Edited by Tuen Koetsier and Luc Bergmans. Amsterdam: Elsevier, 2005.

Scholem, Gershom. *Jewish Gnosticism, Merkabah Mysticism, and the Talmudic Tradition.* New York: Schocken, 1960.

———. *Major Trends in Jewish Mysticism.* New York: Schocken, 1995.

Schuchard, Marsha Keith. *Restoring the Temple of Vision: Cabalistic Freemasonry and Stuart Culture.* Brill's Studies in Intellectual History 110. Leiden: Brill, 2002.

Schumann, Karl. "Rapidità del pensiero e ascensione al Cielo. Alcuni motivi ermetici in Hobbes." *Rivista di Storia in Filosophia* 40 (1985): 203–27.

Schuster, Louis A., Richard C. Marius, and James P. Lusardi, eds. *The Complete Works of Thomas More: Volume 8, Parts I–III.* New Haven: Yale University Press, 1973.

Scott, Tom. *Theology and Revolution in the German Reformation.* London: Macmillan, 1989.

Selderhuis, Herman. *Calvin on the Psalms.* Grand Rapids: Baker Academic, 2007.

Sextus Empiricus. *Against Logicians.* Translated by R. G. Bury. LCL. Cambridge: Harvard University Press, 1935.

———. *Against Physicists. Against Ethicists.* Translated by R. G. Bury. LCL. Cambridge: Harvard University Press, 1936.

———. *Against Professors.* Translated by R. G. Bury. LCL. Cambridge: Harvard University Press, 1949.

———. *Outlines of Pyrrhonism.* Translated by R. G. Bury. LCL. Cambridge: Harvard University Press, 1933.

Seymour, Charles Steve. *A Theodicy of Hell.* Studies in Philosophy and Religion 20. Dordrecht: Kluwer Academic, 2000.

Seznec, Jean. *The Survival of the Pagan Gods: The Mythological Tradition and Its Place in Renaissance Humanism and Art.* Translated by Barbara F. Sessions. Princeton: Princeton University Press, 1953.

Shapin, Steven, and Simon Schaffer. *Leviathan and the Air-Pump: Hobbes, Boyle, and the Experimental Life.* Princeton: Princeton University Press, 1985.

Share, Michael, trans. *Philoponus: Against Proclus; On the Eternity of the World 1–5.* London: Bloomsbury, 2014.

Shizuteru, Uedu, and James W. Heisis. "Ascent and Descent: Zen Buddhism in Comparison with Meister Eckhart, Part One." *Eastern Buddhist* 16.1 (1983): 52–73.

Sider, Ronald J. *Andreas Bodenstein von Karlstadt: The Development of His Thought, 1517–1525.* Studies in Medieval and Reformation Thought 11. Leiden: Brill, 1974.

Siggins, Ian D. Kingston. *Martin Luther's Doctrine of Christ.* New Haven: Yale University Press, 1970.

Sinossoglou, Niketas. *Radical Platonism in Byzantium: Illumination and Utopia in Gemestos Plethon.* Cambridge: Cambridge University Press, 2011.

Skinner, Quentin. "History and Ideology in the English Revolution." *The Historical Journal* 8.2 (1965): 151–78.

Smith, Nigel. "The Charge of Atheism and the Language of Radical Speculation, 1640–1660." Pages 131–58 in *Atheism from the Reformation to the Enlightenment*. Edited by Michael Hunter and David Wootton. Oxford: Oxford University Press, 1992.

———, ed. *A Collection of Ranter Writings: Spiritual Liberty and Sexual Freedom in the English Revolution*. London: Pluto, 2014.

Smith, Steven B. *Modernity and Its Discontents: Making and Unmaking the Bourgeois from Machiavelli to Bellow*. New Haven: Yale University Press, 2016.

Spedding, James, Robert Leslie Ellis, and Douglas Denon Heath, eds. and trans. *The Works of Francis Bacon*. 15 vols. Boston: Houghton & Mifflin, 1857–1874.

Spinka, Matthew. *John Amos Comenius: That Incomparable Moravian*. Chicago: University of Chicago Press, 1943.

Springborg, Patricia. "Hobbes, Heresy, and the Historia Ecclesiastica." *Journal of the History of Ideas* 55.4 (1994): 553–71.

———. "Hobbes on Religion." Pages 346–80 in *The Cambridge Companion to Hobbes*. Edited by Tom Sorell. Cambridge: Cambridge University Press, 1996.

Stayer, James M. *Anabaptists and the Sword*. Lawrence, KS: Coronado, 1976.

———. "Christianity in One City: Anabaptist Münster, 1534–35." Pages 117–34 in *Radical Tendencies in the Reformation: Divergent Perspectives*. Edited by H. J. Hillerbrand. Sixteenth Century Essays and Studies 9. Kirksville, MO: Sixteenth Century Journal Publishers, 1988.

Steiner, Rudolf. *Mystics of the Renaissance and Their Relation to Modern Thought*. New York: Putnam's Sons, 1911.

Stephens, John N. "Heresy in Medieval and Renaissance Florence." *Past & Present* 54 (1972): 25–60.

Sterry, Peter. *The Resurrection Revealed or the Dawning of the Day-star About to Rise and Radiate a Visible Incomparable Glory, etc*. London, 1653.

Stewart, Matthew A. *Nature's God: The Heretical Origins of the American Republic*. New York: Norton, 2014.

———, ed. *Selected Philosophical Papers of Robert Boyle*. Indianapolis: Hackett, 1991.

Stoeffler, F. Ernest. *The Rise of Evangelical Pietism*. Studies in the History of Religions 9. Leiden: Brill, 1965.

Stoyanov, Yuri. *The Other God: Dualist Religions from Antiquity to the Cathar Heresy*. New Haven: Yale University Press, 2000.

Strom, Jonathan. *German Pietism and the Problem of Conversion*. University Park: Pennsylvania State University Press, 2017.

Strong, James, and John McClintock, eds. *The Cyclopedia of Biblical, Theological, and Ecclesiastical Literature*. 10 vols. New York: Harper & Brothers, 1867–1887.

Strype, John. *Annals of the Reformation and Other Various Occurrences in the Church of England, during Queen Elizabeth's Happy Reign*. 4 vols. in 7 parts. Cambridge: Cambridge University Press, 2010.

Sullivan, Francis Patrick, SJ. *Indian Freedom: The Cause of Bartolomé de Las Casas, 1484–1566, A Reader*. Kansas City, MO: Sheed & Ward, 1995.

Szulakowska, Urszula. *The Alchemy of Light: Geometry and Optics in Late Renaissance Alchemical Illustration*. Symbola et Emblemata 10. Leiden: Brill, 2000.

Tarrant, Neil. "Concord and Toleration in the Thought of Francesco Pucci, 1578–81." *Sixteenth Century Journal* 46.4 (2015): 983–1003.

Taylor, A. E. "The Ethical Doctrine of Hobbes." Pages 35–56 in *Hobbes Studies*. Edited by Keith Brown. Cambridge: Harvard University Press, 1965.

Taylor, Charles. *A Secular Age*. Cambridge: Harvard University Press, 2007.

Thompson, Bard. *Humanists and Reformers: A History of the Renaissance and Reformation*. Grand Rapids: Eerdmans, 1996.

Thomson, Ian. "Manuel Chrysoloras and the Early Italian Renaissance." *Greek, Roman, and Byzantine Studies* 7.1 (1966): 63–82.

Tillich, Paul. *A History of Christian Thought: From Its Judaic and Hellenistic Origins to Existentialism*. New York: Simon & Schuster, 1972.

Torrance Kirby, W. J. "Stoic *and* Epicurean? Calvin's Dialectical Account of Providence in the *Institutes*." *International Journal of Systematic Theology* 5.3 (2003): 309–22.

Toulmin, Stephen. *Cosmopolis: The Hidden Agenda of Modernity*. Chicago: University of Chicago Press, 1990.

Trueman, Carl. *The Rise and Triumph of the Modern Self: Cultural Amnesia, Expressive Individualism, and the Road to Sexual Revolution*. Wheaton, IL: Crossway, 2020.

Tuck, Richard. "The 'Christian Atheism' of Thomas Hobbes." Pages 111–30 in *Atheism from the Reformation to the Enlightenment*. Edited by Michael Hunter and David Wootton. Oxford: Oxford University Press, 1992.

Turner, Denys. "Dionysius and Some Late Medieval Mystical Theologians of Northern Europe." Pages 121–36 in *Rethinking Dionysius the Areopagite*. Edited by Sara Coakley and Charles M. Stang. Oxford: Wiley, 2009.

Turretin, Francis. *Institutes of Elenctic Theology*. Translated by George Musgrave Giger. Edited by James T. Dennison Jr. 3 vols. Phillipsburg, NJ: P&R, 1997.

Van Cleve, T. C. *The Emperor Frederick II of Hohenstaufen: Immuntator Mundi*. Oxford: Oxford University Press, 1972.

Vanhaelen, Maude. "Ficino's Commentary on St. Paul's *Epistle to the Romans* (1497): An Anti-Savonarolan Reading of Vision and Prophecy." Pages 205–33 in *The Rebirth of Platonic Theology: Proceedings of a Conference Held at the Harvard University Center for Italian Renaissance Studies (Villa I Tatti) and the Istituto Nazionale di Studi sul Rinascimento (Florence, 26–27 April 2007)*. Edited by James Hankins and Fabrizio Meroi. Florence: Olschki Editore, 2013.

Verastique, Bernardino. *Michoacán and Eden: Vasco de Quiroga and the Evangelization of Western Mexico.* Austin: University of Texas Press, 2000.

Verduin, Leonard. *The Reformers and Their Stepchildren.* Grand Rapids: Eerdmans, 1964.

Versluis, Arthur. "Christian Theosophical Literature of the Seventeenth and Eighteenth Centuries." Pages 217–36 in *Gnosis and Hermeticism from Antiquity to Modern Times.* Edited by Roelof van den Broek and Wouter J. Hanegraaff. Albany: SUNY Press, 1998.

———. *Theosophia: Hidden Dimensions of Christianity.* Hudson, NY: Lindisfarne, 1994.

Vickers, Brian. *Francis Bacon: The Major Works.* Oxford: Oxford University Press, 1996.

Voegelin, Eric. *The New Science of Politics.* Chicago: University of Chicago Press, 1952.

Vogler, Günter. "The Anabaptist Kingdom of Münster in the Tension between Anabaptism and Imperial Policy." Pages 99–116 in *Radical Tendencies in the Reformation: Divergent Perspectives.* Edited by H. J. Hillerbrand. Sixteenth Century Essays and Studies 9. Kirksville, MO: Sixteenth Century Journal Publishers, 1988.

Waite, A. E. *Brotherhood of the Rosy Cross: A History of the Rosicrucians.* London: Rider, 1924.

———, trans. and ed. *The Hermetic and Alchemical Writings of Aureolus Philippus Theophrastus Bombast of Hohenheim, Called Paracelsus the Great.* 2 vols. London: Elliot & Company, 1894.

Walker, D. P. "The *Prisca Theologia* in France." *Journal of the Warburg and Courtauld Institute* 17 (1954): 204–59.

———. *Studies in Musical Science in the Late Renaissance.* Leiden: Brill, 1978.

Walpole, Horace. *The Letters of Horace Walpole, Earl of Oxford, in Four Volumes.* London: John Sharpe, 1818.

Walsh, David. *The Mysticism of Innerworldly Fulfillment: A Study of Jacob Boehme.* Gainesville: University of Florida Press, 1983.

Ward, Seth, and John Wilkins. *Vindiciae academiarum Containing Some Briefe Animadversions upon Mr Websters Book Stiled. The Examination of Academies: Together with an Appendix Concerning What M. Hobbs and M. Dell Have Published on This Argument.* Oxford: Lichfield, 1654.

Waring, A. Graham. Introduction to *On Religion: Speeches to Its Cultured Despisers,* by Friedrich Schleiermacher. New York: Unger, 1955.

Warren, James. *Epicurus and Democritean Ethics: An Archaeology of Ataraxia.* Cambridge: Cambridge University Press, 2002.

Warrender, Howard. *The Political Philosophy of Hobbes: His Theory of Obligation.* Oxford: Clarendon, 1957.

Weber, Max. *The Sociology of Religion.* Translated by Ephraism Fischoff. 2nd ed. Boston: Beacon, 1993.

Webster, Charles. "Essay Review: The Origins of the Royal Society: The Royal Society: Concept and Creation." *History of Science* 6 (1967): 106–28.

———. *Paracelsus: Medicine, Magic, and Mission at the End of Time.* New Haven: Yale University Press, 2008.

Weeks, Andrew. *Boehme: An Intellectual Biography of the Seventeenth-Century Philosopher and Mystic.* Albany: SUNY Press, 1991.

———. *German Mysticism from Hildegard of Bingen to Ludwig Wittgenstein: A Literary and Intellectual History.* Albany: SUNY Press, 1993.

———. *Paracelsus: Speculative Theory and the Crisis of the Early Reformation.* Albany: SUNY Press, 1997.

Weinstein, Donald. *Savonarola: The Rise and Fall of a Renaissance Prophet.* New Haven: Yale University Press, 2011.

———. *Savonarola and Florence: Prophecy and Patriotism in the Renaissance.* Princeton: Princeton University Press, 1970.

Wenger, J. C., ed. *Complete Works of Menno Simon.* Translated by Leonard Verduin. Scottdale, PA: Mennonite Publishing House, 1984.

West, Delno C., and August Kling. *The "Libro de las Profecías" of Christopher Columbus.* Gainesville: University of Florida Press, 1991.

West, Delno C., and Sandra Zimdars-Swartz. *Joachim of Fiore: A Study in Spiritual Perception and History.* Bloomington: Indiana University Press, 1983.

White, Andrew D. *A History of the Warfare of Science with Theology in Christendom.* 2 vols. New York: Appleton, 1896–1897.

Wilberding, James, trans. *Philoponus: Against Proclus; On the Eternity of the World 12–18.* London: Bloomsbury, 2014.

Wilders, John, ed. *Samuel Butler: Hudibras.* Oxford: Oxford University Press, 1967.

Willard, Thomas. "*De furore Brittanico*: The Rosicrucian Manifestos in Britain." *Aries* 14.1 (2014): 32–61.

Williams, George Huntston. *The Radical Reformation.* 3rd ed. Kirksville, MO: Truman State University Press, 2000.

Williams, George Huntston, and Angel M. Mergal, eds. *Spiritual and Anabaptist Writers.* Library of Christian Classics 25. Philadelphia: Westminster, 1957.

Williams, Gwyn A. *When Was Wales? A History of the Welsh.* London: Penguin, 1985.

Wilson, Catherine. *Epicureanism at the Origins of Modernity.* Oxford: Oxford University Press, 2008.

Wilson, Peter Lamborn. "Oneiriconographia: Entering Poliphilo's Utopian Dreamscape—a Review Essay." *Alexandria* 5 (2000): 399–49.

Wingren, Gustaf. *Luther on Vocation.* Translated by Carl C. Rasmussen. Eugene, OR: Wipf & Stock, 2004.

Winstanley, Gerrard. "New Law of Righteousness." In *The Works of Gerrard Winstanley*. Edited by George H. Sabine. Ithaca: Cornell University Press, 1941.

Wood, Anthony. *The History and Antiquities of the University of Oxford*. Edited by John Gutch. 2 vols. Oxford, 1796.

Wood, James. *The Broken Estate: Essays on Literature and Belief.* New York: Random House, 1999.

Woodhouse, C. M. *Gemistos Plethon: The Last of the Hellenes*. Oxford: Clarendon, 1986.

Woolf, Bertram Lee, ed. *Reformation Writings of Martin Luther.* 2 vols. New York: Philosophical Library, 1953.

Wootton, David. *Galileo: Watcher of the Skies*. New Haven: Yale University Press, 2010.

———. "Lucien Febvre and the Problem of Unbelief in the Early Modern Period." *Journal of Modern History* 60 (1988): 695–730.

———. "New Histories of Atheism." Pages 13–54 in *Atheism from the Reformation to the Enlightenment*. Edited by Michael Hunter and David Wootton. Oxford: Oxford University Press, 1992.

Yates, Frances A. *Giordano Bruno and the Hermetic Tradition*. Chicago: University of Chicago Press, 1991.

———. *The Occult Philosophy in the Elizabethan Age*. London: Routledge, 2001.

———. *The Rosicrucian Enlightenment*. London: Routledge, 1972.

Yoder, John Howard. *The Schleitheim Confession*. Scottdale, PA: Herald, 1977.

Young, J. T. *Faith, Medical Alchemy and Natural Philosophy: Johann Moriaen, Reformed Intelligencer and the Hartlib Circle*. London: Routledge, 1998.

Zavala, Silvio. *Sir Thomas More in New Spain: A Utopian Adventure in the Renaissance*. London: Canning House, 1955.

Index of Authors

Index of Subjects